Foreign Investment and the Environment in International Law

Conflicts between foreign investment law and environmental law are becoming increasingly frequent. On the one hand, the rise of environmental regulation poses significant challenges to foreign investors in several industries. On the other, the surge in investment arbitration proceedings is making States aware of the important litigation risks that may result from the adoption of environmental regulation.

This study of the relationship between these two areas of law adopts both a policy and a practical perspective. It identifies the major challenges facing States, foreign investors and their legal advisers as a result of the potential friction between investment law and environmental law, and provides a detailed analysis of all the major legal issues on the basis of a comprehensive study of the jurisprudence from investment tribunals, human rights courts and bodies, the ICJ, the WTO, the ITLOS, the CJEU and other adjudication mechanisms.

JORGE E. VIÑUALES is the Pictet Chair of International Environmental Law and Assistant Professor of Public International Law at the Graduate Institute of International and Development Studies, Geneva. He is also the Director of the Programme on Institutions for Sustainable Development at the Centre for International Environmental Studies.

CAMBRIDGE STUDIES IN INTERNATIONAL AND COMPARATIVE LAW

Established in 1946, this series produces high quality scholarship in the fields of public and private international law and comparative law. Although these are distinct legal sub-disciplines, developments since 1946 confirm their interrelation.

Comparative law is increasingly used as a tool in the making of law at national, regional and international levels. Private international law is now often affected by international conventions, and the issues faced by classical conflicts rules are frequently dealt with by substantive harmonisation of law under international auspices. Mixed international arbitrations, especially those involving state economic activity, raise mixed questions of public and private international law, while in many fields (such as the protection of human rights and democratic standards, investment guarantees and international criminal law) international and national systems interact. National constitutional arrangements relating to 'foreign affairs', and to the implementation of international norms, are a focus of attention.

The Series welcomes works of a theoretical or interdisciplinary character, and those focusing on the new approaches to international or comparative law or conflicts of law. Studies of particular institutions or problems are equally welcome, as are translations of the best work published in other languages.

General Editors James Crawford SC FBA
        Whewell Professor of International Law, Faculty of Law,
        University of Cambridge

        John S. Bell FBA
        Professor of Law, Faculty of Law, University of Cambridge

A list of books in the series can be found at the end of this volume.

Foreign Investment and the Environment in International Law

Jorge E. Viñuales

CAMBRIDGE
UNIVERSITY PRESS

CAMBRIDGE UNIVERSITY PRESS
Cambridge, New York, Melbourne, Madrid, Cape Town,
Singapore, São Paulo, Delhi, Mexico City

Cambridge University Press
The Edinburgh Building, Cambridge CB2 8RU, UK

Published in the United States of America by Cambridge University Press, New York

www.cambridge.org
Information on this title: www.cambridge.org/9781107006386

First published 2012

Printed and Bound in Great Britain by the MPG Books Group

A catalogue record for this publication is available from the British Library

Library of Congress Cataloguing in Publication data
Viñuales, Jorge E.
Foreign investment and the environment in international law / Jorge E. Viñuales.
    pages   cm. – (Cambridge studies in international and comparative law ; 94)
Includes bibliographical references and index.
ISBN 978-1-107-00638-6
1. Investments, Foreign–Law and legislation.   2. Environmental law, International.
I. Title.
K3830.V56 2012
346′.092–dc23

                                                                2012014613

ISBN 978-1-107-00638-6 Hardback

A Joséphine

Contents

Abbreviations

Abbreviation	Full reference
AAU	assigned amount unit
ABS	access and benefit sharing
ALI	American Law Institute
BEE	black economic empowerment
BIT	Bilateral Investment Treaty
CAO	Complaince Advisor/Ombudsman
CCS	carbon capture and storage
CDM	clean development mechanism
CER	Certified Emission Reductions
CFC	chlorofluorocarbon
CFR	United States Code of Federal Regulations
CMLR	Common Market Law Reports
CSS	Commission on Sustainable Development
CWA	Clean Water Act (US)
ECJ	European Court of Justice
ECtHR	European Court of Human Rights
EEZ	exclusive economic zone
EIA	environmental impact assessment
EPA	Environmental Protection Agency (US)
EPL	Environmental Policy and Law
ERU	emission reduction units
FET	fair and equitable treatment
FIC	Foreign Investment Commission (Chile)
FTA	free trade agreement
GEF	Global Environmental Facility
GIS	green investment scheme
GMO	genetically modified organism

HBFC	hydrobromofluorocarbon
HCFC	hydrochlorofluorocarbon
HRC	UN Human Rights Committee
IBRD	International Bank for Reconstruction and Development
ICC	International Chamber of Commerce
ICJ	International Court of Justice
IComm HR	Inter-American Commission on Human Rights
ICSID	International Centre for Settlement of Investment Disputes
ICtHR	Inter-American Court of Human Rights
IFC	International Finance Corporation
IIA	international investment and free trade agreement
ILM	International Legal Materials
ITLOS	International Tribunal for the Law of the Sea
JI	joint implementation
LCIA	London Court of International Arbitration
MDG	Millennium Development Goals
MEA	multilateral environmental agreements
MFN	most-favoured nation
MII	Multilateral Investment Treaty
NAP	national allocation plan
NCP	National Contact Points
OAS	Organisation of American States
OECD	Organisation for Economic Co-operation and Development
OJ	Official Journal of the European Union
PCA	Permanent Court of Arbitration
PCF	Prototype Carbon Fund
PES	payments-for-ecosystem-services
PIC	prior informed consent
PPM	production processes and methods
PPP	public private partnerships
RIAA	Reports of International Arbitral Awards
RMU	removal unit
SCC	Stockholm Chamber of Commerce
SGRP	System-wide Genetic Resources Programme of the Treaty on Plant Genetic Resources
SRI	sustainable and responsible investment

TAC	total allowable catch
TFDD	www.transboundarywaters.orst.edu
TREM	trade-related environmental measure
TURF	territorial use right in fisheries
UNCITRAL	United Nations Commission on International Trade Law
UNDESA	United Nations Department of Economic and Social Affairs
UNDP	United Nations Development Programme
UNEP	United Nations Environment Programme
UNTS	United Nations Treaty Series
WB	World Bank
WSSD	World Summit on Sustainable Development
WTO	World Trade Organization

Table of cases

International Court of Justice/Permanent Court of International Justice

International Tribunal for the Law of the Sea and UNCLOS-related arbitral tribunals

European Court of Human Rights

Inter-American Court of Human Rights

Inter-American Commission on Human Rights

African Commission on Human and Peoples' Rights

European Community Courts

Tribunal of the Southern Africa Development Community

Human Rights Committee

World Heritage Committee

Aarhus Convention (NCP)

World Bank Inspection Panel

IFC CAO

Domestic case-law

Domestic determinations (National Contact Points under the OECD Guidelines)

Table of treaties

Date	Full reference	Abbreviation	Pages
19 March 1902	Convention for the Protection of Birds useful to Agriculture, B7 p. 902:22.	None	10
11 January 1909	Treaty between Great Britain [Canada] and the United States relating to Boundary Waters and Boundary Questions, (1910) 4 AJIL suppl. 239	Boundary Waters Treaty	161
7 July 1911	Convention between the United States, Great Britain, Japan and Russia providing for the Preservation and Protection of the Fur Seals, 37 Stat. 1542.	Fur Seals Convention	10
12 October 1940	Convention on Nature Protection and Wild Life Preservation in the Western Hemisphere, 56 Stat. 1354, TS 981	Western Hemisphere Convention	36, 37, 190, 192, 200

Date	Full reference	Abbreviation	Pages
3 February 1944	Treaty between the United States of America and Mexico relating to the Utilization of the Waters of the Colorado and Tijuana Rivers and of the Rio Grande, 3 UNTS 314	1944 Water Utilisation Treaty	161, 169
2 December 1946	International Convention for the Regulation of Whaling with Schedule of Whaling Regulations, 161 UNTS 361.	Whaling Convention	10, 190
12 August 1949	Geneva Convention Relative to the Treatment of Prisoners of War, 75 UNTS 31	Third Geneva Convention	164
12 August 1949	Geneva Convention Relative to the Treatment of Civilian Persons in Time of War, 75 UNTS 287	Fourth Geneva Convention	164
4 November 1950	Convention for the Protection of Human Rights and Fundamental Freedoms, 213 UNTS 221	ECHR	89, 112, 167, 224, 230–1, 243–4, 248, 326, 344, 356, 376–7
20 March 1952	Protocol to the Convention for the Protection of Human Rights and Fundamental Freedoms, ETS 9	Protocol I	89, 207, 230, 244, 245

Date	Full reference	Abbreviation	Pages
10 June 1958	Convention on the Recognition and Enforcement of Foreign Arbitral Awards, 330 UNTS 38	New York Convention	92, 291
8 November 1959	Agreement between the Republic of Sudan and the United Arab Republic for the Utilization of the Nile Waters, 453 UNTS 51	Nile Treaty	161, 163
4 January 1960	Convention Establishing the European Free Trade Association (EFTA), 370 UNTS 3	EFTA Convention	323
19 November 1960	Indus Waters Treaty between the Government of India, the Government of Pakistan and the International Bank for Reconstruction and Development, 419 UNTS 126	Indus Waters Treaty	161
18 March 1965	Convention on the Settlement of Investment Disputes between States and Nationals of other States, 575 UNTS 159	ICSID Convention	87, 93, 105, 107, 287–9, 291
16 December 1966	International Covenant on Civil and Political Rights, 999 UNTS 171	ICCPR	82, 164, 167, 190, 197, 207–8, 229, 344, 356, 388
16 December 1966	International Covenant on Economic, Social and Cultural Rights, 993 UNTS 3	ICESCR	165, 190, 209, 224, 229, 248, 388

Date	Full reference	Abbreviation	Pages
15 September 1968 (revised on 11 July 2003)	African Convention on the Conservation of Nature and Natural Resources, 1001 UNTS 3	African Conservation Convention	190, 192
23 May 1969	Vienna Convention on the Law of Treaties, 1155 UNTS 331	VCLT	38, 112, 142, 146, 151–2, 154–6, 171–2, 180, 220–1
22 November 1969	American Convention on Human Rights, 1144 UNTS 123	ACHR	165, 167, 178, 191, 197, 205–6, 214, 245, 344
2 February 1971	Convention on Wetlands of International Importance especially as Waterfowl Habitat, 996 UNTS 245	Ramsar Convention	35, 49, 113, 190, 192, 196, 201–3, 218
16 November 1972	Convention for the Protection of the World Cultural and Natural Heritage, 1037 UNTS 151	World Heritage Convention	4, 10, 36, 40, 67, 112, 126, 147, 153, 190–2, 196, 199–204, 215–16, 218–19, 221, 235, 282, 288, 300
29 December 1972 (modified on 7 November 1996)	Convention for the Prevention of Marine Pollution by Dumping of Wastes and Other Matter, as modified by the Protocol of 7 November 1996, 1046 UNTS 120	London Convention	10, 122, 228
17 February 1973 (modified on 17 February 1978)	International Convention for the Prevention of Pollution from Ships, as modified by the	MARPOL	10

Date	Full reference	Abbreviation	Pages
	Protocol of 1978 relating thereto, UNTS 1340 I-22484		
3 March 1973	Convention on International Trade in Endangered Species of Wild Fauna and Flora, 983 UNTS 243	CITES	32, 190, 193, 194
6 August 1977	Protocol Additional to the Geneva Conventions of 12 August 1949, and Relating to the Protection of Victims of International Armed Conflicts, 1125 UNTS 3	Protocol I 1977	164
12 August 1977	Protocol Additional to the Geneva Conventions of 12 August 1949, and Relating to the Protection of Victims of Non-International Armed Conflicts, 1125 UNTS 609	Protocol II 1977	164
22 November 1978 (modified on 16 October 1993)	Agreement between the United States of American and Canada on Great Lakes Water Quality, TFDD	Great Lakes Water Quality Agreement	162, 163
23 June 1979	Convention on the Conservation of Migratory Species of Wild Animals, 1651 UNTS 356	CMS Convention	49

Date	Full reference	Abbreviation	Pages
19 September 1979	Convention on the Conservation of European Wildlife and Natural Habitats, ETS No. 104	Bern Convention	190, 192, 207
26 October 1979	Convention on the Physical Protection of Nuclear Material, 1456 UNTS 124	None	85
13 November 1979	Convention on Long-Range Transboundary Air Pollution, 1302 UNTS 217	LRTAP Convention	66, 109, 136, 224, 227
18 December 1979	Convention on the Elimination of All Forms of Discrimination Against Women, 1249 UNTS 13	CEDAW	164
20 May 1980	Convention for the Conservation of Antarctic Marine Living Resources, 1329 UNTS 47	CCAMLR	194
19 June 1980	Convention on the Law Applicable to Contractual Obligations, OJ 1980 L 266/1	Rome Convention	340
27 June 1981	African Charter on Human and Peoples' Rights, 21 ILM 58 (1982)	African Charter	167, 191, 197, 209, 224, 230, 245
10 December 1982	United Nations Convention on the Law of the Sea, 1833 UNTS 397	UNCLOS	85, 121, 136, 193, 228, 241, 242

Date	Full reference	Abbreviation	Pages
22 March 1985	Vienna Convention for the Protection of the Ozone Layer, 1513 UNTS 293	Ozone Convention	84, 227
8 July 1985	Protocol on the Reduction of Sulphur Emissions or their Transboundary Fluxes, 27 ILM 707	Sulphur Protocol I	227
9 July 1985	ASEAN Agreement on the Conservation of Nature and Natural Resources, 15 EPL 64	Kuala Lumpur Agreement	190
24 October 1986	Treaty on the Lesotho Highlands Water Project, TFDD	Lesotho Treaty	161
10 April 1987	Agreement between the United Mexican States and the Republic of Guatemala on the Protection and Improvement of the Environment in the Border Area, TFDD	Nicaragua–Mexico Agreement	162
16 September 1987	Montreal Protocol on Substances that Deplete the Ozone Layer, 1522 UNTS 29	Montreal Protocol	66, 137, 227
31 October 1988	Protocol concerning the Control of Emissions of Nitrogen Oxides or their Transboundary Fluxes, 28 ILM 214	NOx Protocol	227
16 November 1988	Additional Protocol to the American Convention on Human Rights in the	Protocol of San Salvador	197, 224, 230

Date	Full reference	Abbreviation	Pages
	Area of Economic, Social and Cultural Rights, OAS Treaty Series No. 69		
22 March 1989	Basel Convention on the Control of Transboundary Movements of Hazardous Wastes and their Disposal, 1673 UNTS 57	Basel Convention	32, 34, 49–50, 67, 137, 150, 211–12, 223, 225–6, 239–41, 248–52
27 June 1989	Convention (No. 169) concerning Indigenous and Tribal Peoples in Independent Countries, 28 ILM 1382 (1989)	ILO Convention 169	167, 174, 191, 197
20 November 1989	Convention on the Rights of the Child, 1577 UNTS 3	CRC	164
8 October 1990	Convention between the Federal Republic of Germany and the Czech and Slovak Federal Republic and the European Economic Community on the International Commission for the Protection of the Elbe, TFDD	Convention on the Protection of the Elbe	173
30 January 1991	Bamako Convention on the Ban on the Import into Africa and the Control of Transboundary Movement and Management of Hazardous Wastes within Africa, 30 ILM 773	Bamako Convention	224–6, 239, 248

Date	Full reference	Abbreviation	Pages
4 August 1995	Agreement for the Implementation of the Provisions of the United Nations Conventions on the Law of the Sea of 10 December 1982 relating to the Conservation and Management of Straddling Fish Stocks and Highly Migratory Fish Stocks, S. Treaty Doc. No. 104–24, 2167 UNTS 88	UN Fish Stocks Agreement	11, 194
21 May 1997	United Nations Convention on the Law of the Non-Navigational Uses of International Watercourses, 36 ILM 700 (not yet in force)	UN Watercourses Convention	159–60, 162
11 December 1997	Kyoto Protocol to the United Nations Framework Convention on Climate Change, Kyoto, 2303 UNTS 148	Kyoto Protocol	13, 23, 28, 35, 42, 46–7, 50–4, 58, 96, 253–7, 259, 261–4, 273–6
22 January 1998	Convention on the Protection of the Rhine (France, Germany, Luxembourg, Netherlands, Switzerland, European Union), TFDD	Rhine Convention	162

Date	Full reference	Abbreviation	Pages
24 June 1998	Protocol on Heavy Metals to the LRTAP Convention, available at: www.unece.org/env/lrtap/hm_h1.html	HM Protocol	224, 227
24 June 1998	Protocol on Persistent Organic Pollutants to the LRTAP Convention, 37 ILM513	Aarhus POP Protocol	109, 112, 224, 227, 233, 249
25 June 1998	Convention on Access to Information, Public Participation in Decision-making and Access to Justice in Environmental Matters, 2161 UNTS 447	Aarhus Convention	4, 40, 62, 82, 166, 224, 231, 234, 235, 271–3, 356, 360
10 September 1998	Rotterdam Convention on the Prior Informed Consent Procedure for Certain Hazardous Chemicals and Pesticides in International Trade, 2244 UNTS 337	PIC Convention	149, 223, 225–6, 239
17 June 1999	Protocol on Water and Health to the 1992 Convention on the Protection and Use of Transboundary Watercourses and International Lakes, 2331 UNTS 202	Protocol on Water and Health	82, 164
29 January 2000	Cartagena Protocol on Biosafety to the	Biosafety Protocol	149, 190, 194, 225–6, 239–40

Date	Full reference	Abbreviation	Pages
	Convention on Biological Diversity, 39 ILM 1027		
22 May 2001	Stockholm Convention on Persistent Organic Pollutants, 40 ILM 532	POP Convention	67, 149, 223, 226, 233, 235, 247–8
3 November 2001	International Treaty on Plant Genetic Resources for Food and Agriculture, 2400 UNTS 379	Treaty on Plant Genetic Resources	194
12 December 2001	Responsibility of States for Internationally Wrongful Acts, GA Res. 56/83, UN Doc. A/RES/56/83	ILC Articles	181, 332, 381–2, 384, 387, 389–90
5 August 2004	Dominican Republic–Central America–US Free Trade Agreement (initially concluded by and between the United States, Costa Rica, El Salvador, Guatemala, Honduras and Nicaragua, later joined by the Dominican Republic), 43 ILM 514	CAFTA-DR	139, 176, 202, 236, 285
23 May 2007	COMESA Common Investment Area Agreement	COMESA CIAA	328
15 October 2008	Economic Partnership Agreement between the Cariforum States	CARIFORUM-EPA	138

Date	Full reference	Abbreviation	Pages
	and the European Community and its Member States, OJ 2008 L 289/I/3		
16 October 2010	The Nagoya – Kuala Lumpur Supplementary Protocol on Liability and Redress to the Cartagena Protocol on Biosafety, available at: bch.cbd. int/protocol/ NKL_text.shtml	None	190
29 October 2010	Nagoya Protocol on Access to Genetic Resources and the Fair and Equitable Sharing of the Benefits arising from their Utilization to the Convention on Biological Diversity, available at: www. cbd.int/abs/doc/ protocol/nagoya-protocol-en.pdf	ABS Protocol	55, 70, 150, 190, 194–6
October 2011	Instrument for the Establishment of the Restructured Global Environmental Facility	None	12, 42, 43

Introductory observations

Investment lawyers and environmental lawyers barely speak to each other. Their lack of communication is mostly the result of either mutual disinterest or mutual distrust; and it has had an important consequence, namely that the relationship between two thriving fields of international law – international investment law and international environmental law – has only recently started to be elucidated.

The purpose of the present study is to make, in this context, one basic theoretical point, with two important practical implications. The theoretical point is that, as both international investment law and international environmental law develop and become more precise and demanding, their interactions will intensify, both in terms of synergies and conflicts. The first practical implication is that the operations of investors in an array of sectors, ranging from the extractive industries, to energy production, to waste treatment, will likely be affected. Sometimes, environmental regulation will create new markets, as is the case with a variety of 'clean' technologies. In other cases, environmental regulation will adversely affect the operations of foreign investors, particularly in those areas of environmental regulation where a treaty requires or encourages States to take certain measures. The potential impact of such treaties has been overlooked. For many years, environmental treaties, often couched in broad or even vague terms, did not seem to be relevant for the operations of investors. Today, many of these treaties are 'waking up'. The increasing environmental awareness of growing sectors of the world's population is breathing new life into previously 'dormant environment clauses'. From the perspective of investors, it becomes more and more important to assess the risks posed by environmental measures as well as the legal remedies available to counter potential abuses. This leads to the second practical implication identified above, namely that the regulatory powers of the State in the environmental arena are increasingly besieged by the legal strait-jacket imposed by investment disciplines. States would be ill-advised to underestimate the litigation risk arising from these disciplines, which by most measures can go as far as representing billions of dollars. From the perspective of States, it is thus critical to assess the regulatory space that they will keep for environmental protection purposes. The future importance of these two practical implications must be assessed in the light of the current move towards a green economy. Realising the green economy will indeed take both investment and regulation.[1]

This book is an attempt to identify and analyse the most pressing legal issues raised by the interactions between foreign investment and environmental protection in contemporary international law. As such, it does not seek to provide an analysis of the investment–environment equation from an economic or a political perspective. Such aspects are covered in more detail in a companion volume to this book forthcoming with the same publisher.[2] I have endeavoured to state the current state of international law on the issues covered,[3] avoiding as much as possible the implicit bias sometimes underlying purely environmental or purely investment perspectives. I believe that the protection of the environment is probably the foremost challenge of our time, but I also believe that, as far as international law is concerned, such protection is best served by disentangling law from hope. Just as international environmental law is in many respects economic law, in the meaning of the law governing the activities of economic operators, international investment law is also environmental law, to the extent that investment disciplines, properly interpreted and applied, may help channel much needed resources towards pro-environment projects.

The book is structured into three parts, each consisting of five chapters. Part I sets the overall analytical framework. It begins with two theoretical chapters, one mapping the evolving relationship between environmental and investment law and the other conceptualising the dual nature of this relationship, synergistic and conflicting. The third and fourth chapters provide overviews of the main

---

[1] See United Nations Environment Programme, *Towards a Green Economy: Pathways to Sustainable Development and Poverty Eradication* (2011).

[2] P.-M. Dupuy and J. E. Viñuales (eds.), *Harnessing Foreign Investment to Promote Environmental Protection: Incentives and Safeguards* (Cambridge University Press, forthcoming).

[3] The study takes into account, to the best of my knowledge, developments until 1 December 2011.

instruments that have been developed to create synergies between foreign investment and environmental protection as well as to establish some 'soft' safeguards against the potential risks entailed by the operations of multinational companies abroad. These chapters are of rather descriptive nature, because their contents and implications will be analysed in detail in the aforementioned companion volume. The fifth chapter of Part I begins the technical analysis of the relations between environmental and investment law by focusing on a variety of issues (jurisdiction, applicable law, procedure, damages) raised by the incorporation of environmental considerations into investment proceedings.[4]

Part II takes the perspective of an environmental lawyer. It looks at the impact of different substantive areas of international environmental law on foreign investment schemes. In other terms, it assesses the consistency of foreign investment transactions – and their international legal protection – with the international legal framework for the protection of the environment. Chapter 6 analyses the available legal techniques that can be used to determine normative priority in case of conflicts between two norms of international law (environmental law vs. investment law). As such, it sets the scene for the analysis of such 'normative conflicts' in the four areas of substantive environmental regulation where they have arisen so far or where they are most likely to arise in the future: the regulation of freshwater resources (Chapter 7); the protection of biological and cultural diversity (Chapter 8); the regulation of dangerous substances and activities (Chapter 9); and climate change regulation (Chapter 10). To clarify the approach followed in these chapters, three additional observations appear necessary. First, each chapter begins with an analysis of collision points, which is intended to: (i) identify those obligations arising from international environmental law with the highest impact (actual or potential) on foreign investment law; and (ii) serve as a sort of primer of the relevant area of international environmental law for readers unfamiliar with it. The impact of international environmental law is analysed from the traditional inter-State perspective and from that of 'human rights approaches' to environmental protection. Second, each chapter follows with an analysis of the relevant international jurisprudence. This

---

[4] Chapter 5, as well as a few other sections of this book, draw upon J. E. Viñuales, 'Foreign Investment and the Environmental in International Law: An Ambiguous Relationship' (2009) 80 *British Yearbook of International Law* 244.

discussion draws on the case-law of investment tribunals as well as on that of several adjudicatory and quasi-adjudicatory bodies, including the International Court of Justice, the European Court of Human Rights, the Inter-American Court of Human Rights, the Inter-American Commission on Human Rights, the African Commission on Human and Peoples' Rights, the United Nations Human Rights Committee, the International Tribunal for the Law of the Sea, the Court of Justice of the European Union, the WTO Dispute Settlement Body, the World Bank's Inspection Panel and Compliance Advisor/Ombudsman, the World Heritage Committee or the Compliance Committee of the Aarhus Convention. This broader body of case-law has received little attention from investment lawyers, despite its significance for the analysis of frictions between investment and non-investment obligations. Third, each chapter concludes with a discussion of certain theoretical and practical problems underlying the understanding of normative conflicts, particularly as regards the link between domestic environmental measures and (broad) international environmental obligations.

Part III adopts the perspective of an investment lawyer and looks at the impact of foreign investment law on domestic environmental measures. It begins with a chapter setting out the main techniques available to solve conflicts between norms stemming from different legal orders (Chapter 11) and then analyses the consistency of domestic environmental measures *tour à tour* with expropriation clauses (Chapter 12), non-discrimination standards (Chapter 13) and stability/ due process commitments (Chapter 14). Each chapter starts with a concise overview of the applicable investment disciplines – again, both for conceptual purposes and as a primer for unfamiliar readers – and then analyses the main legal issues raised by the adoption of domestic environmental measures in the light of the relevant case-law. The last chapter (Chapter 15) discusses three cross-cutting 'defence arguments' based on environmental considerations, namely the police powers doctrine, the margin of appreciation doctrine and emergency/ necessity clauses.

From a theoretical perspective, Parts II and III can be seen as two alternative 'front lines' where the struggle for the integration of international environmental law and international investment law is taking place. The most wide-ranging – but perhaps also the most difficult – struggle is the one described in Part II. It requires a change of mindset, particularly as regards the impact of international environmental norms and their reception within specialised investment fora. A fuller understanding of the impact of international environmental norms requires the clarification of the link between such norms and domestic environmental measures. If such link were clear, collisions between environmental measures and investment disciplines would take the form of normative conflicts, which, in turn, would call for a different legal treatment by investment tribunals than that accorded to mere legitimacy conflicts. As long as the link remains unclear, environmental considerations will have to evolve within the bounds set by investment disciplines. Part III analyses these bounds in detail and shows that the space granted to environmental considerations is expanding. As such, the struggle described in Part III can to some extent be seen as an intermediate stage in the integration process, particularly because some of the additional space carved out in investment disciplines for environmental considerations responds to the informal influence of international environmental law. This informal impact will be highlighted, as relevant, in the analysis conducted in Part III.

Overall, the picture that emerges from this book is one where environmental considerations are increasingly present in investment disputes. From mutual ignorance or disinterest, to basic mutual acknowledgment, to growing acceptance and perhaps even integration at some point in the future, the relationship between foreign investment and environmental protection is evolving. This book is an attempt to conceptualise this evolution from the stand-point of international law.

Part I

Setting the framework

1   Changing winds – three signs

This opening chapter maps the contours of the changing relationship between environmental and investment law. It focuses on three indicators or 'signs'. First, international negotiations clearly suggest that the private sector – a proxy for foreign investment – has a growing role in the overall strategy to protect the environment. From a primary focus on environmental protection, to one on sustainable (economic and social) development, to the current shift towards a green economy, the role of the private sector in global environmental governance has moved from marginal to central (Section 1.1). Second, the changing perception of foreign investment in environmental treaties is to some extent mirrored by the increasing attention paid to environmental considerations in investment treaties (Section 1.2). Third, the growing number of investment disputes with environmental components provides still another signal of a changing relationship with important practical consequences (Section 1.3).

1.1   The first sign – conceptual evolution

Since its modern inception in the late 1960s, international environmental regulation has been confronted with the need to integrate considerations of growth and development. In its early days in the nineteenth century and through most of the twentieth century, international environmental regulation was piecemeal, dealing only with some specific issues such as shared water resources,[1] transboundary damages[2] or the

---

[1] See, e.g., *Lac Lanoux (Spain v. France)*, Award (16 November 1957), RIAA, vol. 12 (1957), 281–317.
[2] See, e.g., *Trail Smelter (United States of America v. Canada)*, Awards (16 April 1938 and 11 March 1941), RIAA, vol. 3 (1941), 1905–82.

management of useful living resources[3] (sealing,[4] whaling,[5] etc.). The underlying rationale of these early examples of what today would be seen as environmental regulation was the orderly exploitation of a given natural resource. Economic considerations clearly prevailed over environmental protection.

This view changed considerably over the 1960s and the beginning of the 1970s. The environmental concerns voiced in a number of influential writings,[6] punctuated by several events (e.g., the grounding of the Liberian tanker, *Torrey Canyon*, or the mercury poisoning of the Minamata population in Japan), made the message carried by the emerging environmental movement increasingly powerful. At the time, international environmental law was in its infancy and the main goal was to identify those environmental issues which required action.[7] The primary concerns of these early efforts were 'first generation' environmental issues, such as combating pollution[8] or conserving endangered species and fragile habitats.[9] Perhaps because of the sense of alert and urgency in protecting the environment prevailing at the time, the results of the United Nations Conference on the Human Environment

---

[3] See, e.g., Convention for the Protection of Birds useful to Agriculture, 19 March 1902, B7 902:22.

[4] See, e.g., Convention between the United States, Great Britain, Japan and Russia providing for the Preservation and Protection of the Fur Seals, 7 July 1911, 37 Stat. 1542.

[5] See, e.g., International Convention for the Regulation of Whaling with Schedule of Whaling Regulations, 2 December 1946, 161 UNTS 361.

[6] See R. Carson, *Silent Spring* (Boston, MA: Houghton Mifflin, 1962); K. E. Boulding, 'The Economics of the Coming Spaceship Earth', in H. Jarrett (ed.), *Environmental Quality in a Growing Economy* (Baltimore, MD: John Hopkins University Press, 1966) 3; M. Nicholson, *The Environmental Revolution: A Guide for the New Masters of the World* (London: Hodder & Stoughton, 1969); B. Commoner, *The Closing Circle: Nature, Man, and Technology* (New York, NY: Alfred Knopf, 1971); Donella H. Meadows, Dennis L. Meadows, J. Randers and W. W. Berens, *The Limits to Growth: A Report for the Club of Rome's Project on the Predicament of Mankind* (New York, NY: Universe Books, 1972).

[7] Report of the United Nations Conference on the Human Environment, UN GAOR, 27th Sess, 21st plen. mtg UN Doc. A/CONF.48/14/Rev. 1 (1973), pp. 2–7.

[8] See, e.g., Convention for the Prevention of Marine Pollution by Dumping of Wastes and Other Matter, 29 December 1972, as modified by the Protocol of 7 November 1996, 1046 UNTS 120; International Convention for the Prevention of Pollution from Ships, 17 February 1973, as modified by the Protocol of 1978 relating thereto, 17 February 1978, UNTS 1340 I-22484.

[9] See, e.g., Convention on Wetlands of International Importance especially as Waterfowl Habitat, 2 February 1971, 996 UNTS 245; Convention concerning the Protection of the World Cultural and Natural Heritage, 16 November 1972, 1037 UNTS 151; Convention on International Trade in Endangered Species of Wild Fauna and Flora, 3 March 1973, 983 UNTS 243.

('Stockholm Conference') emphasised environmental protection as the priority, even to the potential detriment of economic development. The tension between these two terms has shaped the evolution of international environmental law ever since.

This became clear twenty years later at the 1992 Rio Conference on Environment and Development (the 'Earth Summit'). At Rio, the focus was on comprehensive normative development (illustrated by the adoption of some major conventions[10]) and on the need to reconcile environmental protection with economic development, which resulted in the affirmation of the concept of sustainable development.[11] This concept offered a consensual solution to the trade-off between protecting the environment and promoting growth and development.[12] Yet, the 'environment–development equation' proved to be a resilient beast, lurking in the shadows of most major environmental negotiations. In those cases where conflicts between the two terms of the equation were singled out, the attention tended to focus mostly on trade restrictions based on environmental considerations[13] rather than on the potential conflicts between the protection of foreign investment and that of the environment. However, the unifying concept of sustainable development is no longer perceived as a sufficient tool to manage potential conflicts between economic and environmental

---

[10] At this time, two major treaties were adopted, namely the United Nations Framework Convention on Climate Change, 9 May 1992, 31 ILM 849, and the Convention on Biological Diversity, 5 June 1992, 1760 UNTS 79, in addition to other important instruments. Following the Rio Conference two other important treaties were adopted, namely the United Nations Convention to Combat Desertification in those Countries Experiencing Serious Drought and/or Desertification, Particularly in Africa, 17 June 1994, UN Doc. A/AC.241/15/Rev. 7 (1994), 33 ILM 1328 and the Agreement for the Implementation of the Provisions of the United Nations Conventions on the Law of the Sea of 10 December 1982 Relating to the Conservation and Management of Straddling Fish Stocks and Highly Migratory Fish Stocks, 4 August 1995, S. Treaty Doc. No. 104–24, 2167 UNTS 88.

[11] On the origins of this concept, see International Union for Conservation of Nature, United Nations Environment Programme and World Wildlife Fund, *World Conservation Strategy. Living Resource Conservation for Sustainable Development*, 1980; Report of the World Commission on Environment and Development: Our Common Future, UN Doc. A/42/427, Annex, 4 August 1987 ('Our Common Future').

[12] See, generally, D. B. Magraw and L. D. Hawke, 'Sustainable Development', in D. Bodansky, J. Brunnée and E. Hey (eds.), *The Oxford Handbook of International Environmental Law* (Oxford University Press 2007), p. 613.

[13] See, e.g., D. Bodansky and J. C. Lawrence, 'Trade and Environment', in D. Bethlehem, D. McRae, R. Deufeld and I. van Damme (eds.), *The Oxford Handbook of International Trade Law* (Oxford University Press, 2009), pp. 505 ff.

considerations. As one commentator has noted, sustainable development is a multilevel concept, with different meanings at different
levels.[14] At a superficial level, sustainable development can be defined,
along the lines of the well-known Brundtland Report, as development
that meets the needs of the present without compromising the needs of
future generations.[15] Such a broad definition is admittedly helpful in
gathering consensus from different constituencies in an international
negotiation. But it provides little guidance, if any, on how the two
terms of the environment–development equation should be reconciled
in case of conflict.[16]

A more recent strategy to reconcile these two terms has been to factor
in the role of the private sector in protecting the environment. At the
2002 Johannesburg Conference, also known as the World Summit on
Sustainable Development ('WSSD'), this role was seen as one of the keys
for the implementation of the framework adopted in the previous
decade, particularly in connection with issues relating to water, energy,
health, agriculture and biodiversity, the so-called WEHAB agenda.[17] The
legal instruments to 'unleash' the private sector included, *inter alia*,
public–private partnerships (PPPs),[18] environmental project finance
(e.g., GEF-leveraged finance)[19] and market mechanisms (e.g., the flexible

---

[14] See A. Dobson, *Fairness and Futurity: Essays on Environmental Sustainability and Social Justice*
(Oxford University Press 1999), pp. 23ff.

[15] Our Common Future, above n. 11, para. 1.

[16] See, e.g., *Gabčíkovo-Nagymaros Project (Hungary v. Slovakia)*, ICJ Reports 1997, 7
('*Gabčíkovo-Nagymaros*'), paras. 140–1 (referring to the need for the parties to find an
'agreed solution'); *Iron Rhine ('IJzeren Rijn') Railway Arbitration (Belgium v. Netherlands)*,
RIAA, vol. 27 (2005) 25 ('*Iron Rhine Arbitration*'), paras. 59–60 (noting that '[t]he mere
invocation of such matters [the principle of sustainable development] does not, of
course, provide the answers in this arbitration to what may or may not be done,
where, by whom and at whose costs'); *Pulp Mills in the River Uruguay (Argentina
v. Uruguay)*, Judgment (20 April 2010), General List No. 135 ('*Pulp Mills* case'),
paras. 75–7 (referring to the duty of co-operation) and para. 177 (stating that
sustainable development requires a balance between the use of the waters and the
protection of rivers).

[17] N. Schrijver, 'The Evolution of Sustainable Development in International Law: Inception,
Meaning and Status', in *Recueil de cours de l'Acadamie de droit international*, vol. 329, (2008),
p. 93.

[18] C. Streck, 'The World Summit on Sustainable Development: Partnerships as New Tools
in Environmental Governance' (2002) 13 *Yearbook of International Environmental Law*
63, 67.

[19] See Instrument for the Establishment of the Restructured Global Environmental Facility
(October 2011), available at: www.thegef.org/gef/instrument.

mechanisms created by the Kyoto Protocol[20] or an array of 'payments for ecosystem services' or 'PES' schemes[21]).

This strategy seems now to be taking a new turn. In December 2009, the UN General Assembly adopted a resolution calling for the organisation of another world environmental summit in 2012.[22] This conference, the Earth Summit 2012 (informally referred to as 'Rio plus 20'), is expected to address two main 'themes' identified by the enabling resolution, namely the move to a 'green economy' and the 'institutional framework' for sustainable development.[23] The concept of a green economy goes beyond the traditional understanding of sustainable development. States are no longer urged to respect the environment while doing 'as well' in economic terms; they are now urged to build their economic models on environmental considerations in order to do 'better' in economic terms. Being 'green' is no longer presented as a matter of responsibility, but as one of profitability and competitiveness in the economy of the future. The green economy concept is thus premised on the idea that it is not sufficient to 'integrate' or 'mainstream' environmental considerations into economic activities. More radically, a 'new economic paradigm' must be designed to fit the new environmental imperatives.[24] These imperatives will, according to the green economy discourse, dictate the rules of the future marketplace, creating new business opportunities and rendering previous ones obsolete. For large sectors of the economy, it will not be simply a matter of adapting to new conditions but rather one of abandoning certain forms of production or lines of business increasingly at odds with environmental trends, in order to pursue new and perhaps entirely different opportunities. In this context, foreign investment in sectors with a strategic importance for environmental protection, such as energy and water efficiency, waste treatment, renewable energies and the like, is a key component of the move towards a green economy.[25] Yet, the expected renewal of production processes is unlikely to go unchallenged. In fact,

---

[20] Kyoto Protocol to the United Nations Framework Convention on Climate Change, Kyoto, 11 December 1997, 2303 UNTS 148 ('Kyoto Protocol'), Articles 6, 12 and 17.

[21] Forest Trends, The Katoomba Group and United Nations Environment Programme, *Payments for Ecosystem Services. Getting Started: A Primer* (Nairobi: UNON/Publishing Services Section, 2008).

[22] UN Doc. A/RES/64/236.   [23] *Ibid.*, para. 20(a).

[24] United Nations Environment Programme, *Towards a Green Economy: Pathways to Sustainable Development and Poverty Eradication* (UNEP, 2011), p. 14.

[25] *Ibid.*, p. 14 (highlighting a 'gross misallocation of capital' because relatively little capital has been invested in 'renewable energy, energy efficiency, public transportation,

the transition will likely be painful and entail a considerable amount of legal battle. As discussed next, to clarify the legal situation of both States and investors, environmental considerations are being increasingly introduced in the wording of investment and free trade agreements.

1.2   The second sign – integrating the environment into investment treaties

In the last two decades the space devoted to environmental considerations in both investment and free trade agreements ('IIAs') has significantly expanded. According to a report published by the Organisation for Economic Co-operation and Development ('OECD') in 2011 and covering 1,623 IIAs (approximately 50 per cent of existing IIAs) only 8.2 per cent of IIAs analysed include express references to environmental concerns.[26] However, if a time dimension is added, the overall picture changes quite drastically. Indeed, the OECD Report shows that, since the mid 1990s 'the proportion of newly concluded IIAs that contain environmental language began to increase moderately, and, from about 2002 onwards, steeply ... reaching a peak in 2008, when 89% of newly concluded treaties contain[ed] reference to environmental concerns'.[27] This result must be nuanced to the extent that, as noted by the Report, 'the treaty sample in recent years is not complete because of lags in including treaties in online databases'.[28] Yet, the overall trend seems clear. The stark contrast between earlier IIAs and those IIAs concluded in the last decade confirms the hypothesis that the interactions between environmental and investment law are increasing. Mirroring to some extent the growing role of foreign investment within global environmental governance, some room is also being carved out in IIAs for environmental considerations. There are important variations according to several criteria. For present purposes, it seems useful to focus on two of them: (i) variations according to countries; and (ii) types of environmental clauses.

---

sustainable agriculture, ecosystem and biodiversity protection, and land and water conservation').
[26] K. Gordon and J. Pohl, 'Environmental Concerns in International Investment Agreements: A Survey' (2011) OECD Working Papers on International Investment No. 2011/1 ('OECD Report'), p. 8.
[27] *Ibid.*, p. 8.   [28] *Ibid.*, p. 7.

Regarding the first criterion, the OECD Report shows wide variations in treaty practice from one country to another. Whereas countries such as Egypt, Germany or the United Kingdom have a very low propensity to include environmental language in their IIAs,[29] other countries, such as Canada, New Zealand, Japan, the United States or Finland, have a much higher propensity to do so.[30] There are also significant differences among IIAs concluded between OECD countries, IIAs concluded between non-OECD countries, and IIAs concluded between an OECD and a non-OECD country. The percentage of IIAs including environmental language in this last group is significantly higher (9.5 per cent) than in the first (6 per cent) and second (3.4 per cent) groups. These results can be contrasted with the findings of a report commissioned by the UN Special Representative for Human Rights and Business on the use of stabilisation clauses in investment contracts.[31] According to the UN Report, contracts between investors and non-OECD countries are more likely to include more protective stabilisation clauses than contracts with OECD countries.[32] Thus, whereas foreign investors in non-OECD countries are receiving broader contractual guarantees in connection with the stability of the legal framework (including environmental and health regulations), the IIAs concluded by OECD countries with some of these non-OECD countries give these latter a larger room for manoeuvre with respect to environmental regulation. A possible explanation of this contrast is that the very fact that IIAs are more environmentally permissive may be pushing investors to seek stronger contractual protections. However, this explanation is based on the assumption that the environmental language included in IIAs between OECD and non-OECD countries is indeed more permissive. To see whether this is the case, it is necessary to clarify the type of environmental provisions included in IIAs.

According to the OECD Report, there are seven categories of recurring environmental provisions in IIAs:

---

[29] For each of these countries, less than 1 per cent of the IIAs include environmental language. See *ibid.*, p. 9.

[30] Approximately 83 per cent of Canada's IIAs contain environmental language. The percentages for other countries are: New Zealand (75 per cent), Japan (61 per cent), United States (34 per cent), Finland (26 per cent), *ibid.*, p. 9.

[31] A. Shemberg, *Stabilization Clauses and Human Rights: A Research Project Conducted for IFC and the United Nations Special Representative to the Secretary General on Business and Human Rights*, 11 March 2008 ('UN Report'), available at: www.ifc.org (accessed on 4 January 2012).

[32] *Ibid.*, p. 26.

[1] General language in preambles that mentions environmental concerns and establishes protection of the environment as a concern of the parties to the treaty . . .

[2] Reserving policy space for environmental regulation . . .

[3] Reserving policy space for environmental regulation for more specific, limited subject matters (performance requirements and national treatment) . . .

[4] [P]rovisions that clarify the understanding of the parties that non-discriminatory environmental regulation does not constitute 'indirect expropriation' . . .

[5] [P]rovisions that discourage the loosening of environmental regulation for the purpose of attracting investment . . .

[6] [P]rovisions related to the recourse to environmental experts by arbitration tribunals . . .

[7] [P]rovisions that encourage strengthening of environmental regulation and cooperation[33]

The frequency of these provisions varies from one country to another and over time. The most common category (82 (62 per cent) of the 133 IIAs including environmental language) is the general reservation of policy space for environmental regulation (category 2), which has, indeed, a potentially permissive effect. Based on the information provided in Annex 2 of the OECD Report, the share of IIAs between OECD and non-OECD countries reserving environmental regulatory space is slightly higher (64 per cent).[34] More specific (categories 3 and 4) and more progressive (category 7) provisions are far rarer (14 per cent for category 3; 9 per cent for category 4; and 18 per cent for category 7). Within the sub-set on IIAs between OECD and non-OECD countries, these percentages are, again, slightly higher (15 per cent for category 3; 11 per cent for category 4; and 19 per cent for category 7). The legal significance of these provisions will be discussed in some detail in Chapters 6 and 11. Overall, however, these results suggest that IIAs are increasingly sensitive to environmental considerations, but that the current approach tends to privilege broad and to some extent uncertain clauses. This may explain – together with variables such as political risk, the level of administrative efficiency or differences in bargaining power – why investment contracts with non-OECD countries include more protective clauses. But the very fact that both States and investors are increasingly referring to environmental considerations in treaty and contract clauses

---

[33] OECD Report, above n. 26, 11 (the numbering has been added and italics omitted).
[34] My estimation based on the information in *ibid.*, Annex 2.

provides a clear indication that such considerations are playing a grow-ing role within the realm of foreign investment law. As discussed next, this conclusion is further supported by the evolution of the investment case-law.

1.3   The third sign – the environment breaks into investment disputes

Trends in the investment case-law are difficult to measure precisely. One reason for this is that a significant share of investment disputes is not public and, even when some information about confidential disputes is disclosed to the public, it is often insufficient to determine the nature of the dispute. Another reason is that, irrespective of the information available, it is particularly challenging to qualify a dispute as 'environmental' or 'environment-related'. As will be discussed in Part II, international environmental law regulates a wide range of questions, and the 'environmental' nature of such questions or even of some of the regulations applicable to them is sometimes debatable.

Yet, this is not to say that no conclusions can be derived from the information available as to the role of environmental considerations in investment disputes over the years. There is indeed some evidence that the number of investment disputes with environmental components has increased in the last two decades. By 'environmental components' I refer to disputes that arise from the operations of investors (i) in environ-mental markets (e.g., land-filling, waste treatment, garbage collection, pesticides/chemicals, energy efficiency, emissions reduction, biodiver-sity compensation, etc.) and/or (ii) in other activities, where their impact on the environment or on certain minorities is part of the dispute (e.g., tourism, extractive industries, pesticides/chemicals, water extrac-tion or distribution) and/or (iii) where the application of domestic or international environmental law is at stake.

The development of the investment case-law suggests that invest-ment disputes with environmental components are becoming more frequent. The overwhelming majority of such disputes arose in the last two decades. I have been able to locate only one investment dispute decided before 1990[35] and three others decided during

---

[35] *International Bank of Washington v. OPIC* (1972) 11 ILM 1216 (dispute concerning an alleged indirect expropriation as a result of forestry regulation).

the 1990s.[36] Except for these cases, all other disputes were decided after 2000. Assuming an average of eight to ten years between the emergence of the dispute and its final outcome, the case-law suggests that most environment-related investment disputes arose from the 1990s onwards. This increase seems consistent with the development of international environmental law and could potentially be linked to the environmental stimulus, both at the national and the international levels, given by the 1992 Earth Summit. Overall, in the period from 2000 until December 2011, twenty-four investment disputes with environmental components were decided by an arbitral tribunal or solved in another manner (settlement or discontinuance).[37] The analysis shows some variation from year to year, with an increase in the last two years, as displayed below:[38]

Environment-related disputes decided in 2000	Environmental component(s)
Compañía del Desarrollo de Santa Elena SA v. Republic of Costa Rica, ICSID Case No. ARB/96/1, Award (17 February 2000)	Dispute concerning the expropriation of land to establish a natural preserve
Metalclad Corporation v. United Mexican States, ICSID Case No. ARB(AF)/97/1, Award (25 August 2000)	Dispute concerning the refusal of a permit to build a landfill and the subsequent reclassification of the land as an ecological preserve
S. D. Myers Inc. v. Canada, NAFTA (UNCITRAL), Partial Award (13 November 2000)	Dispute concerning trade measures interfering with the investor's waste treatment activities

---

[36] *Southern Pacific Properties (Middle East) Limited (SPP) v. Arab Republic of Egypt*, ICSID Case No. ARB/84/3, Award (20 May 1992) (dispute concerning the cancellation of a tourism concession affecting a UNESCO protected site); *Ethyl Corporation v. Government of Canada*, NAFTA (UNCITRAL), Preliminary Award on Jurisdiction (24 June 1998) (dispute concerning a Canadian environmental regulation banning trade in a gasoline additive); *Robert Azinian, Kenneth Davitian and Ellen Baca v. United Mexican States*, ICSID Case No. ARB (AF)/97/2, Award (1 November 1999) (dispute concerning the cancellation of a concession relating to waste collection and disposal).

[37] A broader definition of environmental components would result in the inclusion of other disputes (e.g., water-distribution cases such as *Aguas del Tunari SA v. Republic of Bolivia*, ICSID Case No. ARB/02/3, Decision on Objections to Jurisdiction (21 October 2005) or *Biwater Gauff (Tanz.) Ltd v. United Republic of Tanzania*, ICSID Case No. ARB/05/22, Award (24 July 2008)). Also, if cases that did not proceed to the merits were excluded (e.g., *Empresa Lucchetti SA and Lucchetti Peru SA v. Republic of Peru* ICSID Case No. ARB/03/4, Award (7 February 2005) or *Canadian Cattlemen for Fair Trade v. United States of America*, NAFTA (UNCITRAL) Award on Jurisdiction (28 January 2008) the set would be smaller.

[38] Years where no environment-related dispute was decided are not included in the chart.

Emilio Agustín Maffezini v. *Kingdom of Spain*, ICSID Case No. ARB/97/7, Award (13 November 2000)

Dispute concerning a chemical plant, the construction of which started before completion of an environmental impact assessment

Environment-related disputes decided in 2003

Técnicas Medioambientales Tecmed SA v. *United Mexican States*, ICSID Case No. ARB(AF)/00/2, Award (29 May 2003)

Environmental component(s)

Dispute concerning the non-renewal of the operational permit of a waste treatment facility.

Environment-related disputes decided in 2004

Waste Management Inc. v. *United Mexican States*, ICSID Case No. ARB(AF)/00/3, Award (30 April 2004)

Environmental component(s)

Dispute concerning the operation of a landfill

MTD Equity Sdn Bhd and MTD Chile SA v. *Republic of Chile*, ICSID Case No. ARB/01/7, Award (25 May 2004)

Dispute concerning the refusal of a permit based on local zoning regulations

Environment-related disputes decided in 2005

Empresa Lucchetti SA and Lucchetti Peru SA v. *Republic of Peru*, ICSID Case No. ARB/03/4, Award (7 February 2005)

Environmental component(s)

Dispute concerning the annulment of permits necessary for the operation of a food factory on the basis of environmental reasons

Methanex Corporation v. *United States of America*, NAFTA (UNCITRAL), Award (3 August 2005)

Dispute concerning the adoption of an environmental regulation indirectly banning the product of the investor

Environment-related disputes decided in 2007

Bayview Irrigation District et al. v. *United Mexican States*, ICSID Case No. ARB(AF)/05/1, Award (19 June 2007)

Environmental component(s)

Dispute concerning water rights arising from a treaty between the United States and Mexico

Parkerings-Compagniet AS v. *Republic of Lithuania*, ICSID Case No. ARB/05/8, Award (11 September 2007)

Dispute concerning the construction of a parking lot affecting a UNESCO protected site

Environment-related disputes decided in 2008

Canadian Cattlemen for Fair Trade v. *United States of America*, NAFTA (UNCITRAL), Award on Jurisdiction (28 January 2008)

Environmental component(s)

Dispute concerning certain bans and other restrictions on the imports of Canadian cattle under the US Animal Health Protection Act

Plama Consortium Ltd v. *Republic of Bulgaria*, ICSID Case No. ARB/03/24, Award (27 August 2008)	Dispute concerning a change in the domestic environmental laws rendering the investor liable for environmental remediation

Environment-related disputes decided in 2009	**Environmental component(s)**
Glamis Gold Ltd v. *United States of America*, NAFTA (UNCITRAL), Award (16 May 2009)	Dispute concerning delays and legislative/regulatory action, based on considerations of environmental and cultural protection, that thwarted the investor's mining operations

Environment-related disputes decided in 2010	**Environmental component(s)**
Georg Nepolsky v. *The Czech Republic*, UNCITRAL, Award (February 2010)	Dispute concerning a water extraction concession
Suez, Sociedad General de Aguas de Barcelona SA and InterAguas Servicios Integrales del Agua SA v. *The Argentine Republic*, ICSID Case No. ARB/03/17, Decision on Liability (31 July 2010)	Dispute concerning a water distribution concession with consequences for the right to water
Suez, Sociedad General de Aguas de Barcelona, SA and Vivendi Universal SA v. *The Argentine Republic*, ICSID Case No. ARB/03/19, Decision on Liability (31 July 2010)	Dispute concerning a water distribution concession with consequences for the right to water
Chemtura Corporation (formerly Crompton Corporation) v. *Government of Canada*, UNCITRAL, Award (2 August 2010)	Dispute concerning a phase-out of certain pesticides on health/environmental grounds
Piero Foresti, Laura de Carli and others v. *Republic of South Africa*, ICSID Case No. ARB(AF)/07/1, Award (4 August 2010)	Dispute concerning the effects of post-apartheid redistribution policies based on economic, social and cultural rights

Environment-related disputes decided in 2011	**Environmental component(s)**
Grand River Enterprises Six Nations Ltd et al. v. *United States of America*, NAFTA (UNCITRAL), Award (12 January 2011)	Dispute concerning alleged special economic rights held by indigenous peoples
Vattenfall AB, Vattenfal Europe AG, Vattenfall Europe Generation AG v. *Federal Republic of Germany*, ICSID Case No. ARB/09/6, Award (11 March 2011)	Dispute concerning the delays and the refusal of operational and water permits for the operation of a coal-fired electricity generation plant

Commerce Group Corp and San Sebastian Gold Mines Inc. v. *Republic of El Salvador*, ICSID Case No ARB/09/17, Award (14 March 2011)	Dispute concerning the refusal of an environmental permit to conduct gold mining operations
Dow Agrosciences LLC v. *Government of Canada*, NAFTA (UNCITRAL), (settled on 25 May 2011)	Dispute concerning a phase-out of a pesticide on health/environmental grounds
Vito G. Gallo v. *Government of Canada*, NAFTA (UNCITRAL), Award (15 September 2011)	Dispute concerning the cancellation of permits to convert an abandoned mine into a landfill

If pending disputes are taken into account, the evolution in the last two years seems to reflect the beginning of a trend towards a steep increase in the number of investment disputes with environmental components:

Environment-related disputes pending (as of 1 December 2011)	Environmental component(s)
Marion Unglaube v. *Republic of Costa Rica*, ICSID Case No. ARB/08/1	Dispute concerning the creation of a natural preserve in foreign-owned lands
Reinhard Unglaube v. *Republic of Costa Rica*, ICSID Case No. ARB/09/20	Dispute concerning the creation of a natural preserve in foreign-owned lands
Burlington Resources Inc. and others v. *Republic of Ecuador and Empresa Estatal Petróleos del Ecuador (PetroEcuador)*, ICSID Case No. ARB/08/5	Dispute concerning, *inter alia*, indigenous peoples' opposition to the investor's oil extraction activities as a result of their environmental/social consequences
Pac Rim Cayman LLC v. *Republic of El Salvador*, ICSID Case No. ARB/09/12	Dispute concerning the refusal of an environmental permit necessary to conduct gold mining operations
William Ralph Clayton, William Richard Clayton, Douglas Clayton, Daniel Clayton and Bilcon of Delaware Inc. v. *Government of Canada*, NAFTA (UNCITRAL)	Dispute concerning an allegedly flawed environmental assessment of a basalt quarry and marine terminal project
Abengoa SA y COFIDES SA v. *United Mexican States*, ICSID Case No. ARB(AF)/09/2	Dispute concerning the refusal of a construction permit for a waste treatment facility

Chevron Corporation and Texaco Petroleum Company v. *Republic of Ecuador*, PCA Case No. 2009–23 (UNCITRAL)	Dispute concerning the treatment by Ecuadorian courts of an environmental liability claim for damage caused by Texaco during its oil extraction operations
Renco Group Inc. v. *Republic of Peru*, Notice of Intent to Commence Arbitration, 29 December 2010	Dispute relating to the investor's environmental liability arising from the acquisition of a metallurgical plant
Niko Resources (Bangladesh) Ltd v. *People's Republic of Bangladesh, Bangladesh Petroleum Exploration and Production Company Limited ('Bapex') and Bangladesh Oil Gas and Mineral Corporation ('Petrobangla')*, ICSID Cases No. ARB/10/11 and ARB/10/18	Dispute relating to governmental action linked to the investor's environmental liability for two gas blow-outs
Naftrac Ltd v. *National Environmental Investment Agency (Ukraine)*, PCA Arbitration (Optional Environmental Rules)	Dispute concerning a Kyoto joint implementation project
Accession Eastern Europe Capital AB and Mezzanine Management Sweden AB v. *Republic of Bulgaria*, ICSID Case No. ARB/11/3	Dispute concerning the cancellation of waste-collection and street-cleaning contracts

In addition, at the time of writing, a number of other investment claims with environmental components were reportedly being considered by investors,[39] which further supports the idea of a trend towards an increase in this type of disputes.

---

[39] See *Peter A. Allard* v. *Government of Barbados*, Notice of Dispute (8 September 2009), available at: graemehall.com/legal/papers/BIT-Complaint.pdf (status unknown); J. Hepburn, 'Renewable Energy Arbitration Claims on Horizon, but States take Differing Approaches to Public Disclosure' (7 September 2011) (discussing disputes concerning Canada, the Czech Republic and Spain for changes in incentives for the production of renewable energy); G. Lopez and L.-E. Peterson, 'Investor in Waste Management Project in Mexico puts Government on Notice of Treaty Breaches' (7 September 2011)(discussing a notice of dispute filed by an investor, Inter-Nexus, alleging the misallocation by Mexican authorities of funds that, according to the budget, were earmarked for the investor's landfill); J. Hepburn, 'Swedish Energy Company Reportedly Planning New ICSID Arbitration over German Nuclear Phase-out' (2 November 2011). The three articles are available at: www.iareporter.com (accessed on 4 January 2012).

The evolution of the investment case-law also shows some variation across countries. Most claims were brought against Latin American countries (Argentina, Chile, Costa Rica, El Salvador, Mexico and Peru) in connection with a variety of environmental issues. Among these, Mexico is the most frequent respondent, with five cases (four concerning waste disposal/treatment and the other water rights). The United States and Canada have also been respondents in several cases (the four cases against the United States concern chemical regulation, animal safety and minority rights and the five cases against Canada concern waste and chemical regulation). Most (but not all) of the cases brought against Mexico, Canada and the United States are based on the provisions of the NAFTA.[40] Western European countries (Germany and Spain) have been respondents in two cases and Eastern European countries (Bulgaria, the Czech Republic and Lithuania) in four. African countries (Egypt and South Africa) have been respondents in two cases.

Finally, the types of questions arising in the case-law seem no longer limited to first generation environmental issues, such as waste management, pollution or the protection of species/habitats, but they increasingly include second generation issues (e.g., climate change) arising from more recent environmental regulatory developments. By way of illustration, according to the information publicly available, the dispute brought by Naftrac against the Ukraine concerns a project undertaken under the joint implementation mechanism established by Article 6 of the Kyoto Protocol.[41] In a similar vein, some of the claims being considered by investors against Canada, Spain and the Czech Republic concern massive investments in the production of electricity from renewable sources, induced by the development of clean energy policies in the last decade. The investment case-law thus seems to reflect a growing sensitivity to the development of international and domestic environmental law, thereby supporting the hypothesis that the relationship between environmental and investment law is evolving.

---

[40] North American Free Trade Agreement, 17 December 1992, 32 ILM 296.
[41] Kyoto Protocol, above n. 20.

2 Conceptualising interactions

The evolving relationship between foreign investment and environmental protection has two dimensions, a synergistic one and a conflicting one. This chapter begins with some illustrations of this dual nature, as it arises in practice (Section 2.1), and then sets out the analytical framework that will be applied in the remainder of this book. After a brief discussion of synergies (Section 2.2), it analyses the two types of conflicts that may arise between environmental and investment law (Section 2.3) as well as the relevant regulatory levels and substantive areas (Section 2.4).

2.1 Foreign investment and the environment

Despite the many attempts at reconciling environmental protection with growth/development, neither the sustainable development concept nor the green economy concept offer any guarantee that profitability and sustainability will go hand in hand in the future. Specifically, one must not overlook the fact that foreign investment in developing countries[1] may constitute both a vector of sustainable development, most notably through financial and technology transfers, and a threat to the environment, when its production processes and methods are risky or harmful. In practice, both dimensions are often combined.

One interesting illustration of this latter point is offered by the so-called race-to-the-bottom argument. The basic idea is that States wishing to attract foreign investment to further their development will

---

[1] In 2009, for the first time ever, emerging markets received more inflows of foreign direct investment than developed countries. See L. Kekic, 'The Global Economic Crisis and FDI Flows to Emerging Markets' (October 2009) *Columbia FDI Perspectives* No. 15.

have an incentive to lower their environmental protection standards.[2] In such a situation, other States may be led to do the same in order to avoid a competitive disadvantage, with a resulting overall decline of environmental protection. This would be a problem for both developed and developing countries, although for different reasons. Whereas the former fear the delocalisation of firms driven by the adoption of relatively less costly environmental regulations abroad, the latter have expressed concern over the environmental damage that may result from the activities of foreign investors located in their territory. A prominent example of such risks is given by the Bhopal tragedy, on 3 December 1984, when the accidental release of approximately 42 tonnes of toxic methyl isocyanate (MIC) gas from a Union Carbide pesticide plant located in the Indian city of Bhopal killed and injured several thousand people. The link between the accident and poor (or poorly applied/ enforced) regulation is difficult to establish. The Bhopal tragedy has nevertheless become a common reference in discussions of the risks associated with the transfer of dangerous activities to developing countries.[3]

The perception of the desirability of foreign investment may also change throughout the life of an investment. Numerous illustrations of this phenomenon can be provided. For instance, if one looks at cases of water and sewerage concessions, the initial perception of foreign investors is often positive, as a necessary contribution to the modernisation of the water distribution infrastructure. However, after some time, this initially positive perception may evolve towards a negative one, for a variety of justified or unjustified reasons, ranging from the imposition of high or simply unpopular tariffs to the occurrence of a crisis or to a sudden change in the government of the host country, to name but a few. Such changes have given rise to foreign investment disputes in a number of cases.[4] Another example of perception shifts concerns waste

---

[2] This argument has received particular attention in the context of environmental regulatory competition within the United States. See, e.g., R. L. Revesz, 'Rehabilitating Interstate Competition: Rethinking the Race-to-the-Bottom Rationale for Federal Environmental Regulation' (1992) 67 New York University Law Review 1210.

[3] S. Jasanoff (ed.), Learning from Disaster: Risk Management after Bhopal (Philadelphia, PA: University of Pennsylvania Press, 1994).

[4] See, e.g., Aguas del Tunari SA v. Republic of Bolivia, ICSID Case No. ARB/02/3, Decision on Objections to Jurisdiction (21 October 2005) ('Aguas del Tunari')(later settled); Biwater Gauff (Tanz.) Ltd v. United Republic of Tanzania, ICSID Case No. ARB/05/22, Award (24 July 2008) ('Biwater v. Tanzania'); Compañía de Aguas del Aconquija SA and Vivendi Universal SA v. Argentine Republic, ICSID Case No. ARB/97/3, Award (20 August 2007) ('Vivendi II').

disposal/treatment facilities or related services operated by foreign investors. A number of developing countries or of their political subdivisions have outsourced such activities to foreign investors, often because investors can more easily mobilise the necessary capital and technology to set up such facilities or provide such services. But, again, throughout the life of the investment, the perception may change from a positive to a negative one and give rise to an investment dispute.[5]

As the foregoing examples suggest, the relations between foreign investment and environmental protection are complex and raise a number of difficult issues. It is, for instance, unclear what would happen with investments in environmentally sensitive sectors, such as energy production, water distribution, waste treatment or chemical safety, if the host State's environmental regulations were to become more stringent during the life of the investment. In other cases international investment law could be used to protect the environment, for instance, by requiring a State to respect its own environmental laws upon which an investment is based.[6] Overall, what these examples show is that the relationship between foreign investment and environmental protection has two dimensions, one in which the two terms appear as mutually supportive and another in which they seem to conflict. The emerging international regulation reflects the dual nature of this relationship.

---

[5] See, e.g., *Metalclad Corporation* v. *United Mexican States*, ICSID Case No. ARB(AF)/97/1, Award (25 August 2000) ('*Metalclad* v. *Mexico*'); *Técnicas Medioambientales Tecmed SA* v. *United Mexican States*, ICSID Case No. ARB(AF)/00/2, Award (29 May 2003) ('*Tecmed* v. *Mexico*'); *Abengoa SA y COFIDES SA* v. *United Mexican States*, ICSID Case No. ARB(AF)/09/2 ('*Abengoa* v. *Mexico*') (pending).

[6] See, e.g., the case brought by a Canadian investor against Barbados for failure to enforce its own environmental law (adopted in accordance with international environmental law) in connection with the protection of a natural ecosystem. The investor, who acquired 34.25 acres of natural wetlands and subsequently developed it into an ecotourism facility, claims that, through its acts and omissions, Barbados failed *inter alia*, (i) to prevent the repeated discharge of raw sewage into wetlands, and (ii) to investigate or prosecute sources of runoff of grease, oil, pesticides and herbicides from neighbouring areas, and poachers that have threatened the wildlife within the ecosystem. The text of the notice of arbitration is available at graemehall.com/legal/papers/BIT-Complaint.pdf (accessed on 4 January 2012). See also G. Lopez and L.-E. Peterson, 'Investor in Waste Management Project in Mexico puts Government on Notice of Treaty Breaches' (7 September 2011)(discussing a notice of dispute sent by an investor, Inter-Nexus, alleging the misallocation by Mexican authorities of funds that, according to the budget, were earmarked for the investor's landfill). Irrespective of whether these claims prosper, their interest lies in the way they have been formulated, which illustrates a novel form of complementariness between investment law and environmental law.

2.2 Synergies

The mutually supportive dimension of foreign investment and environmental protection is at the heart of the concept of sustainable development. When considered from this perspective, however, sustainable development appears mainly as a policy goal, the operational contours of which are circumscribed in political declarations, recommendations and soft-law instruments.[7] The main addressees of the international policy instruments dealing with sustainable development are States. Instruments such as Agenda 21, adopted at the 1992 Rio Conference on Environment and Development ('Earth Summit'),[8] or the Plan of Implementation adopted at the 2002 World Summit on Sustainable Development,[9] provide policy guidance to foster sustainable development.

However, as discussed in Chapter 1, these instruments also provide some guidance to private and non-State actors.[10] In addition to the instruments mentioned earlier, numerous other 'guidelines', 'recommendations', 'principles' and 'codes' have been developed by international organisations, non-governmental organisations or industry groups to regulate the environmental dimensions of foreign investment.[11] One of the objectives of these instruments is to reconcile profitability with environmental protection, much as the concept of sustainable development (and more recently that of a green economy) aims at reconciling environmental protection with economic and social development. For instance, the OECD Statement on 'Harnessing Freedom of Investment for Green Growth', adopted in April 2011,[12] is an attempt at spelling out the legal implications of this idea. Specifically, the first paragraph of the statement reads '[country] delegates believe that their governments' environmental and investment policy goals are compatible. They also

---

[7] See N. Schrijver, 'The Evolution of Sustainable Development in International Law: Inception, Meaning and Status', in *Recueil de cours de l'Académie de droit international*, vol. 329, (2008), Chapters 1–3.

[8] Report of the United Nations Conference on Environment and Development, A/CONF.151/26/Rev.1 (Vol. 1), Resolution 1, Annex 2: Agenda 21 ('Agenda 21').

[9] Report of the World Summit on Sustainable Development, A/CONF.199/20, Part I, Item 2: Plan of Implementation of the World Summit on Sustainable Development ('Plan of Implementation').

[10] See, e.g., Agenda 21, Chapter 30; Plan of Implementation, paras. 7(j), 9(g), 20(t), 25(g), 43(a) and 49.

[11] E. Morgera, *Corporate Accountability in International Environmental Law* (Oxford University Press, 2009)

[12] OECD, 'Harnessing Freedom of Investment for Green Growth', Freedom of Investment Roundtable, 14 April 2011 ('OECD Statement').

consider that those goals can be made mutually reinforcing and that this mutual supportiveness should be fostered.' Yet, as discussed in Chapter 4, some of these instruments also operate as 'safeguards' or 'soft-control mechanisms' in that they set standards applicable to the behaviour of companies or of their financiers, and in some cases establish mechanisms to review complaints for breaches of such standards.

In addition to the policy initiatives mentioned so far, there are other forms of fostering mutual supportiveness between foreign investment and environmental protection. Two major examples are the project-based flexibility mechanisms established by Articles 6 (joint implementation) and 12 (clean development mechanism) of the Kyoto Protocol.[13] States that have undertaken quantified emission reduction commitments under Article 3.1 and Annex B of the Kyoto Protocol can earn emission credits by conducting certain projects that reduce emissions in other countries. By providing for such a possibility, these mechanisms induce 'green' investment in transitional and/or developing countries, thereby constituting an additional vector of sustainable development. This said, while such instruments suggest that foreign investment and environmental protection are not antagonistic terms, one must not underestimate the potential for conflicts to arise between the two.

2.3 Conflicts

2.3.1 Basic definitions

The potentially conflicting dimension of the relations between investment and environmental protection calls for a variety of legal techniques through which conflicts can be managed. In order to analyse the operation of these techniques, it is first necessary to introduce a distinction between two fundamental types of conflicts arising from the interactions between foreign investment and environmental regulation. On the one hand, conflicts may arise between one international obligation stemming from international investment law and another international obligation stemming from international environmental law. This scenario shall be referred to as a 'normative conflict'. On the other hand, conflicts may arise between norms or measures stemming from different legal systems. Although many scenarios are possible, in the context of foreign investment disputes the most common one is that of

[13] Kyoto Protocol to the United Nations Framework Convention on Climate Change, Kyoto, 11 December 1997, 2303 UNTS 148 ('Kyoto Protocol').

an environmental measure adversely affecting the interests of a foreign investor, who claims that the measure is in breach of an international investment obligation of the host State. This type of conflict shall be referred to as a 'legitimacy conflict' between investment protection and environmental considerations.

In the following sections, the theoretical underpinnings of this distinction are discussed (Section 2.3.2) and then applied to a number of examples to illustrate its practical operation (Section 2.3.3).

2.3.2   Normative and legitimacy conflicts in theory

Conflicts between different norms can be characterised from two perspectives, logical and legal. From a *logical perspective*, it is possible to spell out what constitutes a conflict between two or more propositions that 'perform a normative function, namely, that comman[d], permi[t] or prohibi[t] an act or an attitude'.[14] Technically, 'a conflict arises when it is impossible to comply with all the requirements of two norms'.[15] To 'comply' means here to perform the act required by a norm or to abstain from performing the act prohibited by a norm, but it can also mean (by extension) to 'make use' (or 'not make use') of a permission granted by a norm.[16] The expression 'all the requirements of the norm' refers to the different conditions that trigger the command, prohibition or permission of a norm. More specifically, it refers to the 'personal, temporal and spatial spheres of application' of a norm,[17] its 'object' (understood as 'a person or thing affected by the act referred to in the norm'[18]) and the 'conditions' set for the obligation (command or prohibition) or the permission to be triggered. Following this analysis 'a conflict of norms arises when two norms cannot be complied with

---

[14] S. A. Sadat-Akhavi, *Methods of Resolving Conflicts between Treaties* (Leiden: Martinus Nijhoff, 2003), p. 5. The monograph written by Sadat-Akhavi (a revised doctoral dissertation defended at the Graduate Institute, Geneva, in 2001) displays a tight conceptual analysis drawing on the traditions of analytical philosophy and deontic logic, as acknowledged by the author. Reference is indeed made to some of the founding works of deontic logic, such as the works of the Finnish philosopher Georg Henrik von Wright (see his 'Deontic Logic' (1951) 60 *Mind* 1; 'A Note on Deontic Logic and Derived Obligation' (1956) 65 *Mind* 507; 'Is There a Logic of Norms' (1991) 4 *Ratio Juris* 270); or of the Argentine philosopher Carlos E. Alchourrón (see C. E. Alchourrón and E. Bulygin, *Normative Systems* (New York, NY: Springer, 1971)); C. E. Alchourrón, 'Conflicts of Norms and the Revision of Normative Systems' (1991) 10 *Law and Philosophy* 417). The following conceptualisation of conflicts from the perspective of deontic logic as applied to law follows the analysis of Sadat-Akhavi.

[15] Sadat-Akhavi, *Methods of Resolving Conflicts between Treaties* above n. 14, p. 23.

[16] *Ibid.*, pp. 5–6.   [17] *Ibid.*, p. 6.   [18] *Ibid.*, p. 6.

by all addressees of the norm, at all times and in all spaces covered by the norm, with regard to all objects of the norm, and under all conditions specified by the norm'.[19]

From this logical perspective, conflicts can be organised according to a variety of criteria. Among these criteria, it is useful to look in more detail at how the norms in conflict are 'formulated' (command, prohibition, permission). Based on the formulation of the norms involved it is possible to distinguish four main types of conflicts: (i) when the same act is subject to different types of norms (a norm commanding an act and a norm prohibiting the same act,[20] a norm permitting an act and a norm prohibiting the same act,[21] a norm permitting to perform or not an act and a norm commanding the same act[22]); (ii) when one norm requires an act, whereas the other requires or permits a contrary act (i.e., an act that, albeit different, cannot be performed at the same time);[23] (iii) when one norm prohibits a necessary condition for the triggering of the command, prohibition or permission set out in another norm (thus effectively banning the operation of such other command, prohibition or permission);[24] and (iv) when one norm prohibits a necessary consequence of another norm[25] (thus effectively banning the operation of the latter norm).[26]

Despite its sophistication, the preceding analysis has the defects of its very qualities. In particular, the analysis applies to any set of normative propositions, including moral, religious and legal sets of norms. Indeed,

---

[19] *Ibid.*, p. 7.

[20] E.g., 'the contracting parties shall not permit the export of ozone depleting substances to third States' vs. 'the contracting parties shall not restrict in any way the export of goods produced by an investor of the other contracting party'.

[21] E.g., 'the contracting parties may restrict the export of ozone depleting substances to third States' vs. 'the contracting parties shall not restrict in any way the export of goods produced by an investor of the other contracting party'.

[22] E.g., 'the contracting parties may restrict the export of ozone depleting substances to third States' (which also implies that they may not do so) vs. 'the contracting parties shall restrict the export of ozone depleting substances to third States'.

[23] E.g., 'the contracting parties shall preserve biological resources *in situ* (where they are located)' vs. 'the contracting parties may preserve biological resources *ex situ* (e.g., in samples held in a laboratory)'.

[24] E.g., 'the access of duly registered foreign investors to electricity markets shall not be restricted' vs. 'the State may deny registration to foreign investors active in the energy sector'.

[25] E.g., 'the contracting parties shall ensure that the natural course of the River X is not modified' vs. 'the contracting parties undertake to divert the waters of River X as part of the system of dams envisioned in this treaty'.

[26] Sadat-Akhavi, *Methods of Resolving Conflicts between Treaties*, above n. 14, pp. 9–10.

if one remains at the level of the 'formulation' of the norms in conflict, the analysis cannot adequately reflect the particular arrangements of legal orders,[27] let alone those of a specific legal order. This is only natural as deontic logic aims at the highest level of abstraction in its attempt at explaining normativity. However, to understand how these conceptual remarks can shed light on the conflicts between environmental and investment protection, it is necessary to come closer to the way in which legal orders (and particularly the international legal order) work.

This *legal perspective* focuses on the relevance of the following elements for the analysis of conflicts between norms: (i) the architecture of the legal order; (ii) the norms (conflict norms *lato sensu*) governing the effects deployed within such order by norms of other legal orders; (iii) the peculiarity of investor–State disputes; and (iv) the link between an international norm and a domestic norm requiring, prohibiting or permitting the same act. Let us discuss these elements one by one.

If one considers, following the dualist tradition, that a domestic norm has no legal effect in international law, there cannot strictly speaking be a conflict between such domestic norm and an international norm, because the status of the domestic norm prevents it from standing at the same level (i.e., applying to the same situation) as the international norm. Similarly, a conflict between a binding command and a non-binding prohibition of the same act is not a conflict from a legal standpoint (while it may be one from a purely logical standpoint). Conversely, from a monist perspective, conflicts between international and domestic norms would be possible, as both types of norms deploy legal effects.

Whether a norm deploys legal effects or not depends on the extent to which it is recognised by the legal order of reference. To continue with the previous example, international norms prevail over domestic norms only if (and to the extent that) a conflict norm so specifies[28] and such conflict norm is taken as the reference point.[29] Yet, from the perspective

---

[27] Even if one does not accept the existence of a legal order or a legal system, but only of a relatively autonomous (or self-referring) set of norms, the following analysis remains applicable.

[28] Such a norm – either international or domestic – could simply state that 'international law or part of it prevails over domestic law or parts of it', but it could also state that from the perspective of international law 'domestic law is only a fact', i.e., it has no binding character in international law, or that 'domestic law has only the legal effects recognised by international law' or, still, that 'domestic law does not release a State from its international obligations'.

[29] Typically by an international adjudicatory or quasi-adjudicatory body, but also, under some circumstances, by a domestic court.

of an international adjudicatory and quasi-adjudicatory body, it is clear that the norms performing this 'function' are different from those performing the 'function' of allocating priority to different norms of 'international' law. Moreover, although some conflict norms (such as the *lex posterior* and the *lex specialis* principles) may apply to all norms and fields of international law with little or no distinction, the 'scope' of other conflict norms will largely depend upon the colliding norms that are governed by them (or more generally the fields of international law at stake). By way of illustration, Article 104 of the NAFTA[30] is relevant only for conflicts among specific international norms, i.e., those arising from the NAFTA, the CITES, the Basel Convention[31] and some other agreements explicitly identified.

Furthermore, the peculiar 'mixed' nature of investor–State disputes adds additional legal complexity to the determination of conflicts. Conflict norms would normally solve conflicts between two norms applicable to both parties. However, a regular feature of investor–State disputes is that the investor is not bound by the international environmental norms governing the conduct of the host State. In some cases, the applicable environmental norm may not even be binding for the investor's home State. Yet, a conflict may arise nevertheless because the host State itself is bound by two conflicting norms governing its conduct.

The analysis of the conflicts becomes even more complex when the link between one of the conflicting norms (e.g., a domestic environmental measure in conflict with an investment treaty) and another international norm (e.g., a provision in an environmental treaty supporting such domestic measure) is brought into the picture. This issue has received some attention in the context of domestic measures in breach of trade disciplines. The debate over mandatory/discretionary (domestic) measures sheds some light on the different dimensions of this link,[32] although it is limited to links between domestic measures (e.g., enabling legislation and executive implementing measures) and, significantly, it does not take into account the implications of linking a domestic measure to an international norm. This is important because, depending on

---

[30] North American Free Trade Agreement, US–Canada–Mexico, 17 December 1992, 32 ILM 296 ('NAFTA').

[31] Basel Convention on the Control of Transboundary Movements of Hazardous Wastes and their Disposal, 22 March 1989, 1673 UNTS 57 ('Basel Convention').

[32] S. Lester 'A Framework for Thinking about the "Discretion" in the Mandatory/ Discretionary Distinction' (2011) 14 *Journal of International Economic Law* 369.

the strength of the link, the nature of the conflict may be different calling for the use of different conflict norms.

The different sets of conflict norms will be discussed later in this book. At this stage, the main point is that the sets of conflict norms applicable to norms within one legal order and those applicable to norms from two distinct legal orders are different. The difference between the two sets of conflict norms provides the theoretical underpinnings of the distinction between 'normative conflicts' (conflicts between norms of the same legal order) and 'legitimacy conflicts' (conflicts between norms of different legal orders). As a result, the need to distinguish between these two broad types of conflicts is not only analytically useful but also legally necessary.

This distinction is also applicable to conflicts between norms arising from other branches of international law. Its application would be useful to avoid a common misunderstanding underlying the analysis of the relations between environmental regulation and trade and invest-ment disciplines. It is sometimes considered that these latter disciplines set the bounds within which environmental regulation must evolve. For instance, the OECD Statement on 'Harnessing Freedom of Investment for Green Growth' states in its fourth paragraph that 'governments should review their new proposed environmental measures for compliance with investment law obligations'.[33] Whereas, broadly speaking, one would tend to agree with this statement, on closer examination this statement could potentially mean that investment disciplines prevail over new inconsistent environmental regulation, even when the latter is required by an international environmental norm. The formulation retained by the delegates takes up the wording of the draft submitted to them by the OECD secretariat, which had been the object of some criticism during the consultation phase on this point.[34] The use of the distinction

---

[33] OECD Statement, above n. 12, para. 4.

[34] See my comments on this relationship (Viñuales, 'Comments', para. 9) as well as the comments of Professor Shotaro Hamamoto (Hamamoto, 'Comments', Section III), available at: www.oecd.org/dataoecd/6/62/47090812.pdf (accessed on 4 January 2012). The background paper prepared by the OECD Secretariat also seemed sensitive to this view when it referred, with approval, to the statement in the International Law Commission, 'Report of the Study Group on the Fragmentation of International Law', finalised by Martin Koskenniemi (13 April 2006), Doc. A/CN.4/L.682 and Corrigendum (11 August 2006), Doc. A/CN.4/L.682/ ('Report on Fragmentation') to the effect that 'the question of the normative weight to be given to particular rights and obligations at the moment they appear to clash with other rights and obligations can only be argued on a case-by-case basis', Background paper II: 'Green Growth: Relations between International Environmental Law and International Investment Law', para. 77, available at: www.oecd.org/dataoecd/8/3/46905672.pdf (accessed on 4 January 2012).

between normative and legitimacy conflicts, with the ensuing conflict techniques applicable to each of these types of conflicts, would clarify the basic proposition that, as a matter of principle, neither investment (or trade) disciplines prevail over international environmental norms nor do the latter prevail over the former. The solution is to be found on a case-by-case basis through the use of the appropriate conflict techniques.

With these theoretical observations in mind, let us now discuss how the distinction between normative and legitimacy conflicts operates in treaty practice.

2.3.3   Normative and legitimacy conflicts in treaty practice

When one looks at the practice of international environmental law and international investment law, it is often difficult to determine whether two or more norms are in conflict or to identify the specific type of conflict. This is largely because the formulation of such norms (whether they are to be seen as commands, prohibitions or permissions) is unclear. In order for a 'normative conflict' to exist, an international environmental norm must require a State to adopt certain conduct (command), or not to adopt such conduct (prohibition), or authorise the adoption or not of this conduct (permission). There are, however, different degrees in which an international environmental norm may do so. Let us elaborate on this point in the light of those environmental norms that have been or could likely be invoked in the context of investment disputes.

First, the norm in question may clearly prohibit certain acts. For instance, pursuant to Article 4(5) of the Basel Convention '[a] Party shall not permit hazardous wastes or other wastes to be exported to a non-Party or to be imported from a non-Party'.[35] Were a host State to enact regulations preventing exports to non-parties, such behaviour could squarely be characterised as an application of an international environmental obligation.[36] In a similar vein, a provision such as the one contained in Annex II of the Aarhus Protocol[37] clearly commands the reassessment of certain

---

[35] Basel Convention, above n. 31, Article 4(5).

[36] In *S. D. Myers* v. *Canada*, the respondent argued that it had acted in accordance with Article 4(5) of the Basel Convention. See *S. D. Myers Inc.* v. *Canada,* NAFTA (UNCITRAL), Partial Award (13 November 2000)('*S. D. Myers* v. *Canada*'). See, specifically, Counter-Memorial, 5 October 1999, para. 106, available at: www.naftaclaims.com (accessed on 4 January 2012).

[37] Protocol on Persistent Organic Pollutants to the LRTAP Convention, 24 June 1998, 37 ILM 513.

uses of lindane, although such reassessment may also be triggered by domestic health and environmental considerations.[38]

However, many environmental conventions contain less clear requirements. For instance, Article 3(1) of the Kyoto Protocol provides:

The Parties included in Annex I shall, individually or jointly, ensure that their aggregate anthropogenic carbon dioxide equivalent emissions of the greenhouse gases listed in Annex A do not exceed their assigned amounts, calculated pursuant to their quantified emission limitation and reduction commitments inscribed in Annex B and in accordance with the provisions of this Article, with a view to reducing their overall emissions of such gases by at least 5 per cent below 1990 levels in the commitment period 2008 to 2012.[39]

In this case, although there is a specific emissions objective for States that have undertaken quantified targets (a command to respect these quantified commitments), the means to achieve those objectives are left to each State. It would therefore be less clear whether a specific measure adopted by a State in furtherance of its obligations under the Kyoto Protocol could be characterised as strictly required by an international environmental obligation.

A somewhat less stringent variant of this type of requirement appears in a number of international treaties dealing with the protection of habitats and biological diversity. For instance, paragraphs 1 and 4 of Article 2 of the Ramsar Convention require States to designate (at least) one or more suitable wetland(s) within their territory for inclusion in the list of wetlands of international importance.[40] A number of consequences follow from the voluntary act of designation, including the formulation and implementation of plans to promote the conservation of listed wetlands[41] or the creation of nature reserves on wetlands.[42] Whereas the designation of one wetland in its territory is mandatory under the Convention, the State has considerable discretion in the selection of particular zones as protected wetlands as well as in the specific measures to be adopted for their protection. Were a State to select a zone near the location of an industrial plant owned by a foreign investor and thereafter adopt stringent regulations restricting the activities of this investor, it would be unclear whether such conduct

---

[38] See *Chemtura Corporation (formerly Crompton Corporation)* v. *Government of Canada*, UNCITRAL, Award (2 August 2010)('*Chemtura* v. *Canada*'), paras. 131 and 137–42.
[39] Kyoto Protocol, above n. 13, Article 3(1).
[40] Convention on Wetlands of International Importance especially as Waterfowl Habitat, 2 February 1971, 996 UNTS 245, Article 2(1) and (4).
[41] *Ibid.*, Article 3(1).   [42] *Ibid.*, Article 4(1).

is commanded by international environmental law.[43] Conversely, if a State failed to adopt or implement stringent environmental regulations, or established only a limited protection framework, it would be unclear whether such conduct would be in breach of international environmental law.

Even less clear are the requirements established by the Convention on Biological Diversity or by the Western Hemisphere Convention. Article 6 of the Convention on Biological Diversity states:

Each Contracting Party shall, in accordance with its particular conditions and capabilities:

(a) Develop national strategies, plans or programmes for the conservation and sustainable use of biological diversity or adapt for this purpose existing strategies, plans or programmes which shall reflect, inter alia, the measures set out in this Convention relevant to the Contracting Party concerned; and

(b) Integrate, as far as possible and as appropriate, the conservation and sustainable use of biological diversity into relevant sectoral or cross-sectoral plans, programmes and policies.[44]

The Western Hemisphere Convention is even less precise as to the specific obligations undertaken by the States parties:

The Contracting Governments will explore at once the possibility of establishing in their territories national parks, national reserves, nature monuments, and strict wilderness reserves as defined in the preceding article. In all cases where such establishment is feasible, the creation thereof shall be begun as soon as possible after the effective date of the present Convention ... [t]he Contracting Governments agree to adopt, or to propose such adoption to their respective appropriate law-making bodies, suitable laws and regulations for the protection and preservation of flora and fauna within their national boundaries but not included in the national parks, national reserves, nature monuments, or strict wilderness reserves referred to in Article II hereof. Such regulations shall contain

---

[43] This issue arose in *Empresa Lucchetti* v. *Peru*, in connection with the construction and operation of a pasta factory near a protected wetland (Pantanos de Villa). However, the tribunal found that it lacked jurisdiction over the dispute, a decision that was confirmed on annulment. See *Empresa Lucchetti SA and Lucchetti Peru SA* v. *Republic of Peru*, ICSID Case No. ARB/03/4, Award (7 February 2005)('*Lucchetti* v. *Peru – Jurisdiction*'); *Industria Nacional de Alimentos SA and Indalsa Perú SA* v. *Republic of Peru*, ICSID Case No. ARB/03/4, Decision on Annulment (5 September 2007)('*Lucchetti* v. *Peru – Annulment*'). A similar issue arose in *Southern Pacific Properties (Middle East) Limited (SPP)* v. *Arab Republic of Egypt*, ICSID Case No. ARB/84/3, Award (20 May 1992)('*SPP* v. *Egypt*'), para. 154, in connection with a site protected under the World Heritage Convention.

[44] Convention on Biological Diversity, 5 June 1992, 1760 UNTS 79, Article 6.

proper provisions for the taking of the specimens of flora and fauna for scientific study and investigation by properly accredited individuals and agencies.[45]

Thus formulated, these provisions leave such a broad discretion to States that it is difficult to determine the degree to which they command or prohibit certain acts. One could alternatively consider that the measure in question is at least authorised by the international norm in question. But such an approach does not necessarily takes us further. Indeed, as discussed in Chapters 7 to 10, the difficulty that arises in practice with these and other more ambiguous norms is that there exists a variety of ways to comply with them, some of which conflict with investment disciplines. As a result of the ambiguities of these norms, the measures taken under their umbrella could be reasonably considered, depending on the perspective that one adopts, either as conduct required (through commands or prohibitions) or authorised by an international norm or, conversely, as an essentially domestic initiative.

A similar analysis could also be conducted with respect to investment protection standards. From the specific provisions on direct expropriation or on performance requirements, to the less precise protections such as the national treatment and most-favoured nation clauses, to the broad provisions on full protection and security or fair and equitable treatment, the requirements of investment protection are increasingly vague, and they would have largely remained so if it had not been for the contribution of the case-law arising from investment disputes.[46]

The preceding observations help understand more fully the practical operation of the distinction between normative and legitimacy conflicts. As a result of the varying degree of precision with which different environmental norms are formulated, as illustrated by the abovementioned examples, normative and legitimacy conflicts may enter into subtle interactions. For instance, the conflict arising in a situation where a State has adopted an adverse environmental measure based on Article 6 of the Convention on Biological Diversity would in practice be very similar to one in which the environmental measure makes no reference to such article or, still, to one in which the host State is not a party to that convention. In the same vein, the conflict arising from

---

[45] Convention on Nature Protection and Wild Life Preservation in the Western Hemisphere, 12 October 1940, 56 Stat. 1354, TS 981 ('Western Hemisphere Convention'), Article II(1) and V(1).

[46] For overviews of the foreign investment case-law, see E. Gaillard, *La jurisprudence du CIRDI*, 2 vols. (Paris: Pédane, 2004–10); R. Happ and N. Rubins, *Digest of ICSID Awards and Decisions 2003–2007* (Oxford University Press, 2009).

a measure adopted pursuant to Annex II of the Aarhus Protocol would also be very similar, despite the more specific content of Annex II, to a conflict where the measure has been adopted on the basis of domestic environmental and health considerations. At the margin, the distinction between normative and legitimacy conflicts turns on whether an international environmental norm can reasonably be considered to govern the conduct of the host State, as opposed to serve as a mere source of inspiration. The boundary between normative and legitimacy conflicts is even thinner if an international environmental norm is invoked as an interpretation tool, as in this case it would be intervening as applicable law and not simply as inspirational guidance. Indeed, Article 31(3)(c) of the VCLT refers to 'any relevant rules of international law applicable in the relations between the parties'[47] as a tool for systemic integration.

Despite the thin boundary between normative and legitimacy conflicts, the distinction remains important because the rules applicable to solving normative conflicts are different from those applicable to solving legitimacy conflicts. The former set of rules consists, essentially, of specific conflict rules contained in treaties and general conflict rules arising from general international law.[48] These rules are technically not applicable to legitimacy conflicts, in which the 'opponents' are an international instrument (most often an investment treaty) and a national instrument (most often environment-related domestic law or measures).[49] Legitimacy conflicts call for a more composite set of conflict rules, including specific conflict rules in treaties, rules governing the relations between international and domestic laws, rules of conflicts of laws *stricto sensu* (private international law), rules governing the hierarchy of norms within a domestic legal system or rules defining the scope of the State's regulatory powers. These two different sets of conflict rules will be discussed in detail in Chapters 6 and 11.

---

[47] Vienna Convention on the Law of Treaties, 23 May 1969, 1155 UNTS 331 ('VCLT'), Article 31(3)(c).

[48] See Report on Fragmentation, above n. 34, para. 18.

[49] The international law component of a legitimacy conflict could also be an international environmental norm. See, e.g., *SPP* v. *Egypt*, above n. 43; *Peter A. Allard* v. *Barbados*. Other examples could be derived from investment-related cases before regional human rights courts. For instance, in the *Awas Tingni* case, the Inter-American Court of Human Rights upheld the customary right to property of an indigenous community over its ancestral land against the right of property of an investor, to whom Nicaragua had granted a concession over the same lands. See *Mayagna (Sumo) Awas Tingni Community* v. *Nicaragua*, ICtHR, Series C No. 79, Judgment (31 August 2001), para. 164.

2.4   Levels and sectors

2.4.1   Levels

Environmental and investment protection interact at three regulatory levels: international law, domestic law, contractual arrangements. In this study, the analysis will focus on the issues that arise at the level of international law. Matters of domestic law and contractual arrangements will not receive systematic treatment. They will, however, be discussed in some detail when their analysis appears important for the understanding of some aspects of international law. For example, some attention will be given to contractual arrangements as a strategy for environmental protection in Chapters 3 and 4. In addition, the structure of foreign investment schemes heavily depends on contractual arrangements, which, understandably, are of great importance from the perspective of investment protection. This contractual dimension of investment protection will be taken into account in the analysis of legitimacy conflicts conducted in Part III of this book, especially in connection with stabilisation clauses.

2.4.2   Sectors

The interactions between environmental and investment protection touch upon different sectors of substantive environmental regulation. The selection of the most relevant points of interaction is important for Part II. In this context, Chapters 7 to 10 attempt to meet three basic requirements, namely: (i) to encompass a wide range of issues while keeping in perspective the main substantive fields of international environmental regulation; (ii) to cover the most relevant issues that have arisen in the practice of investment tribunals as well as, when useful, of other adjudicatory and quasi-adjudicatory bodies; and (iii) to integrate the two main approaches used in international environmental governance, namely the basic 'regulatory approach' imposing environmental obligations on States and the 'human-rights approach' introducing a number of substantive and procedural human rights with environmental components.

The first requirement that Chapters 7 to 10 seek to address is the need to explore the potential tensions between, on the one hand, investment protection and, on the other hand, each one of the four main substantive areas of international environmental regulation. Some accounts of international environmental law may give the impression that it is little more than a collection of exotic issues, ranging from the regulation of whales, to that of ozone depletion, wetlands, nuclear energy or oil pollution. Yet, the broad range of issues encompassed by the 'continent' of international environmental law can be divided into 'sub-continents' to facilitate the understanding of the regulation of different substantive areas. For instance, the *Oxford Handbook of International Environmental Law* identifies four broad areas of international environmental regulation (oceans and freshwater, biological resources, protection of the atmosphere, and dangerous substances and activities).[50] This distinction is analytically useful because it goes beyond the all-encompassing reference to 'environmental' regulation without falling into a casuistic issue-by-issue analysis. It is also useful to identify the general legal background of the specific issues analysed in Chapters 7 to 10, which cover the four 'sub-continents' of international environmental law.

Within the bounds set by these four areas of substantive regulation, the selection of the issues analysed in Chapters 7 to 10 results from a comprehensive review of the questions of international environmental law that have arisen, are pending or could potentially arise in the practice of investment tribunals. In addition, Chapters 7 to 10 also draw on the practice of several other adjudicatory and quasi-adjudicatory bodies, including the International Court of Justice, the European Court of Human Rights, the Inter-American Court of Human Rights, the Inter-American Commission on Human Rights, the African Commission on Human and Peoples' Rights, the United Nations Human Rights Committee, the International Tribunal for the Law of the Sea, the Court of Justice of the European Union, the WTO Dispute Settlement Body, the World Bank's Inspection Panel and Compliance/Advisor Ombudsman, the World Heritage Committee or the Compliance Committee of the Aarhus Convention, in order to extract relevant insights that can illuminate the management of normative conflicts.

Resorting to the practice of adjudicatory and quasi-adjudicatory bodies specialised in human rights is also necessary to take into account the human rights dimensions of environmental protection. In this regard, Chapters 7 to 10 begin by giving an overview of the major collision points between environmental and investment protection from the perspective of both the regulatory and the human rights approaches.

---

[50] D. Bodansky, J. Brunnée and E. Hey (eds.), *The Oxford Handbook of International Environmental Law* (Oxford University Press, 2007), Part III.

3 Synergies – harnessing foreign investment to promote environmental protection

As noted in Chapter 2, the mutually supportive dimension of foreign investment and environmental protection can be seen mainly as a policy goal. However, a number of instruments have been developed in international and transnational law to give this policy goal a more concrete form. These instruments have been studied in some detail in the literature, and they are addressed at length in a forthcoming companion volume to this book.[1] This chapter therefore provides only a brief survey of such instruments, highlighting the synergies sought between foreign investment and the protection of the environment. The chapter is organised in two sections. The first section discusses the two main 'forms' taken by such instruments, namely environmental project finance and public private partnerships (PPPs) (Section 3.1). The second section focuses on the two main substantive areas where such instruments have developed in the last two decades, namely climate change and biodiversity conservation (Section 3.2). Overall, these analytical distinctions are only different prisms (form and substance) through which to observe one and the same reality, i.e., investment in pro-environment activities.

---

[1] See P.-M. Dupuy and J. E. Viñuales (eds.), *Harnessing Foreign Investment to Promote Environmental Protection: Incentives and Safeguards* (Cambridge University Press, forthcoming), Part II, chapters by M.-J. Langer (environmental finance), D. Firger (climate-related instruments), R. Pavoni (biodiversity-related instruments), S. Surminsky (climate-related insurance) and K. Athanasakou (trade in environmental goods and services).

3.1   The form of synergies – environmental project finance and PPPs

3.1.1   Environmental project finance

Environmental finance is a world in itself. In the last years, the allocation of public and private funds in accordance with environmental as well as other 'socially responsible' criteria has grown in importance. According to one estimate, the 'Sustainable and Responsible Investment' ('SRI') market amounted to some €7.6 trillion under management in 2010.[2] For a large part, these funds are structurally similar to other funds allocated to more conventional activities. They differ, essentially, in some of the criteria used for the selection of the assets, projects or activities. A discussion of these criteria is provided in Chapter 4, in connection with environmental standards.

The focus of this section is, instead, on some structures that have been created for the specific purpose of financing pro-environment projects and/or helping channel private funds towards such projects. Not every environmental fund established by treaty pursues this objective. In fact, most of them are limited to helping developing countries participate in treaty bodies or implement their commitments through financial assistance.[3] Only some of these instruments seek to harness foreign investment to promote environmental protection. They take, in essence, either the form of an environmental fund, such as the Global Environmental Facility ('GEF') (Section 3.1.1.1), or that of a market mechanism, such as the flexible mechanisms established by the Kyoto Protocol[4] (Section 3.1.1.2). Some mechanisms, such as the Prototype Carbon Fund ('PCF'), combine these two approaches (Section 3.1.1.3).

3.1.1.1   Environmental funds – the example of the GEF

The operation of environmental funds can be illustrated by reference to the GEF. The GEF was created in 1991 and thoroughly restructured in 1994.[5]

---

[2] European Social Investment Forum (EUROSIF), *European SRI Study* (2010), p. 59.
[3] L. Boisson de Chazournes, 'Technical and Financial Assistance', in D. Bodansky, J. Brunnée and E. Hey (eds.), *The Oxford Handbook of International Environmental Law* (Oxford University Press, 2007) p. 947.
[4] Kyoto Protocol to the United Nations Framework Convention on Climate Change, Kyoto, 11 December 1997, 2303 UNTS 148 ('Kyoto Protocol').
[5] See Instrument for the Establishment of the Restructured Global Environmental Facility (October 2011). The text of the 'Instrument' is reproduced at pp. 9–41 of the 2011 publication. We will use 'Instrument' to refer to this text and 'Instrument Documents' to refer to other documents reproduced in the 2011 publication.

It has been subsequently amended several times, lastly in May 2010. It is a separate international organisation with its own bodies (e.g., the Assembly, the Council, the Secretariat and a Scientific and Advisory Panel) but its funding activities are run through a number of 'Implementing Agencies' (mainly the World Bank, the United Nations Environment Programme (UNEP) and the United Nations Development Progamme (UNDP), but also seven other entities, including regional development banks). Its purpose is to provide 'new and additional grant and concessional funding to meet the agreed incremental costs of measures to achieve agreed global environmental benefits' in six 'focal areas', namely biodiversity, climate change, international water management, land degradation, ozone depletion and persistent organic pollutants.[6] The GEF intervenes in these areas not only in the capacity of an independent financial agency but also as the financial mechanism of certain environmental treaties. Much has been written about the GEF's role in financing environmental projects.[7] The following discussion focuses on one specific aspect of this role, its connection with (private) foreign investment.

The importance of engaging the private sector in pro-environment activities was recognised since the inception of the GEF. Paragraph 28 of the Instrument stated indeed that '[t]he Implementing Agencies may make arrangements for GEF project preparation and execution by ... private sector entities'. In an information document prepared by the Secretariat in October 1995 and entitled 'Engaging the Private Sector' it was noted that 'the challenge for the GEF [was] to find effective modalities to influence ("leverage") ... [private] investment flows in ways that are beneficial to the global environment'.[8] Over the years, the GEF developed a 'Strategy to Engage with the Private Sector' embodied in a number of documents, including a set of 'Principles for Engaging the Private Sector'[9] and additional action to 'enhance' the initial strategy.[10]

---

[6] Instrument, above n. 5, para. 2.

[7] See, e.g., A. S. Miller, 'The Global Environmental Facility and the Search for Financial Strategies to Foster Sustainable Development' (1999–2000) 24 *Vermont Law Review* 1229; C. Streck, 'The Global Environmental Facility – A Role Model for International Environmental Governance?' (2001) 1 *Global Environmental Politics* 71; R. Clemençon, 'What Future for the Global Environmental Facility?' (2006) 15 *The Journal of Environment and Development* 50.

[8] GEF, 'Engaging the Private Sector', 5 October 1995, GEF/C.6/Inf.4, para 7 ('Engaging the Private Sector').

[9] GEF, 'Principles for Engaging the Private Sector', 16 April 2004, GEF/C.23/11 ('GEF Principles').

[10] GEF, 'Revised Strategy for Enhancing Engagement with the Private Sector', 7 October 2011, GEF/C.41/09 ('GEF Revised Strategy'), Annex 1.

From these documents and the practice that ensued within their framework, four types of engagement can be identified.

The first type, characterised as 'indirect engagement', consists in promoting the activities of pro-environment firms by creating certain market conditions in countries receiving GEF funds. The GEF Principles illustrate this form of engagement as follows:

> renewable energy firms ... are able to take advantage of the outputs of a GEF-funded barrier-removal project – outputs such as a more equitable energy pricing regime, publicly available information on renewable energy resources, and agreed standards for industrial inputs and renewable energy equipment.[11]

Indirect engagement does not involve disbursing funds to the private sector. It focuses instead on creating environmental markets where pro-environment firms can prosper.

The second type of engagement ('direct engagement') is for the GEF to provide funds to a private company (or group thereof) to cover the incremental costs of a given project. Direct engagement was identified already in 1995 as a manner to foster investment in risky environments or uncertain sectors or, still, to induce companies to conduct their business in a more environmentally friendly way.[12] However, when compared to indirect engagement, direct engagement presents a number of difficulties. As noted in the GEF Principles, it is necessary 'to ensure that any individual firm is sustainable as a *business* before considering it as a potential GEF recipient'.[13] In addition, it is also necessary 'to ensure that the *public* funding of the GEF still creates a genuine public asset and not just a private one', that it 'does not distort market incentives, and does not unfairly favour the selected firm over unselected ones'.[14] To address these additional difficulties, a set of 'Operational Policies' was adopted in 2008.[15] According to the GEF Revised Strategy, the main instruments of direct engagement used by the GEF include targeted equity participations in private firms with particularly innovative approaches to one of the GEF's focal areas, revolving loan funds and, especially, loan guarantees, which help private firms secure funding from banks and other private lenders.[16]

---

[11] GEF Principles, above n. 9, para. 8(a).

[12] Engaging the Private Sector, above n. 8, paras. 8, 10 and 14.

[13] GEF Principles, above n. 9, para. 10 (italics original).

[14] *Ibid.*, para. 10 (italics original).

[15] GEF, 'Operational Policies and Guidance for the Use of Non-grant Instruments', 26 March 2008, GEF/C.33/12 ('Operational Policies'). Non-grant instruments include loans, loan guarantees and equity participations.

[16] GEF Revised Strategy, above n. 10, para. 20.

This latter point illustrates the third type of private sector engagement, namely as fund providers or 'co-financiers' in GEF-leveraged projects. The rationale for this engagement is described in the GEF Revised Strategy as follows:

[w]hen the GEF becomes a partner through the use of a non-grant instrument, we lower the risks for commercial financial institutions and private investors to participate, thus increasing the level of funding available for projects consistent with the GEF mission.[17]

This type of engagement is particularly important in the context of the move towards a green economy, characterised by the development of clean technologies.[18]

Finally, the fourth type of engagement is by opening the possibility of procurement in GEF-funded projects to private companies. The GEF may facilitate such involvement, for example, by advertising more widely GEF-funded projects that require procurement.[19]

After the adoption of the GEF's Resource Allocation Framework in 2006, the second type of engagement has become more difficult, because the needs of the private sector have not always been sufficiently taken into account in country allocations.[20] Currently, the GEF envisages private sector involvement mostly through the first and the third types of engagement. In particular, implementing agencies are being encouraged to identify certain PPPs that could receive funding and attract co-financing by other lenders.[21]

3.1.1.2 Market mechanisms

Market mechanisms will be discussed in more detail in Section 3.2 below. Yet, it seems useful to characterise here the type of 'synergy' between foreign investment and environmental protection that they are intended to provide. Unlike environmental funds, market mechanisms do not disburse funds or provide guarantees to either States or private companies. Their purpose is to create an incentive for States or private companies to conduct certain types of pro-environment transactions. They do so by creating an environmental market. From the perspective of a foreign investor, the type of incentive could be characterised as a variant of 'indirect engagement' in the meaning discussed above.

---

[17] *Ibid.*, para. 23.   [18] *Ibid.*, para. 40.   [19] GEF Principles, above n. 9, para. 10.
[20] GEF Revised Strategy, above n. 10, para. 35.   [21] *Ibid.*, para. 32.

In the case of the flexible mechanisms of the Kyoto Protocol, the market is created by the existence of a cap on the emissions of certain greenhouse gases (Annex A) by certain countries (Annex B). The right to emit a ton of carbon dioxide equivalent thus acquires value for States subject to the cap, because these 'emission rights' can be used to comply with an international obligation. This, in turn, is implemented by domestic or community legislation (e.g., the European ETS Directive[22]) extending the market of emission rights to the private sector. For a private company an emission right is valuable not only because it can be used to comply with a legal obligation but also for other purposes, such as branding, hedging or simply to avoid investing in a restructuring of its production methods.

Similarly, certain 'ecosystem services' (e.g., carbon capture and storage by trees, water purification and replenishment or flood control by wetlands, biodiversity conservation by tropical forests) can be structured in a way that allows them to be marketed. Depending on the structure given to such services, the market will have different features. Some countries, such as Brazil and Ecuador, have set up funds where public and private investors can invest in preserving the tropical forests.[23] In the context of the climate change negotiations, a forest conservation mechanism (the so-called REDD-plus ('reduced emissions from deforestation, forest degradation and enhancement')[24]) is being developed to channel public and private funds for the purpose of avoiding deforestation, with the ensuing gains in terms of avoided emissions and biodiversity conservation.

3.1.1.3 Hybrid approaches – the PCF

The Prototype Carbon Fund ('PCF') was established by the World Bank in 1999[25] as a PPP comprising six governments and sixteen companies and with an initial capital of US $180 million. A brief reference to its features and operation seems warranted for two reasons. First, the

---

[22] Directive 2003/87/EC of the European Parliament and of the Council of 13 October 2003 establishing a scheme for greenhouse gas emission allowance trading within the Community and amending Council Directive 96/61/EC, OJ 2003 L 87, (consolidated version) ('ETS Directive').

[23] See www.amazonfund.org and www.sosyasuni.org (accessed on 4 January 2012).

[24] 'The Cancun Agreements: Outcome of the work of the Ad Hoc Working Group on Long-term Cooperative Action under the Convention', Decision 1/CP.16, 15 March 2011, FCCC/CP/2010/7/Add.1 ('Decision 1/CP.16'), Chapter III, Section C.

[25] IBRD, Amended and Restated Instrument Establishing the Prototype Carbon Fund, Resolution No. 99–1 ('PCF Resolution').

PCF is both an environmental fund and a component of a market mechanism. Indeed, some of the fund providers are private investors and the PCF funds are channelled towards the Kyoto flexible mechanisms. Second, the PCF provides an illustration of a generation of other hybrid funds established at the domestic level and linked to the Kyoto flexible mechanisms.[26]

The objectives of the PCF are defined in the PCF resolution: (i) to demonstrate how projects to reduce emission can contribute to developing and transitional countries; (ii) to gain and disseminate knowledge on how to conduct such projects; and, more significantly for present purposes, (iii) 'to demonstrate how the IBRD can work in partnership with the public and private sectors to mobilize new resources for its borrowing member countries while addressing global environmental concerns'.[27] The funds are contributed by both public and private 'Participants'[28] and they can be used in projects that generate emissions reductions. Participants receive in exchange an agreed amount of carbon credits recognised under the Kyoto Protocol.[29] Thus, a 'Private Sector Participant', such as Electrabel or Mitsubishi Corporation, can derive from its contribution to the fund a benefit in terms of emission reduction units (ERUs) or certified emission reductions (CERs). According to the most recent annual report, the PCF portfolio comprises twenty-four projects, the majority of which were channelled through the clean development mechanism (CDM) towards East Asia and the Pacific.[30] However, the funding mobilised by the PCF – both public and private – is quite limited (US $172 million).

3.1.2 Environmental PPPs

As discussed in Chapter 1, the idea of private sector involvement in addressing environmental challenges gained ground throughout the 1990s[31] and was officially endorsed by some initiatives of the UN Secretary-General,[32]

---

[26] World Bank, 'Annual Report. Carbon Finance for Sustainable Development' (2010) ('Carbon Finance'), pp. 23–77.

[27] PCF Resolution, above n. 25, Preamble, para. (B) and Section 3.1.

[28] Ibid., Section 4.1.   [29] Ibid., Section 3.2.

[30] Carbon Finance, above n. 26, pp. 24–6.

[31] Report of the United Nations Conference on Environment and Development, A/CONF.151/26/Rev.l (Vol. l), Resolution 1, Annex 2: Agenda 21 ('Agenda 21'), Chapter 30.

[32] Report of the Secretary-General: Renewing the United Nations: A Programme for Reform, 14 July 1997, UN Doc. A/51/1950, paras. 59–60; Report of the Secretary General: Enhanced Cooperation between the UN and All Relevant Partners, in particular the Private Sector, 10 August 2005, UN Doc. A/60/214.

in the United Nations Millennium Declaration[33] and, most significantly, at the World Summit on Sustainable Development, held at Johannesburg (South Africa) in 2002 ('WSSD').[34] PPPs can be used as project finance vehicles, as is currently the case of the GEF[35] or of the PCF, itself a PPP. So far, tapping into the financial resources of the private sector has been perhaps the most important use of PPPs. Yet, PPPs can also provide a vehicle for projects jointly undertaken in the field. The so-called 'Type II outcomes' of the WSSD covered indeed 'commitments to specific targets and objectives for the implementation of sustainable development made by a coalition of actors',[36] including the private sector.

According to the WSSD preparatory documents, the main characteristics of these PPPs included the following: participation (public sector, civil society, business); interdependence (as no sector can alone tackle the relevant issues); openness and flexibility (more adapted to the changing nature of the relevant issues); subsidiarity (governance by those best equipped and closer to the problem); and complementarity (synergies among participants).[37] The overall supervision of the Partnerships for Sustainable Development Programme was entrusted to the Commission on Sustainable Development ('CSS') established in 1992 at the Rio Conference on Environment and Development (the 'Earth Summit'). Over the years, more than 300 partnerships have been registered with the CSS, mostly in the areas of water, energy and education.[38] Most of these partnerships have a global (180), regional (69) or subregional (79) geographic scope.[39] According to the 2008 report on the implementation of this programme, the progress reported so far is mostly of an organisational nature, with little concrete results on environmental indicators.[40]

---

[33] United Nations Millennium Declaration, UNGA Res. 55/2, 8 September 2000, para. 20.

[34] Report of the World Summit on Sustainable Development, A/CONF.199/20, Part I, Item 2: Plan of Implementation of the World Summit on Sustainable Development ('Plan of Implementation'), paras. 7(j), 9(g), 20(t), 25(g), 43(a) and 49.

[35] GEF Revised Strategy, above n. 10, paras. 28–34, 39.

[36] C. Streck, 'The World Summit on Sustainable Development: Partnerships as New Tools in Environmental Governance' (2002) 13 Yearbook of International Environmental Law 63, 67.

[37] Ibid., 70–1.

[38] See webapps01.un.org/dsd/partnerships/public/partnerships/stats/primary_theme.jpg (accessed on 4 January 2012).

[39] See webapps01.un.org/dsd/partnerships/public/partnerships/stats/geographic_scope.jpg (accessed on 4 January 2012).

[40] Report of the Secretary-General: Partnerships for Sustainable Development, 6 February 2008, UN Doc. E/CN.17/2008/10, paras. 36–40, 50–3.

In addition to these PPPs, a number of initiatives have been jointly undertaken by the bodies of some environmental treaties and some private companies.[41] From an analytical perspective, these PPPs can be organised under three main (and sometimes overlapping) categories. First, many of these PPPs are intended to mobilise the financial resources of the private sector to help implement an environmental treaty. An example of this category is the 'Danone–Evian Fund for Water Resources' established in 2002 following an agreement between the Secretariat of the Ramsar Convention[42] and the Danone Group.[43] One recent development of this PPP is the creation of 'Water Protection Schools' in order, *inter alia*, to 'develop the sharing of expertise on the sustainable and collaborative protection of water resources'.[44] The second category covers PPPs set up for communication purposes. One of the major objectives pursued by private companies when entering into PPPs is improving their corporate image. Thus, in the Ramsar–Danone PPP, the funds committed by the company were in exchange for the use of the Ramsar logo.[45] In some cases, however, the communication campaign aims at increasing awareness of the environmental treaty. For example the Secretariat of the CMS Convention[46] entered into a PPP with the German air carrier Lufthansa to show a documentary on the activities of the convention in certain Lufthansa flights.[47] The third category includes initiatives to foster private sector compliance with the obligations of an environmental treaty or even with standards that go beyond what is strictly required by the treaty. An example is the 'Mobile Phone Partnership Initiative'[48] jointly undertaken by the Secretariat of the Basel Convention and a number of private companies for the

---

[41] E. Morgera, *Corporate Accountability in International Environmental Law* (Oxford University Press, 2009) pp. 251–4.

[42] Convention on Wetlands of International Importance especially as Waterfowl Habitat, 2 February 1971, 996 UNTS 245 ('Ramsar Convention').

[43] Action Programme for Water Resource and Water Quality Protection in Wetlands of International Importance, Memorandum of Understanding, 27 January 1998. The initial instrument has been subsequently completed and amended by a number of other instruments. See www.ramsar.org (accessed on 4 January 2012).

[44] Memorandum of Understanding 'Ecole de protection de l'eau', 27 July 2007, Preamble, Recital 2, available at: www.ramsar.org (accessed on 4 January 2012).

[45] *Ibid.*, Preamble, Recital 3, and Article III.

[46] Convention on the Conservation of Migratory Species of Wild Animals, 23 June 1979, 1651 UNTS 356 ('CMS Convention').

[47] Morgera, *Corporate Accountability in International Environmental Law*, above n. 41, p. 253.

[48] 'Sustainable Partnership for the Environmentally Sound Management of End-of-life Mobile Telephones', Decision VI/31, 10 February 2003, UNEP/CHW.6/40.

'environmentally sound management of used and end-of-life mobile phones' not covered by the Convention's definition of waste. On the basis of this initiative, the Basel Convention has been developing in the last years a set of 'Guidelines' on this question.[49]

3.2   The substance of synergies – climate change and biodiversity as examples

Synergies between foreign investment and environmental protection have been explored in many areas. For example, the portfolio of the GEF has been divided into a number of 'focal areas', namely climate change, biodiversity conservation, management of international waters, land degradation, persistent organic pollutants and ozone depletion. The substance of synergies could also be characterised by reference to specific forms of assistance, such as capacity building and/or technology transfer. This section, however, focuses on two main substantive areas: climate change and biodiversity conservation. This choice is based on two considerations. First, it is in these areas that the most innovative synergy mechanisms have been developed. Second, these two areas have received the lion's share in terms of both GEF's funds and leveraged (public and private) financing. Taking the GEF's allocation of funds as a proxy, out of the US $8.6 billion directly invested by the GEF as of 2009, US $5.5 billion has gone to climate change and biodiversity related projects. Moreover, out of the US $36.1 billion leveraged thanks to GEF involvement, US $24.8 billion has flowed into these two areas.[50] In the following paragraphs, I first discuss the flexible mechanisms introduced by the climate change regime (Section 3.2.1) and then focus on a variety of 'payment-for-ecosystem-services' ('PES') schemes used to support biodiversity conservation (Section 3.2.2).

3.2.1   Foreign investment in climate change initiatives

The so-called 'flexible mechanisms' introduced by the Kyoto Protocol have received ample attention in the literature.[51] This section concentrates on how these mechanisms can mobilise foreign investment

---

[49] 'Guidance Document on the Environmentally Sound Management of Used and End-of-life Mobile Phones', 14 July 2011, UNEP/CHW.10/INF/27.

[50] GEF Fact Sheets: About the GEF (2009), pp. 1, 5 and 9, available at: www.thegef.org/gef/node/1540 (accessed on 4 January 2012).

[51] See, in particular, D. Freestone and C. Streck (eds.), *Legal Aspects of Carbon Trading* (Oxford University Press, 2009).

into pro-environment projects. Whereas the so-called 'project-based mechanisms' channel foreign investment directly into projects with emissions-reduction potential (Section 3.2.1.1), 'emissions trading schemes' do so indirectly by creating a market for emissions-reduction units (Section 3.2.1.2).

3.2.1.1 Project-based mechanisms

The Kyoto Protocol provides for two project-based mechanisms, in Articles 6 (joint implementation or 'JI') and 12 (clean development mechanism or 'CDM') respectively. The rationale of these mechanisms is that carbon credits can be generated more efficiently in those places where there is a larger room for improvement of production methods, i.e., transition economies and developing countries, by transferring technology in exchange for carbon credits. From the perspective of foreign investors, the incentive provided by these channels is therefore to 'produce' more cheaply certain goods or assets ('emissions-reduction units' or 'ERUs' for JI projects and 'certified emission reductions' or 'CERs' for CDM projects) and then sell them to companies or States that need them to comply with legal obligations or other commitments. As with any investment, there are some risks associated with these transactions,[52] such as the possibility that the project yields less carbon credits than expected, the value of the credits decreases in international markets or the host State interferes with the transaction. Yet the use of these mechanisms may provide, in addition to the generation of carbon credits, advantages such as facilitated project finance (e.g., through the GEF or the PCF) or access to a strategic market (e.g., China, India, Brazil, Ukraine, Russia, etc.). Most of these different parameters (value of assets produced, facilitated access to finance, regulatory risk) vary according to the mechanism used (JI or CDM).

As a general matter, CDM projects tend to be more sought after than JI projects, because they yield more valuable units, they provide better access to environmental funds, they present less exposure to the host State's regulatory framework and they can be undertaken in strategically more attractive countries. From an environmental perspective, however, their performance is not necessarily higher, as there are serious doubts as to whether the CDM is actually achieving its emissions-reduction and technology transfer objectives. Regarding emissions

---

[52] J. Lin, 'Private Actors in International and Domestic Emissions Trading Schemes', in Freestone and Streck, *Legal Aspects of Carbon Trading*, above n. 51, pp. 138–52.

reduction, there has been much discussion in the last few years regarding the 'additionality' of the carbon credits produced by the CDM. A CDM project can only result in CERs if the emissions reductions achieved are 'additional' to a business-as-usual scenario or, in other terms, if such reductions would not have happened in the absence of the CDM project. Yet, some studies have shown that CDM has created perverse incentives to manipulate the emissions baseline against which reductions are measured and even to breathe new life into agonising polluting industries such as the HCFC-22 industry.[53] As to the transfers of technology initially envisioned, the objective has been fulfilled only partially. CDM flows have gone for the most part to China, Brazil and India but the level of technology transfer for these countries has been found to be lower than average.[54] This does not necessarily mean that no technology transfer is taking place but only that there is little renewal in the technologies being transferred over time.[55]

Compared to CDM, JI projects are less demanding in terms of additionality because, unlike CDM credits, any reductions derived from a JI project are deducted from the allowances of the host country. Thus, any ERUs generated through a JI project amount to a 'trade' from one country subject to a cap (Annex B of the Kyoto Protocol) to another, and not to a carbon credit generated in addition to the Kyoto cap. This said, from the perspective of a foreign investor, JI projects may be somewhat less attractive than CDM projects because ERUs tend to trade at a lower price than CERs and their generation is largely subject to the regulatory powers of the host State.[56]

More recently, several steps have been taken to introduce a new project-based mechanism focusing on carbon credits derived from avoided deforestation, the so-called REDD-plus scheme.[57] As deforestation is one of the major causes of global emissions as well as one of the cheapest ones to avoid, there has been much discussion about how

---

[53] M. Wara, 'Measuring the Clean Development Mechanism's Performance and Potential' (2007) 55 *UCLA Law Review* 1759.

[54] S. Seres, 'Analysis of Technology Transfer in CDM Projects' (2008), pp. 10, 15, available at: cdm.unfccc.int/Reference/Reports/TTreport/TTrep08.pdf (accessed on 4 January 2012).

[55] *Ibid.*, p. 16.

[56] A. Hobley and C. Robers, 'Joint Implementation Transactions: An Overview', in Freestone and Streck, *Legal Aspects of Carbon Trading*, above n. 51, pp. 198–9.

[57] See above n. 24; C. Parker, A. Mitchell, M. Trivedi, N. Mardas and K. Sosis, *The Little REDD Book: A Guide to Governmental and Non-Governmental Proposals for Reducing Emissions from Deforestation and Degradation* (2009), available at: www.unfccc.int (accessed on 14 March 2012).

to curb the economic incentives underlying deforestation. It is believed that deforestation can be avoided by rendering more (or as) profitable – through financial transfers – a scenario in which forests are preserved (instead of cut down to use the land for other purposes). In such a scenario, public and private fund providers would be investing in the continued provision of certain ecosystem services (e.g., carbon capture and storage by forests) and may also receive carbon credits, although, at the time of writing, this latter possibility was still unclear. As a synergy mechanism, REDD-plus concerns both climate change mitigation and biodiversity conservation.

3.2.1.2   Emissions trading

Emissions trading schemes – either domestic or international – contribute to the channeling of foreign investment into pro-environment projects by creating a market for the end-products of such projects, i.e., carbon credits. Although the mere possibility of trading carbon credits is, as such, a positive incentive to invest in generating them, the relationship between trading and investment is of a rather indirect nature. The recognition of certain project-based credits – and therefore their value – may indeed be limited in some trading schemes on the basis of criteria such as the type of project (e.g., the acceptance of credits from changes in land use is restricted in the ETS Directive),[58] the useful life of the credit (e.g., their validity beyond a given 'commitment period')[59] or, simply, the amount of project-based credits that can be used by a given company to fulfil its regulatory obligations.[60] Furthermore, the value of some credits (typically initial allowances) may be politically limited, if there is a perception that they do not correspond to any genuine efforts to reduce emissions.

This latter concern has arisen in connection with the allowances of countries like Russia or Ukraine, whose initial Kyoto shares were rather generous, especially taking into account the economic downturn they

---

[58] ETS Directive, above n. 22, Article 11a(3) second paragraph and Article 28(1)(f). See also Directive 2004/101/EC of the European Parliament and of the Council of 27 October 2004 amending Directive 2003/87/EC establishing a scheme for greenhouse gas emission allowance trading within the Community, in respect of the Kyoto Protocol's project mechanisms, OJ 2004 L338/18, ('Linking Directive'), Article 11a(3)(b).

[59] Wara, 'Measuring the Clean Development Mechanism's Performance and Potential', above n. 53, 1777–8. See, however, ETS Directive, above n. 22, Article 11a.

[60] ETS Directive, above n. 22, Article 11a(8). See also, the current debate on the reform of the Swiss climate legislation at www.bafu.admin.ch/klima/00493/06577/11706/index.html?lang=fr (accessed on 4 January 2012).

experienced during the 1990s. As noted by one commentator, 'concerns that their surpluses resulted from the state of their economies rather than genuinely planned emission reduction policies undermined the perception of the environmental integrity of the [emissions trading] mechanism'.[61] To address this problem of perception, an interesting technique has been developed, the so-called 'green investment schemes' or 'GIS'. Under these schemes, the buying and selling countries agree to devote the proceeds of a sale of emissions allowances (technically 'assigned amount units' or 'AAUs') to an environmental project. Such a project can seek emissions reductions (so-called 'hard greening') or pursue another environmental objective (e.g., education, transparency, adaptation, etc.). In this way, AAUs from transitional countries are made more environmentally attractive and developed States acquiring them can more easily justify resort to such carbon credits. Whereas, as a rule, GIS are used in inter-State emissions trading, private investors could also participate in this mechanism if, for example, they are allowed to use AAUs to comply with their obligations or if they expect to sell the AAUs thus acquired to a country. The risks involved in such transactions (e.g., that the funds are not used as agreed, with the resulting loss of value of the credits purchased)[62] must be managed contractually, as GIS are not regulated by the Kyoto Protocol. The attractiveness of GIS is, however, linked to the useful life of AAUs, which is currently limited to the first commitment period of the Kyoto Protocol (2008–12).[63]

3.2.2 Foreign investment in biodiversity-related activities

The term 'payments for ecosystem services' or 'PES' broadly refers to a variety of techniques that seek synergies between public and private investment and the protection of 'natural infrastructures'. These techniques share the same assumption, namely that forests, wetlands and other ecosystems provide services that can be economically valued. A UNEP-prepared report identifies five main types of PES relating to the protection of biodiversity:[64] (i) purchase of biodiversity rich land for purposes of conservation; (ii) equity support of enterprises active in the conservation of biodiversity; (iii) payment for access to certain biological

---

[61] S. Simonetti and R. de Witt Wijnen, 'International Emissions Trading and Green Investment Schemes', in Freestone and Streck, *Legal Aspects of Carbon Trading*, above n. 51, p. 164.

[62] *Ibid.*, p. 172.   [63] *Ibid.*, pp. 170–1.

[64] Forest Trends, The Katoomba Group and United Nations Environment Programme, *Payments for Ecosystem Services. Getting Started: A Primer* (2008) ('UNEP Report'), p. 6.

resources (e.g., for bioprospecting purposes); (iv) payments to induce land-owners to manage lands in certain pro-environment ways; and (v) tradable biodiversity rights or credits. In the following pages, the three latter mechanisms, which better reflect the technique of PPPs or market mechanisms as applied to the protection of biodiversity, are briefly surveyed.

3.2.2.1 Access and benefit sharing arrangements

In the last twenty years, a system of access and benefit sharing ('ABS') arrangements has been organised under the aegis of Articles 15, 16 and 19 of the Convention on Biological Diversity,[65] as further specified by the so-called 'Bonn Guidelines' (2002)[66] and, more recently, by the adoption of the Nagoya ABS Protocol.[67] This system grants source States broad discretion to regulate the conditions for access as well as to negotiate 'agreed terms' with investors seeking access to genetic resources.[68]

Investors frequently enter into agreements to obtain bioprospecting rights or research permits in exchange for some form of benefit sharing, which may include monetary payments, the sharing of intellectual property rights and/or other forms of technology transfer.[69] These agreements have two dimensions. On the one hand, they seek to create a synergy between the interests of investors, those of the source State and those of other stakeholders, such as affected indigenous peoples. On the other hand, they set a framework to control the bioprospecting activities of the investor in the territory of the source State.

One oft-cited example is the agreement between Merck Pharmaceuticals and the National Biodiversity Institute of Costa Rica (INBio) in late

---

[65] Convention on Biological Diversity, 5 June 1992, 1760 UNTS 79.

[66] Bonn Guidelines on Access to Genetic Resources and Fair and Equitable Sharing of the Benefits Arising out of their Utilization, UN Doc. UNEP/CBD/COP/6/24 (2002) ('Bonn Guidelines').

[67] Nagoya Protocol on Access to Genetic Resources and the Fair and Equitable Sharing of the Benefits Arising from their Utilization to the Convention on Biological Diversity, 29 October 2010 (not in force), available at: www.cbd.int/abs/doc/protocol/nagaya-protocol-en.pdf.

[68] O. Rukundo and J. Cabrera, 'Investment Promotion and Protection in the UNCBD: An Emerging Access and Benefit Sharing Regime', in M.-C. Cordonnier Segger, M. W. Gehring and A. Newcombe (eds.), *Sustainable Development in World Investment Law* (Alphen aan den Rijn: Wolters Kluwer, 2011), p. 721.

[69] R. Lewis-Lettington and S. Mwanyiki, *Case Studies on Access and Benefit Sharing* (Rome: International Plant Genetic Resources Institute, 2006), discussing the experience of ten source countries.

1991.[70] Under this agreement, INBio would provide some 10,000 samples of plants, animals and soils to Merck for its exclusive research use over two years, in exchange for a lump sum amount, some laboratory equipment and, most remarkably, a right to royalties for drugs developed on the basis of these samples. Over the years, INBio has entered into several agreements with other foreign investors and institutions, including some foreign universities such as Cornell and the University of Strathclyde.[71]

Some countries have developed model ABS agreements. For example, the Australian government has drawn up two templates,[72] one for transactions where Australia is the source country (access provider agreement) and the other for Australian companies seeking access to biological resources abroad (user agreement). Pursuant to Section 3 of both templates, the investor ('access party') must pay an access fee ('threshold payments') and share duplicates of the samples taken (Schedule 3) and, normally, it will also be required to share benefits through various forms of technology transfers in accordance with the Bonn Guidelines (Schedule 4). More than fifty other model and actual ABS agreements are available on the database compiled by the World Intellectual Property Organisation's Committee on Genetic Resouces, Traditional Knowledge and Folklore.[73]

3.2.2.2   Land use inducements

Some of the most significant land use inducement mechanisms include the REDD-plus scheme and a number of environmental funds (e.g., the Amazon Fund or the Yasuní Initiative). The purpose of these schemes is to modify the economic incentives underlying non-sustainable or environmentally detrimental uses of land. The aforementioned report by UNEP identifies five types of land use inducement schemes:

Conservation easements (owner is paid to use and manage a defined piece of land only for conservation purposes; restrictions are usually in perpetuity and transferable upon sale of the land)

   Conservation land lease (owner is paid to use and manage a defined piece of land for conservation purposes, for a defined period of time)

---

[70] M. D. Coughlin, 'Using the Merck-INBio Agreement to Clarify the Convention on Biological Diversity' (1993) 31 *Columbia Journal of Transnational Law* 337.

[71] Lewis-Lettington and Mwanyiki, *Care Studies on Access and Benefit Sharing* above n. 69, p. 10.

[72] See www.environment.gov.au/biodiversity/science/access/model-agreements/index.html (accessed on 4 January 2012).

[73] See www.wipo.int/tk/en/databases/contracts/ (accessed on 4 January 2012).

Conservation concession (public forest agency is paid to maintain a defined area under conservation uses only; comparable to a forest logging concession)

Community concession in public protected areas (individuals or communities are allocated use rights to a defined area of forest or grassland in return for a commitment to protect the area from practices that harm biodiversity)

Management contracts for habitat or species conservation on private farms, forests, or grazing lands (contract that details biodiversity management activities, and payments linked to the achievement of specified objectives)[74]

These five types of PES have, as their primary goal, the conservation of biodiversity. The description is, however, too general to see why foreign investment into such schemes may be induced for profitability – rather than conservation – considerations.

To understand this latter point, a brief discussion of a specific case appears useful. In the early 1990s, Nestlé Waters developed a scheme to change agricultural practices in an area surrounding the water source of one of its most successful natural mineral water brands (Vittel).[75] The problem was largely a regulatory one. French legislation imposed a number of stringent requirements for the use of the Vittel brand. In particular, the composition of the source water (an aquifer serving the 'Grand Source' from which Vittel water is derived) had to be very stable and could not be achieved by post-extraction treatment. The composition of Vittel water is very low in nitrates (less that 4.5 mg/l, by contrast with up to 15 mg/l for other 'natural mineral waters' or even 50 mg/l for tub water). Yet, the increasing use of the lands surrounding the source for agricultural purposes was affecting the composition of the groundwater with the potential consequence that Nestlé would no longer be allowed to commercialise the water under its 'Vittel' brand. To address this situation Nestlé analysed several options and eventually opted for inducing farmers to change their practices through a PES scheme. The agreement involved incentives such as subsidies to farmers, additional resources to help farmers finance the acquisition of new farm equipment or free technical assistance to accompany the transition.[76] In addition to these financial incentives, extensive efforts were made to establish a co-operative relationship with farmers, which, according to the director of the entity that led the process, was a decisive factor.[77]

---

[74] UNEP Report, above n. 64, p. 6.

[75] D. Perrot-Maître, 'The Vittel Payments for Ecosystem Services: a "Perfect" PES Case?', IISD Project Paper No. 3 (2006).

[76] Ibid., 15.   [77] Ibid., 19.

Nestlé has pursued similar strategies in connection with other natural mineral waters (Perrier and Contrex) extracted in France.

3.2.2.3   Tradable rights

Tradable rights have also been used to protect biodiversity. One example is provided by the ERUs that can be derived from activities relating to land use. Under the Kyoto Protocol, some of these activities (e.g., reforestation and aforestation) can yield carbon credits (e.g., ERUs, CERs or removal units, also called 'RMUs'). Also, activities relating to avoided deforestation under the REDD-plus scheme could potentially yield some form of carbon credits still to be defined.

Beyond the climate change regime, another example of the tradable rights approach can be found in US regulations under Section 404(b)(1) of the Clean Water Act ('CWA').[78] Under the CWA, dredged or fill material cannot be discharged into a watercourse unless the entity responsible is authorised to do so. Any such discharge is moreover subject to two additional requirements, namely to avoid or minimise adverse impacts on wetlands and to compensate for unavoidable impacts. One form of compensation is to acquire 'compensatory mitigation credits'. These credits are sold by companies or agencies operating so-called 'mitigation banks'. A mitigation bank is a wetland that has been restored or preserved and that is currently managed to ensure the continual provision of its ecosystem services. The entity managing the bank has to meet a number of regulatory standards and can sell credits to other companies that are required to compensate for the adverse impacts of their activities elsewhere in the watershed. According to the US Environmental Protection Agency (EPA), this 'form of "third party" compensatory mitigation ... has been a very attractive feature for Section 404 permit-holders, who would otherwise be responsible for the design, construction, monitoring, ecological success, and long-term protection of the site'.[79] For the purpose of this section, the EPA scheme illustrates how the protection of wetlands can become a business venture.

---

[78] Compensatory Mitigation for Losses of Aquatic Resources, 40 CFR Part 230 Subpart J, and 33 CFR 332. See Environmental Protection Agency (EPA), Wetlands Compensatory Mitigation, available at: www.epa.gov/owow/wetlands/pdf/CMitigation.pdf (accessed on 4 January 2012).

[79] EPA, Mitigation Banking Factsheet, available at: www.epa.gov/owow/wetlands/facts/fact16.html (accessed on 4 January 2012).

4   Conflicts I – soft control mechanisms

This chapter provides a concise description of certain mechanisms that have been developed over the years to provide some measure of control over the activities of multinational corporations beyond their home countries. The term 'soft control mechanisms' encompasses a diverse array of tools, ranging from simple guidelines or codes to contractual techniques to fact-finding mechanisms. Some of these mechanisms amount to quasi-adjudicatory systems, where the actions of a corporation or of a lending institution are scrutinised to assess their conformity with human rights and environmental standards. The description provided in this chapter is, however, limited because such mechanisms have already received ample attention in the literature,[1] and they will be

---

[1] See S. Coonrod, 'The United Nations Code of Conduct for Transnational Corporations' (1977) 18 *Harvard International Law Journal* 273; A. Gowlland Gualtieri, 'The Environmental Accountability of the World Bank to Non-State Actors: Insights from the Inspection Panel' (2001) 72 *British Yearbook of International Law* 213; D. Ong, 'The Impact of Environmental Law on Corporate Governance: International and Comparative Perspectives' (2001) 12 *European Journal of International Law* 685; C. Freeman, C. Heydenreich and S. Lillywhite, *Guide to the OECD Guidelines for Multinational Enterprises' Complaints Procedure: Lessons from Past NGO Complaints* (2006), available at: www.oecolwatch.org (accessed on 4 January 2012); J. Zerk, *Multinationals and Corporate Social Responsibility* (Cambridge University Press, 2006); B. J. Richardson, 'Financing Sustainability: The New Transnational Governance of Socially Responsible Investment' (2006) 17 *Yearbook of International Environmental Law* 73; B. J. Richardson, *Socially Responsible Investment Law: Regulating the Unseen Polluters* (Oxford University Press, 2008); E. Morgera, *Corporate Accountability in International Environmental Law* (Oxford University Press, 2009); R. B. Stewart, 'A New Generation of Environmental Regulation' (2001) 29 *Capital University Law Review* 21; E. W. Orts and K. Deketelaere (eds.), *Environmental Contracts: Comparative Approaches to Regulatory Innovation in the United States and Europe* (The Hague: Kluwer Law International 2001); C. O'Faircheallaigh, *Environmental Agreements in Canada: Aboriginal Participation, EIA Follow-up and Environmental Management of Major Projects* (Calgary AB: Canadian Institute of Resources Law; 2006); N. Affolder, 'Rethinking Environmental Contracting' (2010) 21 *Journal of Environmental Law and Practice* 115.

analysed in detail in a companion volume to this book.[2] The discussion focuses on three main categories of mechanisms, namely standards of conduct (Section 4.1), contractual approaches (Section 4.2) and accountability mechanisms (Section 4.3).

4.1 Standards of conduct

The first step in the efforts to develop an international framework applicable to the activities of multinational corporations was to adopt basic standards of conduct. The initial approach was to adopt standards directly applicable to the operations of multinational companies (Section 4.1.1). Over time, another body of standards has also emerged affecting such operations only indirectly, by targeting financial intermediaries (Section 4.1.2).[3] In discussing these standards, particular attention will be paid to their sources in international environmental law. Reference to these sources seems useful to understand why the contents of such standards converge to a considerable extent.[4]

4.1.1 Direct standards affecting multinational enterprises

4.1.1.1 Overview

The most prominent illustrations of direct standards are perhaps the efforts undertaken within the framework of the United Nations and the Organisation for Economic Co-operation and Development (OECD). Historically, the two processes were linked because the OECD initiative was undertaken by developed countries at a time when a UN draft Code of Conduct on Transnational Corporations was the object of vivid debates between developed and developing countries.[5] Whereas the main outcome of the OECD process was the 'Guidelines for Multinational Enterprises',[6] the UN process led to the elaboration of a

---

[2] See P.-M. Dupuy and J. E. Vinuales (eds.), *Harnessing Foreign Investment to Promote Environmental Protection: Incentives and Safeguards* (Cambridge University Press, forthcoming), Part III, chapters by E. Morgera (accountability mechanisms), N. Affolder (environmental contracts), and B. Richardson (SRI codes).

[3] Richardson, 'Financing Sustainability', above n. 1, 74.

[4] On the converging contents of these standards, see Morgera, *Corporate Accountability in International Environmental Law* above n. 1, Chapter 8.

[5] *Ibid.*, p. 102.

[6] OECD, Guidelines for Multinational Enterprises, Annex I to the Declaration on International Investment and Multinational Enterprises, 25 May 2011 ('OECD Guidelines'); E. Morgera, 'An Environmental Outlook on the OECD Guidelines for Multinational Enterprises: Comparative Advantage, Legitimacy, and Outstanding

series of documents and frameworks,[7] of which only the 'UN Global Compact'[8] will be discussed here.

Both instruments operate as normative frameworks that seek to influence the behaviour of multinational corporations in a number of areas, including environmental protection. The OECD Guidelines were adopted in 1976 and subsequently updated five times, most recently in May 2011. The chapter on environmental protection was added in 1991, largely as a result of the Bhopal catastrophe. It now contains eight recommendations focusing on environmental matters. As to the UN Global Compact, it was launched in July 2000, addressing four areas potentially affected by the activities of businesses, namely human rights, labour standards, environment and corruption. The Global Compact is structured as a public–private partnership and operates essentially as a policy network with more than 7,700 participants worldwide, including some 5,300 businesses. It was established as a tool to channel the activities of the private sector towards the accomplishment of the Millennium Development Goals (MDGs) adopted by the United Nations General Assembly in 2000.[9]

As discussed next, these instruments take very different approaches to the soft control of foreign investors. Such differences concern, essentially, (i) the regulatory angle of each of the two instruments; (ii) their environmental standards; and (iii) their enforcement.

4.1.1.2 The OECD Guidelines

Regarding the regulatory angle adopted by the OECD Guidelines, they must be seen as 'recommendations jointly addressed by governments to multinational enterprises'.[10] They apply to multinational companies (broadly defined to include both parent companies and/or local entities[11])

Questions in the Lead Up to the 2006 Review' (2006) 18 *Georgetown International Environmental Law Review* 751.

[7] Morgera, above n. 1, *Corporate Accountability in International Environmental Law*, pp. 77–101 (discussing the UN Draft Code of Conduct, the UN Global Compact and the Norms on the Responsibilities of Transnational Corporations and Other Business Enterprises with regard to Human Rights).

[8] UN Global Compact, available at: www.globalcompact.org (accessed on 4 January 2012). On the operation of the Global Compact, see UN Global Compact Office, *United Nations Guide to the Global Compact: A Practical Understanding of the Vision and the Nine Principles*; B. King, 'The UN Global Compact: Responsibility for Human Rights, Labour Relations, and the Environment in Developing Nations' (2001) 34 *Cornell International Law Journal* 481.

[9] United Nations Millennium Declaration, UN Doc. A/RES/55/2 Millennium (18 September 2000).

[10] OECD Guidelines, above n. 6, Chapter I, para. 1.   [11] *Ibid.*, Chapter I, para. 4.

operating 'in or from' the territories of adhering countries.[12] Their observance by covered enterprises is 'voluntary and not legally enforceable'.[13] There are, however, three caveats to their applicability. First, the standards set out in the Guidelines 'may also be regulated by national law or international commitments',[14] in which case their observance may be required by law. Second, adhering States make a binding commitment to implement them in accordance with the Decision of the OECD Council on the OECD Guidelines for Multinational Enterprises.[15] This decision requires adhering States to implement into their domestic legislation the system of accountability described in Part II of the Guidelines.[16] Third, when the domestic laws and regulations of the host States where covered enterprises operate are inconsistent with the Guidelines, enterprises 'should seek ways to honour such principles and standards to the fullest extent which does not place them in violation of domestic law'.[17]

With respect to the contents of the Guidelines, Chapter VI ('Environment') sets out eight principles derived from the Rio Declaration,[18] the Aarhus Convention[19] and the ISO Environmental Management standards[20] (the so-called '14000 family').[21] Accordingly, the three main pillars underlying these eight principles are sound environmental management, environmental transparency and prevention *lato sensu* (encompassing self-assessment, precaution and efficiency). These pillars appear in more than one principle and they are often intertwined within the same principle. However, they can be broadly located as follows: sound environmental management (principle 1); environmental transparency (principle 2); and prevention *lato sensu* (principles 3 to 8).

---

[12] OECD, Declaration on International Investment and Multinational Enterprises, 25 May 2011 ('OECD Declaration'), para. I. There are currently forty-two adhering countries. According to the website of the OECD Guidelines, they cover 85 per cent of total foreign direct investment. See www.oecd.org (accessed on 4 January 2012).

[13] OECD Guidelines, above n. 6, Chapter I, para. 1.

[14] *Ibid.*, Chapter I, para. 1.   [15] *Ibid.*, Preface, para. 1.

[16] See Section 4.3.   [17] OECD Guidelines, above n. 6, Chapter I, para. 2.

[18] Rio Declaration on Environment and Development, 13 June 1992, UN Doc. A/CONF.151/26 ('Rio Declaration').

[19] Convention on Access to Information, Public Participation in Decision-making and Access to Justice in Environmental Matters, 25 June 1998, 2161 UNTS 447 ('Aarhus Convention').

[20] See the website of the International Organisation for Standardisation ('ISO'), www.iso.org (accessed on 4 January 2012).

[21] OECD Guidelines, above n. 6, Chapter IV, Commentary, para. 60.

As to the enforcement of these standards, Part II of the OECD Guidelines provides for a rather sophisticated system of accountability based on the establishment of National Contact Points in each adhering country, which may entertain complaints relating to the violation of the Guidelines in 'specific instances'. This system will be analysed in Section 4.3.1.3 below.

4.1.1.3   The UN Global Compact

The regulatory approach followed by the UN Global Compact is very different from that of the OECD Guidelines. Rather than 'recommending' standards, enterprises are invited to adhere voluntarily, through a letter of intent, to one or more of the ten principles included in the Global Compact. It thus takes a 'collaborative' or 'partnership' approach rather than a 'regulatory' one.[22] As noted in the introductory brochure available on the Global Compact's website: '[t]he UN Global Compact is not a regulatory instrument, but rather a voluntary initiative that relies on public accountability, transparency and disclosure to complement regulation and to provide a space for innovation and collective action.'[23] Importantly, companies do not undertake any obligation by signing up to the Global Compact. At best, they are expected to file reports showing the actions taken to align with the principles to which they have subscribed.[24] In exchange, companies may present themselves as supporters of the Global Compact.

Regarding the environmental contents of the UN Global Compact, they consist of three principles (7 to 9) derived from the Rio Declaration[25] and Agenda 21.[26] Principle 7 states that '[b]usinesses should support a precautionary approach to environmental challenges'. Precaution is defined by reference to Principle 15 of the Rio Declaration, according to which 'where there are threats of serious or irreversible damage, lack of full scientific certainty shall not be used as a reason for postponing cost-effective measures to prevent environmental degradation'.[27] Principle 8

---

[22] Morgera, *Corporate Accountability in International Environmental Law* above n. 1, p. 89.

[23] UN Global Compact Brochure, available at: www.unglobalcompact.org (accessed on 4 January 2012), p. 2.

[24] UN Global Compact, Policy for the Communication of Progress ('COP Policy'), para. 2.1., available at: www.unglobalcompact.org (accessed on 4 January 2012).

[25] Rio Declaration, above n. 18.

[26] Report of the United Nations Conference on Environment and Development, A/CONF.151/26/Rev.1 (Vol. 1), Resolution 1, Annex 2: Agenda 21 ('Agenda 21').

[27] See www.unglobalcompact.org/AboutTheGC/TheTenPrinciples/principle7.html (accessed on 4 January 2012).

provides that '[b]usinesses should undertake initiatives to promote greater environmental responsibility'. Characterised by reference to Principle 2 of the Rio Declaration and Chapter 30 of Agenda 21,[28] this broad principle encompasses elements of prevention, management and transparency. As to Principle 9, it states that '[b]usinesses should encourage the development and diffusion of environmentally friendly technologies'. These technologies are characterised by reference to Chapter 34 of Agenda 21,[29] as those technologies that 'protect the environment, are less polluting, use all resources in a more sustainable manner, recycle more of their wastes and products, and handle residual wastes in a more acceptable manner than the technologies for which they were substitutes.'[30] Principle 9 goes beyond Principle 6(b) of the OECD Guidelines in that it encourages companies not only to develop but also to 'diffuse' environmentally friendly technologies.

With respect to the enforcement of these principles, the collaborative approach pursued by the UN Global Compact seems inconsistent with a strong accountability mechanism. As noted above, companies are expected to submit progress reports. Since August 2005, compliance with this expectation has started to be monitored under the so-called 'Integrity Measures'. According to the level of compliance, a company may be listed as 'non-communicating' (if it has missed one reporting deadline) or as 'expelled' from the list (if a further reporting year elapses without submission of a report).[31] As of 2010, only 23 per cent of the companies listed appeared as 'non-communicating'. Among these, the non-communicating status was twice as frequent in smaller companies (less than 250 employees) than in larger companies (more than 250 employees).[32] A non-communicating company may however regain 'active company' status by simply 'posting a link to or description of their COP [report]'. As to 'expelled' companies, as of January 2011, more than 2,000 companies (representing 24 per cent of all the companies that have joined the Global Compact) had been expelled from the

---

[28] See www.unglobalcompact.org/AboutTheGC/TheTenPrinciples/principle8.html (accessed on 4 January 2012).

[29] See www.unglobalcompact.org/AboutTheGC/TheTenPrinciples/principle9.html (accessed on 4 January 2012).

[30] Agenda 21, above n. 26, para. 34.1.

[31] UN Global Compact, Note on Integrity Measures (updated as of 12 April 2010) ('Integrity Measures'), Section 3, para. 2, available at: www.unglobalcompact.org (accessed on 4 January 2012).

[32] UN Global Compact, Annual Review 2010, p. 18, available at: www.unglobalcompact.org (accessed on 4 January 2012).

list. Most of these were companies with less than 250 employees, but more than a quarter of them were companies with between 251 to 49,999 employees.[33] Expelled companies are allowed to reapply for listing if they attach a report to their application.[34] The Global Compact office may take additional measures in case of 'systematic or egregious abuses', as discussed in Section 4.3.1.2.

4.1.2   Indirect standards affecting financial intermediaries

4.1.2.1   Overview

Indirect standards encompass a number of principles and policy instruments aimed at regulating the activities of financial intermediaries, including the World Bank's International Finance Corporation (IFC) and private financial institutions (commercial banks, investment banks, insurance companies and pension funds).[35] Among the numerous instruments falling under this category, one may mention the IFC's Performance Standards on Social and Environmental Sustainability,[36] the Equator Principles,[37] the UNEPFI-led Statement by Financial Institutions on the Environment and Sustainable Development,[38] the UN Principles of Responsible Investment[39] and many others.

Despite some variation from one instrument to another, they all operate by setting social and environmental standards for project financing by public, institutional or private financiers. Thus, access to funding by promoters of infrastructure or other projects with significant implications for the environment is subject to the respect of a number of environmental

---

[33] *Ibid.*, p. 19.

[34] Integrity Measures, above n. 31, Section 3, para. 3.

[35] See Richardson, 'Financing Sustainability', above n. 1; Richardson, *Socially Responsible Investment Law*, above n. 1.

[36] International Finance Corporation (IFC), *Performance Standards on Social and Environmental Sustainability*, adopted on 21 February 2006, ('Performance Standards') available at www.ifc.org/sustainability (accessed on 4 January 2012). On the operation of the Standards, see E. Morgera, 'Significant Trends in Corporate Environmental Accountability: The New Performance Standards of the International Financial Corporation' (2007) 18 *Colorado Journal of International Law and Policy* 151.

[37] Equator Principles, available at: www.equator-principles.com (accessed on 4 January 2012). On the operation of these principles, see B. J. Richardson, 'The Equator Principles: The Voluntary Approach to Environmentally Sustainable Finance' (2005) 14 *European Environmental Law Review* 280.

[38] UNEP Finance Initiative, 'Statement by Financial Institutions on the Environment and Sustainable Development', available at: www.unepfi.org (accessed on 4 January 2012).

[39] United Nations Principles of Responsible Investment, available at: www.unpri.org/principles (accessed on 4 January 2012).

standards. As discussed next in connection with the role of the IFC,[40] the contents of these standards are based, sometimes explicitly, on international environmental law.

4.1.2.2   The IFC Performance Standards

The IFC Performance Standards were developed through a process that lasted some fifteen years as a means to ensure that both the IFC and its clients ('IFC-funded projects') conduct their activities in a manner that is socially and environmentally responsible. Initially limited to a vague reference to 'appropriate World Bank environmental policies and guidelines',[41] the policy was expanded twice, in 1998 and 2003, before taking its present form in February 2006. The operation of the Performance Standards is based on a combination of: (i) eight standards focusing on social and environmental protection; and (ii) a rather sophisticated enforcement mechanism through the Compliance Advisor Ombudsman ('CAO').

Regarding the standards, they consist, as noted by Morgera,[42] of a general cross-cutting standard requiring two key components, namely environmental impact assessment and environmental management systems, and seven area-specific standards. Of these latter, three are of a chiefly environmental nature, namely Standards 3 (pollution prevention and abatement), 6 (biodiversity conservation and sustainable natural resource management) and 8 (cultural heritage), whereas the others are mostly concerned with stakeholders, through 'labour and working conditions' (Standard 2), 'community health, safety and security' (Standard 4), 'land acquisition and involuntary resettlement' (Standard 5) and 'indigenous peoples' rights, (Standard 7). The grounding of these standards in international environmental law is sometimes explicit. For example, Standard 3 (pollution prevention and abatement) explicitly refers[43] to the LRTAP Convention,[44] the Montreal Protocol,[45] the

---

[40] The IFC has played a trend-setting role in this area. See Morgera, *Corporate Accountability in International Environmental Law*, above n. 1, pp. 169–70.

[41] IFC, Environmental Analysis and Review of International Finance Corporation Projects. Procedure for Environmental Review of the International Finance Corporation (8 September 1993), reproduced in Morgera, *Corporate Accountability in International Environmental Law* above n. 1, p. 147.

[42] Morgera, *Corporate Accountability in International Environmental Law*, above n. 1, pp. 148–9.

[43] Performance Standards, above n. 36, Standard 3, paras. 4–6.

[44] Convention on Long-Range Transboundary Air Pollution, 13 November 1979, 1302 UNTS 217 ('LRTAP Convention').

[45] Montreal Protocol on Substances that Deplete the Ozone Layer, 16 September 1987, 1522 UNTS 29 ('Montreal Protocol').

Basel Convention[46] and the POP Convention.[47] Similarly, Standard 6 (biodiversity conservation and sustainable natural resource management) explicitly refers to the Convention on Biological Diversity,[48] while Standard 8 (cultural heritage) is explicitly grounded on both the CBD and the World Heritage Convention.[49] Overall, these standards can be seen as expressions of the three pillars mentioned in connection with the OECD Guidelines, namely environmental management, transparency and prevention *lato sensu*. The IFC Standards go well beyond the OECD standards in some respects, most notably with regard to the protection of other stakeholders.

Concerning the enforcement mechanism, as further discussed in Sections 4.3.1.4 and 4.3.2.1, those affected by an IFC-financed project can bring a complaint before the CAO for breach of the IFC Performance Standards. In case of breach, sanctions may go as far as the suspension of the funding of the project. According to the information available on its website, the CAO has handled (or is handling) several dozens of cases so far, either in its capacity of Ombudsman (disputes between the IFC's 'client' and complaining stakeholders) and/or in its compliance role (audits of the IFC itself).

4.2 Contractual approaches

Contractual approaches to environmental governance encompass a variety of heterogeneous instruments, ranging from environmental public–private partnerships (PPPs), to credit facility agreements with environmental clauses, to an array of agreements between a company (or industry sector) and some public constituencies (federal or local governments, regulators, indigenous peoples, etc.) providing for environmental performance requirements ('environmental contracting'). Some of these contractual techniques, such as PPPs or credit facility agreements, have already been referred to, either as examples of 'synergies' between

---

[46] Basel Convention on the Control of Transboundary Movements of Hazardous Wastes and their Disposal, 22 March 1989, 1673 UNTS 57 ('Basel Convention').

[47] Stockholm Convention on Persistent Organic Pollutants, 22 May 2001, 40 ILM 532 (2001) ('POP Convention').

[48] Convention on Biological Diversity, 5 June 1992, 1760 UNTS 79 ('CBD'). See Performance Standards, above n. 36, Standard 6, para. 1.

[49] Convention for the Protection of the World Cultural and Natural Heritage, 16 November 1972, 1037 UNTS 151 ('World Heritage Convention'). See Performance Standards, above n. 36, Standard 8, para. 1.

foreign investment and environmental protection[50] or in connection with the environmental standards used by providers of project finance.[51] This section focuses on quasi-regulatory contractual approaches. For the purpose of this brief introductory discussion, rather than reviewing the literature on this issue[52] it seems more useful to characterise the angle from which the governance of private sector conduct is approached (Section 4.2.1) and the main components of these environmental contracts (Section 4.2.2).

4.2.1   Regulatory angle

The diversity of instruments encompassed by the concept of environmental contracting makes it difficult to circumscribe its specific regulatory angle. As noted by one commentator, '[e]nvironmental agreements occupy an amorphous and ill-defined space between command and control regulation and voluntary initiatives'.[53]

When one or more regulators are a party to the contract, the situation is closer to command and control regulation. This quasi-regulatory approach can be pursued at the level of one specific project or company ('micro-contracts') or at an industry wide level ('macro-contracts').[54] Stewart gives several examples of environmental micro-contracts in the United States and some of environmental macro-contracts in Europe.[55] From the perspective of the relations between foreign investment and environmental law, these types of environmental contracts can be seen as part of the regulatory framework of the host State or, depending on the circumstances, as specific assurances given to the investor. When the regulator is not a party, environmental contracting is closer to either private contracts with environmental clauses (as in credit facility agreements subject to the IFC Performance Standards or to other similar standards such as the Equator Principles) or to voluntary CSR initiatives. These latter instruments, which may involve companies, indigenous peoples and/or other civil society groups, are more difficult to characterise from a foreign investment perspective.

---

[50] See Chapter 3.   [51] See Section 4.1.2.

[52] Stewart, 'A New Generation of Environmental Regulation', above n. 1; Orts and Deketelaere, *Environmental Contracts*, above n. 1; O'Faircheallaigh, *Environmental Agreements in Canada*, above n. 1; Affolder, 'Rethinking Environmental Contracting', above n. 1.

[53] Affolder, 'Rethinking Environmental Contracting', above n. 1, 156.

[54] Stewart, 'A New Generation of Environmental Regulation', above n. 1, 60.

[55] *Ibid.*, 64–77, 80–6.

Depending on the factual configuration, they may be considered as a component of an overall investment scheme.

The nature of the contract is also significant to determine whether it should be seen as an alternative to the applicable default regime or simply as a supplement to it. It is unclear to what extent such contracts can depart from the existing regulatory framework.[56] In practice, the ambiguities surrounding the exact legal effects of commitments undertaken by regulators and, particularly, their consistency with a regulator's mandate may be a source of investment disputes. It seems clear, however, that when the regulator is not a party, the environmental contract cannot derogate from the existing framework. In this latter case, the purpose of the contract will be to supplement the regulatory framework on some specific questions. This may be necessary for a number of reasons, including stakeholders' mistrust of government regulators, the inadequacy of the regulatory framework to deal with certain issues or simply the need to implement verbal promises made by investors.

4.2.2 Components of environmental contracts

The contents of environmental contracts vary from one case to the other. In a number of contracts concluded in connection with the operation of extractive industries in Canada, the main focus has been on strengthening participation of civil society and establishing adequate means to monitor and enforce the environmental commitments undertaken by the investor.[57] For example, the environmental agreement concluded in the context of the Ekati diamond mine, in Northern Canada,[58] requires the investor: (i) to establish environmental management plans as well as a closure and reclamation plan (Articles VI and VIII); (ii) to meet certain environmental monitoring obligations regarding water and wildlife (Article VII); (iii) to submit detailed compliance reports (Article V); and (iv) to post a security bond of several million dollars to back compliance (Article XIII).[59] Most importantly, it sets up

---

[56] *Ibid.*, 62.

[57] Affolder, 'Rethinking Environmental Contracting' above n. 1, 168–70.

[58] Environmental Agreement between Her Majesty the Queen in Right of Canada as represented by the Minister of Indian Affairs and Northern Development and the Government of the Northwest Territories as represented by the Minister of Resources, Wildlife and Economic Development, and BHP Diamonds Inc, 6 January 1997 ('Ekati Environmental Agreement'), available at: www.monitoringagency.net (accessed on 4 January 2012).

[59] Affolder, 'Rethinking Environmental Contracting', above n. 1, 165.

a monitoring agency, consisting of members appointed by Aboriginal communities, governmental agencies and subdivisions, and the company concerned, to oversee the implementation of the contract. These components can also be found, to a varying extent, in other environmental agreements concluded in connection with mining projects in Northern Canada.[60]

Another context where environmental contracting has developed considerably is the protection of biodiversity. So-called 'transnational conservation contracts'[61] can be seen both as a way to develop synergies between foreign investment and conservation, and as a technique to regulate the activities of foreign investors in this area. Depending on the type of agreement, the balance between the synergistic aspect and the regulatory aspect will be different. An example of a type of agreement with a strong regulatory component is provided by 'access and benefit sharing' (ABS) agreements regarding bioprospecting activities by the pharmaceutical, biotechnology and agro-technology industries. A report prepared by the CBD Secretariat notes that such agreements most often consist of 'an inter-locking web of agreements between the various involved parties',[62] which include companies, government agencies and territorial subdivisions, indigenous peoples, academic institutions and/or other civil society groups. In some cases, a framework agreement is complemented by more specific agreements. In addition, depending on the sector, different types of agreements (focusing on research, transfer of materials, licensing and commercialisation, confidentiality) may intervene at different phases of the project. The broad framework applicable to such agreements has been identified in the ABS Protocol to the CBD adopted in October 2010 at Nagoya, but not yet in force.[63] Article 19 of this Protocol 'encourages' States parties to develop model contractual clauses for these agreements. Moreover, pursuant to Article 18, States parties are required to:

---

[60] Ibid., 169 (referring to the Voisey Bay nickel mining project and the Diavik and Snap Lake diamond mines).

[61] The term has been coined by Affolder, 'Rethinking Environmental Contracting' above n. 1.

[62] S. Laird and R. Wynberg, 'Access and Benefit-Sharing in Practice: Trends in Partnerships across Sectors', CBD Technical Series No. 38, 2008.

[63] Nagoya Protocol on Access to Genetic Resources and the Fair and Equitable Sharing of Benefits Arising from their Utilization to the Convention on Biological Diversity, 29 October 2010 ('ABS Protocol'). The ABS Protocol takes up the contents of the 'Bonn Guidelines on Access to Genetic Resources and Fair and Equitable Sharing of the Benefits Arising out of their Utilisations', UN Doc. UNEP/CBD/COP/6/24 (2002).

encourage providers and users of genetic resources and/or traditional knowledge associated with genetic resources to include provisions in mutually agreed terms to cover, where appropriate, dispute resolution including:

(a) The jurisdiction to which they will subject any dispute resolution processes;
(b) The applicable law; and/or
(c) Options for alternative dispute resolution, such as mediation or arbitration.

Such 'encouragement' is backed by the obligation of State parties to provide judicial recourse under their legal systems in case of dispute. This latter point takes us to the discussion of the different accountability mechanisms short of access to jurisdictional remedies that are available to implement the standards and contracts seen so far.

4.3 Accountability mechanisms

The concept of 'accountability' broadly refers to 'the way in which public and private actors are considered answerable for their decisions and operations, and are expected to explain them when they are asked by stakeholders'.[64] The mechanisms surveyed in this section provide means for companies – including foreign investors – to be held answerable for their activities and to explain themselves before different constituencies.

Among the various accountability mechanisms, some may lead to a finding of liability, whereas some others are of a less 'legalised' nature, with milder consequences for the companies concerned. Here, I will only focus on these latter 'softer' accountability mechanisms, leaving the analysis of adjudication mechanisms to Chapter 5. Within the category of soft accountability mechanisms, an additional distinction can be made between those mechanisms directly involving companies as a party to the procedure and those other mechanisms where companies are only indirectly concerned.[65] The operation of the mechanisms of the first category is premised on the existence of standards applicable to the conduct of companies and, as a rule, these mechanisms can be triggered by civil society groups (Section 4.3.1). The second category is premised on standards applicable to an entity, such as the State or a multilateral funding agency, in connection with its dealings with the private sector (Section 4.3.2). In the following Sections, I provide an overview of these

---

[64] Morgera, *Corporate Accountability in International Environmental Law*, above n. 1, p. 19.
[65] *Ibid.*, p. 224.

different mechanisms. A detailed account of their operation is, however, beyond the scope of this book. The discussion will be therefore limited to their basic features.

4.3.1   Controlling companies – direct mechanisms

The accountability mechanisms available to subject multinational companies – including foreign investors – to some measure of control are of different sorts. Some are project-specific and are based on an agreement between the company and other constituencies, including regulators and/or civil society groups (e.g., contractual monitoring agencies or 'watchdogs') (Section 4.3.2.1). Others are a component of a broader system to which companies may choose whether to adhere or not (e.g., complaints before the Global Compact Office) (Section 4.3.1.2). Others, still, are also a component of a broader system, but choice whether to adhere or not is not free, either because this choice lies with the company's home State (e.g., OECD Specific Instances) (Section 4.3.1.3) or because adherence is a requirement to obtaining project funding (e.g., CAO Ombudsman procedure) (Section 4.3.1.4).

4.3.1.1   Contractually agreed 'watchdogs'

A recurrent feature of environmental contracts in the area of extractive industries is the creation of a project-specific monitoring agency or 'watchdog'. This watchdog does not, as such, operate as an accountability mechanism but rather as a component thereof, with varying degrees of involvement in case of dispute.

By way of illustration, in the Ekati Environmental Agreement, referred to above,[66] there is a detailed provision (Article V) setting up an 'Independent Environmental Monitoring Agency'. The mandate of this 'agency' includes 'to serve as a public watchdog of the regulatory process and the implementation of this Agreement' (Article 5.2(b)) and, for this purpose, 'to compile and analyze available relevant Environmental Quality data, in order to review, report, or make recommendations concerning', inter alia, the environmental performance of the investor (Article 5.2(c)) as well as 'to participate as an intervenor in regulatory and other legal processes respecting environmental matters' (Article 5.2(d)), including the contractual dispute resolution process (Articles 5.2(h) and XV). Yet, the agency is not entitled to trigger the dispute resolution mechanisms (negotiation, mediation, arbitration) set

---

[66] See above n. 58.

out in Article XV of the agreement. The primary responsibility for enforcing the agreement remains therefore with the federal and local authorities (Article 15.5(b)), although the agency may 'intervene' in the dispute resolution procedures (Article 15.3.). As noted by Affolder, in practice, this limitation has created a significant 'accountability deficit', which other provisions of the agreement cannot easily fill.[67]

In other agreements studied by Affolder, such as the Snap Lake Environmental Agreement[68] or the Diavik Environmental Agreement,[69] an ad hoc watchdog has also been established. For example, Article IV of the Snap Lake Environmental Agreement provides for the creation of both multi-project and *ad interim* agencies. The mandate of the latter includes to 'serve as a public watchdog of the regulatory process and the implementation of this Agreement' (Article 4.2(f)), to 'review and monitor the environmental performance of the Project using western science and traditional knowledge' (Article 4.2(d)) and to 'make recommendations to any body having regulatory or management responsibility for a matter, for the achievement of the purposes and guiding principles in this Agreement' (Article 4.2(j) and 4.3). Yet, Article 11.3 makes it clear that '[n]othing in this Agreement shall be construed as limiting the Minister or any other regulatory authority in the exercise of statutory powers and duties'. In a similar vein, Article IV of the Diavik Environmental Agreement sets up an 'Environmental Monitoring Advisory Board' in the form of a non-profit organisation under Canadian law (Article 4.1(a)). The mandate of this board is also to 'serve as a public watchdog' (Article 4(2)(c)), to review compliance with environmental requirements (Article 4(2)(d)) and to 'make recommendations' either to the investor or to the regulatory authorities in connection with

---

[67] Affolder, 'Rethinking Environmental Contracting', above n. 1, 168.

[68] Environmental Agreement between Her Majesty the Queen in Right of Canada as represented by the Minister of Indian Affairs and Northern Development and the Government of the Northwest Territories as represented by the Minister of Resources, Wildlife and Economic Development, and De Beers Canada Mining Inc. and the Dogrib Treaty 11 Council, Lutsel K'E Dene Band, Yellowknives Dene First Nation and North Slave Métis Alliance, 31 May 2004 ('Snap Lake Environmental Agreement'), available at: www.slema.ca (accessed on 4 January 2012).

[69] Environmental Agreement between Her Majesty the Queen in Right of Canada as represented by the Minister of Indian Affairs and Northern Development and the Government of the Northwest Territories as represented by the Minister of Resources, Wildlife and Economic Development, and Diavik Diamond Mines Inc. and the Dogrib Treaty 11 Council, Lutsel K'E Dene Band, Yellowknives Dene First Nation, North Slave Métis Alliance, and Kitikmeot Inuit Association, 8 March 2000 ('Diavik Environmental Agreement'), available at: www.diavik.ca (accessed on 4 January 2012).

these matters (Article 4(2)(e)). Moreover, the agreement includes a provision (Article 13.3) similar to Article 11.3 of the Snap Lake Environmental Agreement.

Overall, these examples suggest that contractually agreed watchdogs are mostly intended as a supplement to the normal regulatory process and not as a substitute.

4.3.1.2   Complaints before the Global Compact Office

Although the Global Compact does not adopt a regulatory approach, a mild compliance procedure has been established in case of allegations of 'systematic or egregious abuses'.[70] The system is broadly similar to – albeit more loosely structured than – the 'Specific Instances' mechanism established in Part II of the OECD Guidelines.

A written complaint may be brought before the Global Compact Office by any 'stakeholder',[71] including civil society groups. Upon receipt of a complaint, the Office will conduct a *prima facie* assessment of whether it is frivolous or credible and, as the case may be, discard it or continue with the procedure. In the latter case, the Office may take a number of measures, including to request comments from the company concerned, to provide guidance and assistance to such company, to engage in good offices, or to refer the matter to the Global Compact Board or even to UN bodies 'for advice, assistance or action'.[72] Given that the Office has no other sanction power than changing the status of a company to 'non-communicating' or 'expelled', referral to a body with more ample powers is perhaps the most significant tool available to induce compliance.

A number of complaints have been filed in the last two years (seventeen in 2009 and twenty-one in 2010).[73] Most of them were not pursued, typically because they were found to be 'out of scope' (either *ratione materiae* – i.e., not relating to the Global Compact's ten principles – or *ratione personae* – i.e., concerning companies not adhering to the Global Compact). The few matters pursued (only two in 2009 and three in 2010)

---

[70] Integrity Measures, above n. 31, Section 4.
[71] Although the requirement to be a 'stakeholder' is not made explicit in the Integrity Measures, it has been applied in practice. See UN Global Compact, 'Annual Review 2009', p. 20 (noting that, out of the seventeen complaints filed in 2009 '2 matters were raised by concerned individuals who were not stakeholders and thus, formal dialogue facilitation would not have been appropriate'), available at www.unglobalcompact.org (accessed on 4 January 2012).
[72] Integrity Measures, above n. 31, Section 4.
[73] Annual Review 2009, above n. 71, p. 20; Annual Review 2010, above n. 32, p. 42.

were handled through 'dialogue facilitation', which would suggest that the outcome was neither a change of status nor a referral to other bodies.

4.3.1.3 OECD Specific Instances

Part II of the OECD Guidelines sets out a rather sophisticated account-ability mechanism for the implementation of the substantive standards of Part I.[74] Indeed, States adhering to the guidelines are required to establish 'national contact points' (NCPs),[75] the function of which is, *inter alia*, to receive complaints from civil society groups relating to the implementation of the Guidelines by multinational corporations ('Specific Instances').[76] Upon reception of a complaint, NCPs '[m]ake an initial assessment of whether the issues raised merit further examin-ation'[77] and, if so, they 'offer good offices to help the parties involved to resolve the issues'.[78] If no agreement is reached, NCPs 'issue a statement, and make recommendations as appropriate, on the implementation of the Guidelines'.[79]

So far, some 170 Specific Instances have been brought before different NCPs,[80] including some forty (24 per cent) concerning environmental questions. Of these, only fifteen had resulted in the issuance of a statement.[81] A review of these cases concluded that 'the practice in

---

[74] OECD, Part II: Implementation Procedures of the OECD Guidelines for Multinational Enterprises, consisting of a 'Decision of the OECD Council on the OECD Guidelines on Multinational Enterprises' ('Council Decision') and a 'Procedural Guidance' document ('Procedural Guidance').

[75] Council Decision, above n. 74, para. I.1.

[76] Procedural Guidance, above n. 74, para. I.C.

[77] *Ibid.*, para. I.C.1.   [78] *Ibid.*, para. I.C.2.   [79] *Ibid.*, para. I.C.3.

[80] OECD, Specific Instances considered by National Contact Points, 7 October 2009 ('Specific Instances Report'), available at: www.oecd.org/dataoecd/15/43/33914891.pdf (accessed on 4 January 2012).

[81] See *Statement from the Swedish NCP concerning Atlas Copco and Sandvik* (June 2003) ('*Atlas Copco* case'); *Statement by the Chilean NCP on the case of Marine Harvest Chile SA* (6 November 2003) ('*Marine Harvest* case'); *Statement by the Netherlands NCP on Chemie Pharmacie Holland* (May 2004); *Recommendations of the French NCP to EDF and its partners regarding the 'Nam Theun 2' Project in Laos/Recommandations du PCN français à l'intention de l'entreprise EDF et de ses partenaires au sujet de la mise en œuvre du projet 'Nam Theun 2' au Laos* (26 May 2005)('*Nam Theun 2* case'); Press release concerning the activities of the Forrest Group in the Democratic Republic of Congo/Communiqué concernant les activités du groupe Forrest en RD Congo (8 November 2005); *Statements concerning Ivanhoe Mines Ltd in Burma and Ascendant Copper Corporation in Ecuador/Constatations concernant Ivanhoe Mines Ltd en Birmanie et Ascendant Copper Corporation en Équateur* (2006); *Statement by the Finnish NCP on the Orion paper mill factory project and Finnvera Oyj* (12 October 2006); *ANZ specific instance: Statement by the Australian NCP* (13 October 2006); Press release by the Finnish NCP on

the procedures, timelines, and final outcomes of the NCPs is highly heterogeneous'.[82] However, a number of significant insights into the relationship between foreign investment and environmental protection can be derived from this practice. For example, in some cases, NCPs have suggested that the social and environmental standards applicable to OECD-based multinational companies are not necessarily those of the host State but those arising from the OECD Guidelines[83] or even those from the home State.[84] NCPs have also considered that multinational companies may be accountable for the actions of their local subcontractors in the countries where they operate to the extent that they can, in practice, influence the conduct of such subcontractors.[85] Still another interesting contribution made by an NCP was recommending the establishment of a project specific watchdog with a mandate similar to those discussed in Section 4.3.1.1. above.[86]

In some cases, the NCP procedures have been combined with other – potentially more powerful – mechanisms, such as judicial[87] or diplomatic means of dispute settlement. By way of illustration of this latter point, some complaints were brought before NCPs in connection with the exploitation of natural resources in the Democratic Republic of Congo,[88] which in turn triggered the establishment, in 2000, of a 'Panel of Experts on the Illegal Exploitation of Natural Resources and Other Forms of Wealth of the Democratic Republic of the Congo' by the United Nations Security Council.[89]

Metsä-Botnia in Uruguay (22 December 2006) ('*Botnia* case'); *Statement by the Swedish NCP on the CEDHA complaint against Nordea* (24 January 2008); *Statement by the Netherlands NCP on the complaint against Pilipinas Shell Petroleum Corporation* (14 July 2009)('*Pilipinas Shell Petroleum* case'); *Final statement by the UK NCP on the complaint from Survival International against Vedanta Resources plc* (25 September 2009) ('*Vedanta* case'); *Statement by the Netherlands NCP on complaint by Shehri-CBE concerning Makro-Habib Pakistan Limited* (February 2010); *Follow up to the revised final statement by the UK NCP on the complaint from Corner House et al. against BTC Corporation* (5 October 2011). All available at: www.oecd.org/document/59/0,3746,en_2649_34889_2489211_1_1_1,00.html (accessed on 4 January 2012).

[82] Morgera, *Corporate Accountability in International Environmental Law*, above n. 1, p. 237.

[83] *Pilipinas Shell Petroleum* case, above n. 81, 11; *Vedanta* case, above n. 81, para. 56.

[84] *Nam Theun 2* case, above n. 81, Recommendation 2; *Marine Harvest* case, above n. 81, Recommendation 7(f).

[85] *Atlas Copco* case, above n. 81, 2.

[86] Morgera, *Corporate Accountability in International Environmental Law*, above n. 1, p. 237.

[87] See, e.g., *Botnia* case, above n. 81, which is related to the dispute before the International Court of Justice in *Pulp Mills in the River Uruguay (Argentina v. Uruguay)*, Judgment (20 April 2010), General List No. 135.

[88] O. K. Fauchald, 'International Investment Law and Environmental Protection' (2006) 17 *Yearbook of International Environmental Law* 3, 43ff.

[89] UN Doc. S/PRST/2000/20.

The Panel issued its first 'final' report in 2002, finding that eighty-five named enterprises were in violation of the Guidelines.[90] Eventually, however, the follow-up of these cases was mostly[91] left to the NCPs of the relevant home countries, and very few cases were actually continued, allegedly for lack of sufficiently detailed information.[92]

4.3.1.4 The CAO Ombudsman procedure

One approach to ensure that projects funded by the IFC do not lead to violations of the IFC performance standards is to provide a channel for affected parties to bring a complaint before an independent body, the Compliance Advisor Ombudsman ('CAO'). The processes triggered by such complaints differ in their object and structure. In this Section, the discussion focuses on CAO's 'Ombudsman' role. Although such role may concern failures by the IFC itself or its staff, the complaint procedure may also target the conduct of the project's 'sponsors'. According to the Glossary included in CAO's Operational Guidelines, the term sponsor refers to:

the project sponsor of an IFC/MIGA [Multilateral Investment Guarantee Agency] project. However, the term is used broadly to refer to the party that is most appropriate to address the issues raised in the complaint, including the borrower of IFC funds or the recipient of IFC equity, the investor covered by a MIGA guarantee, and/or the entity that is implementing/has implemented the project in question.[93]

Thus, this procedure can directly involve companies as recipients of IFC funding. Moreover, the intervention of the Ombudsman may facilitate the conclusion of an agreement between the complainants and the private companies involved in the project or may even lead to the issuance of recommendations directly addressed to the private company.

---

[90] Final Report (1) of the Panel of Experts on the Illegal Exploitation of Natural Resources and Other Forms of Wealth of the Democratic Republic of the Congo, S/2002/1146 (2002), paras. 170–8 and Annex III, referred to by Fauchald, 'International Investment Law and Environmental Protection', above n. 88, 43.

[91] The UN Security Council followed up on those cases where the illegal resource exploitation was closely linked to illegal import of arms into the Congo. See UN Doc. S/RES/1533 (2004) establishing a committee to examine such cases. This committee took a number of measures, but none of the multinational enterprises subject to the OECD Guidelines seems to have been targeted. See *ibid.*, p. 44, at footnote 180.

[92] Fauchald, 'International Investment Law and Environmental Protection', above n. 88, 44–5.

[93] CAO, Operational Guidelines, p. 36, available at: www.cao-ombudsman.org (accessed on 4 January 2012) ('CAO Guidelines').

Three requirements must be met to bring a complaint before the CAO. First, the complaint must 'relate to any aspect of the planning, implementation, or impact of IFC/MIGA projects'.[94] This requirement has been deemed to be satisfied even if the IFC has withdrawn from the project.[95] Second, the complaint must be related to social and/or environmental issues.[96] Third, the complainant, which may be '[a]ny individual, group, community, entity or other party' (or a representative acting on their behalf), must be 'affected – or potentially affected – by the social and/or environmental impacts of [the project]'.[97] The Operational Guidelines expressly mention that '[i]f prospective complainants are from outside the country where the project is located, complaints should be lodged jointly with a local entity'.[98] According to CAO's website, some seventy complaints have been brought so far under the Ombudsman procedure.

In some cases, the intervention of the Ombudsman has helped the parties (typically affected communities and the company undertaking the project) to reach an agreed solution. For example, Morgera reports that the Ombudsman facilitated a number of agreements in the context of a complaint brought against the Baku–Tbilisi–Ceyhan (BTC) Pipeline project.[99] In some other cases, the Ombudsman has issued recommendations directly addressed to the investor. Thus, in a complaint brought against a mining project in Bolivia, the Ombudsman issued an assessment report including recommendations as to the steps that the company involved had to take to improve its social and environmental performance and to continue to receive IFC support.[100] In a similar vein, the Ombudsman formulated a number of recommendations to a private company involved in a hydropower project in India.[101] These recommendations were clearly addressed to the company. By way of

---

[94] Ibid., para. 2.2.1.

[95] Assessment by the Office of the Compliance Advisor/Ombudsman in relation to a complaint filed against IFC's investment in ENDESA Pangue SA (May 2003), p. 26, available at: www.cao-ombudsman.org (accessed on 4 January 2012).

[96] CAO Guidelines, above n. 93, para. 2.2.1.

[97] Ibid., para. 2.2.2.   [98] Ibid., para. 2.2.2.

[99] Morgera, Corporate Accountability in International Environmental Law, above n. 1, p. 221. More than twenty complaints have been brought in Georgia and Turkey in connection with different aspects of the BTC Pipeline project, which links Baku (Azerbaijan) to Ceyhan (Turkey), through Tbilisi (Georgia).

[100] Assessment Report on the complaint concerning COMSUR/Don Mario Mine (November 2003), 18–20, referred to in Morgera, Corporate Accountability in International Environmental Law, above n. 1, p. 217.

[101] Assessment Report of the complaint regarding Allain Duhangan Hydropower Project (March 2005) ('AD Hydro Project'), referred to in ibid., p. 220.

illustration, the Ombudsman recommended that the company 'should ask ERM to undertake an independent study of water demand and vulnerability for the village of Jagatsuk'.[102] As discussed next, such 'assessment reports' must be analysed in the broader context of complaint procedures focusing on the 'compliance' of the IFC itself with its performance standards.

4.3.2 Controlling the controllers – indirect mechanisms

Even in those cases where corporate activities cannot be targeted as such by a complaint, it may still be possible to challenge such activities indirectly, as a component of a complaint for regulatory failure or negligence either by a multilateral agency providing funding for the project or by the host State. In the first case, what is at stake is not the conduct of the company but a breach of the social and environmental standards applicable to the conduct of the financier itself (Section 4.3.2.1). In the second case, it is the conduct of the State (either its inaction or, in some cases, its complicity with corporate misbehaviour) which is claimed to be in breach of its international human rights or environmental obligations (Section 4.3.2.2).

4.3.2.1 Controlling financiers – the WB Inspection Panel and IFC compliance

Since the early 1990s, a number of mechanisms have been set up to ensure that multilateral funding agencies such as the World Bank, the IFC or similar regional agencies comply with certain social and environmental standards in performing their activities.[103] The relevance of these mechanisms to influence indirectly the situation of foreign investors depends on the type of projects funded by these agencies. As a general rule, the World Bank funds projects undertaken by States, whereas the IFC funds projects undertaken by the private sector, including foreign investors.[104] The compliance procedure applicable to the latter's projects (CAO) is *a priori* more relevant for present purposes. However, some discussion of the compliance mechanism applicable to the activities of the World Bank (WB Inspection Panel) seems warranted because the World Bank may be involved in different ways in foreign

---

[102] *AD Hydro Project*, 8.
[103] Morgera, *Corporate Accountability in International Environmental Law*, above n. 1, pp. 216–17.
[104] Gowlland Gualtieri, 'The Environmental Accountability of the World Bank to Non-State Actors', above n. 1, 227.

investment transactions[105] and, more generally, because the WB Inspection Panel provided the template for subsequent mechanisms.

The Panel was established in 1993 following allegations that the Bank's activities had adverse environmental effects. Most notably, the United States conditioned its financial contribution on the creation of an oversight structure to scrutinise the activities of the Bank.[106] The legal foundations of the Panel lie in a 'Resolution' adopted in September 1993[107] as well as two 'Clarifications' adopted in 1996[108] and 1999,[109] respectively. The essence of the mechanism is to provide 'a forum for non-state entities to hold the World Bank accountable for the way in which it conducts its project lending activities with regard to, *inter alia*, environmental conservation'.[110]

'Affected parties' (two or more persons) who are in the borrower's territory[111] may request the Panel to investigate a serious violation by the Bank of its operational policies and/or procedures with respect to the design, appraisal and/or implementation of projects (procurement action is not covered) provided that the alleged violation has or is likely to have a material adverse effect on the complainant.[112]

As an accountability mechanism, the mandate of the Panel is significantly limited in that it only targets the activities of the Bank and not those of borrowers. This is an important difference between the Panel and the CAO, and it is due to the fact that 'borrowers' are States. Both the Resolution and the Clarifications make this point clear. The Resolution expressly excludes from the Panel's scope '[c]omplaints with respect to actions which are the responsibility of other parties, such as a borrower, or potential borrower, and which do not involve any action or omission on the part of the Bank'.[113] The 1999 Clarification emphasises that the

---

[105] *Ibid.*, 227.   [106] *Ibid.*, 225-6.

[107] Resolution No. IBRD 93-10, 22 September 1993; Resolution No. IDA 93-6, 22 September 1993 ('Resolution') reproduced as Appendix VI to Inspection Panel, 'Accountability at the World Bank. The Inspection Panel at 15 Years (2009)' ('IP at 15'), pp. 202-6, available at: www.inspectionpanel.org (accessed on 4 January 2012).

[108] 1996 Clarification of Certain Aspects of the Resolution ('1996 Clarification'), reproduced as Appendix VII, *ibid.*, pp. 207-8.

[109] 1999 Clarification of Certain Aspects of the Resolution ('1999 Clarification'), reproduced as Appendix VIII, *ibid.*, pp. 209-12.

[110] Gowlland Gualtieri, 'The Environmental Accountability of the World Bank to Non-State Actors', above n. 1, 215.

[111] Resolution, above n. 107, para. 12; 1996 Clarification, above n. 108, 'Eligibility and Access'; 1999 Clarification, above n. 109, para. 9(a).

[112] Resolution, above n. 107, para. 13, 14(b); 1996 Clarification, above n. 108, 'Eligibility and Access'; 1999 Clarification, above n. 109, para. 9(b), (d).

[113] Resolution, above n. 107, para. 14(a).

Panel must neither address failures attributable to State borrowers nor create the impression that such failures are being scrutinised.[114]

One area where the Panel may express its view, albeit indirectly, on the conduct of the borrower is public participation. Although 'action plans' agreed by the Bank and the borrower, in consultation with complainants, are 'outside the purview of the Resolution' (and therefore of the Panel), the Panel 'may submit to the Executive Directors for their consideration a report on their view of the adequacy of consultations with affected parties in the preparation of the action plans'.[115] This is perhaps the main entry point for the Panel's assessment of the accountability of borrowers. The relevant decisions of the Panel in this connection will be discussed in Chapter 7.[116]

Another indirect procedure is the 'compliance role' of the CAO in connection with the IFC. Chapter 3 of CAO's Operational Guidelines sets out a 'compliance auditing' procedure of the social and environmental performance of the IFC/MIGA at the project level. Significantly, however, the guidelines note that '[i]n many cases ... it will be necessary to review the actions of the project sponsors and verify outcomes in the field, in assessing the performance of the project and implementation of measures to meet the relevant requirements'.[117] One of the avenues to launch a compliance audit is a request of the CAO Ombudsman 'where no resolution was possible'.[118] Thus, as far as the accountability of the private sector is concerned, the compliance procedure is mainly a supplement of the Ombudsman procedure, discussed in Section 4.3.1.4.

4.3.2.2   Controlling regulators – human rights bodies and non-compliance procedures

Other indirect mechanisms focus on the duty of States, in accordance with international human rights and environmental law, to regulate the activities of third parties, including foreign investors. We enter here the traditional province of public international law. A variety of adjudicatory and quasi-adjudicatory mechanisms have been established to review State compliance with human rights and environmental standards.

---

[114] 1999 Clarification, above n. 109, para. 3(iii)–(iv), 4, 12, 13, 15.
[115] 1999 Clarification, above n. 109, para. 15, 16.   [116] See sub-section 7.2.4.
[117] CAO Guidelines, above n. 93, para. 3.1.   [118] *Ibid.*, para. 3.3.1.

In the area of human rights,[119] these mechanisms include regional courts, such as the European Court of Human Rights or the Inter-American Court of Human Rights, regional commissions, such as the Inter-American Commission on Human Rights or the African Commission on Human and People's Rights, or certain quasi-adjudicatory bodies focusing on one 'category' of human rights, such as the Human Rights Committee set up by the ICCPR.[120]

As to environmental treaties, although some of them give the possibility of resorting to judicial mechanisms of dispute settlement,[121] a different approach to compliance has favoured the development, over the years, of so-called 'non-compliance procedures', the purpose of which is to manage non-compliance as a process, by providing assistance to non-complying States and only adopting sanctions as a last resort.[122] Some non-compliance procedures can be triggered by individuals or NGOs.[123]

The contribution of these mechanisms to the relationship between foreign investment law and international environmental law will be discussed in detail in Chapters 7 to 10.

---

[119] See, e.g., P.-M. Dupuy, F. Francioni and E.-U. Petersmann (eds.), *Human Rights in International Investment Law and Arbitration* (Oxford University Press, 2009), Chapters 10–12.

[120] International Covenant on Civil and Political Rights, 16 December 1966, 999 UNTS 171.

[121] See Chapter 5, Section 5.1.

[122] For an overview of the operation of NCPs including up-to-date case studies and comparative analysis, see T. Treves, L. Pineschi, A. Tanzi, C. Pitea, C. Ragni and F. Romanin Jaceur (eds.), *Non-Compliance Procedures and Mechanisms and the Effectiveness of International Environmental Agreements* (The Hague: T. M. C. Assers Press 2009).

[123] Aarhus Convention, above n. 19, and the Decision I/7, 2 April 2004, UN Doc. ECE/MP.PP/2/ Add.8, Addendum, 1, Annex, paras. 18–24; Protocol on Water and Health to the 1992 Convention on the Protection and Use of Transboundary Watercourses and International Lakes, 17 June 1999, 2331 UNTS 202 and the Decision I/2, 3 July 2007, UN Doc. ECE/MP.WH/2/ Add.3, EUR/06/5069385/1/Add.3, para. 16. See also North American Agreement on Environmental Cooperation, 17 December 1992, 32 ILM 1519, Article 14(1).

5   Conflicts II – adjudication mechanisms

In addition to the soft-control mechanisms reviewed in the preceding chapter, conflicts between environmental and investment protection have arisen in a growing number of cases before international courts and tribunals. These cases will be analysed in detail in Parts II and III of this study. Their significance must be appraised in the light of the considerable development, in the last several years, of international environmental litigation,[1] itself a component of the more general trend towards the judicialisation of international disputes. After some brief general observations (Section 5.1), this chapter analyses the extent to which investment tribunals may take environmental considerations into account as regards matters of jurisdiction (Section 5.2), applicable law (Section 5.3), procedure (Section 5.4) and damages (Section 5.5).

5.1   The adjudication of environment-related disputes

In the last decades, an increasing number of international disputes with environmental components have been brought before domestic[2] and

---

[1] T. Stephens, *International Courts and Environmental Protection* (Cambridge University Press, 2009).

[2] See, e.g., *Amoco Cadiz*, District Court of Chicago (18 April 1984) 2 Lloyds Rep 304; *In re Union Carbide Corp Gas Plant Disaster*, 634 F. Supat 842 (SDNY 1986), aff'd, 809 F.2d 195 (2d Cir. 1987); *Aguinda* v. *Texaco*, No. 93 Civ 7527 (VLB), 1994 US Dist. (SDNY 11 April 1994) ('*Aguinda* v. *Texaco*'); *Wiwa* v. *Royal Dutch Petroleum Co.*, No. CIV.A.96–8386 2003)(SDNY 1996); *Beanal* v. *Freeport-McMoRan, Inc.*, 969 F. Supat 362 (E.D. La. 1997) (No. 96–1474); *Sarei* v. *Rio Tinto plc*, 221 F. Supat 2d 1116 (C.D. Cal. 2001) ('*Sarei* v. *Rio Tinto*'); *Flores* v. *Southern Peru Copper Corat*, 2002 US Dist. (SDNY 2002); *Bano* v. *Union Carbide Corat*, No. 99 Civ. 11329 (JFK) (SDNY 18 March 2003), all referred to in E. Morgera, *Corporate Accountability in International Environmental Law* (Oxford University Press 2009), Chapter 6.

international courts and tribunals. Although it is difficult to define the degree to which a dispute is 'environmental', as the mere presence of an environmental component does not necessarily define the nature of the dispute, one can safely state that many disputes with important environmental components have been brought before forums such as the International Court of Justice ('ICJ'), the International Tribunal for the Law of the Sea ('ITLOS'), arbitral tribunals organised under the aegis of the Permanent Court of Arbitration ('PCA'), human rights courts, the WTO dispute settlement body or investment tribunals. It is not the purpose of this chapter to review this case-law,[3] as only some of these decisions are relevant for the understanding of the interface between environmental and investment protection and they will be discussed in subsequent chapters. Rather, this section is intended to place the discussion of the role played by investment tribunals in the broader context of international environmental adjudication.

A first observation in this regard is that environmental adjudication has not taken place within an adjudication system specialised in environmental disputes. Although the establishment of such a system has been attempted in several forms, including the creation of a specialised court,[4] a special chamber[5] or at least a specific set of arbitration rules,[6] these efforts have met with little success in practice. Moreover, limited use has been made of mechanisms set out in multilateral environmental agreements ('MEAs'), such as clauses providing for optional ('opt-in'[7]

---

[3] See Stephens, *International Courts and Environmental Protection*, above n. 1.

[4] *Ibid.*, pp. 56–61.

[5] A 'Chamber for Environmental Matters' was created in 1993 pursuant to Article 26(1) of the Statute of the International Court of Justice (Press Release 93/20, Constitution of a Chamber of the Court for the Environmental Matters, 19 July 1993). This Chamber was never put to use and, eventually, in 2006, the Court decided not to reconstitute it. Another example is the 'Chamber for Marine Environmental Disputes' established by the ITLOS in 1997 pursuant to Article 15(1) of its Statute (Press Release ITLOS/Press 5, 3 March 1997).

[6] Permanent Court of Arbitration (PCA), Optional Rules for Arbitration of Disputes relating to the Environment and/or Natural Resources ('PCA Optional Rules'). I am aware of only one case where these rules applied: *Naftrac Limited v. National Environmental Investment Agency (Ukraine)*, PCA (Optional Environmental Rules) Arbitration ('*Naftrac v. Ukraine*') (pending), case reported in L.-E. Peterson, IAR, Vol. 3, No. 16, 20 October 2010, available at www.iareporter.com (accessed on 4 January 2012).

[7] See, e.g., Vienna Convention for the Protection of the Ozone Layer, 22 March 1985, 1513 UNTS 293 ('Ozone Convention'), Article 11(3); United Nations Framework Convention on Climate Change, 9 May 1992, 31 ILM 849 ('UNFCCC'), Article 14(2); Convention on Biological Diversity, 5 June 1992, 31 ILM 82 ('CBD'), Article 27(3).

or 'opt-out'[8]) or compulsory arbitral or judicial dispute settlement.[9] Thus, environmental questions have been handled by other tribunals, as components of disputes of a different and/or more general character.

As a rule, such other tribunals have no particular constraints when it comes to hearing disputes with environmental components. For example, the ICJ can take cognisance of an environmental question arising within a dispute submitted to it in much the same way as it could take cognisance of a question concerning the application of international investment law, international human rights law or international humanitarian law. Similarly, while the power of a human rights court to take cognisance of a claim relating to environmental degradation is not unlimited,[10] this is not because of jurisdictional or other legal limitations specifically attached to environmental claims but, rather, the general framework governing the powers of such courts. This said, because of their substantive focus, some specialised tribunals seem to be more receptive to environmental questions than others. It is perhaps because of the broader synergies between environmental protection and human rights protection that human rights

---

[8] See, e.g., Convention on the Physical Protection of Nuclear Material, 26 October 1979, 1456 UNTS 124, Article 17(3). In practical terms, any treaty that admits reservations to a dispute settlement clause contains an opt-out clause.

[9] See, e.g., United Nations Convention on the Law of the Sea, 16 December 1982, 1833 UNTS 3 ('UNCLOS'), Article 287; Convention for the Protection of the Marine Environment of the North-East Atlantic, 22 September 1992, 2354 UNTS 67 ('OSPAR Convention'), Article 32. Although the use of these mechanisms is still limited, it seems to be expanding. In addition to a number of requests for provisional measures, a chamber of ITLOS has issued an advisory opinion of some importance for the protection of the marine environment. See (a) provisional measures: *Southern Bluefin Tuna* cases (*New Zealand* v. *Japan*; *Australia* v. *Japan*), Provisional Measures, ITLOS Nos. 3 and 4 (27 August 1999) ('*Bluefin Tuna - ITLOS*'); *MOX Plant* case (*Ireland* v. *United Kingdom*), Provisional Measures, ITLOS Case No. 10, Order (3 December 2001) ('*MOX Plant - ITLOS*'); (b) advisory opinion: *Responsibilities and obligations of States sponsoring persons and entities with respect to activities in the Area*, ITLOS (Seabed Disputes Chamber), Case No. 17, Advisory Opinion (1 February 2011). Moreover, one pending case before an arbitral tribunal based on Article 287 and Annex VII of UNCLOS has an important environmental component: *The Republic of Mauritius* v. *The United Kingdom of Great Britain and Northern Ireland*, Annex VII UNCLOS Arbitration (PCA hosted) (pending).

[10] See *Fadeyeva* v. *Russia*, ECtHR Application no. 55723/00, Judgment (9 June 2005), para. 68 stating that 'Article 8 has been relied on in various cases involving environmental concern, yet it is not violated every time that environmental deterioration occurs: no right to nature preservation is as such included among the rights and freedoms guaranteed by the Convention ... Thus, in order to raise an issue under Article 8 the interference must directly affect the applicant's home, family or private life'.

courts have made significant room for environmental adjudication. Conversely, the higher likelihood of tensions between, on the one hand, environmental protection and, on the other hand, trade liberalisation or investment protection, may render the WTO dispute settlement body or investment tribunals relatively less receptive to environmental protection than human rights courts.

A third observation is that the specific features of international environmental law or of environmental claims may also play a role in whether (and in the extent to which) environmental questions are discussed by these forums. But the constraints potentially derived from such features must be distinguished from the legal framework circumscribing the powers of a given forum to hear a particular claim or take cognisance of a given argument.

Thus, from an analytical perspective, one can distinguish between (i) constraints arising from the specific features of international environmental law or, more generally, of environmental claims, and (ii) constraints arising from the legal framework circumscribing the powers of a given forum, including limitations arising from narrower synergies between environmental protection and the area of specialisation of a given tribunal. The discussion in this chapter focuses on the constraints of the second type that affect the integration of environmental law into investment proceedings. Constraints of the first type are discussed at length in Chapters 7 to 10.

5.2 Jurisdictional matters

5.2.1 Jurisdictional bases in investment arbitration

The jurisdiction of an investment tribunal is based on the consent of the parties to a dispute. Such consent may arise from three main sources: a contract, domestic law and/or a treaty. There is a vast literature covering the different dimensions of this question.[11] The present section is only intended to provide some minimal background to facilitate the understanding of subsequent sections.

Often, consent to arbitration is given by means of a compromissory clause in an investment contract between the investor and the host State applicable to disputes that may arise in the future. Several arbitration institutions, including the International Centre for the Settlement of

---

[11] See, e.g., R. Dolzer and C. Schreuer, *Principles of International Investment Law* (Oxford University Press, 2008), pp. 238–53.

Investment Disputes ('ICSID'),[12] the PCA or the International Chamber of Commerce ('ICC'), propose model clauses for submitting disputes to arbitration under their rules. Some clauses are broad and cover 'any dispute arising out of or relating to' the contract. Other clauses refer to 'any dispute, controversy, or claim arising out of or relating to the interpretation, application or performance of this agreement, including its existence, validity, or termination'. Some clauses specify that the consent to jurisdiction shall only extend to certain matters, or shall not extend to certain others. Until the late 1980s, these clauses were the prevailing source of consent to arbitration.

This started to change with the development of bilateral or multilateral investment treaties ('BITs' or 'MITs') containing investor–State arbitration clauses. The turning point is often associated with the *AAPL* v. *Sri Lanka* case,[13] where the tribunal based its jurisdiction directly on the arbitration clause contained in the applicable BIT. In subsequent years, the idea that arbitration proceedings could be brought against a State even in the absence of privity of contract became widespread.[14] Although it is difficult to estimate the relative share of contractual and treaty-based consent, it is now commonplace to invoke arbitration clauses in BITs or in investment treaties such as the NAFTA[15] or the ECT.[16] The formulation of these clauses varies. For example, Articles 1116(1) and 1117(1) of the NAFTA specify the types of claims that can be brought to arbitration, essentially claims for breach of the provisions of Section A of Chapter 11. Article 1120(1) then offers three alternatives (ICSID Arbitration Rules, ICSID Additional Facility Rules and UNCITRAL Arbitration Rules) subject to some conditions. The system is completed by a firm consent clause stating that '[e]ach Party consents to the submission of a claim to arbitration in accordance with the procedures set out in this Agreement'.[17] Another example is provided by Article 8 of the

---

[12] Established by the Convention on the Settlement of Investment Disputes between States and Nationals of other States, 18 March 1965, 575 UNTS 159 ('ICSID Convention').

[13] *Asia Agricultural Products Ltd* v. *Sri Lanka*, ICSID Case No. ARB/87/3, Award (27 June 1990) ('*AAPL* v. *Sri Lanka*').

[14] See, e.g., J. Paulsson, 'Arbitration without Privity' (1995) 10 *ICSID Review-Foreign Investment Law Journal* 232.

[15] North American Free Trade Agreement, 17 December 1992, 32 ILM 296 ('NAFTA'), Articles 1120 and 1122.

[16] Energy Charter Treaty, 17 December 1994, 2080 UNTS 95 ('ECT'), Article 26(3)(a).

[17] Other treaties follow a similar approach. See, e.g., ECT, above n. 16, Articles 26(1) and 26(3)(a) or the US Model BIT 2004, Article 24(1) and 25 reprinted as Annex 8 in Dolzer and Scheuer, *Principles of International Investment Law*, above n. 11, pp. 385–419.

UK Model BIT 2005. This provision refers to '[d]isputes between a national or company of one Contracting Party and the other Contracting Party concerning an obligation of the latter under this Agreement in relation to an investment of the former'.[18] This clause clearly limits the grounds for claims to alleged breaches of the treaty, thus excluding other norms of international law. Examples of broader provisions include Article 9(1) of the Chinese Model BIT 2003, which refers to '[a]ny legal dispute between an investor of one Contracting Party and the other Contracting Party in connection with an investment in the territory of the other Contracting Party',[19] or Article 11(1) of the German Model BIT 2005, which refers to '[d]ivergencies concerning investments between a Contracting State and an investor of the other Contracting State'.[20] Arbitration clauses in BITs are seen as unilateral offers of arbitration, which become binding when an investor either accepts them expressly (e.g., by letter) or implicitly (by submitting a request for arbitration). The attempts at expanding the scope or the availability of arbitration through the use of most-favoured nation ('MFN') clauses and the simultaneous references to contract and treaty clauses have given rise to complex legal questions both in theory and practice.

A third basis of consent to arbitration can be found in the domestic legislation of host States. In order to attract foreign investment, States may make a unilateral offer of arbitration in a provision of their domestic investment laws. As with arbitration clauses contained in treaties, unilateral offers become binding when the investor accepts them either explicitly or implicitly. One illustration of this third hypothesis is given by the *SPP* v. *Egypt* case, where the tribunal based its jurisdiction on Article 8 of Egypt's Law No. 43.[21] However, such provisions are interpreted rather restrictively.[22]

---

[18] UK Model BIT, reprinted as Annex 7 in Dolzer and Scheuer, *Principles of International Investment Law*, above n. 11, pp. 376–84.

[19] China Model BIT 2003, Article 9(1), reprinted as Annex 4 in Dolzer and Scheuer, *Principles of International Investment Law*, above n. 11, pp. 352–9.

[20] German Model BIT, Article 11(1), reprinted as Annex 6 in Dolzer and Scheuer, *Principles of International Investment Law*, above n. 11, pp. 368–75.

[21] *Southern Pacific Properties (Middle East) Limited (SPP)* v. *Arab Republic of Egypt*, ICSID Case No. ARB/84/3, Award (20 May 1992)('*SPP* v. *Egypt*'), paras. 10–24.

[22] See, e.g., *Mobil Corporation Venezuela Holdings Bv and others* v. *The Bolivarian Republic of Venezuela*, ICSID Case No. ARB/07/27, Decision on Jurisdiction (10 June 2010), paras. 67–141 (interpreting Article 22 of Venezuela's Investment Law by analogy with unilateral declarations accepting the jurisdiction of the ICJ under Article 36(2) of the Court's Statute and rejecting Article 22 as a basis for consent).

The preceding observations provide the background for the analysis of the impact of environmental considerations on jurisdictional matters. In this regard, two main hypotheses can be distinguished: the possibility of bringing environmental claims before investment tribunals and the role of environmental law in determining the scope of protected investments under a given investment treaty.

5.2.2   Environmental claims

5.2.2.1   Environmental claims as investment claims

An investment protection standard may be breached as a result of conduct of the host State in violation of an environmental norm, either domestic or international. This could be the case where the investment heavily depends upon the host State's implementation of environmental law.

An example is provided by the notice of arbitration filed by a Canadian national, Peter A. Allard, against Barbados,[23] for failure to enforce applicable international and domestic environmental law in connection with the protection of a natural wetlands ecosystem. According to the investor, the profitability of its investment (an ecotourism facility) was reduced as a result, *inter alia*, of 'Barbados actions and omissions' which 'have severely damaged the natural ecosystem that [the investor's facility] relies upon to attract visitors'.[24] These and other actions and omissions would allegedly amount to a breach of the fair and equitable treatment, full protection and security, and expropriation clauses of the Canada–Barbados BIT.[25]

Another illustration is the claim brought before the European Court of Human Rights ('ECtHR') in the case *Atanasov* v. *Bulgaria*.[26] In this case, the applicant claimed that a reclamation scheme of a pond previously used by a copper mine had had adverse effects on his right to private and family life[27] as well as on his right to the enjoyment of his property[28]

---

[23] *Peter A. Allard* v. *Government of Barbados*, Notice of Dispute (*'Allard* v. *Barbados'*), available at: graemehall.com/legal/papers/BIT-Complaint.pdf (accessed on 4 January 2012).

[24] *Ibid.*, para. 16.

[25] *Ibid.*, paras. 14–21, referring to the Agreement between the Government of Canada and the Government of Barbados for the Promotion and Reciprocal Protection of Investments ('Canada–Barbados BIT'), Articles II(2), and VIII(1).

[26] *Ivan Atanasov* v. *Bulgaria*, ECtHR Application no. 12853/03, Judgment (12 December 2010) (*'Atanasov* v. *Bulgaria'*).

[27] Convention for the Protection of Human Rights and Fundamental Freedoms, 4 November 1950, Europ.T.S. No. 5, 213 UNTS 221 ('ECHR'), Article 8.

[28] Protocol to the Convention for the Protection of Human Rights and Fundamental Freedoms, 20 March 1952, ETS 9 ('Protocol I to the ECHR' or 'Protocol I'), Article 1.

because the scheme did not conform to basic environmental standards. The ECtHR rejected both arguments, but noted that a severe nuisance (in this case the nuisance came allegedly from the lack of implementation of environmental standards by the host State) could result in a partial expropriation.[29] Although the case was brought before the ECtHR, it is, on its facts, sufficiently similar to an investment claim to serve as an illustration of the basic point under consideration.

Still another example would be a situation where the uneven enforcement of environmental standards on different foreign and/or domestic investors would fall foul of the MFN or national treatment clauses contained in an investment treaty. For instance, one could think of a case where mandatory emissions targets for companies in electricity generation are unevenly enforced. In this hypothesis, the affected investor could bring a claim for breach of investment disciplines arguing that the host State is not enforcing its environmental laws on the investor's competitors. This is not to say that such claim would be justified, an issue that would depend on the circumstances of each case. Some aspects of this question have been discussed in the case law of the European Court of Justice, particularly in the *Arcelor* case,[30] which will be analysed in Chapter 10.

For the purpose of establishing jurisdiction, this type of claim would not present any significant specificity and must therefore be treated as a regular investment claim. A number of issues may arise, however, with respect to applicable law, as will be discussed later.

5.2.2.2   Environmental claims as independent heads of claim

The situation is different when an environmental claim is brought as an independent head of claim, i.e., when the investor claims that the conduct of the host State is in breach of an environmental norm arising from a different instrument than the one (primarily) covered by the arbitration clause.

In *Biloune* v. *Ghana*,[31] the claimant had asked an investment tribunal organised under the UNCITRAL Arbitration Rules to examine a claim for violation of international human rights law by the host State. The

---

[29] *Atanasov* v. *Bulgaria*, above n. 26, para. 83.
[30] *Société Arcelor Atlantique et Lorraine et al.* v. *Premier Ministre, Ministre de l'Economie, des Finances et de l'Industrie, Ministre de l'Ecologie et du Développement Durable*, ECJ Case C-127/07, Judgment (16 December 2008).
[31] *Antoine Biloune* v. *Ghana Investment Centre*, UNCITRAL, Award on Jurisdiction and Liability (27 October 1989), 95 ILR 183 ('*Biloune* v. *Ghana*').

tribunal considered that it did not have jurisdiction to examine such issues as an independent head of claim but only within the context of specific investment claims:

> This Tribunal's competence is limited to commercial disputes arising under a contract entered into in the context of Ghana's Investment Code. As noted, the Government agreed to arbitrate only disputes 'in respect of' the foreign investment. Thus, other matters – however compelling the claim or wrongful the alleged act – are outside this Tribunal's jurisdiction. Under the facts of this case it must be concluded that, while the acts alleged to violate the international human rights of Mr Biloune may be relevant in considering the investment dispute under arbitration, this Tribunal lacks jurisdiction to address, as an independent cause of action, a claim of violation of human rights.[32]

The decision of the tribunal suggests that, as a rule, an investment tribunal would not have jurisdiction over a claim brought solely for breach of an environmental norm, irrespective of any breach of an investment discipline contained in the instrument covered (primarily) by the arbitration clause. This conclusion seems consistent with the approach followed by some treaties according to which the availability of arbitration is limited to certain causes of action. As discussed in Section 5.2.1, provisions such as Articles 1116(1) and 1117(1) of the NAFTA, Article 26(1)–(3) of the ECT or, to a lesser extent, Articles 24(1) and 25 of the US Model BIT 2004, specify what types of claims can be brought to arbitration.

The foregoing examples also suggest that the question whether an investment tribunal may assert jurisdiction over an environmental claim brought as an independent head of claim depends upon the scope of the arbitration clause and the substantive provisions contained in the applicable treaty. The conjunction of these two elements was discussed by the ICJ in the *Pulp Mills* case.[33] Argentina argued that the compromissory clause contained in Article 60 of the 1975 Statute of the River Uruguay,[34] read in the light of Articles 1 and 41 of the said statute, which Argentina characterised as 'referral clauses', gave the Court jurisdiction over breaches of obligations arising from multilateral

---

[32] *Ibid.*, paras. 202–3.

[33] *Pulp Mills in the River Uruguay (Argentina v. Uruguay)*, Judgment (20 April 2010), General List No. 135 ('*Pulp Mills* case').

[34] This clause was indeed broadly stated, providing that '[a]ny dispute concerning the interpretation or application of the Treaty [the Montevideo Treaty of 1961] and the Statute which cannot be settled by direct negotiations may be submitted by either party to the International Court of Justice', *ibid.*, para. 48.

environmental treaties and general international law. The Court rejected this argument on the grounds that Articles 1 and 41 of said statute could not operate as referral clauses.[35] However, the reasoning of the Court suggests *a contrario* that, under a relatively broad jurisdictional treaty clause, an investor could bring an independent environmental claim if the treaty in question contains a referral clause. As will be discussed later,[36] investment treaties and free trade agreements ('FTAs') may incorporate environmental protection standards either in their text or in parallel agreements. Moreover, the current attempts at expanding the operation of investment clauses (e.g., MFN or fair and equitable treatment ('FET')) beyond the limits of their initial purposes could potentially go as far as paving the way for such clauses to be used to import environmental standards, at least under some specific circumstances.[37] Yet, were an investor to bring a claim under such circumstances, the claim would operate as an investment claim, much in the same way as a claim for breach of the FET standard imported through an MFN clause in the applicable treaty is technically based on the latter clause.

5.2.2.3   Environmental counterclaims

As rule, rather than bringing a counterclaim, States tend to bring environmental claims against investors before their own courts. A State may nevertheless decide to bring a counterclaim within an investment proceeding to facilitate the set-off of the opposing claims[38] or to benefit from the more sophisticated international regime for the recognition and enforcement of arbitral awards.[39] Whether (and to what extent) a State is entitled to bring such a counterclaim is a complex question, with ramifications for both jurisdiction and applicable law.

The basic requirements for a State counterclaim in investment arbitration can be found in provisions such as Article 46 of the ICSID

---

[35] *Ibid.*, paras. 48–63.   [36] See Chapters 6 and 11.

[37] One such attempt was made by the claimants, without success, in *Grand River Enterprises Six Nations, Ltd. et al.* v. *United States of America*, NAFTA (UNCITRAL), Award (12 January 2011) ('*Grand River* v. *United States*'), para. 219.

[38] Similarly, an investor may decide not to challenge the jurisdiction of a tribunal with respect to an environmental counterclaim brought by a State, if in doing so, (i) it precludes the State from bringing such claim before its domestic courts and/or (ii) it facilitates the set-off of any amount for which the investor could be liable with the amount resulting from the State's breach of an investment discipline, particularly if the enforcement of the award against said State would be difficult from a practical standpoint.

[39] Convention on the Recognition and Enforcement of Foreign Arbitral Awards, 10 June 1958, 330 UNTS 38 ('New York Convention').

Convention or Article 21(3) of the revised (2010) UNCITRAL Arbitration Rules. These requirements are as follows: (i) the counterclaim arises directly out of the subject-matter of the dispute ('connection'); (ii) it falls within the scope of the consent of the parties ('consent'); and (for ICSID arbitration) (iii) it falls within the scope of jurisdiction of ICSID (in essence Article 25 of the ICSID Convention). Underlying these requirements is the assumption that investment disputes would normally arise from a contract, although nothing prevents them from accommodating a counterclaim in an arbitration based solely on an investment treaty. From the perspective of a potential environmental counterclaim, two main questions arise.

The first question is whether the requirement that the counter claim arises directly out of the subject-matter of the dispute could be met. The answer will, of course, depend on the circumstances of the case, but an important element to be taken into account is the existence of legal obligations (e.g., environmental provisions in a contract or obligations arising from domestic environmental law) capable of founding such a counterclaim. If this is not the case (e.g., in the context of a treaty arbitration where the choice of law provision in the treaty does not refer to domestic law), then either the counterclaim will have no legal grounds[40] or the link between the counterclaim and the subject-matter will be more difficult to establish. If the tribunal interprets the 'connection' requirement narrowly, as it did in *Saluka* v. *Czech Republic*,[41] environmental counterclaims may be very difficult to bring in a treaty

---

[40] As a general rule, international law (including investment and environmental treaties) does not create obligations for investors. A number of domestic claims have sought to apply international environmental law to companies, with very limited success. See *Aguinda* v. *Texaco*, above n. 2, 22–3; *Sarei* v. *Rio Tinto*, above n. 2, 127. Attempts have also been made in connection with human rights law. On the question of whether the US Alien Tort Claims Act can be used to hold corporations accountable for wrongdealing abroad, different federal Circuit courts have expressed different views, either rejecting this principle (*Doe I* v. *Nestlé*, No. 2:05-cv-05133, 121–60 (C.D. Cal. 8 September 2010); *Kiobel* v. *Royal Dutch Petroleum*, No. 06–4800-cv, 06–4876-cv, 2010 WL 3611392 (2d Cir. 17 September 2010)) or accepting the possibility (*Flomo* v. *Firestone Natural Rubber Co.*, No. 10–3675, 2011 WL 2675924 (7th Cir. 11 July 2011); *Doe VIII* v. *Exxon Mobil Corp.*, Nos. 09–7125, 09–7127, 09–7134, 09–7135, 2011 WL 2652384 (D.C. Cir. 8 July 2011)). The US Supreme Court is expected to clarify this issue in the pending petition for *certiorari* in the *Kiobel* case.

[41] *Saluka Investments BV* v. *The Czech Republic*, UNCITRAL, Decision on Jurisdiction over the Czech Republic's Counterclaim (7 May 2004) ('*Saluka* v. *Czech Republic* – Jurisdiction'), paras. 65, 79 (referring to the test of the 'indivisible whole' used in an early contract arbitration, *Klöckner Industrie-Anglagen GmbH et al.* v. *United Republic of Cameroon and Société Camerounaise des Engrais*, ICSID Case No. ARB/81/2, Award (21 October 1983)).

arbitration. Conversely, a broader interpretation of this connection[42] would facilitate the admission not only of contract-based environmental counterclaims but also of treaty-based environmental counterclaims (grounded in domestic environmental law).

The second question relates to the basis of consent to arbitration. In contract arbitrations, the investor's consent is normally given in an arbitration clause. The scope of this clause may vary, but regular arbitration clauses applying to 'any dispute arising from or in connection with the contract' are broad enough to cover counterclaims based on contractual environmental terms and, perhaps also, on domestic environmental law. A more difficult question is whether the consent to arbitration given by an investor in a letter accepting a unilateral offer of arbitration (made by the State in an investment law or in a treaty) or, more generally, through the filing of an arbitration request, would be sufficiently broad to cover environmental counterclaims. As with contractual arbitration clauses, the solution heavily depends on the specific wording of the arbitration clause.[43] However, this second hypothesis presents an additional difficulty, namely the interpretation of the scope of the consent given by the investor, either explicitly (through a letter) or implicitly (through a request for a arbitration). As noted by Lalive and Halonen, '[a]s the BIT itself imposes no obligations on investors in the vast majority of cases, the arbitration agreement should refer to disputes that can also be brought under domestic law for counter-claims to be within the tribunal's jurisdiction'.[44] This reasoning also applies to environmental counterclaims. A possible caveat would include cases where the investor has undertaken to respect certain environmental standards (e.g., those contained in corporate social responsibility instruments) as part of the procedure to receive an investment licence or funding. Under these circumstances, it could be argued that the treaty implicitly considers domestic law as applicable and that such environmental standards are incorporated into domestic law. The conditions for such an implicit reference to domestic law are further discussed in the following section.

---

[42] Such a broader interpretation has been persuasively advocated by P. Lalive and L. Halonen, 'On the Availability of Counterclaims in Investment Treaty Arbitration' (2011) 2 *Czech Yearbook of International Law* 141, 153ff.

[43] *Saluka* v. *Czech Republic* – Jurisdiction, above n. 41, para. 39.

[44] Lalive and Halonen, 'On the Availability of Counterclaims in Investment Treaty Arbitration', above n. 42, 146.

5.2.3   Investments in accordance with (environmental) law

The incorporation of environmental considerations may also have an impact on determining the existence of a protected investment, either in connection with the definition of the rights or entitlements that can amount to a protected investment (Section 5.2.3.1) or, conversely, with respect to the limits of protection of certain investments contrary to environmental law (Section 5.2.3.2).

5.2.3.1   Environmental rights as investments

The first scenario can be illustrated by reference to the case *Bayview* v. *Mexico*,[45] where the US-based claimants argued that the diversion by Mexico of the waters of the Rio Grande River amounted to a breach of Chapter 11 of the NAFTA. This argument supposed that water rights held by the US claimants in the US territory could constitute a protected investment under the NAFTA. However, in a submission made before the tribunal on the basis of Article 1128 of the NAFTA, the US government itself argued against this proposition.[46] Eventually, the tribunal concluded that such water rights were not protected under Article 1101 of the NAFTA. The tribunal noted, in this regard, that:

[I]n order to be an 'investor' within the meaning of NAFTA Art. 1101(a), an enterprise must make an investment in another NAFTA State, and not in its own. Adopting the terminology of the *Methanex* v. *United States* Tribunal, it is necessary that the measures of which complaint is made should affect an investment that has a 'legally significant connection' with the State creating and applying those measures. The simple fact that an enterprise in a NAFTA State is affected by measures taken in another NAFTA State is not sufficient to establish the right of that enterprise to protection under NAFTA Chapter Eleven: it is the relationship, the legally significant connection, with the State taking those measures that establishes the right to protection, not the bare fact that the enterprise is affected by the measures.[47]

In a subsequent award rendered in the case *Canadian Cattlemen* v. *United States*[48] a NAFTA tribunal confirmed this stance concluding that it could not assert jurisdiction 'where all of the Claimants' investments at issue

---

[45] *Bayview Irrigation District et al.* v. *United Mexican States*, ICSID Case No. ARB(AF)/05/1, Award (19 June 2007) ('*Bayview* v. *Mexico*').

[46] *Bayview* v. *Mexico*, Submission of the United States of America, 27 November 2006, para. 14, available at: www.naftaclaims.com (accessed on 4 January 2012).

[47] *Bayview* v. *Mexico*, above n. 45, para. 101.

[48] *Canadian Cattlemen for Fair Trade* v. *United States of America*, NAFTA (UNCITRAL), Award on Jurisdiction (28 January 2008).

are located in the Canadian portion of the North American Free Trade Area and the Claimants do not seek to make, are not making and have not made any investment in the territory of the United States of America'.[49] This view was further confirmed in *Grand River* v. *United States*,[50] where three of the claimants argued unsuccessfully that their cigarette export business from Canada amounted to an investment in the United States. It seems therefore well established that, at least in the NAFTA context, only those investments that have a 'legally significant connection' (meaning, in essence, that are located in the territory of the host State) are protected under Chapter 11 of the NAFTA. This conclusion is important for disputes that may arise as a result of long-arm environmental statutes, which strongly affect investments made in either Canada or Mexico, but whose main market is in the United States.

Environmental law can also have an impact on the definition of a protected investment by creating a specific form of asset that would constitute the return on the investment scheme. Despite the limited information publicly available, a possible illustration is provided by the *Naftrac* v. *Ukraine* case[51] where, according to reports, the investor claims, *inter alia*, that it was deprived of the emission reduction units ('ERUs') that it would have received if it had not been unlawfully excluded from a joint implementation project undertaken under the umbrella of Article 6 of the Kyoto Protocol.[52] The obtaining of ERUs is, however, not guaranteed, as it supposes that after verification of the project some reduction in emissions (as compared with a business as usual scenario) has been achieved. Moreover, ERUs are, technically, the result of a conversion of the units assigned as part of the cap appearing in Annex B of the Kyoto Protocol. Assigned amount units ('AAUs') are debited from the account of the relevant country (Ukraine) and credited to the account of the acquiror as ERUs. These different steps are based on the specific regulations issued by the bodies established by the Kyoto Protocol as well as, to some extent, on the domestic law of member States. The investment made by the investor (at least as far as ERUs are concerned) would therefore have no existence beyond the Kyoto regulatory framework.

5.2.3.2   Investments contrary to environmental law

The lack of protection of investments in breach of domestic laws has more often been argued in investment cases, although not in connection

---

[49] *Ibid.*, para. 233.   [50] *Grand River* v. *United States*, above n. 37, paras. 81–122.

[51] *Naftrac* v. *Ukraine*, above n. 6.

[52] Kyoto Protocol to the United Nations Framework Convention on Climate Change, 11 December 1997, 2303 UNTS 148 ('Kyoto Protocol'), Article 6.

with violations of domestic environmental laws. A number of investment treaties subject the definition of protected investments to their conformity with the laws of the host State.[53] As a result, domestic environmental laws may have an impact on whether an investment is protected.[54] This qualification may, under some circumstances, be relevant for the determination of a tribunal's jurisdiction.

Most tribunals have considered that such a reference to the host State's laws concerns the validity of an investment and not the definition of the term investment itself. As noted by the tribunal in *Salini v. Morocco*, the provisions in BITs requiring the conformity of the investments with the host State's laws refer 'to the validity of the investment and not to its definition. More specifically, [such provisions seek] to prevent the Bilateral Treaty from protecting investments that should not be protected because they would be illegal'.[55] However, in a growing number of cases, the legality of an investment has been considered as a jurisdictional obstacle.

In *Inceysa v. El Salvador*,[56] the respondent argued that it had not consented to the protection of investments procured by fraud, forgery or corruption.[57] The applicable BIT did not qualify the definition of investment in the provision defining this term but contained a reference to compliance with national laws in the provisions dealing with admission and protection. The tribunal concluded that, under the circumstances, it did not have jurisdiction to hear the claim because the respondent had not consented to extend the protections of the treaty or those of its domestic code to an investment made in an openly illegal manner.[58]

A similar conclusion was reached in *Fraport v. Philippines*.[59] The respondent had argued, in essence, that 'the protections afforded by the BIT at

---

[53] See, e.g., Egypt–Pakistan BIT (2000), Article 1(1); Bahrain–Thailand BIT (2002), Article 2, reproduced in A. Joubin-Bret, 'Admission and Establishment in the Context of Investment Protection', in A. Reinisch (ed.), *Standards of Investment Protection* (Oxford University Press, 2008), p. 17.

[54] *Ibid.*, 19.

[55] *Salini Costruttori SpA and Italstrade SpA v. Morocco*, ICSID Case No. ARB/00/4 Decision on Jurisdiction (23 July 2001), para. 46, reproduced in Dolzer and Scheuer, *Principles of International Investment Law*, above n. 11, p. 113.

[56] *Inceysa Vallisoletane, SL v. El Salvador*, ICSID Case No. ARB/03/26, Award (2 August 2006) ('*Inceysa v. El Salvador*').

[57] *Ibid.*, para. 45.   [58] *Ibid.*, paras. 257, 264.

[59] *Fraport AG Frankfurt Airport Services Worldwide v. Republic of the Philippines*, ICSID Case No. ARB/03/25, Award (16 August 2007) ('*Fraport v. Philippines*'). Note, however, that this award was subsequently annulled on the grounds that the tribunal had departed from a fundamental rule of procedure, *Fraport AG Frankfurt Airport Services Worldwide v. Republic of the Philippines*, ICSID Case No. ARB/03/25, Decision on the Application for Annulment (17 December 2010) ('*Fraport Annulment*'), paras. 218–47.

issue [did] not extend to investments made in violation of Philippine law'
and that such conclusion applied even once an investment had been
admitted if the investment was 'implemented in a manner that materi-
ally violates the host State's laws that directly regulate the investment or
the investment activities'.[60] The domestic laws at issue restricted foreign
ownership and control of corporations engaging in certain activities. In
its analysis, the tribunal distinguished between initial and subsequent
illegality, considering that, whereas the latter could only operate as a
substantive defence, the former could potentially limit jurisdiction.[61] This
was so irrespective of whether the investment had been accompanied by
some explicit agreement with or communication from the host State,[62]
as even where the host State had issued an authorisation, a potential
estoppel argument could be dismissed if the arrangements making an
investment illegal were covert.[63] That was, as a matter of fact, the conclusion of the tribunal in this case.[64]

A question that arises in connection with the illegality *ab initio* of an
investment is whether any illegality (as long as it is initial) excludes the
jurisdiction of the tribunal or whether only some forms of illegality have
this effect. In *Saba Fakes* v. *Turkey*, the tribunal considered that only the
illegality arising from a violation of the host State's law relating to the
admission of investments would have such effect.[65] The tribunal noted
that 'it would run counter to the object and purpose of investment
protection treaties to deny substantive protection to those investments
that would violate domestic laws that are unrelated to the very nature of
investment regulation'.[66] This view has been criticised for being too
restrictive.[67] In this regard, three observations appear necessary. First,
as a general matter the tribunal seems to acknowledge that at least some
form of illegality *ab initio* of an investment may prevent a tribunal from
exercising jurisdiction. Second, it is unclear what domestic laws are

---

[60] *Fraport* v. *Philippines*, above n. 59, paras. 285–6, 344.

[61] *Ibid.*, para. 345.   [62] *Ibid.*, para. 343.

[63] *Ibid.*, paras. 346–7. Such conclusion is exceptional. Where the actions of the host
State's own authorities were themselves illegal, an objection to jurisdiction based on the
non-conformity of the investment with laws of the host State would normally fail. See
Ioannis Kardassopoulos v. *Georgia*, ICSID Case No. ARB/05/18, Decision on Jurisdiction
(6 July 2007), para. 182.

[64] *Fraport* v. *Philippines*, above n. 59, para. 404.

[65] *Saba Fakes* v. *Turkey*, ICSID Case No. ARB/07/20, Award (12 July 2010)('*Saba Fakes* v. *Turkey*').

[66] *Ibid.*, para. 119.

[67] S. Manciaux, 'Chronique des sentences arbitrales' (2011) 138 *Journal de droit international*
565, at 581.

related to the 'very nature of investment regulation'. Whereas, under the tribunal's analysis, an investment code requiring a licensing proce-dure for an investment to be made would clearly be 'related' to the core definition of investment, some other regulations (e.g., some environ-mental regulations) that do not focus primarily on investments but, more generally, on the legality of 'any' economic activity in a given sector, should also be relevant.[68] Some of these other regulations, despite their generality, may go to the very core of investment regula-tion and, as a consequence, may have to be taken into account at the jurisdictional level. Third, some recent decisions seem to acknowledge that the relevant law for the assessment of the legality/illegality *ab initio* of an investment is broader than the mere investment codes.[69] Thus, environmental law may play a role in determining the legality of an investment for jurisdictional purposes.

The significance of this body of case-law for the relations between foreign investment and environmental protection should not be under-estimated. One could imagine, for instance, a case where a landfill or a chemical production plant has been established in a developing country in violation of local laws requiring the conduct of an environ-mental impact assessment, especially if the investor has resorted to corruption or other unacceptable means prohibited by international public policy.[70] Even if establishing such facts could be difficult in

---

[68] Sornarajah refers in this connection to an investment dispute arising from a sand-mining concession in Fraser Island (Australia) near the Great Barrier Reef. The Australian authorities terminated the concession on environmental grounds. The legality of this action was confirmed by the Australian High Court. See *Dillingham-Moore* v. *Murphyores* (1979) 136 CLR 1, referred to in M. Sornarajah, *The International Law on Foreign Investment* (Cambridge University Press, 2010), pp. 109–10. Many readings of this case are possible. For present purposes, suffice it to say that the case illustrates the direct relevance of environmental law for the 'very nature of investment regulation'. Sornarajah further refers to an OPIC arbitration (*International Bank of Washington* v. *OPIC* (1972) 11 ILM 1216) as authority for the 'general acceptance that a state has a right to cancel agreements or investment projects which cause significant environmental harm', *ibid.*, p. 110.

[69] *Inmaris Perestroika Sailing Maritime Services GmbH* v. *Ukraine*, ICSID Case No. ARB/08/8, Decision on Jurisdiction (8 March 2010), paras. 135–45 (reviewing a variety of domestic laws and rejecting the respondent's objection on the facts); *Gustav F. W. Hamester GmbH & Co. KG* v. *Ghana*, ICSID Case No. ARB/07/24, Award (10 June 2010), paras. 125–39 (reviewing a broader set of laws and rejecting the respondent's objection on the facts).

[70] In *Inceysa* v. *El Salvador*, the tribunal considered that Inceysa's investment was contrary to international public policy and that asserting jurisdiction over such investment would also constitute a violation of international public policy. See above n. 56, paras. 245–52. On the treatment of fraud see also *Société d'Investigation de Recherche et d'Exploitation Minière (SIREXM)* v. *Burkina Faso*, ICSID Case No. ARB/97/1, Award (19 January 2000), para. 6.33; *World Duty Free Co. Ltd* v. *Republic of Kenya*, ICSID Case No. ARB/00/7,

practice, treating this issue before reaching the merits phase (either as a jurisdictional or an admissibility question) would increase the efficiency of investment arbitration proceedings, saving some of the scarce resources that developing countries can devote to such proceedings.

5.3   Applicable law

5.3.1   Preliminary observations

The question of the law applicable to investment disputes is different from, although related to, the question of the scope of jurisdiction.[71] Even in cases where an independent human rights or environmental claim has been deemed to be outside the scope of jurisdiction of the tribunal, human rights or environmental rules may remain relevant for the consideration of an investment claim.[72] The potential confusion between jurisdiction and applicable law stems, *inter alia*, from the diversity of the provisions from which the applicable law can be determined, and the fact that, in some treaties, the same provision deals with both jurisdiction and governing law.[73]

As noted in Chapter 2, the legal framework potentially applicable to an investment consists of three main layers, namely contractual provisions (if the investment has been made through a contract with the host State or its instrumentalities), domestic law (of the host State or, potentially, of another State), and international law (treaty law or customary international law). Environmental considerations may be included in a clause of the investment contract (and/or of a related agreement, such as a credit facility agreement), in domestic regulations or in the applicable investment treaty. Environmental protection standards may also arise from an applicable environmental treaty or, exceptionally, from general international law.[74] The specific body of norms (contractual, domestic, international) which will be applicable for the determination of a given dispute as well as the precise articulation of such norms will depend upon the law possibly chosen by the parties or indicated by other means

Award (4 October 2006), para. 156; *Plama Consortium Ltd* v. *Republic of Bulgaria*, ICSID Case No. ARB/03/24, Award (27 August 2008), para. 141.

[71] *Pulp Mills* case, above n. 33, para. 66.   [72] *Biloune* v. *Ghana*, above n. 31, paras. 202–3.

[73] See, e.g., Article 26 of the ECT, which defines both the scope of jurisdiction of (paras. 1 and 2) and the law applicable by (para. 6) arbitral tribunals constituted under para. 4.

[74] *Legality of the Threat or Use of Nuclear Weapons*, ICJ Reports 1996, 226 ('*Legality of Nuclear Weapons*'), para. 29 (affirming the prevention principle); *Pulp Mills* case, above n. 33, para. 204 (asserting a requirement for a prior environmental impact assessment).

(mainly a default clause)(Section 5.3.2), and the relevance of potentially applicable norms in the light of the scope of the dispute (Section 5.3.3). These two aspects must not be considered as a sequential test but merely as two questions that help organise the process of determining the applicable law.

5.3.2   Choice of law and other indications

Concerning the first issue, indications as to the applicable law may appear in different forms including in a choice of law clause contained in an investment contract between a foreign investor and the host State (Section 5.3.2.1), in a choice of law provision contained in an investment treaty between the host State and the investor's home State (a choice that the investor accepts in availing itself of the treaty's arbitration clause) (Section 5.3.2.2), in an 'indirect' reference to the applicable law in the form of a provision in a treaty or in an investment code specifying that only investments made in accordance with the host State's laws are protected (Section 5.3.2.3) or in a default clause contained in the rules governing the arbitration proceedings (Section 5.3.2.4).

5.3.2.1   Choice of law clause in an investment contract

When there is a choice of law, the applicable law is quite often that of the host State, although it may also be that of the investor's home State, that of a third State or another body of law such as international law.[75]

The place occupied by environmental laws in this choice raises a number of questions. The most basic one is whether environmental laws are included in the scope of the choice. Whereas the answer will normally be affirmative when the parties have chosen the laws of the host State, the situation is less clear when the laws chosen are those of the investor's home State or of a third State, to the extent that environmental law could take the form of either private or public law and that there are limitations in the application of a foreign public law.[76]

Where the parties have chosen a foreign law to govern contractual matters, an argument could be made in favour of applying the environmental laws of the host State if and to the extent that they can be considered as *lois de police* or overriding norms. The application of the

---

[75] For examples, see Dolzer and Schreuer, *Principles of International Investment Law*, above n. 11, pp. 265ff; D. Bishop, J. Crawford and M. Reisman, *Foreign Investment Disputes: Cases, Materials and Commentaries* (The Hague: Kluwer Law International 2005), pp. 255ff.

[76] See H. Batiffol and P. Lagarde, *Droit international privé*, Vol. I (Paris: LDGJ, 1974), paras. 245–6; IDI, 'The Application of Foreign Public Law', Session of Wiesbaden, 1975.

environmental laws of the investor's home State or of a potentially affected third State is more difficult to determine. In practice, the overriding character of *lois de police* and their application by arbitral tribunals seem to be in decline. As a result, the application of *lois de police* will often turn on the specifics of the case.[77]

5.3.2.2   Choice of law provision in an investment treaty

The inclusion of a choice of law provision in an investment treaty is frequent in practice. Indeed, MITs and BITs often include provisions specifying the law applicable for the resolution of disputes.

For instance, Article 1131(1) of the NAFTA states: 'A Tribunal established under this Section shall decide the issues in dispute in accordance with this Agreement and applicable rules of international law.'[78] Similarly, Article 26(6) of the ECT states: 'A tribunal established under paragraph (4) [arbitral tribunal] shall decide the issues in dispute in accordance with this Treaty and applicable rules and principles of international law.'[79] Turning to BITs, the Canadian Model BIT 2004 states in Article 40(1): 'A Tribunal established under this Section shall decide the issues in dispute in accordance with this Agreement and applicable rules of international law.' Similarly, the Chinese Model BIT 2003 states in Article 9(3) that 'the arbitration award [of the investment tribunal] shall be based on the law of the Contracting Party to the dispute including its rules on the conflict of laws, the provisions of this Agreement as well as the universally accepted principles of international law'.[80] Still another example is provided by Article 30 of the US Model BIT 2004, which is much more detailed than most other BITs:

1. Subject to paragraph 3, when a claim is submitted under Article 24(1)(a) (i)(A) or Article 24(1)(b)(i)(A) [claims for breach of an investment protection brought, respectively, by a foreign entity or by a local entity under foreign control], the tribunal shall decide the issues in dispute in accordance with this Treaty and applicable rules of international law.

2. Subject to paragraph 3 and the other terms of this Section, when a claim is submitted under Article 24(1)(a)(i)(B) or (C), or Article 24(1)(b)(i) (B) or (C) [the same as above except for the cause of action, which is,

---

[77] See L. Radicati di Brozolo, 'Arbitrage commercial international et lois de police. Considérations sur les conflits de juridictions dans le commerce international', (in *Recueil des cours de L'Académie de droit international* Vol. 315 (2005), pp. 265, at 402.

[78] NAFTA, above n. 15, Article 1131(1).

[79] ECT, above n. 16, Article 26(6).   [80] China Model BIT 2003, above n. 19.

respectively, breach of an investment authorisation or an investment agreement], the tribunal shall apply:

(a) the rules of law specified in the pertinent investment authorization or investment agreement, or as the disputing parties may otherwise agree; or

(b) if the rules of law have not been specified or otherwise agreed:
    (i) the law of the respondent, including its laws on the conflict of laws; and
    (ii) such rules of international law as may be applicable.

3. A joint decision of the Parties, each acting through its representative designated for purposes of this Article, declaring their interpretation of a provision of this Treaty shall be binding on a tribunal, and any decision or award issued by a tribunal must be consistent with that joint decision.[81]

In all these examples, some room is left for the potential application of environmental norms stemming from both domestic and international law. As noted by two commentators with respect to the potential application of human rights law: 'human rights [and by analogy environmental] provisions are applicable to the extent to which they are included in the parties' choice of law'.[82]

One potentially important issue arising from the scope of the choice-of-law clause in a BIT relates to the possibility for a State to bring a counterclaim against an investor for breach of the domestic environmental laws. The admissibility of such a counterclaim will depend on a variety of factors, including the scope of the jurisdictional and the choice-of-law clauses as well as the facts of the case.[83] Assuming *ratio arguendi* that neither the jurisdictional clause nor the facts preclude such possibility, an independent environmental counterclaim could be brought only if the applicable treaty directs the arbitral tribunal to apply domestic (environmental) law. This hypothesis would be similar to a case where a treaty with a broad arbitration clause directs the tribunal to apply the provisions of investment contracts. In both cases, the investor would be subject to substantive obligations (arising, respectively, from the host State's law or from a contract) capable of founding a State counterclaim. These substantive obligations would not be present if the applicable law is limited to the provisions of the treaty and/or

---

[81] US Model BIT 2004, above n. 17.

[82] See C. Reiner and C. Schreuer, 'Human Rights and International Investment Arbitration', in P.-M. Dupuy, F. Francioni and E.-U. Petersmann (eds.), *Human Rights in International Investment Law and Arbitration* (Oxford University Press, 2009) p. 84.

[83] See Section 5.2.2.3.

international law, as private investors have no obligations under either treaties or customary international law.[84]

5.3.2.3 References to the validity of an investment

This hypothesis has already been discussed in some detail in connection with jurisdictional matters. In essence, the reference in an investment treaty to investments made 'in accordance with the laws' of the host State is, as a rule, considered through the lens of the 'validity' theory. Thus, where the operation of an investment is (or becomes) in breach of the host State's environmental laws, an investment tribunal would tend to recognise that the host State could avail itself of this circumstance in the form of a substantive defence. The technical operation of such a defence is not entirely clear and could be spelled out in at least three manners, depending on the circumstances of the case.

Let us assume, for the purposes of the analysis, that, as a result of an investor's breach of the domestic environmental regulations, a State adopts a measure adversely affecting the interests of the investor. Let us also assume that the investor brings only treaty claims under a treaty providing that the dispute will be decided solely on the basis of its provisions and other relevant rules of international law. In this first situation, the non-conformity of the investment with local environmental regulations would be a mere fact relevant to assess whether the adverse measures were justified or not, which is in turn important for determining whether an investment protection clause in the treaty has been breached or not.

A second situation would arise where the treaty does not contain a provision excluding the applicability of domestic law[85] or where the choice of law provision expressly mentions the applicability of the host State's domestic laws. In such a hypothesis, the domestic environmental laws could be applied as law instead of as facts. In *Maffezini* v. *Spain*,[86] the choice of law clause in the Argentina–Spain BIT expressly mentioned the applicability of 'the law of the Contracting Party in whose territory

---

[84] See above n. 40.

[85] Although this is not a choice of law *stricto sensu*, the initiation of arbitration proceedings by an investor based on the arbitration clause in a treaty containing such a reference to the validity of investments can arguably amount to consent by the investor to the application of the relevant domestic laws.

[86] *Emilio Agustín Maffezini* v. *Kingdom of Spain*, ICSID Case No. ARB/97/7, Award (13 November 2000) ('*Maffezini* v. *Spain* – Award').

the investment was made'.[87] Maffezini argued that the Spanish authorities had forced him to proceed with the construction of a chemical
plant even before the implications of the environmental impact assessment ('EIA') conducted as part of the process were known, and that they
had then asked for additional information in this connection. Spain
replied that Maffezini was well aware of the standards for the conduct
of an EIA under Spanish and European law and had nevertheless decided
to start the construction works before the conclusion of the EIA. After
reviewing the arguments of the parties, the tribunal concluded that the
Spanish authorities had strictly abided by the applicable domestic and
European environmental laws on this point.[88]

The third situation would arise where the violation of the domestic
laws by the investor is so glaring that it brings into operation the rules
on international public policy.[89] Of course, it is unclear whether certain
environmental norms are or could be part of international public policy.
However, this is by no means impossible, in light of the increasing
environmental awareness in the population of many countries as well
as of the morally unacceptable effects that a violation of certain environmental norms, such as the prohibition of indiscriminate disposal of radioactive or other highly toxic waste, could have on the local population.

5.3.2.4 Default rules

The arbitration rules most frequently used in investment proceedings,
namely the ICSID and UNCITRAL Arbitration Rules,[90] as well as other
rules increasingly in use, such as those of the LCIA,[91] the ICC,[92] the PCA[93]
or the Stockholm Chamber of Commerce,[94] contain provisions indicating how the applicable law must be determined in the absence of a
choice of law by the parties. Article 42(1) of the ICSID Convention goes

---

[87] *Emilio Agustín Maffezini* v. *Kingdom of Spain*, ICSID Case No. ARB/97/7, Decision on
Jurisdiction (25 January 2000) ('*Maffezini* v. *Spain* – Jurisdiction'), para. 19.

[88] *Maffezini* v. *Spain* – Award, above n. 86, para. 71.

[89] See P. Lalive, 'Ordre public transnational (ou réellement international) et arbitrage
international' (1986) 3 *Revue de l'arbitrage* 329.

[90] UNCITRAL Arbitration Rules, 1976 ('UNCITRAL Rules', subsequently revised in 2010),
Article 33(1).

[91] London Court of International Arbitration (LCIA), Arbitration Rules ('LCIA Rules'),
Article 22.3.

[92] International Chamber of Commerce (ICC), Arbitration Rules (January 2009)('ICC Rules'),
Article 17(1)–(2).

[93] Permanent Court of Arbitration (PCA), Optional Rules for Arbitrating Disputes between
two Parties of which only one is a State ('PCA Rules'), Article 33(1).

[94] Stockholm Chamber of Commerce (SCC), Arbitration Rules 2010, Article 22(1).

a step further because, unlike the provisions contained in other arbitration rules, it expressly identifies the applicable law:

The Tribunal shall decide a dispute in accordance with such rules of law as may be agreed by the parties. In the absence of such agreement, the Tribunal shall apply the law of the Contracting State party to the dispute (including its rules on the conflict of laws) and such rules of international law as may be applicable.

Thus, in the absence of a choice of law clause, the laws of the host State and the rules of international law will be applicable. There has been some discussion as to the meaning of the term 'and' in Article 42(1).[95] This answer heavily depends upon the specific legal question at issue. Three basic scenarios can be identified.

First, the two bodies of law may have to be 'separately' applied, for instance, when the investor has brought both contract claims, which will then be governed by the contract and the host State's laws, and treaty claims, which will be decided on the basis of the treaty as well as other relevant rules of international law. As noted by the Ad Hoc Committee in *Vivendi* v. *Argentina*:

[W]hether there has been a breach of the BIT and whether there has been a breach of contract are different questions. Each of these claims will be determined by reference to its own proper or applicable law – in the case of the BIT, by international law; in the case of the Concession Contract, by the proper law of the contract, in other words, the law of Tucumán [a province of Argentina]. For example, in the case of a claim based on a treaty, international law rules of attribution apply, with the result that the state of Argentina is internationally responsible for the acts of its provincial authorities.[96]

In this first scenario, international environmental law may be applicable to assess a treaty claim (e.g., whether the conduct of a State allegedly in breach of an investment discipline was required by an international obligation of that State arising from an environmental treaty), whereas domestic environmental law may apply to assess a contract claim (e.g., whether termination of an investment contract by the host State was justified by the investor's violation of domestic environmental law).

---

[95] See E. Gaillard and Y. Banifatemi, 'The Meaning of "and" in Article 42(1), second sentence, of the Washington Convention: The Role of International Law in the ICSID Choice of Law Process' (2003) 18 *ICSID Review: Foreign Investment Law Journal* 375.

[96] *Compañía de Aguas del Aconquija SA and Vivendi Universal SA* v. *Argentine Republic*, ICSID Case No. ARB/97/03, Decision on Annulment (3 July 2002) ('*Vivendi* v. *Argentina* – Annulment'), para. 96. See further Z. Douglas, *The International Law of Investment Claims* (Cambridge University Press, 2009) 41.

Second, in deciding treaty claims (whether or not they have been brought together with contract claims), the tribunal may have to consider the operation of domestic laws. Domestic environmental laws may then be indirectly relevant to decide a treaty claim. For instance, in *Azurix* v. *Argentina*, the claimant had brought treaty claims in connection with a water concession contract. As part of its defence, Argentina argued that, in the absence of choice of law by the parties, Argentine law was applicable to the dispute. The application of Argentine law was relevant, *inter alia*, in connection with the standards of quality of the water distributed by the investor. In its award, the tribunal noted that domestic law was relevant for the assessment of the treaty claims, but only as 'an element of the inquiry':

> Azurix's claim has been advanced under the BIT and, as stated by the Annulment Committee in Vivendi II, the Tribunal's inquiry is governed by the ICSID Convention, by the BIT and by applicable international law. While the Tribunal's inquiry will be guided by this statement, this does not mean that the law of Argentina should be disregarded. On the contrary, the law of Argentina should be helpful in the carrying out of the Tribunal's inquiry into the alleged breaches of the Concession Agreement to which Argentina's law applies, but it is only an element of the inquiry because of the treaty nature of the claims under consideration.[97]

As this passage suggests, there is some ambiguity as to the precise status of domestic law. Traditionally, international law views domestic laws as facts, although quite particular ones, in that they may be necessary for the operation of international law. For instance, in the *Pulp Mills* case, after concluding that the requirement to conduct an environmental impact assessment prior to the execution of a project is part of general international law, the ICJ added that general international law does not specify the scope and content of environmental impact assessments and, for this reason, in the absence of a treaty clause to such effect, 'it is for each State to determine in its domestic legislation or in the authorization process for the project, the specific content of the environmental impact assessment required in each case'.[98] An alternative view is that tribunals select a given set of norms from both domestic and international law and then apply such set as a distinct body of law. This is how the tribunal in *CMS* v. *Argentina* seems

[97] *Azurix Corporation v. The Argentine Republic*, ICSID Case No. ARB/01/12, Award (14 July 2006) ('*Azurix* v. *Argentina*'), para. 67.
[98] *Pulp Mills* case, above n. 33, para. 205.

to have proceeded when it circumscribed the applicable law as follows: 'there is a close interaction between the legislation and the regulations governing the gas privatization, the License and international law, as embodied both in the Treaty and in customary international law. All of these rules are inseparable and will, to the extent justified, be applied by the Tribunal'.[99]

Third, in those cases where the same legal question is regulated by both domestic and international law, it may be necessary to determine the relative hierarchy of each body of law[100] or even of different norms within the same body of law.[101] Such conflicts will be analysed in Chapter 11, when discussing the legal techniques available to address them.

5.3.3   Relevance

Let us now turn to the issue of relevance. The scope of the dispute imposes 'relevance boundaries' on the selection of the applicable norms. The fact that a provision in an investment contract or in a BIT or a default rule contained in the rules governing the arbitration may point to international law as the applicable law does not mean that any rule of international law will be relevant for the determination of the case. Relevance is a complex concept, as there are different ways to characterise it and there may also be different degrees of relevance. Arbitral tribunals, as other international jurisdictions, have wide discretion in determining whether and to what extent a given norm is relevant.[102] In conducting such analysis they are guided by several considerations. Let us mention three of them, namely the boundaries of the dispute (Section 5.3.3.1), the pleas of the parties (Section 5.3.3.2) and some specific uses of environmental norms (Section 5.3.3.3).

---

[99] *CMS Gas Transmission Company* v. *Argentine Republic*, ICSID Case No. ARB/01/08, Award (12 May 2005) ('*CMS* v. *Argentina* – Award'), para. 117. For a theoretical account of this approach, see F. Grisel, *L'arbitrage international ou le droit contre l'ordre juridique*. Ph.D. dissertation, Université Paris I Pantheon-Sarbonn (2010).

[100] *Compañía del Desarrollo de Santa Elena SA* v. *Republic of Costa Rica*, ICSID Case No. ARB/96/1, Award (17 February 2000) ('*CDSE* v. *Costa Rica*'), paras. 64–5.

[101] *S. D. Myers Inc.* v. *Canada*, NAFTA (UNCITRAL), Partial Award (13 November 2000) ('*S. D. Myers* v. *Canada*'), paras. 214–15 and 255–6.

[102] This is a consequence of the *iura novit curia* principle. See O. Spiermann, 'Applicable Law', in P. Muchlinsky, F. Ortino and C. Schreuer (eds.), *The Oxford Handbook of International Investment Law* (Oxford University Press 2008), pp. 90–2.

5.3.3.1   Boundaries of the dispute

The starting-point for determining the boundaries of relevance is the definition of the dispute over which a tribunal has asserted jurisdiction. For instance, if the parties have brought treaty (as opposed to contract) claims, the relevance of the contractual layer as well as of the domestic norms governing the contract will be lower. As noted by the tribunal in *Bayindir* v. *Pakistan*:

> As a threshold matter, the Tribunal recalls that its jurisdiction covers treaty and not contract claims. This does not mean that it cannot consider contract matters. It can and must do so to the extent necessary to rule on the treaty claims. It takes contract matters, including the contract's governing municipal law, into account as facts as far as they are relevant to the outcome of the treaty claims. Doing so, it exercises treaty not contract jurisdiction.[103]

This point has already been discussed above in the paragraphs devoted to choice-of-law clauses and default rules, particularly in connection with the *Azurix* v. *Argentina* case.[104]

5.3.3.2   The pleas of the parties

Another indication of the relevance of a given (set of) norm(s) is provided, quite naturally, by the pleadings of the parties. For instance, in *Chemtura* v. *Canada*,[105] the respondent specifically referred to the provisions of the Aarhus Protocol on Persistant Organic Pollutants to the LRTAP Convention ('Aarhus POP Protocol')[106] to justify the launching of a special review of lindane, which eventually led to the suspension of the registration of certain lindane-based products manufactured by the claimant.[107] In its award, the tribunal accepted the argument of the respondent, considering that the Aarhus POP Protocol had indeed been at the origin of the special review process.[108]

---

[103] *Bayindir Insaat Turizm Ticaret ve Sanayi A Ş* v. *Pakistan*, ICSID Case No. ARB/03/29, Award (27 August 2009) ('*Bayindir* v. *Pakistan*'), para. 135. The tribunal in *Bayindir* v. *Pakistan* relied on the reasoning of the tribunal in *Compañía de Aguas del Aconquija SA and Vivendi Universal SA* v. *Argentine Republic*, ICSID Case No. ARB/97/3, Award (20 August 2007) ('*Vivendi II*'), para. 7.3.9.

[104] *Azurix* v. *Argentina*, above n. 97.

[105] *Chemtura Corporation (formerly Crompton Corporation)* v. *Government of Canada*, UNCITRAL, Award (2 August 2010) ('*Chemtura* v. *Canada*').

[106] Protocol on Persistent Organic Pollutants to the LTRAP Convention 24 June 1998, 37 ILM 513 ('Aarhus POP Protocol').

[107] *Chemtura* v. *Canada*, above n. 105, para. 131.   [108] *Ibid.*, paras. 139–41.

Beyond this basic hypothesis, the effect of the parties' pleadings on the tribunal's room for manoeuvre is difficult to determine conceptually. In *Klöckner* v. *Cameroon*, the Ad Hoc Committee made a distinction between arguments that are within the 'legal framework established by the Claimant and Respondent' and those that are 'beyond':

> As for the Tribunal itself [the one that had issued the award under review], when in the course of its deliberations it reached the provisional conclusion that the true legal basis for its decision could well be different from either of the parties' respective arguments, it was not, subject to what will be said below, in principle prohibited from choosing its own argument. Whether to reopen the proceeding before reaching a decision and allow the parties to put forward their views on the arbitrators' 'new' thesis is rather a question of expedience. The real question is whether, by formulating its own theory and argument, the Tribunal goes beyond the 'legal framework' established by the Claimant and Respondent.[109]

The tribunal gave an example of this '*hors sujet*' by referring to a hypothetical case in which the tribunal would have 'rendered its decision on the basis of tort while the pleas of the parties were based on contract'.[110] Aside from such extreme cases, the tribunal considered that 'arbitrators must be free to rely on arguments which strike them as the best ones, even if those arguments were not developed by the parties (although they could have been)'.[111]

Thus, a tribunal would have some freedom to introduce environmental questions even if the parties have not focused on such questions in their pleadings. Conversely, when such questions have been raised and the tribunal does not deem them relevant for the resolution of the case, it would also have some leeway to leave them aside. In practice, however, a tribunal would be well advised to give the parties an opportunity to comment on such issues and/or to explain why it does not consider certain arguments relevant.

This latter issue can be illustrated by reference to the decision of the tribunal in *Glamis* v. *United States*.[112] The case concerned an open-pit gold mining project, the development of which was prevented for

---

[109] *Klöckner Industrie-Anlagen GmbH et al.* v. *United Republic of Cameroon and Société Camerounaise des Engrais*, ICSID Case No. ARB/81/2, Decision on Annulment (3 May 1985) ('*Klöckner v. Cameroon*'), para. 91.

[110] *Ibid.*, para. 91.

[111] *Ibid.*, para. 91. However, the tribunal added a caveat at paras. 91–2.

[112] *Glamis Gold Ltd* v. *United States of America*, NAFTA (UNCITRAL), Award (16 May 2009) ('*Glamis v. United States*').

environmental and human rights reasons.[113] Several groups sought to intervene invoking domestic/international environmental and other norms.[114] These arguments were to some extent echoed in the respondent's briefs.[115] It was therefore understandable that, until the very moment when the tribunal issued its award, some commentators referred to the potential of such decision for clarifying the relations between foreign investment and the environment. For those groups and commentators, it came as a disappointment to see the tribunal's explanations as to why it preferred not to decide the most controversial issues touching on the environmental and human rights dimensions of the dispute. The tribunal gave the following explanation for proceeding as it did:

The Tribunal is aware that the decision in this proceeding has been awaited by private and public entities concerned with environmental regulation, the interests of indigenous peoples, and the tension sometimes seen between private rights in property and the need of the State to regulate the use of property. These issues were extensively argued in this case and considered by the Tribunal. However, given the Tribunal's holdings, the Tribunal is not required to decide many of the most controversial issues raised in this proceeding. The Tribunal observes that a few awards have made statements not required by the case before it. The Tribunal does not agree with this tendency; it believes that its case-specific mandate and the respect demanded for the difficult task faced squarely by some future tribunal instead argues for it to confine its decision to the issues presented.[116]

An alternative way to handle considerations that the tribunal deems of limited relevance would be to mention them without, however, integrating them into the analysis.[117]

---

[113] See C. Knight, 'A Regulatory Minefield: Can the Department of Interior say "No" to a Hardrock Mine?' (2002) 73 *University of Colorado Law Review* 619.

[114] Quechan Indian Nation Amicus Application & Submission, 19 August 2004; Friends of the Earth Amicus Application, 30 September 2005; Friends of the Earth Amicus Submission, 30 September 2005; Sierra Club & Earthworks Application for Leave to File a Non-Party Submission, 16 October 2006; Submission of Non-Disputing Parties Sierra Club & Earthworks, 16 October 2006; Quechan Indian Nation Application for Leave to File Supplementary Non-Party Submission, 16 October 2006; Supplemental Submission of Non-Disputing Party Quechan Indian Nation, 16 October 2006, all available at www.naftaclaims.com (accessed on 4 January 2012).

[115] Respondent's Counter-Memorial, 19 September 2006, 33ff, available at www.naftaclaims.com (accessed on 4 January 2012).

[116] *Glamis* v. *United States*, above n. 112, para. 8.

[117] This path was arguably followed in a water-related case, *Biwater Gauff (Tanz.) Ltd* v. *United Republic of Tanzania*, ICSID Case No. ARB/05/22, Award (24 July 2008) ('*Biwater* v. *Tanzania*'), para. 392.

5.3.3.3   Specific uses of environmental norms

A given norm may be relevant for different purposes, including: (i) as the norm governing a particular conduct; (ii) as an interpretation tool; or (iii) as mere inspirational guidance.

An illustration of (i) is provided by the *SPP* v. *Egypt* case, where the tribunal considered that the World Heritage Convention governed the respondent's conduct. The tribunal noted, in this regard, that there was no doubt that 'the UNESCO Convention [was] relevant: the Claimants themselves acknowledged during the proceedings before the French *Cour d'Appel* that the Convention obligated the Respondent to abstain from acts or contracts contrary to the Convention'.[118] Also, in *Chemtura* v. *Canada*, the tribunal considered that the Aarhus POP Protocol, and more specifically the undertaking to reassess the restricted uses of lindane contemplated in its Annex II, governed the conduct of Canada.[119]

Regarding (ii), environmental norms may also be relevant for the purpose of interpreting the scope of an investment discipline. For instance, in *Parkerings* v. *Lithuania*, the tribunal interpreted the MFN clause of the applicable BIT in the light of the World Heritage Convention to conclude that two foreign investors were not in a like position.[120] In a similar vein, in the *Pulp Mills* case, the ICJ excluded the application, as such, of the multilateral environmental agreements and principles of general international law invoked by Argentina, while stressing that such agreements and principles remained relevant to interpret the provisions of the Statute of the River Uruguay.[121]

Finally, environmental or human rights law may be relevant as an inspirational source (iii). An example would be the *Tecmed* v. *Mexico* case, where the tribunal turned to the case-law of the European Court of Human Rights (ECtHR), despite the fact that Mexico was not a party to the European Convention on Human Rights (ECHR), for intellectual guidance in applying the expropriation clause of the applicable BIT.[122]

---

[118] *SPP* v. *Egypt*, above n. 21, para. 78.

[119] *Chemtura* v. *Canada*, above n. 105, paras. 139–41.

[120] *Parkerings-Compagniet AS* v. *Republic of Lithuania*, ICSID Case No. ARB/05/8, Award (11 September 2007) ('*Parkerings* v. *Lithuania*'), para. 392.

[121] *Pulp Mills* case, above n. 33, paras. 64–6.

[122] *Técnicas Medioambientales Tecmed SA* v. *United Mexican States*, ICSID Case No. ARB(AF)/00/2, Award (29 May 2003) ('*Tecmed* v. *Mexico*'), para. 122. Unless the approach of the ECtHR were to be considered as a reflection of international customary law or of general principles of law, the reasoning of the tribunal could not be deemed to be an application of Article 31(3)(c) of the Vienna Convention on the Law of Treaties, 23 May 1969, 1155 UNTS 331 ('VCLT').

5.4   Procedural matters

The range of procedural issues potentially influenced by the incorporation of environmental matters in international proceedings is broad enough to have triggered several initiatives, including some attempts to establish an international environmental court, the creation of a special chamber of the ICJ focusing on environmental matters or the adoption by the PCA of a specific set of arbitration rules for natural resource and environmental disputes. In the context of investment proceedings, the procedural issues most directly affected by environmental considerations can be organised under two broad categories: the role of non-disputing parties (Section 5.4.1) and the additional challenges relating to evidentiary procedures (Section 5.4.2).

5.4.1   Role of non-disputing parties

It is useful to look, first, at how environmental considerations can be introduced into a foreign investment dispute (Section 5.4.1.1), before assessing the reasons explaining the intervention of non-disputing parties in investment proceedings (Section 5.4.1.2) and the legal framework applicable to such intervention (Section 5.4.1.3).

5.4.1.1   Raising environmental issues

How can environmental considerations be introduced into a foreign investment dispute? The basic answer is that the parties to a dispute may refer to all those considerations that they deem relevant in support of their case. Despite the fact that, in practice, host States will be the ones most likely to find support for their argumentation in environmental considerations, such considerations may also serve to buttress the legal case of an investor. As already mentioned, in *Allard* v. *Barbados* the investor refers, in support of its investment claims, to both domestic and international environmental law, including the Ramsar Convention[123] and the Convention on Biological Diversity.[124]

Second, environmental considerations could be introduced by the tribunal itself. This point has been discussed in the context of issues relating to both jurisdictional matters and applicable law. A tribunal

---

[123] Convention on Wetlands of International Importance especially as Waterfowl Habitat, 2 February 1971, 996 UNTS 245 ('Ramsar Convention').

[124] CBD, above n. 7.

may deem it appropriate to use environmental norms as mere guidance, as interpretation tools or, exceptionally, as applicable primary rules governing the conduct of (one of) the parties to the dispute. The basis for such application varies according to the use. As a rule, the maxim *iura novit curia* would provide a sufficient basis for the first two uses, whereas the third use (the actual application of an environmental norm) would normally require an additional element (i.e., a referral clause, a particularly broad jurisdictional clause or, simply, the inclusion of environmental obligations in the instrument primarily concerned by the jurisdictional clause). In addition, the tribunal itself could invite the parties to state their position with respect to the applicability of some environmental obligations that have not been referred to in the pleas of the parties. The tribunal could do so on the basis of its inherent powers.[125] The procedural situation would then be similar to one in which environmental considerations have been introduced in the pleas of the parties, unless both parties take the position that such norms are not applicable. In this latter case, the tribunal would need one of the additional elements identified above to ground its reference to environmental norms.

The third and remaining procedural access point is the submission of a non-disputing party. Such submissions have significantly increased in the last several years in both investment[126] and other international proceedings.[127] As noted above, the analysis conducted

---

[125] See C. Brown, *A Common Law of International Adjudication* (Oxford University Press 2007) pp. 55ff.

[126] In the context of investment disputes conducted under the aegis of ICSID, the following cases have triggered environment-related interventions by non-disputing parties: *Piero Foresti, Laura de Carli and others v. Republic of South Africa*, ICSID Case No. ARB(AF)/07/1 ('*Foresti v. South Africa*'); *Suez, Sociedad General de Aguas de Barcelona, SA and Vivendi Universal, SA v. The Argentine Republic*, ICSID Case No. ARB/03/19, Decision on Liability ('*Suez v. Argentina – 03/19*'); *Suez, Sociedad General de Aguas de Barcelona SA and InterAguas Servicios Integrales del Agua SA v. The Argentine Republic*, ICSID Case No. ARB/03/17, Decision on Liability ('*Suez v. Argentina – 03/17*'); *Biwater v. Tanzania*, above n. 117; *Aguas del Tunari SA v. Republic of Bolivia*, ICSID Case No. ARB/02/3, Decision on Objections to Jurisdiction, 21 October 2005 ('*Aguas del Tunari*')(later settled). In the context of NAFTA investment disputes, the following cases have triggered environment-related interventions by non-disputing parties: *Methanex Corporation v. United States of America*, NAFTA (UNCITRAL), Award (3 August 2005) ('*Methanex v. United States*'); *Glamis v. United States*, above n. 112.

[127] Even limiting the analysis to *amicus curiae* intervention, the examples of such interventions are numerous. See D. Shelton, 'The Participation of Nongovernmental Organizations in International Judicial Proceedings' (1994) 88 *American Journal of International Law* 611.

here focuses on two aspects of the role of non-disputing parties in environment-related disputes: the reasons explaining such intervention (Section 5.4.1.2) and the emerging legal framework applicable to it (Section 5.4.1.3).[128]

5.4.1.2   Reasons for third-party intervention

The reasons underlying third-party intervention can be better understood by reference to the historical roots of this phenomenon in the early history of the English legal system.[129] This affiliation has two interesting implications for the understanding of the role of this institution.

First, *amicus* intervention provided an avenue to bring points of law or fact to the attention of courts in an epoch characterised by considerable uncertainty as to the contents of the law.[130] Nowadays, the centre of gravity of such function would be instead on points of fact (e.g., informing the tribunal of the specific environmental consequences of a given project) or, to a lesser extent, on legal questions requiring specific knowledge (e.g., the application of certain environmental conventions to the issues under consideration). One difficulty with such function stems, however, from the potential inclination of *amici curiae* to forgo objectivity in favour of advocating a broader cause.[131]

The second and related implication of the origins of *amicus* intervention concerns its potential contribution to the legitimacy of courts' decisions. To the extent that, in the common law tradition, certain decisions had force of law and, as a result, could potentially modify the legal situation of third parties, *amicus* intervention served to give a voice to such third parties.[132] In the modern law of foreign investment, this function could be illustrated by reference to Article 1128 of the NAFTA, which allows NAFTA member States to intervene in investment proceedings against one of them. Another illustration is the case

---

[128] See B. Stern, 'Civil Society's Voice in the Settlement of International Economic Disputes' (2007) 22 *ICSID Review-Foreign International Law Journal* 280; F. Grisel and J. E. Viñuales, 'L'amicus curiae dans l'arbitrage d'investissement' (2007) 22 *ICSID Review-Foreign Investment Law Journal* 380.

[129] See the note on *amici curiae* in (1921) 34 *Harvard Law Review* 773 ('Harvard Note').

[130] S. Krislov, 'The Amicus Curiae Brief: From Friendship to Advocacy' (1963) 72 *Yale Law Journal* 694, at 694–5.

[131] F. V. Harper and E. D. Etherington, 'Lobbyists before the Court' (1953) 101 *University of Pennsylvania Law Review* 1172.

[132] Krislov, 'The Amicus Curiae Brief', above n. 130, 698.

Foresti v. *South Africa*,[133] where the tribunal took pains to give civil society groups the opportunity to express their views, and even requested feedback from such groups on the adequacy of the intervention framework.[134]

5.4.1.3   Applicable framework

The discussion of *Foresti* v. *South Africa* provides a useful basis for the analysis of the legal framework for *amicus* intervention. The dispute arose from a mining investment made by Italian nationals, who claimed, *inter alia*, that they had been expropriated by South Africa as a result of measures adopted by this State in the context of Black Economic Empowerment ('BEE') policies to eliminate the consequences of the apartheid regime. Given the public ramifications of the dispute, the tribunal anticipated that several civil society groups would likely seek to intervene. It therefore prepared, in agreement with the parties, a short summary of the dispute as well as rules governing *amicus* intervention.[135]

Despite its technical rooting in Rule 41(3) of the ICSID's Additional Facility Arbitration Rules, the document prepared by the tribunal can arguably be seen as a current statement of the basic requirements for the submission of *amicus* briefs:

Non-disputing parties seeking to make a written submission should file a petition with the Tribunal for leave to file a written submission and such petition should include the following information:

- the identity and background of the petitioner, the nature of its membership if it is an organization, and the nature of its relationships, if any, to the Parties to the dispute;
- the nature of the petitioner's interest in the case;
- whether the petitioner has received financial or other material support from any of the Parties or from any person connected with the Parties in this case; and
- the reasons why the Tribunal should accept the petitioner's written submission.[136]

---

[133] *Foresti* v. *South Africa*, above n. 126.
[134] Letter of 5 October 2009 from the Secretary of the Tribunal, available at: www.investmenttreatynews.org/cms/news/archive/2009/10/10/an-icsid-tribunal-introduces-innovative-steps-into-non-disputing-party-procedure.aspx (accessed on 4 January 2012) ('*Foresti* – Letter from Tribunal').
[135] Agreed text for potential non-disputing parties ('*Foresti* v. *South Africa* – Intervention Instructions').
[136] *Foresti* v. *South Africa* – Intervention Instructions, above n. 135, 2.

Thereafter, two petitions were submitted, one from the International Commission of Jurists, a human rights organisation,[137] and another from a group of four non-governmental organisations ('NGOs'), including two focusing on environmental protection.[138]

In its decision granting leave for intervention,[139] the tribunal authorised the petitioners not only to submit written briefs, but also to access redacted versions of documents of the case file, and it even left open the possibility of granting them access to the hearing.[140] Even more noteworthy was the system established by the tribunal to receive feedback from the *amici curiae*:

> In view of the novelty of the NDP procedure, after all submissions, written and oral, have been made the Tribunal will invite the Parties and the NDPs to offer brief comments on the fairness and effectiveness of the procedures adopted for NDP participation in this case. The Tribunal will then include a section in the award, recording views (both concordant and divergent) on the fairness and efficacy of NDP participation in this case and on any lessons learned from it.[141]

The introduction by the tribunal of this additional step was likely due to the exceptionally sensitive context of the case, in which procedural openness could no doubt add legitimacy to any future decision made by the tribunal on the merits of the dispute.[142] It must be noted, in addition, that the procedure established by the tribunal was not exactly novel. Although neither the access to the file nor the potential access to the hearing had been previously granted to NGOs acting as *amici curiae*, the requirements set out by the tribunal for *amicus* intervention are fundamentally the same as those established by previous tribunals and international instruments.[143]

---

[137] Petition for Participation as Non-disputing Party pursuant to Article 41(3) of the ICSID Arbitration (Additional Facility) Rules, presented by the International Commission of Jurists, available at: www.icj.org/IMG/ICJ_Petition_Foresti_v_RSA_19_Aug2009.pdf (accessed on 4 January 2012).

[138] Petition for Limited Participation as Non-Disputing Parties in Terms of Articles 41(3), 27, 39, and 35 of the Additional Facility Rules, presented by the Centre for Applied Legal Studies (CALS), the Center for International Environmental Law (CIEL), the International Centre for the Legal Protection of Human Rights (INTERIGHTS), and the Legal Resources Centre (LRC), available at: www.interights.org/view-document/index.htm?id=543 (accessed on 4 January 2012).

[139] *Foresti* – Letter from Tribunal, above n. 134.

[140] *Ibid.*, 1–2.   [141] *Ibid.*, 2 *in fine*.

[142] The case did not reach the merits. See *Foresti v. South Africa*, above n. 126, Award (4 August 2010) ('*Foresti v. South Africa* – Award').

[143] See the remarks of the tribunals in *Suez v. Argentina* – 03/19, above n. 126, Order in Response to a Petition for Transparency and Participation as *Amicus Curiae*, 19 May 2005

In essence, *amicus* intervention is allowed if the petitioner can make (i) a substantive (points of law or fact) and a (ii) procedural (enhancing legitimacy) contribution to the proceedings,[144] (iii) without severely encroaching on the parties due process and confidentiality rights (proportionality). Whereas the first two requirements are the same for the three types of requests (written intervention, access to documents, access to the hearing) usually made by *amici curiae*, the 'no-disturbance' requirement is more demanding with respect to two of these requests (access to documents and to the hearing).[145]

Environment-related disputes, such as those concerning water services, natural resources extraction, waste treatment facilities or regulated substances, are particularly prone to present broader public considerations, which a tribunal should take into account in reaching a decision. An important function of *amicus* intervention in this context is therefore to assist the tribunal in understanding such broader public repercussions as well as to enhance the legitimacy of arbitration proceedings by presenting the perspective of civil society. In order to perform such function, however, *amici curiae* must be both competent and representative of relevant constituencies. Representativeness further supposes the absence of bias arising from any relevant relation with one of the parties, especially financial relations. Such are, in a nutshell, the conceptual underpinnings of the requirements set for *amicus* intervention.

5.4.2   Evidentiary issues

Environment-related disputes present some specific challenges in terms of evidence as a result of both the highly technical nature and the

---

('Order I'), paras. 17–29; *Suez* v. *Argentina* – 03/19, above n. 126, Order in Response to a Petition by Five Non-Governmental Organizations for Permission as *Amicus Curiae*, 12 February 2007 ('Order II'), para. 15; *Suez* v. *Argentina* – 03/17, above n. 126, Order in Response to a Petition for Participation as *Amicus Curiae*, 17 March 2006 ('Order'), para. 17–34; *Biwater* v. *Tanzania*, above n. 117, Procedural Order No. 5 ('Order 5'), paras. 46–61. See also ICSID Arbitration Rules (2006), Article 37(2). In *Suez* v. *Argentina* – 03/19, the tribunal took position on the conditions that it had set, prior to the entry into force of the new Article 37(2) of the ICSID Arbitration Rules, for the admission of *amicus* briefs and found them to be in accordance with the new rules, Order II, para. 15. For a survey of codification efforts regarding *amicus* intervention see Grisel and Viñuales, 'L'amicus curiae dans l'arbitrage d'investissement' above n. 128, 402–13.

[144] The tribunal in *Biwater* v. *Tanzania* seemed to imply that either one of these two conditions (substantive contribution and legitimacy enhancement) would be sufficient, Order 5, above n. 143, para. 54.

[145] ICSID Arbitration Rules (2006), Article 32(2); *Suez* v. *Argentina* – 03/19, Order I, above n. 143, para. 6; *Suez* v. *Argentina* – 03/17, Order, above n. 143, para. 7.

considerable scientific uncertainty often associated with environmental issues. In order to deliberate the merits of an investment dispute with environmental components, tribunals must not only understand in some detail complex environmental processes but may also have to take position on a scientific debate where the views of the experts presented by the parties are often at odds. This can be challenging for judges or arbitrators who, as a rule, do not have a sufficient scientific background to understand the intricacies of such complex processes.[146] In order to respond to such challenge, international courts and tribunals can follow four main approaches:[147] to downplay the need for an explicit decision on the scientific merits of each position (Section 5.4.2.1); to appoint an independent expert to assist the tribunal (Section 5.4.2.2); to adjust the burden or the standard of proof (Section 5.4.2.3); or to defer to the scientific assessment made by specialised agencies. Here, I focus on the first three avenues, leaving the fourth for the discussion of the margin of appreciation doctrine in Chapter 15.

5.4.2.1   Downplaying the role of science

The first approach can be illustrated by reference to a number of international proceedings where the adjudicators were asked by the parties, either explicitly or (more often) implicitly, to take a position on a scientific debate.

In *Gabčíkovo-Nagymaros*,[148] Hungary argued, to justify its non-performance of a treaty with Slovakia for the construction of a system of dams, that if it had conducted the works as planned 'the environment – and in particular the drinking water resources – in the area would have been exposed to serious dangers'.[149] In the course of the proceedings, both Hungary and Slovakia presented what the Court itself qualified as an impressive amount of scientific material to buttress their respective arguments. In its decision, however, the Court considered that 'it [was] not necessary in order to

---

[146] This point was underlined in the Joint-Dissenting Opinion of Judges Al-Khasawneh and Simma in the *Pulp Mills* case, above n. 33, para. 2 (stating that 'the Court has evaluated the scientific evidence brought before it by the Parties in ways that we consider flawed methodologically').

[147] On these and other techniques see M. Orellana, 'The Role of Science in Investment Arbitrations Concerning Public Health and the Environment' (2006) 17 *Yearbook of International Environmental Law* 48; C. Forster, *Science and the Precautionary Principle in International Courts and Tribunals* (Cambridge University Press, 2011).

[148] *Gabčíkovo-Nagymaros Project (Hungary v. Slovakia)*, ICJ Reports 1997, 7 ('*Gabčíkovo-Nagymaros*').

[149] *Ibid.*, para. 55.

respond to the questions put to it in the Special Agreement for it to determine which of those points of view is scientifically better founded'.[150]

This may appear as an exceptional solution to the extent that the Court was able to decide the issue for which the scientific evidence had been adduced on the basis of different legal grounds. But such a way of proceeding is not uncommon. To take another example, the panel established by the WTO to decide the *EC Asbestos* case noted, in the same vein:

> In relation to the scientific information submitted by the parties and the experts, the Panel feels bound to point out that it is not its function to settle a scientific debate, not being composed of experts in the field or the possible human health risks posed by asbestos. Consequently, the Panel does not intend to set itself up as arbiter of the opinions expressed by the scientific community.[151]

It seems reasonable not to require international adjudicators to take a position in an unsettled or at least arguable scientific debate. But the problem with this solution is that it is sometimes impossible to decide a legal dispute without forming a general opinion on the scientific debate underlying it, and that adjudicators do in practice form such an opinion, whether or not it is spelled out in the final decision. An alternative way of proceeding would consist of providing adjudicators with the assistance they need to reach a reasonable and informed opinion on the science underlying the law.

5.4.2.2   Scientific assistance

A number of arbitration and procedural rules contain specific provisions allowing the tribunal to appoint its own expert. For instance, Article 27(1) of the UNCITRAL Arbitration Rules states that:

> The arbitral tribunal may appoint one or more experts to report to it, in writing, on specific issues to be determined by the tribunal. A copy of the expert's terms of reference, established by the arbitral tribunal, shall be communicated to the parties.[152]

---

[150]   *Ibid.*, para. 55.

[151]   *European Communities – Measures Affecting Asbestos and Asbestos-Containing Products*, Panel Report, Doc. WT/DS135/R (18 September 2000), para. 8.181. See also *Continental Shelf (Libya v. Malta)*, ICJ Reports 1985, 36, para. 41; (*Bluefin Tuna* – ITLOS, above n. 9, para. 40, 65, referred to by Orellana, 'The Role of Science in Investment Arbitrations' above n. 147, 52–3.

[152]   UNCITRAL Rules, above n. 90, Article 27(1).

Similarly, the IBA Rules on the Taking of Evidence in International Commercial Arbitration, frequently used in investment cases, provide in Article 6(1):

The Arbitral Tribunal, after having consulted with the Parties, may appoint one or more independent Tribunal-Appointed Experts to report to it on specific issues designated by the Arbitral Tribunal. The Arbitral Tribunal shall establish the terms of reference for any Tribunal-Appointed Expert report after having consulted with the Parties. A copy of the final terms of reference shall be sent by the Arbitral Tribunal to the Parties.[153]

Still another illustration of this possibility is provided by Article 27(1) of the PCA Optional Rules:

After having obtained the views of the parties, the arbitral tribunal may upon notice to the parties appoint one or more experts to report to it, in writing, on specific issues to be determined by the tribunal. A copy of the expert's terms of reference, established by the arbitral tribunal, shall be communicated to the parties.[154]

Article 24(4) of the PCA Optional Rules also provides an alternative method to assist tribunals, namely the possibility to ask the parties to provide non-technical summaries or explanations of the scientific or technological issues relevant to assess the merits of the dispute. Although not expressly mentioned in other arbitration and procedural rules, such possibility is arguably encompassed by the tribunals' general procedural powers.[155]

5.4.2.3   Adjustments to evidentiary standards

This approach is more controversial, as deviations from the basic rules governing the burden and the standard of proof in international

---

[153] International Bar Association (IBA), Rules on the Taking of Evidence in International Commercial Arbitration ('IBA Evidence Rules'), Article 6(1).

[154] PCA Optional Rules, above n. 6, Article 27(1). Other examples of this type of provision include the following: ICJ Statute, Article 50; WTO Understanding on Rules and Procedures Governing the Settlement of Disputes, Article 13(2); UNCLOS above n. 9, Article 289; NAFTA, above n. 15, Article 1133. In their Joint Dissenting Opinion in the *Pulp Mills* case, judges Al-Khasawneh and Simma regretted, in particular, that the Court did not resort to the possibility offered by Article 50 of the Court's Statute, above n. 146, para. 8.

[155] See L. Craig, W. W. Park and J. Paulsson, International Chamber of Commerce Arbitration (2000) 300ff; D. Caron, L. M. Caplan and M. Pellonpaa, *The UNCITRAL Arbitration Rules. A Commentary* (Oxford University Press, 2006), pp. 25ff; C. Schreuer, L. Malintoppi, A. Reinisch and A. Sinclair, *The ICSID Convention. A Commentary* (Cambridge University Press, 2nd edn, 2009), pp. 672ff.

adjudication[156] should be admitted only under particular circumstances.[157] The difficulties involved in establishing environmental risk or harm in international proceedings may, however, justify some adjustment of those basic rules. In this regard, two main avenues could be followed.

The first possibility would be to shift the burden of proof by means of a treaty provision. For instance, under the London Dumping Convention, as amended by the 1996 Protocol, it is for the party dumping industrial waste (or other substances) at sea to prove that such dumping does not harm the environment.[158] A conventional shift of the burden of proof has also been proposed by the European Community within the context of the Doha round in connection with the relations between trade restrictions in multilateral environmental agreements and the general exceptions clause in Article XX of the GATT.[159] According to this proposal, a trade restriction based on a multilateral environmental agreement would be presumed to fall within the general exceptions clause in Article XX unless otherwise established by the party affected by the measure.[160] This solution can be seen as an application of one of the formulations of the precautionary principle.[161] In the absence of an agreement along the lines of the foregoing examples, a shift of the burden of proof seems unlikely in the present state of international law. In the *Pulp Mills* case, Argentina argued that the Statute of the River Uruguay implicitly adopted a precautionary approach whereby the burden of proving that the mills would not cause significant damage

---

[156] See C. Santulli, *Droit du contentieux international* (Paris: Montchrestien, 2005), paras. 846–68; Brown, *A Common Law of International Adjudication*, above n. 125, pp. 92–101. See, also, PCA Optional Rules, above n. 6, Article 24(1); UNCITRAL Rules, above n. 90, Article 24(1), with identical language; *Bayindir* v. *Pakistan*, above n. 103, paras. 140–3; *Pulp Mills* case, above n. 33, para. 162.

[157] See the reasoning of the ICJ in the *Corfu Channel* case with respect to the use of circumstantial evidence: *Corfu Channel case (UK v. Albania)*, ICJ Reports 1949, 4, at 18.

[158] Convention for the Prevention of Marine Pollution by Dumping of Wastes and Other Matter, 29 December 1972, as modified by the Protocol of 7 November 1996, 1046 UNTS 120, Article 4(1).

[159] General Agreement on Tariffs and Trade, 1947, incorporated into the General Agreement on Tariffs and Trade, 15 April 1994, 1867 UNTS 187 ('GATT'), Article XX(b) and (g).

[160] Committee on Trade and Environment, Resolving the Relationship Between the WTO Rules and Multilateral Environmental Agreements, Communication by the European Communities of 19 October 2000, WT/CTE/W/170, paras. 10, 15.

[161] D. Bodansky, 'Deconstructing the Precautionary Principle' in D. Caron and H. N. Scheiber (eds.), *Bringing New Ocean Waters* (Leiden: Martinus Nijhoff, 2004) p. 381.

to the environment was on Uruguay.[162] The ICJ rejected this argument stating that 'while a precautionary approach may be relevant in the interpretation and application of the provisions of the Statute, it does not follow that it operates as a reversal of the burden of proof'.[163]

The second possibility would be to maintain the burden of proof on the party alleging a fact while relaxing the standard for proving such fact. For instance, in the *EC – Hormones* case,[164] the WTO Appellate Body confirmed that, under the SPS Agreement,[165] the claimant only needs to make a *prima facie* showing that the respondent is in breach of its obligations, after which the burden of proving an exception shifts to the respondent.[166] ITLOS has followed an arguably similar approach in the *Southern Bluefin Tuna* cases, in that it seems to apply precautionary reasoning to compensate for the absence of conclusive indications on a fact alleged by the petitioner.[167] However, this approach has not been followed consistently.[168]

5.5   Damages

The question whether a breach of investment disciplines (particularly a taking) based on environmental (or human rights) reasons should be subject to a requirement for compensation or not has attracted some attention from legal commentators.[169] Broadly speaking, there are two opposite approaches. The first approach considers environmental justifications as irrelevant (Section 5.5.1), whereas the second approach holds that some deprivations of property based on environmental considerations are non-compensable (Section 5.5.2). Between these two stances, some middle-ground positions can be identified in some cases (Section 5.5.3).

---

[162] *Pulp Mills* case, above n. 33, para. 160.   [163] *Ibid.*, para. 164.

[164] *European Communities Measures concerning Meat and Meat Products (Hormones)*, 16 January 1998, WT/DS26/AB/R, WT/DS48/AB/R ('*EC – Hormones*').

[165] Agreement on Sanitary and Phytosanitary Measures, 15 April 1994, 1867 UNTS 493 ('SPS Agreement').

[166] *EC – Hormones*, above n. 164, para. 109.

[167] The standard of proof applied seems to be lower than the one applicable for provisional measures. See *Bluefin Tuna – ITLOS*, above n. 9, paras. 79–80; *Land Reclamation by Singapore in and around the Straits of Johor (Malaysia v. Singapore)*, Provisional Measures, ITLOS Case No. 12, Order (8 October 2003) ('*Land Reclamation – ITLOS*'), paras. 93–6.

[168] *MOX Plant – ITLOS* above n. 9, paras. 69–81.

[169] S. Robert-Cuendet, *Droits de l'investisseur étranger et protection de l'environnement: Contribution à l'analyse de l'expropriation indirecte* (Leiden : Martinus Nijhoff, 2010).

5.5.1   The irrelevance thesis

The first approach focuses on the sole effects of a deprivation of property. It holds that such taking must be compensated irrespective of its reasons. The awards in *CDSE* v. *Costa Rica*[170] and *Metalclad* v. *Mexico*[171] illustrate this first stance. The dispute in *CDSE* v. *Costa Rica* concerned the amount due for the direct expropriation of a land that the claimant had acquired in order to build a resort. The respondent had invoked a number of domestic and international environmental instruments to challenge the calculation of the amount of compensation. The tribunal held the following view:

> While an expropriation or taking for environmental reasons may be classified as a taking for a public purpose, and thus may be legitimate, the fact that the property was taken for this reason does not affect either the nature or the measure of compensation to be paid for the taking. That is, the purpose of protecting the environment for which the property was taken does not alter the legal character of the taking for which adequate compensation must be paid. The international source of the obligation to protect the environment makes no difference.[172]

This stance was confirmed in *Metalclad* v. *Mexico*,[173] this time with respect to an indirect taking. The claimant argued that Mexico had breached Articles 1105 (minimum standard of treatment) and 1110 (expropriation) as a result of the acts and omissions of the municipal authorities in connection with the construction of a waste disposal landfill. Indeed, whereas the federal government had granted a permit for the project and represented that no further permits were required, the local authorities declined to grant a second construction permit and subsequently declared the area to be an ecological preserve. The tribunal held that, irrespective of the environmental reasons invoked by Mexico, the measures amounted to both a breach of the minimum standard of treatment and a compensable expropriation:

> Although not strictly necessary for its conclusion, the Tribunal also identifies as a further ground for a finding of expropriation the Ecological Decree issued by the Governor of SLP on September 20, 1997. This Decree covers an area of 188,758 hectares within the 'Real de Guadalcazar' that includes the landfill site, and created therein an ecological preserve. This Decree had the effect of barring

---

[170] *CDSE* v. *Costa Rica*, above n. 100.
[171] *Metalclad Corporation* v. *United Mexican States*, ICSID Case No. ARB(AF) 197/Award (25 August 2000) ('*Metalclad* v. *Mexico*').
[172] *Ibid.*, para. 71.   [173] *Metalclad* v. *Mexico*, above n. 171.

forever the operation of the landfill ... The Tribunal is not persuaded by Mexico's representation to the contrary. The Ninth Article, for instance, forbids any work inconsistent with the Ecological Decree's management program. The management program is defined by the Fifth Article as one of diagnosing the ecological problems of the cacti reserve and of ensuring its ecological preservation. In addition, the Fourteenth Article of the Decree forbids any conduct that might involve the discharge of polluting agents on the reserve soil, subsoil, running water or water deposits and prohibits the undertaking of any potentially polluting activities. The Fifteenth Article of the Ecological Decree also forbids any activity requiring permits or licenses unless such activity is related to the exploration, extraction or utilization of natural resources ... The Tribunal need not decide or consider the motivation or intent of the adoption of the Ecological Decree. Indeed, a finding of expropriation on the basis of the Ecological Decree is not essential to the Tribunal's finding of a violation of NAFTA Article 1110. However, the Tribunal considers that the implementation of the Ecological Decree would, in and of itself, constitute an act tantamount to expropriation.[174]

These cases would suggest that international obligations (or related considerations) other than those arising from investment treaties are simply not relevant for the assessment of compensation for expropriation. However, other tribunals have followed an entirely different approach.

5.5.2 The police powers thesis

Some tribunals have held that deprivations of property resulting from environmental measures (targeted or general[175]) are not compensable or, more precisely, that they do not even constitute an expropriation.

A clear formulation of this stance appears in the decision of the tribunal in a dispute without environmental dimensions, namely *Saluka* v. *Czech Republic*,[176] where the tribunal made the following statement:

In the opinion of the Tribunal, the principle that a State does not commit an expropriation and is thus not liable to pay compensation to a dispossessed alien investor when it adopts general regulations that are 'commonly accepted as within the police powers of States' forms part of customary law today.[177]

The same stance was adopted by the tribunal in *Chemtura* v. *Canada*, this time specifically in connection with a targeted environmental measure:

[T]he Tribunal considers in any event that the measures challenged by the Claimant constituted a valid exercise of the Respondent's police powers. As

---

[174] *Ibid.*, para. 109–11.   [175] See Chapter 12.
[176] *Saluka Investments BV* v. *The Czech Republic*, UNCITRAL, Partial Award (17 March 2006) ('*Saluka* v. *Czech Republic*').
[177] *Ibid.*, para. 262.

discussed in detail in connection with Article 1105 of NAFTA, the PMRA took measures within its mandate, in a non-discriminatory manner, motivated by the increasing awareness of the dangers presented by lindane for human health and the environment. A measure adopted under such circumstances is a valid exercise of the State's police powers and, as a result, does not constitute an expropriation.[178]

While it is accurate to say that the doctrine of police powers focuses only on liability and not on compensation, in some cases where there has been an expropriation environmental considerations may also play the additional role of limiting compensation. In *SPP v. Egypt*,[179] the tribunal concluded that Egypt had expropriated property from the investors. However, in assessing compensation, the tribunal excluded the amount of damages corresponding to the period after the emergence of Egypt's obligations of protection in accordance with the World Heritage Convention. The tribunal reasoned as follows:

Even if the Tribunal were disposed to accept the validity of the Claimant's DCF calculations, it could only award lucrum cessans until 1979, when the obligations resulting from the UNESCO Convention with respect to the Pyramids Plateau became binding on the Respondent. From that date forward, the Claimant's activities on the Pyramids Plateau would have been in conflict with the Convention and therefore in violation of international law, and any profits that might have resulted from such activities are consequently non-compensable.[180]

This is a clear statement in favour of incorporating environmental considerations in the calculation of compensation. The question then becomes how exactly such incorporation should be operated.

5.5.3   Middle grounds

A number of tribunals have followed approaches that can be situated between the two preceding stances. The reasoning of the tribunals in *Methanex v. United States*[181] and *MTD v. Chile*[182] in connection with the police powers and margin of appreciation doctrines will be discussed in detail in Chapters 12 and 15. Here, the analysis will be limited to those aspects of these decisions that could assist in clarifying the impact of environmental considerations on the assessment of damage.

---

[178] *Chemtura v. Canada*, above n. 105, para. 266, referring to para. 262 of *Saluka v. Czech Republic*.

[179] *SPP v. Egypt*, above n. 21.   [180] *Ibid.*, paras. 191, 250.

[181] *Methanex v. United States*, above n. 126.

[182] *MTD Equity Sdn Bhd and MTD Chile SA v. Republic of Chile*, ICSID Case No. ARB/01/7, Award (25 May 2004) ('*MTD v. Chile – Award*').

In *Methanex* v. *United States*, the tribunal took a stance that, in essence, corresponds to the police powers thesis. It concluded indeed that the measures adopted by the Californian authorities banning MTBE (methyl tertiary butyl ether) fell within the scope of the State's police powers and, as a result, were not an expropriation in the meaning of Article 1110 of the NAFTA. What is interesting for the issue of compensation is the caveat introduced by the tribunal regarding situations where the host State has given specific assurances that an adverse regulation will not be adopted. A situation could arise where the State has given such specific assurances to an investor on the basis of its contemporaneous scientific understanding of an environmental question. One could think, for instance, of topics on which the scientific community is divided, or of fields where a major scientific or technological breakthrough permits the replacement of a lesser evil (i.e., a very important product with some undesirable consequences but with no serious substitute)[183] with a new healthier product. After new developments in the scientific understanding of the question, the State decides, despite its previous assurances, to adopt a measure that makes the investor's business less profitable or even unviable. The question would then be how to balance environmental and investment protection. Admittedly, the solution will heavily depend on the specific facts of the case as well as on the ability of counsel to mobilise such facts in support of a claim. But broadly speaking, there are two possible solutions.

The first solution would be to bring the situation under the umbrella of the police powers doctrine and conclude that the measures are not an expropriation. A similar reasoning could also intervene *mutatis mutandis* in connection with a claim for breach of the FET standard if the possibility of a change in the scientific understanding of a product was reasonably predictable, as may be the case for heavily regulated products.

The second (alternative) solution would be to conclude that, as a result of the assurances given to the investor, the measures are not covered by the police powers doctrine and constitute an expropriation. What is unclear is whether the amount of compensation could be adjusted to take into account the specific circumstances in which the expropriation intervened. There are different ways to incorporate such considerations in the assessment of compensation.

[183] An example is the continuing use of DDT, one of the most widely known persistent organic pollutants, in some developing countries, as an effective way to fight malaria. See 'WHO gives Indoor Use of DDT a Clean Bill of Health for Controlling Malaria', press release of 15 September 2006, available at: www.who.int (accessed on 4 January 2012).

One approach would be to reduce the amount of compensation to take into account the degree of diligence or reasonableness of the investor. In *MTD v. Chile*, the tribunal considered that the investor, which had acted negligently in assessing regulatory risks, had to bear part of the damages that it had suffered. The tribunal reasoned that such damage was attributable to business risk because the investor could have mitigated it if it had deployed better business judgment.[184]

Another approach, in the context of the hypothetical situation described above, would be to assess the value of the expropriated asset as a going concern and/or of the *lucrum cessans* resulting from the expropriation by reference to a shorter time horizon. The time horizon may be limited by reference to international legal developments, as in *SPP v. Egypt*,[185] or by the specific characteristics of some markets.[186] Markets in highly regulated products or activities sometimes face fast-moving scientific and technological environments, which may limit their lifespan. Indeed, specific assurances are not insurance against all odds. It may also happen that the investor knew, at the time it invested, that a market was still profitable in some countries but not in others, as a result of different perceptions of a health or an environmental risk. An apposite illustration would be tobacco-related investments made in emerging markets based on specific assurances of the host State. In such cases, the reasoning of the tribunal in *Tecmed v. Mexico*, which distinguished environmental risks from the socio-political reaction attached to their perception by the population,[187] would be problematic. A risk may indeed exist despite the fact that the affected population is not actively aware of it. Moreover, the perception of the relevant population, irrespective of whether the environmental risk is high or low, is an important factor in assessing the value of an investment, to the extent that such perception affects the current and future demand for an

---

[184] *MTD v. Chile* – Award, above n. 182, paras. 242–3. The damages assessment of the tribunal withstood an annulment challenge, see *MTD Equity Sdn Bhd and MTD Chile SA v. Chile*, ICSID Case No ARB/01/7, Decision on Annulment (16 February 2007) ('*MTD v. Chile* – Annulment'), para. 101.

[185] *SPP v. Egypt*, above n. 21, para. 191. Interestingly, the *SPP v. Egypt* decision also leaves open the possibility of adjusting compensation on the basis of other factors, such as the potential benefits (monetary or other) derived by one of the parties. The existence of such benefits was invoked by the respondent as a mitigation factor but eventually rejected by the tribunal. *Ibid.*, paras. 245–9.

[186] *Ibid.*, para. 251.

[187] *Tecmed v. Mexico*, above n. 122, paras. 132–51. See the discussion of this point in Chapter 12, Section 12.3.2.

investor's product. An example could be provided by investments relating to genetically modified organisms ('GMOs'), irrespective of the scientific position that one may take as to the risks associated with GMOs.

Thus, environmental considerations could indeed affect the reasoning of a tribunal regarding the assessment of compensation. Technically, tribunals have considerable room for manoeuvre in selecting the appropriate standard of compensation and, even when they retain the fair market value approach, either for expropriation or for other breaches, they still have considerable leeway in deciding which valuation techniques are the most appropriate to calculate such value.[188]

---

[188] P.-Y. Tschanz and J. E. Viñuales, 'Compensation for Non-Expropriatory Breaches of International Investment Law – The Contribution of the Argentine Awards' (2009) 6 *Journal of International Arbitration* 729.

Part II

Normative conflicts

6 Normative priority in international law

Normative priority in international law is determined through a variety of means, which can all be traced back to different types of conflict norms. What all the conflict norms relevant to tackle normative conflicts have in common are: (i) their grounding in public international law, and (ii) their basic 'function', namely to solve conflicts between different norms of international law.

Aside from these two common features, these norms differ considerably as to their 'scope'. Some conflict norms have narrowly defined scopes, which limit their operation to the resolution of normative conflicts between specific norms or sets of norms, whereas others have much broader scopes and can therefore be used to solve conflicts irrespective of the branches of international law to which the conflicting norms belong. I will refer to the former as 'specific conflict norms' and the latter as 'general conflict norms'.

In this chapter, after a brief discussion of how the issue of fragmentation affects the relationship between international investment law and international environmental law (Section 6.1), I analyse the palette of specific (Section 6.2) and general (Section 6.3) conflict norms available to manage normative conflicts between these two branches of international law. The chapter is not intended to provide a general presentation of these conflict norms, which have already received some attention from legal commentators,[1] but rather to analyse how such norms

---

[1] See Conclusions of the Work of the Study Group on the Fragmentation of International Law: Difficulties arising from the Diversification and Expansion of International Law (2006) ('Conclusions – Fragmentation'), adopted by the International Law Commission at its fifty-eighth session in 2006, and submitted to the General Assembly in its general report on the works of the said session (Doc. A/61/10/, para. 251). See also the Report, finalised by Marti Koskenniemi, dated 13 April 2006 (Doc. A/CN.4/L.682) and the Corrigendum of 11 August 2006 (Doc. A/CN.4/L.682/Corr.1) ('Report - Fragmentation');

operate in the specific context of normative conflicts between international investment law and international environmental law.

6.1   Fragmentation as it concerns the relations between environmental and investment protection

International environmental law and international investment law have traditionally evolved without paying much attention to each other. Until recently, the instruments dealing with each of these two branches of international law made little reference, if any, to the instruments relevant to the other, or even to the goals pursued by such instruments. For most of the history of both international environmental law and international investment law, fragmentation meant, indeed, not only specialisation but also mutual ignorance or, at least, mutual disinterest.[2]

As noted in Chapter 1, the normative development of these two branches of international law is changing their relations. As with the relations between trade and environmental law, discussed in some detail in the ILC Report on the Fragmentation of International Law,[3] the potential for normative conflicts between environmental and investment law is attracting growing attention. Some commentators have focused on how fragmentation affects, specifically, international investment law[4] or international environmental law.[5] In the context of this broader debate, three main considerations are relevant for the present analysis.

First, the process whereby an area of international law becomes increasingly specialised has many dimensions. In addition to 'functional' specialisation,[6] understood as either the pursuit of a particular policy objective or as the provision of a response tailored to a particular area of concern (e.g., the protection of foreign investors or of the environment), significant attention must be paid to the level of specificity in the formulation of the

---

E. Roucounas, 'Engagements parallèles et contradictoires', in *Recueil des cours de l'Académie de droit international*, Vol. 206 (1987), pp. 9–288; S. A. Sadat-Akhavi, *Methods of Resolving Conflicts between Treaties* (Leiden: Martinus Nijhoff, 2003); J. Pauwelyn, *Conflict of Norms in Public International Law: How WTO Law Relates to other Rules of International Law* (Cambridge University Press, 2003).

[2] Report – Fragmentation, above n. 1, para. 8.

[3] See, e.g., *ibid.*, paras. 24, 55, 146, 168, 170 and 443–50.

[4] A. van Aaken, 'Fragmentation of International Law: The Case of International Investment Law' (2006) 17 *Finnish Yearbook of International Law* 91.

[5] T. Stephens, *International Courts and Environmental Protection* (Cambridge University Press, 2009), Chapter 10.

[6] Report – Fragmentation, above n. 1, paras. 7, 8 and 15.

relevant norms as well as to the timing/pace of the process. Functional specialisation does not necessarily entail increased specificity in the formulation of norms, as norms concerning one particular area of concern may be broadly formulated. Moreover, the timing/pace of both specialisation and specificity in different fields of international law have a bearing on the dynamics of their interactions. The three aspects of specialisation ('functional specialisation', 'specificity of formulation' and 'timing/pace') are relevant to understand the changing interactions between international environmental law and international investment law.

Second, the common use made by academics and practitioners of a given designation such as 'international environmental law' or 'international investment law' must not lead one to overestimate the legal relevance of such designations. The ILC Report on Fragmentation rightly points out that these designations 'are only informal labels that describe the instruments from the perspective of different interests or different policy objectives'.[7] This is not to say that such designations have no relevance at all, as they may be taken into account in a variety of contexts, such as the exclusion of a category of disputes from a jurisdictional basis or the applicability of a given provision.[8] Yet, the instruments covered by the broad expression 'environmental law' are, arguably, much more diverse (and even conflicting[9]) than those referred to as 'investment law'.[10] International environmental law is not one 'country' within the community represented by public international law but rather a 'continent', itself divided into numerous, more specific regimes of diverse natures. In order to take into account such diversity, it is therefore useful to go beyond the designation 'environmental law' and to focus on more specific regulatory areas ('freshwater', 'biological and cultural diversity', 'dangerous substances and activities', 'climate change'), as discussed in Chapter 2. The different aspects of specialisation mentioned in the preceding paragraph have evolved differently in each of these more specific regulatory areas. These differing paths have, in turn, had repercussions on the interactions between international environmental law and international investment law.

---

[7] *Ibid.*, para. 21.
[8] See, e.g., North American Free Trade Agreement, 17 December 1992, 32 ILM 296 ('NAFTA'), Article 104(2) *in fine.*
[9] R. Wolfrum and N. Matz, *Conflicts in International Environmental Law* (Berlin: Springer Verlag, 2003).
[10] J. W. Salacuse, 'The Treatification of International Investment Law' (2007) 13 *NAFTA: Law and Business Review of the Americas* 155; S. Schill, *The Multilateralization of International Investment Law* (Cambridge University Press, 2010).

Third, it is also useful to take into account the institutional manifestations of the 'identity' of both international environmental law and international investment law.[11] The institutional links between two or more treaties (arising from techniques such as the framework–protocol approach,[12] the adoption of 'side-agreements',[13] the 'package deal' approach[14] or, simply, the convergence of goals leading to increased institutional co-operation[15]) may influence their respective normative environments and, thereby, also the interpretation of the provisions of such treaties.[16] This is particularly the case when there is an institutional asymmetry between different sets of treaties, as is the case with international investment law, which benefits from a system of specialised adjudicatory bodies, and international environmental law, which lacks such bodies.

The foregoing considerations must be taken into account in assessing the operation of both specific and general conflict norms to manage normative conflicts between environmental and investment protection. Indeed, these questions make the operation of conflict norms more difficult, thus maintaining considerable room for legal uncertainty.

6.2 Specific conflict norms

The evolving relationship between international environmental law and international investment law, with the increasing likelihood of normative conflicts that it entails, already started to be noticed in the 1990s.[17] As will be discussed in the context of legitimacy conflicts, the environmental provisions contained in investment and free trade agreements

---

[11] Report – Fragmentation, above n. 1, paras. 255–6.

[12] See, e.g., Convention on Long-Range Transboundary Air Pollution, 13 November 1979, 1302 UNTS 217 ('LRTAP Convention') and its eight protocols.

[13] See, e.g., North American Agreement on Environmental Cooperation, 17 December 1992, 32 ILM 1519 ('NAAEC') (environmental side agreement to the NAFTA).

[14] See, e.g., United Nations Convention on the Law of the Sea, 10 December 1982, 1833 UNTS 397 ('UNCLOS').

[15] UNDESA et al., 'Synergies Success Stories – Enhancing Cooperation and Coordination among the Basel, Rotterdam and Stockholm Conventions', March 2011, available at: chm.pops.int (accessed on 4 January 2012).

[16] Report – Fragmentation, above n. 1, Section F.

[17] The following discussion is based on a survey by the Organisation for Economic Co-operation and Development (OECD) focusing on a sample of 269 investment and free trade agreements concluded by the thirty OECD members (as well as the 9 non-member adherents): OECD, International Investment Law: Understanding Concepts and Tracking Innovation (Paris: OECD, 2008)('OECD 2008 Study').

focus mainly on the scope for domestic environmental regulation. There are, however, some investment and free trade agreements that contain specific language on the relations between international investment law and international environmental law.

Among the first treaties to include such language, one must mention the NAFTA. Article 104 of the NAFTA states that:

1. In the event of any inconsistency between this Agreement and the specific trade obligations set out in:
    a) the Convention on International Trade in Endangered Species of Wild Fauna and Flora, done at Washington, March 3, 1973, as amended June 22, 1979,
    b) the Montreal Protocol on Substances that Deplete the Ozone Layer, done at Montreal, September 16, 1987, as amended June 29, 1990,
    c) the Basel Convention on the Control of Transboundary Movements of Hazardous Wastes and Their Disposal, done at Basel, March 22, 1989, on its entry into force for Canada, Mexico and the United States, or
    d) the agreements set out in Annex 104.1,
        such obligations shall prevail to the extent of the inconsistency, provided that where a Party has a choice among equally effective and reasonably available means of complying with such obligations, the Party chooses the alternative that is the least inconsistent with the other provisions of this Agreement.
2. The Parties may agree in writing to modify Annex 104.1 to include any amendment to an agreement referred to in paragraph 1, and any other environmental or conservation agreement.

The annex to this provision guided the reasoning of the tribunal in *S. D. Myers* v. *Canada* with respect to the relations between the Basel Convention and the NAFTA. The tribunal noted in this regard that:

The drafters of the NAFTA evidentially considered which earlier environmental treaties would prevail over the specific rules of the NAFTA in case of conflict. Annex 104 provided that the Basel Convention would have priority if and when it was ratified by the NAFTA Parties... Even if the Basel Convention were to have been ratified by the NAFTA Parties, it should not be presumed that CANADA would have been able to use it to justify the breach of a specific NAFTA provision because... *where a party has a choice among equally effective and reasonably available alternatives for complying... with a Basel Convention obligation, it is obliged to choose the alternative that is... least inconsistent... with the NAFTA.* If one such alternative were to involve no inconsistency with the Basel Convention, clearly this should be followed.[18]

---

[18] *S. D. Myers Inc.* v. *Canada*, NAFTA (UNCITRAL), Partial Award (13 November 2000) ('*S. D. Myers* v. *Canada*'), paras. 214–15 (italics original) and 255–6.

The NAFTA also contains other references potentially relevant for the relations between international investment law and international environmental law. Its Preamble expressly refers to the need to act 'in a manner consistent with environmental protection and conservation', to 'promote sustainable development' and to 'strengthen the development and enforcement of environmental laws and regulations'.[19] Moreover, the States parties to the NAFTA concluded a side agreement focusing specifically on environmental co-operation.[20]

Another provision addressing a potential conflict between international investment law and international environmental law is Article 72(c) of the CARIFORUM – European Union Economic Partnership Agreement (EPA) signed on 15 October 2008,[21] which reads as follows: '[i]nvestors do not manage or operate their investments in a manner that circumvents international environmental or labour obligations arising from agreements to which the EC Party and the Signatory CARIFORUM States are parties.' This provision is less clear than Article 104 of the NAFTA because it does not state that the environmental instruments identified in it prevail over the obligations of the States parties relating to economic co-operation. Rather, it stresses the importance of certain environmental treaties in connection with the activities contemplated in the Partnership Agreement. A similar, albeit less assertive, approach is followed in article 69 of the EU–Russia Agreement on Partnership and Co-operation, which states, in relevant part:

1. Bearing in mind the European Energy Charter and the Declaration of the Lucerne Conference of 1993, the Parties shall develop and strengthen their co-operation on environment and human health.
2. Co-operation shall aim at combating the deterioration of the environment and in particular: . . .
   – waste reduction, recycling and safe disposal, implementation of the Basle Convention;
   – implementation of the Espoo Convention on Environmental Impact Assessment in a transboundary context.[22]

Again, the focus of this provision is on the implementation of environmental treaties and not on solving conflicts between international

---

[19] NAFTA, above n. 8, Preamble.   [20] NAAEC, above n. 13.

[21] Economic Partnership Agreement between the Cariforum States and the European Community and its Member States, 15 October 2008, OJ 2008 L 289/I/3.

[22] Agreement on Partnership and Cooperation establishing a Partnership between the European Communities and their Member States, of one part, and the Russian Federation, of the other part, of 26 June 1994, reproduced in *OECD 2008 Study*, above n. 17, pp. 223–4.

investment law and international environmental law. A similar focus appears in Article 5(3) of the Belgian/Luxembourg Model BIT, according to which: '[t]he Contracting Parties reaffirm their commitments under the international environmental agreements, which they have accepted. They shall strive to ensure that such commitments are fully recognised and implemented by their domestic legislation.'[23] This approach is not limited to the treaty practice of the European Union or of some European States. It also seems to characterise the practice of the United States regarding the conclusion of free trade agreements ('FTAs').

Indeed, several FTAs concluded by the United States, including the CAFTA-DR[24] or those with Australia, Chile, Morocco, Oman, Peru or Singapore, contain a specific provision on 'Relationship to Environmental Agreements'. With some variation in wording from one treaty to the other, this provision essentially stresses the importance of environmental agreements and the need to enhance the mutual supportiveness between environmental and trade agreements. For example, Article 17.12.1 of CAFTA-DR provides that:

[t]he Parties recognise that multilateral environmental agreements to which they are all party play an important role in protecting the environment globally and domestically and that their respective implementation of these agreements is critical to achieving the environmental objectives of these agreements. The Parties further recognise that this Chapter and the ECA [side environmental agreement] can contribute to realising the goals of those agreements. Accordingly, the Parties shall continue to seek means to enhance the mutual supportiveness of multilateral environmental agreements to which they are all party.[25]

In the same vein, Article 18.8 of the US–Singapore FTA provides that:

The Parties recognise the critical role of multilateral environmental agreements in addressing some environmental challenges, including through the use of carefully tailored trade measures to achieve specific environmental goals and objectives. Recognising that WTO Members have agreed in paragraph 31 of the Ministerial Declaration adopted on 14 November 2001 in Doha to negotiations on the relationship between existing WTO rules and specific trade obligations set

---

[23] Belgian/Luxembourg Model BIT, art 5(3), reproduced in *OECD 2008 Study*, above n. 17, p. 177.

[24] Dominican Republic–Central America–US Free Trade Agreement, 5 August 2004, 43 ILM 514, reproduced in *OECD 2008 Study*, above n. 17, p. 214 ('CAFTA-DR').

[25] CAFTA-DR.

out in multilateral environmental agreements, the Parties shall consult on the extent to which the outcome of those negotiations applies to this Agreement.[26]

Other FTAs concluded by the United States contain comparable provisions.[27]

Without minimising the normative significance of such provisions, upon closer examination, most of them appear to be insufficient to solve potential conflicts between international investment law and international environmental law. If their scope is evaluated in the light of the criteria set by the ILC Group on Fragmentation for the elaboration of conflict clauses,[28] arguably none of the aforementioned provisions would reach the bar, except perhaps for Article 104 of the NAFTA. Moreover, despite some developments in the last five years, specific conflict rules are still relatively rare in treaty practice, particularly in BITs. In order to supplement the operation of such conflict rules, tribunals may therefore need additional guidance from more general conflict rules.

6.3   General conflict norms

There are several approaches in general international law to solving conflicts between two or more international obligations. Such approaches may be based on the following considerations: the order in which norms grounded on different sources are applied in practice (Section 6.3.1); the relative substantive hierarchy of different norms (Section 6.3.2); priority by reason of the degree of specificity of different norms (Section 6.3.3); priority by reason of the temporal relations between norms (Section 6.3.4); and interpretation techniques (Section 6.3.5).

6.3.1   Sequential application

The first approach concerns the relations between norms grounded on different formal sources of international law. Whereas it is generally

---

[26] US–Singapore FTA, reproduced in *OECD 2008 Study*, above n. 17, p. 212.

[27] US–Australia FTA, Article 19.8; US–Chile FTA, Article 19.9; US–Morocco FTA, Article 17.7; US–Oman FTA, Article 17.9; US–Peru FTA, Article 18.12, reproduced in *OECD 2008 Study*, above n. 17, pp. 206–12.

[28] Conflict clauses '(a) ... may not affect the rights of third parties; (b) They should be as clear and specific as possible. In particular, they should be directed to specific provisions of the treaty and they should not undermine the object and purpose of the treaty; (c) They should, as appropriate, be linked with means of dispute settlement', Conclusions – Fragmentation, above n. 1, para. 30.

admitted in public international law that there is no hierarchy among formal sources, the application of norms arising from different sources follows a certain logic.[29]

According to this logic, both treaty and customary law are considered to be principal sources of international law, whereas general principles of law are treated as subsidiary sources.[30] Despite their great importance in practice, especially in the investment field,[31] judicial decisions and the teachings of the most highly qualified publicists are only auxiliary sources, in that they help identify the contents of norms founded on formal sources.[32] Finally, the possibility for a tribunal to judge *ex aequo et bono* should be seen as an alternative formal source of international law, based on the consent of the parties to a dispute.[33]

In practice, it would be highly unlikely, although theoretically possible, that a normative conflict between a rule arising from a treaty and one arising from general principles of law be solved in favour of the latter. Normative conflicts will, as a rule, arise between either two treaty (or customary) norms or between a treaty norm and a norm of customary international law. This is all the more so that most international investment law and international environmental law is based on treaties, the contents of customary rules being often controversial.[34] Such more specific normative conflicts could be addressed by reference to the different substantive hierarchy of the norms involved, their relative degree of specificity, their temporal relations or through interpretation techniques.[35]

6.3.2   Lex superior

In contemporary international law, the existence of hierarchical relations between norms depends upon the contents of such norms.[36]

---

[29] Conclusions – Fragmentation, above n. 1, para. 31; G. Abi-Saab, 'Les sources du droit international: essai de deconstruction', in R. Rama Montaldo (ed.), *International Law in an Evolving World: Liber Amicorum Jiménez de Aréchaga*, Vol. I (Montevideo: Fundación de Cultura Universitaria, 1994), p. 29.

[30] Abi-Saab, 'Les sources du droit international', above n. 29, 33.

[31] G. Kaufmann-Kohler, 'Arbitral Precedent: Dream, Necessity or Excuse?' (2007) 23 *Arbitration International* 357.

[32] Abi-Saab, 'Les sources du droit international', above n. 29, p. 34.   [33] *Ibid.*, p. 35.

[34] P.-M. Dupuy, 'Formation of Customary International Law and General Principles', in D. Bodansky, J. Brunnée and H. Hey (eds.), *The Oxford Handbook of International Environmental Law* (Oxford University Press, 2007), p. 453.

[35] Report – Fragmentation, above n. 1, para. 18.

[36] See, generally, D. Shelton, 'Normative Hierarchy in International Law' (2006) 100 *American Journal of International Law* 291; P. Weil, 'Towards Relative Normativity in International Law?' (1983) 77 *American Journal of International Law* 413.

A norm is in a hierarchical relation in respect of another if it (or a specific conflict rule) expressly states so or if it possesses a given character that as such carries hierarchical effect.

For instance, a norm will be hierarchically inferior to another if it (or a specific conflict rule) expressly states so. This hypothesis has been studied in connection with specific conflict rules, which in some cases give priority to international environmental norms over investment disciplines. Conversely, a norm (or a specific conflict rule referring to such norm) may assert priority over another with an ensuing hierarchical effect. An example where such assertion of hierarchy has been widely recognised is Article 103 of the Charter of the United Nations,[37] which confers material hierarchy to any obligation arising from the Charter over any obligation arising from other agreements. Certain norms, referred to as peremptory norms or *ius cogens*, possess a particular character that excludes any derogation from them, except for potential derogations stemming from a norm with the same character.[38]

There has been some discussion as to whether at least some international environmental norms are of a peremptory nature.[39] However, there does not seem to be sufficient evidence to conclude that in the current state of international law this is the case; most of the arguments advanced to support *ius cogens* status are purely theoretical or have been disproved by subsequent developments.[40] This is not to say that environmental norms cannot display some hierarchical effects through other channels.

For instance, environmental norms can help characterise certain interests as essential, which in turn would open the way for the

---

[37] See Conclusions – Fragmentation, above n. 1, paras. 34–6 and 40–1; Report – Fragmentation, above n. 1, paras. 328–60; R. Bernhardt, 'Article 103', in B. Simma (ed.), *The Charter of the United Nations: A Commentary* (Oxford University Press, 2nd edn, 2002), pp. 1293ff. See, however, *Kadi & Al Barakaat v. Council of the European Union*, ECJ Joined cases C-402/05 P & C-415/05 P, 3 CMLR 41 (2008).

[38] This characterisation is provided in Article 53 of the Vienna Convention on the Law of Treaties, 23 May 1969, 1155 UNTS 331 ('VCLT'). On the concept of *ius cogens*, see Conclusions – Fragmentation, above n. 1, paras. 32–3, 38 and 40–1; Report – Fragmentation, above n. 1, paras. 361–79; A. Verdross, '*Jus dispositivum* and *jus cogens* in International Law' (1966) 60 *American Journal of International Law* 55; A. Orakhelashvili, *Peremptory Norms in International Law* (Oxford University Press, 2006).

[39] E. Kornicker, *Ius cogens und Umweltvölkerrecht. Kriterien, Quellen und Rechtsforgen zwingender Völkerrechtsnormen und deren Anwendung auf das Umweltvölkerrecht* (Basel: Helbing & Lichtenhahn, 1997); Orakhelashvili, *Peremptory Norms in International Law*, above n. 38, p. 65.

[40] M. Fitzmaurice, 'International Protection of the Environment', in *Recueil des cours de l'Académie de droit international*, Vol. 293 (2001), pp. 132ff.

invocation of necessity or public emergency clauses. In the *Gabčíkovo-Nagymaros* case, the ICJ preferred not to discuss the question of whether a peremptory norm had arisen that commanded the protection of the environment.[41] Yet, it considered that the protection of the environment amounted to an essential interest. To justify this latter conclusion, the ICJ referred to its Advisory Opinion in *Legality of Nuclear Weapons*, issued the previous year, where the Court had asserted the customary nature of States' obligation to ensure that activities within their jurisdiction and control respect the environment of other States or of areas beyond national control.[42]

The importance attached to certain interests, and specifically to the protection of the environment, is also relevant in connection with the interpretation of certain treaty clauses to accommodate environmental or human rights considerations. In the *Gabčíkovo-Nagymaros* case, the ICJ discussed this point by reference to Articles 15, 19 and 20 of the treaty in question, which contemplated the possibility of adapting the project to take into account emerging norms of international law.[43] However, the Court asserted the need for adaptation of treaty clauses in stronger and more general terms when it stated that:

Throughout the ages, mankind has, for economic and other reasons, constantly interfered with nature. In the past, this was often done without consideration of the effects upon the environment. Owing to new scientific insights and to a growing awareness of the risks for mankind – for present and future generations – of pursuit of such interventions at an unconsidered and unabated pace, new norms and standards have been developed, set forth in a great number of instruments during the last two decades. Such new norms have to be taken into consideration, and such new standards given proper weight, not only when States contemplate new activities but also when continuing with activities begun in the past. This need to reconcile economic development with protection of the environment is aptly expressed in the concept of sustainable development.[44]

In his Separate Opinion, Vice President Weeramantry distilled from this passage a new and additional interpretation rule, as will be discussed in Section 6.3.5.

---

[41] *Gabčíkovo-Nagymaros Project (Hungary v. Slovakia)*, ICJ Reports 1997, 7 ('*Gabčíkovo-Nagymaros*'), para. 112.

[42] *Ibid.*, para. 53, referring to *Legality of the Threat or Use of Nuclear Weapons*, ICJ Reports 1996, 226 ('*Legality of Nuclear Weapons*'), para. 29.

[43] *Gabčíkovo-Nagymaros*, above n. 41, para. 112.   [44] *Ibid.*, para. 140.

Despite the possibility of such hierarchical effects, as a rule, absent an amendment to the UN Charter introducing environmental obligations or the emergence of a peremptory environmental norm, normative conflicts will most likely be solved by reference to either a specific conflict rule or some other general methods discussed next.

6.3.3   Lex specialis

Another frequently used approach is to compare the degree of specificity of the norms potentially applicable to the same situation, an approach often referred to as the principle *lex specialis derogat legi generalis*.[45] This principle rests on the idea that 'special law, being more concrete, often takes better account of the particular features of the context in which it is to be applied than any applicable general law. Its application may also often create a more equitable result and it may often better reflect the intent of the legal subjects'.[46] Thus, the rationale for justifying the prevalence of a special rule over a general one is that special rules are assumed to be better adapted to a specific situation than rules governing a much broader range of situations.

However, the level of specificity or generality of a norm may be difficult to assess. For instance, Article 15(5) of the Convention on Biological Diversity provides that '[a]ccess to genetic resources shall be subject to prior informed consent of the Contracting Party providing such resources, unless otherwise determined by that Party'.[47] This norm could conflict with an investment discipline, such as a treaty clause providing for fair and equitable treatment or the international minimum standard of treatment, which are themselves very general and have sometimes been characterised as blanket standards encompassing breaches that do not fall under more specific disciplines.[48] A situation could arise in which an investor, having established a laboratory in a developing country with the consent of the host State, suddenly sees its operating licence revoked on the grounds that such consent was not sufficiently informed. In such a situation, it would be difficult to reach a conclusion on the basis of the *lex specialis* principle. Indeed, if one looks at the rationale of this principle, it would not be unreasonable to argue that Article 15(5) is more specifically adapted than any investment

---

[45] Conclusions – Fragmentation, above n. 1, paras. 5–16; Report – Fragmentation, above n. 1, paras. 46–222.

[46] Conclusions – Fragmentation, above n. 1, para. 7.

[47] Convention on Biological Diversity, 5 June 1992, 1760 UNTS 79 ('CBD'), Article 15(5).

[48] See, e.g., *S. D. Myers v. Canada*, above n. 18, para. 259.

protection accorded in general terms for any type of investment. And yet, depending on the facts of the dispute, one could also make a persuasive case in favour of protecting the investment based on good faith or proportionality considerations. As discussed in Chapter 5, the fact that the dispute is heard by an investment tribunal does not exclude the potential application of international environmental law, nor does it preclude the admissibility of an environmental claim. International investment law may be argued to be a highly specialised field,[49] but this is not a reason to exclude environmental matters from the consideration of investment tribunals. In other terms, the fact that international investment law may be considered as a specialised field does not mean that investment disciplines must be treated as *lex specialis* in case of a normative conflict. Yet, in practice, investment tribunals may be inclined to do so.

Underlying these difficulties is the question of whether the *lex specialis* principle is adapted to solve conflicts between norms (or regimes) pursuing different policy goals, such as those arising from international investment law and international environmental law (or even within one such branch of international law[50]). In such case, considerations of specificity may lose their conflict-solving power or they may have to be 'converted' into levels of relevance. In this latter case, the question would become one of deciding which goal is the most 'specifically' relevant for solving the dispute. This, in turn, may heavily depend on the legal framework circumscribing the powers of a given forum as well as on potential idiosyncrasies. Investment tribunals may indeed be inclined to consider investment disciplines as the *lex specialis* for solving an 'investment' dispute. This choice may partly be a result of the greater familiarity that investment tribunals have with investment disciplines (as compared with international environmental norms). But it may also stem from the fact that, in order to assert its jurisdiction, an investment tribunal may need to qualify the dispute between the parties as 'arising out of' or 'relating to' an investment, thereby stressing the investment component of the dispute at the expense of the environmental one, and, by the same token, paving the way for considering investment disciplines as the *lex specialis*.

---

[49] *Ahmadou Sadio Diallo (Republic of Guinea v. Democratic Republic of the Congo)*, Preliminary Objections, Judgment of 24 May 2007, General List No. 103 ('*Diallo* case'), paras. 88 and 90.

[50] Wolfrum and Matz, *Conflicts in International Environmental Law*, above n. 9, pp. 8ff.

The preceding observations highlight some of the difficulties raised by the use of the *lex specialis* principle to solve conflicts between branches of international law that, until recently, had evolved in relative autarchy.

6.3.4   Lex posterior

Another potentially relevant approach is to focus on the temporal dimension of norms. According to this approach, commonly referred to as *lex posterior derogat legi priori*, later norms should in principle supersede earlier norms.[51] The use of this principle is conditioned by three main considerations.

First, as noted by the ILC Group on Fragmentation, the *lex posterior* principle cannot be 'automatically extended to the case where the parties to the subsequent treaty are not identical to the parties of the earlier treaty'.[52] The Group further noted:

In case of conflicts or overlaps between treaties in different regimes, the question of which of them is later in time would not necessarily express any presumption of priority between them. Instead, States bound by the treaty obligations should try to implement them as far as possible with the view of mutual accommodation and in accordance with the principle of harmonization.[53]

Second, where the conflict arises between provisions in treaties that belong to different regimes 'special attention should be given to the independence of the means of settlement chosen'.[54] This is particularly relevant in connection with the potential formal or informal bias of international courts and tribunals created under the aegis of a field-specific treaty or system of treaties, such as regional human rights courts or the WTO dispute settlement body, in favour of their own regime.[55] As noted when discussing the *lex specialis* principle, aside from the higher familiarity of specialised tribunals – such as investment tribunals – with the law that they are regularly called to apply, investment tribunals are constituted on the basis of an investment instrument (a treaty, a domestic law, a contract) for the purpose of deciding a specific investment dispute. This, in turn, may introduce an implicit bias in favour of investment law.

---

[51] VCLT, above n. 38, Article 30; Conclusions – Fragmentation, above n. 1, paras. 24–30; Report – Fragmentation, above n. 1, paras. 223–323.

[52] Conclusions – Fragmentation, above n. 1, para. 25.

[53] *Ibid.*, para. 26.   [54] *Ibid.*, para. 28.

[55] The Group on Fragmentation refers, in this regard, to a case before the ECtHR, *Slivenko and others* v. *Latvia*, Decision as to the Admissibility of 23 January 2002, ECtHR 2002-II, 482-3, paras. 60–1. See Conclusions – Fragmentation, above n. 1, para. 25, note 17.

Third, the relative autarchy in which international investment law and international environmental law developed, as well as the law-making techniques used in this latter field (particularly the framework–protocol approach and the use of 'administrative law' secreted by the bodies established by environmental treaties[56]) make it difficult to determine which obligation is prior/posterior. For instance, would the obligation imposed on States by Article 4(1) of the UNFCCC[57] (which was concluded in 1992, entered into force in 1994, and was later developed in the decisions of the Conference of the Parties – particularly the Cancún Agreements of December 2010[58]) prevail over a BIT concluded in 2005? Another example is the relative uncertainty regarding when certain environmental norms – that are already in force – become effective obligations. In *SPP* v. *Egypt*,[59] the tribunal considered that Articles 4, 5(d), and 11 of the World Heritage Convention,[60] despite being in force for Egypt since 1975, had only created an effective obligation in 1979, at the time of the inclusion of the relevant site in the UNESCO list.[61] This understanding of the World Heritage Convention is controversial. Some distinguished commentators have noted, indeed, that the obligation to protect world heritage under the Convention is independent of the actual listing of a site in the list held by the World Heritage Committee.[62]

These three considerations significantly limit the suitability of the *lex posterior* principle for dealing with normative conflicts between environmental and investment law. One avenue that has been suggested[63] to

---

[56] On these two techniques, see J. E. Viñuales, 'Legal Techniques for Dealing with Scientific Uncertainty in Environmental Law' (2010) 43 *Vanderbilt Journal of Transnational Law* 437, at 452–4 and 456–9.

[57] United Nations Framework Convention on Climate Change, 9 May 1992, 31 ILM 849 ('UNFCCC').

[58] 'The Cancun Agreements: Outcome of the work of the Ad Hoc Working Group on Long-term Cooperative Action under the Convention', Decision 1/CP.16, 15 March 2011, FCCC/CP/2010/7/Add.1 ('Cancún Agreements'). On the relations between these agreements and the UNFCCC, see J. E. Viñuales, 'Du bon dosage du droit international: les négociations climatiques en perspective' (2010) 56 *Annuaire français de droit international* 437, at 450–7.

[59] *Southern Pacific Properties (Middle East) Limited (SPP)* v. *Arab Republic of Egypt*, ICSID Case No. ARB/84/3, Award (20 May 1992) ('*SPP* v. *Egypt*').

[60] Convention for the Protection of the World Cultural and Natural Heritage, 16 November 1972, 1037 UNTS 151 ('World Heritage Convention').

[61] *Ibid.*, para. 154.

[62] F. Francioni and F. Lenzerini 'The Destruction of the Buddhas of Bamiyan and International Law' (2003) 14 *European Journal of International Law* 619, 631.

[63] Report – Fragmentation, above n. 1, paras. 272–82. Although the Report – Fragmentation discusses these 'open-ended' conflict norms in the context of temporal priority, the proposal seems to be considered rather as an interpretation technique.

deal with comparable conflicts (between trade disciplines and environmental norms) is the use of 'open-ended' conflict norms that are midway between specific conflict norms (discussed above) and the general conflict norms discussed in this section. This proposal amounts, in essence, to incorporating into treaties with significant potential for conflict – such as multilateral environmental treaties – clauses guiding the interpretation towards a mutually supportive outcome.

6.3.5 *Interpretation techniques*

Interpretation techniques may operate not only in conflict solving but also, and more importantly, in conflict characterisation. As noted by the ILC Group on Fragmentation:

> Whether there is a conflict and what can be done with prima facie conflicts depends on the way the relevant rules are interpreted ... Interpretation does not intervene only once it has already been ascertained that there is conflict. Rules appear to be compatible or in conflict as a result of interpretation.[64]

In the context of investment disputes with environmental components, the use of interpretation techniques at the conflict characterisation phase is important because it allows tribunals to avoid making controversial statements on the relative hierarchy of investment and environmental protection.[65] In fact, some of the approaches already discussed in connection with conflict rules can also be seen as involving interpretation techniques to the extent that they seek to circumscribe the contours of investment disciplines so as to carve out some space for environmental regulation. The following paragraphs discuss three main interpretation techniques: specific systemic integration or 'mutual supportiveness' (Section 6.3.5.1); general systemic integration (Section 6.3.5.2); and the seldom analysed principle of contemporaneity in the application of environmental norms (Section 6.3.5.3).

6.3.5.1 Mutual supportiveness as interpretive guidance

In a number of international instruments, the concept of mutual supportiveness has been used as a tool for preventing conflicts between trade and environmental requirements. The so-called 'principle of mutual supportiveness' seeks, indeed, to articulate multilateral environmental

---

[64] Report – Fragmentation, above n. 1, para. 412.
[65] J. E. Viñuales, 'Conflit de normes en droit international: normes environnementales vs. protection des investissements', in Société française pour le droit international (SFDI), *Le droit international face aux enjeux environnementaux* (Paris: Pédone, 2010), p. 407.

agreements with international trade agreements through a harmonising interpretation.[66] It could, by analogy, be used for the relations between investment and environmental agreements.

Reference to mutual supportiveness usually appears in the form of one or more Recitals in the Preamble of the relevant treaties or, exceptionally, also in the form of a specific provision. One early formulation of mutual supportiveness appears in the Preamble of the Marrakesh Agreement, which recognises the need to foster trade relations 'while allowing for the optimal use of the world's resources in accordance with the objective of sustainable development, seeking both to protect and preserve the environment'.[67] Paragraph 6 of the Doha Declaration states, with reference to the Marrakesh Agreement, that 'the aims of upholding and safeguarding an open and non-discriminatory multilateral trading system, and acting for the protection of the environment and the promotion of sustainable development can and must be mutually supportive'.[68] Other formulations have been used in the Preambles of environmental agreements, including those of the PIC Convention,[69] the POP Convention[70] and, most notably, the Biosafety Protocol.[71] The last three Recitals of the Preamble of the Biosafety Protocol '[r]econi[se] that trade and environment agreements should be mutually supportive with a view to achieving sustainable development', while at the same time '[e]mphasising that this Protocol shall not be interpreted as implying a change in the rights and obligations of a Party under any existing international agreements' nor as 'subordinat[ing] this Protocol to other international agreements'.

---

[66] R. Pavoni, 'Mutual Supportiveness as a Principle of Interpretation and Law-Making: A Watershed for the "WTO-and-Competing-Regimes" Debate?' (2010) 21 *European Journal of International Law* 649. Mutual supportiveness has attracted renewed attention as a result of a much commented case brought before the WTO dispute settlement body: *European Communities – Measures Affecting the Approval and Marketing of Biotech Products*, WT/DS291/R, WT/DS292/R, WT/DS293/R (29 September 2006).

[67] See Agreement establishing the World Trade Organisation, 15 April 1994, 1867 UNTS 154 ('Marrakesh Agreement'), Recital 1.

[68] Ministerial Declaration, adopted at Doha on 14 November 2001, WT/MIN(01)/DEC/1 ('Doha Declaration').

[69] Rotterdam Convention on the Prior Informed Consent Procedure for Certain Hazardous Chemicals and Pesticides in International Trade, 10 September 1998, 2244 UNTS 337 ('PIC Convention'), Preamble, Recital 8.

[70] Stockholm Convention on Persistent Organic Pollutants, 22 May 2001, 40 ILM 532 (2001) ('POP Convention'), Preamble, Recital 9.

[71] Cartagena Protocol on Biosafety to the Convention on Biological Diversity, 29 January 2000, 39 ILM 1027 (2000).

Although these rather broad formulations suggest that mutual supportiveness is mainly a policy goal,[72] this does not mean that references to mutual supportiveness have no legal value. As argued by Pavoni, these references can guide the interpretation of international norms in a way so as to exclude meanings that entail a normative conflict.[73] Moreover, the formulation of mutual supportiveness may become less vague in the future. A step in this direction has been made in Article 4 of the ABS Protocol to the CBD, entitled '[r]elationship with international agreements and instruments', which provides that:

1. The provisions of this Protocol shall not affect the rights and obligations of any Party deriving from any existing international agreement, except where the exercise of those rights and obligations would cause a serious damage or threat to biological diversity. This paragraph is not intended to create a hierarchy between this Protocol and other international instruments ...

2. This Protocol shall be implemented in a mutually supportive manner with other international instruments relevant to this Protocol. Due regard should be paid to useful and relevant ongoing work or practices under such international instruments and relevant international organizations, provided that they are supportive of and do not run counter to the objectives of the Convention and this Protocol.[74]

This provision, which takes up and develops Article 22(1) of the CBD is more directive than previous formulations of mutual supportiveness and comes closer to the more assertive stance taken in Article 11(1) of the Basel Convention. According to this latter provision, the obligation of States parties not to export hazardous waste to (or import from) third parties can be set aside by the conclusion of a more specific agreement with such other party only if the provisions of such agreement 'are not less environmentally sound than those provided for by this Convention'.[75] These more specific formulations of mutual supportiveness come closer to the operation of specific conflict rules.

---

[72] See Chapter 2, Section 2.2.

[73] Pavoni, 'Mutual Supportiveness as a Principle of Interpretation and Law-Making', above n. 66, 650.

[74] Nagoya Protocol on Access to Genetic Resources and the Fair and Equitable Sharing of the Benefits arising from their Utilization to the Convention on Biological Diversity, 29 October 2010 ('ABS Protocol'), Article 4(1) and (4).

[75] Basel Convention on the Control of Transboundary Movements of Hazardous Wastes and their Disposal, 22 March 1989, 1673 UNTS 57 ('Basel Convention'), Article 11(1).

6.3.5.2   General systemic integration

The concept of mutual supportiveness discussed in the preceding section can be seen as a specific application of a general interpretation technique that is receiving increasing attention from legal commentators,[76] namely the principle of 'systemic integration', provided for in Article 31(3)(c) of the VCLT.[77] This provision states that: '[t]here shall be taken into account, together with the context: ... (c) any relevant rules of international law applicable in the relations between the parties'. The underlying rationale of this principle is explained by the ILC Group on Fragmentation as follows:

> All treaty provisions receive their force and validity from general law, and set up rights and obligations that exist alongside rights and obligations established by the other treaty provisions and rules of customary international law. None of such rights or obligations has any intrinsic priority against the others.[78]

The Group further notes that, sometimes, there will be no need to go beyond the framework of the treaty itself for purposes of its interpretation, and adds that: 'Article 31(3)(c) deals with the case where material sources external to the treaty are relevant in its interpretation. These may include other treaties, customary rules or general principles of law.'[79] This latter observation seems important in the light of a number of investment disputes where systemic integration appeared relevant.[80] The following disputes illustrate this point.

One early reference to systemic integration in connection with international environmental law appears in the *Gabčíkovo-Nagymaros* case and, more specifically, in the Separate Opinion of Vice President Weeramantry. As already noted when discussing hierarchical effects among different norms of international law, the ICJ stressed the importance of taking into account new environmental norms in interpreting existing treaties. In his opinion, Vice-President Weeramantry referred

---

[76] Such renewed attention stems primarily from some observations made by the ICJ in the *Oil Platforms case (Islamic Republic of Iran v. United States of America)*, ICJ Reports 2003, 161, para. 41. See C. McLachlan, 'The Principle of Systemic Integration and Article 31 3) c) of the Vienna Convention' (2005) 54 *International and Comparative Law Quarterly* 279; Pavoni, 'Mutual Supportiveness as a Principle of Interpretation and Law-Making', above n. 66, 650.

[77] See above n. 38.   [78] Report – Fragmentation, above n. 1, para. 414.

[79] Conclusions – Fragmentation, above n. 1, para. 18.

[80] For a discussion of the use of Article 31(3)(c) in other international courts and tribunals, see Report – Fragmentation, above n. 1, paras. 433–60; McLachlan, 'The Principle of Systemic Integration', above n. 76, 293–309.

expressly to Article 31(3)(c) of the VCLT as a vector for the 'principle of contemporaneity in the application of environmental norms'. In the *Pulp Mills* case, the Court also referred to this provision in connection with the interpretation of the Statute of the River Uruguay. Implying that the interpretation of treaties in the light of 'any relevant rules of international law applicable in the relations between the parties' was a rule of customary international law, the Court stressed that consideration of such other rules for interpretation purposes had no bearing on the scope of its jurisdiction.[81]

In some investment cases, tribunals have deployed systemic integration reasoning[82] to assess allegations of discrimination against foreign investors. In *S. D. Myers* v. *Canada*, the tribunal interpreted the term 'like circumstances' in Article 1102 of the NAFTA (national treatment) by reference to its 'legal context', which, according to the tribunal, included:

[T]he various provisions of the NAFTA, its companion agreement the NAAEC and principles that are affirmed by the NAAEC (including those of the Rio declaration). The principles that emerge from that context, to repeat, are as follows ... states have the right to establish high levels of environmental protection. They are not obliged to compromise their standards merely to satisfy the political or economic interests of other states ... states should avoid creating distortions to trade ... environmental protection and economic development can and should be mutually supportive.[83]

The preamble of the NAAEC reaffirms 'the Stockholm Declaration on the Human Environment of 1972 and the Rio Declaration on Environment and Development of 1992'.[84] Some parts of these declarations, most notably Principles 21 of the Stockholm Declaration and 2 of the Rio Declaration, are declaratory of customary international law.[85] Thus, the tribunal also included in the legal context of Article 1102 of the NAFTA principles of customary international law. Eventually, the tribunal concluded that the export ban affecting the investor was a breach of Article 1102.[86]

Another illustration is given by *Parkerings* v. *Lithuania*, where the tribunal interpreted the most-favoured nation clause of the applicable

---

[81] *Pulp Mills in the River Uruguay (Argentina* v. *Uruguay)*, Judgment of 20 April 2010, General List No. 135 ('*Pulp Mills* case'), paras. 65–6.

[82] The fact that in most cases tribunals do not refer explicitly to Article 31(3)(c) of the VCLT is immaterial. See Report – Fragmentation, above n. 1, para. 468.

[83] *S. D. Myers* v. *Canada*, above n. 18, para. 247.

[84] NAAEC, above n. 13, Preamble.   [85] *Legality of Nuclear Weapons*, above n. 42, para. 29.

[86] *S. D. Myers* v. *Canada*, above n. 18, paras. 255–6.

investment treaty in the light of different considerations, including the fact that the projects of the two investors did not have the same consequences for a UNESCO protected site. The tribunal noted:

[T]he fact that the [Claimant's] MSCP [multi-storey car park] project in Gedimino extended significantly more into the Old Town as defined by the UNESCO, is decisive. Indeed, the record shows that the opposition raised against the [Claimant's] projected MSCP were important and contributed to the Municipality decision to refuse such a controversial project. The historical and archaeological preservation and environmental protection could be and in this case were a justification for the refusal of the project. The potential negative impact of the [Claimant's] project in the Old Town was increased by its considerable size and its proximity with the culturally sensitive area of the Cathedral. Consequently, [the Claimant's] MSCP in Gedimino was not similar with the MSCP constructed by [the other investor].[87]

The interpretation provided by the tribunal thus carved out some space for the incorporation of environmental considerations in assessing the scope of the MFN (but also the national treatment) clause. After noting the similarities between the MFN and the national treatment clauses, as well as of other non-discrimination standards, the tribunal set out the following test for assessing whether two investors are in like circumstances:

In order to determine whether Parkerings was in *like circumstances* with Pinus Proprius, and thus whether the MFN standard has been violated, the Arbitral Tribunal considers that three conditions should be met:

(i) Pinus Proprius must be a foreign investor;
(ii) Pinus Proprius and Parkerings must be in the same economic or business sector;
(iii) The two investors must be treated differently. The difference of treatment must be due to a measure taken by the State. No policy or purpose behind the said measure must apply to the investment that justifies the different treatments accorded. *A contrario*, a less favourable treatment is acceptable if a State's legitimate objective justifies such different treatment in relation to the specificity of the investment.[88]

Thus, reference to recognised environmental objectives identified in international environmental instruments, such as the World Heritage Convention, could potentially justify differentiated treatment.

---

[87] *Parkerings-Compagniet AS* v. *Republic of Lithuania*, ICSID Case No. ARB/05/8, Award (11 September 2007) ('*Parkerings* v. *Lithuania*'), para. 392.
[88] *Ibid.*, para. 371.

Systemic integration could also be a useful tool for redefining the boundaries of investment disciplines, particularly with respect to its relations with environmental regulation. This issue will be further discussed in connection with the operation of the police powers doctrine.[89] However, the question may also arise in the context of fair and equitable treatment clauses. In *Grand River* v. *United States*, the claimants argued that by reason of their quality of indigenous peoples, the minimun standard of treatment that had to be accorded to them under Article 1105 of the NAFTA was different (higher) than the normal one.[90] The tribunal rejected this argument noting that '[w]hile other legal rules may shape the context in which Article 1105 is applied, they do not alter the content of the customary international law minimum standard of treatment'.[91] More specifically, the tribunal considered that:

[e]ven if one were to indulge a supposition that a customary rule required consultations directly with an individual First Nations investor under the circumstances of this case, it would be difficult to construe such a rule as part of the customary minimum standard of protection that must be accorded to every foreign investment pursuant to Article 1105. The notion of specialized procedural rights protecting some investors, but not others, cannot readily be reconciled with the idea of a minimum customary standard of treatment due to all investments.[92]

The restrictive solution reached by the tribunal requires some clarifications. Although it expressly referred to Article 31 of the VCLT, including paragraph 3(c),[93] the tribunal appears to have followed the argument of the respondent according to which '"relevant rules" under the VCLT cannot override agreed treaty text and the Parties' agreements regarding its interpretation',[94] mainly because of the binding interpretation of Article 1105 adopted by the Free Trade Commission.[95] Yet, if

---

[89] See Chapter 15.

[90] *Grand River Enterprises Six Nations, Ltd, et al.* v. *United States of America*, NAFTA (UNCITRAL), Award (12 January 2011), para. 180. The claimants referred to several instruments at the intersection of human rights and environmental law, including the American Convention on Human Rights (Article 21), the International Labour Organisations' Convention No. 169 (Article 6(1)(a)) and the United Nations Declaration on the Rights of Indigenous Peoples (Article 17), *ibid.*, para. 182(3).

[91] *Ibid.*, para. 181. Although this statement is made in the section of the award laying out the position of the claimant, its formulation indicates that it expresses the position of the tribunal.

[92] *Ibid.*, para. 213.   [93] *Ibid.*, para. 64.

[94] *Ibid.*, para. 68.   [95] *Ibid.*, para. 219.

followed strictly, this conception would deprive Article 31(3)(c) of the VCLT of its main purpose, which is to introduce flexibility in the interpretation of international norms. Whereas the outcome of the tribunal's analysis in this case seems justified, the tribunal's reasoning on the relevance of other norms of international law for interpretation purposes is debatable.

Finally, reference to systemic integration has also been made in the context of some water-related disputes. In the *amicus* brief presented in *Suez* v. *Argentina*,[96] the *amici* exhorted the tribunal to follow this interpretive approach:

> In application of this principle of systemic interpretation, human rights law can add color and texture to the standards of treatment included in a BIT. In addition, systemic interpretation is particularly apt when the terms of a treaty are by their nature open-textured, such as the fair and equitable treatment standard. A contextual interpretation of language in a BIT is also necessary because investment and human rights law seem to encounter frictions at the level of regimes, particularly in regards to quantitative policy space available for social development. Indeed, the 'regulatory chill' that may result from certain interpretations of investment disciplines could reduce the capabilities of States to fulfill their human rights obligations, including their duty to regulate. In that sense, a contextual interpretation leads to normative dialogue, accommodation, and mutual supportiveness among human rights and investment law.[97]

Interestingly, and no doubt aware of the realities of investment arbitration, the *amici curiae* contemplated the possibility of a conflict of norms between human rights (including the right to water) and investment disciplines, but advocated rather for a harmonised reading of the applicable treaty in the light of human rights.[98] This observation is quite perceptive, given the general reluctance of investment tribunals to openly decide potential conflicts between investment protection and public policy objectives. In its decision on liability, the tribunal found no conflict, noting that 'Argentina [was] subject to both international obligations, i.e. human rights *and* treaty obligations, and [had to] respect both of them equally. Under the circumstances of

---

[96] *Suez, Sociedad General de Aguas de Barcelona SA and Vivendi Universal SA* v. *The Argentine Republic*, ICSID Case No. ARB/03/19, Decision on liability (31 August 2010) ('*Suez* v. *Argentina* – 03/19').

[97] *Amicus Curiae* Submission, 4 April 2007 ('*Suez* – Amicus Submission'), para. 15, available at: www.ciel.org/Publications/SUEZ_Amicus_English_4Apr07.pdf (accessed on 4 January 2012).

[98] *Ibid.*, para. 17.

these cases, Argentina's human rights obligations and its investment treaty obligations [were] not inconsistent, contradictory, or mutually exclusive.'[99]

6.3.5.3 The principle of contemporaneity in the application of environmental norms

As noted above in connection with the *Gabčíkovo-Nagymaros* case,[100] the ICJ has suggested that some treaties may have to be interpreted in the light of subsequent international environmental norms. In his Separate Opinion in this case, Vice President Weeramantry went a step further and noted that what he called the 'principle of contemporaneity in the application of environmental norms' was important to 'all treaties dealing with projects impacting on the environment', and that such need was insufficiently taken into account by Article 31(3)(c) of the VCLT.[101] This principle has been used by subsequent tribunals.

In the *Iron-Rhine* arbitration between Belgium and the Netherlands,[102] the tribunal noted that the duty to integrate environmental considerations in planning economic activities (*in casu* the reactivation of a railway passing through Dutch territory) had acquired a customary nature, and that it applied 'not only in autonomous activities but also in activities undertaken in implementation of specific treaties between the Parties'.[103] More specifically referring to the *Gabčíkovo-Nagymaros* case, the tribunal noted that this principle was 'relevant to the interpretation of those treaties in which the answers to the Questions [put to the tribunal] may primarily be sought'.[104]

The principle was also referred to by the ICJ in the *Pulp Mills* case in connection with the interpretation of the Statute of the River Uruguay.[105] In paragraph 204 of its decision, the ICJ referred to a passage of another judgment, rendered the preceding year, where the Court had recognised that 'there are situations in which the parties' intent upon conclusion of the treaty was, *or may be presumed to have been*, to give the terms used – or some of them – a meaning or content capable of

---

[99] *Suez v. Argentina* – 03/19, above n. 96, para. 262 (italics original); see also *Suez, Sociedad General de Aguas de Barcelona SA and InterAguas Servicios Integrales del Agua SA v. The Argentine Republic*, ICSID Case No. ARB/03/17, Decision on liability (31 August 2010) ('*Suez v. Argentina* – 03/17'), para. 240.

[100] *Gabčíkovo-Nagymaros*, above n. 41.   [101] *Ibid.*, Weeramanty, Separate Opinion, 114.

[102] *Iron Rhine (IJzeren Rijn) Railway (Belgium v. Netherlands)*, PCA Case, Award (24 May 2005).

[103] *Ibid.*, para. 59.   [104] *Ibid.*, para. 60.

[105] *Pulp Mills* case, above n. 81, paras. 66, 194, 197 and 204.

evolving, not one fixed once and for all, so as to make allowance for, among other things, developments in international law'.[106]

In the practice of investment tribunals, a similar question has arisen in some water-related disputes where the human right to water appeared relevant for assessing the scope of the investment disciplines invoked by the investors or the necessity defence. This issue will be further discussed in Chapters 7 and 15.

---

[106] *Dispute Regarding Navigational and Related Rights (Costa Rica v. Nicaragua)*, Judgment of 13 July 2009, General list No. 133, para. 64 (italics added).

7   Foreign investment and the international regulation of freshwater

The purpose of this chapter is to analyse the interactions between the international regulation of freshwater resources and international investment law, as a first illustration of a source of normative conflicts. More specifically, the chapter identifies the incidence (actual or potential) of a wide array of international instruments relating to freshwater on the operations of foreign investors. The chapter is divided into three sections. The first section is an attempt to distill from the body of international water law those types of obligations that are most likely to collide with investment disciplines. Section 2 then undertakes an analysis of the decisions of adjudicatory and quasi-adjudicatory bodies that can shed light on the type of normative conflicts under consideration. The third section generalises the insights that can be derived from the analysis of the case-law for future reference.

7.1   International regulation of freshwater – an analysis of collision points

7.1.1   Overview

From a regulatory angle, freshwater is considered as both a resource and a medium. Each of these aspects affects freshwater regulation. The regulation of freshwater as a resource is multifaceted and depends, to a large extent, on the particular uses of freshwater. Generally speaking, one can distinguish among the use of freshwater resources: (i) for basic consumption and sanitation purposes; and (ii) for other uses (mainly food production and industrial processes, including power generation). In order to maintain the quality of water regulations also require that freshwater resources be protected from pollution and discharges (iii).

158

This latter angle serves as the common boundary with the protection of freshwater (more specifically international watercourses) as a medium (iv) hosting a wide range of animal and plant species and complex ecosystems, as well as (v) providing important navigation and communication waterways.

The two aspects (resource and medium), each with its more specific angles, are covered by an array of domestic, regional and international instruments.[1] Leaving aside navigation, which is not directly relevant for present purposes,[2] the international regulation of freshwater focuses content-wise on: (a) allocating jurisdiction over the (domestic) regulation of freshwater resources; (b) formulating principles regarding the distribution of freshwater resources between two or more States (either through general or more specific regimes, these latter being established through regional instruments); (c) protecting the quality of freshwater resources both directly, for its different uses, and indirectly, as a medium containing species and ecosystems; and (d) asserting a right to water with increasingly specific contents and enforcement avenues.

Points (a) and (b) are (together with the regulation of the navigation) the classic province of the international law of watercourses. Both the navigational and the non-navigational uses of international watercourses have been regulated mostly at the regional or bilateral level.[3] Point (c) is the province of international environmental law relating to oceans, seas and freshwater (surface-water and groundwater). Modern treaties relating to the regulation of international

---

[1] See E. Brown Weiss, 'The Evolution of International Water Law', in *Recueil des cours de l'Académie de droit International*, Vol. 331 (2007), pp. 161–404; D. Caponera, *Principles of Water Law and Administration: National and International* (London: Taylor & Francis, 2nd edn, 2007); J. Dellapenna and J. Gupta 'Toward Global Law on Water' (2008) 13 *Global Governance* 437; S. McCaffrey, *The Law of International Watercourses* (Oxford University Press, 2007).

[2] Pollution from navigation is covered by items (iii) and (iv).

[3] Brown Weiss, 'The Evolution of International Water Law', above n. 1, pp. 234–5. Following the work of the International Law Association, in 1971, the UN International Law Commission undertook the codification of the law governing the non-navigational uses of international watercourses. These efforts resulted, some twenty-five years later, in the United Nations Convention on the Law of the Non-Navigational Uses of International Watercourses, 21 May 1997, 36 ILM 700 (not yet in force) ('UN Watercourses Convention'). See S. Bogdanovic, *International Law of Water Resources: Contribution of the International Law Association* (London: Kluwer Law International, 2001). The Commission also adopted, in 2008, the Draft Articles on the Law of Transboundary Aquifers (2008) II (2) *Yearbook of the International Law Commission* (hereafter the 'ILC Aquifers Draft').

watercourses often include provisions for environmental protection. Points (a), (b) and (c) share a common approach that can be characterised, for present purposes, as a 'regulatory approach' because it operates essentially between States (imposing primary obligations on States and, often, establishing inter-State co-operation and dispute settlement mechanisms), whereas point (d) is more limited in scope (as the regulation of freshwater is limited to what is required by human rights) but more sophisticated enforcement-wise (as individuals are granted rights that – as a rule – can be enforced by international adjudicatory and quasi-adjudicatory bodies). The following analysis of the incidence of international water law on foreign investment schemes makes a distinction between a 'regulatory approach' (Section 7.1.2) and a 'human rights approach' (Section 7.1.3).

7.1.2   The regulatory approach

The purpose of this section is not to provide an overview of the historical development of freshwater treaties or customary law, nor to compare the types of agreements currently in force[4] (either agreements focusing on a specific watercourse or those, such as the UN Watercourses Convention or the 1992 UNECE Watercourses Convention,[5] which set out general principles governing the non-navigational uses of international watercourses[6]); rather, this section attempts to capture the main water-related obligations that may encroach on investment disciplines. In this context, three main categories of water-related obligations can be distinguished: (i) obligations concerning water allocation among different parties/uses or water transfers; (ii) obligations concerning the protection of the quality of the water resource or the species and ecosystems hosted by a water-body; and (iii) obligations imposing procedural requirements.

---

[4]   See A. Wolf and J. Hammer 'Patterns in International Water Resource Treaties: The Transboundary Freshwater Dispute Database' (1998) 9 *Colorado Journal of International Environmental Law and Policy* 157, at 168–73; A. Wolf, 'Transboundary Freshwater Dispute Database: International Freshwater Treaties Database', available at: www.transboundarywaters.orst.edu (accessed on 4 January 2012) ('TFDD'); www.ecolex. org (searchable database of environmental treaties; a query using the word water and limited to treaties yields some 400 results).

[5]   Convention on the Protection and Use of Transboundary Watercourses and International Lakes, 18 March 1992, 1936 UNTS 269 ('UNECE Watercourses Convention').

[6]   Brown Weiss, 'The Evolution of International Water Law,' above n. 1, Chapters I and II; McCaffrey, *The Law of International Watercourses*, above n. 1, Chapters 8, and 10 to 13.

Regarding the first category, some treaties regulate the allocation of water among different States[7] and/or uses[8] or the transboundary transfer of bulk water.[9] According to one empirical study,[10] out of a sample of 145 water treaties studied, 54 (37 per cent) define allocations of water (15 of them specify equal portions and 39 provide for specific means of allocation). The uses covered by these treaties range from hydroelectric power (59), to water consumption (53), industrial uses (9) or flood control (13).[11] Some treaties, as well as a variety of other types of agreements,[12] focus specifically on water transfers. For instance, Lesotho transfers bulk water to South Africa in exchange for monetary payments.[13] Other examples include Turkey's water transfers to Israel, Iran's transfers to Kuwait, Malaysia's transfers to Singapore or Bolivia's transfers to Chile.[14] The basic incidence of such treaties on foreign investment schemes is through the regulations that are adopted to implement them. These regulations may take the form of restrictions on water transfers (e.g., export restrictions) or on the amounts of water available for specific uses or for different parties, which, as discussed in Section 7.2, may adversely affect the profitability of an investment.

[7] See, e.g., Treaty between the United States of America and Mexico relating to the Utilization of the Waters of the Colorado and Tijuana Rivers and of the Rio Grande, 3 February 1944, 3 UNTS 314 ('1944 Water Utilisation Treaty'), Article 4; Agreement between the Republic of Sudan and the United Arab Republic for the Utilization of the Nile Waters, 8 November 1959, 453 UNTS 51 ('Nile Treaty'), Article 1 and 2(4); Indus Waters Treaty between the Government of India, the Government of Pakistan and the International Bank for Reconstruction and Development, 19 November 1960, 419 UNTS 126 ('Indus Waters Treaty'), Article II(1) and III(1).

[8] See, e.g., Treaty between Great Britain [Canada] and the United States relating to Boundary Waters and Boundary Questions, 11 January 1909, (1910) 4 *American Journal of International Law* suppl. 239 ('Boundary Waters Treaty'), Article 8; 1944 Water Utilisation Treaty, above n. 7, Article 3; Indus Waters Treaty, above n. 7, Article I(9)–(11), II(2), (3), (5), and III(2).

[9] See, e.g., Boundary Waters Treaty, above n. 8, Article III (restrictions on new diversions); Treaty on the Lesotho Highlands Water Project, 24 October 1986, TFDD ('Lesotho Treaty'), Article 4(1).

[10] Wolf and Hammer, 'Patterns in International Water Resource Treaties', above n. 4, 162–3. See also, I. Dombrowsky, 'Integration in the Management of International Waters: Economic Perspectives on a Global Policy Discourse' (2008) 14 *Global Governance* 455, at 463.

[11] Wolf and Hammer, 'Patterns in International Water Resource Treaties', above n. 4, 161; Dombrowsky, 'Integration in the Management of International Waters', above n. 10, 463.

[12] Brown Weiss, 'Water Transfers and International Trade Law', in E. Brown Weiss, L. Boisson de Chazournes and N. Bernasconi-Osterwalder (eds.), *Fresh Water and International Economic Law* (Oxford University Press, 2005), pp. 61, at 74–6.

[13] Lesotho Treaty, above n. 9, Articles 4(1), 12 and 13.

[14] Brown Weiss, 'Water Transfers and International Trade Law', above n. 12, 75.

When such regulations cannot be linked to a treaty provision, the occurrence of a normative conflict (as opposed to a legitimacy conflict) will be more difficult to establish. However, even in the absence of a specific treaty provision, such flows and transfers of water are still governed by other rules of international law, in particular the principle of 'equitable and reasonable utilization' and the principle of 'no-harm',[15] which a State may invoke as the basis for the adoption of measures. The main question is whether the potential inconsistency of such measures with investment disciplines may be justified by reference to water treaties or customary law.

With respect to the second category of obligations, many modern water treaties, as well as customary international law, provide for some measure of protection of the quality of water-bodies and/or the species and ecosystems hosted by them.[16] According to one empirical study, water quality is, together with water allocation, the most frequently mentioned issue in water treaties.[17] The environmental protection obligations arising from this body of law provide an ample basis for States to adopt specific environmental regulations, which, in turn, may impinge on foreign investors' activities. Current trends affirm the need to protect the 'ecological integrity necessary to sustain ecosystems dependent on particular waters'[18] by ensuring a minimum streamflow,[19] preventing the introduction of alien species[20] or, more generally, of hazardous

---

[15] Helsinki Rules on the Uses of the Waters of International Rivers, adopted at the 52nd conference of the ILA in August 1966 ('Helsinki Rules'), Articles IV and V; UNECE Watercourses Convention, above n. 5, Article 2(2)(c); UN Watercourses Convention, above n. 3, Articles 5–7; ILC Aquifers Draft, above n. 3, Articles 4–6; Berlin Rules on Water Resources, adopted by the ILA on 21 August 2004 ('Berlin Rules'), Articles 12–13 and 16. See McCaffrey, *The Law of International Watercourses*, above n. 1, pp. 384–445.

[16] See, e.g., Agreement between the United States of American and Canada on Great Lakes Water Quality, 22 November 1978 as subsequently amended, TFDD ('Great Lakes Water Quality Agreement'), Articles II–V; Agreement between the United Mexican States and the Republic of Guatemala on the Protection and Improvement of the Environment in the Border Area, 10 April 1987, TFDD ('Nicaragua–Mexico Agreement'), Articles 2, 3, 4(b)–(d), and 5; The Convention on Co-operation for the Protection and Sustainable Use of the River Danube, 29 June 1994, IER 35:0251 ('Danube River Protection Convention'), Articles 5–7; Convention on the Protection of the Rhine, 22 January 1998, TFDD ('Rhine Convention'), Articles 3(1)–(2), 4 and 5(4); Helsinki Rules, above n. 15, Articles IX and X; UNECE Watercourses Convention, above n. 5, Articles 2–3; UN Watercourses Convention, above n. 3, Articles 20–3; ILC Aquifers Draft, above n. 3, Articles 10–12; Berlin Rules, above n. 15, Articles 22–8, 41. See McCaffrey, *The Law of International Watercourses*, above n. 1, pp. 446–62.

[17] Dombrowsky, 'Integration in the Management of International Waters', above n. 10, 463.

[18] Berlin Rules, above n. 15, Article 22.   [19] *Ibid.*, Article 24.   [20] *Ibid.*, Article 25.

substances and other forms of pollution,[21] and this even on a precautionary basis, when there is a 'serious risk of significant adverse effect on or to the sustainable use of waters'.[22] International law sometimes requires States to adopt emission limits or water quality standards. For instance, Article 7(1) of the Danube River Protection Convention requires States parties to 'set emission limits applicable to individual industrial sectors or industries in terms of pollution loads and concentrations'.[23] Similarly, the Great Lakes Water Quality Agreement provides for specific objectives of water quality, set out in Annex I of the treaty, which are to be considered as 'minimum levels of water quality in the boundary waters of the Great Lakes System and are not intended to preclude the establishment of more stringent requirements'.[24] Often, some international bodies (e.g., the 'International Commission' established by the Danube River Protection Convention, or the 'International Joint Commission' and the 'Great Lakes Quality Board' established by the Great Lakes Water Quality Agreement) oversee the implementation of these measures. In addition, water treaties occasionally contain provisions on public or minority participation.[25] These and other procedural requirements raise a separate set of issues which will be discussed here and in Section 7.1.3 in connection with the human rights approach.

From a regulatory perspective, international water law imposes two main types of procedural requirements, i.e., inter-State co-operation and environmental impact assessment. The components of the obligation to co-operate in the management of shared water resources have evolved over time, from mere notification or consultation requirements, to increasingly ambitious forms of joint management, embodied by international river basin commissions with some measure of regulatory powers.[26] As to the need to conduct environmental impact assessments ('EIA') prior to undertaking an activity with potentially harmful effects

---

[21] *Ibid.*, Articles 26 and 27.   [22] *Ibid.*, Article 23.

[23] Annex II to the Danube River Protection Convention, above n. 16, contains a list of industrial sectors and industries, and of hazardous substances and groups of substances.

[24] Great Lakes Water Quality Agreement, above n. 16, Article IV(1)(a). See also, Berlin Rules, above n. 15, Article 28.

[25] See, e.g., Danube River Protection Convention, above n. 16, Article 14; Berlin Rules, above n. 15, Articles 4, 18–20 and 30. Older water treaties are less attentive to participation. See, e.g., Nile Treaty, above n. 7, Article 2(7).

[26] J. Dellapenna, 'Treaties as Instruments for Managing Internationally-Shared Water Resources: Restricted Sovereignty vs. Community of Property' (1994) 26 *Case-Western Reserve Journal of International and Comparative Law* 27, at 42–54.

for a water source, it arises from an array of general[27] and specific treaties,[28] as well as from general international law.[29] It is easy to understand why such procedural requirements may have an impact on the operation of foreign investors. For instance, the violation of a procedural requirement could have entailed, if the International Court of Justice ('ICJ') had accepted Argentina's argument in the *Pulp Mills* case, the dismantlement of a plant built by a foreign investor in Uruguay.[30] A flawed EIA may entail the suspension or termination of an economic activity or liability for the cost of eliminating and/or repairing the damage caused. More generally, the procedural requirements set out in water treaties may introduce important delays in the development of a project. As discussed next, these procedural obligations may be amplified by participatory requirements arising from human rights law.

7.1.3 The human rights approach

A reference to a right to water[31] appears, to varying degrees, in a number of international instruments[32] and is considered as an implicit precondition to the fulfilment of certain human rights.[33] Approaching the protection of freshwater resources from a human rights perspective

---

[27] See, e.g., Convention on Environmental Impact Assessment in a Transboundary Context, 25 February 1991, 1989 UNTS 310; Protocol on Environmental Protection to the Antarctic Treaty, 4 October 1991, 30 ILM 1455 (1991).

[28] See, e.g., Danube River Protection Convention, above n. 16, Article 7(5)(f); Berlin Rules, above n. 15, Articles 29–31.

[29] *Pulp Mills in the River Uruguay (Argentina v. Uruguay)*, Judgment (20 April 2010), General List No. 135 ('*Pulp Mills* case'), para. 204.

[30] *Ibid.*, para. 270.

[31] See, generally, M. Fitzmaurice, 'The Human Right to Water' (2007) 18 *Fordham Environmental Law Review* 537.

[32] See, e.g., Convention on the Elimination of All Forms of Discrimination Against Women, 18 December 1979, 1249 UNTS 13 ('CEDAW'), Article 14.2(h); Convention on the Rights of the Child, 20 November 1989, 1577 UNTS 3 ('CRC'), Article 24.2(c); Protocol on Water and Health to the 1992 Convention on the Protection and Use of Transboundary Watercourses and International Lakes, 17 June 1999, 2331 UNTS 202 ('Protocol on Water and Health'), Articles 5(m) and 9(1)(b); Geneva Convention Relative to the Treatment of Prisoners of War, 12 August 1949, 75 UNTS 31 ('Third Geneva Convention'), Articles 20, 26, 29 and 46; Geneva Convention Relative to the Treatment of Civilian Persons in Time of War, 12 August 1949, 75 UNTS 287 ('Fourth Geneva Convention'), Articles 85, 89 and 127; Protocol Additional to the Geneva Conventions of 12 August 1949, and Relating to the Protection of Victims of International Armed Conflicts, 6 August 1977, 1125 UNTS 3 ('Protocol I 1977'), Articles 54 and 55; Protocol Additional to the Geneva Conventions of 12 August 1949, and Relating to the Protection of Victims of Non-International Armed Conflicts, 12 August 1977, 1125 UNTS 609 ('Protocol II 1977'), Articles 5 and 14.

[33] See, e.g., International Covenant on Civil and Political Rights, 16 December 1966, 999 UNTS 171 ('ICCPR'), Articles 1(2) and 6(1); American Convention on Human

has the advantage of facilitating access to the often more sophisticated international and domestic mechanisms available for the enforcement of human rights, but also the disadvantage that water is only protected to the extent that it is covered by such rights.[34] For present purposes, it seems useful to distinguish between the substantive contents and the procedural contents of the human right to water.

A representative account of the substantive contents of the right to water is provided by General Comment No. 15 of the United Nations Committee on Economic, Social and Cultural Rights ('GC 15').[35] General Comments to the International Covenant on Economic, Social and Cultural Rights ('ICESCR') are authoritative (but not binding) interpretations of the provisions of the ICESCR. GC 15 reads into the ICESCR the existence of an independent right to water implied in Articles 11(1) (right to an adequate standard of living) and 12(2)(b) (right to health). According to paragraph 2 of GC 15: '[t]he human right to water entitles everyone to sufficient, safe, acceptable, physically accessible and affordable water for personal and domestic uses'. In this connection, two main points must be noted. The first is that, despite the relative diversity of angles and scopes of the instruments concerning the right to water, they all share a focus on personal uses of water. The right to water for other uses, either (large-scale) irrigation or industrial processes is not covered by these instruments. The second point is that, within the protected use, GC 15 makes a distinction between 'core obligations', with 'immediate effect',[36] and other obligations, which can be progressively fulfilled. Taking into account this brief characterisation of the right to water, the potential points of collision with investment disciplines are easily discernible. The use of water for industrial processes is not protected.

Rights, 22 November 1969, 1144 UNTS 123 ('ACHR'), Article 4 (read in the light of *Villagrán-Morales et al.* v. *Guatemala (The 'Street Children' Case)*, ICtHR Series C No. 63 (19 November 1999), para. 144); International Covenant on Economic, Social and Cultural Rights, 19 December 1966, 993 UNTS 3 ('ICESCR'), Articles 11 and 1 (read in the light of Committee on Economic, Social and Cultural Rights, General Comment No. 15 (2002); The Right to Water (Articles 11 and 12 of the International Covenant on Economic, Social and Cultural Rights), 26 November 2002, UN ESCOR Doc. E/C.12/2002/11 ('GC 15')).

[34] On the limits of human rights approaches to environmental protection, see, F. Francioni, 'International Human Rights in an Environmental Horizon' (2010) 21 *European Journal of International Law* 41.

[35] See above n. 33.

[36] GC 15, above n. 33, para. 37. The concept of 'core obligations' was introduced by the ESCR Committee in its General Comment No. 3 (1990), The Nature of States Parties' Obligations (Article 2, para. 1), 14 December 1990, UN Doc. E/1991/23, para. 19.

Despite some reference to related concepts such as access to water for food production purposes (which is not necessarily related to agriculture)[37] or for 'securing livelihoods (right to gain a living by work)',[38] a systematic reading of GC 15 suggests that the position of companies is not one of holders of rights but one of subjects of indirect obligations. This is particularly clear from paragraphs 23 and 24 of GC 15, which require States parties 'to prevent third parties from interfering in any way with the enjoyment of the right to water'[39] and '[w]here water services ... are operated or controlled by third parties ... to prevent them from compromising equal, affordable, and physical access to sufficient, safe and acceptable water'.[40] States are thus required to adopt 'the necessary and effective legislative and other measures' to prevent third parties from denying equal access to adequate water or from polluting and inequitably extracting from water resources.[41] As a result, whereas a State may invoke the need to fulfill its obligations to provide access to water when adopting measures that adversely impact the interests of foreign investors, access to water by the latter would only be protected by investment disciplines.

Regarding the procedural content of the human right to water, although its customary grounding is still subject to divergent views,[42] a number of international instruments increasingly state some measure of public participation as part of the right to water.[43] For instance, paragraph 12(c)(iv) of GC 15 mentions, as one of the four components of access to water 'the right to seek, receive and impart information concerning water issues'. Moreover, where water services are operated or controlled by third parties (such as a foreign investor), GC 15 requires States to establish an 'effective regulatory system' including, *inter alia*, 'genuine public participation'.[44] Paragraph 48 of GC 15 further adds that '[t]he right of individuals and groups to participate in decision-making processes that may affect their exercise of the right to water must be an integral part of any policy, programme or strategy concerning water'.[45] More generally, some measure of participation (although not specifically related to water) is also required by the Aarhus Convention[46]

---

[37] GC 15, above n. 33, para. 6.   [38] *Ibid.*, para. 6.   [39] *Ibid.*, para. 23.
[40] *Ibid.*, para. 24.   [41] *Ibid.*, para. 23; Berlin Rules, above n. 15, Article 17(3)(b).
[42] Berlin Rules, above n. 15, commentary ad Article 4.
[43] See above n. 25.   [44] GC 15, above n. 33, para. 24.
[45] See also Berlin Rules, above n. 15, Articles 4, 18, 20 and 30.
[46] Convention on Access to Information, Public Participation in Decision-making and Access to Justice in Environmental Matters, 25 June 1998, 2161 UNTS 447 ('Aarhus Convention').

as well as by a number of provisions in human rights treaties,[47] including Article 27 of the ICCPR,[48] Articles 6, 8 and 10 of the ECHR,[49] Articles 16 and 24 of the African Charter,[50] Article 21 of the ACHR,[51] and Articles 6, 7 and 15 of the ILO Convention 169.[52] When the participatory dimension of the right to water is not (or not sufficiently) taken into account in the process of authorisation of a water-related investment scheme, the activities of the foreign investor may be delayed or even suspended, depending on the circumstances of the case.

7.2   Decisions from adjudicatory and quasi-adjudicatory bodies

7.2.1   Overview

The collision points identified in the preceding section have been discussed to varying extents in the decisions of different adjudicatory and quasi-adjudicatory bodies, including the ICJ, human rights bodies and investment tribunals, but also administrative procedures such as the one before the World Bank Inspection Panel or other similar bodies. The materials that can be derived from this practice are of a composite nature and require some comment.

First, not all of the collision points mentioned in the foregoing sections have been addressed by the case-law and, even for those that have, reference to them is made only indirectly. Second, those cases where the claim was not pursued, either because a settlement intervened or for other reasons, will only be mentioned when they appear useful to illustrate a collision point that could arise again in the future. Third, in some cases, the friction between environmental and investment protection is not clearly formulated as a normative conflict because the regulation challenged cannot easily be linked to an environmental treaty. Fourth, given the different nature and scope of jurisdiction of the international bodies dealing with these issues, the types of normative conflicts at stake also vary. Whereas some involve investment

---

[47] See P. Cullet and A. Gowlland-Gualtieri, 'Local Communities and Water Investments', in Brown Weiss *et al.*, *Fresh Water and International Economic Law*, above n. 12, 303.

[48] Above n. 33.

[49] European Convention for the Protection of Human Rights and Fundamental Freedoms, 4 November 1950, 213 UNTS 221 ('ECHR').

[50] African Charter on Human and Peoples' Rights, 27 June 1981, 21 ILM 58 (1982) ('African Charter').

[51] Above n. 33.

[52] Convention (No. 169) concerning Indigenous and Tribal Peoples in Independent Countries, 27 June 1989, 28 ILM 1382 (1989) ('ILO Convention 169').

disciplines contained in bilateral or multilateral investment treaties, others take the form of a friction between provisions of the same human rights treaty or, exceptionally, between different protected rights within the same treaty provision. The type of normative conflict influences, in turn, the conflict techniques that are used to solve such conflicts. Fifth and finally, reference will also be made to other cases that, albeit not water-related, can shed light on the issues discussed in the case-law reviewed in this section.

In what follows, I analyse *tour à tour* conflicts arising from water allocation (Section 7.2.2), pollution and depletion of water-bodies (Section 7.2.3), participation and procedural requirements (Section 7.2.4) and access to clean and affordable water (Section 7.2.5).

7.2.2 Water allocation

Conflicts over the allocation of water between different parties and/or uses have a long history in international law, especially in connection with delimitation, navigation or water diversion.[53] Also, several investment cases arising from water-related projects, such as the construction of waterways or dams,[54] have dealt with aspects of these transactions (allegedly unpaid amounts, modalities of the public procurement process, responsibility for project delays) that do not raise normative conflicts. Here, the analysis will focus on those cases where such allocation collides (or could potentially collide) with an investment discipline *lato sensu*.

---

[53] See, e.g., *Territorial Jurisdiction of the River Oder Commission (Czechoslovakia, Denmark, France, Germany, United Kingdom, and Sweden v. Poland)*, PCIJ Series A No. 23 (10 September 1929); *Diversion of Water from the Meuse (Netherlands v. Belgium)*, PCIJ Series A/B No. 70 (28 June 1937); *Lac Lanoux Arbitration (Spain v. France)*, RIAA, Vol. 12 (1957), 281–317 (16 November 1957) ('*Lac Lanoux*'); *Gabčíkovo-Nagymaros Project (Hungary v. Slovakia)*, ICJ Reports 1997, 7 ('*Gabčíkovo-Nagymaros*'); *Kasikili/Sedudu Island (Botswana v. Namibia)*, ICJ Reports 1999, 1045; *Land and Maritime Boundary between Cameroon and Nigeria (Cameroon v. Nigeria; Equatorial Guinea intervening)*, ICJ Reports 2002, 303; *Frontier Dispute (Benin v. Niger)*, ICJ Reports 2005, 90; *Dispute regarding Navigational and Related Rights (Costa Rica v. Nicaragua)*, ICJ Reports 2009, p. 213.

[54] See, e.g., *Zhinvali Development Ltd v. Republic of Georgia*, ICSID Case No. ARB/00/1, Award (24 January 2003) (rehabilitation of a hydropower plant); *JacobsGibb Ltd v. Hashemite Kingdom of Jordan*, ICSID (W. Bank) ARB/02/12 (Waterway construction project – discontinued by order of 13 October 2004, following a settlement); *Salini Costruttori SpA and Italstrade SpA v. The Hashemite Kingdom of Jordan*, ICSID Case No. ARB/02/13, Award (31 January 2006) (Dam construction project); *Impregilo SpA v. Islamic Republic of Pakistan*, ICSID Case No. ARB/03/3, Decision on Jurisdiction (22 April 2005)(hydropower project – discontinued by order of 26 September 2005 following a settlement); *ATA Construction, Indus and Trading Co. v. Hashemite Kingdom of Jordan*, ICSID Case No. ARB/08/2, Award (12 May 2010)(regarding liability for the collapse of a dike built by the claimant).

Regarding the question of the allocation of water among different parties, in an investment dispute brought under Chapter 11 of the NAFTA,[55] *Bayview* v. *Mexico*,[56] a group of Texan irrigation districts claimed that Mexico had expropriated their right to a certain amount of water from the Rio Grande resulting from a treaty between the United States and Mexico[57] through the development of a system of dams and reservoirs affecting the flow of the tributaries of the Rio Grande. This argument supposed that such water rights could constitute a protected investment under the NAFTA despite the fact that the claimants were based in the US territory, an allegation that the US government itself opposed in a third-party submission.[58] Eventually, the tribunal concluded that such water rights were not protected under Article 1101 of the NAFTA. The reasoning of the tribunal was based on the idea that, in order to be protected under the NAFTA, an investment must have a 'legally significant connection' with the State adopting the measures challenged.[59] This is an important observation, of relevance not only for disputes arising under the NAFTA but also for other investment disputes that may be brought in connection with measures of water diversion adopted by a foreign State. The situation would likely be different if the investment scheme was operated in the territory of the State adopting the restrictive measures. An apposite illustration of this factual hypothesis is provided by the notice of claim filed, in 1999, by a US investor, Sun Belt Water Inc., against Canada, in connection with a measure adopted by the Canadian province of British Columbia limiting and later suspending the licence of the claimant to operate bulk water transfers.[60] The claim was not pursued further, but, considering it in the light of other analogous (not water-related) cases,[61] the main legal issue would not be whether the scheme

---

[55] North American Free Trade Agreement, 17 December 1992, 32 ILM 296.

[56] *Bayview Irrigation District et al.* v. *United Mexican States*, ICSID Case No. ARB(AF)/05/1, Award (19 June 2007) ('*Bayview* v. *Mexico*').

[57] 1944 Water Utilisation Treaty, above n. 7.

[58] *Bayview* v. *Mexico*, above n. 56. Submission of the United States of America, 27 November 2006, para. 14, available at: www.naftaclaims.com (accessed on 4 January 2012).

[59] *Bayview* v. *Mexico*, above n. 56, para. 101.

[60] *Sun Belt Water Inc.* v. *Her Majesty the Queen (Canada)*, Notice of Claim and Demand for Arbitration, NAFTA, 12 October 1999, available at: www.naftaclaims.com (accessed 21 March 2012) ('*Sun Belt* v. *Canada*').

[61] *S. D. Myers Inc.* v. *Government of Canada*, NAFTA (UNCITRAL), Partial Award (13 November 2000) ('*S. D. Myers* v. *Canada*') (case involving an export restriction of hazardous waste); *Pope & Talbot* v. *Government of Canada*, NAFTA (UNCITRAL), Interim Award on Merits I (26 June 2000), Interim Award on Merits II (10 April 2001) (case involving export

constitutes an investment but rather to what extent a trade restriction may amount to a breach of an investment discipline.

Questions as to the allocation of water may also arise in the context of competing uses and, more specifically, when the same water resources are subject to rival uses. Aside from cases such as *Lac Lanoux*,[62] *Gabčíkovo-Nagymaros*[63] or *Pulp Mills*,[64] where the rights of investors were only indirectly affected through the potential repercussions of an inter-State dispute, there is limited practice in this respect. One can refer, by way of illustration, to a claim brought by a German investor, Georg Nepolsky, against The Czech Republic in connection with a project to sell water from a water-body located below the surface of his land.[65] According to reports, the investor had been awarded some extraction rights by local authorities but these were only a fraction of what he needed to extract on an annual basis to make its operation profitable. Although the claim was abandoned,[66] the dispute provides an interesting set of facts to illustrate how frictions between industrial uses could potentially interfere with other uses (e.g., those covered by the right to water) and raise a normative conflict.[67] Another illustration is the claim brought by a Swedish State-owned energy company, Vattenfall, against Germany in connection with restrictions in the amount of water that the investor's projected power plant could draw from (and discharge into) the Elbe River. The investor claimed that such restrictions amounted to a breach of the Energy Charter Treaty ('ECT').[68] Although the proceedings were confidential, the media released some information about the main stakes of the dispute, including the text of the request

restrictions of softwood lumber); *Merrill & Ring Forestry LP v. Government of Canada*, NAFTA (UNCITRAL), Award (31 March 2010) (case involving export restrictions of logs).

[62] *Lac Lanoux*, above n. 53.   [63] *Gabčíkovo-Nagymaros*, above n. 53.

[64] *Pulp Mills* case, above n. 29.

[65] See *Georg Nepolsky v. The Czech Republic*, UNCITRAL, Award (February 2010). The proceedings were not public but some information has been reported in L.-E. Peterson, 'Tribunal Constituted to Hear Water Extraction Dispute between German Investor and Czech Republic', available at: www.iareporter.com/articles/20090725_5/print (accessed on 4 January 2012).

[66] L.-E. Peterson, 'Water Extraction Claim Dries Up in Absence of Funds: Claimant Ordered to Cover Half of State's Expenses in UNCITRAL Arbitration', available at: www.iareporter.com/articles/20100616_7/print (accessed on 4 January 2012).

[67] Another potential illustration (although there is limited public information available) is *Branimir Mensik v. Slovak Republic*, ICSID Case No. ARB/06/9 (claim involving a mineral water spring project – discontinued by order of 9 December 2008).

[68] Energy Charter Treaty, 17 December 1994, 2080 UNTS 95 ('ECT'). See, e.g., *Vattenfall AB, Vattenfall Europe AG, Vattenfall Europe Generation AG v. Federal Republic of Germany*, ICSID Case No. ARB/09/6 Award (11 March 2011) ('*Vattenfall v. Germany*').

for arbitration.[69] The case was settled before Germany had the opportunity to present an articulated legal response, but some German politicians reportedly decried how Germany was being 'pilloried just for implementing German and EU laws'.[70] If pursued, the dispute could have raised a normative conflict between the ECT and EU environmental law.[71]

7.2.3   Pollution and depletion of water-bodies

Questions of pollution and depletion of water-bodies have been raised in different contexts. As with allocation matters, a number of inter-State disputes indirectly connected with investment schemes have addressed such questions. For instance, in the *Gabčíkovo-Nagymaros* case, Hungary argued that its suspension and later abandonment of the project was motivated by environmental concerns, in particular the potential impact of the works on the acquifer providing freshwater to Budapest.[72] The plea of necessity to justify the breach of the 1977 treaty (which could be seen as the investment term of the conflict) was based on Hungary's essential interest to protect its water resources, which, in turn, was argued by reference, *inter alia*, to a 'right to environment' grounded in international customary law.[73] The ICJ recognised that the protection of the environment could qualify as an essential interest of a State, referring to the customary grounding of the prevention principle,[74] but it rejected Hungary's plea of necessity because other requirements were not met.[75] Moreover, Hungary also sought to justify its breach of the 1977 treaty on the basis of the *inadimplenti non est adimplendum* rule codified in Article 60 of the VCLT.[76] It argued indeed that Czechoslovakia breached the environmental obligations arising under other provisions (Articles 15 and 19) of the 1977 treaty, as well as of other related

[69] See, e.g., S. Knauer, 'Power Plant's Battle goes to International Arbitration', 15 July 2009, available at: www.spiegel.de (accessed on 4 January 2012). See also *Vattenfall* v. *Germany*, Request for Arbitration, 30 March 2009 ('*Vattenfall* – RoA'), available at: ita.law.uvic.ca/documents/VattenfallRequestforArbitration.pdf (accessed on 4 January 2012).

[70] Knauer, 'Power Plant's Battle goes to International Arbitration', above n. 69, quoting a statement of Michael Müller, Germany's Deputy Environment Minister.

[71] *Ibid.*, quoting a Greenpeace expert's statement that the fact that EU environmental protection legislation may be pushed to the sidelines by an international arbitration body is 'completely absurd'.

[72] Memorial of Hungary (2 May 1994)('Memorial – H'), paras. 10.19–10.21; *Gabčíkovo-Nagymaros*, above n. 53, para. 40.

[73] Memorial – H, above n. 72, para. 10.24 and footnote 17.

[74] *Gabčíkovo-Nagymaros*, above n. 53, para. 53.   [75] *Ibid.*, paras. 54–8.

[76] Vienna Convention on the Law of Treaties, 23 May 1969, 1155 UNTS 331 ('VCLT').

agreements, including a water treaty.[77] But the Court considered that the evidence was insufficient to admit this argument.[78] Furthermore, Hungary referred to the emergence of a customary principle of prevention both to buttress its claim of a fundamental change of circumstances (Article 62 of the VCLT) and, especially, as a limit to the performance of the 1977 treaty.[79] The Court rejected both arguments,[80] but it made two observations of some importance for the analysis of normative conflicts. First, the emergence of new norms of environmental law was not considered as a basis for a fundamental change of circumstances mainly because such norms had been foreseen.[81] Thus, the Court left the door half open for the future admission of a similar argument. Second, the Court stressed the need to take into account, in existing treaties, the emergence of new norms of environmental law.[82] This said, according to the Court, this 'incorporation' would in principle require a referral clause in the treaty. The second observation is relevant for another environment-related inter-State dispute.

Indeed, in the *Pulp Mills* case, Argentina argued that the operations of a foreign investor established in the territory of Uruguay were potentially harmful for the quality of the waters[83] and the ecosystems of the River Uruguay.[84] The position of Argentina was based on both a bilateral treaty (the 1975 Statute of the River Uruguay) and a number of international environmental norms arising both from other treaties (through incorporation) and from customary international law.[85] The Court did not accept the incorporation argument,[86] but it acknowledged that such other rules had to be taken into account for the interpretation of the 1975 Statute pursuant to Article 31(3)(c) of the VCLT.[87] Thus, the conflict was eventually framed as a mere question of interpretation between two competing meanings of the relevant provision (Article 41(a)) of the 1975 Statute, one (Argentina's) stressing a higher level of environmental protection and the other (Uruguay's) asserting that some discharges into the river, necessary for the operations of the foreign investor, were consistent with the treaty. The Court premised its analysis of this claim on a reference to the customary status of the principle of prevention of environmental harm and to the need to take into account new norms as

---

[77] Memorial – H, above n. 72, paras. 10.86–10.90; *Gabčíkovo-Nagymaros*, above n. 53, para. 96.
[78] *Gabčíkovo-Nagymaros*, above n. 53, para. 107.
[79] Memorial – H, above n. 72, paras. 10.64 and 10.91–10.96.
[80] *Gabčíkovo-Nagymaros*, above n. 53, paras. 104 and 112.   [81] *Ibid.*, para. 104.
[82] *Ibid.*, para. 112.   [83] *Pulp Mills* case, above n. 29, para. 179.   [84] *Ibid.*, para. 191.
[85] *Ibid.*, para. 22.   [86] *Ibid.*, para. 63.   [87] *Ibid.*, paras. 65–6.

they emerge.[88] However, it found no conclusive evidence that Uruguay had breached this provision.[89] This conclusion was based on the analysis of detailed regulations adopted by CARU, the river commission, governing waste discharges into the river and is therefore of limited general relevance.

Questions of water pollution have also been raised in a number of investor–State disputes.[90] For instance, in *Vattenfall v. Germany*[91] one of the main issues at stake was the discharge into the River Elbe of water used by a power plant at a temperature (30 degrees Celsius) that, according to the German authorities, would have been ecologically disruptive. The water permit granted to the investor carried both intake (of water) and discharge (of waste water) restrictions, pursuant to German and European law. Had the dispute been pursued, a normative conflict between the ECT and other obligations of European and international law could have arisen.[92] The principles developed for conflicts between European State aid rules and investment disciplines could have been relevant in this connection, taking into account that, were a State to assume liability for the environmental damage caused by an investor, it could amount to State aid.[93]

Another example of an investor–State dispute relating to water pollution is the case between Chevron and Ecuador resulting from the investor's oil exploration and exploitation activities in Ecuador's Amazonian rainforest (Chevron acquired the initial investor Texaco).[94] An action has

---

[88] *Ibid.*, paras. 193–4.   [89] *Ibid.*, para. 265.

[90] See also, *Methanex Corporation v. United States of America*, UNCITRAL (NAFTA), Award (9 August 2005) (relevant for legitimacy conflicts).

[91] Knauer, 'Power Plant's Battle goes to International Arbitration', above n. 69.

[92] See, e.g., Convention between the Federal Republic of Germany and the Czech and Slovak Federal Republic and the European Economic Community on the International Commission for the Protection of the Elbe, 8 October 1990, TFDD ('Convention on the Protection of the Elbe'), Articles 1(2)(b), 1(3) and 2(1)(f). The application of European water law by States could be a significant source of normative conflicts, as suggested by the number of cases brought by the European Commission against several European States for failing to properly implement European water law, particularly in connection with water quality standards. See, e.g., *Commission v. Belgium*, ECJ case C-200271122 (16 January 2003); *Commission v. Ireland*, ECJ case C-316/00 (14 November 2002); *Commission v. United Kingdom*, ECJ case C-63/02 (15 October 2002); *Commission v. Germany*, ECJ case C-161/00 (14 May 2002); *Commission v. Italy*, ECJ case C-396/00 (25 April 2002); *Commission v. Greece*, ECJ case C-384-97 (25 May 2000).

[93] *Plama Consortium Ltd v. Republic of Bulgaria*, ICSID Case No. ARB/03/24, Award (27 August 2008), para. 214.

[94] The dispute between Chevron and Ecuador has given rise to a number of domestic disputes (before both Ecuadorian and US courts) and international disputes (two

been brought before Ecuadorian domestic courts claiming that the methods used by Texaco's local subsidiary contaminated the water sources and the aquatic environment of the regions affected,[95] in breach, *inter alia*, of Article 15 of the ILO Convention 169.[96] In the arbitration proceedings, Chevron claims that 'Ecuador ... is colluding with a group of Ecuadorian plaintiffs and US contingency-fee lawyers who sued Chevron in 2003 in the courts of Ecuador seeking damages and other remedies for impacts that they allege were caused by the Consortium's operations'.[97] According to Chevron, such collusion constitutes a breach both of a settlement agreement concluded in 1995 between Ecuador, Petroecuador and Texaco's local subsidiariy, and of several investment disciplines contained in the Ecuador–US BIT.[98] On this basis, Chevron seeks not only compensation from Ecuador but, most importantly, that the tribunal declare that 'Claimants have no liability or responsibility for environmental impact'.[99] Interestingly, in 1994 the Inter-American Commission on Human Rights ('ICommHR') had undertaken a mission in Ecuador to investigate oil pollution in the Ecuadorian jungle and had concluded that '[b]oth the State and the companies conducting oil exploration activities are responsible for these anomalies, and both should be responsible for correcting them. It is the duty of the State to ensure that they are corrected'.[100] In this context, an intricate

separate claims under the Ecuador–US BIT). Here, the focus is on two proceedings: first, the claims brought by Ecuadorian plaintiffs against Texaco before the Superior Court of Nueva Loja in Lago Agrio, Ecuador, on 7 May 2003 ('*Lago Agrio* litigation') (a free English translation is available at: chevrontoxico.com/news-and-multimedia/2003/0501-ecuador-legal-complaint.html, hereafter '*Lago Agrio* – Complaint'); second, the arbitration proceedings initiated by Chevron on 23 September 2009, see *Chevron Corporation and Texaco Petroleum Company* v. *Republic of Ecuador*, PCA Case No. 2009–23 (UNCITRAL Rules) ('*Chevron* v. *Ecuador II*'), Claimant's Notice of Arbitration, available at: www.chevron.com/documents/pdf/EcuadorBITEn.pdf (accessed on 4 January 2012) ('*Chevron* v. *Ecuador II* – NOA'). Following the judgment of the local court condemning Chevron to pay compensation for the environmental damage caused through Texaco's activities in Ecuador, Chevron requested and obtained provisional measures from the arbitral tribunal constituted in *Chevron* v. *Ecuador II*. See Order for Interim Measures (9 February 2011).

[95] *Lago Agrio* – Complaint, above n. 94, section III, para. 1.
[96] *Ibid.*, section V, para. 2.   [97] *Chevron* v. *Ecuador II* – NOA, above n. 94, para. 3.
[98] *Ibid.*, paras. 66–9.   [99] *Ibid.*, para. 76(1).
[100] Inter-American Commission on Human Rights, *Communiqué with Preliminary Findings* 24/94, Quito (11 November 1994). The final report of the ICommHR confirmed these conclusions. See ICommHR, 'Report on the Situation of Human Rights in Ecuador', OEA/ser.L/V/II.96, doc10 rev1 (24 April 1997)('Ecuador Report'), discussed in E. Morgera, *Corporate Accountability in International Environmental Law* (Oxford University Press, 2009), pp. 136ff.

normative conflict could arise between Ecuador's obligation to respect international environmental and human rights law (through its domestic courts) and its obligation to respect investment disciplines (the acts of the judiciary being attributable to the State). Such a conflict could arise both in the pending investment proceeding and before the Ecuadorian courts.

7.2.4 Procedural requirements

Conflicts between investment disciplines *lato sensu* and procedural obligations stemming from international water law can arise in a variety of forms and fora. Here, I concentrate on conflicts regarding two questions: environmental impact assessment and monitoring, and procedural environmental rights (access to information, participation/consultation, access to justice).

The need for a continuing environmental impact assessment ('EIA') of projects or activities that may have consequences for the environment is contemplated in both treaty[101] and customary law.[102] Often, the operations of foreign investors will be subject to this requirement, the conduct of which may render more onerous, delay or even prevent the investment scheme from being pursued. In the *Gabčíkovo-Nagymaros* case, after noting that the 1977 treaty had not been performed as initially envisioned, the ICJ observed that whatever the agreement of the parties on how to pursue the implementation of their joint investment, they were obliged to evaluate and monitor the impact of their activities on water quality and, more generally, on the environment, as required by Articles 15 and 19 of the 1977 treaty.[103] In the *Pulp Mills* case, Argentina claimed that Uruguay had granted preliminary environmental authorisations to foreign investors in breach of both its procedural and substantive environmental obligations arising from the 1975 Statute of the River Uruguay. Specifically, Argentina argued that Uruguay should have informed it (as well as the river commission – CARU) of the planned mills and that the EIA conducted by Uruguay was flawed. The Court considered that, by issuing environmental authorisations without notifying CARU or Argentina,[104] Uruguay had breached its procedural obligations. The claim for breach of substantive

---

[101] See above nn. 27 and 28.   [102] *Pulp Mills* case, above n. 29, para. 204.

[103] *Gabčíkovo-Nagymaros*, above n. 53, para. 140.

[104] *Pulp Mills* case, above n. 29, para. 111. Uruguay's breach of this obligation (Article 7(1) of the 1975 Statute) also entailed a breach of the obligation to notify Argentina (Article 7(2)), *ibid.*, para. 122.

environmental obligations was instead rejected for lack of conclusive evidence.[105] This is important because the Court took this second conclusion into account when determining the relief to be granted for Uruguay's procedural breach. Uruguay was indeed not required to dismantle the mill built by the foreign investor, as Argentina had requested.[106] Had the Court found Uruguay in breach of both procedural and substantive environmental obligations, it would have likely ordered Uruguay to take measures more intrusive from the perspective of the investor, which, in turn, would have provided a basis for a potential investment claim.[107] Moreover, by requiring Uruguay to continue to monitor the operation of the mill in accordance with Article 41 of the Statute,[108] the Court's decision left the door half open for the adoption of more restrictive environmental measures in the future, which, again, may be a source of normative conflicts.

Aside from the two preceding inter-State disputes, the question of EIA as a procedural requirement was also raised in some investor–State disputes. For instance, in *Vattenfall* v. *Germany*, the investor claimed, *inter alia*, that the additional EIA requirements imposed by the local authorities (extending the monitoring period for the fish-stair by one year to two years) were unreasonable and politically motivated, and therefore in breach of the ECT.[109] In the pending case *Pacific Rim* v. *El Salvador*,[110] the investor has argued that the government's delay in approving an EIA and issuing an environmental permit (necessary for the issuance of a mining permit) amounts to a breach of the investment provisions of the CAFTA and of Salvadorian domestic law. Among the grounds that the President of El Salvador mentioned in his public statements for not issuing the permits is the protection of Salvadorian aquifers. The case is still at an early stage in the proceedings and, so far, it is unclear whether El Salvador will invoke international environmental law in its legal defence. Another relevant pending case is *Clayton/Bilcon* v. *Canada*,[111] where the investor claims that excessive delays in the conduct of an EIA

---

[105] *Ibid.*, para. 265.   [106] *Ibid.*, para. 275.

[107] Agreement relating to the Promotion and Protection of Investments between the Oriental Republic of Uruguay and Finland, 21 March 2002.

[108] *Pulp Mills* case, above n. 29, para. 266.

[109] *Vattenfall* – RoA, above n. 69, para. 54 (especially items (i) and (iv)).

[110] *Pac Rim Cayman LLC* v. *Republic of El Salvador*, ICSID Case No. ARB/09/12, Decision on the Respondent's Preliminary Objections under CAFTA Articles 10.20.4 and 10.20.5 (2 August 2010).

[111] *William Ralph Clayton, William Richard Clayton, Douglas Clayton, Daniel Clayton and Bilcon of Delaware, Inc.* v. *Government of Canada*, UNCITRAL (NAFTA) ('*Clayton/Bilcon* v. *Canada*').

amounted to a breach of the NAFTA. In the light of the statement of defence submitted by Canada, the government does not seem to frame the question as a normative conflict, as it only refers to Canadian domestic environmental law and, more fundamentally, its main contention is that no rule of customary international law sets a specific time period for the conclusion of EIAs.[112] Still another example (although not directly related to water) is the *Maffezini v. Spain* case,[113] where the investor argued, *inter alia*, that Spain was responsible for the additional costs of its investment arising from the results of an EIA. Specifically, Maffezini claimed that the Spanish authorities had exercised pressure on him to start the construction of a chemical plant before the results of the ongoing EIA were known and, therefore, any additional investment costs that would arise from the results of the EIA had to be supported by Spain.[114] The tribunal rejected this contention, noting that the Spanish authorities had simply applied domestic and European law and, therefore, there was no breach of the applicable BIT.[115]

With respect to procedural environmental rights, the body of decisions potentially relevant for the analysis of normative conflicts can be organised under three main headings: disclosure requirements, participatory rights and the right to judicial recourse in environmental matters. The question of disclosure requirements arose in *Aguas del Tunari v. Bolivia*,[116] in connection with the way in which the negotiations leading to the conclusion of a water concession contract for the city of Cochabamba had been conducted. However, the dispute was settled before the proceedings reached the merits phase. In another case (although not focusing on water), *Claude Reyes v. Chile*,[117] the refusal by the Foreign Investment Committee, a Chilean state agency, to provide the information requested by the plaintiffs regarding a deforestation project undertaken by a foreign investor, was challenged before the Inter-American Court of Human Rights. The Court considered that Chile had breached Articles 13 (freedom of speech) and 8 (due process) of the

---

[112] *Ibid.*, Statement of Defence, 4 May 2009, paras. 16–41, 52–53, 103–108, available at: www.pca-cpa.org/upload/files/CanadaStatementDefence04May.PDF (last accessed 21 March 2012).

[113] *Emilio Agustín Maffezini v. Kingdom of Spain*, ICSID Case No. ARB/97/7, Award (13 November 2000).

[114] *Ibid.*, para. 44.   [115] *Ibid.*, para. 71.

[116] *Aguas del Tunari SA v. Republic of Bolivia*, ICSID Case No. ARB/02/3, Decision on Respondent's Objections to Jurisdiction (21 October 2005) ('*Aguas del Tunari*'), paras. 62–6.

[117] *Claude Reyes and others v. Chile*, ICtHR Series C No. 151 (19 September 2006) ('*Claude Reyes v. Chile*').

ACHR.[118] Although Chile did not invoke its obligations under the relevant BIT to justify the actions of its agency, during the proceedings, the Executive Vice President of the agency alluded to the need to protect the 'legitimate business expecations' of the investor.[119] Had Chile referred to its obligations arising from a BIT, the case would have raised a clear normative conflict between procedural rights and investment disciplines.[120] Similar conflicts could potentially arise with respect to some investment schemes financed by the World Bank ('WB'). In several cases relating to water resources, the WB Inspection Panel has found breaches to the WB's operating policies and procedures, including those setting disclosure requirements.[121] The constraints faced by the WB under its operating policies and procedures, which increasingly involve the need to respect international environmental and human rights agreements,[122] may lead to the adoption by a State of measures that a foreign investor views as inconsistent with the State's investment disciplines.[123] Regarding participatory rights, the work of the WB Inspection Panel also shed some light on how normative conflicts between procedural environmental obligations and investment disciplines may arise. WB operating policies and procedures provide for some measure of participation by local communities and indigenous peoples in the implementation of the WB-funded projects. The Inspection Panel addressed

---

[118] *Ibid.*, paras. 103 and 143.   [119] *Ibid.*, para. 57(21).

[120] The tension between obligations arising from the ACHR (right to property under Article 21) and from a BIT (Germany/Paraguay) was more clearly framed as a normative conflict in *Sawhoyamaxa Indigenous Community* v. *Paraguay*, ICtHR Series C No. 146 (29 March 2006), para. 140. See P. Nikken, 'Balancing of Human Rights and Investment Law in the Inter-American System of Human Rights', in P.-M. Dupuy, F. Francioni and E.-U. Petersmann (eds.), *Human Rights in International Investment Law and Arbitration* (Oxford University Press, 2009), pp. 259, at 265–6.

[121] *Report and Recommendation – Bangladesh: Jamuna Bridge Project* (Credit 2569-BD) (26 November 1996), paras. 47–8 ('Jamuna Bridge Project'); *Investigation Report – Uganda: Third Power Project* (Credit No. 2268-UG), *Fourth Power Project* (Credit No. 3545-UG) *and Bujagali Hydropower Project* (PRG No. B003-UG)(30 May 2002), para. 332 ('Uganda Power Projects'); *Investigation Report – The Quinhai Project: A Component of the China: Western Poverty Reduction Project* (Credit No. 3255-CHA and Loan No. 4501-CHA)(28 April 2000), paras. 416–22 ('China Western Poverty Reduction Project'). See Cullet and Gowlland-Gualtieri, 'Local Communities and Water Investments', above n. 47, pp. 319–20.

[122] *Investigation Report – Honduras: Land Administration Project* (IDA Credit 3853-HO)(12 June 2007), paras. 256–8.

[123] See, e.g., *Bayindir Insaat Turizm Ticaret ve Sanayi A Ş* v. *Pakistan*, ICSID Case No. ARB/03/29, Award (24 August 2009) (where the claimant unsuccessfully alleged that pressure from the WB had led Pakistan to put an end to a contract for a construction of a motorway).

this issue in several investigations[124] concerning water projects in Nepal,[125] Argentina/Paraguay,[126] Bangladesh,[127] China,[128] Kenya[129] and Uganda,[130] although none was framed as (nor gave rise to) a normative conflict. As to the right to judicial recourse in water-related matters, the question arose in at least two cases before the European Court of Human Rights.[131] Although none of these cases addresses a normative conflict, they illustrate how a right to judicial recourse could be mobilised (successfully or unsuccessfully) to oppose measures adopted by a State in favour of an economic operator.

7.2.5   Access to clean and affordable water

Questions relating to the quality and affordability of water for domestic uses have been raised in a number of investment cases arising from water and sewerage concessions. The underlying facts giving rise to these disputes are often quite similar. In an effort to modernise the water distribution infrastructure, a State (or a political subdivision) calls on a foreign investor (or a consortium) to develop and manage the water distribution system. The initial perception of foreign investors is often positive but, after some time, this perception evolves into a negative one, for a variety of justified or unjustified reasons, ranging from the imposition of high or simply unpopular tariffs to the occurrence of a crisis, to a sudden change in the government of the host country.[132] In this

---

[124] Cullet and Gowlland-Gualtieri, 'Local Communities and Water Investments', above n. 47, pp. 321–2.

[125] *Investigation Report – Nepal: Proposed Arun III Hydroelectric Project* (Credit 2029-NEP)(21 June 1995), paras. 110–13.

[126] *Investigation Report – Paraguay: Reform Project for the Water and Telecommunications Sectors* (Loan No. 3842-PA); *Argentina: Segba V Power Distribution Project* (Loan No. 2854-AR) (24 February 2004), paras. 397–9.

[127] *Jamuna Bridge Project*, above n. 121, paras. 46 and 54.

[128] *China Western Poverty Reduction Project*, above n. 121, paras. 94–5, 116 and 275–6.

[129] *Investigation Report – Kenya: Lake Victoria Environmental Management Project* (IDA Credit 2907-KE) (GEF TF 23819)(15 December 2000), para. 50.

[130] *Uganda Power Projects*, above n. 121, paras. 343–6.

[131] *Zander v. Sweden*, ECtHR No. 14282/88, Judgment (25 November 1993)(application for breach of Article 6(1) granted)('*Zander v. Sweden*'); *Gorriaz Lizarraga and others v. Spain*, ECtHR No. 62543/00, Judgment (27 April 2004) (application for breach of Articles 6(1) and 8 rejected).

[132] See, e.g., *Aguas del Tunari*, above n. 116; *Azurix Corp v. Argentine Republic*, ICSID Case No. ARB/01/12, Award (14 July 2006) ('*Azurix v. Argentina*'); *Compañía de Aguas del Aconquija SA and Vivendi Universal SA v. Argentine Republic*, ICSID Case No. ARB/97/3, Award (20 August 2007) ('*Vivendi II*'); *Biwater Gauff (Tanz.) Ltd v. United Republic of Tanzania*, ICSID Case No. ARB/05/22, Award (24 July 2008)('*Biwater v. Tanzania*').

context, the human right to water has been mobilised against investment disciplines, either to limit the scope of the latter or to trigger the applicability of an emergency/necessity clause.

The first issue was addressed in a number of cases against Argentina. In the two *Suez* v. *Argentina* cases,[133] the respondent argued that investment disciplines were trumped by the human right to water. An *amicus curiae* brief submitted by a group of NGOs also elaborated on this point to highlight the need, pursuant to Article 31(3)(c) of the VCLT, for the tribunal to interpret investment disciplines in the light of other applicable norms of international law, including the right to water.[134] In their decisions on liability, the tribunals avoided making a determination on the relevant hierarchy of investment disciplines and the human right to water. In the view of the tribunals, 'Argentina [was] subject to both international obligations, i.e. human rights *and* treaty obligations, and [had to] respect both of them equally. Under the circumstances of these cases, Argentina's human rights obligations and its investment treaty obligations [were] not inconsistent, contradictory, or mutually exclusive'.[135] Thus, the tribunals considered that any potential normative conflict between the right to water and investment disciplines could be satisfactorily solved by the systemic integration technique provided for in Article 31(3)(c) of the VCLT. Other cases relating to water concessions in Argentina, such as *Azurix* v. *Argentina*[136] and *Vivendi II*,[137] also raised issues of water quality and/or affordability without clearly framing the question as a normative conflict.[138] A possible explanation of the different approach followed in the *Suez* v. *Argentina* cases is given by the context in which these disputes arose. Unlike *Azurix* v. *Argentina*

[133] *Suez, Sociedad General de Aguas de Barcelona SA and Vivendi Universal SA* v. *The Argentine Republic*, ICSID Case No. ARB/03/19, Decision on Liability (31 July 2010)('*Suez* v. *Argentina* – 03/19'); *Suez, Sociedad General de Aguas de Barcelona SA and InterAguas Servicios Integrales del Agua SA* v. *The Argentine Republic*, ICSID Case No. ARB/03/17, Decision on Liability (31 July 2010)('*Suez* v. *Argentina* – 03/17'). Although technically distinct, the two tribunals have the same composition.

[134] *Suez* v. *Argentina* – 03/19, *Amicus Curiae* Submission, 4 April 2007 ('*Suez* – *Amicus* Submission'), 15–17, available at: www.ciel.org/Publications/SUEZ_Amicus_English_4Apr07.pdf (accessed on 4 February 2012).

[135] *Suez* v. *Argentina* – 03/19, above n. 133, para. 262 (italics original). See also, *Suez* v. *Argentina* – 03/17, above n. 133, para. 240.

[136] *Azurix* v. *Argentina*, above n. 132.   [137] *Vivendi II*, above n. 132.

[138] See, e.g., *Azurix* v. *Argentina*, above n. 132, paras. 140–4. It must be noted however that, in *Vivendi II*, the respondent sought to ground the legitimacy of the action of the Tucumán's authorities by reference, *inter alia*, to the 'supply of quality water, a fundamental human need which the state has a responsibility to safeguard', *Vivendi II*, above n. 132, paras. 3.3.3, 3.3.5., 6.5.1(iii) and 6.5.9.

and *Vivendi II*, the *Suez* v. *Argentina* cases were triggered by the measures adopted by Argentina to cope with the 2001–3 economic and social crisis.

Under the circumstances of the crisis, Argentina also argued that the measures allegedly in breach of the relevant BITs were justified on grounds of necessity. The potential application of the customary defence of necessity to protect environmental interests had been recognised by the ICJ in the *Gabčíkovo-Nagymaros* case.[139] Public emergency clauses and the necessity defence had also been invoked in several investment disputes arising from the Argentine crisis of 2001–3.[140] In *Suez* v. *Argentina*, the customary necessity defence was discussed with specific reference to the right to water by both the respondent and the *amici curiae*. The *amicus* brief referred, *inter alia*, to a previous investment case, *LG&E* v. *Argentina*,[141] where the tribunal had noted that 'a state of necessity is identified by those conditions in which a State is threatened by a serious danger ... to the possibility of maintaining its essential services in operation'.[142] However, unlike the respondent, the *amici* stressed the fact that 'necessity does not apply to human rights treaties that provide guarantees to human rights in times of national emergency'.[143] The legal basis of this assertion rests on the idea that the customary law on State responsibility codified in the ILC Articles[144] is strictly limited to so-called secondary rules (e.g., the necessity defence), as opposed to primary rules (e.g., the various obligations of States to implement the right to water). However, primary and secondary norms entertain a much subtler relationship than the one suggested by the aforementioned distinction.[145] Primary norms may, for instance, be instrumental in the recognition of a given value as an 'essential interest' of the State, in the meaning of Article 25 of the ILC Articles on State Responsibility.[146] In the *Suez* v. *Argentina* cases, although the tribunals

---

[139] See *Gabčíkovo-Nagymaros*, above n. 53, para. 53.   [140] See Chapter 15.

[141] *LG&E* v. *Argentine Republic*, ICSID Case No. ARB/02/1, Decision on Liability (13 October 2006).

[142] *Suez – Amicus* Submission, above n. 134, 27–8.   [143] *Ibid.*, 28.

[144] Responsibility of States for Internationally Wrongful Acts, GA Res. 56/83, UN Doc. A/RES/56/83, 12 December 2001 ('ILC Articles').

[145] See E. David, 'Primary and Secondary Rules', in J. Crawford, A. Pellet and S. Olleson (eds.), *The Law of International Responsibility* (Oxford University Press, 2010), pp. 29ff.

[146] Primary norms have already played this role in the crystallisation of environmental protection as an essential interest of States. See J. E. Viñuales, 'The Contribution of the International Court of Justice to the Development of International Environmental Law' (2008) 32 *Fordham International Law Journal* 232, at 248–9.

rejected the necessity defence, they recognised that '[t]he provision of water and sewage services ... certainly was vital to the health and well-being of [the population] and was therefore an essential interest of the Argentine State'.[147] Whereas, technically, the analysis of the necessity defence did not entail an application of the primary obligations arising from the right to water, such obligations were indeed taken into account by the tribunals to the extent that they had been expressly referred to by the respondent.[148] For this reason, the analysis of the tribunals sheds light on how the necessity defence can be used to manage not only legitimacy conflicts but also normative conflicts.

7.3   Assessing contemporary practice

The following assessment summarises the findings of this chapter with respect to the theoretical inquiry on the evolving relationship between international investment law and international environmental law (Section 7.3.1) as well as to the implications for practitioners and policy-makers (Section 7.3.2). Although this section focuses on the decisions relating to the relations between the international regulation of freshwater and investment disciplines, it serves as a prelude to the findings of Chapters 8 to 10.

7.3.1   Conceptual findings

The first conclusion that can be drawn from the foregoing analysis of the case-law is that normative conflicts between the international regulation of freshwater and investment disciplines are still very rare in practice. Seen in the light of the discussion in Chapter 6 of the fragmentation debate, this finding supports a mild view of fragmentation, as 'mutual ignorance' or 'mutual disinterest' between two branches of international law, rather than as colliding sets of norms that would be harmonised through the use of conflict norms. Tensions between these two areas of regulation are seldom framed as normative conflicts and, even when they are pleaded as such (e.g., the *Suez* v. *Argentina* cases) the tribunals are reluctant to treat them as normative conflicts.

This said, the case-law reviewed also suggests that such conflicts could nevertheless arise in the future, in connection with questions such as:

---

[147] See *Suez* v. *Argentina* – 03/17, above n. 133, para. 238; *Suez* v. *Argentina* – 03/19, above n. 133, para 260.

[148] See *Suez* v. *Argentina* – 03/17, above n. 133, para. 232; *Suez* v. *Argentina* – 03/19, above n. 133, para. 252.

(i) water allocation among different users or uses; (ii) pollution or depletion of a water-body; (iii) procedural requirements (such as EIAs or procedural environmental rights) impinging on the development of investment schemes; or (iv) encroachment on the right to water of individuals and minorities. The main variable explaining the likelihood of conflicts seems to be the increasing specificity of international environmental law, which, in some areas, has tightened its grip moving from a set of merely exhortatory norms to a body of actual obligations (commands, prohibitions and, by extension, permissions). The potential conflict between European water law and the ECT preliminarily raised by the *Vattenfall* v. *Germany* case provides an example of this hypothesis. Another example concerns the procedural requirement to conduct an EIA. In the *Pulp Mills* case, the determination of the requirements applicable to the EIA conducted by Uruguay was critical for the Court's finding that no substantive obligation had been breached, which, in turn, paved the way for the dismissal of Argentina's request to dismantle the mill. The Court found the necessary space to reach this solution by making an ambiguous statement, namely that, although the conduct of an EIA is now a requirement under general international law, 'it is for each State to determine in its domestic legislation or in the authorization process for the project, the specific content of the environmental impact assessment required in each case'.[149] Still another illustration of the incidence of increasingly specific environmental norms could be derived from the case-law concerning the right to water, such as the *Suez* v. *Argentina* cases, but also from other cases where the right to water has been upheld as a limit to the activities of economic operators, such as *Zander* v. *Sweden*.[150]

Significantly, this transformation in the incidence of international environmental law has not (or not chiefly) been prompted by the adoption of new treaties but, rather, by the hardening of existing broad provisions through the work of a variety of actors, including adjudicatory and quasi-adjudicatory bodies (e.g., human rights courts or river commissions), interpretive bodies (e.g., the ESCR Committee) or advocacy groups (e.g., NGOs acting as *amici curiae*). The efforts of these different

---

[149] *Pulp Mills* case, above n. 29, para. 205. Read in the context of the pleadings of the parties, this statement should not lead to the conclusion that States have full discretion to determine the contents of an EIA. See A. Boyle, 'Developments in International Law of EIA and their Relation to the Espoo Convention', 5, available at: www.unece.org/fileadmin/DAM/env/eia/documents/mop5/Seminar_Boyle.pdf (accessed on 12 January 2012).

[150] *Zander* v. *Sweden*, above n. 131.

actors both to spell out the specific content of environmental norms and to carve out an environmental dimension in non-environmental norms are transforming the nature of international environmental law. This process should be familiar to investment lawyers. It is indeed through the work of investment tribunals that international investment law has undergone its remarkable transformation from an array of broad standards to a set of specific disciplines.

However, one important difference between the transformation processes undergone, respectively, by international environmental law and international investment law is that, unlike the former, the latter has benefited from a set of specialised tribunals. As discussed in more detail in Chapters 8 to 10, although a similar function has been performed in the environmental field by a variety of other mechanisms, including those mentioned in the preceding section, the end result is not yet entirely satisfactory. Specifically, there is still considerable uncertainty as to the link between broadly stated international environmental norms and the specific domestic measures adopted under their umbrella. This problem introduces an additional layer of complexity, with important practical implications, as discussed next.

7.3.2   Some practical problems

The weakness of the link between international environmental norms and domestic environmental measures presents four main practical problems: domestic measures seldom refer to their grounding in international environmental obligations (Section 7.3.2.1); even when there is a discernible link, respondent States have rarely invoked their international environmental obligations (Section 7.3.2.2); even in those cases where the link is invoked, it remains difficult to establish that the domestic measures challenged by the investor were required (or fully permitted) by an international environmental norm, largely because of the typically broad formulation of such norms (Section 7.3.2.3); even in cases where the link is established, given the (still) relative scarcity of specific conflict norms, normative conflicts would have to be solved on a case-by-case basis through the use of general conflict norms, a process that is made more difficult by the fact that investment tribunals seem reluctant to make open pronouncements on the relative hierarchy of environmental and investment protection (Section 7.3.2.4).

7.3.2.1   The link is unclear

In those cases where a State plans to adopt an environmental measure that may encroach on the profitability of foreign investment schemes, the relevant authorities would be well advised to spell out the link between the measure and the State's obligations under international environmental law. This link sometimes appears in the Preamble of a piece of legislation and/or is apparent from the *travaux préparatoires*. However, a simple reference may not be enough to reduce the litigation risk entailed by such measures.

An additional step could consist of an analysis of the reasons why the State authorities consider that the measure is required or fully author-ised by an environmental treaty. Such analysis could perhaps be sup-ported by more direct interventions from international bodies, such as reports exhorting a country to comply with some specific provisions or even the outcomes of a non-compliance procedure recommending a State to adopt certain measures or, at least, a set of measures consistent with its international environmental obligations. For example, the ICommHR explicitly encouraged Ecuador to take action to protect the rights of the individuals concerned by providing redress mechanisms.[151]

Another useful step would be the conduct of a cost-benefit analysis of the measure discussing in some detail the implications of the different options available to the State to reach the environmental objective pursued. Proportionality and even consultation of the different interests at stake, including those of foreign investors, is a key element both to preserve the business relationship with foreign investors and, as the case may be, to reduce litigation risk. Indeed, proportionality and consult-ation provide a direct response to two legitimate arguments often advanced by investors to neutralise the reference to environmental considerations, namely that there were other equally effective but less restrictive measures or that the process was flawed.

7.3.2.2   Invocation of the link in investment proceedings

The link between the host State's international environmental obliga-tions and the domestic measures challenged by the investor is seldom mentioned by respondent States and, even when they do so, the impli-cations of this link are rarely developed. Although this point is difficult to investigate, because the submissions of the parties are normally

---

[151] Ecuador Report, above n. 100, Chapter VIII (recommendations).

confidential, the summaries of the parties' positions made in the decisions analysed suggest that respondent States seldom (but increasingly) refer to their international environmental (or human rights) obligations to justify their domestic measures.

Based on the information publicly available, the only water-related investment disputes where the link has been raised are the *Suez* v. *Argentina* cases where Argentina contended that the adoption of the measures challenged followed Argentina's obligations to ensure access to water for its population.[152] Aside from this case, it is not unlikely that Germany would have invoked European water law to justify the measures challenged in the *Vattenfall* v. *Germany* case. More generally, international norms protecting the right to water have been invoked in support of the contention that preventing pollution or depletion of a waterbody[153] or ensuring water distribution[154] meet the requirements of some customary defences.

The rare references to international environmental law may be explained by several reasons, including: (i) the special features of international environmental norms in the area of freshwater regulation and, particularly, their limited usefulness to buttress the State's argumentation, either because they are too broad or because they cannot be easily linked to specific measures; (ii) other strategic defence choices; or (iii) simply the lack of familiarity of counsel with the relevant area of law. As will be discussed in the next chapters, a number of cases relating to other areas of environmental protection indicate a growing use of legal justifications based on international environmental law.

7.3.2.3 The vulnerability of the link

The third and related practical problem is the vulnerability of the link. This is in part due to the often broad formulation of international environmental norms, which makes it difficult for States to establish that the domestic measure adopted was commanded, prohibited or fully permitted by an international environmental norm. Such vulnerability has been noticed by investors. As noted in Section 7.3.2.1, it is indeed

---

[152] *Suez* v. *Argentina* – 03/19, above n. 133, para. 252; *Suez* v. *Argentina* – 03/17, above n. 133, para. 232.

[153] See Memorial – H, above n. 72, paras. 10.19 – 21, 10.24, 10–64 and 10.86 – 10.96; *Gabčíkovo-Nagymaros*, above n. 53, paras. 53–8, 96, 104, 107, 112 (in connection with the defences of necessity, *inadimplenti non est adimplendum*, fundamental change of circumstances, and *ius cogens superveniens*).

[154] See above n. 152.

a recurrent feature of investment disputes with environmental components that the link between international environmental law and domestic measures, when referred to at all, is challenged by the investor on two justifiable grounds, namely (i) that the State has gone well beyond what was required by international environmental law while other equally effective but less harmful measures could have been adopted and/or (ii) that the measure has been adopted through a flawed process (even when the link with international environmental law seems clear).

For instance, in *Suez v. Argentina* the investors argued that the 'forced renegotiation' of their contracts imposed by Argentina amounted to a breach of the fair and equitable standard of the applicable BITs.[155] They further argued that Argentina could not avail itself of the necessity defence because, *inter alia*, it could have adopted less restrictive measures to achieve the same end. The investors also mentioned that, in fact, the measures challenged had themselves threatened the provision of water to the Argentine population, by preventing the operation of the water distribution system managed by the investor.[156] The tribunal agreed with the position of the investor on both points,[157] noting with respect to the necessity defence that 'Argentina could have attempted to apply more flexible means to assure the continuation of the water and sewage services to the people of Buenos Aires and at the same time respected its obligations of fair and equitable treatment. The two were by no means mutually exclusive'.[158]

7.3.2.4   The available conflict norms are (still) too general

As discussed in Chapter 6, investment treaties seldom include specific conflict norms applicable to normative conflicts (as opposed to legitimacy conflicts). Introducing specific conflict norms would be useful to provide a higher level of legal certainty to both investors (to clarify the regulatory risk that they assume) and host States (to clarify the room for environmental regulation and the level of litigation risk). The OECD Statement on 'Harnessing Freedom of Investment for Green Growth', adopted in April 2011,[159] calls for States to 'continue to monitor their investment treaty practices with regard to environmental

---

[155] *Suez v. Argentina* – 03/19, above n. 133, paras. 194–9 and 257–65.
[156] *Ibid.*, paras. 254–5.   [157] *Ibid.*, paras. 239–43.   [158] *Ibid.*, para. 260.
[159] Organisation for Economic Co-operation and Development (OECD), 'Harnessing Freedom of Investment for Green Growth, Freedom of Investment Roundtable', 14 April 2011 ('OECD Statement').

goals'.[160] More specifically, the Statement acknowledges that 'specific references to the environment are included in a limited number of investment agreements' although 'the number is increasing', particularly in the treaty practice of States that have faced investment claims.[161]

In the absence of such specific conflict norms, potential normative conflicts will have to be addressed by either general conflict norms or by case-specific ad hoc techniques, which is perhaps less desirable from the perspective of legal certainty. The still limited practice in the area of freshwater regulation suggests that tribunals prefer to use interpretation techniques, as in *Suez* v. *Argentina*, where the tribunals concluded that 'Argentina [was] subject to both international obligations, i.e. human rights *and* treaty obligations, and [had to] respect both of them equally. Under the circumstances of these cases, Argentina's human rights obligations and its investment treaty obligations [were] not inconsistent, contradictory, or mutually exclusive'.[162] It is worth noting that this cautious approach has been followed despite the fact that access to water is widely recognised as a human right or, in other words, that its content is more specific than many international environmental norms. This is significant because it highlights the important role that interpretation techniques (out of the array of general conflict norms) may be called upon to play in future disputes.

---

[160] *Ibid.*, point 2.   [161] *Ibid.*, point 2.
[162] *Suez* v. *Argentina* – 03/19, above n. 133, para. 262 (italics original); *Suez* v. *Argentina* – 03/17, above n. 133, para. 240.

8 Foreign investment and the protection of biological and cultural diversity

This chapter analyses the interactions between the international protection of biological and cultural diversity and international investment law, as the second illustration of a source of normative conflicts. As in the previous chapter, the analysis focuses on the incidence, actual or potential, of an array of international instruments relating to the protection of species, habitats, ecosystems, biodiversity, cultural heritage and cultural rights *lato sensu* on the operations of foreign investors. The chapter is divided into three sections. The first section identifies, in the overall body of law relating to the protection of biological and cultural diversity, those obligations that may potentially conflict with investment disciplines. Section 8.2 analyses the contribution of adjudicatory and quasi-adjudicatory bodies to the understanding of the type of normative conflicts under review. Section 8.3 distils some general insights from the analysis conducted in the first two sections.

8.1 The protection of biological and cultural diversity – an analysis of collision points

8.1.1 Overview

There is a vast body of international law focusing on the protection of species, habitats, ecosystems and, more recently, biological diversity (including genetic resources). Together with the regulation of international watercourses, the protection of species is one of the earliest manifestations of international environmental regulation.[1]

---

[1] P. H. Sand 'The Evolution of International Environmental Law' in D. Bodansky, J. Brunnée and E. Hey (eds.), *The Oxford Handbook of International Environmental Law* (Oxford University Press, 2007), pp. 31ff.

For convenience, one can organise the main instruments of this body of law in accordance with two different criteria. The first is the substantive scope of the relevant instruments. From this perspective, one can distinguish treaties focusing on certain species (e.g., whales[2]) or groups of species (e.g., migratory species[3] or, more broadly, endangered species[4]), treaties relative to certain types of habitats or ecosystems (e.g., wetlands[5] or the Antarctic ecosystem[6]) and treaties pertaining to more complex problems (e.g., biological diversity[7] or desertification[8]). A second useful criterion is the spatial scope of these instruments, which may be bilateral,[9] regional[10] or universal.[11] In addition to these treaties, a number of instruments dealing with the rights of individuals, minorities and peoples[12] provide an

---

[2] International Convention for the Regulation of Whaling with Schedule of Whaling Regulations, 2 December 1946, 161 UNTS 361.

[3] Convention on the Conservation of Migratory Species of Wild Animals, 23 June 1979, 1651 UNTS 356, developed by numerous subsidiary agreements under its Articles IV and V.

[4] Convention on International Trade in Endangered Species of Wild Fauna and Flora, 3 March 1973, 983 UNTS 243 ('CITES').

[5] Convention on Wetlands of International Importance especially as Waterfowl Habitat, 2 February 1971, 996 UNTS 245 ('Ramsar Convention').

[6] Protocol on Environmental Protection to the Antarctic Treaty, 4 October 1991, 30 ILM 1455 (1991).

[7] Convention on Biological Diversity, 5 June 1992, 31 ILM 82 ('CBD'), followed by three protocols: Cartagena Protocol on Biosafety to the Convention on Biological Diversity, 29 January 2000, 39 ILM 1027 (2000) ('Biosafety Protocol'); The Nagoya – Kuala Lumpur Supplementary Protocol on Liability and Redress to the Cartagena Protocol on Biosafety, 16 October 2010 (not yet in force); Nagoya Protocol on Access to Genetic Resources and the Fair and Equitable Sharing of Benefits Arising from their Utilization to the Convention on Biological Diversity, 29 October 2010 ('ABS Protocol') (not yet in force).

[8] United Nations Convention to Combat Desertification in those Countries Experiencing Serious Drought and/or Desertification, Particularly in Africa, 17 June 1994, 33 ILM 1328 ('UNCCD').

[9] For examples, see www.ecolex.org.

[10] Most continents or areas have their own systems, e.g., Convention on Nature Protection and Wildlife Preservation in the Western Hemisphere, 12 October 1940, 161 UNTS 193; African Convention on the Conservation of Nature and Natural Resources, 15 September 1968, 1001 UNTS 3 (revised on 11 July 2003); Convention on the Conservation of European Wildlife and Natural Habitats, 19 September 1979, ETS No. 104 ('Bern Convention'); ASEAN Agreement on the Conservation of Nature and Natural Resources, 9 July 1985, 15 EPL 64 (not yet in force).

[11] See e.g., Ramsar Convention, above n. 5; Convention for the Protection of the World Cultural and Natural Heritage, 16 November 1972, 1037 UNTS 151 ('World Heritage Convention'); CITES, above n. 4; CBD, above n. 7; UNCCD, above n. 8.

[12] See, in particular: International Covenant on Civil and Political Rights, 16 December 1966, 999 UNTS 171 ('ICCPR'), Article 27; International Covenant on Economic, Social and Cultural Rights, 19 December 1966, 993 UNTS 3 ('ICESCR'), Article 15; American

additional layer of protection focusing on the relationship between individuals and/or groups and their environment.

The link between these two angles of protection (biological and
cultural) is particularly clear in the case of indigenous peoples, whose
relationship to their lands, territories and resources is consubstantial
with their cultural identity.[13] The link is also established with respect to
the protection of natural and cultural heritage, by the 1972 World
Heritage Convention.[14] More specifically, treating these two angles of
protection together is useful to capture the manner in which normative
conflicts have arisen in a number of investment disputes.

Although the distinction between the protection of 'biological' and
'cultural' diversity partly overlaps with that between the 'regulatory'
and the 'human rights' approaches to environmental protection, it seems
convenient to address these two latter approaches separately, as several
aspects of the protection of 'biological' and 'cultural' diversity are important from the perspective of both the regulatory and the human rights
approach. Thus, the following analysis of the incidence of the international
protection of biological and cultural diversity on foreign investment
schemes distinguishes between a 'regulatory approach' (Section 8.1.2) and
a 'human rights approach' (Section 8.1.3).

8.1.2   The regulatory approach

This section is not intended to provide an overview of the international
protection of biological[15] and cultural diversity[16] but only, as in the
previous chapter, to capture the main obligations arising from this body

Convention on Human Rights, 22 November 1969, 1144 UNTS 123 ('ACHR'), Article 21;
African Charter on Human and Peoples' Rights, 27 June 1981, 21 ILM 58 (1982) ('African
Charter'), Articles 21 and 24; Convention (No. 169) concerning Indigenous and Tribal
Peoples in Independent Countries, 27 June 1989, 28 ILM 1382 (1989) ('ILO Convention
169'); Declaration on the Rights of Persons Belonging to National or Ethnic, Religious
and Linguistic Minorities, 18 December 1992, UN Doc. A/RES/47/135; United Nations
Declaration on the Rights of Indigenous Peoples, 13 September 2007, UN Doc. A/RES/61/295
('UN Indigenous Peoples Declaration').

[13] Indigenous Peoples and their Relationship to Land, Final working paper prepared by the
Special Rapporteur, Mrs. Erica-Irene A. Daes, 11 June 2001, UN Doc. E/CN.4/Sub.2/2001/21,
para. 12; ILO Convention 169, above n. 12, Article 13; *Mayagna (Sumo) Awas Tingni
Community* v. *Nicaragua*, ICtHR Series C No. 79 (31 August 2001) ('*Awas Tingni*'), para. 149.

[14] World Heritage Convention, above n. 11. See F. Francioni (ed.), *The 1972 Heritage
Convention. A Commentary* (Oxford University Press, 2008).

[15] See M. Bowman, P. Davies and C. Redgwell, *Lyster's International Wildlife Law* (Cambridge
University Press, 2nd edn, 2010).

[16] See F. Francioni and M. Scheinin (eds.), *Cultural Human Rights* (Leiden: Martinus Nijhoff,
2008); J. Anaya, *Indigenous Peoples in International Law* (Oxford University Press, 2004).

of law that may encroach on investment disciplines. In this regard, four main categories of obligations can be distinguished: (i) obligations concerning the protection of certain areas or species; (ii) obligations relating to the international trade of certain species; (iii) obligations relating to the access and benefit sharing of biological and genetic resources; and (iv) procedural requirements.

Regarding the first category, several environmental agreements provide for the protection of certain areas (e.g., through the establishment of natural reserves or other protected areas[17]) and species (e.g., by creating property rights on fisheries[18]). Often, the protection of certain areas is a function of the protection of certain species. Many examples of this category of obligations can be provided. Pursuant to Article 4(1) of the Ramsar Convention, States 'shall promote the conservation of wetlands and waterfowl by establishing nature reserves on wetlands, whether they are included in the List or not, and provide adequately for their wardening'.[19] Similar obligations arise from Article 4 of the World Heritage Convention, Article II(1) of the Convention on Migratory Species, or Article 8(a)–(b) of the CBD. At the regional level, the obligation to establish protected areas is contemplated in Article II(1)–(2) of the Western Hemisphere Convention, Articles 1, 3(1) and 4(4) of the Bern Convention,[20] or Article XII(1) of the African Conservation Convention. The potential incidence of this type of obligations on foreign investment schemes must be appraised in the light of the more specific regulations issued by the bodies responsible for the management of these treaties to implement such obligations. Such regulations focus, *inter alia*, on the contents of the management plans that States are required to submit, the legal status that must be granted to the relevant area to qualify for recognition by an international body, the buffer zones that must be established in the surroundings of the protected area or the requirements in terms of environmental impact assessment and monitoring attached to the creation of such

---

[17] See A. Gillespie, *Protected Areas and International Environmental Law* (Leiden: Martinus Nijhoff, 2007).

[18] See K. M. Wyman, 'The Property Rights Challenge in Marine Fisheries' (2008) 50 *Arizona Law Review* 511; J. L. Jacobson, 'International Fisheries Law in the Year 2010' (1985) 45 *Louisiana Law Review* 1161.

[19] See also, Ramsar Convention, above n. 5, Articles 2(1) and 2(4).

[20] Together with the 'European Diploma' system (Council of Europe, Criteria for the Award of the European Diploma of Protected Areas, www.coe.int) and the Emerald Network (Strasbourg Declaration on the Role of the Bern Convention in the Preservation of Biological Diversity, 30 November 2004).

protected areas.[21] As to the question of fisheries, international law governs mainly the allocation of these resources among States, most notably by the creation of an exclusive economic zone ('EZZ') of 200 nautical miles within which the coastal State exercises regulatory powers,[22] subject to some environmental and conservation obligations,[23] including the establishment by international fisheries commissions of 'total allowable catches' ('TACs'), country quotas and some restrictions on the use of certain fishing techniques.[24] These obligations are implemented by States through a variety of regulatory tools.[25] In this regard, one must distinguish the regulation of wild fisheries from that of aquaculture. Wild fisheries are most often managed by restrictions on the total or individual amount of catches allowed, territorial use rights or 'TURFs' (for sedentary species), restrictions of fishing seasons, restrictions on the techniques used and licensing requirements (for the ownership and use of fishing vessels). Aquaculture is regulated mostly through the lease of an area of the ocean (within the EZZ) and licensing requirements to grow fish.[26] Changes in international requirements (e.g., in-country quotas or fishing techniques) may induce domestic measures (e.g., redistribution of quotas and/or territories, new technological or licensing requirements) that adversely affect the operations of foreign investors.

The second category of obligations focuses on the transboundary movement of certain species of flora and fauna. A number of environmental agreements provide for trade-related environmental measures ('TREMs').[27] For instance, Article III of CITES subjects trade in endangered species (listed in Appendix I) to the issuance of both an export and an import permit which, in turn, can only be granted if certain restrictive

---

[21] See A. Gillespie, 'The Management of Protected Areas of International Significance' (2006) 10 *New Zealand Journal of Environmental Law* 93.

[22] See United Nations Convention on the Law of the Sea, 10 December 1982, 1833 UNTS 397 ('UNCLOS'), Part VI, in particular, Articles 55–7.

[23] See *ibid.*, Part VI, Articles 61–2 and, more generally, Part XII.

[24] See 'Closing the Net: Stopping Illegal Fishing on the High Seas – Final Report of the Ministerially-led Task Force on IUU Fishing on the High Seas', available at: www.data.iucn.org/dbtw-wpd/edocs/2006-024.pdf (accessed on 4 January 2012), p. 47.

[25] Wyman, 'The Property Rights Challenge in Marine Fisheries', above n. 18, 515–20.

[26] See J. Firestone, W. Kempton, A. Krueger and C. E. Loper 'Regulating Offshore Wind Power and Aquaculture: Messages from Land and Sea' (2004) 14 *Cornell Journal of Law and Public Policy* 71, at 101–3.

[27] See WTO/CTE, Matrix on Trade Measures pursuant to Selected Multilateral Environmental Agreement, 14 March 2007, WT/CTE/W/160/Rev.4, TN/TE/S/5/Rev.2 ('CTE MEA Matrix'), Section II.

requirements are met, in particular that the transaction is not 'detrimental to the survival of the species'[28] and that 'the specimen is not to be used for primarily commercial purposes'.[29] Another example is Article 7(1) of the Biosafety Protocol, according to which 'the first intentional transboundary movement of living modified organisms for intentional introduction into the environment of the Party of import' is subject to an advance informed agreement procedure set out in Articles 8 to 10 and 12. These and other more general provisions contained in other treaties, including the CCAMLR,[30] the CBD, or the UN Fish Stocks Agreement,[31] are implemented through the decisions of the body responsible for the treaty in question or other subsidiary bodies in charge of compliance procedures.[32] To the extent that domestic measures giving effect to such obligations and decisions may interfere with the activities of foreign investors engaged in a variety of sectors, such as food production, fishing or forestry, there is a risk of normative conflicts between TREMs and investment disciplines.

The third strand of obligations of some importance for the operation of foreign investors (especially in the agricultural and pharmaceutical industries) are those concerning access to biological and genetic resources and benefit sharing ('ABS'). The main legal sources are the CBD (further developed in its ABS Protocol, adopted in October 2010, which takes up the previous Bonn ABS Guidelines, adopted in 2002[33]) and the specialised regime set out by the Treaty on Plant Genetic Resources.[34] Article 15 of the CBD states the principle of national sovereignty over resources located in a State's territory but adds that '[e]ach Contracting Party shall endeavour to create conditions to facilitate

---

[28] CITES, above n. 4, Article III(2)(a) and (3)(a).

[29] *Ibid.*, Article III(3)(c); Res. Conf 5.10 (Rev COP.15), paras. 2 and 3 (defining 'commercial').

[30] Convention for the Conservation of Antarctic Marine Living Resources, 20 May 1980, 1329 UNTS 47.

[31] The Agreement for the Implementation of the Provisions of the United Nations Convention on the Law of the Sea of 10 December 1982 relating to the Conservation and Management of Straddling Fish Stocks and Highly Migratory Fish Stocks, 4 August 1995, 2167 UNTS 88.

[32] See CTE MEA Matrix, above n. 27, Section II.

[33] Bonn Guidelines on Access to Genetic Resources and Fair and Equitable Sharing of the Benefits Arising out of their Utilisations, UN Doc. UNEP/CBD/COP/6/24 (2002).

[34] International Treaty on Plant Genetic Resources for Food and Agriculture, 3 November 2001, 2400 UNTS 379. On the ABS system of this treaty, see Secretariat of the Centre of the Consultative Group on International Agricultural Research (CGIAR) System-wide Genetic Resources Programme (SGRP), 'The Importance of Recognizing the International Treaty in the CBD's Protocol on Access and Benefit-Sharing', Policy Brief (July 2010), both available at: www.bioversityinternational.org (accessed on 4 January 2012).

access to genetic resources for environmentally sound uses by other Contracting Parties and not to impose restrictions that run counter to the objectives of this Convention'.[35] This provision also states that:

[c]ontracting States shall take legislative, administrative or policy measures … with the aim of sharing in a fair and equitable way the results of research and development and the benefits arising from the commercial and other utilization of genetic resources with the Contracting Party providing such resources. Such sharing shall be upon mutually agreed terms.[36]

The decision on whether to grant access and on what conditions rests upon the host State.[37] The ABS Protocol confirms these principles[38] and provides further detail in connection with a number of issues, such as 'prior informed consent or approval and involvement of indigenous and local communities',[39] informational requirements (the establishment of national focal points as well as co-operation with an ABS Clearing-House),[40] the rules for the establishment of 'mutually agreed terms'[41] and the monitoring/compliance mechanisms.[42] These provisions could justify the adoption of restrictive domestic regulations on access (e.g., differentiating between national and foreign investors, or among foreign investors, depending on the legal framework established in their home States or simply on whether these latter have ratified the CBD or the ABS Protocol), which, depending on the content of the BITs concluded by the host State,[43] may raise a normative conflict with some investment disciplines, including those on the right of establishment, performance requirements or discrimination.[44] However, domestic law could also go beyond the guidance provided in the CBD and the ABS Protocol and, as a result, would not always be sufficiently based on international law. Moreover, to the extent that each State retains the right to regulate this matter as it deems appropriate, even those

---

[35] CBD, above n. 7, Article 15(1)–(2).   [36] *Ibid.*, Article 15(7).
[37] *Ibid.*, Article 15(1).   [38] ABS Protocol, above n. 7, Articles 4 and 5 (1).
[39] *Ibid.*, Articles 5(1 *bis*), 5(2)(a)–(e), 5 *bis* and 6(b).   [40] *Ibid.*, Articles 10 and 11.
[41] *Ibid.*, Article 5(2)(f).   [42] *Ibid.*, Articles 12–14.
[43] Some BITs simply do not grant a right of establishment whereas others grant a right of establishment in the form of a national treatment clause, but limited to some sectors. See R. Dolzer and C. Scheuer, *Principles of International Investment Law* (Oxford University Press, 2008), pp. 80–2; M. Sornarajah, *The International Law on Foreign Investment* (Cambridge University Press, 2010), pp. 97–116.
[44] See O. Rukundo and J. Cabrera, 'Investment Promotion and Protection in the UNCBD: An Emerging Access and Benefit Sharing Regime', in M.-C. Cordonnier Segger, M. W. Gehring and A. Newcombe (eds), *Sustainable Development in World Investment Law* (Alphen aan den Rijn: Wolters Kluwer, 2010), pp. 721ff.

domestic ABS provisions that can be traced back to the CBD and the ABS Protocol would have to be closely scrutinised to determine whether they are required or fully authorised by international law.

The fourth category of obligations concerns procedural requirements. Procedural rights have already been discussed in Chapter 7, where it was noted that there are both instruments of general applicability and instruments more specifically tailored to one area of environmental regulation. With respect to the protection of biological and cultural diversity, a number of participatory requirements have been introduced, particularly in connection with mining operations that may adversely affect protected areas or species, or the minorities living in such areas.[45] For instance, whereas the World Heritage Convention does not specifically provide for a participation requirement, its Operational Guidelines (2008 version) 'encourage' States parties to the WHC 'to ensure the participation of a wide variety of stakeholders ... in the identification, nomination and protection of World Heritage properties'.[46] Similarly, whereas the listing of a protected wetland under the Ramsar Convention is left for States to decide, the Strategic Plan 2009–15 stresses, as its 'Goal 1' of 'wise use' of wetlands, '[t]o work towards achieving the wise use of all wetlands by ensuring that all Contracting Parties develop, adopt and use the necessary and appropriate instruments and measures, with the participation of the local indigenous and non-indigenous population and making use of traditional knowledge'.[47] The CBD goes a step further and requires the prior informed consent of indigenous peoples for certain activities, as mentioned in the preceding paragraph. Participation requirements have therefore played a significant role in the regulatory approach adopted by the World Heritage Convention, the Ramsar Convention and the CBD, and the impact of such requirements on certain types of investment schemes, particularly mining operations, have been substantial.[48]

---

[45] See C. Redgwell, 'The International Law of Public Participation: Protected Areas, Endangered Species, and Biological Diversity', in D. N. Zillman, A. R. Lucas and G. Pring (eds.), *Human Rights in Natural Resource Development* (Oxford University Press, 2002), pp. 187–214.

[46] Operational Guidelines for the Implementation of the World Heritage Convention (January 2008) ('Operational Guidelines'), para. 12. See also, paras. 64, 123, 211(d) and Annex 3 (Guidelines on the Inscription of Specific Types of Properties on the World Heritage List), para. 15(iii).

[47] The Ramsar Strategic Plan 2009–2015, COP Resolution X.1 ('Strategic Plan 2009–2015'), Goals 1 and 4 (para. 4.1.iii).

[48] See e.g., World Heritage Committee, twenty-fourth session (27 November – 2 December 2000), WHC-2000/CONF.204/21, Decision – 24COM VIII.44–49 – World Heritage and Mining (establishing a working group on this topic), and Annex XV.

8.1.3 The human rights approach

The protection of biological and cultural diversity is also contemplated in a number of instruments dealing directly or indirectly with cultural rights.[49] Aside from a limited number of instruments focusing specifically on the rights of indigenous peoples, most notably the ILO Convention 169 and the UN Indigenous Peoples Declaration, some measure of protection of the relationship between minorities and their ancestral environment is provided by other human rights treaties, including Article 27 of the ICCPR, Article 21 of the ACHR and Articles 21 and 24 of the African Charter. Such protection takes the form of prior informed consent or consultation requirements,[50] the right of peoples to their natural resources and to a safe environment[51] and the entitlement of the members of an indigenous community to their ancestral land, protected by the right to property.[52]

As discussed in the following section, these instruments have been invoked to justify State interference with the activities of foreign investors, giving rise to normative conflicts with both investment disciplines and, more generally, with the right to property. In some cases, the normative conflicts have taken different forms, going from the basic case of a conflict between two obligations each arising from a different instrument, to conflicts between obligations arising from different but related instruments, to the exceptional case of a conflict between two equally accepted interpretations of the same provision (the right of a land owner to its property vs. the entitlement of an indigenous community to the same land).[53]

---

[49] See above n. 12.

[50] See e.g., ILO Convention 169, above n. 12, Article 16(2); UN Indigenous Peoples Declaration, above n. 12, Article 19; ICCPR, above n. 12, Article 27 (as subsequently interpreted by the Human Rights Committee). See G. Triggs, 'The Rights of Indigenous Peoples to Participate in Resource Development: An International Legal Perspective', in Zillman et al., Human Rights in Natural Resource Development, above n. 45, pp. 123–54.

[51] See e.g., African Charter, above n. 12, Articles 21 and 24; Additional Protocol to the American Convention on Human Rights in the area of Economic, Social and Cultural Rights, 17 November 1988, OAS Treaty Series No. 69 ('Protocol of San Salvador'), Article 11.

[52] See e.g., ACHR, above n. 12, Article 21 (as subsequently interpreted by the ICtHR); ILO Convention 169, above n. 12, Article 14.

[53] See P. Nikken, 'Balancing of Human Rights and Investment Law in the Inter-American System of Human Rights' in P.-M. Dupuy, F. Francioni and E. U. Petersmann (eds.), Human Rights in International Investment Law and Arbitration (Oxford University Press, 2009), pp. 261ff.

8.2   Decisions from adjudicatory and quasi-adjudicatory bodies

8.2.1   Overview

As in the preceding chapter, the analysis of the relations between the protection of biological and cultural diversity and investment disciplines must go beyond the case-law of investment tribunals and consider also the decisions of other adjudicatory and quasi-adjudicatory bodies. If one looks at this broader body of decisions, the types of environmental obligations that have attracted particular attention are those regarding the protection of certain areas or species (Section 8.2.2) and those protecting the cultural rights of minorities and indigenous peoples (Section 8.2.3). Some other decisions, whether specifically relating to biological and cultural protection or not, may also be relevant to shed light on how other types of obligations (e.g., consultation obligations and trade restrictions) could lead to normative conflicts (Section 8.2.4).

8.2.2   Protected areas and species

Generally speaking, much of the case-law reviewed in connection with pollution of freshwater resources would also be relevant for the present discussion, to the extent that watercourses are not only resources but also a medium where a myriad species evolve as well as a component of complex ecosystems. In this regard, readers are referred to Section 7.2. Here, the discussion will focus on those cases where measures adopted pursuant to an international obligation to protect biological or cultural diversity interfere with an investment discipline.

An early example of how the protection of cultural heritage may collide with investment schemes is provided by the *SPP* v. *Egypt*[54] case, also known as the 'pyramids case'. A foreign investor planned to build a tourist resort near the pyramids, for which it had received the initial approval of Egypt, most notably through an investment agreement concluded in December 1974 and a series of decrees. As the works went on, however, the project encountered increasing political opposition, which eventually led the Egyptian government to declare, in 1978, that the relevant parcels of land were of public utility and not suitable for tourism development. In response, the investor initiated arbitration proceedings claiming that its property had been expropriated in breach of a domestic investment law and of the investment agreement. The case

---

[54] *Southern Pacific Properties (Middle East) Limited (SPP)* v. *Arab Republic of Egypt*, ICSID Case No. ARB/84/3, Award (20 May 1992) ('*SPP* v. *Egypt*').

is of particular interest for our analysis because an eminent tribunal presided over by Eduardo Jiménez de Aréchaga, a former President of the ICJ, analysed the impact of the World Heritage Convention as a potential justification for the acts of Egypt. Significantly, the tribunal had no difficulty in considering that this Convention governed the acts of Egypt,[55] but the incidence of the obligations arising from the Convention were somewhat diluted by the interpretation retained by the tribunal. Specifically, the tribunal concluded that the effect of Articles 4, 5(d) and 11 was to create an obligation that had become binding not on the date of entry into force of the Convention (i.e., 1975) but only on the date in which the World Heritage Committee accepted the nomination.[56] This interpretation, which links the obligation of protection to the inclusion of the relevant sites into the list maintained by the Committee, has been criticised as excessively restrictive. According to some prominent commentators, States have an obligation to protect natural and cultural heritage irrespective of whether a particular site is listed or not.[57] The debate over this question is important to understand the incidence of a number of environmental treaties on the treatment granted to foreign investors. If the 'institutionalist' approach retained by the tribunal in *SPP* v. *Egypt* is followed, then States parties would not be under an actual obligation to protect unlisted sites, at least not in those environmental regimes where a list system is established. As a result, a State's ability to justify its actions by reference to such environmental regimes would be considerably limited. If, on the contrary, a 'conservationist' approach is followed, then measures adopted to protect biological and cultural diversity could be justified by direct reference to obligations arising from international environmental law. The conservationist approach seems to be more in line with the current development of international environmental law, characterised by the emergence of a number of customary norms such as the prevention principle, the requirement to conduct an environmental impact assessment or the principle of contemporaneity in the application of environmental law.[58] Thus, subject to the

---

[55] *Ibid.*, para. 78.   [56] *Ibid.*, para. 154.
[57] See F. Francioni, and F. Lenzerini, 'The Destruction of the Buddhas of Bamiyan and International Law' (2003) 14 *European Journal of International Law* 619, at 631.
[58] *Legality of the Threat or Use of Nuclear Weapons*, ICJ Reports 1996, 226 ('*Legality of Nuclear Weapons*'), para. 29 (prevention principle); *Dispute Regarding Navigational and Related Rights (Costa Rica* v. *Nicaragua)*, Judgment (13 July 2009), para. 64 (contemporaneity of the application of environmental law); *Pulp Mills in the River Uruguay (Argentina* v. *Uruguay)*, General List No. 135, Judgment (20 April 2010) ('*Pulp Mills* case'), paras. 204 (prior environmental impact assessment) and 66, 194, 197 and 204 (contemporaneity of the application of environmental law).

specific circumstances of the case,[59] the conservationist approach provides a more accurate understanding of the link between international and domestic conservation measures.

The existence of a specific link between the measures adopted by the host State and international environmental law is a recurrent problem in investment cases touching on the protection of biological and cultural diversity. In *CDSE* v. *Costa Rica*,[60] the dispute concerned the amount of compensation that the respondent had to pay for the direct expropriation of a biodiversity-rich land that the investor had acquired to develop a resort. The link between the measures taken by the State (and its implications for the value of the investment) and international environmental law were almost completely neglected. We know from an article written by counsel for Costa Rica that, as part of its argumentation, the respondent had referred to a number of environmental treaties, including the CBD and the Western Hemisphere Convention.[61] The tribunal disposed of this argument without even analysing the contents of these treaties, stating that 'the purpose of protecting the environment for which the Property was taken does not alter the legal character of the taking for which adequate compensation must be paid. The international source of the obligation to protect the environment makes no difference' and adding, in a footnote, that '[f]or this reason, the Tribunal does not analyse the detailed evidence submitted regarding what Respondent refers to as its international legal obligation to preserve the unique ecological site that is the Santa Elena Property'.[62] This assertion is premised on the assumption that (domestic or international) environmental law is irrelevant for the determination of quantum. As discussed in Chapter 5, this assumption is ill-founded. This is suggested, *inter alia*, by the *SPP* v. *Egypt* case, where the tribunal excluded from the amount of compensation the damage corresponding to the period after the emergence of Egypt's obligations under the World Heritage Convention, noting that '[f]rom that date forward, the Claimant's activities on the Pyramids Plateau would have been in conflict with the Convention

---

[59] See *Metalclad Corporation* v. *United Mexican States*, ICSID Case No. ARB(AF)/97/1, Award (25 August 2000) ('*Metalclad* v. *Mexico*'), paras. 109–11.

[60] *Compañía del Desarrollo de Santa Elena SA* v. *Costa Rica*, ICSID Case No. ARB/96/1, Award (17 February 2000) ('*CDSE* v. *Costa Rica*').

[61] See C. Brower and J. Wong, 'General Valuation Principles: The Case of Santa Elena', in T. Weiler (ed.), *International Investment Law and Arbitration: Leading Cases from the ICSID, NAFTA, Bilateral Treaties and Customary International Law* (London: Cameron May, 2005), p. 764.

[62] *CDSE* v. *Costa Rica*, above n. 60, para. 71.

and therefore in violation of international law, and any profits that might have resulted from such activities are consequently noncompensable'.[63]

The link between domestic measures and international environmental obligations has also arisen in other investment disputes. In *Lucchetti* v. *Peru*,[64] the dispute concerned measures adopted by the State in connection with the construction and operation of a pasta factory near a wetland (Pantanos de Villa) protected under the Ramsar Convention. However, the potential normative conflict remained unexplored, as the tribunal concluded that it lacked jurisdiction to examine the merits of the dispute.[65] Still another case in which this link was raised is *Glamis* v. *United States*.[66] The dispute concerned an open-pit gold mining project, which was blocked by US federal and Californian authorities on environmental and human rights grounds. Echoing the arguments advanced in a number of third-party interventions, the respondent referred, *inter alia*, to the World Heritage Convention and its implementation statute.[67] Importantly, the respondent specifically stressed that 'the fact that a site is not included on that list [managed by the World Heritage Committee] shall in no way be construed to mean that it does not have an outstanding universal value'.[68] In its long award, the tribunal rejected the investor's claims, but did not elaborate on the impact of the World Heritage Convention.[69] The case nevertheless provides an additional illustration of the significance of the link between an international environmental obligation and a domestic measure. In this regard, the tribunal in *Parkerings* v. *Lithuania*[70] went a step further, deriving from the protection granted by the World Heritage Convention a decisive reason for rejecting the arguments of the investor. At stake was the question whether the claimant's project had been discriminated

---

[63] *SPP* v. *Egypt*, above n. 54, para. 191.

[64] *Empresa Lucchetti SA and Lucchetti Peru SA* v. *Republic of Peru*, ICSID Case No. ARB/03/4, Award (7 February 2005) ('*Lucchetti* v. *Peru*').

[65] The award denying jurisdiction withstood an annulment challenge. See *Industria Nacional de Alimentos SA and Indalsa Perú SA* v. *Republic of Peru*, ICSID Case No. ARB/03/4, Decision on Annulment (5 September 2007).

[66] *Glamis Gold Ltd* v. *United States of America*, NAFTA (UNCITRAL), Award (16 May 2009) ('*Glamis* v. *United States*').

[67] Respondent's Counter-Memorial, (19 September 2006) 33–5, available at: www.naftaclaims.com (accessed on 4 January 2012).

[68] *Ibid.*, 35.

[69] The tribunal expressly refrained from undertaking the analysis suggested in the *amicus* briefs. See *Glamis* v. *United States*, above n. 66, para. 8.

[70] *Parkerings-Compagniet AS* v. *Republic of Lithuania*, ICSID Case No. ARB/05/08, Award (11 September 2007) ('*Parkerings* v. *Lithuania*').

against as compared with a project of another foreign investor. The respondent argued, *inter alia*, that such was not the case because the different impact of each of these projects on the old town of Vilnius, a site included in the World Heritage List, put the projects in a very different situation. The tribunal accepted this argument and concluded that '[t]he historical and archaeological preservation and environmental protection could be and in this case were a justification for the refusal of the project' and that, as a result, the claimant's project 'was not similar with the MSCP constructed by Pinus Propius [the other investor]'.[71]

Beyond the cases discussed so far, the link between international environmental obligations and domestic measures, and the tension between these latter and investment disciplines, appears to be relevant to other cases, pending at the time of writing, such as the *Pac Rim* v. *El Salvador*[72] (concerning mining operations in Salvadorian jungle) or the two *Unglaube* v. *Costa Rica*[73] cases (in which the investors claim that measures adopted by Costa Rica to protect the endangered baula sea turtles amount to a breach of the applicable BIT). Interestingly, the link between international and domestic environmental law could also be relevant for an investor seeking to ground an investment claim for the damage arising from the absence of compliance by a State with its environmental obligations. This is not a merely theoretical hypothesis, as suggested by the notice of arbitration filed by the Canadian owner of an ecotourism facility located in Barbados for the reduced profitability of its investment caused by the non-compliance by Barbados with its domestic and international obligations arising from the CBD and the Ramsar Convention.[74] Another example of this hypothesis is the notice of arbitration filed by an American mining company, Renco Group Inc., against Peru, in connection with environmental remediation obligations. Under the applicable contract, both the investor and Peru had

---

[71] *Ibid.*, para. 392.

[72] *Pac Rim Cayman LLC* v. *Republic of El Salvador*, ICSID Case No. ARB/09/12, Decision on the Respondent's Preliminary Objections under CAFTA Articles 10.20.4 and 10.20.2 (2 August 2010). The tribunal in another mining case against El Salvador under the CAFTA dismissed the claim for lack of jurisdiction: *Commerce Group Corp and San Sebastian Gold Mines, Inc.* v. *Republic of El Salvador*, Award, ICSID Case No ARB/09/17, Award (14 March 2011).

[73] *Marion Unglaube* v. *Republic of Costa Rica*, ICSID Case No. ARB/08/1; *Reinhard Unglaube* v. *Republic of Costa Rica*, ICSID Case No. ARB/09/20 (both pending).

[74] *Peter A. Allard* v. *Government of Barbados*, Notice of Dispute, (8 September 2009) available at: graemehall.com/legal/papers/BIT-Complaint.pdf (last accessed 21 March 2012). See J. E. Viñuales, 'Foreign Investment and the Environment in International Law: An Ambiguous Relationship' (2009) 80 *British Yearbook of International Law* 244, at 255.

obligations of environmental remediation in the site of La Oroya. The investor claims that failure by Peru to do its share amounts to a breach of the US–Peru Trade Promotion Agreement.[75]

The link betwen international and domestic environmental law could be clarified through the action of the World Heritage Committee or other comparable international bodies. Such bodies could indeed be called to intervene in a variety of ways. One way would be to act as *amici curiae*[76] or even as experts. Such was the case in the (non-investment-related) application for provisional measures brought by Costa Rica against Nicaragua, in a dispute pending before the ICJ. In this case the Secretariat of the Ramsar Convention sent an expert mission to the disputed area and established a report concluding that the dredging works conducted by Nicaragua had resulted in serious damage to the protected wetlands.[77] The Ramsar report seemed to play a significant role in the decision of the Court, which granted Costa Rica the right to send civilian personnel to the area to prevent any irreparable damage to the wetland and expressly instructed Costa Rica to 'consult with the Secretariat of the Ramsar Convention in regard to these actions'.[78] These bodies may also be called to consider a situation where the potential operations of foreign investors are seen as a threat to a protected site.[79] In one case concerning the Jabiluka mining proposal, in Australia, the World Heritage Committee received communications from a number of scientists and civil society groups regarding the threat represented by the mining operations for the Kakadu National Park, a site listed in the World Heritage List. The Committee sent a special mission to the site, which confirmed the existence of 'severe ascertained and potential dangers to the cultural and natural values of Kakadu National Park posed primarily by the proposal for uranium mining and milling at Jabiluka' and recommended that 'the proposal to mine and mill uranium at Jabiluka should not proceed'.[80] At an extraordinary session

---

[75] *Renco Group Inc.* v. *Republic of Peru*, Notice of Intent to Commence Arbitraiton, (29 December 2010), (*Renco v. Peru* – NOI'), paras. 43–4, available at: ita.law.uvic.ca/documents/RencoGroupVPeru_NOI.pdf (last accessed 21 March 2012).

[76] On *amicus* intervention, see Chapter 5.

[77] *Certain activities carried out by Nicaragua in the border area (Costa Rica* v. *Nicaragua)*, Provisional measures (8 March 2011) General List No. 50, paras. 33 and 41 ('*Costa Rica* v. *Nicaragua*').

[78] *Ibid.*, para. 81 and para. 2 of the operative part.

[79] See N. Affolder, 'Mining and the World Heritage Convention: Democratic Legitimacy and Treaty Compliance' (2007) 24 *Pace Environmental Law Review* 35.

[80] Reproduced in World Heritage Committee, third extraordinary session (12 July 1999), WHC-99/CONF.205/5Rev. ('WHC Session 1999'), para. III.4.

convened in July 1999, the Committee examined the possibilty of upgrading the status of the site to the List of World Heritage in Danger but, upon strong opposition from Australia, such listing was not made. In its decision, the Committee stressed that 'it is the clear responsibility of the Australian Government to regulate the activities of a private company, such as Energy Resources of Australia, Inc, in relation to the proposed mining and milling activities at Jabiluka to ensure the protection of the World Heritage values of Kakadu National Park'.[81] It is not for the Committee to examine other constraints on the projects, such as investment disciplines. As it noted in connection with the New World mine project, near the Yellowstone National Park (United States):

[w]hether the State Party should grant a permit to the mining company or not is entirely a domestic decision of the State Party ... there is no wording in the Convention or the Operational Guidelines which could lead to an interference in sovereignty ... [however] even if the State Party did not request action, the Committee still had an independent responsibility to take action based on the information it had gathered.[82]

However, were a State to adopt measures pursuant to a recommendation from an international body such as the World Heritage Committee, the link between such measures and the State's international obligations would be much clearer. This, in turn, could have significant legal consequences, as illustrated by the *SPP* v. *Egypt* case.

8.2.3   Protection of minorities and indigenous peoples

A number of decisions from human rights bodies can also illuminate the relations between international environmental obligations and investment disciplines. As noted in Section 8.1.3, certain human rights treaties provide some measure of protection of the relations between minorities or indigenous peoples and their environment. The most developed case-law in this regard is that of the Inter-American Court of Human Rights ('ICtHR'), although some interesting elements can also be derived from certain decisions of the European Court of Human Rights ('ECtHR'), the UN Human Rights Committee ('HRC'), and the African Commission on Human and Peoples' Rights ('African Commission').

The case-law of the ICtHR is of particular interest because it raises a peculiar type of normative conflict, namely one between two similarly

---

[81] *Ibid.*, para. XI(2)(c).

[82] World Heritage Committee, nineteenth extraordinary session (4–9 December 1995), WHC-96/CONF.203/4, p. 21.

accepted interpretations of the right to property enshrined in Article 21 of the ACHR. To analyse this type of normative conflict, it is first necessary to look at how the ICtHR understands the concept of property protected by the Convention. In its first case raising the protection of property, *Ivcher-Bronstein* v. *Peru*,[83] the ICtHR took a broad view of the concept of property enshrined in Article 21 of the ACHR. According to the ICtHR '[p]roperty may be defined as those material objects that may be appropriated, and also any right that may form part of a person's patrimony; this concept includes all movable and immovable property, corporal and incorporeal elements, and any other intangible object of any value'.[84] Under such a broad definition, a foreign investor's private property rights or its rights under a concession agreement would be covered, at least when the investor is a physical person.[85] Yet, at the same time, the ICtHR has also considered that Article 21 protects the entitlements of indigenous peoples to their ancestral lands.[86] A situation could therefore arise where the protection of the right to property of a foreign investor (either property over the land or concession rights) conflicts with the right to property of indigenous peoples. The ICtHR examined at least three cases where such a conflict was present. In the *Awas Tigni* case, Nicaragua had granted concession rights to a foreign investor the exercise of which encroached on the enjoyment by an indigenous community of its ancestral land. Based on a broad interpretation of Article 21 of the ACHR, the ICtHR concluded that Nicaragua was under an obligation 'to abstain from acts which might lead the agents of the State itself, or third parties acting with its acquiescence or its tolerance, to affect the existence, value, use or enjoyment of the property located in the geographic area where the members of the Awas Tingni Community live and carry out their activities'.[87] Some four years later, in the *Yakye Axa* case,[88] the Court noted that the 'restriction of the right of private individuals to private property might be necessary to attain the collective objective of preserving cultural identities in a democratic and pluralist society', and it even went as far as to add that a

---

[83] *Ivcher-Bronstein* v. *Peru*, ICtHR Series C No. 74 (6 February 2001) ('*Ivcher-Bronstein* v. *Peru*').

[84] *Ibid.*, para. 122.

[85] In the Inter-American system, there is limited scope for claims by legal persons. See Nikken, 'Balancing of Human Rights and Investment Law', above n. 53, 255–9.

[86] *Awas Tingni*, above n. 13, para. 149 and 153.

[87] *Ibid.*, para. 164.

[88] *Indigenous Community Yakye Axa* v. *Paraguay*, ICtHR Series C No. 125 (17 June 2005) ('*Yakye Axa*').

restriction would be 'proportional, if fair compensation is paid to those affected pursuant to Article 21(2) of the Convention'.[89] The conflict between different rights of property was even more clearly stated in the *Sawhoyamaxa* case.[90] Although the Court refused to decide whether communal property prevailed over private property or vice versa,[91] it nevertheless made it clear that '[t]he restitution of traditional lands ... is the reparation measure that best complies with the *restitutio in integrum* principle' and ordered the State to adopt any measures necessary to ensure that the indigenous community could enjoy ownership rights over their ancestral lands.[92]

The approach followed in these cases is important for the analysis of normative conflicts because it suggests that, to comply with Article 21 of the ACHR (or, arguably, also with a similar provision), a State may be required to impose restrictions on the property rights (investment) of a foreign investor. The investor could, as the case may be, bring a claim for breach of an investment discipline before an investment tribunal, but the measure taken by the State would be shielded to some extent by the fact that it was taken pursuant to an international obligation or even a judgment from an international court. In some cases, the investment tribunal seized of the matter may be asked to grant additional compensation for the damage suffered by the investor. However, because of their link with human rights obligations, the measures taken by the host State may be considered by the investment tribunal as not in breach of a BIT or at least, if a small compensation has been paid, as sufficiently compensated. This is problematic because human rights courts tend to be less generous than investment tribunals in assessing the amount of monetary damages that would re-establish a balance between the different interests. The case-law of the ECtHR confirms the latter point. In a number of cases brought by land-owners against Turkey as a result of the reclassification of certain lands as State forests, the ECtHR has considered that 'economic imperatives and even some fundamental rights, such as the right to property, should not be accorded primacy against considerations of environmental protection'.[93]

---

[89] *Ibid.*, para. 148.

[90] *Sawhoyamaxa Indigenous Community v Paraguay*, ICtHR Series C No. 146 (29 March 2006) ('*Sawhoyamaxa* case').

[91] *Ibid.*, para. 136.   [92] *Ibid.*, para. 210.

[93] See *Turgut v. Turkey*, ECtHR Application No. 1411/03, Judgment – Merits (8 July 2008), para. 90 (unofficial translation of the French text).

Although fair compensation must be paid, in practice, this has meant less than the full value of the property.[94]

Conflicts between different forms of the right to property *lato sensu* have been discussed, albeit only indirectly, in some decisions from the HRC and the African Commission. In the context of the ICCPR, the protection of the relationship between a minority (including indigenous peoples[95]) and its community land has been addressed through the lens of Article 27 of the ICCPR.[96] A number of individual complaints have been submitted to the HRC alleging a breach of Article 27 as a result of the conduct of economic activities in communal lands with the approval of the State. In *Ominayak v. Canada*,[97] a group of Lubicon Lake Cree Indians argued that leases granted by the provice of Alberta, Canada, to certain companies for purposes of oil and gas exploration in their communal lands threatened their traditional way of life. Because Canada proposed measures to rectify the situation, the HRC offered almost no analysis of the conflict between minority rights and the rights arising from the leases.[98] More fundamentally, the State did not (and could not, under the text of the ICCPR) refer to a need to respect the leases granted to oil companies as an argument to justify its actions. However, the short individual opinion appended by Nisuke Ando offers

---

[94] *Ibid.*, Judgment – Just Satisfaction (13 October 2009), para. 14. This case has influenced the outcomes of many other related cases. See, most recently, *Sarisoy v. Turkey*, Application No. 19641/05, Judgment (13 September 2011); *Ali Kılıc and others v. Turkey*, Application No. 13178/05 Judgment (13 September 2011); *Erkmen and others v. Turkey*, Application No. 6950/05, Judgment – Merits (16 March 2010), Just Satisfaction (13 September 2011). Another example with an environmental component is *Theodoraki v. Greece*, ECtHR Application No. 9368/06, Judgment (2 December 2010). In this case, two hotel developers claimed that their right to property (Article 1 of Protocol 1 to the ECHR) had been breached by reason of the measures adopted by Greece to protect endangered loggerhead turtles pursuant to the Bern Convention. The ECtHR concluded that the measures amounted indeed to a deprivation of the right to property of the plaintiffs but accorded only €3.7 million as fair compensation, instead of the €47 million requested.

[95] HRC, General Comment No. 23: The rights of minorities (Art. 27), 4 August 1994, CCPR/C/21/Rev.1/Add.5 ('GC 23'), para. 3.2 and 7.

[96] Other provisions of the ICCPR could also be used. For instance, in *Hopu v. France*, the HRC considered that a plan to build a hotel in Tahiti on the traditional burial lands of a minority (which had been expropriated in 1961) would violate the rights to family and privacy (Articles 17(1) and 23(1)) of the ICCPR. This alternative avenue was necessary because France has made a reservation to Article 27 of the ICCPR. See *Francis Hopu and Tepoaitu Bessert v. France*, HRC Communication No. 549/1993 (29 July 1997)('Hopu v. France').

[97] *Bernard Ominayak and the Lubicon Band v. Canada*, HRC Communication No. 167/1984 (26 March 1990)('*Ominayak v. Canada*').

[98] *Ibid.*, para. 33.

some insights on this conflict. Ando stressed that he did not 'oppose the adoption of the Human Rights Committee's views, as they may serve as a warning against the exploitation of natural resources which might cause irreparable damage to the environment of the earth that must be preserved for future generations'. However, in his view 'the right to enjoy one's own culture should not be understood to imply that the Band's traditional way of life must be preserved intact *at all costs*'.[99] This more reserved view of the conflict seems to have prevailed in subsequent decisions. In *Länsman* v. *Finland*,[100] the plaintiffs argued that mining operations conducted with the approval of the State in a mountainous region of cultural value to an indigenous people (the mountain at stake had spiritual value for the community and that was where they conducted their reindeer herding practices) constituted a breach of Article 27 of ICCPR. The HRC rejected the claim considering that the impact of the mining activities was not substantial enough to amount to a denial of the right of the members of the minority to enjoy their own culture,[101] but it noted, in connection with future mining activities, that 'if mining activities in the Angeli area were to be approved on a large scale and significantly expanded by those companies to which exploitation permits have been issued, then this may constitute a violation of the authors' rights under article 27'.[102] The latter paragraph served as the basis for another individual complaint submitted by the same minority this time in connection with permits granted to certain companies to conduct logging activities and the construction of roads.[103] This complaint was also rejected on similar grounds but the HRC noted, again, that 'if logging plans were to be approved on a scale larger than already agreed to for future years in the area in question or if ... the effects of logging already planned were more serious than can be foreseen at present, then it may have to be considered whether it would constitute a violation of ... article 27'.[104] Aware of the mining operations that had been challenged in the preceding complaint, the HRC further noted that 'the State party must bear in mind when taking steps

---

[99] Individual Opinion of Nisuke Ando, *Ominayak* v. *Canada*, above n. 97, Appendix I (emphasis original).

[100] *Ilmari Länsman and others* v. *Finland*, HRC Communication No. 511/1992 (8 November 1995)('*Länsman* v. *Finland*').

[101] *Ibid.*, paras. 9.5 and 9.6.   [102] *Ibid.*, para. 9.8.

[103] *Jouni E. Länsman et al.* v. *Finland*, HRC Communication No. 671/1995 (30 October 1996) ('*Länsman* v. *Finland II*').

[104] *Ibid.*, para. 10.7.

affecting the rights under article 27, that though different activities in themselves may not constitute a violation of this article, such activities, taken together, may erode the rights of Sami people to enjoy their own culture'.[105]

A stronger stance was taken by the African Commission in the *Ogoni* case.[106] At stake were the environmental and health consequences of the oil development activities conducted by a State-owned oil company and a foreign investor, with the approval of Nigeria. The plaintiffs claimed that such practices had led to widespread pollution of their land in violation, *inter alia*, of the collective rights provided in Articles 21 (right to natural resources) and 24 (right to a satisfactory environment) of the African Charter. The Commission concluded that Nigeria had violated both (as well as other) provisions. Among the reasons it gave for its conclusion, the Commission noted that Article 24 'requires a State to take reasonable and other measures to prevent pollution and ecological degradation, to promote conservation, and to secure an ecologically sustainable development and use of natural resources'.[107] It also noted, in connection with Article 21, that '[c]ontrary to its Charter obligations ... the Nigerian Government ha[d] given the green light to private actors, and the oil Companies in particular, to devastatingly affect the well-being of the Ogonis'[108] and that '[b]y any measure of standards, its practice falls short of the minimum conduct expected from governments, and therefore, is in violation of Article 21 of the African Charter'.[109] In the light of such a strong statement, the chances of success of the foreign investor involved in this case in an investment dispute brought against Nigeria for measures adopted pursuant to the decision of the African Commission would likely be very limited.

A similar analysis could be conducted not only in situations where other human rights bodies have taken a strong stance but also where a State has adopted measures pursuant to a number of domestic and

---

[105] *Ibid.*, para. 10.7.

[106] *Social and Economic Rights Action Center and the Center for Economic and Social Rights* v. *Nigeria*, ACHPR Communication 155/96, 15th Activity Report of the Acomm HRP (2001–2002) ('*Ogoni* case'). Some domestic claims have been brought in connection with the Ogoni dispute. See *Wiwa* v. *Royal Dutch Petroleum Co.*, No. CIV.A.96–8386 2003(SDNY 1996); *Kiobel* v. *Royal Dutch Petroleum*, No. 06–4800-cv, 06–4876-cv, 2010 WL 3611392 (2d Cir. 17 September 2010) (currently pending before the US Supreme Court).

[107] *Ibid.*, para. 52. The Commission also read in Article 12 of the ICESCR an unstated obligation requiring States 'to take necessary steps for the improvement of all aspects of environmental and industrial hygiene'.

[108] *Ibid.*, para. 58.   [109] *Ibid.*, para. 58.

international human rights obligations irrespective of any decision from a human rights body. The first hypothesis could arguably be illustrated with the case of oil pollution in Ecuador. The Inter-American Commission on Human Rights ('ICommHR') long warned against the adverse environmental and health consequences of oil exploration and exploitation activities in the Ecuadorian jungle.[110] The reports of the ICommHR in this connection could play a significant role in assessing the merits of the pending *Chevron* v. *Ecuador* case,[111] despite the fact that the claimants formulated their case mainly as a claim for denial of justice.[112] The second hypothesis could be illustrated by reference to a number of disputes arising from land and resource redistribution policies in Southern Africa. In *Funnekotter* v. *Zimbabwe*,[113] a group of Dutch farmers claimed that the State had, *inter alia*, expropriated their lands without paying sufficient compensation. The political context in which the dispute arose, in particular the poor human rights record of the Zimbabwean dictatorship and the forceful character of the appropriation of the land, limits the general relevance of this case for the analysis of other disputes relating to land reform policies. It is, however, noteworthy that Zimbabwe argued that, given the land reform and redistribution context in which the measures challenged had been adopted, it was entitled to pay reduced compensation.[114] The tribunal rejected this

---

[110] See ICommHR, 'Report on the Situation of Human Rights in Ecuador', OEA/ser.L/V/II.96, doc10 rev1 (24 April 1997)('Ecuador Report').

[111] As noted in Chapter 7, the dispute between Chevron and Ecuador has given rise to a number of domestic cases (before both Ecuadorian and United States' courts) and international disputes (two separate claims under the Ecuador–US BIT). Here, we refer to the second (and still pending) arbitration procedure: *Chevron Corporation and Texaco Petroleum Company* v. *Republic of Ecuador*, PCA Case No 2009–23 (UNCITRAL Rules) ('*Chevron* v. *Ecuador II*'), Claimant's Notice of Arbitration ('*Chevron* v. *Ecuador II* – NOA'), available at: www.chevron.com/documents/pdf/EcuadorBITEn.pdf (accessed on 4 January 2012). A comparable hypothesis concerns gold-mining activities in Peru and, more specifically, in the site of La Oroya. A claim for environmental damage has been filed by affected individuals before a US domestic court against an American investor, Renco Group Inc. A claim against Peru has also been lodged with the Inter-American Commission on Human Rights in connection with the same factual situation. The investor has, in turn, filed an investment claim against Peru seeking to limit its exposure. See *Investment Arbitration Reporter*, Vol. 4, No. 7, 20 May 2011, Sections 5–6.

[112] Following the judgment of the Ecuadorian court in the so-called '*Lago Agrio* litigation' condemning Chevron to pay compensation for the environmental damage caused by Texaco, Chevron requested and obtained an order for provisional measures from an investment tribunal. See *Chevron* v. *Ecuador II*, Order for Interim Measures (9 February 2011).

[113] *Bernardus Henricus Funnekotter and others* v. *Republic of Zimbabwe*, ICSID Case No. ARB/05/6, Award (22 April 2009) ('*Funnekotter* v. *Zimbabwe*').

[114] *Ibid.*, paras. 100, 108, 121 and 124.

argument.[115] In *Foresti v. South Africa*,[116] a group of Italian investors challenged a set of black economic empowerment ('BEE') policies adopted by South Africa to eliminate (or reduce) the consequences of the apartheid regime. Given the public ramifications of the dispute, a number of civil society groups sought to intervene, stressing the grounding of BEE policies in international and domestic human rights law.[117] However, the tribunal did not reach the merits of the dispute, as the case was discontinued.[118]

8.2.4   Other environmental obligations

A number of cases have shed light on the incidence of other environmental obligations on investment disciplines. Here I focus on three main areas of tension, namely environmental obligations relating to trade restrictions, access and benefit sharing (ABS) and other participatory rights.

As noted above, some environmental treaties focusing on the protection of biological diversity contain trade-related environmental measures ('TREMs'). I am not aware of any investment case in which such provisions have come into play, but their potential operation can be analysed in the light of some cases dealing with other types of TREMs, such as those contemplated in the Basel Convention on Hazardous Waste[119] or in some bilateral agreements. In *S D. Myers v. Canada*,[120] a US waste disposal company claimed that measures taken by Canada banning the export of waste to the United States (where the investor's

---

[115] Other cases touching on the relationship between land reform policies and investment disciplines include *Mike Campbell (Pvt) Ltd and others v. Republic of Zimbabwe*, SADC (T) Case No. 2/2007, Judgment (28 November 2008), *Guenther Kessl and others v. (Namibian) Ministry of Lands and Resettlement and others*, Namibia High Court (P) A 27/2006, Judgment (6 March 2008). See L.-E. Peterson and R. Garland, 'Bilateral Investment Treaties and Land Reform in Southern Africa', Report prepared for Rights & Democracy (June 2010).

[116] *Piero Foresti, Laura de Carli and others v. Republic of South Africa*, ICSID Case No. ARB(AF)/07/1 ('*Foresti v. South Africa*').

[117] Two petitions were submitted, one from the International Commission of Jurists, a human rights organisation, and another from a group of four non-governmental organisation ('NGOs'), including two focusing on environmental protection. See respectively: www.icj.org/IMG/ICJ_Petition_Foresti_v_RSA_19_Aug2009.pdf and www.interights.org/view-document/index.htm?id=543 (both accessed on 4 January 2012).

[118] *Foresti v. South Africa*, above n. 116, Award (4 August 2010).

[119] Basel Convention on the Control of Transboundary Movements of Hazardous Wastes and Their Disposal, 22 March 1989, 1673 UNTS 57 ('Basel Convention').

[120] *S. D. Myers Inc. v. Canada*, NAFTA (UNCITRAL), Partial Award (13 November 2000) ('*S. D. Myers v. Canada*').

waste treatment plant was located) were in breach of the investment disciplines of Chapter 11 of the NAFTA. To justify these measures Canada invoked, *inter alia*, its obligation under Article 4(5) of the Basel Convention to prohibit the export of hazardous waste to countries that are not a party to the Convention (the United States has signed but not ratified the Convention). In its discussion of the impact of the Basel Convention on the legal position of the parties, the tribunal focused on three elements. First, it analysed the scope of the obligation provided in Article 4(5) of the Basel Convention in the light of Article 11 of the same instrument, which creates an exception to Article 4(5) when a State party has concluded a treaty with a non-party subjecting movements to standards that are not 'less environmentally sound' than those of the Convention. According to the tribunal, this exception applied in the instant case.[121] Second, the tribunal specified the rules that would apply to solve a potential conflict between the Basel Convention and the NAFTA noting, with reference to Annex 104 of the latter, that the NAFTA drafters expressly intended that the Basel Convention would prevail, but only to the extent that Canada had no 'equally effective and reasonably available alternatives' for complying with the Basel Convention.[122] Third, combining the two preceding elements, the tribunal concluded that the obligation arising from Article 4(5) did not apply and that, even if it had applied, Canada had less harmful means than the export ban to comply with the Basel Convention.[123] A similar situation was examined by the tribunal in *Pope & Talbot* v. *Canada*.[124] In this case, the investor claimed that the manner in which Canada had implemented the Softwood Lumber Agreement concluded in 1996 between the United States and Canada (limiting the exports of Canadian softwood lumber to the United States) was in breach of certain investment disciplines of Chapter 11 of the NAFTA. Although the claims were not framed as a normative conflict, this case is interesting because it stresses, again, the importance of the link between an international obligation (an export restriction albeit not for environmental reasons) and the measures adopted pursuant to it. Although the tribunal rejected all the claims except for the one based on administrative

---

[121] *Ibid.*, para. 213.

[122] *Ibid.*, para. 215, referring to the wording of Annex 104 of the NAFTA.

[123] *Ibid.*, paras. 255–6.

[124] *Pope & Talbot* v. *Canada*, NAFTA (UNCITRAL), Interim Award on Merits I (26 June 2000), Interim Award on Merits II (10 April 2001) (respectively '*Pope & Talbot* – Interim Award I' and '*Pope & Talbot* – Interim Award II').

mistreatment (in breach of Article 1105 of the NAFTA), this case suggests that measures going beyond what is specifically required by the international obligation in question could be in breach of an investment discipline if there is no reasonable relationship between the domestic measure and the international obligation.[125]

Regarding the incidence of environmental obligations relating to ABS, although I am not aware of any international decisions examining a normative conflict between such obligations and investment disciplines, some insights can be derived from investment cases dealing with analogous situations. For instance, in *MTD* v. *Chile*[126] inconsistent behaviour on the part of the Chilean authorities was found to be a breach of the fair and equitable treatment standard of the applicable BIT, despite the fact that the investor had been negligent in assessing the zoning requirements relevant for its investment. Whereas the Chilean Foreign Investment Commission ('FIC') had approved the investment plan of the investor, the Minister of Urban Development rejected the application made by MTD for the necessary zoning changes on the grounds that the project fell foul of the urban development policy of the Santiago area.[127] A similar situation could arise in connection with ABS obligations if, for example, the investment authorities of a State were to give the green light to a bioprospecting investment without co-ordinating its decision with the authorities in charge of the administration of the ABS procedure and, particularly, of the prior informed consent mechanism. If one were to follow the reasoning of the tribunal in *MTD* v. *Chile*, such an inconsistent behaviour would potentially amount to a breach of investment disciplines. However, aside from the fact that the tribunal's reasoning on this point is debatable,[128] a highly specialised bioprospecting investor would find it difficult to argue that it was not (and should not be) aware of the rules on prior informed consent.

The latter point leads to a third type of environmental obligation that could potentially encroach on investment disciplines: consultation requirements *lato sensu*. Such requirements will most likely arise from

---

[125] *Pope & Talbot* – Interim Award II, above n. 124, para. 87 (finding a reasonable relationship).

[126] *MTD Equity Sdn Bhd and MTD Chile SA* v. *Republic of Chile*, ICSID Case No. ARB/01/7, Award (25 May 2004) ('*MTD* v. *Chile*').

[127] *Ibid.*, paras. 164–5.

[128] See *MTD Equity Sdn Bhd and MTD Chile SA* v. *Republic of Chile*, ICSID Case No. ARB/01/7, Decision on Annulment (16 February 2007), para. 89.

human rights instruments. As noted in Chapter 7, in *Claude Reyes* v. *Chile*[129] the applicants challenged before the ICtHR the refusal by the Chilean FIC to provide information regarding a deforestation project undertaken by a foreign investor. In the course of the proceedings, the Executive Vice President of the FIC referred to the need to protect the 'legitimate business expectations' of the investor,[130] although Chile did not raise this argument to justify the action of its agency. In all events, the Court concluded that Chile had violated Articles 13 (freedom of speech) and 8 (due process) of the ACHR,[131] suggesting that the protection of foreign investors would not be a sufficient justification for limiting certain human rights enshrined in the ACHR. Participatory rights could also be invoked by foreign investors to buttress their claim for breach of an investment discipline. In *Grand River* v. *United States*,[132] the claimants were, *inter alia*, a group of people belonging to First Nations. They claimed that measures taken by the United States pursuant to a settlement agreement between a number of US States and cigarettes manufacturers were in breach of Article 1105 of the NAFTA. More specifically, they argued that Article 1105 had to be construed in the light of a number of treaty and customary rules on human rights and the rights of indigenous peoples (including a duty of consultation) that protected the traditional commercial activities of such groups.[133] The tribunal was not persuaded by this argument, concluding that the obligation to take into account other rules of international law does not 'provide a license to import into NAFTA legal elements from other treaties, or to allow alteration of an interpretation established through the normal interpretive processes of the Vienna Convention'[134] and that, even if a duty of consultation existed in customary international law, it would not assist an individual investor and would not require a different standard to be applied under Article 1105 of the NAFTA.[135]

8.3   Assessing contemporary practice

As in the previous chapter, the following assessment seeks to distil from the foregoing analysis some general insights on the evolving relationship between international investment law and international

---

[129] *Claude Reyes and others* v. *Chile*, ICtHR Series C No 151 (19 September 2006) ('*Claude Reyes* v. *Chile*').

[130] *Ibid.*, para. 57(21).   [131] *Ibid.*, paras. 103 and 143.

[132] *Grand River Enterprises Six Nations, Ltd, et al.* v. *United States of America*, NAFTA (UNCITRAL), Award (12 January 2011) ('*Grand River* v. *United States*').

[133] *Ibid.*, paras. 66–7 and 190.   [134] *Ibid.*, para. 71.   [135] *Ibid.*, para. 210–16.

environmental law (Section 8.3.1) and on the practical implications of this trend (Section 8.3.2). Much of what has been said in connection with the international regulation of freshwater is also relevant for this chapter. For this reason, the focus will be on the particular features of normative conflicts between investment disciplines and the legal protection of biological and cultural diversity.

8.3.1   Conceptual findings

The starting-point of the discussion is, as before, that normative conflicts in this specific area are still rare, although less infrequent than in the freshwater context. 'Mutual ignorance' or 'disinterest' between these areas of international regulation has been mitigated by the rather direct impact of natural preserves and indigenous peoples' protection on the activities of the tourism and extractive industries. Cases such as *SPP* v. *Egypt*,[136] *CDSE* v. *Costa Rica*,[137] *Glamis* v. *United States*,[138] and, from a different perspective, *Awas Tingni*,[139] *Yakye Axa*,[140] *Sawhoyamaxa*,[141] *Claude Reyes* v. *Chile*[142] or *Kakadu National Park*,[143] are all premised on (and to some extent address) normative conflicts. The context of each of these cases is, of course, different, but they all highlight the increasing importance of international environmental law for the operation of investment schemes affecting biological and/or cultural diversity. The creation of protected areas and the protection of minorities are having a growing impact on investment-related disputes, whether these are seen from the perspective of investment tribunals or from that of adjudicatory or quasi-adjudicatory bodies focusing on human rights (e.g., the ICtHR, the African Commission or the HRC) and environmental law (e.g., the World Heritage Committee).

The increasing importance of biological and cultural protection is also of some interest to understand the implications of the potential idiosyncrasies of certain tribunals. With the exception of cases such as *SPP* v. *Egypt*[144] or *Parkerings* v. *Lithuania*,[145] investment tribunals are reluctant to fully consider the implications of international environmental law for the disputes they are tasked to decide. Such reluctance may take different forms. In *Glamis* v. *United States*, it took the form of a paragraph in the first pages of the award downplaying the relevance of such considerations for deciding the specific dispute submitted to the tribunal:

[136] See above n. 54.   [137] See above n. 60.   [138] See above n. 66.   [139] See above n. 13.
[140] See above n. 88.   [141] See above n. 90.   [142] See above n. 129.
[143] See above n. 80.   [144] See above n. 54   [145] See above n. 70.

The Tribunal is aware that the decision in this proceeding has been awaited by private and public entities concerned with environmental regulation, the interests of indigenous peoples, and the tension sometimes seen between private rights in property and the need of the State to regulate the use of property. These issues were extensively argued in this case and considered by the Tribunal. However, given the Tribunal's holdings, the Tribunal is not required to decide many of the most controversial issues raised in this proceeding.[146]

Reluctance seems to have reached the level of disinterest or even misunderstanding in *CDSE* v. *Costa Rica*, where arguments based on international environmental law were disposed of by the tribunal in little more than a footnote.[147] On the other end of the spectrum, the ICtHR has gone as far as to suggest that States may have to expropriate private land owners to ensure indigenous communities' full enjoyment of their property rights over their ancestral lands.[148] In the same vein, the special mission sent by the World Heritage Committee to assess the situation of the Kakadu National Park, in Australia, assertively recommended that 'the proposal to mine and mill uranium at Jabiluka should not proceed'.[149] In the light of these elements, it would be difficult to conclude that tribunals' idiosyncrasies have no impact on how international environmental law develops.

8.3.2   Some practical problems

The four practical problems arising from the link between international environmental norms and domestic measures that were discussed in Chapter 7 are also relevant for the present discussion. The more developed jurisdictional and quasi-jurisdictional practice relating to the protection of biological and cultural property is useful in this connection, as it provides clearer illustrations of these practical problems as well as of the potential tools to address them. As in the previous chapter, the discussion will be structured as follows: (i) the lack of clarity of the link between international environmental obligations and domestic measures (Section 8.3.2.1); (ii) the invocation of this link in investment proceedings (Section 8.3.2.2); (iii) the vulnerability of the link (Section 8.3.2.3); and (iv) the applicable conflict norms (Section 8.3.2.4).

---

[146] *Glamis* v. *United States*, above n. 66, para. 8.
[147] *CDSE* v. *Costa Rica*, above n. 60, para. 71.
[148] *Sawhoyamaxa* case, above n. 90, para. 210.
[149] WHC Session 1999, above n. 80, para. III.4.

8.3.2.1   The link is unclear

As noted in Chapter 7, when a host State plans to adopt an environmental measure, it would be well advised to clarify the link between such regulation and its international environmental commitments.

Clarifying that the action is taken within the framework of international environmental law would be useful from the perspective of both investors and host States. Investors' expectations as to the environmental regulatory framework in which their activities will evolve would be guided by the international environmental commitments assumed by the host States. Even when such commitments are 'dormant' (i.e., when the relevant treaty formulates broad commitments the effect of which is to permit the adoption (or not) of measures to be chosen by each State), the very existence of such broad permissive commitments sends a signal to investors that potentially more demanding measures may be forthcoming. The investor may then adapt its behaviour, either by abandoning the investment scheme or by structuring it in a way as to reduce its regulatory risk. It may also choose to disregard such risk, as in *MTD* v. *Chile*,[150] where the investor conducted a flawed due diligence assessment neglecting the zoning requirements applicable to its investment. In all events, the existence of prior international commitments will provide an indication, a 'warning', on the evolution of the regulatory framework to which the investment may be subject in the future. As such, it gives investors the opportunity to introduce this element into their calculations and, by the same token, converts what could potentially have been presented as 'political risk' into regular 'commercial risk'. Similarly, spelling out the link between a domestic measure and international environmental law gives host States the advantage of reducing their investment-related litigation risk resulting from the enactment of environmental regulation.

I have already mentioned, in Chapter 7, the steps that can be taken to clarify the link. These include express references to international environmental law in the text of the measure adopted, the conduct of a cost–benefit (proportionality) analysis explicitly taking into account the impact on foreign investors, the establishment of consultation channels to get foreign investors involved and resort to international bodies to clarify the link. This latter instrument is of particular relevance in the area of biodiversity and cultural protection given the availability of a

---

[150] See above n. 126.

number of international adjudicatory and quasi-adjudicatory bodies that could potentially step in. Examples of this hypothesis include the intervention of the World Heritage Committee in the case of the *Kakadu National Park*, the different cases mentioned above decided by the ICtHR in the area of property rights over ancestral lands, some cases decided by HRC where the possibility of more intrusive action by the State was left open,[151] the involvement of the Ramsar Secretariat in the *Costa Rica v. Nicaragua* case (albeit this case is not investment-related)[152] or the potential use of the reports of the ICommHR regarding Ecuador in the context of the pending *Chevron v. Ecuador* investment dispute.[153]

8.3.2.2 Invocation of the link in investment proceedings

The link between domestic measures and a State's international environmental commitments is more frequently mentioned by respondent States in the area of biodiversity and cultural protection than in that of freshwater regulation. Examples include *SPP v. Egypt*, *CDSE v. Costa Rica*, and *Glamis v. United States*.

However, the practical impact of such references is uneven. I have already referred to the reluctance of investment tribunals to fully integrate such arguments in their awards (e.g., *Glamis v. United States*; *CDSE v. Costa Rica*). Even in *SPP v. Egypt*, where the tribunal had no difficulty in concluding that the World Heritage Convention was fully applicable,[154] the 'institutionalist' (as opposed to the 'conservationist') approach eventually retained by the tribunal considerably limited the impact of the obligations set out in the Convention. Yet, practitioners would be ill-advised to derive from these cases the impression that international environmental law has little room to intervene in investment proceedings. As suggested by other portions of the award in *SPP v. Egypt* (section on quantum) as well as by cases such as *Parkerings v. Lithuania*[155] and others that will be discussed in Chapter 9, the operation of international environmental law may have a decisive effect either in limiting compensation or in excluding liability altogether.

8.3.2.3 The vulnerability of the link

Given the broad manner in which international environmental norms are formulated (see Chapter 2), even in those cases where the measure

---

[151] See e.g., *Länsman v. Finland*, above n. 100, para. 9.8; *Länsman v. Finland II*, above n. 103, para. 10.7.

[152] See above n. 77.   [153] See above n. 111.

[154] *SPP v. Egypt*, above n. 54, para. 78.   [155] *Parkerings v. Lithuania*, above n. 70, para. 74.

refers to its international basis and the respondent State includes this point in its pleadings, the link remains vulnerable. As noted in Chapter 7, the vulnerability of the link has been noticed by investors and is often challenged by reference to considerations of proportionality and due process. In the area of biodiversity and cultural protection, additional difficulties arise from the 'executable' character of a given obligation or, more generally, from some ways of 'recycling' international environmental obligations within investment disciplines.

In *SPP* v. *Egypt*, the 'institutionalist' interpretation retained by the tribunal had the effect of depriving Articles 4, 5(d) and 11 of the World Heritage Convention of their 'executable' character until the World Heritage Committee had accepted the nomination of the site by Egypt. In practice, following this approach amounted to breaking the link between the domestic measures challenged and Egypt's international environmental obligations and, as a result, to concluding that Egypt had breached its investment obligations. Whereas the overall outcome appeared justified under the circumstances of the case, it would be problematic to generalise this 'institutionalist' interpretation of list-based environmental treaties. As noted earlier in this chapter, obligations to identify and protect certain sites contained in environmental treaties should be seen as specific applications of the principle of prevention, the requirement to conduct a prior environmental impact assessment and the principle of contemporaneity in the application of environmental law. This is especially so considering that this question may become a relatively common feature of investment disputes touching on biodiversity and cultural protection.[156]

More generally, the implications of the link between domestic measures and international environmental obligations should be carefully balanced in a manner that preserves the *effet utile* of both environmental treaties and investment disciplines. A notorious example of an ill-suited balance is *CDSE* v. *Costa Rica*, where the tribunal reduced the relevance of several environmental treaties invoked by the respondent to the mere satisfaction of the public purpose requirement of the applicable expropriation clause. Stating that this solution is ill-suited does not mean that no compensation was due under the circumstances of the case (a direct expropriation). Quite to the contrary, it is widely acknowledged that, while host States are permitted under international law to expropriate private property, they can only do so under certain conditions, including the payment of an

---

[156] See, e.g., *Lucchetti* v. *Peru*, above n. 64.

appropriate compensation. Under some circumstances, a host State may even be required to expropriate private property in order to comply with an international obligation, as suggested by the ICtHR in the *Sawhoyamaxa* case.[157] The question is rather to what extent international environmental obligations must be taken into account in the determination of the amount of compensation. I have discussed this issue in Chapter 5. Let me add here one additional point, namely the need to pay due attention to the international environmental commitments undertaken prior to the moment when the investment was made. The existence of such prior commitments would, to some extent, justify treating allegedly 'political' risk as 'commercial' risk. This is why it is important to clarify the link between domestic measures and international environmental commitments.

8.3.2.4   The available conflict norms are (still) too general

As discussed in Chapters 6 and 7, the introduction of specific conflict norms applicable to normative conflicts in investment treaties is (still) rare, albeit growing. No significant difference exists, in this regard, between the areas of freshwater and biodiversity/cultural protection. However, biodiversity and cultural protection presents some specific features with respect to the potential operation of general conflict norms. Let me discuss two of these features.

The first question concerns the tension between the 'institutionalist' and the 'conservationist' interpretations of list-based environmental treaties. Although, technically, the moment when an obligation emerges should not be confused with the moment at which it becomes 'executable', in practice, it is unclear when exactly an obligation is deemed to 'exist', as illustrated by the *SPP* v. *Egypt* case. The difference between emergence and executability could raise some difficulties for the use of the *lex posterior* principle, especially when a site has been nominated and introduced in the relevant list after the entry into force of an investment treaty, which would itself come after the entry into force of the list-based environmental treaty. Similarly, the ambiguity between emergence and executability could raise some problems in the context of a strict interpretation[158] of Article 31(3)(c) of the VCLT.[159] It is indeed unclear

---

[157] *Sawhoyamaxa* case, above n. 90, para. 210.

[158] For a restrictive interpretation of this provision see *European Communities – Measures Affecting the Approval and Marketing of Biotech Products*, WT/DS291/R, WT/DS292/R, WT/DS293/R, 29 September 2006, para. 7.74 and 7.75.

[159] Vienna Convention on the Law of Treaties, 23 May 1969, 1155 UNTS 331 ('VCLT').

whether an obligation that is not yet 'executable' can be considered as 'applicable' in the meaning of Article 31(3)(c) of the VCLT. To take an example, had the old town of Vilnius not been a listed site under the World Heritage Convention, it is unclear whether the tribunal in *Parkerings* v. *Lithuania* would have interpreted the MFN clause in the applicable investment treaty in the same manner.

The second, more general, question relates to 'dormant' environmental commitments stemming from early environmental treaties focusing on the protection of flora and fauna (see Section 8.1). When host States adopt domestic environmental measures that fall under the general scope of a 'dormant' environmental commitment but are not specifically linked to it, the impact of such commitments is unclear. If the link has not been invoked or is weak (for the reasons discussed in the previous sub-sections) the potential tension between environmental and investment protection may be framed as a legitimacy conflict rather than as a normative conflict, which, in turn, would change the set of applicable conflict norms from those discussed in Chapter 6 to those analysed in Chapter 11.

9   Foreign investment and the international regulation of dangerous substances and activities

This chapter analyses the incidence of several international instruments regulating dangerous substances and activities on the operations of foreign investors. As with the two preceding chapters, it is structured in three sections. The first section identifies those types of international environmental obligations likely to conflict with investment disciplines. The second section discusses the contribution of the case-law to the understanding of normative conflicts between the aforementioned obligations and investment disciplines. Drawing upon this analysis, the third section identifies some more general insights that appear useful for future reference.

9.1   The regulation of dangerous substances and activities – an analysis of collision points

9.1.1   Overview

The broad foundation of the international regulation of dangerous substances and activities is the principle of prevention, which requires States to adopt measures in order to prevent harm to the environment.[1] At the international level, efforts to implement this principle have led to the adoption of an array of legal instruments. At the global level, following the 1992 Conference on Environment and Development and the detailed action plan adopted at this conference, 'Agenda 21',[2] two

---

[1] Rio Declaration on Environment and Development, 13 June 1992, UN Doc. A/CONF.151/26 ('Rio Declaration'), Principle 2; *Legality of the Threat or Use of Nuclear Weapons*, ICJ Reports 1996, 226 ('*Legality of Nuclear Weapons*'), para. 29.

[2] Report of the United Nations Conference on Environment and Development, A/CONF.151/26/Rev.1 (Vol. 1), Resolution 1, Annex 2: Agenda 21 ('Agenda 21').

main initiatives were launched in connection with the regulation of chemicals. First, pursuant to Chapter 19 of Agenda 21, an Intergovernmental Forum on Chemical Safety (IFCS) was established in 1994[3] in order to foster chemical co-operation among States. Second, in 1995, a number of international organisations, including the OECD, UNEP and FAO, established an Inter-Organisation Programme for the Sound Management of Chemicals (IOMC).[4] More recently, the combined efforts of IFCS and IOMC have led to the adoption of a Strategic Approach to International Chemicals Management (SAICM).[5] Another important development at the global level is the adoption of three major conventions relevant for the regulation of dangerous substances and activities: the 1989 Basel Convention;[6] the 1998 PIC Convention;[7] and the 2001 POP Convention.[8]

In some cases, regulatory efforts have been undertaken at the regional level. The OECD has taken several steps for the identification of chemicals requiring regulation as well as for the mutual recognition of chemical testing data by OECD countries.[9] Also, in the context of the European Union, several texts have been developed in this regard, including the so-called 'Seveso II Directive' (on industrial accidents)[10] and the 'REACH' Regulation (on chemical regulation).[11] A number of treaties relevant to this subject-matter have also been concluded either

[3] See www.who.int/ifcs/page2/en/index.html (accessed on 4 January 2012).

[4] See www.who.int/iomc/en/ (accessed on 4 January 2012).

[5] See www.saicm.org (accessed on 4 January 2012).

[6] Basel Convention on the Control of Transboundary Movements of Hazardous Wastes and their Disposal, of 22 March 1989, 1673 UNTS 57 ('Basel Convention').

[7] Rotterdam Convention on the Prior Informed Consent Procedure for Certain Hazardous Chemicals and Pesticides in International Trade, 10 September 1998, 2244 UNTS 337 ('PIC Convention').

[8] Stockholm Convention on Persistent Organic Pollutants, 22 May 2001, 40 ILM 532 (2001) ('POP Convention').

[9] Decision concerning the Mutual Acceptance of Data in the Assessment of Chemicals, OECD Doc. C(81)30, as amended by OECD Doc. C(97)186; Decision concerning the Adherence of Non-Member Countries to the Council Acts Related to the Mutual Acceptance of Data in the Assessment of Chemicals, OECD Doc. C(97)114.

[10] Council Directive 96/82/EC of 9 December 1996 on the control of major-accident hazards involving dangerous substances, OJ 1997 L 10/14, ('Seveso II').

[11] Regulation (EC) No. 1907/2006 of the European Parliament and of the Council of 18 December 2006 concerning the Registration, Evaluation, Authorisation and Restriction of Chemicals (REACH), establishing a European Chemicals Agency, amending Directive 1999/45/EC and repealing Council Regulation (EEC) No. 793/93 and Commission Regulation (EC) No. 1488/94 as well as Council Directive 76/769/EEC and Commission Directives 91/155/EEC, 93/105/EC and 2000/21/EC, OJ 2007 L 136/3 ('REACH' Regulation).

within a regional co-operation context, e.g., UNECE,[12] or with respect to some specific area, e.g., the provisions on land-based pollution of some regional seas conventions[13] or the regional instruments on the transboundary movement of waste.[14]

In addition to these regulatory layers, several human rights instruments – global and regional – are relevant for the regulation of hazardous substances and activities, as they provide, *inter alia*, for a right to health[15] or a right to a safe environment.[16] And even when no such provision is included, the interpretation of some human rights has been broadened in a way so as to incorporate some environmental components.[17]

The diverse nature of the legal framework created by these and other instruments[18] makes it difficult to identify those specific obligations that could most likely have a bearing on the operations of foreign

---

[12] The United Nations Economic Commission for Europe has been very active in promoting environmental co-operation among its members. Importantly, the treaties concluded within this context are sometimes open to other States. Regarding the regulation of dangerous substances and activities, five treaty systems are particularly noteworthy: Convention on Long-Range Transboundary Air Pollution, 13 November 1979, 1302 UNTS 217 ('LRTAP Convention'), with its eight protocols (including the Protocol on Persistent Organic Pollutants, 24 June 1998, 37 ILM 513 ('Aarhus POP Protocol') and the Protocol on Heavy Metals ('HM Protocol') 24 June 1998: available at: www.unece.org/env/lrtap/ hm_h1.html (accessed 21 March 2012); Convention on Environmental Impact Assessment in a Transboundary Context, 25 February 1991, 1989 UNTS 310 ('Espoo Convention'); Convention on the Transboundary Effects of Industrial Accidents, 17 March 1992, 2105 UNTS 457 ('IA Convention'); Convention on the Protection and Use of Transboundary Watercourses and International Lakes, 18 March 1992, 1936 UNTS 269 ('UNECE Water Convention'); Convention on Access to Information, Public Participation in Decision-making and Access to Justice in Environmental Matters, 25 June 1998, 2161 UNTS 447 ('Aarhus Convention').

[13] See, e.g., Convention for the Protection of the Marine Environment of the North-East Atlantic, 22 September 1992, 2354 UNTS 67 ('OSPAR Convention').

[14] See, e.g., Bamako Convention on the ban on the Import into Africa and the Control of Transboundary Movement and Management of Hazardous Wastes within Africa, 30 January 1991, 30 ILM 773 ('Bamako Convention').

[15] International Covenant on Economic, Social and Cultural Rights, 16 December 1966, 993 UNTS 3 ('ICESCR'), Article 12.

[16] Additional Protocol to the American Convention on Human Rights in the Area of Economic, Social and Cultural Rights, 17 November 1988, OAS Treaty Series No. 69 ('Protocol of San Salvador'), Article 11; African Charter on Human and Peoples' Rights, 27 June 1981, OAU Doc. CAB/LEG/67/3 rev. 5, 21 ILM 58 (1982) ('African Charter'), Article 24.

[17] Convention for the Protection of Human Rights and Fundamental Freedoms, 4 November 1950, 213 UNTS 221 ('ECHR'), Article 8.

[18] See D. Wirth, 'Hazardous Substances and Activities', in D. Bodansky, J. Brunnée and E. Hey (eds.), *The Oxford Handbook of International Environmental Law* (Oxford University Press, 2007), pp. 394–422.

investors. A simpler – and analytically more useful – approach is to focus on the type of obligations that can be derived from these instruments. As in previous chapters, I will distinguish between a 'regulatory approach' (Section 9.1.2) and a 'human rights approach' (Section 9.1.3).

9.1.2   The regulatory approach

From a regulatory perspective, the potentially most important collision points between international environmental law and investment disciplines arise from three main types of obligations. The first two types relate to the movement/trade and production/use/release of dangerous substances, respectively. The third type concerns the prevention of harm to the environment through a variety of safety measures.

The need to regulate movements of chemicals and hazardous waste must be assessed in the light of two important considerations. First, the production of dangerous chemical substances and the treatment of hazardous waste have in many cases been relocated from developed to developing countries, with potentially lower regulatory standards and/ or a lower level of enforcement. Second, the disposal of some types of waste may be very expensive if conducted in accordance with ecologically reasonable standards. In the past, this had the unfortunate consequence that hazardous waste was shipped to countries in the global South, particularly in Africa, where it was disposed of without any treatment or safeguard, at a lower cost. These two considerations help understand the regulatory approach followed by treaties such as the Basel Convention, the Bamako Convention, the PIC Convention or (by analogy) the Biosafety Protocol.[19] Under these instruments, the transboundary movement of hazardous waste, chemicals or living modified organisms, respectively, has been managed through a combination of export/import restrictions and prior informed consent ('PIC') procedures. The objective pursued by these procedures is two-fold: to discourage the generation of waste at the source (by an increase in the cost of treatment)[20] and to ensure that States exposed to dangerous substances are capable of managing them properly.[21] The use of export bans is not infrequent in multilateral environmental agreements. For instance, Article 4(5) of the Basel Convention bans the export of

---

[19] Cartagena Protocol on Biosafety to the Convention on Biological Diversity, 29 January 2000, 39 ILM 1027 (2000) ('Biosafety Protocol').

[20] Basel Convention, above n. 6, Article 4(2)(a) and (d); Bamako Convention, above n. 14, Article 4(3)(c).

[21] Basel Convention, above n. 6, Article 4(2)(e) and (g).

hazardous waste[22] to non-parties (except for cases where the export is governed by a treaty applying similar standards[23]) and even to parties where there is sufficient reason to conclude that the waste will not be treated properly.[24] Between parties, the transboundary movement is subject to a PIC procedure.[25] The Bamako Convention follows a similar, albeit more stringent,[26] approach, banning imports of hazardous waste from developed countries[27] and providing for a PIC procedure for movements among parties.[28] The PIC Convention introduces an institutional PIC procedure applicable to the trade in regulated chemicals (i.e., those included in Annex III to the Convention),[29] as does the Biosafety Protocol with respect to living modified organisms for intentional introduction into the environment of the importing party.[30] The impact of this type of provision on foreign investors may be significant, as the export bans or restrictions can increase the cost or even block the operations of certain businesses, as suggested in a number of investment cases discussed in Section 9.2.

The second type of obligations with a potentially important impact on investment schemes concerns the production/use/release of dangerous substances. The operation of these obligations can be illustrated by reference to three major environmental treaties. A ban on the production and use of certain chemicals (produced either intentionally or unintentionally, as by-products) was introduced by the POP Convention and subsequently expanded to a broader list of chemicals in 2009 and 2011.[31] Pursuant to Article 3(1)(a)(i) of the POP Convention, States parties 'shall ... [p]rohibit and/or take the legal and administrative measures necessary to eliminate [their] production and use of the chemicals listed in Annex A subject to the provisions of that Annex'. The POP Convention also restricts the use (without eliminating it) of certain chemicals, such as the insecticide DDT, listed in Annex B.[32] The use of DDT is only allowed in accordance with the recommendations of the World Health

---

[22] Characterised on the basis of three sets of cross-cutting criteria, provided in Annexes I–III to the Basel Convention.

[23] *Ibid.*, Article 11.   [24] *Ibid.*, Article 4(2)(e).   [25] *Ibid.*, Article 6.

[26] Bamako Convention, above n. 14, Article 4(1).

[27] *Ibid.*, Article 4(1).   [28] *Ibid.*, Article 6.

[29] PIC Convention, above n. 7, Articles 10–11. This treaty does not ban, however, trade with non-parties. *Ibid.*, Article 10(9).

[30] Biosafety Protocol, above n. 19, Articles 7–10 and 12.

[31] See Decisions SC-4/10 to SC-4/18, 8 May 2009, UNEP/POPS/COP.4/38 and Decision SC-5/3, 29 May 2011, UNEP/POPS/COP.5/36.

[32] POP Convention, above n. 8, Article 3(1)(b).

Organization,[33] which considers DDT, despite its toxicity, as the most effective agent to combat malaria in some developing countries.[34] Another important treaty in this regard is the LRTAP Convention and its protocols. Different types of obligations arise from some of these protocols for the reduction and control of transboundary air pollution, including the use of certain technologies,[35] the adoption of quantified emissions-reduction commitments[36] and the periodic review of such obligations.[37] Of particular mention is the Aarhus POP Protocol,[38] which was at stake in one investment dispute brought under the NAFTA. Pursuant to Article 3(1)(a) of this Protocol, each State party undertakes '[t]o eliminate the production and use of the substances listed in annex I in accordance with the implementation requirements specified therein'. Also, pursuant to Article 3(1)(c), the use of certain substances listed in Annex II of the Protocol is restricted as provided in such annex. The third major illustration of the type of obligations under discussion is the Montreal Protocol[39] to the Vienna Convention on the Protection of the Ozone Layer.[40] Articles 2A to 2I introduce a system of time-scaled emissions-reduction commitments for a number of ozone depleting substances, such as chlorofluorocarbons ('CFCs'), halons, hydrochloro-fluorocarbons ('HCFCs') or hydrobromofluorocarbons ('HBFCs'). These provisions replace and expand the initial commitments set out in Article 2(1)–(4) of the protocol.

---

[33] *Ibid.*, Annex B, Part II, para. 2.

[34] See 'WHO gives Indoor Use of DDT a Clean Bill of Health for Controlling Malaria', Press Release, 15 September 2006, available at: www.who.int/mediacentre/news/releases/2006/pr50/en/print.html (accessed on 4 January 2012).

[35] See, e.g., Protocol concerning the Control of Emissions of Nitrogen Oxides or their Transboundary Fluxes, 31 October 1988, 28 ILM 214 ('NOx Protocol'), Article 2(2)(c); Protocol concerning the Control of Emissions of Volatile Organic Compounds or their Transboundary Fluxes, 18 November 1991, 31 ILM 573 ('VOC Protocol'), Article 2(3)(a)(iii) and 2(3)(b); Protocol to the LRTAP Convention on Further Reduction of Sulphur Emissions, 14 June 1994, 33 ILM 1540 ('Sulphur Protocol II'), Article 2(4); HM Protocol, above n. 12, Article 3(2)(a) and (c) and Annex IV.

[36] See, e.g., Protocol on the Reduction of Sulphur Emissions or their Transboundary Fluxes, 8 July 1985, 27 ILM 707 ('Sulphur Protocol I'), Article 2; NOx Protocol, above n. 35, Article 2(1); VOC Protocol, above n. 35, Article 2(2); Sulphur Protocol II, above n. 35, Article 2(2) and Annex II; HM Protocol, above n. 12, Article 3(1) and Annex I.

[37] See, e.g., NOx Protocol, above n. 35, Article 5(1); VOC Protocol, above n. 35, Article 6(1); Sulphur Protocol II, above n. 35, Article 2(8) and 8; HM Protocol, above n. 12, Article 10.

[38] Aarhus POP Protocol, above n. 12.

[39] Montreal Protocol on Substances that Deplete the Ozone Layer, 16 September 1987, 1522 UNTS 29 ('Montreal Protocol')

[40] Vienna Convention for the Protection of the Ozone Layer, 22 March 1985, 1513 UNTS 293.

The third type of obligations of some importance for the operation of investment schemes relates to the prevention of harm to the environment through safety standards. The specific features of these standards are sometimes difficult to pinpoint because such standards are, in many respects, the flip-side of the obligations banning or restricting the pollution of certain protected areas[41] or resources (either as such or as a medium hosting species and ecosystems)[42] or, still, to respect, protect or fulfil certain human rights (see Section 9.1.3). One could refer, for instance, to the general obligation imposed by Article 192 of UNCLOS[43] to protect the marine environment, as further specified in Part XII of UNCLOS and in specific treaties supplementing this general duty.[44] To illustrate this third type of obligations, it is therefore useful to refer to some of its most representative examples, such as the safety standards arising from the IA Convention,[45] the ILO Convention on the Prevention of Major Industrial Accidents ('ILO Convention 174'),[46] the IAEA Convention on Nuclear Safety[47] as well as from a number of regulations and guidelines, including the safety standards/codes issued by the IAEA,[48] the OECD[49] or the ILO.[50] By way of illustration, the IA Convention focuses on 'the prevention of, preparedness for and response to industrial accidents capable of causing transboundary effects'[51] and, as part of its prevention system, States must identify 'hazardous activities' within their jurisdiction[52] for which they have an obligation to 'take

---

[41] See Chapter 8.   [42] See Chapter 7.

[43] United Nations Convention on the Law of the Sea, 10 December 1982, 1833 UNTS 397 ('UNCLOS').

[44] See, e.g., Convention for the Prevention of Marine Pollution by Dumping of Wastes and other Matter, 29 December 1972, as modified by the Protocol of 7 November 1996, 1046 UNTS 120; International Convention for the Prevention of Pollution from Ships, 1973, as modified by the Protocol of 1978 relating thereto, 17 February 1978, UNTS 1340 I-22484.

[45] IA Convention, above n. 12.

[46] International Labour Organisation (ILO), Convention on the Prevention of Major Industrial Accidents (No. 74), 22 June 1993, 1967 UNTS 231.

[47] International Atomic Energy Agency (IAEA), Convention on Nuclear Safety, 17 June 1994, 1963 UNTS 293.

[48] For the list of safety standards published by the IAEA, see www-ns.iaea.org (accessed on 4 January 2012).

[49] See, e.g., OECD, 'Guiding Principles for Chemical Accident Prevention, Preparedness, and Response' (2003).

[50] See, e.g., ILO, 'Prevention of Major Industrial Accidents', Code of Practice (1991).

[51] IA Convention, above n. 12, Article 2(1).

[52] Ibid., Article 4. The term 'hazardous activity' is defined in Article 1(b) and in the 'Guidelines to Facilitate the Identification of Hazardous Activities for the Purposes of the Convention', Decision 2000/3, Annex, Report of the First Meeting, 22 February 2000, ECE/CP.TEIA/2.

appropriate measures for the prevention of industrial accidents, including measures to induce action by operators to reduce the risk of industrial accidents'.[53] Annex IV to the Convention provides examples of the
types of preventive measures that may be adopted by States pursuant to
this obligation. They include the adoption of 'safety measures and safety
standards', the introduction of 'licensing and authorisation systems',
the application of the 'most appropriate technology' standard or the
'establishment of internal managerial structures and practices designed
to implement and maintain safety regulations effectively'.[54] All these
actions may involve some measure of interference with the activities of
foreign investors, with the ensuing potential for normative conflicts
between the IA Convention and investment disciplines.

9.1.3 The human rights approach

From a human rights perspective, States have a positive obligation to
protect individuals from actions of third parties, such as economic
operators, which may encroach on certain human rights. Of particular
relevance, in this context, are the right to health and the right to a safe
environment. However, other human rights, including the right to private and family life and cultural rights,[55] have also been brought to bear.
Moreover, procedural rights may also have an impact on the development of investment schemes, as discussed in previous chapters.

Regarding, first, the right to health, it is enshrined in Article 12 of
the ICESCR,[56] and it has been expansively interpreted in the General
Comment issued by the ESCR Committee to include 'not only [the right]
to timely and appropriate health care but also to the underlying deter-
minants of health, such as access to safe and potable water and adequate
sanitation, an adequate supply of safe food, nutrition and housing,
healthy occupational and environmental conditions, and access to
health-related education and information'.[57] Thus interpreted, this right
could be mobilised in support of governmental measures raising the
standards of protection of a number of environmental parameters.

---

[53] IA Convention, above n. 12, Article 6(1).
[54] Ibid., Annex IV, paras. 2, 3, 6 and 8, respectively.
[55] See, e.g., International Covenant on Civil and Political Rights, 16 December 1966,
999 UNTS 171 ('ICCPR'), Article 27. On the relevance of Article 27, see Section 8.2.3.
[56] ICESCR, above n. 15.
[57] ESCR Committee, General Comment 14: The Right to the Highest Attainable Standard
of Health (Article 12), 11 August 2000, UN Doc. E/c.12/2000/4 ('General Comment 14'),
para. 11.

With respect to the right to a safe environment, it has been expressly stated both in Article 11 of the Protocol of San Salvador and in Article 24 of the African Charter. From an individual's perspective, the two provisions present some enforcement problems. Article 24 of the African Charter grants this right to '[a]ll peoples' (other provisions of the Charter refer to '[e]very individual'), while Article 11 of the Protocol of San Salvador cannot serve as a basis for an individual complaint before the Inter-American Commission or the Court.[58] Yet, the potential of these provisions as international legal grounds for governmental action towards the realisation of a right to a safe environment must not be underestimated. The Protocol of San Salvador expressly refers to the 'obligation to adopt measures' and the 'obligation to enact domestic legislation',[59] and Article 11(2) makes it an obligation ('shall') for States to 'promote the protection, preservation, and improvement of the environment'. As to the African Charter, the right to a safe environment has been specifically addressed in a communication concerning the activities of foreign investors, as discussed in Section 9.2.

Beyond these two specific rights, one may also mention the right to private and family life enshrined in Article 8 of the ECHR.[60] Although the use of this right for purposes of environmental protection has some limitations,[61] the European Court of Human Rights ('ECtHR') has elaborated considerably on the positive obligations entailed by this provision in connection with the activities of third parties, such as economic operators. States are required to take measures in order to ensure that the activities of third parties do not encroach on the right to private and family life of affected individuals.[62] For instance, States are expected to regulate industrial activities causing emissions or other disturbances or to ensure that sufficient information is made available to individuals about the environmental hazards to which they are exposed. Conversely, the protection of the environment may justify certain restrictions to Article 8, particularly those arising from planning policies. More generally, the preservation of the environment may also justify restrictions of the right to property (of economic operators) enshrined in Article 1 of Protocol I to the ECHR.[63]

---

[58] See Protocol of San Salvador, above n. 16, Article 19(6) *a contrario*.

[59] *Ibid.*, Articles 1 and 2, respectively.   [60] ECHR, above n. 17.

[61] *Fadeyeva* v. *Russia*, ECtHR Application No. *55723/00*, Judgment (9 June 2005) (*Fadeyeva* v. *Russia*), para 68.

[62] Council of Europe, 'Manual on Human Rights and the Environment' (2006) ('Manual'), Chapter 2.

[63] Protocol to the Convention for the Protection of Human Rights and Fundamental Freedoms, 20 March 1952, ETS 9. See Manual, above n. 62, Chapter 3.

The brief discussion of the obligations that flow from Article 8 of the ECHR is also relevant with respect to procedural rights. Beyond the procedural requirements that may be read into some human rights provisions, such as the right to water, the right to enjoy one's culture or the right to private and family life, a sophisticated set of procedural rights has been established by the Aarhus Convention.[64] The Convention obliges States to introduce into their domestic systems three clusters of environmental procedural rights, namely rights to access environmental information,[65] rights to participate in the decision-making procedure of certain activities, measures and policies with environmental implications[66] and the right to judicial review of decisions relating to the two preceding clusters.[67] Although these clusters of rights apply to all environmental matters, they seem of particular relevance for the regulation of dangerous substances and activities. States have sometimes been reluctant to encumber, through the implementation of participatory rights, the activities of economic operators. This has, in turn, given rise to a significant number of individual complaints brought before the non-compliance procedure established by the Aarhus Convention.[68]

9.2 Decisions from adjudicatory and quasi-adjudicatory bodies

9.2.1 Overview

The lion's share of the investment-related case-law raising matters of environmental protection concerns the regulation of dangerous substances and activities. This should be of no surprise to either investment or environmental lawyers to the extent that the bulk of environmental regulation as it developed from the the late 1960s onwards was geared towards the control of the unintended consequences of industrial and chemical products and processes. At the same time, most of the regulations and measures taken by States in this connection had no clear link with international obligations relating to dangerous substances and activities. This link has become increasingly discernible with the

---

[64] Aarhus Convention, above n. 12.

[65] Ibid., Articles 4 and 5. Article 2(3) defines the term 'environmental information' broadly.

[66] Ibid., Articles 6, 7 and 8. Two standards are used to identify the activities, measures or policies subject to participatory requirements. See 'The Aarhus Convention: An Implementation Guide', available at: www.unece.org (accessed on 15 March 2012), pp. 94, 115.

[67] Aarhus Convention, above n. 12, Article 9.

[68] Ibid., Article 15 and 'Review of Compliance', Decision I/7, UN Doc. ECE/MP.PP/2/Add.8, 2 April 2004, Addendum, p.1 ('Decision I/7').

emergence of the principle of prevention mentioned in Section 9.1.1. However, the environmental regulations at stake in most of the relevant case-law are still of a predominantly domestic nature or, at least, they only entertain loose relations with the broad principle of prevention or with other international environmental norms.

As a result, before undertaking the analysis of the case law, three caveats must be introduced. First, given the predominantly domestic character of the environmental measures concerned and their relative disconnection with international environmental obligations, normative conflicts are rare as compared with legitimacy conflicts. In this section, I will nevertheless focus on normative conflicts, actual or potential, referring to cases raising legitimacy conflicts only peripherally. These latter will be discussed in detail in Part III. Second, out of the normative conflicts that could be discussed, the focus will be on those arising from the international obligations identified in Section 9.1 as potential collision points. This is because there are many international instruments that have an indirect bearing on the regulation of dangerous substances and activities (e.g., by preventing the pollution of water or by protecting the natural environment), and their incidence on investment schemes has already been discussed in the two preceding chapters. Third, there are a number of decisions of human rights adjudicatory and quasi-adjudicatory bodies that touch upon the object of this chapter in different ways. Although some of these decisions have already been discussed, their relevance to the object of this chapter will be recalled when necessary.

With these caveats in mind, in the following paragraphs I analyse the case-law relating to administrative permits (Section 9.2.2), safety standards (Section 9.2.3), restrictions of movement (Section 9.2.4) and the protection of the rights of individuals and minorities (Section 9.2.5).

9.2.2   Administrative permits

Administrative permits are required by domestic law to build and operate certain types of facilities, such as landfills, waste treatment and/or chemical plants. Although the granting, refusal or withdrawal of such permits are, as a rule, a matter of pure domestic law,[69] international

---

[69] Other cases in which this question has arisen (but without a discussion of the links to international environmental law) include: *Robert Azinian, Kenneth Davitian and Ellen Baca* v. *United Mexican States*, ICSID Case No. ARB(AF)/97/2, Award (1 November 1999) ('*Azinian* v. *Mexico*'); *Metalclad Corporation* v. *United Mexican States*, ICSID Case No. ARB(AF)/

environmental law may have an impact (i) on how the applicable procedure is conducted or (ii) on the reasons why a permit may be refused or
withdrawn.

Concerning questions of process, in *Chemtura* v. *Canada*[70] the investor
claimed that a review procedure of the effects of lindane on human
health and the environment, which eventually led to the suspension
of the investor's authorisation to produce and commercialise lindane-
based pesticides, had been launched for purely trade purposes.
According to the claimant, the absence of any genuine health or environmental motive made this procedure and its consequences a breach of the
NAFTA. The tribunal rejected this argument noting that the launching of
the special review procedure was consistent with Canada's obligations
under Annex II of the Aarhus POP Protocol. According to the tribunal
'the evidence on the record … show[ed] that the Special Review was
undertaken by the PMRA [Canada's environmental agency] in pursuance
of its mandate and as a result of Canada's international obligations'.[71]
Read in context, the reference to Canada's international obligations
(which was further supported by the subsequent inclusion of lindane
as a restricted substance under the POP Convention) had the effect of
excluding any doubts as to the legitimacy of the review process, despite
the trade ramifications of the issue.

Another example of the incidence of international environmental law
on process can be derived from the *Pulp Mills* case brought before the
International Court of Justice ('ICJ').[72] In this case, Argentina contended
that Uruguay had authorised the construction of two large pulp mills on
the shore of the River Uruguay, which marks the border with Argentina,
in breach of both the 1975 Statute of the River Uruguay and a number of
environmental treaties. As part of the background of the dispute, it must
be noted that the scheme authorised by Uruguay was the largest foreign

---

97/1, Award (25 August 2000) ('*Metalclad* v. *Mexico*'); *Técnicas Medioambientales Tecmed
SA* v. *United Mexican States*, ICSID Case No. ARB(AF)/00/2, Award (29 May 2003) ('*Tecmed* v.
Mexico'). A number of pending cases provide, according to the information publicly
available, additional illustrations of claims relating to domestic permits with no explicit
link to international environmental obligations: *Abengoa SA y COFIDES SA* v. *United Mexican
States*, ICSID Case No. ARB(AF)/09/2; *Apotex Inc.* v. *United States of America*, NAFTA (UNCITRAL),
Notice of Arbitration (10 December 2008); *Accession Eastern Europe Capital AB and Mezzanine
Management Sweden AB* v. *Republic of Bulgaria*, ICSID Case No. ARB/11/3 (pending).

[70] *Chemtura Corporation (formerly Crompton Corporation)* v. *Government of Canada*, UNCITRAL,
Award (2 August 2010) ('*Chemtura* v. *Canada*').

[71] *Ibid*, para. 138.

[72] *Pulp Mills in the River Uruguay (Argentina* v. *Uruguay)*, Judgment of 20 April 2010, General
List No. 135 ('*Pulp Mills* case').

investment transaction in the country's history, and that the operation of the mill entailed discharges into the river as well as odours reaching the Argentine town of Gualeguaychú, a popular holiday destination. The Court admitted Argentina's contention to some extent concluding that, in granting the construction permits without following the consultation mechanism laid out in Articles 7 to 12 of the 1975 Statute, Uruguay had breached its procedural obligations. However, the Court rejected Argentina's argument that procedural and substantive obligations were so closely related that the breach of the former automatically entailed the breach of the latter. It reasoned that:

> there is indeed a functional link, in regard to prevention, between the two categories of obligations laid down by the 1975 Statute, but that link does not prevent the States parties from being required to answer for those obligations separately, according to their specific content, and to assume, if necessary, the responsibility resulting from the breach of them, according to the circumstances.[73]

Uruguay could therefore breach its procedural obligations without breaching its substantive environmental obligations. This had important consequences for the determination of the reparation due by Uruguay. The Court considered that, in the absence of a breach of substantive obligations, there was no basis to require the dismantling of the mill or to award compensation to Argentina.[74] But the reasoning of the Court on this point suggests that, had the operation of the pulp mill led to a breach of substantive obligations, the dismantling of the mill might have consti-tuted an appropriate remedy.[75] This, in turn, could have compelled Uruguay to take measures – even short of dismantling the mill – that would encroach on the investment disciplines protecting the owner of the mill, such as adjustments to production processes making the operations less profitable or introducing delays.

The potential normative conflicts arising from EIA requirements can be further illustrated by an individual complaint brought against the Slovak Republic through the non-compliance procedure of the Aarhus Convention.[76] A group of environmental NGOs claimed that Slovakia had breached its obligations under Article 6 of the Aarhus Convention by granting permits for the construction of two nuclear reactors by a

---

[73] *Ibid.*, para. 79.   [74] *Ibid.*, paras. 275–6.   [75] *Ibid.*, para. 275.

[76] *Findings and Recommendations with regard to Communication ACCC/C/2009/41 concerning compliance by Slovakia* (17 December 2010)('*Committee Findings (Slovakia)*') available at www.unece.org/env/pp/pubcom.htm (accessed on 4 January 2012).

consortium led by an Italian investor without allowing for sufficient public participation. The Committee concluded that Slovakia had indeed breached Article 6(4) and 6(10) of the Convention, noting, *inter alia*, that it was 'not sufficient to provide for public participation only at the stage of the EIA [environmental impact assessment] procedure, unless it [was] also part of the permitting procedure'.[77] On this basis, the Committee recommended that Slovakia review its procedures to allow for more public participation.[78] The implementation of such a recommendation could potentially raise normative conflicts between investment disciplines and the international obligations of Slovakia (or other States) under the Aarhus Convention.

Turning now to the second question identified at the beginning of this section, international environmental obligations may also have a bearing on the reasons why a permit is refused or withdrawn. For instance, in *Chemtura* v. *Canada*, the results of the special review undertaken by the Canadian environmental agency led to the conclusion that lindane indeed posed significant health and environmental risks. As a result, the investor's authorisations to produce and commercialise lindane-based products were suspended. In order to justify the withdrawal of the registrations, Canada argued during the proceeding that lindane had been banned or restricted in many countries as well as by a variety of international instruments, most recently the POP Convention. The tribunal took this element into account in reasoning that the concerns shown by Canada were justified. It referred, *inter alia*, to the ban imposed by the European Community on plant protection products containing lindane, to the list of chemicals for priority action under the OSPAR Convention and, more significantly, to the inclusion of lindane in the list of chemicals designated for elimination under the POP Convention.[79]

Another relevant case in this same connection is *Glamis* v. *United States*, where the Californian and federal authorities blocked an open-pit gold mining project on the basis of environmental concerns. The decisions were, however, based on domestic law, and the reference to international obligations concerned the World Heritage Convention[80] rather

---

[77] *Ibid.*, para. 64.   [78] *Ibid.*, para. 70.

[79] *Chemtura* v. *Canada*, above n. 70, para. 135–6.

[80] Convention on the Protection of the World Cultural and National Heritage, 16 November 1972, 1037 UNTS 152 ('World Heritage Convention'). See Respondent's Counter-Memorial, 19 September 2006, 33–5, available at: www.naftaclaims.com (accessed on 4 January 2012). The tribunal did not elaborate on this point.

than the regulatory framework of dangerous substances and activities.[81] This case has been discussed in Chapter 8.

9.2.3   Safety standards

The administrative procedures discussed above are based, to a large extent, on the need to ensure that dangerous substances and activities are subject to safety standards. The connection between domestic standards and the principle of prevention is often unclear or too distant. Even the connection with more specific international environmental instruments, such as treaties or guidelines, may be difficult to establish. For example, in the *Pulp Mills* case, Argentina sought to establish a link between this principle and the need to conduct a prior environmental impact assessment (EIA) meeting international (as opposed to domestic) standards.[82] The Court accepted only the first part of the argument, recognising the existence of a customary requirement to conduct a prior EIA,[83] but adding that the content and standards applicable to EIAs were a matter of domestic (as opposed to international) law.[84] This said, in those cases where a link between international and domestic standards can be shown, measures adopted pursuant to such standards may raise normative conflicts with investment disciplines in at least three ways: (i) by prohibiting the continuation of certain activities (or the use of certain products) that were previously authorised; (ii) by increasing the cost of operations; and (iii) by adding additional layers of protection of consumers. These three potential types of conflicts may overlap to some extent, but each has a distinct meaning, as suggested by the following illustrations.

Regarding the suspension of activities,[85] in *Chemtura* v. *Canada*, one important issue was the impact of evolving safety standards relating to

---

[81] Another potentially relevant case concerns mining in the Salvadorian jungle: *Pac Rim Cayman LLC* v. *Republic of El Salvador*, ICSID Case No. ARB/09/12, Decision on the Respondent's Preliminary Objections under CAFTA, Articles 10.20.4 and 10.20.2 (2 August 2010).

[82] *Pulp Mills* case, above n. 72, para 203.   [83] *Ibid.*, para. 204.   [84] *Ibid.*, para. 205.

[85] Similar conflicts may arise in case of pollution by an investor. In this case, a State (or a group of individuals) may seek compensation for environmental damage. This issue has been discussed in Chapter 5 (environmental counterclaims) and will be further analysed in Chapter 14 (denial of justice). Based on the limited public information, possible examples include *Chevron Corporation and Texaco Petroleum Company* v. *Republic of Ecuador*, PCA Case No 2009–23 (UNCITRAL) ('*Chevron* v. *Ecuador II*'); *Niko Resources (Bangladesh) Ltd* v. *People's Republic of Bangladesh, Bangladesh Petroleum Exploration and Production Company Limited ('Bapex') and Bangladesh Oil Gas and Mineral Corporation ('Petrobangla')*, ICSID Case Nos. ARB/10/11 and ARB/10/18 ('*Niko* v. *Bangladesh*'); *The Renco Group* v. *Republic of Peru*, United States–Peru Trade Promotion Agreement, *Notice of Intent to Commence Arbitration,*

persistent organic pollutants. *In casu* the Canadian environmental agency had taken measures adverse to the interests of the investor on the basis of the application of higher safety standards; these, in turn, were the result of both the special review of lindane and the steps taken at the international level in connection with this substance. The tribunal clearly stated that its task was not to settle the scientific debate on the impact of lindane,[86] but only to determine whether the measures taken by Canada were justified under the circumstances. As part of this assessment, the tribunal took into account the evolving nature of safety standards in three main ways. First, the tribunal noted that the claimant's position as to the health and environmental effects of lindane was itself ambiguous.[87] Indeed during the proceedings the claimant had not argued that lindane was safe, but only that it could still be used for some purposes or that it could have been phased out from the market over a longer period of time. Second, the tribunal clearly noted that 'irrespective of the state of the science ... the Tribunal [could] not ignore the fact that lindane has raised increasingly serious concerns both in other countries and at the international level since the 1970s'.[88] On this premise, the tribunal referred to a number of international instruments restricting the use of lindane. Third, regarding the manner in which the Canadian authority had conducted its scientific inquiry (particularly with respect to occupational risk assessment), the tribunal noted that 'as a sophisticated registrant experienced in a highly-regulated industry, the Claimant could not reasonably ignore the PMRA's practices and the importance of the evaluation of exposure risks within such practices'.[89] This statement must be understood in the light of the claimant's contention that the Canadian authority had applied an unnecessarily demanding standard to assess the occupational risk presented by the claimant's lindane-based products. This contention was rejected by the tribunal on the grounds that the risk factor applied by the Canadian authority was within scientifically acceptable bounds.[90] Based on these reasons, the tribunal dismissed the claim for breach of Article 1105 of the NAFTA. For present purposes, this case illustrates how safety standards may encroach on investment disciplines and,

29 December 2010, ('*Renco v. Peru*') available at: ita.law.unw.ca/documents/Rencogro VPeru_NOI.pdf (pending).

[86] *Chemtura* v. *Canada*, above n. 70, para. 134.   [87] *Ibid.*, para. 133.

[88] *Ibid.*, para. 135.   [89] *Ibid.*, para. 149.   [90] *Ibid.*, para. 154.

more significantly, how the international support enjoyed by such standards may have an impact on the way in which (loosely framed) normative conflicts may be solved.[91]

Even when the introduction of a new safety standard does not put an end to certain industrial activities, it may nevertheless hamper their operation and/or make it more costly. Such was one of the components of the claim in *Vattenfall* v. *Germany*,[92] as noted in Chapter 7 and further discussed in Chapter 10. The State-owned Swedish energy company Vattenfall brought an investment claim against Germany in connection with delays and conditions imposed by a German territorial subdivision for the issuance of permits to operate a coal-fired power plant. These additional conditions related to safety standards applicable to the protection of the River Elbe as well as to the need to reduce emissions of greenhouse gases from the plant, through the construction of a carbon capture and storage ('CCS') plant. The legal basis for such standards remained unclear because the dispute was settled before the filing of a brief articulating Germany's legal position. However, according to reports, such standards were, at least in part, grounded in European environmental law.[93] Thus, some measure of conflict between an international environmental obligation (arising from European law) and investment protection disciplines (arising from the Energy Charter Treaty[94]) could have arisen in this case, comparable to conflicts between other obligations of European law (e.g., those regarding State aid) and investment disciplines.[95] The reasoning of the tribunal in *Chemtura* v. *Canada* may also be relevant for solving this type of conflicts to the extent that investors in highly regulated industries cannot ignore that regulatory changes are part of their commercial risk.

---

[91] Another potentially relevant case, presenting a factual configuration similar to the one in *Chemtura* v. *Canada* (it concerns a ban on the registration of products based on active ingredient 2,4-D), was eventually discontinued following a setttlement. See *Dow Agrosciences LLC* v. *Government of Canada*, NAFTA (UNCITRAL).

[92] *Vattenfall AB, Vattenfal Europe AG, Vattenfall Europe Generation AG* v. *Federal Republic of Germany*, ICSID Case No. ARB/09/6, Award (11 March 2011)('*Vattenfall* v. *Germany*'). See S. Knauer, 'Power Plant's Battle goes to International Arbitration', 15 July 2009, available at: www.spiegel.de (accessed on 4 January 2012); *Vattenfall* v. *Germany*, Request for Arbitration, 30 March 2009 ('*Vattenfall* – RoA'), available at: ita.law.uvic.ca/documents/VattenfallRequestforArbitration.pdf (accessed on 4 January 2012).

[93] The German deputy minister for the environment reportedly complained about Germany's being 'pilloried just for implementing German and EU laws', quoted in Knauer 'Power Plants Battle goes to International Arbitration' above n. 92.

[94] Energy Charter Treaty, 17 December 1994, 2080 UNTS 95.

[95] This issue is further discussed in Chapter 10 in connection with climate change policies.

With respect to the introduction by States of additional layers of consumer protection, such as labelling requirements, the question has been mainly discussed in the context of trade disciplines,[96] but it has also arisen in some recent investment disputes. In *Phillip Morris v. Uruguay*,[97] the investor claims that a domestic legislation imposing additional labelling requirements for the commercialisation of cigarettes constitutes a violation of the Switzerland–Uruguay BIT. Given the well established risks of smoking, Uruguay could resort to many public health arguments to seek to justify its measure, including international health standards relating to smoking. A similar situation could arise in connection with the commercialisation of genetically modified organisms ('GMOs'). Under the Biosafety Protocol, States are entitled to adopt certain measures, such as the labelling of GMOs, to provide additional protection to their consumers.[98] Such measures may, however, collide with investment disciplines, as they have – according to a WTO panel – done with trade disciplines.[99]

9.2.4   Restriction of movement

As noted in Section 9.1.2, restrictions on the transboundary movement of chemicals or hazardous waste are a regular feature of environmental treaties such as the PIC Convention, the Basel Convention or the Bamako Convention. Such environmental restrictions have most often been analysed from the perspective of international trade.[100] In the *EC – Biotech* case, a WTO panel concluded that measures banning the approval and commercialisation of biotech products adopted by the European Community as well as by some European countries on health and environmental grounds were in breach, *inter alia*, of certain provisions of the Agreement on Sanitary and Phytosanitary Measures ('SPS Agreement').[101] The respondents referred to the Convention on Biological Diversity ('CBD')

---

[96] See, e.g., A. Appleton (ed.), *Environmental Labelling Programmes: Trade Law Implications* (London: Kluwer International, 1997).

[97] *FTR Holding SA (Switzerland), Philip Morris Products SA (Switzerland) and Abal Hermanos SA (Uruguay) v. Oriental Republic of Uruguay*, ICSID Case No. ARB/10/7 (pending)('*Phillip Morris v. Uruguay*').

[98] Biosafety Protocol, above n. 19, Annexes A, letter (l), and B, letter (k).

[99] See *European Communities – Measures Affecting the Approval and Marketing of Biotech Products*, Reports of the Panel WT/DS291/R, WT/DS292/R, WT/DS293/R (29 September 2006) ('*EC – Biotech*').

[100] On the issue of trade-related environmental measures or 'TREMs', see WTO/CTE, Matrix on Trade Measures pursuant to Selected Multilateral Environmental Agreement, 14 March 2007, WT/CTE/W/160/Rev.4, TN/TE/S/5/Rev.2 ('CTE MEA Matrix'), Section II.

[101] *EC – Biotech*, above n. 99, para. 3.2(a).

and its Biosafety Protocol as relevant international obligations to be taken into account in the interpretation of the SPS Agreement, pursuant to Article 31(3)(c) of the Vienna Convention on the Law of Treaties.[102] The panel rejected this argument on the basis of a restrictive interpretation of the wording of Article 31(3)(c). Specifically, the panel considered that such instruments could only be taken into account if all WTO members have also ratified them. As neither the CBD nor the Biosafety Protocol had been ratified by the United States, these instruments were not 'applicable in the relations between the parties'.[103]

However, such focus on trade must not lead us to overlook the fact that restrictions on the movement of chemicals or hazardous waste may also have an impact on the operations of foreign investors, particularly when cross-border movements are an important feature of the investor's business model.[104] Such was the case in S. D. Myers v. Canada.[105] The investor was a provider of waste treatment services (PCB remediation). It had incorporated an entity in Canada, Myers Canada, but its waste treatment facility was located on US soil. As a result, the cross-border movements of waste were a critical component of the investor's operations. Canada had signed and ratified the Basel Convention, under which shipments of waste to States that are not parties to the Convention are, in principle, prohibited (Article 4(5)).[106] The United States had signed but not ratified this Convention; thus, in principle, it fell under the scope of the prohibition in Article 4(5) of the Convention. Yet, the relations between Canada and the United States regarding waste movements were also governed by a Transboundary Agreement concluded in 1986. This is the broad context in which the measures challenged by the investor intervened. In November 1995, a ministerial order prohibited cross-border shipments of PCB. This order was in force for a period of eighteen months (from November 1995 to February 1997). The investor

---

[102] *Ibid.*, paras. 7.53–7.55.   [103] *Ibid.*, paras. 7.74–7.75.

[104] Other investment disputes concerning (non-environmental) trade restrictions include: *Pope & Talbot* v. *Government of Canada*, NAFTA (UNCITRAL), Interim Award on Merits I (26 June 2000), Interim Award on Merits II (10 April 2001) (case concerning restrictions on the export of softwood lumber); *Merrill & Ring Forestry LP* v. *Government of Canada*, NAFTA (UNCITRAL), Award (31 March 2010) (case concerning restrictions on the export of logs); *Canadian Cattlemen for Fair Trade* v. *United States* of America, NAFTA (UNCITRAL), Award on Jurisdiction (28 January 2008) (case concerning a US ban on Canadian exports of cattle after the discovery of bovine spongiform encephalopathy in a cow in Alberta).

[105] *S. D. Myers Inc.* v. *Government of Canada*, NAFTA (UNCITRAL), Partial Award (13 November 2000) ('*S. D. Myers* v. *Canada*').

[106] Basel Convention, above n. 6, Article 4(5).

complained that this measure amounted to a breach of several investment disciplines of Chapter 11 of the NAFTA. Canada argued, *inter alia*,
that the order was consistent with its obligations under the Basel
Convention not to export hazardous waste to States that were not a
party to this Convention.[107] It further argued that such international
obligations prevailed over its obligations under the NAFTA to the extent
that there was any inconsistency.[108] Thus, Canada's defence clearly
framed the question as a normative conflict. However, the tribunal
rejected Canada's arguments for three main reasons. First, the tribunal
considered that Canada was not under an international obligation to
ban exports of PCB because Article 11 of the Basel Convention introduces
an exception to the prohibition in Article 4(5) where the parties
concerned have concluded a bilateral agreement that applies environmental standards equivalent to those of the Convention.[109] Second, the
provision of the NAFTA stating that the Basel Convention prevails over
the NAFTA (Article 104 and the corresponding Annex) was technically
not applicable because the United States was not a party to the
Basel Convention.[110] Third, even if such provision were to apply, the
measure adopted by Canada could still breach the investment disciplines provided in the NAFTA, because Canada was required to choose the
measure that was 'the least inconsistent with the other provisions of
[the NAFTA]'.[111]

Restrictions on the movement of dangerous substances may also arise
in other circumstances, as illustrated by the *MOX Plant* case.[112] The case
concerned the operation permit granted by the UK to a plutonium
recycling plant located in Sellafield, on the coast of the Irish Sea. Ireland
claimed, *inter alia*, that the operation of the plant was inconsistent with
the UK's obligations under the UNCLOS[113] to protect and preserve the
marine environment and requested provisional measures. One of the
issues raised by Ireland was the risk posed by the marine transport of

---

[107] *S. D. Myers* v. *Canada*, above n. 105, para. 153.
[108] *Ibid.*, para. 150.   [109] *Ibid.*, para. 213.   [110] *Ibid.*, para. 214.
[111] *Ibid.*, para. 215 referring to Annex 104 of the NAFTA (the text quoted here is that of
Article 104 of the NAFTA).
[112] The MOX Plant affair gave rise to proceedings before the International Tribunal for
the Law of the Sea (ITLOS), an arbitral tribunal constituted in accordance with
Annex VII of UNCLOS, an arbitration tribunal constituted pursuant to the OSPAR
Convention and the European Court of Justice. Here, we focus on the first proceeding:
The Mox Plant Case (Ireland v. *United Kingdom)*(Provisional Measures) ITLOS Case No. 10,
Order (3 December 2001) ('*MOX Plant – ITLOS*').
[113] See above n. 43.

radioactive material to or from the Sellafield plant. According to Ireland, the UK had failed to 'assess the potential effects on the marine environment of the Irish Sea of international movements of radioactive materials to be transported to and from the MOX plant' in breach of Article 206 of UNCLOS.[114] Overall, the tribunal rejected Ireland's request but ordered the two States to co-operate 'in order to ... monitor risks or the effects of the operation of the MOX Plant for the Irish Sea ... [and to] devise, as appropriate, measures to prevent pollution of the marine environment which might result from the operation of the MOX Plant'.[115] Significantly, however, the tribunal placed on the record the UK's undertaking that 'there [would] be no additional marine transports of radioactive material either to or from Sellafield as a result of the commissioning of the MOX plant'.[116] In this context, if the operator of the plant[117] needed to proceed to additional movements of radioactive material (an activity that would seem to be precluded by the UK's unilateral act[118]) a potential conflict could arise with investment disciplines. Of course, such a conflict is merely theoretical, but it helps illustrate a more specific type of normative conflict arising between an investment discipline and an environmental obligation stemming from a unilateral act.

9.2.5   Protection of the rights of individuals and minorities

The rights of individuals and minorities have been invoked in a variety of contexts in connection with the effects of investment schemes. In a number of cases, individuals and NGOs have used the procedures available to bring claims or complaints before certain adjudicatory and quasi-adjudicatory bodies for breach of their human rights. Although technically these are not investment cases, they are relevant for present purposes because the underlying question in most cases is the relation between, on the one hand, the international protection of the rights of

---

[114] *MOX Plant – ITLOS*, above n. 112, para. 26(4)(c).

[115] *Ibid.*, para. 89.   [116] *Ibid.*, paras. 78–80.

[117] In this particular case, the operator of the plant was the British government, but the situation could arise in factual circumstances where the operator is a foreign investor.

[118] See *Legal Status of Eastern Greenland (Norway/Denmark)*, PCIJ Series A/B, No. 53 (5 April 1933) 69–73; *Nuclear Tests (Australia v. France)*, Judgment, ICJ Reports 1974, 253, paras. 43–6; *Nuclear Tests (New Zealand v. France)*, Judgment, ICJ Reports 1974, 457, paras. 45–9; *Armed Activities on the Territory of the Congo (New Application: 2002) (Democratic Republic of the Congo v. Rwanda)*, Jurisdiction and Admissibility, Judgment, ICJ Reports 2006, 6, paras. 46–9; *Sovereignty over Pedra Branca/Pulau Batu Puteh, Middle Rocks and South Ledge (Malaysia/Singapore)*, Judgment, ICJ Reports 2008, 12, para. 229.

these individuals and minorities and, on the other hand, the operations of economic actors. The following paragraphs discuss *tour à tour* the case-law developed in the European, American and African human rights treaty systems.

Regarding, first, the case-law of the ECtHR, the main question facing the Court in this context is whether the relevant authorities have remained within the broad bounds of their margin of appreciation in striking a balance among the different interests involved. Such margin of appreciation, which will be further discussed in Chapter 15, can operate to limit the scope of Article 8 of the ECHR (thereby extending the room for manoeuvre granted by a State to economic operators) or, conversely, to introduce limitations to the property rights of economic operators (thereby extending the scope for environmental protection required by Article 8). However, the ECtHR does not frame these issues as normative conflicts but, rather, as the interpretation of the scope of one specific provision (e.g., Article 8) in the light of the margin of appreciation of States.

In several cases the Court reached the conclusion that the respondent State had overstepped its powers (in breach of Article 8) by failing to regulate harmful activities conducted by economic operators. For instance, in *Lopez Ostra v. Spain*,[119] the Court took the view that, by allowing an illegal waste-treatment plant to cause nuisance and health problems to local residents, Spain had failed to strike a fair balance between the interests of the affected individuals and the interest of the community to have the waste (from the operation of tanneries) treated.[120] Similarly, in *Guerra v. Italy*[121] the Court considered that Italy's failure to ensure that local residents received sufficient information on the risks presented by the operation of a chemical plant amounted to a breach of Article 8 of the ECHR.[122] More recently, in cases such as *Taskin v. Turkey*[123] or *Tătar v. Romania*,[124] the ECtHR has further clarified the obligations of

---

[119] *Lopez-Ostra v. Spain*, ECtHR Application no. 16798/90, Judgment (9 December 1994)('*Lopez Ostra v. Spain*').

[120] *Ibid.*, paras. 51–8.

[121] *Guerra and Others v. Italy*, ECtHR Application No. 14967/89, Judgment (19 February 1998) ('*Guerra v. Italy*').

[122] *Ibid.*, paras. 56–60.

[123] *Taskin and others v. Turkey*, ECtHR Application No. 46117/99, Judgment (10 November 2004, Final 30 March 2005)('*Taskin v. Turkey*'). *In casu*, a permit to operate a gold mine was found to be in breach of Article 8 of the ECHR because the government authorised the continuation of the activities despite the injunctions issued by domestic courts, *ibid.*, paras. 111–26.

[124] *Tătar v. Romania*, ECtHR Application No. 67021/01, Judgment (27 January 2009, Final 6 July 2009)('*Tătar v. Romania*'). This case also concerned permits to operate a gold mine

States arising from Article 8 of the ECHR in connection with potentially harmful activities conducted by third parties. States have a 'positive obligation ... to take reasonable and appropriate measures to secure the applicant's rights under paragraph 1 of Article 8'.[125] Thus, States are not only required to abstain from interfering with the right provided in Article 8 of the ECHR, but they must also take positive measures to ensure the respect of such right by third parties.[126] In these and other cases,[127] one important element influencing the conclusions reached by the ECtHR was the existence of some form of legal irregularity (operation without licence, lack of transparency, contradictions between judicial and administrative authorities, absence of an EIA) at the domestic level. In cases where no such irregularities were present[128] or where there was no clear link between them and the interference with the right of the applicant,[129] the Court has rejected the claim for breach of Article 8 of the ECHR. By deciding whether the State has remained within the bounds of its margin of appreciation or not, the Court has therefore been led to strike a balance between environmental and economic interests, a balance which is also relevant to assess the relations between the different provisions protecting these interests. Such a balance could also be struck from another (in many respects similar) perspective, namely through the assessment of the proportionality of an environmental measure interfering with the right to property.[130] This hypothesis could be framed as a normative conflict when a State invokes an international norm that expressly authorises the adoption of measures for environmental purposes (e.g., the second paragraph of Article 1 of Protocol No. 1 to the ECHR) interpreting it in the light of obligations such as those arising under Article 8 of the ECHR. I have not found cases where the ECtHR specifically addressed this situation. However, to the extent that the Court has viewed

---

near the applicants' residence. The Court concluded that Romania's inaction (its failure to evaluate the environmental impact of the gold mining operations and to provide adequate information to the affected individuals) amounted to a breach of Article 8 of the ECHR, *ibid.*, paras. 112, 122 and 124.

[125] *Taskin v. Turkey*, above n. 123, para. 113.   [126] *Tătar v. Romania*, above n. 124, para. 87.

[127] See, e.g., *Fadeyeva v. Russia*, above n. 61, para. 86.

[128] *Hatton et al. v. United Kingdom*, ECtHR Application No. 36022/97, Judgment (8 July 2003) ('*Hatton v. UK*'), paras. 119–29.

[129] *Ivan Atanasov v. Bulgaria*, ECtHR Application No. 12853/03, Judgment (12 December 2010) ('*Atanasov v. Bulgaria*'), paras. 77–9.

[130] See, e.g., *Pine Valley Developments Ltd and others v. Ireland*, ECtHR Application No. 12742/87, Judgment (29 November 1991)('*Pine Valley v. Ireland*'), paras. 55–60; *Fredin v. Sweden*, ECtHR Application No. 12033/86, Judgment (18 February 1991)('*Fredin v. Sweden*'), paras. 41–56.

purely domestic considerations as sufficient to justify restrictions on the right to property,[131] one would expect, *a fortiori*, that restrictions based on Article 8 would not violate Article 1 of Protocol No. 1 to the ECHR.

A similar issue has arisen in the context of the American treaty system. As discussed in Chapter 8, the protection of the right to property of a foreign investor (land property or concession rights) under Article 21 of the American Convention on Human Rights ('ACHR')[132] could conflict with the protection of the entitlement of indigenous peoples to their communal land under the same provision. The ICtHR addressed aspects of this question in at least three cases.[133] Although these cases have a different focus, they are relevant to some extent because the protection of communal property involves some measure of protection against polluting activities. The most interesting contribution of this case-law for present purposes were the ICtHR's statements that 'restriction of the right of private individuals to private property might be necessary to attain the collective objective of preserving cultural identities in a democratic and pluralist society' and that it would be 'proportional, if fair compensation is paid to those affected pursuant to Article 21(2) of the Convention'.[134]

In the African context, the African Commission addressed the environmental and health consequences of the activities of foreign investors in the oil sector in the *Ogoni* case.[135] The oil exploration activities conducted jointly by a foreign investor and a national oil company with the support of Nigeria had resulted in widespread pollution of the land and water bodies, in violation, *inter alia*, of the right to a satisfactory environment provided in Article 24 of the African Charter. The Commission considered (in the same line as the ECtHR) that States have an obligation to take positive measures to ensure that the rights of individuals are protected against the activities of third parties. However, the broader environmental scope of Article 24 of the African Charter

---

[131] *Pine Valley* v. *Ireland*, above n. 130, paras. 57 and 59; *Fredin* v. *Sweden*, above n. 130, para. 48.

[132] American Convention on Human Rights, 22 November 1969, 1144 UNTS 123.

[133] *Mayagna (Sumo) Awas Tingni Community* v. *Nicaragua*, ICtHR Series C No. 79 (31 August 2001) ('*Awas Tingni*'); *Indigenous Community Yakye Axa* v. *Paraguay*, ICtHR Series C No. 125 (17 June 2005) ('*Yakye Axa*'); *Sawhoyamaxa Indigenous Community* v. *Paraguay*, ICtHR Series C No. 146 (29 March 2006) ('*Sawhoyamaxa* case').

[134] *Yakye Axa*, above n. 133, para. 148.

[135] *Social and Economic Rights Action Center and the Center for Economic and Social Rights* v. *Nigeria*, ACHPR Communication 155/96, 15th Activity Report of the Acomm HRP (2001–2002) ('*Ogoni* case').

allowed the Commission to go further than the case-law of the ECtHR and conclude that Article 24 'requir[ed] a State to take reasonable and other measures to prevent pollution and ecological degradation, to promote conservation, and to secure an ecologically sustainable development and use of natural resources'.[136]

9.3 Assessing contemporary practice

As in previous chapters, this section generalises a number of insights arising from the foregoing analysis. Overall, much of what has been said in the context of freshwater and biodiversity/cultural protection is relevant for the present discussion. Thus, as in Chapter 8, I will focus on the specific features of the international regulation of dangerous substances and activities from a conceptual (Section 9.3.1) and a practical perspective (Section 9.3.2).

9.3.1   Conceptual findings

As in the other areas of international environmental law discussed, normative conflicts between investment disciplines and the regulation of dangerous substances and activities are still rare. Such conflicts are, however, relatively more likely to arise in the future, as suggested by the growing number of cases and, more importantly, by the specific characteristics of this area of international environmental law.

Regarding the growing case-law relating to this area of conflict, in addition to the cases discussed in Chapters 7 and 8 relating to the health threats posed by extractive industries, several investment (and investment-related) disputes touch upon the international regulation of dangerous substances and activities. Prominent examples include: investor–State disputes such as *S. D. Myers* v. *Canada*[137] or *Chemtura* v. *Canada*,[138] human rights cases such as *Lopez Ostra* v. *Spain*,[139] *Guerra* v. *Italy*,[140] *Taskin* v. *Turkey*,[141] *Tătar* v. *Romania*[142] or the *Ogoni* case;[143] cases brought before non-compliance procedures such as the one concerning the operations of Enel in Slovakia;[144] and inter-State cases such as the *MOX Plant* case[145] and the *Pulp Mills* case.[146] This case-law is interesting because it illustrates the

---

[136] *Ibid.*, para. 52.   [137] See above n. 105.   [138] See above n. 70.
[139] See above n. 119.   [140] See above n. 121.   [141] See above n. 123.
[142] See above n. 124.   [143] See above n. 135.
[144] See *Committee Findings (Slovakia)*, above n. 76.
[145] See above n. 112.   [146] See above n. 72.

diversity of collision points identified in Section 9.1 as well as some of the problems that may arise in addressing normative conflicts in this area.

One of the main problems is establishing a link between a domestic measure and international environmental law, as discussed in Section 9.3.2. There are also other problems that stem from the specific characteristics of the regulation of dangerous substances and activities. The looming changes in the regulatory framework are not merely an abstract danger associated with 'dormant' clauses in a prior environmental treaty but, rather, an essential feature of the market conditions in which investors operate. Many environmental treaties in this area specifically direct States to take intrusive measures such as requiring new permits, restricting movements, updating safety measures and even eliminating the production and/or use of certain substances. These measures may be adopted as a result of the inclusion of new chemicals in an international listing of banned substances (see, e.g., the last two conferences of the parties of the POP Convention[147]). There is limited room for an investor operating in an affected industry to argue that such changes are to be seen as a manifestation of political risk. First, the understanding of the risks associated with certain substances and activities evolve at the pace of scientific and technical discoveries, and it is therefore subject to change. Second, and related, investors in highly regulated industries such as pharmaceuticals, chemicals, waste treatment and other hazardous activities cannot ignore the fact that regulatory changes are likely to be introduced if the understanding of the risks associated with certain substances or activities changes, as it often does. In other words, regulatory change is a fact of life in these industries, particularly when such change results from developments at the international level reflecting a wide recognition of the risks posed by a given substance/activity. As discussed next, these specific features have significant practical consequences.

9.3.2   Some practical problems

This Section addresses the four practical problems identified in the two preceding chapters in connection with the clarity of the link between international environmental obligations and domestic regulation (Section 9.3.2.1), the use of this link in investment proceedings (Section 9.3.2.2), the vulnerability of the link (Section 9.3.2.3) and the

---

[147] See above n. 31. The listing of lindane in May 2009 as part of the restricted substances under the POP Convention was discussed in *Chemtura v. Canada*, above n. 70, para. 135.

adequacy of the available conflict norms (Section 9.3.2.4). In analysing these problems, particular attention is paid to the implications of the specific features of the regulation of dangerous substances and activities.

9.3.2.1   The link is unclear

The domestic framework relating to the regulation of dangerous substances and activities is, as a rule, more sophisticated than what is required by international environmental law. States have reached agreement with respect to some transboundary problems such as acid deposition, ozone depletion, movements of hazardous waste and the restriction/elimination of certain chemical substances (currently twenty-two under the POP Convention). Beyond this threshold, international co-ordination is mostly embodied in soft-law instruments and chemical dialogues. This has some implications for the link between domestic measures and international environmental commitments. Four basic scenarios can be identified.

First, the domestic measure may be required by a specific international obligation leaving the host State limited room for manoeuvre. The obligation to prohibit the exports/imports of certain hazardous waste[148] or that commanding the elimination of both the production and the use of certain chemicals[149] are specific in nature and, as a result, a simple reference to them in the Preamble (or elsewhere) of the domestic measure should be sufficient to establish the link.

Second, the domestic measure may be linked to a broadly formulated clause directing States to take measures to achieve certain goals or impose certain standards. One illustration is Article 6(1) of the IA Convention, which requires States to 'take appropriate measures for the prevention of industrial accidents, including measures to induce action by operators to reduce the risk of industrial accidents'.[150] Another illustration is provided by some provisions in human rights instruments, such as Article 12 of the ICESCR[151] or Article 8 of the ECHR,[152] which involve an obligation for States to take positive measures to regulate the operations of third parties (including foreign investors) that may have an impact on human

---

[148] Basel Convention, above n. 6, Article 4(5). The effect of this provision had been discussed by the Canadian government in the context of the dispute underlying the case *S. D. Myers* v. *Canada*, above n. 105, paras. 121 and 186. See also, Bamako Convention, above n. 14, Article 4(1).

[149] POP Convention, above n. 8, Article 3(1)(a)(i).

[150] IA Convention, above n. 12, Article 6(1).   [151] See above n. 15.   [152] See above n. 17.

rights.[153] Such a link is significantly more vulnerable, as discussed in Chapters 7 and 8 in connection with analogous hypotheses. The steps suggested in Chapter 7 (cost–benefit analyses, consultations, resort to international bodies) would therefore be useful to strengthen the link between the domestic measure and the host State's international environmental obligations.

The third and fourth scenarios relate to the analysis of legitimacy conflicts (as opposed to normative conflicts). The third scenario covers situations where the domestic measure is based on a non-binding international instrument, such as a soft-law instrument (e.g., Chapter 19 of Agenda 21) or a memorandum of understanding.[154] The fourth scenario concerns cases in which the domestic measure has no link to an international instrument. Although from a strictly legal standpoint there is no difference between the third and fourth scenarios, they do differ in terms of legitimacy, as discussed in Part III.

9.3.2.2   Invocation of the link in investment proceedings

In at least two cases, the link between the challenged domestic measures and international environmental law was fully argued by the respondent States.

In *S. D. Myers* v. *Canada*, the respondent invoked its obligations under the Basel Convention to justify the ban on the exports of PCB.[155] However, one must not overestimate the place occupied by this argument in Canada's defence. As is apparent from Canada's briefs[156] the argument based on the applicability of Article 4(5) of the Basel Convention received only a few paragraphs,[157] and it was made in order to stress the need for the tribunal to interpret the NAFTA in the light of Canada's other international obligations.

In *Chemtura* v. *Canada*, the respondent also referred to its international environmental obligations and, more specifically, to its obligation under Annex II of the Aarhus POP Protocol to proceed to a reassessment of

---

[153] See, e.g., *Taskin* v. *Turkey*, above n. 123, para. 113.

[154] See, e.g., the 'Record of Understanding' referred to in *Chemtura* v. *Canada*, above n. 70, paras. 17, 175 and 178.

[155] *S. D. Myers* v. *Canada*, above n. 105, para. 150.

[156] Canada's Counter-Memorial on the Merits (5 October 1999) ('Canada's C.-M.'). See also Canada's Supplemental Memorial on the Merits (15 December 1999) ('Canada's Supplemental Memorial'), para. 82; Canada's Reply to the Investor Supplemental Memorial (24 January 2000) ('Canada's Reply'), para. 18–24. All available at: www.naftaclaims.com (accessed on 4 January 2012).

[157] Canada's C.-M., above n. 156, paras. 104–12 (factual section) and 200–3 (legal discussion).

lindane.[158] The basic contention was that no disingenuous behaviour in breach of the international minimum standard of treatment can be established when a State simply performs an act required by its international environmental obligations. A similar contention had been advanced in *S. D. Myers* v. *Canada*, where the respondent argued that 'the conduct complained of as an alleged breach of the minimum standard of treatment, even if true, is hardly of the malicious or arbitrary type necessary to breach the NAFTA provision; the action was taken consistent with Canada's international legal obligations under the Basel Convention'.[159]

Thus, in both cases, the link between domestic measures and international environmental law was invoked not to neutralise the application of an investment discipline but rather to argue in favour of a specific interpretation of such discipline. The impact of these contentions differed from one case to the other. Whereas the tribunal in *S. D. Myers* v. *Canada* rejected the argument, the tribunal in *Chemtura* v. *Canada* admitted it. This latter point serves as a prelude to the discussion of the vulnerability of the link between domestic measures and international commitments.

9.3.2.3   The vulnerability of the link

As noted in previous chapters, even when a link can be established, its operation remains vulnerable on grounds of proportionality and due process. Regulatory changes based on health and environmental grounds are difficult to challenge as a matter of principle, given the wide recognition of the need to protect people against harmful substances and hazardous activities. However, even necessary measures can be challenged for being disproportionally adverse to the interests of investors or adopted following a flawed process. The awards of the tribunal in *S. D. Myers* v. *Canada* and *Chemtura* v. *Canada* shed some light on how these two issues may be tackled in future investment disputes.

In *S. D. Myers* v. *Canada*, the challenge to the link was successful. As mentioned earlier in this chapter, the tribunal considered that, as a general matter:

Even if the Basel Convention were to have been ratified by the NAFTA Parties, it should not be presumed that CANADA would have been able to use it to justify the breach of a specific NAFTA provision because ...*where a party has a choice*

---

[158] *Chemtura* v. *Canada*, above n. 70, para. 131.
[159] Canada's Supplemental Memorial, above n. 156, para. 82.

among equally effective and reasonably available alternatives for complying....with a Basel Convention obligation, it is obliged to choose the alternative that is ...least inconsistent... with the NAFTA. If one such alternative were to involve no inconsistency with the Basel Convention, clearly this should be followed.[160]

In other words, if the hierarchy mentioned in Article 104 (and its Annex) of the NAFTA had been technically applicable (which the tribunal excluded[161]), an issue of proportionality may have arisen despite the link between the measure challenged and the Basel Convention.

A different approach was followed by the tribunal in *Chemtura v. Canada.* One of the questions that the tribunal had to decide was whether the process that led to the suspension of the claimant's registered products was flawed. This question had different dimensions. One aspect concerned the scientific basis of the decision. Although the tribunal specifically avoided taking a stance on the scientific aspects of the dispute, it did note that the use by Canada of higher safety standards (*in casu* a higher uncertainty factor for the assessment of the occupational risk presented by the products) remained within acceptable bounds and, as a result, was not sufficient to conclude to a breach of the minimum standard of treatment.[162] The other dimensions of the claimant's due process contention concerned the alleged opacity of the process and certain delays. The tribunal rejected both arguments on the basis of certain circumstances of the case that are difficult to generalise.[163]

9.3.2.4 The adequacy of the available conflict norms

Although the broad conclusions reached in Chapters 6, 7 and 8 (in essence, the scarcity of specific conflict norms and the inadequacy of general conflict norms) are also applicable in the present context, three issues deserve some additional comment.

First, it is worth noting that in *S. D. Myers v. Canada* the operation of a specific conflict norm (Article 104 – and its Annex – of the NAFTA) was addressed at two levels. On the one hand, the respondent argued that by virtue of this provision the Basel Convention prevailed over the NAFTA. But this contention was rejected by the tribunal on the grounds that, in

---

[160] *S. D. Myers v. Canada*, above n. 105, para. 215 (italics original, referring to Article 104 of the NAFTA).

[161] *Ibid.*, para. 214.

[162] *Chemtura v. Canada*, above n. 70, paras. 153–4.

[163] *Ibid.*, particularly paras. 155–62 (timing of the review of lindane), 184–93 (phase-out conditions) and 200–25 (allegedly excessive delays in the registration of replacement products).

order for Article 104 of the NAFTA to deploy its effect, the United States had to be a party to the Basel Convention,[164] which, in turn, precluded the very argument made by Canada (which assumed the United States to be a third party). Yet, Canada's defence also invoked Article 104 of the NAFTA to carve out some space for environmental regulation within the investment disciplines of NAFTA.[165] Through this approach, Canada was, in fact, stressing the importance of the Basel Convention as part of the normative context of the NAFTA or, in other words, asserting the need for systemic integration.

Second and related, irrespective of whether a specific conflict norm is technically applicable or not, the very existence of such a norm suggests the relative importance attached by the parties to the international obligations under consideration. As discussed in Chapter 6 in connection with the *lex superior* approach, there are different ways in which norms can display some hierarchical effects. A tribunal facing a normative conflict between an investment discipline and an environmental norm explicitly considered as superior by a technically inapplicable conflict norm would in all likelihood take this relative hierarchy into account in applying general conflict rules and, specifically, interpretive techniques.

Third, the relative importance attached to international norms regulating dangerous substances and activities as well as the particular features of the markets in which investors in these industries operate (the inherently moving regulatory landscape that they face) have an impact on the use of the *lex posterior* and *lex specialis* approaches. To the extent that subsequent norms are seen as the manifestation of an evolving scientific and technical understanding of the risks associated with certain substances and activities, such norms would have a claim to priority on the basis both of the time factor and of their higher specificity, as an updated (and therefore more accurate) reflection of an evolving understanding.

---

[164] *S. D. Myers* v. *Canada*, above n. 105, para. 214.
[165] Canada's C.-M., above n. 156, paras. 200–3.

10 Foreign investment and the climate change regime

This chapter analyses the interactions between the international regulation of climate change and international investment law, as the fourth and final illustration of a source of normative conflicts. As in previous chapters, the analysis focuses on the incidence, actual or potential, of a number of international instruments (particularly the UNFCCC,[1] the Kyoto Protocol,[2] an array of decisions adopted under these two treaties and some relevant human rights treaties) on the operations of foreign investors. The chapter is divided into three sections. The first section identifies the most likely collision points between the international climate change regime and investment disciplines. Section 10.2 analyses the still limited contribution of adjudicatory and quasi-adjudicatory bodies to the understanding of this type of normative conflicts. Section 10.3 generalises the insights derived from the previous sections.

10.1 Climate change policies – an analysis of collision points

10.1.1 Overview

The term 'climate change policies' encompasses a wide array of international, regional, national and sub-national instruments that have been developed over the last two decades. As a rule, climate change policies follow a regulatory approach as opposed to a human rights-based one. This is because it is still very difficult to conceptualise the legal relationship between the effects of climate change and their incidence on human

---

[1] United Nations Framework Convention on Climate Change, 9 May 1992, 31 ILM 849 ('UNFCCC').
[2] Kyoto Protocol to the United Nations Framework Convention on Climate Change, Kyoto, 11 December 1997, 2303 UNTS 148 ('Kyoto Protocol').

rights. However, in the last five years, there have been important attempts at using human rights to strengthen the obligations of States in connection with the mitigation of emissions of greenhouse gases (GHG) and the adaptation to the consequences of climate change (the effects of climate change and of the response measures). After a brief survey of the main collision points that can be identified from a regulatory perspective (Section 10.1.2), I discuss the emerging human rights approach to climate change issues (Section 10.1.3).

10.1.2   The regulatory approach

From a regulatory stand-point, the two main international instruments regulating the activities of States in connection with climate change are, at present, the UNFCCC and the Kyoto Protocol. As in previous chapters, the purpose of this section is not to provide an introduction to the international regulation of climate change,[3] but only to discuss ways in which this framework may conflict with investment disciplines.[4] After a brief review of the relevant international provisions, I analyse three main types of climate policies potentially interfering with investment schemes.

The specific mitigation and adaptation obligations imposed on States by the UNFCCC and the Kyoto Protocol are difficult to circumscribe precisely. This is not because the relevant provisions are unclear. Article 4 of the UNFCCC provides for a variety of obligations in connection with mitigation of GHG,[5] transfers of financial resources and technology,[6]

---

[3] See D. Bodansky, 'The United Nations Framework Convention on Climate Change: A Commentary' (1993) 18 *Yale Journal of International Law* 451; J. Depledge, 'Tracing the Origins of the Kyoto Protocol: An Article-by-Article Textual History', Technical Paper, FCCC/TP/2000/2 (2000); F. Yamin and J. Depledge, *The International Climate Change Regime* (Cambridge University Press, 2004); D. Freestone and C. Streck, *Legal Aspects of Carbon Trading* (Oxford University Press 2009).

[4] See D. M. Firger and M. B. Gerrard, 'Harmonizing Climate Change Policy and International Investment Law' (2010/11) 3 *Yearbook of International Investment Law and Policy* 517; K. Miles, 'Arbitrating Climate Change: Regulatory Regimes and Investor-State Disputes' (2010) 1 *Climate Law* 63; L. Johnson, 'International Investment Agreements and Climate Change: The Potential for Investor-State Conflicts and Possible Strategies for Minimizing It' (2009) 39 *Environmental Law Reporter* 11147; F. Baetens, 'The Kyoto Protocol in Investor-State Arbitration: Reconciling Climate Change and Investment Protection Objectives', in M.-C. Cordonnier-Segger, M. W. Gehring and A. Newcombe (eds.), *Sustainable Development in World Investment Law* (Alphen aan den Rijn: Wolters Kluwer, 2011), pp. 683–715.

[5] See, e.g., Article 4(1)(b) and (d), applicable to both Annex I and non-Annex I parties, or Article 4(2)(a), applicable to Annex I parties only.

[6] See, e.g., Article 4(3) and (5), applicable to Annex II parties only.

and adaptation.[7] The Kyoto Protocol is even more precise, at least with respect to the obligations of States included in Annex I of the UNFCCC.[8] Specifically, Article 3 and Annex B of the Kyoto Protocol provide for quantified emissions-reduction commitments for Annex I parties. The difficulty of circumscribing such obligations lies, however, in the fact that they were specifically designed to leave to States parties the choice of the means used to abide by their commitments. Thus, when a State adopts a particular measure to reduce its emissions, it is unclear whether such a measure is 'required' to comply with the Kyoto Protocol or the UNFCCC or whether it has a purely domestic (as opposed to an international) grounding. As in the hypotheses discussed in the previous chapters, the existence of a specific link between the measures adopted by the host State and international environmental law is likely to pose significant problems in investment disputes involving issues of climate change regulation. However, this is not to say that when States introduce climate-related measures they are not acting in pursuance of their international obligations. Moreover, the specific features of the measures adopted are very important for their legal assessment. In what follows, I briefly discuss three main approaches that have been used so far to implement the UNFCCC and/or the Kyoto Protocol, namely cap-and-trade systems, command-and-control regulation and certain differentiation devices (taxes and subsidies).[9]

Some States (e.g., New Zealand[10]), as well as some groups of States (e.g., European Union[11]) or of sub-federal entities (e.g., the US states participating in the RGGI[12] or the Canadian province of British

---

[7] See, e.g., Article 4(1)(e), applicable to both Annex I and non-Annex I parties or Article 4(4), applicable to Annex II parties only.

[8] Regarding non-Annex I parties, Article 10 of the Kyoto Protocol simply refers back to Article 4(1) of the UNFCCC.

[9] For an overview of the palette of measures, see Intergovernmental Panel on Climate Change (IPCC), 'Climate Change 2007: Mitigation of Climate Change. Contribution of Working Group III to the Fourth Assessment Report (2007)' ('IPCC') Sections 13.1.2 (Criteria for policy choice) and 13.2 (National policy instruments, their implementation and interaction), pp. 750–68, available at: www.ipcc.ch (accessed on 4 January 2012).

[10] Climate Change Response (Emissions Trading) Amendment Act 2008, Public Act 2008 No. 85, 25 September 2008.

[11] Directive 2003/87/EC of the European Parliament and of the Council of 13 October 2003 establishing a scheme for greenhouse gas emission allowance trading within the Community and amending Council Directive 96/61/E, OJ 2003 L 0087 (consolidated version) ('ETS Directive').

[12] Memorandum of Understanding, 20 December 2005 ('RGGI MOU') and Revised Model Rule, 31 December 2008 ('RGGI RMR'), both available at: www.rggi.org (accessed on 4 January 2012). A federal cap-and-trade system was envisioned in the draft Clean Energy and Security Act, which was later abandoned by the US Senate.

Columbia[13]) have implemented mechanisms known as 'cap-and-trade'.[14] The specific features of these mechanisms may vary considerably from one case to the other. But their basic structure can be pinned down to four components. First, an overall cap in the GHG emissions of the participating entities (States, federated States and/or companies) is set. Second, the available emissions are distributed among these entities (either given away or auctioned), which results in emissions-reduction commitments for each one of them. Third, participating entities are authorised to trade their emissions entitlements. Fourth, participating entities may also acquire other types of emissions-reduction quotas beyond the cap (typically project-based certified emissions-reduction units[15]). Each one of these four components may interfere with the operations of foreign investors. An investor may challenge its inclusion among the participating entities or the specific quota that has been allocated to it. Investors may also challenge measures that interfere with the trading of the emission entitlements or with the acquisition of such entitlements through projects aimed at reducing emissions in foreign countries. It has been persuasively argued that one of the main reasons why the acquisition of project-based emissions-reduction units has been pursued through the clean development mechanism ('CDM') established by the Kyoto Protocol rather than through the joint implementation mechanism ('JI') is the host country's stronger involvement in the regulation of the latter, which entails a higher risk of project disruption.[16] For each of these hypotheses, one may refer to concrete cases involving potential normative conflicts, as discussed in Section 10.2.

Climate-related command-and-control regulation often concerns technical requirements for the production of certain goods or operational requirements for certain activities. The examples of command-and-control regulations relevant for climate change mitigation and adaptation are numerous, and they are not limited to measures specifically targeting GHG but concern, more generally, issues such as energy efficiency and construction standards.[17] For instance, among the various

---

[13] Bill 18 – 2008: Greenhouse Gas Reduction (Cap and Trade) Act, 2008 Legislative Session: 4th Session, 38th Parliament, passed on third reading.

[14] IPCC, above n. 9, Section 13.2.1.3 (Tradable permits), pp. 756–9.

[15] See, e.g., Kyoto Protocol, above n. 2, Article 12 (relative to the establishment of a 'Clean Development Mechanism' or 'CDM'); ETS Directive, above n. 11, Article 11a; RGGI RMR, above n. 12, Section XX-10(3)(b)(1).

[16] A. Hobley and C. Robers 'Joint Implementation Transactions: An Overview', in Freestone and Streck, *Legal Aspects of Carbon Trading* above n. 3, pp. 198–9.

[17] IPCC, above n. 9, Section 13.2.1.1. (Regulations and Standards), pp. 753–5.

components forming the 'EU Climate and Energy Package' introduced in April 2009,[18] one finds, together with the amended ETS Directive, also some pieces of command-and-control legislation such as the 'Fuel Specification Directive' (setting technical specifications for fuels on health and environmental grounds)[19] or the 'Passenger Car Regulation' (setting binding standards for CO2 emissions from new passenger cars).[20] Importantly, the link between these and other measures and the UNFCCC or the Kyoto Protocol is sometimes unclear. One may refer, in this connection, to the 'Emission Standards for New Motor Vehicles or New Motor Vehicle Engines' enacted by the United States as a matter of domestic policy.[21] The potential collision of such measures with the activities of foreign investors in the car or electricity industries is sufficiently clear not to require additional comment.

The third approach taken by climate policies can be generally referred to as differentiation measures. These measures may take a variety of forms. In fact, cap-and-trade systems and command-and-control regulations may, depending on the circumstances, be considered as differentiation measures. Here, however, I focus on carbon taxes/duties[22] and climate-related subsidies.[23] Regarding the first category, taxes vary considerably as to their object and modalities.[24] According to the IPCC '[m]ost environmentally related taxes with implications for

---

[18] See K. Kulovesi, E. Morgera and M. Muñoz 'The EU's Climate and Energy Package: Environmental Integration and International Dimensions', Working Paper Series of the Europa Institute, University of Edinburgh, available at: www.law.ed.ac.uk/europa/ (accessed on 4 January 2012).

[19] Directive 2009/30/EC of the European Parliament and of the Council of 23 April 2009 amending Directive 98/70/EC as regards the specification of petrol, diesel and gas-oil and introducing a mechanism to monitor and reduce greenhouse gas emissions and amending Council Directive 1999/32/EC as regards the specification of fuel used by inland waterway vessels and repealing Directive 93/12/EEC, OJ 2009 L 140/88 ('Fuel Specification Directive').

[20] Regulation (EC) No. 443/2009 of the European Parliament and of the Council of 23 April 2009 setting emission performance standards for new passenger cars as part of the Community's integrated approach to reduce CO_2 emissions from light-duty vehicles, OJ 2009 L 140/1 ('Passenger Car Regulation').

[21] See 42 USC § 7521.

[22] IPCC, above n. 9, Section 13.2.1.2 (Taxes and Charges), pp. 755–6.

[23] IPCC, above n. 9, Section 13.2.1.5 (Subsidies and Incentives), pp. 760–2; R. Howse 'Climate Mitigation Subsidies and the WTO Legal Framework: A Policy Analysis', *International Institute for Sustainable Development*, (May 2010).

[24] IPCC, 'Climate Change 2001: Mitigation. Contribution of Working Group III to the Third Assessment Report', (2001), Section 6.2.2.2.1 (Collection Point and Tax Base), available at: www.ipcc.org (accessed on 4 January 2012); G. E. Metcalf and D. Weisbach, 'The Design of a Carbon Tax' (2009) 33 *Harvard Environmental Law Review* 499.

GHG emissions in OECD countries are levied on energy products (150 taxes) and on motor vehicles (125 taxes), rather than on CO_2 emission directly', although 'there is some experience with the direct taxation of CO_2 emissions'.[25] From a legal standpoint, modalities are particularly important,[26] as they may introduce differentiation among different economic operators and thus amount to a potential breach of investment and/or trade disciplines.[27] Differentiation is, arguably, also the major concern in connection with the introduction of subsidies or other incentive measures. This second category of measures may include support for research and development, investment tax credits or schemes for price support (e.g., for electricity production from renewable energy sources).[28] Investors not benefiting from such subsidies may bring a claim for breach of non-discrimination standards. In addition, the main advantage of subsidies (i.e., that they are politically easier to introduce than taxes) may turn into a major disadvantage when the time comes for a subsidy to be withdrawn,[29] as, again, the investors affected by such withdrawal may seek to recover any losses by bringing an investment claim. Collisions between climate policies and investment disciplines may arise in a variety of contexts such as the introduction of a subsidy in favour of climate-friendly technologies (e.g., solar panels or wind turbine producers), the withdrawal of subsidies for fossil fuel production and/or consumption (in order to make the renewable energy industry more competitive) or the subsequent withdrawal or reduction of subsidies initially granted to an investor in renewable energy (e.g., feed-in tariffs).

10.1.3   The human rights approach

Reference to human rights approaches in the context of climate policies has been made from two main perspectives.

First, it has been argued that the moral concept of human rights (by contrast with specific human rights provisions) must be taken into account for distributional purposes, i.e., to justify certain distributions

---

[25] IPCC, above n. 9, p. 756; see also, Metcalf and Weisbach, 'The Design of a Carbon Tax', above n. 24, 508.

[26] For instance, Metcalf and Weisbach suggest that by taxing a few thousand tax payers in the United States a well-designed carbon tax could capture more than 80 per cent of American emissions. Metcalf and Weisbach, 'The Design of a Carbon Tax' above n. 24, 501 and Part III.C.

[27] Miles, 'Arbitrating Climate Change' above n. 4, 77–80.

[28] IPCC, above n. 9, p. 761.   [29] Ibid., p. 761.

of the rights to emissions 'rights'.[30] It is from this perspective that a distinction between 'luxury emissions' and 'subsistence emissions' (based on human rights) has been advocated.[31] It is also from this perspective that the allocation of a certain share of emissions to developing countries in pursuance of the 'right to development' has been argued for[32] or that different paths to convergence in the well-known 'Contraction & Convergence' model[33] could be justified. Despite the political potential of these initiatives, from a legal stand-point their reliance on human rights law provisions is not entirely clear and, in all events, not sufficiently spelled out to assess how the relations between climate change policies and investment disciplines could be affected.

The second perspective seeks to mobilise human rights provisions and mechanisms to strengthen the implementation of climate policies. The objectives pursued are diverse and range from holding companies/States liable through tort litigation or, exceptionally, human rights claims,[34] to the broadening of human rights provisions to incorporate climate change components,[35] to more general attempts at spelling out, in terms of human rights obligations, some of the corollaries of the obligations assumed by States under the UNFCCC and the Kyoto Protocol.[36]

---

[30] International Council on Human Rights Policy (ICHRP), 'Climate Change and Human Rights. A Rough Guide' (2008), pp. 9–11.

[31] H. Shue 'Subsistence Emissions and Luxury Emissions' (1993) 15 *Law & Policy* 39.

[32] See, e.g., P. Baer, T. Athanasiou, S. Kartha and E. Kemp-Benedict, *The Right to Development in a Climate Constrained World* (Berlin: Heinrich Boll Stiftung, 2008).

[33] The current C&C model is based on a 450 ppm 'contraction budget' which would be reached by the progressive convergence of emissions reduction in different countries by 2030. The different paths towards convergence (defined by contraction rates that must account for equity considerations) would reach a goal of equal emissions per capita in the target date (2030). See www.gci.org.uk (accessed on 4 January 2012).

[34] See, e.g., Inuit Circumpolar Conference, 'Petition to the Inter American Commission on Human Rights Seeking Relief from Violations Resulting from Global Warming Caused by Acts and Omissions of the United States', (2005) ('Inuit Petition'), available at: www.earthjustice.org (accessed on 4 January 2012); W. C. G. Burns and H. M. Osofsky, *Adjudicating Climate Change: Sub-National, National, and Supra-National Approaches* (Cambridge University Press, 2010).

[35] On 'broadening', see J. E. Viñuales and S. Chuffart, 'From the Other Shore: Economic, Social and Cultural Rights from an International Environmental Law Perspective', in E. Reidel, C. Golay, C. Mahon and G. Giacca (eds.), *Contemporary Issues in the Realization of Economic, Social and Cultural Rights* (Oxford University Press, forthcoming).

[36] See Office of the High Commissioner for Human Rights (OHCHR), Report of the Office of the United Nations Hight Commissioner for Human Rights on the Relationship Between Climate Change and Human Rights, 15 January 2009, UN Doc. A/HRC/10/61 ('OHCHR Report').

Although this area of practice is still in its infancy, it is likely to develop in the next years, with essentially two significant consequences for present purposes. First, increasing access to information and participatory requirements may potentially affect not only the time-frame of the approval and development of investment schemes but also the likelihood of climate-related litigation against investors. Second, the use of human rights provisions to clarify the obligations of States in connection with mitigation and adaptation may potentially strengthen the link, referred to above, between the measures adopted by the host State and international environmental law. In turn, the potential collisions between, on the one hand, climate policies adopted pursuant to international environmental and human rights law, and, on the other hand, investment disciplines, may give rise to normative conflicts.

10.2   Decisions from adjudicatory and quasi-adjudicatory bodies

10.2.1   Overview

Despite the increasing number of climate change-related claims initiated at the domestic level,[37] the number of cases brought before international adjudicatory and quasi-adjudicatory bodies is still limited. Moreover, there is little public information available regarding climate-related investment or commercial proceedings. Therefore, in seeking to distil from the existing international case-law some guidance for managing normative conflicts, the analysis must be extended to a number of decisions rendered in other contexts (e.g., the judicial bodies of the European Union, some committees established by environmental treaties, as well as some loosely connected investment cases) involving potentially relevant findings, reasoning or, at least, illustrations of how such conflicts may arise. From an analytical standpoint, these cases can be organised by the type of collision point: conflicts arising from cap-and-trade systems (Section 10.2.2); command-and-control regulation (Section 10.2.3); differentiation measures (Section 10.2.4); and breaches of human rights (normally formulated as either tort claims or violations of participatory rights) (Section 10.2.5).

---

[37] Burns and Osofsky, *Adjudicating Climate Change*, above n. 34.

10.2.2   Cap-and-trade systems

There is a substantial case-law interpreting different aspects of the ETS Directive and its implementation by member States.[38] Commentators have tended to analyse these cases according to the party which initiated the action (i.e., a State, the European Commission or a private company)[39] or to the legal means used (i.e. Article 234, 230 or 226 EC).[40] Whereas these distinctions may be justified in the context of those analyses, here a different analytical approach will be used, based on the four basic components of cap-and-trade systems mentioned in Section 10.1.2. Conflicts between cap-and-trade systems and investment schemes may arise in connection with an investor's inclusion among the participating entities or with the amount of allowances allocated to it. Collisions may also occur when a State interferes with the trading of emission rights or with the acquisition of such rights through project-based mechanisms. In analysing these cases, I will pay attention to the link between international environmental obligations (UNFCCC/Kyoto Protocol), the ETS Directive and domestic measures.

The question of the inclusion of an investor in the ETS arose in the challenges brought by Arcelor, a large steel producer, against the ETS Directive and the French implementing measures. The validity of the ETS Directive was discussed by the European Court of Justice ('ECJ') in a reference procedure initiated by the French Conseil d'Etat[41] and, to a limited extent, in the context of an action for annulment brought by Arcelor.[42] The main question submitted to the ECJ in these two cases was one of differentiation, namely whether the ETS Directive can validly cover the steel sector while leaving outside of its scope the chemical and aluminium sectors. Although the cases did not concern the application of a BIT, they did touch upon the relations between, on the one hand, measures adopted by the European institutions and France

---

[38] N. S. Ghaleigh, 'Emissions Trading before the European Court of Justice: Market Making in Luxembourg', in Freestone and Streck, *Legal Aspects of Carbon Trading*, above n. 3, pp. 367ff; J. van Zeben 'The European Emissions Trading Scheme Case Law' (2009) 18 *Review of European Community and International Environmental Law* 119.

[39] van Zeben, 'The European Emissions Trading Scheme Case Law', above n. 38.

[40] Ghaleigh, 'Emissions Trading before the European Court of Justice' above n. 38.

[41] *Société Arcelor Atlantique et Lorraine et al.* v. *Premier Ministre, Ministre de l'Economie, des Finances et de l'Industrie, Ministre de l'Ecologie et du Développement Durable*, ECJ Case C-127/07, Judgment (16 December 2008)('*Arcelor* reference').

[42] *Arcelor SA* v. *European Parliament and Council*, ECJ Case T-16/04, Judgment (2 March 2010) ('*Arcelor* annulment').

pursuant to the UNFCCC and the Kyoto Protocol[43] and, on the other hand, a number of investment disciplines *lato sensu*, including non-discrimination (equal treatment), the right to property, the right to the pursuit of an economic activity and the right of establishment.[44] The reasoning of the ECJ is interesting for present purposes in two main respects. First, despite the wide discretion left by the UNFCCC and the Kyoto Protocol to States, the link between these treaties and the ETS Directive is made explicit. Second, the ECJ discussed in some detail the reasons justifying differential treatment under the ETS Directive, as discussed in more detail in Section 10.2.4. In essence, the Court considered that the three sectors at stake, i.e., steel, chemicals and aluminium, were 'in a comparable position',[45] but that the European Community had proved that the differentiated treatment was nevertheless justified[46] as a valid exercise of the Community's 'broad discretion'[47] based on 'objective criteria appropriate to the aim pursued'.[48]

Collisions between environmental and investment protection may also occur in connection with the amount of emissions allowances allocated to a given investor. In *US Steel Kosice* v. *Commission*,[49] the main steel producer in the Slovak Republic complained about pressure allegedly put on Slovakia by the Commission authorities to reduce the amount of emissions allowances in its national allocation plan (NAP). According to the investor, the decisions challenged had a direct legal effect on its operations because a large part of the allowances (some 10,000 kilotons per year) were earmarked for the investor and an overall reduction in the allowances distributed by the plan necessarily entailed a reduction of its part of allowances.[50] The Court dismissed

---

[43] *Arcelor* reference, above n. 41, paras. 3–19; *Arcelor* annulment, above n. 42, para. 3.

[44] *Arcelor* reference, above n. 41, para. 23; *Arcelor* annulment, above n. 42, para. 36.

[45] *Arcelor* reference, above n. 41, para. 38.

[46] *Ibid.*, paras. 69 and 72.   [47] *Ibid*, para. 57.   [48] *Ibid.*, para. 58.

[49] *US Steel Kosice* v. *Commission*, CFI Case T-489/04, Order (1 October 2007) ('*US Steel I*'); *US Steel Kosice* v. *Commission*, CFI Case T-27/07, Order (1 October 2007) ('*US Steel II*'); *US Steel Kosice* v. *Commission*, ECJ Case C-6/08 P (19 June 2008) ('*US Steel II Appeal*').

[50] *US Steel I*, above n. 49, paras. 16 and 28; *US Steel II*, above n. 49, para. 42. Similar claims have been brought by other companies. See *Fels-Werke and others* v. *Commission*, CFI Case T-28/07, Order (11 September 2007) (claim relating to the German national allocation plan); *Saint-Gobain Glass Deutschland* v. *Commission*, ECJ Case C-503/07, Order (14 November 2007) (claim relating to the Serman national allocation plan, appeal); *Cemex UK Cement* v. *Commission*, CFI Case T-13/07, Order (6 November 2007) (claim relating to the British national allocation plan); *Gorazdze Cement* v. *Commission*, CFI Case T-193/07, Order (23 September 2008) (claim relating to the Polish national allocation plan); *Lafarge Cement* v. *Commission*, CFI Case T-195/07, Order (23 September 2008) (claim relating to the Polish national allocation plan); *Dyckerhoff Polska* v. *Commission*, CFI Case T-196/07, Order

the claims considering that the applicant had not established that the challenged decisions had a direct legal effect on it. The Court stressed that the final word regarding the allocation of the allowances covered by the NAP lied with the Slovak Republic[51] and, therefore, if the applicant wished to challenge the specific allocation made in the NAP, it had to proceed at the national level.[52] Despite the mostly procedural nature of the reasoning of the Court in these cases, it is interesting to note that the State's margin for manoeuvre in making the final allocation creates some space for a potential claim for breach of investment disciplines. The connection with current case-law is, in fact, quite close. In *US Steel II*, the Commission considered that the large amount of allowances earmarked for the steel producer could have been in breach of the European State aid provisions;[53] the Commission therefore pressed the Slovak Republic to amend its NAP. Yet, this factual configuration (the reduction of advantages granted or promised to investors as part of a State's reforms in view of its accession to the EU) has already given rise to a number of investment disputes against Eastern European countries.[54]

Collisions at the level of the actual trading of emissions can also occur, much in the same way as restrictions from capital and exchange controls. Such restrictions can be imposed through the non-compliance procedure established pursuant to Article 18 of the Kyoto Protocol. A failure by Greece to establish a system capable of estimating emissions and absorption by sinks, as well as to report such information, was found to be in 'non-compliance' of Greece's obligations under the Kyoto Protocol.[55] As a result, the Enforcement Branch of the Compliance

(23 September 2008) (claim relating to the Polish national allocation plan); *Grupa Ozarow* v. *Commission*, CFI Case T-197/07, Order (28 September 2008) (claim relating to the Polish national allocation plan); *Cementownia 'Warta'* v. *Commission*, CFI Case T-198/07, Order (28 September 2008) (claim relating to the Polish national allocation plan); *Cementownia 'Odra'* v. *Commission*, CFI Case T-199/07, Order (28 September 2008) (claim relating to the Polish national allocation plan); *Cemex Polska* v. *Commission*, CFI Case T-203/07, Order (28 September 2008) (claim relating to the Polish national allocation plan); *Buzzi Unicen* v. *Commission*, CFI Case T-241/07, Order (27 October 2008) (claim relating to the Italian national allocation plan). Cases referred to in van Zeben, 'The European Emissions Trading Scheme Case Law' above n. 38, 124.

[51] *US Steel I*, above n. 49, para. 48; *US Steel II*, above n. 49, para. 60.

[52] *US Steel II*, above n. 49, para. 77.   [53] *Ibid*, para. 22.

[54] See, e.g., *Electrabel SA* v. *Republic of Hungary*, ICSID Case No. ARB/07/19 (pending); *AES Summit Generation Limited and AES-Tisza Erőmű Kft.* v. *Republic of* Hungary, ICSID Case No. ARB/07/22, Award (23 September 2010) ('*AES* v. *Hungary*'); *Ioan Micula, Viorel Micula and others* v. *Republic of Romania*, ICSID Case No. ARB/05/20 (pending).

[55] Decision CC-2007-1-6/Greece/EB, para. 5.

Committee, *inter alia*, suspended Greece's eligibility for participation in the flexible mechanisms set up by the Protocol, including emissions trading (Article 17).[56] It is unclear what consequences may arise for economic operators from such a suspension, and this will largely depend upon the organisation of the emissions trading system in Greece. However, holders of emissions rights could be affected either directly (by being prevented from trading) or indirectly (by a decrease in demand from the Greek government) by a measure of this type.[57] From a legal stand-point, the binding character of the decisions of the Compliance Committee is unclear. Article 18 of the Kyoto Protocol expressly requires ratification for the creation of a system capable of taking binding decisions. Yet, the NCP was established by a mere decision of the meeting of the Parties, which carries no binding effect.[58] Were an investment claim to be brought against a country for restrictions to emissions trading arising from a decision of the Compliance Committee, the fact that the conditions set by Article 18 of the Kyoto Protocol have not been met could render more difficult the justification of the restrictions, despite the clear link with the obligations arising from the Protocol.

Finally, collisions may also occur in connection with the acquisition of emissions rights through project-based mechanisms such as the JI and the CDM. This possibility is particularly clear with respect to JI projects, because under this mechanism the emissions rights derived from the investment are issued directly by the host State. Technically, the host State is required to convert an amount of 'assigned amount units' ('AAUs') given to it as part of Kyoto allowances into 'emission reduction units' ('ERUs'), and then transfer these latter from its account to the account of the investor. However, these operations are mostly based on domestic law. JI projects can be conducted through the so-called 'track I' and 'track II' procedures. The main difference between the two is that in 'track II' projects, most of the procedures are governed by international (as opposed to domestic) regulations. That has led some observers to consider that 'track II' projects are fundamentally similar, from this

---

[56] Decision CC-2007-1-8/Greece/EB, para. 5; Decision CC-2007-1-6/Greece/EB, para. 18.

[57] A practical illustration (from a different but closely related context) is provided by the restrictions imposed on Bulgaria (June 2010) and Romania (July 2011) to transfer emission reduction units on the grounds that their GHG Registries were not in conformity with the applicable UN rules. See 'ERU Supply under Threat from UN Investigation', (2011) 8/7 *CDM & JI Monitor*.

[58] J. Brunnee, 'COPing with Consent: Law-making under Multilateral Environmental Agreements' (2002) 15 *Leiden Journal of International Law* 1, at 23–30; Yamin and Depledge, *The International Climate Change Regime*, above n. 3, pp. 405–7, 546.

perspective, to CDM projects, which are almost entirely governed by international regulations. However, JI (even 'track II') and CDM crucially differ as to the entity which issues the emissions rights developed through the investment. Whereas in CDM projects, these rights (called 'certified emissions reduction units' or 'CERs') are issued by an international body (the CDM Executive Board), in JI projects the issuing entity is the host State. A potential illustration of the risks entailed in project-based mechanisms is the case *Naftrac v. Ukraine*.[59] On the basis of the limited information publicly available,[60] it would appear that this case relates, *inter alia*, to the acquisition of ERUs through a gas efficiency project in Ukraine channelled through the JI mechanism. According to the project design document,[61] the project concerned more specifically the reduction of methane leakages in the gas distribution system – managed by Naftrac – in the City of Makiivka and was pursued under JI track II. The investor claims, apparently, that it suffered losses resulting from its exclusion from the project before it could be completed. According to the investor, had the project been completed, it would have acquired ERUs that it could have thereafter sold in carbon markets. The Ukrainian Agency replied that the investor did not meet the applicable licensing and regulatory requirements. In the absence of more detailed information (particularly as to the treaty or contract bases of the investor's claim, or as to the link between the measures taken by the Ukrainian Agency and the requirements governing JI track II projects) it is difficult to determine whether this case raises a normative conflict. It nevertheless provides a good illustration of how such conflicts could arise.

10.2.3   Command-and-control regulation

Some climate change regulation takes the form of command-and-control regulation. Command-and-control approaches are common in most other areas of environmental law, and the issues potentially raised by this type of climate change regulation present no significant differences from those raised by other environmental regulations of this kind. Moreover, given the links of the climate change problem with many other environmental problems, regulations concerning matters

---

[59] *Naftrac Limited* v. *National Environmental Investment Agency (Ukraine)*, PCA (Optional Environmental Rules) Arbitration (pending) ('*Naftrac v. Ukraine*').

[60] See L.-E. Peterson, (20 October 2010) 3(16) *International Arbitration Reporter*, available at: www.iareporter.com (accessed on 4 January 2012).

[61] Available at: www.sgsqualitynetwork.com (accessed on 4 January 2012).

such as fuel additives, construction requirements, waste treatment and even forest management may be considered, at least to some extent, as climate policies or measures. Normative conflicts arising from such regulations (when they implement international obligations) have been already discussed at length in the preceding chapters. Many other cases, brought before the domestic courts of a variety of countries, have received sustained analysis by other commentators.[62] Here, the focus is on one illustration that has received some attention in the literature, namely the claim brought by the State-owned Swedish company Vattenfall against Germany for breach of the Energy Charter Treaty ('ECT').[63]

The claim concerned delays and conditions imposed by a German territorial subdivision for the issuance of permits to operate a coal-fired power plant. The request for arbitration referred to the impact of the Fourth Assessment Report of the IPCC on local politicians as one of the reasons for the alleged German failures.[64] According to the claimant, this led to the imposition of additional conditions for the issuance of the necessary permits, including the installation of a carbon capture and storage plant at the expense of the investor.[65] At the time, German politicians reportedly decried how Germany was being 'pilloried just for implementing German and EU laws'.[66] The case was subsequently settled, so one can only make conjectures as to how a potential normative conflict between the ECT and EU environmental law would have been framed and addressed. However, in light of the diverse components of the EU Climate and Energy Package, which has been expressly introduced as a set of measures for the implementation of the EC's international obligations in the area of climate change, the potential for normative conflicts between these latter obligations (as implemented in EU and domestic law) and investment disciplines should not be underestimated.

---

[62] Burns and Osofsky, *Adjudicating Climate Change*, above n. 34.
[63] Energy Charter Treaty, 17 December 1994, 2080 UNTS 95 ('ECT'). See *Vattenfall AB, Vattenfall Europe AG, Vattenfall Europe Generation AG* v. *Federal Republic of Germany*, ICSID Case No. ARB/09/6, Award (11 March 2011) ('*Vattenfall* v. *Germany*'). See S. Knauer, 'Power Plant's Battle goes to International Arbitration', 15 July 2009, available at: www.spiegel.de (accessed on 4 January 2012); *Vattenfall* v. *Germany*, Request for Arbitration, 30 March 2009 ('*Vattenfall* – RoA'), available at: ita.law.uvic.ca/documents/VattenfallRequestforArbitration.pdf (accessed on 4 January 2012).
[64] *Vattenfall* – RoA, above n. 63, para. 16.   [65] *Ibid.*, para. 20.
[66] Knauer, 'Power Plants Battle goes to International Arbitration' above n. 63, quoting a statement of Michael Müller, Germany's deputy environment minister.

10.2.4 Differentiation (subsidies and duties)

Some climate policies and measures seek to introduce differences in the treatment of carbon-intensive activities as compared to carbon-efficient ones. Differentiation may take a variety of forms, including subsidies to 'climate friendly' technologies or activities, taxes on carbon intensive activities or end-products, or the inclusion (or exclusion) of a given investor in/from a cap-and-trade system. The decisions of international courts and tribunals specifically dealing with these types of measures in connection with investment schemes are still rare. However, some guidance as to the potential normative conflicts arising from differentiation can be derived from other decisions.

Concerning the question of differentiation by means of subsidies, a potentially relevant case is *AES v. Hungary*.[67] In this case, the investors claimed, *inter alia*, that they had been treated in an unreasonable and discriminatory manner, in breach of the ECT, as a result of Hungary's reintroduction of administrative prices (set by Decree) for the purchase of electricity from the investors' plants. The administrative prices were indeed lower than the purchase prices set by an agreement with the Hungarian government concluded in 2001, and the manner in which they were calculated (by generator) was unfavourable to the claimants, as compared to other local and foreign generators.[68] The reasoning of the tribunal is interesting in four main respects. First, in analysing the reasonableness of the measure, the tribunal suggested that a measure adopted at the national level to comply with European law (*in casu* State aid rules but one could also think of European environmental law) would 'no doubt' constitute a 'rational public policy measure'.[69] However, to the extent that the record did not establish that Hungary had specifically acted pursuant to a decision of the European Commission, the tribunal considered that Hungary could not avail itself of this argument. This reasoning leads to the second point, namely the question of the specific link between an international obligation and national implementing measures. The arbitrators disagreed as to the nature of the link, with the majority stressing the need for a 'formal' decision of the European Commission for the link to exist,[70] while the remaining

---

[67] *AES v. Hungary*, above n. 54. Another case that may be significant for the analysis of differentiation in this context is the dispute between the United States and China over Chinese subsidies to producers of wind energy equipment. See www.globalsubsidies.org/subsidy-watch/news/wto-subsidy-dispute-round-0 (accessed on 4 January 2012).

[68] *AES v. Hungary*, above n. 54, paras. 10.3.45 and 10.3.46.

[69] *Ibid.*, para. 10.3.16.   [70] *Ibid.*, paras. 10.3.16–10.3.18.

arbitrator considered the pressure exercised by the European Commission as sufficient to accept Hungary's argument.[71] But, despite such disagreement, the tribunal unanimously considered that the administrative prices were within the palette of reasonable measures that Hungary could adopt to pursue its policy objective.[72] Third, the tribunal admitted that excessive rates of return may be reasonably adjusted in light of subsequent circumstances: 'the Tribunal . . . is of the view that it is a perfectly valid and rational policy objective for a government to address luxury profits. And while such price regimes may not be seen as desirable in certain quarters, this does not mean that such a policy is irrational.'[73] Fourth, and finally, the tribunal concluded that there was no discrimination because a single methodology had been applied to the calculation of prices. This approach leaves some room for reasonable differentiation,[74] as will be discussed in connection with the *Arcelor* case. Overall, the reasoning of the tribunal in *AES* v. *Hungary* could be relevant for the analysis of future disputes concerning not only the elimination of subsidies for fossil fuels but also the potential reduction of prices set under schemes for the production of electricity from renewable sources,[75] which are two key areas of climate policy.

Another case relating to differentiation through subsidies is *EnBW Energie Baden-Württenberg* v. *Commission*.[76] The claim was brought by the third largest energy group in Germany against the decision of the European Commission on the German NAP. According to the claimant, the specific allocation of emissions allowances made by the NAP conferred an unfair advantage on the claimant's main competitor, RWE Power AG, because the application of the so-called 'transfer rule' (i.e., the transfer of the allowances of a closed installation to new installations open by the same group within three months) resulted in an excessive amount of allowances being allocated to RWE. To the extent that the Commission had not questioned the NAP on this point, the claimant argued that the decision amounted to a violation of the ETS Directive, European State aid rules and the claimant's freedom of

---

[71] *Ibid.*, para. 10.3.19.   [72] *Ibid.*, para. 10.3.35.

[73] *Ibid.*, para. 10.3.34.   [74] *Ibid.*, para. 10.3.47.

[75] See J. Hepburn, 'Renewable Energy Arbitration Claims on Horizon, but States take Differing Approaches to Public Disclosure' (7 September 2011) (discussing disputes concerning Canada, the Czech Republic and Spain for changes in incentives for the production of renewable energy), available at: www.iareporter.com (accessed on 4 January 2012).

[76] *EnBW Energie Baden-Württenberg* v. *Commission*, CFI Case T-387/04, Order (30 April 2007) ('*EnBW Energie*').

establishment.[77] The peculiarity of this case (as compared to other challenges brought by private parties against decisions of the Commission on the NAP of a given country) lies in the attempts by the claimant to characterise the act challenged as a decision authorising State aid. However, as with the other cases brought by private parties in this specific context, the Court of First Instance considered the application inadmissible for lack of *locus standi*[78] and, therefore, did not address the issue of differentiation.

The absence of specific reasoning on differentiation in most cases brought by private parties in this context makes the *Arcelor* case, in which this issue was discussed, all the more significant. As noted above, the main issue in this case was the additional burden for companies in the steel sector resulting from their inclusion in the European cap-and-trade system. The ECJ accepted that the steel, chemical and aluminium sectors were in a comparable position and that they had been treated differently. However, the Court concluded that such differential treatment was justified under the circumstances. The Court's reasoning in this regard is interesting in a number of ways. The Court stated that 'the quantity of CO2 emitted by each sector [is not] essential for assessing their comparability'[79] and, yet, it later found that the differential treatment of the steel and aluminium sectors was objectively justified because '[t]he difference in the levels of direct emissions between the two sectors concerned is so substantial'.[80]

There is no contradiction between these two statements because there is a significant difference between considering that two sectors are not in a comparable position (because of their different emissions) and finding that, despite the comparable position of the two sectors, a differential measure is justified. This difference lies in the allocation of the burden of proof. The burden of proving comparable positions (or 'likeness') lies with the claimants. By contrast, the burden of proving that there are justified grounds to treat two comparable situations differently lies with the respondent.[81] The practical relevance of this allocation depends, admittedly, on the standard of proof applied at each stage. In the *Arcelor* case, although the ECJ placed the burden of proving that the differentiation was justified by objective criteria on the EC, the standard of proof was arguably not very demanding. In practice, this had the effect of shifting the burden of proof back to the claimant. Indeed,

---

[77] *Ibid.*, paras. 36–8.   [78] *Ibid.*, paras. 112–13.
[79] *Arcelor* reference, above n. 41, para. 37.   [80] *Ibid.*, para. 72.   [81] *Ibid.*, para. 48.

the EC sought to justify the differential treatment of the steel and chemical sectors by reference to administrative complexity (according to the EC, the number of chemical installations concerned, 34,000, was far too high to be included in the first phase of the ETS Directive, which covered some 10,000 installations overall), while Arcelor countered that nearly 60 per cent of the total CO_2 emissions of the chemical sector stemmed from ninety-six installations. Yet, the ECJ seemed to revert the burden of proof to the claimants when it concluded that 'the data produced by the applicants ... do not enable the Court to verify the assertion that a small number of installations in the chemical sector were responsible for a large part of the total CO_2 emissions'.[82]

With respect to the criteria for differentiating between two sectors in a comparable situation, i.e., the criteria circumscribing the boundaries of EC discretion, the ECJ noted that the choice must be based on 'objective criteria appropriate to the aim pursued by the legislation ... taking into account all the facts and the technical and scientific data available at the time of adoption of the act in question'[83] as well as 'all the interests involved'.[84] In particular, the Court noted that the EC's 'exercise of its discretion must not produce results that are manifestly less appropriate than those that would be produced by other measures that were also suitable for those objectives'.[85] In stating the latter point, the ECJ adopted a position arguably similar to that of the tribunals in *AES* v. *Hungary* and in *S. D. Myers* v. *Canada*.[86] Indeed, in *AES* v. *Hungary*, the tribunal stressed the fact that, in adopting the decrees challenged by the investor, Hungary had 'approached the generators to renegotiate the [price purchase agreements]' and '[g]iven that no agreement was reached, and in the absence of a specific commitment to the Claimants that administrative pricing was never going to be reintroduced, the Hungarian parliament voted for the reintroduction of administrative pricing, which parliament considered to be the best option at the moment'.[87] Similarly, the tribunal in *S. D. Myers* looked at whether the objectives pursued by the measure challenged could have been attained by measures less harmful for the interests of the investor before concluding that the measure under review was unnecessarily restrictive.[88]

---

[82] *Ibid.*, para. 68.   [83] *Ibid.*, para. 58.   [84] *Ibid.*, para. 59.   [85] *Ibid.*, para. 59.

[86] *S. D. Myers Inc.* v. *Government of Canada*, NAFTA (UNCITRAL), Partial Award (13 November 2000) ('*S. D. Myers* v. *Canada*').

[87] *AES* v. *Hungary*, above n. 54, para. 10.3.35.

[88] *S. D. Myers* v. *Canada*, above n. 86, paras. 255–6.

10.2.5 The use of a human rights approach

In the discussion of collision points, I identified two main avenues through which the connection between human rights and climate change policies could have an impact on investment schemes. First, by strengthening the access to environmental information, public participation in decision-making and access to justice, human rights may affect the approval and development of certain investment schemes, particularly in the energy sector. Second, human rights provisions could be used to clarify the link, often indirect, between broadly formulated international obligations and domestic measures. Whereas, so far, the latter hypothesis has not been explored by international adjudicatory or quasi-adjudicatory bodies,[89] the former one seems to have received some attention in the work of the Compliance Committee established by the Aarhus Convention.[90] The non-compliance procedure managed by the Compliance Committee is open to individual complaints from the public[91] regarding alleged violations by States parties (or the European Community) of their obligations under the Convention. In the last six years, no less than fifty-eight such applications have been filed in connection with a variety of environmental issues, including the construction of power plants.[92]

The potential impact of the non-compliance procedure on investment schemes can be illustrated by reference to an application brought by a group of NGOs against the Slovak Republic for the alleged failure to ensure public participation in the decision-making procedure leading to the construction of a nuclear power plant.[93] Pursuant to Article 6(1) and

---

[89] See, however, the Inuit Petition, above n. 34. At the national level, see *Native Village of Kivalina and City of Kivalina* v. *ExxonMobil Corporation et al., Order granting Defendant's Motion to Dismiss for Lack of Subject Matter Jurisdiction* (Case No: C 08–1138 SBA), 30 September 2009.

[90] Convention on Access to Information, Public Participation in Decision-making and Access to Justice in Environmental Matters, 25 June 1998, 2161 UNTS 447 ('Aarhus Convention'), Article 15; 'Review of Compliance', Decision I/7, UN Doc. ECE/MP.PP/2/ Add.8, 2 April 2004, Addendum, p.1 ('Decision I/7').

[91] Decision I/7, above n. 90 Annex, paras. 18–24. As with most other non-compliance procedures, the procedure can also be triggered either by other States parties or by the Secretariat of the Convention. See *ibid.*, Annex, paras. 15–17. For an example of a case referred by a State, see Doc. ACCC/C/2004/3 (Ukraine). So far, no case has been referred by the Secretariat.

[92] See, e.g., ACCC/C/2005/12 (Albania), ACCC/C/2007/21 (European Community), ACCC/C/2009/37 (Belarus), ACCC/C/2009/41 (Slovakia), available at: www.unece.org/env/ pp/pubcom.htm (accessed on 4 January 2012).

[93] *Findings and Recommendations with regard to Communication ACCC/C/2009/41 concerning compliance by Slovakia*, 17 December 2010 ('*Committee Findings (Slovakia)*'), paras. 1 and 2, available at www.unece.org/env/pp/pubcom.htm (accessed on 4 January 2012). The

Annex I(1) of the Aarhus Convention, the construction and operation of nuclear power plants qualify as activities requiring public participation in procedures for the granting of an authorisation. The case concerned the completion of construction work and the putting into operation of two additional nuclear reactors by a consortium between the Italian company Enel Spa and Slovak Slovenské Elektrané as ('ENEL/SE'). In May 2008, ENEL/SE applied for the required permits, which were granted on 14 August 2008. Before the permits were granted, two environmental NGOs filed statements urging the Slovak authorities to conduct an environmental impact assessment ('EIA') prior to issuing any permits. However, their statements were rejected on the grounds that the organisations did not meet the (very demanding) criteria required to participate in the procedure. The construction works started in November 2008. Around the same date, the Slovak authorities decided to conduct an EIA limited to the operation of the reactors and not covering certain construction changes authorised by the permits. In the meantime, the NGOs had filed an administrative appeal against the issuance of the permits arguing that a necessary component, the EIA, was missing. The appeal was rejected at the administrative level, and the NGOs turned to the Slovak courts. At the time that the application was filed with the Aarhus Compliance Committee, the local court proceedings were still pending.[94] Despite this fact, the Compliance Committee proceeded to the examination of the communication, reasoning that:

> for a major installation ..., when a permit has been granted and the construction is carried out, there may be considerable pressure on a court not to stop the activity and not to annul the permit decision for lack of public participation. Even if it were to do so, the construction in itself is likely to cause significant environmental effects.[95]

As a result of its examination, the Compliance Committee considered that it was 'not sufficient to provide for public participation only at the stage of the EIA procedure, unless it [was] also part of the permitting procedure'.[96] On this basis, the Committee concluded that the Slovak authorities had failed to comply with Articles 6(4) and 6(10) of the Aarhus Convention[97] and recommended that the Slovak Republic 'review its legal framework so as to ensure that early and effective public

---

following discussion is based on Viñuales and Chuffart, 'From the Other Shore', above n. 35, 16–17.

[94] Committee Findings (Slovakia), above n. 93, para. 45.

[95] Ibid., para. 46.   [96] Ibid., para. 64.   [97] Ibid., paras. 64 and 68.

participation is provided'.[98] The State was, moreover, invited to 'submit to the Committee a progress report on 1 December 2011 and an implementation report on 1 December 2012'.[99]

Although the impact of such a decision on the activities of the foreign investor are still to be determined,[100] were the State to suspend the works and require additional public participation,[101] a normative conflict could arise between the standards laid out in the Aarhus Convention and the investment disciplines provided, for instance, in the ECT (which both Italy and the Slovak Republic have ratified). The same could happen, more generally, in connection with other investment schemes, particularly in the energy sector, as a result of the strengthening of participatory rights.

10.3   Assessing contemporary practice

This section discusses the implications of the preceding analysis for the management of future normative conflicts between international climate change regulation and investment disciplines. After a brief presentation of the main conceptual findings (Section 10.3.1), I focus on a number of practical problems that may arise in this connection (Section 10.3.2).

10.3.1   Conceptual findings

The review of the case-law in Section 10.2 shows that, so far, normative conflicts between investment disciplines and either the UNFCCC or the Kyoto Protocol have not yet arisen. There are, of course, cases where such conflicts could potentially arise (or at least could have arisen). One example is *Vattenfall* v. *Germany*,[102] although the dispute was settled before Germany had the opportunity to present its legal defence. Another illustration is the pending *Naftrac* v. *Ukraine*,[103] which could potentially involve the application by Ukraine of regulations concerning

---

[98] *Ibid.*, para. 70.   [99] *Ibid.*, para. 70.

[100] On the effectiveness of the Committee's recommendations, see 'National Implementation Report', available at www.unece.org/env/pp/reports%20implementation.htm (accessed on 4 January 2012).

[101] The occurrence of delays has been considered as a potential breach of investment disciplines. See *S. D. Myers* v. *Canada*, above n. 86, paras. 256, 268 and 283; *Chemtura Corporation (formerly Crompton Corporation)* v. *Government of Canada*, UNCITRAL, Award (2 August 2010) ('*Chemtura* v. *Canada*'), paras. 217–20.

[102] See above n. 63.   [103] See above n. 59.

the JI mechanism. But the information publicly available is not sufficient to conclude that a normative conflict has arisen.

Yet, limiting normative conflicts in this area to potential clashes between investment disciplines and either the UNFCCC or the Kyoto Protocol would be misleading. These two treaties are but the tip of the climate regulation ice-berg. One could refer, for instance, to the *Arcelor* case,[104] where an international instrument (a European Directive) specifically adopted to implement the Kyoto Protocol clashed with certain economic freedoms recognised by European law. From the perspective of this broader understanding of normative conflicts in this area, the number of relevant disputes grows considerably, encompassing a significant body of cases before the judicial bodies of the European Union.[105] Normative conflicts in this area must be more broadly conceived because climate policies may be very diverse in nature, ranging from the familiar cap-and-trade systems to a broader array of command-and-control regulation, taxes and subsidies (see Section 10.1). Disputes relating to electricity generation schemes, automobile production, steel production, etc., may well raise a normative conflict if the measure challenged is linked, even indirectly, to a State's efforts to mitigate emissions deployed within the framework of the UNFCCC or the Kyoto Protocol. To identify the proper set of relevant disputes it is therefore necessary to clarify the link between domestic measures and international obligations in the area of climate change.

In this context, the question of the link presents several practical problems that will be analysed below. These include, *inter alia*, the approach followed by both the UNFCCC and the Kyoto Protocol, which leave the choice of the implementation measures for States to decide. Even when States' obligations are specified in the decisions adopted by the conference of the parties to the UNFCCC (or the meeting of the parties to the Kyoto Protocol), such decisions are not binding on States. Similarly, the voluntary commitments that a State may advance as part of the negotiations are of a purely political nature and not binding under international law. More generally, the measures that a State may adopt can affect a wide spectrum of industries. Let me discuss these difficulties in more detail.

10.3.2 Some practical problems

This section addresses three basic practical problems already identified in previous chapters: the link between domestic measures and

---

[104] See above n. 41.   [105] See above n. 42, 49 and 50.

international obligations (Section 10.3.2.1); the vulnerability of such link (Section 10.3.2.3); and the adequacy of the available conflict norms (Section 10.3.2.4). The invocation of the link will not be addressed because of the absence of specific practice in this regard. In analysing these problems, I will highlight the specific features of climate change regulation.

10.3.2.1   Building a link with international obligations

Some pieces of legislation make their grounding on the UNFCCC or the Kyoto Protocol explicit. A prominent example is the ETS Directive. But even when they do so, the very nature of the international obligations in this area makes it difficult to establish that a measure is commanded (or that some activities are prohibited) or fully authorised by international law. However, there are several techniques through which the link could be strengthened, in addition to those already discussed in previous chapters (i.e. cost–benefit analyses,[106] consultations,[107] decisions from international bodies[108]).

The first possibility is the use of decisions from the conference of the parties to the UNFCCC (or the meeting of the parties to the Kyoto Protocol) as interpretive guidance of the international commitments undertaken by the State. Much of the past and present developments of the international climate change regime (in particular the so-called 'Marrakesh Agreements' of 2001 and the more recent 'Cancun Agreements' of 2010) have taken the form of decisions. Although these decisions are technically not binding, they could be treated as subsequent practice relevant for the interpretation of the binding provisions of both the UNFCCC and the Kyoto Protocol.[109]

The second possibility would be to refer to the 'voluntary' commitments undertaken by States, either in the form of emissions or efficiency targets or in the form of projected measures.[110] The 'voluntary' nature of such commitments does not necessarily mean that they are deprived of

---

[106] *Arcelor* reference, above n. 41.

[107] *AES v. Hungary*, above n. 54, para. 10.3.35.

[108] *Ibid.*, paras. 10.3.16–10.3.19. Another illustration is the case against Greece brought before the non-compliance procedure of the Kyoto Protocol. See above nn. 55 and 56.

[109] J. E. Viñuales, 'Du bon dosage du droit international: les négociations climatiques en perspective' (2010) 56 *Annuaire de droit international* 437, at 447–9, 455–7.

[110] See unfccc.int/meetings/cop_15/copenhagen_accord/items/5264.php (objectives communicated by States included in Annex I to the UNFCCC) and unfccc.int/meetings/cop_15/copenhagen_accord/items/5265.php (objectives/actions communicated by States not included in Annex I to the UNFCCC) (accessed on 4 January 2012).

any legal effect. They could, for instance, be considered as an expression of the understanding of States regarding the contents of their obligations under the UNFCCC or, at least, as part of the practice relevant for the interpretation of such obligations.[111]

Third, reference to human rights provisions could also be useful to clarify the link between a domestic measure and the host State's international environmental obligations. More specifically, human rights provisions would serve the purpose of clarifying the obligations of States under the UNFCCC or the Kyoto Protocol, thereby clarifying also the extent to which a given measure is required or fully authorised by international law. This avenue has been explored, with limited success, in the Inuit petition before the ICommHR.[112] However, the elaboration of the link between human rights provisions and the obligations of States under the UNFCCC and the Kyoto Protocol remains to be done.

10.3.2.2   The vulnerability of the link

As pointed out in previous chapters, even when a link between the challenged domestic measure and the host State's international obligations can be established, questions of proportionality and due process may render such link vulnerable.

In the area of climate change, the question of proportionality was discussed in both *AES* v. *Hungary*[113] and the *Arcelor* case.[114] In *AES* v. *Hungary*, the tribunal had to determine whether the reintroduction of administrative prices (set by decree, as opposed to the prices set by agreement with the claimant) had been a rational policy. In concluding that it had, the tribunal took into account several elements, including the government's attempts to negotiate lower prices with the investors, the deliberations of the Hungarian Parliament[115] and, more importantly for present purposes, the fact that acting pursuant to European law (and by extension also with international law) would 'no doubt' constitute a 'rational public policy measure'.[116] Thus, there would be a sort of presumption of proportionality when the actions have been taken pursuant to a community (or international) obligation. Under the specific circumstances of the case, the arbitrators disagreed as to whether Hungary's actions were indeed required by European law. The majority considered that, for such a link to be established, a decision from the European

---

[111] Viñuales, 'Du bon dosage du droit international', above n. 109, 448–9.
[112] See above n. 34.   [113] See *AES* v. *Hungary*, above n. 54.
[114] See *Arcelor* reference, above n. 41.   [115] *AES* v. *Hungary*, above n. 54, para. 10.3.35.
[116] *Ibid.*, para. 10.3.16; *Chemtura* v. *Canada*, above n. 101, para. 138.

Commission (as opposed to mere pressure) was needed.[117] They nevertheless considered that it had been proportional (the tribunal uses the terms 'perfectly valid and rational policy objective') for the government to seek to reduce 'luxury profits'.[118] In *Arcelor*, the question of proportionality was addressed as part of the ECJ's assessment of whether the differentiation introduced by the ETS Directive among different industry sectors was proportional. It noted that the exercise of governmental discretion (at the EC level) 'must not produce results that are manifestly less appropriate than those that would be produced by other measures that were also suitable for those objectives'.[119] On the basis of its assessment, it concluded that given the complexities involved in introducing the European cap-and-trade system and the legitimate choice to move progressively, it was not disproportionate to include the steel industry (and not the chemical and aluminium industries) in the first phase of operation of the ETS.[120]

With respect to due process, as already noted above in connection with the *AES* v. *Hungary* case, the efforts of the Hungarian government to seek an agreement with the claimants before introducing administrative prices was taken into account by the tribunal in determining the reasonableness of the measures adopted. Another case where the issue of due process may be potentially relevant is *Naftrac* v. *Ukraine*,[121] but the information publicly available is not sufficient to take the analysis further.

10.3.2.3   The adequacy of the available conflict norms

As with the regulatory areas discussed in previous chapters, the present area is also characterised by the scarcity of specific conflict norms and the inadequacy of general conflict norms. One specific point that may be worth noting in this connection is the potential role of the general principles enshrined in Article 3 of the UNFCCC.

An interesting example of the role of such principles is provided by Article 3(5) of the UNFCCC, which states that '[m]easures taken to combat climate change, including unilateral ones, should not constitute a means of arbitrary or unjustifiable discrimination or a disguised restriction on international trade'. In the context of the debate on the legality of carbon neutralisation measures, this specific application of the

---

[117] *AES* v. *Hungary*, above n. 54, paras. 10.3.16 –10.3.18.
[118] *Ibid.*, para. 10.3.34.   [119] *Arcelor* reference, above n. 41, para. 59.
[120] *Ibid.*, paras. 69–71.   [121] See above n. 59.

mutual supportiveness principle was taken up in Section E of Chapter III (mitigation) of the Cancun Agreements.[122] The third Recital of the Preamble of this section states indeed that 'responses to climate change should be coordinated with social and economic development in an integrated manner, with a view to avoiding adverse impacts on the latter'. And the text goes further 'reaffirming' the text of Article 3(5) of the UNFCCC.[123]

The impact this principle could have in the context of a trade (and by extension also an investment) dispute should not be underestimated. An idiosyncratic forum may find in such a statement support for limiting the consideration of international environmental law in the context of trade and investment proceedings. States should be aware of the dormant effects of such statements and, depending on their needs and strategy, they should also be ready to introduce statements that clarify the relations between investment disciplines and the international climate change regulation.

---

[122] Decision 1/CP.16, *The Cancun Agreements: Outcome of the Work of the Ad Hoc Working Group on Long-term Cooperative Action under the Convention*, 15 March 2011, FCCC/CP/2010/7/ Add.1, Chapter III, Section E (echoing UNFCCC, above n. 1, Article 3(5)).

[123] *Ibid.*, para. 90.

Part III

Legitimacy conflicts

11 Normative priority between different legal systems

The function and the scope of the set of conflict norms reviewed in this chapter are different from those of the conflict norms applicable to normative conflicts. Unlike the latter, the former regulate normative priority between norms belonging to different legal systems and their scope therefore tends to be broader.[1] These conflict norms are also diverse in nature, reflecting the diversity of forms that such conflicts may take. In this chapter, I first identify the main types of legitimacy conflicts that may arise between environmental and investment protection (Section 11.1). This discussion is followed by an analysis of the specific conflict norms currently in existence (Section 11.2) as well as of a number of legal tools (including conflict norms *stricto sensu*, but also 'doctrines' or legal defences) that serve the function of allocating normative priority among norms from different legal systems (Section 11.3). Interpretation techniques, which are also relevant for the determination of the scope of investment disciplines in the context of a legitimacy conflict, are not taken up in this chapter. Despite their importance, their operation in the present context is essentially as conflict characterisation techniques rather than as general conflict norms.[2]

11.1 Legitimacy conflicts

Legitimacy conflicts can take different forms according to: (i) the legal systems at stake; (ii) the substance of the contending norms; and (iii) the manner in which the conflict is framed.

---

[1] However, some general conflict norms discussed in Chapter 6 may also be relevant here because some forms of reasoning about normative priority exist in different legal systems.

[2] See Chapter 6, Section 6.3.5.

From the perspective of the first criterion, a legitimacy conflict may involve one norm of international law and another of domestic law or norms from two different domestic legal systems. In the first case, the applicable conflict norms are those concerning the relations between international and domestic law (norms informing the dualistic, monistic or mixed nature of such relations)(Section 11.3.1). In the second case, the main set of applicable conflict norms will be the body of private international law or choice-of-law rules (*'normes de conflit des lois et de juridictions'*) (Section 11.3.2). In investment disputes, the first case is more frequent.

From the perspective of the second criterion, several types of legitimacy conflicts can be identified. For present purposes, it is sufficient to distinguish, within conflicts between one international norm and one domestic norm, two basic scenarios. On the one hand, a legitimacy conflict may arise between a norm from international investment law and a domestic environmental measure. This is the most frequent occurrence.[3] On the other hand, the reverse is also possible, namely a conflict between one norm of international environmental law and a domestic investment measure.[4] The applicable conflict norms consist of a growing number of specific provisions in free-trade agreements ('FTAs') and, to a lesser extent, of bilateral (or multilateral) investment treaties ('BITs' or 'MITs') carving out space for environmental regulation (Section 11.2).

A third criterion is the manner in which the conflict is framed. Among the many forms in which such conflicts are argued by the parties and framed by the tribunal for their resolution, the most frequent ones are those involving the concept of State regulatory powers or some more specific legal concepts manifesting these powers such as the police powers

---

[3] See, e.g., *Robert Azinian, Kenneth Davitian and Ellen Baca* v. *United Mexican States*, ICSID Case No. ARB(AF)/97/2, Award (1 November 1999) (*'Azinian* v. *Mexico'*); *Metalclad Corporation* v. *United Mexican States*, ICSID Case No. ARB(AF)/97/1, Award (25 August 2000) (*'Metalclad* v. *Mexico'*); *Compañía del Desarrollo de Santa Elena SA* v. *Republic of Costa Rica*, ICSID Case No. ARB/96/1, Award (17 February 2000) (*'CDSE* v. *Costa Rica'*); *Methanex Corporation* v. *United States of America*, NAFTA (UNCITRAL), Award (3 August 2005) (*'Methanex* v. *United States'*); *Técnicas Medioambientales Tecmed SA* v. *United Mexican States*, ICSID Case No. ARB(AF)/00/2, Award (29 May 2003) (*'Tecmed* v. *Mexico'*); *Glamis Gold Ltd* v. *United States of America*, NAFTA (UNCITRAL), Award (16 May 2009) (*'Glamis* v. *United States'*); *Chemtura Corporation (formerly Crompton Corporation)* v. *Government of Canada*, UNCITRAL, Award (2 August 2010) (*'Chemtura* v. *Canada'*).

[4] *Southern Pacific Properties (Middle East) Limited (SPP)* v. *Arab Republic of Egypt*, ICSID Case No. ARB/84/3, Award (20 May 1992) (*'SPP* v. *Egypt'*) (to the extent of the clash between the investment law of Egypt and the World Heritage Convention); *Grand River Enterprises Six Nations, Ltd, et al.* v. *United States of America*, NAFTA (UNCITRAL), Award (12 January 2011) (*'Grand River* v. *United States'*) (only to the extent that one may consider that the international law relating to minorities was applied).

doctrine,[5] the margin of appreciation doctrine,[6] and emergency and necessity clauses.[7] These concepts will be analysed in detail in Chapter 15.

11.2 Specific conflict norms

11.2.1 Types of specific conflict norms

As noted in Chapter 6 in connection with normative conflicts, environmental considerations are increasingly being taken into account in the drafting of agreements. The OECD's survey of 269 investment and free trade agreements found indeed that FTAs tend to include express language on environmental issues, whereas these references are rather exceptional in BITs.[8]

Such language mostly concerns the scope for domestic environmental regulation in three main forms: the assertion of a right to adopt environmental regulations (type (i)); the statement that it is inappropriate for States to lower environmental regulations to attract foreign investment (type (ii)); and certain environmental exceptions either general or specific (in connection with some investment disciplines, such as those on expropriation or on performance requirements) (type iii).

11.2.2 Some illustrations

One of the earliest manifestations of the trend towards the introduction of environmental considerations in trade and investment treaties appears in the text of the NAFTA.[9] Chapter 11 of the NAFTA contains the three types of environmental clauses identified above. Article 1114 reads as follows:

> 1. Nothing in this Chapter shall be construed to prevent a Party from adopting, maintaining or enforcing any measure otherwise consistent with this Chapter that it considers appropriate to ensure that investment activity in its territory is undertaken in a manner sensitive to environmental concerns.

---

[5] See, e.g., *Methanex* v. *United States*, above n. 3; *Chemtura* v. *Canada*, above n. 3.
[6] See, e.g., *Chemtura* v. *Canada*, above n. 3.
[7] See, e.g., *Suez, Sociedad General de Aguas de Barcelona SA and InterAguas Servicios Integrales del Agua SA* v. *The Argentine Republic*, ICSID Case No. ARB/03/17 ('*Suez* v. *Argentina* – 03/17'); *Suez, Sociedad General de Aguas de Barcelona, SA and Vivendi Universal, SA* v. *The Argentine Republic*, ICSID Case No. ARB/03/19 ('*Suez* v. *Argentina* – 03/19').
[8] OECD, *International Investment Law: Understanding Concepts and Tracking Innovation*, (Paris: OECD, 2008) ('*OECD 2008 Study*'), pp. 141ff.
[9] North American Free Trade Agreement, 17 December 1992, 32 ILM 296 ('NAFTA'), Articles 1120 and 1122.

2. The Parties recognize that it is inappropriate to encourage investment by relaxing domestic health, safety or environmental measures. Accordingly, a Party should not waive or otherwise derogate from, or offer to waive or otherwise derogate from, such measures as an encouragement for the establishment, acquisition, expansion or retention in its territory of an investment of an investor. If a Party considers that another Party has offered such an encouragement, it may request consultations with the other Party and the two Parties shall consult with a view to avoiding any such encouragement.

This provision circumscribes the boundaries of the environmental regulation of foreign investment. An exercise of regulatory power that unreasonably interferes with foreign investment would not be 'consistent' with Chapter 11 of the NAFTA. Conversely, regulatory competition through the relaxation of environmental standards would be 'inappropriate'. This latter component is strengthened by the mechanisms established in the NAAEC,[10] which contemplates both non-compliance and individual complaint procedures in case a State party does not respect its own environmental regulations.[11] Chapter 11 of the NAFTA also contains specific environmental exceptions to the prohibition of performance requirements. Article 1106(2) provides, in relevant part, that '[a] measure that requires an investment to use technology to meet generally applicable health, safety or environmental requirements shall not be construed to be inconsistent with paragraph 1(f) [protection against forced transfer of technology]'. In addition, Article 1106(6) provides for a more general exception to the prohibition of performance requirements:

Provided that such measures are not applied in an arbitrary or unjustifiable manner, or do not constitute a disguised restriction on international trade or investment, nothing in paragraph 1b) or c) or 3a) or b) shall be construed to prevent any Party from adopting or maintaining measures, including environmental measures: a) necessary to secure compliance with laws and regulations that are not inconsistent with the provisions of this Agreement; b) necessary to protect human, animal or plant life or health; or c) necessary for the conservation of living or non-living exhaustible natural resources.

Another early manifestation of the same trend appears in the Energy Charter Treaty ('ECT'), concluded shortly after the NAFTA, which also

---

[10] North American Agreement on Environmental Cooperation, 17 December 1992, 32 ILM 1519 ('NAAEC').
[11] *Ibid.*, Article 14.

addresses the relations between environment and investment, albeit with a somewhat different accent. Article 19(1) of the ECT emphasises that the protection of the environment should not be pursued through economically inefficient measures:

In pursuit of sustainable development and taking into account its obligations under those international agreements concerning the environment to which it is party, each Contracting Party shall strive to minimize in an economically efficient manner harmful Environmental Impacts occurring either within or outside its Area from all operations within the Energy Cycle in its Area, taking proper account of safety.[12]

These provisions suggest that by the early 1990s environmental protection had gained considerable strength, not only politically but also legally.

Later generations of BITs or FTAs have further developed this approach expressly addressing the relations between foreign investment and environmental protection. For example, the investment chapter of CAFTA–DR[13] contains specific provisions on issues such as performance requirements,[14] the adoption, maintenance and enforcement of environmental regulations[15] and the scope of indirect expropriation.[16] In a similar vein, several model BITs have also incorporated express references to the relations between foreign investment and environmental protection. Examples include the 2004 model BIT of the United States[17] and Canada,[18] as well as the current model BIT of Belgium/Luxembourg,[19] Finland,[20] the Netherlands[21] and Sweden.[22]

---

[12] Energy Charter Treaty, 17 December 1994, 2080 UNTS 95 ('ECT'). The requirements of Article 19 of the ECT are further developed by the Energy Charter Protocol on Energy Efficiency and Related Environmental Aspects ('PEEREA'), negotiated, opened for signature and entered into force at the same time as the ECT, on 17 December 1994, 2081 UNTS 3.

[13] Dominican Republic–Central America–United States Free Trade Agreement, 5 August 2004 (initially concluded on 28 May 2004, by and between the United States, Costa Rica, El Salvador, Guatemala, Honduras and Nicaragua, later joined by the Dominican Republic), 43 ILM 514 ('CAFTA-DR').

[14] *Ibid.*, Article 10.9(3).   [15] *Ibid.*, Article 10.11.   [16] *Ibid.*, Annex 10-B, Section 4(b).

[17] United States' 2004 Model BIT, Preamble, Articles 8, 12 and 32, and Annex B (expropriation), reproduced in *OECD 2008 Study*, above n. 8, pp. 183–5.

[18] Canada's 2004 Model BIT, Articles 10 and 11, reproduced in *OECD 2008 Study*, above n. 8, pp. 178–179.

[19] Belgium/Luxembourg's Model BIT, Preamble, reproduced in *OECD 2008 Study*, above n. 8, p. 180.

[20] Finland's 2004 Model BIT, Article 5, reproduced in *OECD 2008 Study*, above n. 8, pp. 176–7.

[21] The Netherlands' 2004 Model BIT, Preamble, reproduced in *OECD 2008 Study*, above n. 8, p. 182.

[22] Sweden's 2003 Model BIT, Preamble, reproduced in *OECD 2008 Study*, above n. 8, p. 182.

11.2.3   Effects

The potential effects of some of these clauses must not be underestimated, especially when they are formulated as exceptions to specific investment protection clauses (type (iii)). The basic operation of such clauses could be quite radical and simply neutralise the very existence of a conflict, therefore excluding the liability of the host State.

The impact of broadly formulated clauses (types (i) and (ii)), such as Article 1114 of the NAFTA or Article 19(1) of the ECT, is more difficult to assess. Such treaty clauses would, for instance, provide limited assurance to a State contemplating the adoption of domestic environmental regulations with potentially adverse effects on foreign investors established in its territory. To take one example, as discussed in Chapter 10, the implementation of the international climate change regime may increasingly require countries to adopt far-reaching environmental measures to curb emissions. Such measures may in turn affect the profitability of foreign investments made prior to their adoption. But not every type of measure will entail the same litigation risk. Some measures may appear more compatible than others with the obligations assumed by a State in connection with the protection of foreign investment, and therefore present a lower litigation risk. Given the substantial amounts often at stake in foreign investment proceedings, a State may be well advised to undertake an assessment of potential litigation risks, and provisions like those referred to above would be of little help in conducting such an assessment. Similarly, on the assumption that the host State would take an adverse environmental measure, such provisions would provide limited guidance to a foreign firm (or its legal counsel) in assessing the probability of recovering an investment made in an environmentally sensitive sector. Such provisions would be of limited use even for arbitral tribunals tasked with solving an investment dispute with environmental dimensions, particularly when the dispute has a significant public dimension and the tribunal is, as is often the case, reluctant to make an open pronouncement on the relative hierarchy between investment protection and environmental considerations.

It is therefore important to discuss which additional approaches could be used to deal with potential conflicts between investment and environmental protection.

11.3   General conflict norms

There are different approaches to solving legitimacy conflicts: (i) rules governing the relations between international and domestic law; (ii) rules governing conflicts of laws belonging to different domestic legal systems or within one domestic system; (iii) rules governing the scope of the State's regulatory powers. In this Section, the discussion focuses only on (i) and (ii). Point (iii) is only briefly noted, as it will be analysed in detail in Chapter 15.

11.3.1   Relations between domestic and international law

The relationship between international and domestic law is a traditional subject of study by international law scholars.[23] The purpose of the following remarks is limited to an assessment of the relevance of this relationship in the specific context of legitimacy conflicts between investment and environmental protection. As noted when discussing the law applicable to investment disputes, there is some controversy as to the specific relations between international and domestic law. But such divergence of views does not affect one fundamental point, namely that when there is inconsistency between domestic and international law, international courts and tribunals give priority to the latter.

An apposite illustration is provided by the decision of the tribunal in *SPP v. Egypt*.[24] In this case, brought under the aegis of ICSID,[25] the investor claimed that its property had been expropriated in breach of a domestic law and an investment agreement of 1974. The parties disagreed on the law applicable to the dispute. The respondent argued that the parties had implicitly agreed to apply Egyptian law and, therefore, under Article 42(1) first sentence of the ICSID Convention, the dispute

---

[23] See H. Triepel, *Völkerrecht und Landesrecht* (Leipzig: Hirschfeld, 1899); H. Triepel, 'Les rapports entre le droit interne et le droit international', in *Recueil des cours de l'Académie de droit international*, Vol. 1 (1923) pp. 73–122; D. Anzilotti, 'Il diritto internazionale nei giudizi interni', in D. Anzilotti (ed.), *Scritti di diritto internazionale pubblico*, Vol. 1, (Padova: Cedam, 1956); D. Anzilotti, *Cours de droit international* (Paris: Sirey, 1929) 49; H. Kelsen, 'Les rapports de système entre le droit interne et le droit international', in *Recueil des cours de l'Académie de droit international*, Vol. 14 (1926) pp. 227–332; H. Kelsen, 'La transformation du droit international en droit interne' (1936) 43 *Revue générale de droit international public* 5. For a recent and targeted study see M. Sasson, *Substantive Law in Investment Treaty Arbitration. The Unsettled Relationship between International Law and Municipal Law* (Alphen aan den Rijn: Kluwer Law International, 2010).

[24] *SPP v. Egypt*, above n. 4.

[25] Convention on the Settlement of Investment Disputes between States and Nationals of other States, 18 March 1965, 575 UNTS 159, ('ICSID Convention').

was to be exclusively governed by Egyptian law. The respondent further argued that international law could apply only to the extent that it had been incorporated in Egyptian law, as was the case with the World Heritage Convention.[26] The claimants countered that there was no such implicit choice of law and, as a result, international law was applicable in accordance with Article 42(1) second sentence of the ICSID Convention.[27] The tribunal considered that both Egyptian law and international law, including the World Heritage Convention, were applicable to the dispute.[28] It further stated that:

When municipal law contains a lacuna, or international law is violated by the exclusive application of municipal law, the Tribunal is bound in accordance with Article 42 of the Washington Convention to apply directly the relevant principles and rules of international law.[29]

This position, which ascribes a supplemental and corrective role to international law over domestic law, has received considerable support in the investment case-law.[30] Under the specific circumstances of the *SPP* v. *Egypt* case, the application of international law was important because the host State had argued, *inter alia*, that the allegedly expropriatory acts had been adopted pursuant to its obligations under the World Heritage Convention. Egypt had ratified the World Heritage Convention in 1975, i.e., some three years before the adoption of the measures challenged, in 1978. However, the World Heritage Committee had not registered the sites proposed by Egypt for the Committee's list of protected sites until 1979. Based on this latter fact, the tribunal considered that the obligation to protect the site had not arisen until 1979, i.e., after the date of the expropriatory acts. Thus, these acts could not be justified as conduct required by the provisions of the World Heritage Convention.[31] More importantly for present purposes, the tribunal considered that from 1979 onwards the obligations of Egypt under the World Heritage Convention prevailed over the protections granted to investors. As a result, the compensation due to the investor could not take into account gains that would have accrued after the emergence of the obligation under the World Heritage Convention.[32]

---

[26] *SPP* v. *Egypt*, above n. 4, para. 75–6. See Convention for the Protection of the World Cultural and Natural Heritage, 16 November 1972, 1037 UNTS 151 ('World Heritage Convention').

[27] *Ibid.*, para. 77.   [28] *Ibid.*, paras. 78–80.   [29] *Ibid.*, para. 84.

[30] See R. Dolzer and C. Schreuer, *Principles of International Invesment Law* (Oxford University Press, 2008) pp. 269–70.

[31] *SPP* v. *Egypt*, above n. 4, para. 154.   [32] *Ibid.*, para. 191.

The priority of international environmental law over domestic investment disciplines was implied in this conclusion.

The corrective role of international law was also discussed in *CDSE* v. *Costa Rica*, a dispute concerning the expropriation of a biodiversity-rich land to establish a nature preserve. At stake were the different approaches to the valuation of the property expropriated arising, respectively, from the laws of Costa Rica and from international law. The tribunal applied the second sentence of Article 42(1) of the ICSID Convention and concluded that international investment law was controlling:

> This leaves the Tribunal in a position in which it must rest on the second sentence of Article 42(1) ('In the absence of such agreement . . .') and thus apply the law of Costa Rica and such rules of international law as may be applicable. No difficulty arises in this connection. The Tribunal is satisfied that the rules and principles of Costa Rican law which it must take into account, relating to the appraisal and valuation of expropriated property, are generally consistent with the accepted principles of public international law on the same subject. To the extent that there may be any inconsistency between the two bodies of law, the rules of public international law must prevail. Were this not so in relation to takings of property, the protection of international law would be denied to the foreign investor and the purpose of the ICSID Convention would, in this respect, be frustrated . . . [t]he parties' divergent positions lead, in substance, to the same conclusion, namely, that, in the end, international law is controlling. The Tribunal is satisfied that, under the second sentence of Article 42(1), the arbitration is governed by international law.[33]

Although the tribunal referred to the rules on 'appraisal and valuation of expropriated property', which have apparently nothing to do with environmental matters, it is important to note that the respondent's arguments on quantum were partly based on its domestic environmental laws. According to the respondent, such laws restricted and even prohibited the commercial development of the expropriated site, with obvious consequences for the estimation of the fair market value of the property.[34] Moreover, we know from an article published by counsel for Costa Rica that the respondent had invoked several environmental treaties as part of its argumentation on quantum,[35] which were dismissed

---

[33] *CDSE* v. *Costa Rica*, above n. 3, paras. 64–5.

[34] *Ibid.*, paras. 34–5.

[35] C. Brower and J. Wong, 'General Valuation Principles: The Case of Santa Elena', in T. Weiler (ed.), *International Investment Law and Arbitration: Leading Cases from the ICSID, NAFTA, Bilateral Treaties and Customary International Law* (London: Cameron May, 2005), p. 764.

rather hastily by the tribunal.[36] The tribunal's conclusion in this case would suggest that an act of expropriation for environmental purposes is subject to the rules on compensation arising from international investment law, irrespective of whether domestic valuation and environmental laws would lead to a different result.

A different conclusion as to the relations between international investment law and domestic (and European) environmental law was reached by the tribunal in *Maffezini v. Spain*.[37] In this case, the tribunal seemed to give priority to the standards for the conduct of environmental impact assessments emanating from both Spanish and European law. The reasoning of the tribunal suggests that, to the extent that they abided by the applicable environmental laws, the Spanish authorities were not in breach of the applicable BIT.[38]

11.3.2   Conflicts of (domestic) laws

Legitimacy conflicts may also arise between norms stemming from different domestic systems (or within a decentralised – federal – domestic system). There are essentially two methods to determine the applicable law in such cases.

First, the traditional private international law methods will be applicable to assess whether and to what extent a foreign law (or the law of a territorial subdivision, in some federal States like the United States) is applicable to the substance of the dispute. As was discussed in Section 5.3.2.4, the main arbitration rules give tribunals some discretion in the selection of the applicable law, *inter alia*, by allowing tribunals to use the conflict of laws rules that they deem appropriate.[39]

Second, domestic norms may be applicable as a result of their higher substantive hierarchy, as is the case of *lois de police* or other overriding or mandatory norms. At least some environmental laws, either from

---

[36] *CDSE v. Costa Rica*, above n. 3, para. 71 (and footnote 32).

[37] *Emilio Agustín Maffezini v. Kingdom of Spain*, ICSID Case No. ARB/97/7, Award (13 November 2000) ('*Maffezini v. Spain* – Award'), paras. 65–71.

[38] *Ibid.*, para. 71. However, the reasoning of the tribunal seems to depend much more on the factual record (the absence of pressure from the Spanish authorities for Maffezini to start the construction of the contemplated chemical plant before having presented a satisfactory EIA) and, potentially, on the grounding in international law of the need to conduct an EIA prior to any project with potential environmental consequences. See on this latter point, *Pulp Mills in the River Uruguay (Argentina v. Uruguay)*, Judgment (20 April 2010), General List No. 135 ('*Pulp Mills* case'), para. 204.

[39] See Section 5.3.

the State where the legal seat of the arbitration is located or from a foreign State,[40] may qualify as *lois de police* and therefore be potentially applicable irrespective of the choice of the parties to a dispute. As with the applicability of competition law, which has received sustained attention,[41] arbitration tribunals have some leeway in deciding whether or not the environmental *lois de police* of the host State or of other States may be applicable.[42] Some commentators have even argued that arbitral tribunals would have the obligation to apply such *lois de police*.[43] In practice, the limits of arbitral tribunals' discretion are basically the causes of annulment of the award set out, as the case may be, in Article 52 of the ICSID Convention,[44] in Article V of the New York Convention[45] or in the relevant provisions of the arbitration laws of the State where the legal seat of the arbitration proceedings has been located.

11.3.3 Regulatory powers as general conflict norms

Reference to the State's regulatory powers has emerged in recent years as one of the most important techniques for solving conflicts between investment protection standards and environmental, health or human rights considerations. Although the doctrine of regulatory powers is not as such a conflict rule, it may operate as one to the extent that it shields certain measures taken by the State from being considered as a breach of investment protections.

The scope of the State's regulatory powers is difficult to determine precisely. Commentators and tribunals have often sought to circumscribe this doctrine by reference to more specific formulations of the underlying concept. Among the many legal expressions of a State's regulatory powers, three are of particular relevance for solving legitimacy conflicts: (i) the police powers doctrine; (ii) the margin of appreciation doctrine; and (iii) emergency and necessity clauses. Despite the many differences among these three legal concepts or 'doctrines', they

---

[40] See P. Mayer, 'Lois de police étrangères' (1981) 108 *Journal de droit international* 277.

[41] P. Landolt, *Modernised EC Competition Law in International Arbitration* (London: Kluwer, 2006), Chapter 6.

[42] L. Radicati di Brozolo, 'Arbitrage commercial international et lois de police. Considérations sur les conflits de juridictions dans le commerce international', in *Recueil des cours de l'Académie de droit international*, Vol. 315 (2005), p. 402.

[43] J.-B. Racine, *L'arbitrage commercial international et l'ordre public* (Paris: LGDJ, 1999) p. 162.

[44] ICSID Convention, above n. 25, Article 52.

[45] Convention on the Recognition and Enforcement of Foreign Arbitral Awards, 10 June 1958, 330 UNTS 38 ('New York Convention'), Article V.

all share a focus on the balancing of two competing considerations, normally two interests (each protected by a different – international or domestic – norm). It is in this sense that such concepts or doctrines can be considered to perform the function of a general conflict norm. A detailed discussion of these concepts is provided in Chapter 15.

12 Environmental measures and expropriation clauses

This chapter analyses a number of questions that may arise in the context of legitimacy conflicts between environmental measures and expropriation clauses. The subject of expropriation (either 'direct' or 'indirect') in international investment law has received ample attention in the literature[1] and does not require further comment here. Environmental expropriation as such has also received sustained attention.[2] However, with some exceptions, the literature focuses on specific cases[3]

---

[1] See, e.g., R. Dolzer, 'Indirect Expropriation of Alien Property' (1986) 1 *ICSID Review – Foreign Investment Law Journal* 41; M. Reisman and R. Sloane, 'Indirect Expropriation and its Valuation in the BIT Generation' (2003) 74 *British Yearbook of International Law* 115; Y. Fortier and S. Drymer, 'Indirect Expropriation in the Law of International Investment: I Know It When I See It, or Caveat Investor' (2004) 19 *ICSID Review – Foreign Investment Law Journal* 293; C. McLachlan, L. Shore and M. Weiniger, *International Investment Arbitration: Substantive Principles* (Oxford University Press, 2007) pp. 291–313; M. Sornarajah, *The International Law on Foreign Investment* (Cambridge University Press, 3rd edn, 2010) Chapter 10, especially pp. 400ff.

[2] See, e.g., OECD, Foreign Direct Investment and the Environment: An Overview of the Literature (1997) DAFFE/MAI(97)33/REV1; T. Wälde and A. Kolo, 'Environmental Regulation, Investment Protection and "Regulatory Taking" in International Law' (2001) 50 *International and Comparative Law Quarterly* 811; K. Tienhaara, *The Expropriation of Environmental Governance* (Cambridge University Press, 2009); S. Robert-Cuendet, *Droits de l'investisseur étranger et protection de l'environnement: Contribution à l'analyse de l'expropriation indirecte* (Leiden: Martinus Nijhoff, 2010); M. Paparinskis, 'Regulatory Expropriation and Sustainable Development', in M.-C. Cordonnier-Segger, M. Gehring and A. Newcombe (eds.), *Sustainable Development in World Investment Law* (Alphen aan den Rijn: Wolters Kluwer, 2011) pp. 299–327.

[3] See, e.g., C. Brower, 'International Decisions: S.D. Myers, Inc. v. Canada' (2004) 98 *American Journal of International Law* 339; C. Brower and J. Wong, 'General Valuation Principles: The Case of Santa Elena', in T. Weiler (ed.), *International Investment Law and Arbitration: Leading Cases from the ICSID, NAFTA, Bilateral Treaties and Customary International Law* (London: Cameron May, 2005) pp. 747–75; J. Coe and N. Rubins, 'Regulatory Expropriation and the Tecmed Case: Context and Contributions', in Weiler, *International Investment Law and Arbitration*, above, pp. 597–667; T. Weiler, 'Good Faith and Regulatory

or contexts,[4] and it does not take into account some recent practice that signals that the case-law in this area is reaching maturity. For this reason, some additional comment on this topic seems warranted. In the following pages, after an overview of the main strands of cases touching on the relations between environmental measures and expropriation (Section 12.1), I analyse *tour à tour* direct environmental expropriations (Section 12.2), targeted environmental measures (Section 12.3) and regulatory environmental measures (Section 12.4).

12.1   Three strands of cases

Within the vast body of cases dealing with takings of alien property, a first fundamental distinction is generally made between direct expropriation, which entails the formal transfer of title to the State, and indirect expropriation, which does not. Concerning 'direct expropriation', there has been some discussion as to whether a distinction is necessary between 'lawful' and 'unlawful' direct expropriation. From a practical perspective, such a distinction would mainly be relevant for the purpose of calculating the amount of compensation due to the investor, as the right of States to expropriate is widely recognised.[5] As to indirect expropriation, it has multiple faces, and terms such as 'regulatory expropriation' (or 'taking'), 'creeping expropriation', 'constructive taking' or, still, 'disguised expropriation' have been used to describe them.

From an analytical standpoint, a second basic distinction must be introduced between two major types of indirect expropriation. The one

---

Transparency: The Story of Metalclad v. Mexico', in Weiler, *International Investment Law and Arbitration*, above, pp. 701–45.

[4] Mostly in the context of the Iran–US Claims Tribunal and the NAFTA. See, e.g., G. H. Aldrich, *The Jurisprudence of the Iran–United States Claims Tribunal* (Oxford: Clarendon Press, 1996); S. Gaines, 'The Masked Ball of NAFTA Chapter 11: Foreign Investors, Local Environmentalists, Government Officials, and Disguised Motives', in J. Kirton and V. MacLaren (eds.), *Linking Trade, Environment, and Social Cohesion: NAFTA Experiences, Global Challenges* (Aldershot: Ashgate, 2002), pp. 103–29; J. Soloway, 'Environmental Expropriation under NAFTA Chapter 11: The Phantom Menace', in Kirton and MacLaren, *Linking Trade, Environment, and Social Cohesion*: above, pp. 131–44; V. Been and J. Beauvais, 'The Global Fifth Amendment? NAFTA's Investment Protections and the Misguided Quest for an International "Regulatory Takings" Doctrine' (2003) 78 *New York University Law Review* 30; S. Baughen, 'Expropriation and Environmental Regulation: The Lessons of NAFTA Chapter Eleven (2006) 18 *Journal of Environmental Law* 207; J. Lawrence, 'Chicken Little Revisited: NAFTA Regulatory Expropriations after Methanex' (2006) 41 *Georgia Law Review* 261.

[5] See R. Dolzer and C. Schreuer, *Principles of International Investment Law* (Oxford University Press, 2008), pp. 90–2.

most frequently discussed is 'regulatory' expropriation, i.e., the substantial deprivation of the value of property resulting from the adoption of a measure of general application but without formal transfer of title. The other form of indirect expropriation, which can be called 'targeted', concerns cases where the measure is not general but individual and specific (e.g., suspension or revocation of a licence, termination of a contract, targeted restriction of the operations, etc.). The treatment of such measures is, in practice, different from that of general measures, because the impact of the measure on the investor differs significantly. Importantly, targeted measures may be a mere extension of a measure of general application (e.g., the suspension of a licence to operate may be the direct application of a new law). In such a case, some of the legal tools available for shielding regulatory expropriation may also be available in the context of claims for targeted expropriation.

Third, the evolution of the case-law suggests that the legal framework applicable to targeted and regulatory expropriation in an environmental context is not identical to that applicable in a non-environmental context. The existence of some differences between these two frameworks seems to be the result of the increasing awareness of the need to protect the environment, which, in turn, is reflected by the adoption of environmental treaties and soft-law instruments as well as by the growing scope of the State's regulatory powers in this area. In other words, the potential differences that may be signalled between the environmental and the non-environmental contexts are not the result of a different definition of indirect expropriation or of additional exceptions, but of the broader availability of existing defence arguments.

In the following sections, these three analytical distinctions are used to explore the case-law on direct, targeted and regulatory expropriation in the area of environmental protection.

12.2   Direct environmental expropriation

In the area of environmental protection, direct expropriation does not seem to be the rule. Most cases of alleged expropriation arise, indeed, from targeted or regulatory measures. The limited case-law arising from direct environmental takings concerns expropriation decrees for the purpose of creating a natural preserve or a buffer zone or, sometimes, a protected cultural site.

A well-known example is the *CDSE* v. *Costa Rica* case, where the host State expropriated a parcel of land owned by the claimant to create a nature preserve.[6] Article 1 of the expropriation decree of 5 May 1978 left no ambiguity as to the direct nature of the taking. It stated, in relevant part, that 'the property owned by the Compañia de Desarrollo Santa Elena S.A. described in the third whereas clause of this decree, is hereby expropriated'.[7] The dispute hinged rather on the amount of compensation. In this connection, the tribunal stated that the environmental purpose pursued by the expropriation made no difference to the obligation to pay compensation:

> Expropriatory environmental measures – no matter how laudable and beneficial to society as a whole – are, in this respect, similar to any other expropriatory measures that a state may take in order to implement its policies: where property is expropriated, even for environmental purposes, whether domestic or international, the state's obligation to pay compensation remains.[8]

The position of the tribunal has two components: the principle that, as a rule, direct takings – even for environmental reasons – must be compensated; and the extent to which environmental reasons must be taken into account in calculating the amount of compensation. Only the first component[9] seems consistent with the case-law from other international jurisdictions. In *Lithgow* v. *United Kingdom*, a case concerning a formal taking of property (albeit not for environmental reasons), the ECtHR stated that 'under the legal systems of the Contracting States, the taking of property in the public interest without payment of compensation is treated as justifiable only in exceptional circumstances not relevant for present purposes'.[10]

In fact, even in exceptional circumstances, the ECtHR has generally considered that at least some compensation must be paid. The amount of compensation may be reduced as long as it remains 'reasonably related' to the value of the property taken or, stated in other terms, as long as the applicant does not bear a disproportionate burden. In *Scordino* v. *Italy*, the ECtHR summarised its case-law on this question stating that '[l]egitimate objectives in the "public interest", such as those pursued in measures of economic reform or measures designed to achieve greater social justice, may call for less than reimbursement of

---

[6] *Compañia del Desarrollo de Santa Elena SA* v. *Republic of Costa Rica*, ICSID Case No. ARB/96/1, Award (17 February 2000) ('*CDSE* v. *Costa Rica*').

[7] Reproduced in Brower and Wong, 'General Valuation Principles', above n. 3, 750.

[8] *CDSE* v. *Costa Rica*, above n. 6, para. 62.   [9] On the second component, see Section 5.5.

[10] *Lithgow and others* v. *United Kingdom*, ECtHR Application No. 9006/80; 9262/81; 9263/81; 9265/81;9266/81; 9313/81; 9405/81, Judgment (8 July 1986), para. 120.

the full market value'.[11] Yet, an excessive reduction of the compensation awarded may amount to an indirect or de facto taking. In *Aka* v. *Turkey*, the applicant's land had been expropriated by the government for the purpose of building a dam. The amount of compensation per se was not disputed, but the long delay in the payment of such amount had reduced its value. The Court considered that:

the difference between the value of the amounts due to Mr Aka when his land was expropriated and when actually paid – which difference was due solely to failings on the part of the expropriating authority – caused him to sustain a separate loss which, coupled with the loss of his land, upset the fair balance that should have been maintained between the protection of the right to property and the demands of the general interest.[12]

Thus, although States have considerable leeway in determining the amount and conditions of compensation, their discretion is not unbounded.

12.3   Targeted environmental measures

12.3.1   Targeted measures v. general regulation

Whether or not a targeted measure amounts to an expropriation depends on the circumstances of the case. However, the case-law suggests that, other things being equal, targeted measures substantially depriving the affected investment of its value are more likely to be considered as tantamount to expropriation than general regulatory measures.

For instance, out of the ten types of indirect taking identified by Sornarajah, only one (taxation) could be categorised as 'regulatory' (as opposed to targeted).[13] This conclusion is further suggested by a review of the case-law of the Iran–United States Claims Tribunal, where most indirect takings were the result of targeted measures.[14] Similarly, in the ICSID context, many awards characterising the measures challenged as

---

[11] *Scordino* v. *Italy (No. 1)*, ECtHR Application No. 36813/97, Judgment (29 March 2006), paras. 95 and 97–8.

[12] *Aka* v. *Turkey*, ECtHR Application No. 107/1997/891/1103, Judgment (23 September 1998), para. 72.

[13] Sornarajah, *The International Law on Foreign Investment*, above n. 1, 375.

[14] Aldrich distinguishes cases that amounted to an expropriation (aside from formal nationalisations, these are all targeted measures) from cases where no taking was found (including 'lawful regulations'). See Aldrich, *The Jurisprudence of the Iran–United States Claims Tribunal*, above n. 4, Chapter 5.

tantamount to expropriation concerned targeted measures (at least as the decisive measure for the finding of expropriation).[15] Given the variability of facts of the different cases that one could refer to in this connection, it is, however, difficult to derive from this observation specific legal consequences.

Generally speaking, the main reason underlying this pattern seems to be the recognition that regulation should, in principle, not be considered expropriatory.[16] Additional reasons include: (i) the similar effects of direct takings and targeted measures (by contrast with those of regulatory measures); (ii) the clearer contradiction between specific assurances given to the investors and subsequent (contrary) targeted measures (the contrary character of subsequent general measures is, as a rule, more difficult to show); and (iii) the more difficult use, in the context of targeted measures, of defences based on the regulatory powers of the State (e.g., the police powers doctrine, the margin of appreciation doctrine, and emergency and necessity clauses).

---

[15] For cases (ICSID and non-ICSID) potentially relevant from an environmental perspective, see, e.g., *Southern Pacific Properties (Middle East) Limited (SPP) v. Egypt*, ICSID Case No. ARB/84/3, Award (20 May 1992) ('*SPP v. Egypt*'); *Metalclad Corporation v. United Mexican States*, ICSID Case No. ARB(AF)/97/1, Award (25 August 2000) ('*Metalclad v. Mexico*'); *Técnicas Medioambientales Tecmed SA v. United Mexican States*, ICSID Case No. ARB(AF)/00/2, Award (29 May 2003) ('*Tecmed v. Mexico*'); *Compañía de Aguas del Aconquija SA and Vivendi Universal SA v. Argentine Republic*, ICSID Case No. ARB/97/3, Award (20 August 2007) ('*Vivendi II*'); *Biwater Gauff (Tanz.) Ltd v. United Republic of Tanzania*, ICSID Case No. ARB/05/22, Award (24 July 2008) ('*Biwater v. Tanzania*'). See also, *Middle East Cement Shipping and Handling Co SA v. Egypt*, ICSID Case No. ARB/99/6, Award (12 April 2002). In a number of cases, tribunals have avoided a finding of expropriation but have awarded compensation in accordance with the rules and methodologies used in the context of expropriation. See P.-Y. Tschanz and J. E. Viñuales, 'Compensation for Non-Expropriatory Breaches of International Investment Law: The Contribution of the Argentine Awards' (2009) 6 *Journal of International Arbitration* 729.

[16] See P. Jessup, 'Confiscation' (1933) 21 *American Society of International Law Proceedings* 40; Sornarajah, *The International Law on Foreign Investment*, above n. 1, p. 374; Aldrich, *The Jurisprudence of the Iran–United States Claims Tribunal*, above n. 4, pp. 208–10 (through a reference to *Emanuel Too v. United States of America*, Award No. 460–880–2 (29 December 1989), Iran–US CTR, vol. 23, 378); McLachlan, Shore and Weiniger, *International Investment Arbitration*, above n. 1, pp. 306–8 (stating that regulation is not, as such, exempted from constituting an expropriation but that their non-discriminatory character is usually influential in rejecting expropriation); Dolzer and Schreuer, *Principles of International Investment Law*, above n. 5, 109ff (these authors note that '[e]mphasis on the host state's sovereignty supports the argument that the investor should not expect compensation for a measure of general application', but their position is nuanced and fact-dependent); A. Newcombe and L. Paradell, *Law and Practice of Investment Treaties* (Alphen aan den Rijn: Kluwer Law International, 2009) pp. 357–8.

One may ask whether these potential reasons operate in a similar manner irrespective of the environmental or non-environmental context of the dispute or, conversely, whether their operation is to some extent facilitated in the environmental context. A review of the case-law suggests that the environmental context of a dispute has an influence on the assessment of targeted measures as expropriatory or not. More specifically, the environmental context facilitates the operation of some specific and general conflict norms (or similar techniques) relevant in this regard.

12.3.2   Targeted environmental measures amounting to an expropriation

The literature on indirect expropriation sometimes refers, in connection with targeted environmental measures, to the *CDSE* v. *Costa Rica* case,[17] a case in which environmental considerations were disposed of in little more than a footnote. But such reference is technically inaccurate. As discussed in Section 12.2., this case involved compensation for a direct (and not a targeted or a regulatory) expropriation. Whereas the need to compensate in the event of a direct expropriation is widely recognised, such principle does not necessarily extend to indirect (targeted) takings or, at least, not to the same extent. The three most significant cases to explore this question are *SPP* v. *Egypt*, *Metalclad* v. *Mexico* and *Tecmed* v. *Mexico*.[18]

In *SPP* v. *Egypt*, the tribunal concluded that the withdrawal of the government's approval of a tourist project had amounted to an indirect expropriation of the claimant's investment.[19] The tribunal emphasised the proximity between the measure and a State's exercise of its right of eminent domain, and it concluded that compensation was due.[20] Yet, environmental considerations were taken into account in determining the amount of compensation. Although the tribunal noted that the obligation to pay compensation (in the context of a direct expropriation) applied even when the protection of antiquities was involved,[21] the amount of compensation claimed by the investor and, specifically, the *lucrum cessans* component (representing future profits) was reduced because, from 1979 onwards:

---

[17] *CDSE* v. *Costa Rica*, above n. 6.   [18] See above n. 15.
[19] *SPP* v. *Egypt*, above n. 15, para. 160–73.
[20] *Ibid.*, paras. 158–9 and 179.   [21] *Ibid.*, para. 159.

the Claimant's activities on the Pyramids Plateau would have been in conflict with the Convention [World Heritage Convention] and therefore in violation of international law, and any profits that might have resulted from such activities are consequently non-compensable.[22]

Similarly, in other cases relating to targeted environmental measures tribunals have concluded to the existence of an indirect expropriation, despite the environmental purposes pursued by the measures.

In *Metalclad* v. *Mexico*, the tribunal concluded that Mexico had committed an indirect expropriation by two distinct sets of measures, some targeted (described in paragraph 104 of the award[23]) and some regulatory (the ecological decree[24]). The compensation awarded by the tribunal did not take into account the environmental dimension of the case, but remains interesting in two respects. First, the main reason why the environmental dimension was not taken into account seems to have been that the local government's perception of the environmental risks posed by the investor's facility had no basis.[25] Second, the tribunal did not award any future profits because it considered that, as the landfill had never operated, the granting of future profits would have been speculative. Interestingly, the tribunal found support for this conclusion in a case before the Iran–United States Claims Tribunal where the tribunal had reasoned that profits dependent on 'as yet unobtained preferential treatment of the government ... [made] any prediction of them ... entirely speculative'.[26] This reasoning is consistent with the idea, developed in Chapter 5, that future profits in highly regulated industries are largely dependent on the evolution of the regulatory framework, which, in turn, is not only a natural feature of such markets, but it is also dependent (as are future profits) on scientific and technological change.

In a similar vein, the tribunal in *Tecmed* v. *Mexico* considered that a targeted measure (the non-renewal of an operation permit) amounted to an expropriation under the applicable investment treaty.[27] Despite the fact that the investor was responsible for several deficiencies with potential health and environmental implications, on the balance of the evidence the tribunal found that such deficiencies had not been the decisive trigger of the non-renewal of the permit. Such trigger was instead to be found in the social unrest provoked by the operation of

---

[22] *Ibid.*, para. 191.   [23] *Metalclad* v. *Mexico*, above n. 15, para. 104.
[24] *Ibid.*, para. 109.   [25] *Ibid.*, para. 106.
[26] *Ibid.*, para. 122.   [27] *Tecmed* v. *Mexico*, above n. 15, para. 151.

the landfill.[28] However, the tribunal explicitly noted that the environmental context (not only the effects) of the adoption of the measure had to be taken into account in assessing whether such measure amounted to a compensable expropriation. More specifically, although the tribunal noted that the regulatory character of a measure (the tribunal did not have a general regulation in mind[29]) was not as such an impediment to its expropriatory effect,[30] it considered that it had to examine 'whether the Resolution [the environmental targeted measure], due to its characteristics and considering not only its effects, is an expropriatory decision'.[31] It then sought guidance in the case-law of the European Court of Human Rights ('ECtHR') in order to give some room, through the use of the ECtHR's proportionality test, to considerations other than the sole effects of the measure.[32] But, as already noted, the tribunal eventually concluded that the environmental basis of the targeted measure was too thin to be the actual trigger of the non-renewal of the permit.

These three early cases relating to the effects of targeted environmental measures do not necessarily reflect the current state of the law. As discussed next, more recent cases shed a different light on this question. In addition, as further discussed in Section 12.4, the adoption of general environmental regulation is increasingly recognised as not giving rise to liability for breach of expropriation clauses, thus excluding the payment of compensation.

12.3.3 Targeted environmental measures not amounting to an expropriation

In a number of cases involving environment-related targeted measures (ranging from zoning requirements to the suspension of pesticides registrations to measures allegedly necessary to implement the right to water) tribunals have rejected a claim for expropriation. The decisive reasons underlying the decisions of these tribunals are not always the result of environmental considerations, but they remain informative because they suggest: (i) that a targeted environmental measure may sometimes not amount to an expropriation; (ii) that the police powers doctrine may not only shield measures of general application but also targeted environmental measures; and (iii) that determination of the value of an investment (and therefore the application of the substantial

---

[28] *Ibid.*, para. 127.   [29] *Ibid.*, para. 119.   [30] *Ibid.*, para. 121.
[31] *Ibid.*, para. 118.   [32] *Ibid.*, para. 122.

deprivation test) may be influenced by the environmental regulatory context in which the investor operates.

A first illustration of this trend is provided by *MTD* v. *Chile*.[33] In this case, the claimant argued, *inter alia*, that the denial of a permit, based on zoning requirements, amounted to an indirect expropriation in the circumstances of the case. More specifically, the claimant argued that:

> after receiving authorization to ... [make its investment] from the State; [it] was [then] forced to halt the execution of its project because it was informed that it lacked a necessary permit; [it] attempted to obtain such permit but the attempts were rebuffed; as a result it was unable to continue with the Project and essentially lost the value of its investment.[34]

This case raised one potentially frequent problem encountered by foreign investors when dealing with different sections of the host State's administration, namely the possible lack of co-ordination or even inconsistency between the actions attributable to the State. The issuance of environmental permits is often in the hands of State agencies that are separate and, sometimes, have little contact with investment agencies. When an investor has made an investment in reliance of an investment authorisation and, later on, an environmental permit required for starting the operations is denied, one would tend to consider that the expectations of the investor should be in some way protected. But granting such protection does not necessarily mean granting an expropriation claim. In *MTD* v. *Chile* the tribunal rejected the expropriation claim, noting that the investor did not have a right to a modification in the laws of the host State (*in casu* the zoning requirements) and adding that, in this case, the problem had not been the non-renewal or the cancellation of a licence to operate but rather the fact that the State had acted in an inconsistent manner by granting, in the first place, the authorisation to invest.[35] Importantly, there is no reason for the risk of inconsistency to be borne by the sole State. Investors are required to assess the regulatory environment of the country in which they invest and part of such assessment is the need to obtain environmental or (as in this case) zoning permits. A reasonable investor would be expected to be aware of such potential complications and to take them into account when calculating its 'commercial' risk. In *MTD* v. *Chile*, not only did the tribunal reject the expropriation claim, but it also reduced the

---

[33] *MTD Equity Sdn Bhd and MTD Chile SA* v. *Republic of Chile*, ICSID Case No. ARB/01/7, Award (25 May 2004) ('*MTD* v. *Chile*').

[34] *Ibid.*, para. 207.   [35] *Ibid.*, para. 214.

compensation awarded for other breaches to account for the investor's negligence.[36] Moreover, environmental permits are not granted unconditionally. If, before obtaining the required permit, an investor decides nevertheless to proceed with its investment (or with some substantial works relating to it) and, in the end, the permit is not granted, the investor must assume the consequences of its decision.[37]

Another more recent case where the tribunal rejected an expropriation claim relating to a targeted environmental measure is *Chemtura v. Canada*.[38] In this case, the claimant argued that the suspension, by the Canadian environmental agency, of the claimant's authorisation to produce and commercialise certain lindane-based pesticides amounted to an indirect expropriation under Article 1110 of the NAFTA.[39] The tribunal rejected the claim confirming that targeted environmental measures do not necessarily amount to an expropriation. The tribunal gave two main reasons for its conclusion. First, it considered that the measure did not have the effect of substantially depriving the investor of the value of its investment. Significantly, the investor did not argue that the totality of its investment in Canada (the shares of Chemtura Canada) had been expropriated but rather than its lindane 'line of business' (a limited portion of the overall business) had been deprived of its value. The tribunal noted the following in this connection:

applying a percentage or threshold approach to the overall assets held by the investor in the host State would preclude the deprivation from being 'substantial', whereas applying the same assessment to the specific asset in question would lead to the opposite conclusion. Given the diversity of situations that may arise in practice, it is preferable to examine each situation in the light of its own specific circumstances.[40]

Under the specific circumstances of the case, the tribunal found that no substantial deprivation had occurred.[41] This finding was premised on the fact that both parties agreed that the investment potentially

---

[36] *Ibid.*, paras. 242–3.
[37] See *Emilio Agustín Maffezini* v. *Kingdom of Spain*, ICSID Case No. ARB/97/7, Award (13 November 2000), para. 71.
[38] *Chemtura Corporation (formerly Crompton Corporation)* v. *Government of Canada*, UNCITRAL, Award (2 August 2010) (*'Chemtura v. Canada'*).
[39] North American Free Trade Agreement, 17 December 1992, 32 ILM 296 ('NAFTA').
[40] *Ibid.*, para. 249. See also, *GAMI Investments Inc.* v. *United Mexican States*, NAFTA (UNCITRAL), Award (15 November 2004), para. 125 (highlighting the identification of the 'affected property').
[41] *Ibid.*, paras. 259–63.

expropriated were the shares of Chemtura Canada, and not a mere part of them.[42] In order to identify the 'baseline' for assessing whether a deprivation has been substantial or not, the award in *Chemtura v. Canada* thus suggests that one may look to the investment identified for jurisdictional purposes. This path had already been followed by the tribunal in *Azurix v. Argentina*, which accepted a broad definition of investment for jurisdictional purposes and then, applying the investment thus defined as a baseline, rejected the existence of a substantial deprivation.[43] An additional indication of what should be the baseline is given by the connections between the different assets of the investor located in the host State. To the extent that such connections are taken into account to assess damages for expropriation,[44] there is no reason why such connections should not be taken into account to identify the investment scheme that must be used as the 'baseline' for assessing the extent of the deprivation.[45] The practical importance of this issue must not be underestimated, as many investors in markets subject to environmental regulation are not active in a single line of business and, given the dynamics of environmental regulation (which follows the understanding of risks), targeted or even regulatory measures will normally affect only some of the products produced by diversified investors. The second reason given by the tribunal to reject the expropriation claim was that the measure under review (albeit targeted) was but a normal exercise of the State's regulatory powers.[46] Thus, the tribunal clarified that the police powers doctrine may apply also to targeted measures.[47]

---

[42] *Ibid.*, para. 258.

[43] *Azurix Corp v. Argentina*, ICSID Case No. ARB/01/12, Decision on Jurisdiction (8 December 2003), paras. 59–65; *Azurix Corp v. Argentina*, Award, ICSID Case No. ARB/01/12, Award (23 June 2006), para. 322.

[44] *Tecmed v. Mexico*, above n. 15, para. 117.

[45] *Fredin v. Sweeden* (No. 1), ECtHR Application No. 12033/86, Judgment (18 February 1991), para. 45. See Newcombe and Paradell, *Law and Practice of Investment Treaties*, above n. 16, pp. 348ff referring to the US doctrine of the 'parcel as a whole', which prevents the property owner from dividing its array of property rights to argue that one component has been fully expropriated (*Tahoe-Sierra Preservation Council, Inc. v. Tahoe Regional Planning Agency* (2002) 122 S. Ct. 1465). The economic connections among different assets of the investor were also taken into account by the tribunal in *Telenor v. Hungary* in determining the 'investment' that had allegedly been expropriated. It must be noted, however, that Hungary did not dispute the claimant's contention that its investment consisted of different components economically related, so the tribunal did not assess the claimant's argument. See *Telenor Mobile Communications AS v. Hungary*, ICSID Case No. ARB/04/15, Award (22 June 2006) ('*Telenor v. Hungary*'), para. 60–2 and 67.

[46] *Chemtura v. Canada*, above n. 38, para. 266.

[47] On the police powers doctrine, see Chapter 15.

The reasoning of the tribunal in *Suez* v. *Argentina* – 03/17[48] is also relevant for the assessment of the expropriatory nature of targeted measures. In this case, the claimant argued, *inter alia*, that the refusal by the Argentine province of Santa Fe to revise the water tariffs as well as the subsequent termination of contract amounted to an indirect expropriation. The tribunal rejected the expropriation claim for lack of substantial deprivation, but it added as an *obiter dictum* that, whereas the police powers may have shielded the general regulations adopted by Argentina, it could not have covered the two targeted measures under review, which had only intervened after Argentina had exercised its police powers.[49] However, what according to the tribunal seems to lie beyond the scope of the police powers doctrine is not any targeted measure but only the 'deliberate refusal to respect a specific commitment made to a foreign investment'.[50] Thus, when no such commitment has been given, as is the case of the granting of an environmental authorisation, which depends upon meeting certain conditions, the police powers would remain applicable.[51] This should be particularly the case when the targeted measure has been adopted to implement a general regulatory measure.

12.4   Regulatory environmental measures

12.4.1   Rule or exception?

As already noted, it is commonly recognised that States have the power to adopt general regulations and that, even when such regulations adversely affect the interests of investors, the resulting damage is as a rule non compensable.[52] In a number of cases involving environmental regulations of general application,[53] tribunals have indeed considered

---

[48] *Suez, Sociedad General de Aguas de Barcelona SA and InterAguas Servicios Integrales del Agua SA* v. *The Argentine Republic*, ICSID Case No. ARB/03/17 ('*Suez* v. *Argentina* – 03/17').

[49] *Ibid.*, para. 149.   [50] *Ibid.*, para. 149.

[51] This is further consistent with *Saluka* v. *Czech Republic*, where the tribunal considered that a targeted measure (the decision of a banking regulator) was shielded by the police powers doctrine. See *Saluka Investments BV* v. *The Czech Republic*, UNCITRAL, Partial Award, 17 March 2006 ('*Saluka* v. *Czech Republic*'), paras. 262 and 275.

[52] See above n. 16.

[53] *S. D. Myers Inc.* v. *Canada*, NAFTA (UNCITRAL), Partial Award (13 November 2000) ('*S. D. Myers* v. *Canada*'), para. 281; *Methanex Corporation* v. *United States of America*, NAFTA (UNCITRAL), Award (3 August 2005) ('*Methanex* v. *United States*'), Part IV, Ch. D, para. 7; *Glamis Gold Ltd* v. *United States of America*, NAFTA (UNCITRAL), Award (16 May 2009) ('*Glamis* v. *United States*'), paras. 356 and 361 (focusing the inquiry on the effects of regulatory – rather than targeted – measures); *Chemtura* v. *Canada*, above n. 38, para. 266.

that no expropriation had taken place and, consequently, that no compensation was due. However, it is not entirely clear whether this generally acknowledged rule constitutes a principle or an exception (or the nature of such an exception). This ambiguity has, in turn, a bearing on the allocation of the burden of proof.

The case-law touching on this specific issue is not always conceptually clear. Tribunals have considered that nothing in the nature of general (environmental) regulations places them per se beyond the scope of expropriation clauses.[54] But what is the exact meaning of such an observation? One could consider that nothing prevents general regulations from amounting to indirect expropriations if not the fact that the claimant will probably find it much more difficult to establish the conditions required for an expropriation claim. From this perspective, a showing by the investor that a general regulation has caused a substantial deprivation of the value of the investment would shift the burden of proof to the host State to establish that it was acting under one exception. Such an understanding would, in fact, amount to treating targeted and general regulatory measures on the same footing, considering them expropriatory unless a specific exception (e.g., the police powers doctrine) is available.

However, this latter view is highly problematic from the perspective of both law and practice. First, given that regulatory powers are an essential component of sovereignty, such a view would be inconsistent with the well established principle that limitations to State sovereignty are not to be presumed.[55] Second, in practice, regulatory change is not the exception but the rule, particularly when it comes to the highly regulated markets in which investors in the energy, mining, chemical and other similar sectors operate. The normal course of a regulated market is that general regulations will evolve over time.[56] The better view is

---

Other relevant cases, albeit concerning regulations of a non-environmental nature, include *Telenor* v. *Hungary*, above n. 45, para. 64; *Saluka* v. *Czech Republic*, above n. 51, para. 262.

[54] *S. D. Myers* v. *Canada*, above n. 53, para. 281 *in fine*.

[55] This fundamental principle has been recognised in both general international law and international economic law. See, e.g., *SS Wimbledon*, PCIJ, Series A, No. 1 (17 August 1923), 24–5; *SS Lotus*, PCIJ, Series A, No. 10 (7 September 1927), 18; *Free Zones of Upper Savoy and the District of Gex*, PCIJ, Series A/B, No. 46 (7 June 1932), 167. More recently, see R. Howse, 'The Appellate Body Rulings in the Shrimp/Turtle Case: A New Legal Baseline for the Trade and Environment Debate' (2002) 27 *Columbia Journal of Environmental Law* 491, at 519.

[56] *Methanex* v. *United States*, above n. 53, Part IV, Ch. D, para. 9; *Chemtura* v. *Canada*, above n. 38, para. 149.

therefore that changes in general regulations are the rule and that only exceptionally will they amount to an expropriation. This view is further consistent with a fair allocation between 'commercial' risk (borne by the investor) and 'political' risk (borne by the State).

Under this second view, the investor bears the burden of proving (i) that regulatory changes had the effect of substantially depriving the investment of its value, and (ii) that such changes cannot be regarded as part of its commercial risk or, alternatively to showing (ii), (iii) that despite being part of its commercial risk the regulatory change was effected in contradiction with prior specific assurances given to the investor. Only then the burden of proof is shifted to the State, which may then establish the availability of a specific exception (e.g., Article 1114 of the NAFTA) or of a general exception, such as the police powers doctrine or emergency and necessity clauses. The term 'exception' or 'defence' in connection with these different legal tools is used here in a non-technical manner. It is only intended to convey the idea that the State is required to make a certain showing. On the one hand, the operation of specific exceptions (e.g., Article 1114 of the NAFTA) as well as of certain general exceptions (e.g., the police powers doctrine) amounts to establishing the 'normality' of the regulatory change (or, in other words, that such change is part of the investor's commercial risk).[57] On the other hand, the operation of emergency and necessity clauses focuses on establishing that, despite the 'exceptional' character of a regulatory change, it should nevertheless be regarded as justified under the circumstances.

12.4.2 Reasons why environmental regulation rarely amounts to an expropriation

Different factors must be assessed in determining whether environmental regulations should be characterised as an expropriation or not. These range from the availability of specific exceptions in the applicable treaty, to a number of more general factors, such as the laudable motives behind the regulation, its non-discriminatory character, the imperious need for it or its limited effects on the value of the investment. In this Section, I analyse four of them: the extent of the deprivation (Section 12.4.2.1); the use of the police powers doctrine (Section 12.4.2.2);

---

[57] *Telenor* v. *Hungary*, above n. 45, para. 64; *Chemtura* v. *Canada*, above n. 38, para. 266. The police powers doctrine may also be used to justify exceptionality. See *Suez* v. *Argentina* – 03/17, above n. 48, paras. 146–50.

the relevance of purpose (Section 12.4.2.3); and the impact of specific assurances (Section 12.4.2.4).

12.4.2.1   The extent of the deprivation

The most important reason why, in practice, environmental regulations challenged by investors have not been considered to amount to an expropriation is the absence of a substantial deprivation. Several tribunals have indeed rejected a claim of expropriation relating to the effects of an environmental regulation because the investor had failed to establish that it had been substantially deprived of the value of its investment.

A key issue in assessing this question is the identification of the 'baseline' or the 'affected property' that must be taken into account to measure whether the deprivation of value has been substantial. This question has been discussed in Section 12.3.3. The two basic considerations that must guide this determination are: (i) the investment that has been identified for the purpose of establishing jurisdiction; and (ii) the connections between the different assets held by the investor in the territory of the host State (whether severance would accurately reflect the reality of the investment situation or whether it would be purely conceptual or artificial). As already noted, these two criteria have been used not only in the case-law of investment tribunals, but also in that of the ECtHR as well as in the domestic legal system of the United States.

Once the baseline has been identified, the following step is to assess whether the investment has been substantially deprived of its value as a result of the regulatory measure. The burden of proving this requirement lies with the claimant.[58] The criteria that can be used to conduct this assessment in an environmental context do not differ from those used in non-environmental contexts,[59] although their operation (and more generally the overall application of the 'sole effects doctrine') in an environmental context has been considered unsatisfactory by some

---

[58] This is a simple application of the basic principle that *actori incumbit probatio*. See C. Brown, *A Common Law of International Adjudication* (Oxford University Press, 2007), pp. 92–7; PCA Optional Rules, Article 24(1); UNCITRAL Arbitration Rules, Article 24(1); *Bayindir Insaat Turizm Ticaret ve Sanayi A Ş v. Pakistan*, ICSID Case No. ARB/03/29, Award (27 August 2009) ('*Bayindir v. Pakistan*'), paras. 140–3; *Pulp Mills in the River Uruguay (Argentina v. Uruguay)*, Judgment (20 April 2010), General List No. 135 ('*Pulp Mills* case'), para. 162.

[59] *Chemtura v. Canada*, above n. 38, paras. 245–7 (referring to *Pope & Talbot Inc. v. Canada*, NAFTA (UNCITRAL), Interim Award on Merits I (26 June 2000)).

commentators.[60] They include questions relating to: (i) the control of the investment scheme;[61](ii) the interference (short of control or supervision) of the State with the operations of the investment scheme;[62] and (iii) the duration of the interference. Typically, a general regulation will be less likely to meet any of these criteria than one or more targeted measures. For this reason, the application of the basic test in the case of environmental regulation tends to exclude a finding of substantial deprivation. In at least three cases, namely *S. D. Myers v. Canada*, *Glamis v. United States* and *Chemtura v. Canada*, the failure of the claimant to establish this point was indeed dispositive of the expropriation claim.[63] However, the test is not a rigid one. As noted by the tribunal in *Chemtura v. Canada* in connection with a disagreement between the parties as to the operation of the criteria for assessing a substantial deprivation:

> the divergence of views between the Parties regarding the use of the criteria mentioned in *Pope & Talbot* is not fundamental. Indeed, the Respondent has not seriously argued that each such criterion or at least some of them must be present for a deprivation to be 'substantial'. The criteria must thus guide the inquiry of the Tribunal when it seeks to determine whether the effects of the measures challenged are to 'substantially' deprive the investor of the benefit of its investment. *This is a matter of degree and not one of specific conditions.*[64]

Thus, an environmental regulation of general application is not per se exempted from constituting an expropriatory measure; it is simply very unlikely to be so. This is a consequence of the very criteria developed by investment tribunals to assess whether a deprivation has been substantial. These criteria seem quite fair and balanced, as they have served to identify both expropriatory acts (most often targeted measures) to the benefit of investors as well as non-expropriatory acts, to the benefit of host States. Therefore, neither States nor investors should be allowed to 'cherry-pick' within this set of criteria those which appear the most favourable for their arguments, while disregarding the others. Whereas tribunals are not required to apply each and every one of these criteria, they do have to take them into account in forming their overall opinion of the impact of a given measure on the value of an investment.

---

[60] Robert-Cuendet, *Droits de l'investisseur étranger et protection de l'environnement*, above n. 2, pp. 158–94.

[61] *Chemtura v. Canada*, above n. 38, para. 245.   [62] *Ibid.*, para. 245.

[63] *S. D. Myers v. Canada*, above n. 53, paras. 284–8; *Glamis v. United States*, above n. 53, paras. 534–6; *Chemtura v. Canada*, above n. 38, paras. 259–65.

[64] *Chemtura v. Canada*, above n. 38, para. 247 (italics added).

12.4.2.2   The use of the police powers doctrine

In a number of cases,[65] the host State has also invoked the police powers doctrine to justify its regulations. As discussed in more detail in Chapter 15, a consistent line of cases can now be referred to in support of the application of such doctrine to justify environmental regulations. In *Methanex v. United States*, a case concerning the adoption by Californian authorities of an environmental regulation affecting the operations of a Canadian investor, the tribunal stated that:

> [A]s a matter of general international law, a non-discriminatory regulation for a public purpose, which is enacted in accordance with due process and, which affects, inter alios, a foreign investor or investment is not deemed expropriatory and compensable unless specific commitments had been given by the regulating government to the then putative foreign investor contemplating investment that the government would refrain from such regulation.[66]

This statement was subsequently confirmed by the tribunals in *Saluka v. Czech Republic* (in connection with a decision of a banking regulator),[67] and in *Chemtura v. Canada* (in connection with the cancellation of the authorisation to produce and commercialise certain pesticides).[68] Importantly, in these three cases, the police powers doctrine was not referred to in *obiter dicta* but was actually applied to reject the expropriation claim.

12.4.2.3   The relevance of purpose

The importance of the effects (rather than the purpose) of a regulatory measure for assessing whether it amounts to an expropriation has sometimes been highlighted in the practice of investment tribunals. In *Tecmed v. Mexico*, the tribunal noted that '[t]he government's intention is less important than the effects of the measures on the owner of the assets or on the benefits arising from such assets'.[69] However, one must not conclude from this view that the purpose of a measure is irrelevant,

---

[65] See above nn. 48 and 53.

[66] *Methanex v. United States*, above n. 53, Part IV, Ch. D, paras. 7 and 15.

[67] *Saluka v. Czech Republic*, above n. 51, paras. 262 and 275.

[68] *Chemtura v. Canada*, above n. 38, para. 266.

[69] *Tecmed v. Mexico*, above n. 15, para. 116. The literature often refers to *CDSE v. Costa Rica*, but, as already noted, such reference is inaccurate to the extent that this case involved a direct or formal taking. Beyond the environmental context, see *Tippetts, Abbett, McCarthy, Stratton v. TAMS-AFFA Consulting Engineers of Iran, the Government of the Islamic Republic of Iran*, Award (22 June 1984), Iran–US CTR, Vol. 6, 219, at 225, stating that '[t]he intent of the government is less important than the effects of the measures on the owner'.

either in theory or in practice. Purpose may have an impact at different levels,[70] including: (i) as a condition for the operation of a specific conflict norm; (ii) for the assessment of whether a measure is to be seen as part of 'commercial' or 'political' risk; and (iii) for the assessment of proportionality in connection with either liability or quantum.

Regarding, first, the operation of specific conflict norms, some trade and/or investment treaties provide for specific exceptions when a regulation pursues an environmental purpose. Examples of such provisions have been mentioned in Chapter 11, by reference to the NAFTA, the ECT[71] and some other investment treaties. Reference to purpose is not always explicit. For instance, Article 19(1) of the ECT requires States parties to 'strive to minimize in an economically efficient manner harmful Environmental Impacts'. A State invoking such provision would likely need to establish that the regulatory measure it adopted was aimed at minimising harmful environmental impact. Similarly, Article 1114(1) of the NAFTA provides that '[n]othing in this Chapter [Chapter 11] shall be construed to prevent a Party from adopting, maintaining or enforcing any measure otherwise consistent with this Chapter that it considers appropriate to ensure that investment activity in its territory is undertaken in a manner sensitive to environmental concerns'. For a State to avail itself of this provision, it would be necessary to show that the purpose of the regulation (or at least one of its purposes) was 'to ensure that investment activity ... is undertaken in a manner sensitive to environmental concerns'. Reference to the environmental purpose of a measure may be more explicit. By way of illustration, Annex B.13(1) of the Canadian Model BIT 2004 provides that:

Except in rare circumstances, such as when a measure or series of measures are so severe in the light of their purpose that they cannot be reasonably viewed as having been adopted and applied in good faith, non-discriminatory measures of a Party that are designed and applied to protect legitimate public welfare objectives, such as health, safety and the environment, do not constitute indirect expropriation.[72]

---

[70] Purpose may also operate as a decisive factor in excluding compensation. See the practice (particularly in the United States) reviewed by Paparinskis, 'Regulatory Expropriation and Sustainable Development', above n. 2, pp. 313–15.

[71] Energy Charter Treaty, 17 December 1994, 2080 UNTS 95 ('ECT').

[72] Reproduced in OECD, *International Investment Law: Understanding Concepts and Tracking Innovation*, (Paris: OECD, 2008) ('*OECD 2008 Study*'), p. 179. See also, US Model BIT 2004, Annex B (Expropriation), letter b), reproduced in *ibid.*, pp. 184–5.

The concept of 'rare circumstances' is not defined, but one may think of cases where specific assurances have been given to an investor and where the circumstances of the case are such that the investor's reliance on these assurances appears reasonable. Provisions referring to the environmental purpose of a measure may be difficult to interpret to the extent that a measure may have more than one purpose. The question arose in a dispute between the United States and Canada over the application of the 2006 Softwood Lumber Agreement ('SLA').[73] Article XVII(2)(c) of the SLA exempted measures taken by Canada 'for the purpose of forest or environmental management, protection, or conservation' from the anti-circumvention clause in Article XVII(1). In assessing whether Canada could avail itself of this environmental exception, the tribunal reasoned that when a measure has more than one purpose, it is the 'primary purpose' that must be taken into account to determine whether the requirements of the exception are met.[74]

The second avenue through which the environmental purpose of a regulation may influence its conformity with investment disciplines is by indicating that the regulation is part of the commercial (and not the political) risk assumed by the investor. The basic idea is that an investor operating in a highly regulated industry may find it difficult to prove that a regulation adopted for a genuine environmental purpose was not a normal part of the evolving regulatory landscape of the industry, i.e., part of its commercial risk.[75] The investor may of course challenge the regulation on the grounds that it does not genuinely pursue an environmental purpose, but such an allegation may trigger the application of a higher standard of proof. For instance, in *Chemtura* v. *Canada*, the tribunal had to determine whether the Canadian environmental agency had acted in bad faith or at least in a disingenuous manner in launching a scientific review of the effects of lindane. The tribunal noted, in this connection that:

[a]lthough the Claimant has avoided formulating this allegation in such terms, the underlying idea is that the PMRA [Canadian environmental regulator] acted

---

[73] *United States of America* v. *Canada*, LCIA Case No. 81010, Award (28 January 2011)('*Softwood lumber* dispute').

[74] *Ibid.*, para. 315.

[75] The ECtHR presumes that an interference with property has a legitimate aim when such interference arises from the implementation of social and economic laws. The burden of proving that the State has acted 'manifestly without reasonable foundation' lies with the applicant. See D. J. Harris, M. O'Boyle, E. P. Bates and C. M. Buckley, *Law of the European Convention on Human Rights* (Oxford University Press, 2nd edn, 2009), p. 668.

in bad faith and launched a review process for reasons unrelated to its mandate and to the international obligations of Canada. The burden of proving these facts rests on the Claimant, in accordance with well established principles on the allocation of the burden of proof, and the standard of proof for allegations of bad faith or disingenuous behaviour is a demanding one.[76]

The failure of the claimant to establish that the Canadian agency had not acted within its mandate (health and environmental protection) or in pursuance of Canada's international obligations was decisive to reject the claim (for breach of Article 1105 of the NAFTA). The tribunal took into account, among other elements, that 'as a sophisticated registrant experienced in a highly-regulated industry, the Claimant could not reasonably ignore the PMRA's practices and the importance of the evaluation of exposure risks within such practices'.[77] Despite the relative difficulty for an investor to establish that the measure is a manifestation of political (rather than commercial) risk, this is by no means impossible. In *S. D. Myers* v. *Canada*, the investor successfully persuaded the tribunal that the environmental purpose pursued by the ban of PCBs exports was, at best, indirect. The tribunal concluded indeed that '[t]he evidence establishe[d] that Canada's policy was shaped to a very great extent by the desire and intent to protect and promote the market share of [Canadian] enterprises'[78] and that 'there was no legitimate environmental reason for introducing the ban'.[79] Although the tribunal rejected the investor's expropriation claim, its finding as to the real purpose behind the measure was decisive in reaching the conclusion that Canada had breached Article 1102 of the NAFTA.[80] Summarising, the environmental purpose of a regulation is an indication of its legitimacy and, as such, it may render it more difficult (but not impossible) for an investor to show that the measure challenged was a manifestation of political risk rather than mere commercial risk.

The third avenue identified above is the impact of an environmental purpose in the assessment of proportionality, in connection with either liability or quantum. Some courts, such as the ECtHR, apply a 'fair balance test' to determine whether a measure interferes with the right to property.[81] In *Tecmed* v. *Mexico*, despite the fact that the tribunal

---

[76] *Chemtura* v. *Canada*, above n. 38, para. 137.

[77] *Ibid.*, para. 149; *Methanex* v. *United States*, above n. 53, Part IV, Ch. D, para. 9.

[78] *S. D. Myers* v. *Canada*, above n. 53, para. 162.   [79] *Ibid.*, para. 195.

[80] *Ibid.*, paras. 252–7; *Tecmed* v. *Mexico*, above n. 15, para. 127.

[81] On the contents and sources of the 'fair balance test' used by the EctHR, see Harris *et al.*, *Law of the European Convention on Human Rights*, above n. 75, pp. 674–5.

premised its analysis on the idea that '[u]nder international law ... the government's intention is less important than the effects of the measures',[82] it then applied a proportionality test imported from the case-law of the ECtHR. In so doing, the tribunal reintroduced the purpose of the measure (by contrast with the government's intent) as one of the terms of the 'reasonable relationship of proportionality between the means employed and the aim sought to be realised [by the measure]'.[83] To appreciate the importance of purpose in the reasoning of the tribunal, one can refer to paragraph 128 of the award, where the tribunal noted that its assessment focused on:

the extent to which such political circumstances [community pressure against the investor] – that in the opinion of the Arbitral Tribunal, on the basis of the evidence submitted, do not seem to go beyond the circumstances arising from community pressure – are the basis of the Resolution [measure challenged], in order to assess whether the Resolution is proportional to such circumstances and to other circumstances, and to the neutralization of the economic and commercial value of the Claimant's investment caused by the Resolution.[84]

Had the tribunal considered, instead, that the measure challenged genuinely pursued an environmental objective (e.g., cessation of the operations of the investor due to its grave breaches of environmental standards), the expropriation claim could have been decided differently.

12.4.2.4   The impact of specific assurances

One important question in assessing whether an environmental regulation amounts to an expropriation is whether the investor received specific assurances that no such regulation would be adopted.

The tribunal in *Methanex* v. *United States* specifically mentioned, as an exception to the application of the police powers doctrine, an hypothesis in which the investor would have received 'specific commitments ... by the regulating government to the then putative foreign investor contemplating investment that the government would refrain from such

---

[82] *Tecmed* v. *Mexico*, above n. 15, para. 116.

[83] *Ibid.*, para. 122, quoting the reasoning of the ECtHR in *James and others* v. *United Kingdom*, ECtHR Application No. 8793/79, Judgment (21 February 1986). Other investment cases referring to the case-law of the ECtHR for the assessment of an expropriation claim include: *Ronald S. Lauder* v. *Czech Republic*, UNCITRAL, Award (3 September 2001), para. 200; *International Thunderbird Gaming Corporation* v. *United Mexican States*, NAFTA (UNCITRAL), Award (26 January 2006) ('*Thunderbird* v. *Mexico*'), Separate Opinion (T. Wälde), para. 13 (making an analogy between investment arbitration and human rights adjudication before the ECtHR or the ICtHR).

[84] *Tecmed* v. *Mexico*, above n. 15, para. 128.

regulation'.[85] It then considered that, under the circumstances of the case, no such commitments had been given and, therefore, the measure was a valid exercise of the police powers doctrine.[86]

The main argument to consider whether such specific assurances were given is one of good faith.[87] In practice, specific assurances raise three distinct issues, namely: (i) what should be understood by specific assurances; (ii) who has the burden of proving them; and (iii) whether, if proven, they necessarily lead to a finding of expropriation. These three issues will be discussed in detail in Chapter 15.

---

[85] *Methanex v. United States*, above n. 53, Part IV, Ch. D, para. 7.
[86] *Ibid.*, paras. 9–18.   [87] *Thunderbird v. Mexico*, above n. 83, para. 147.

13 Environmental measures and non-discrimination standards

This chapter analyses the relations between non-discrimination standards arising from investment treaties and domestic environmental measures adverse to the interests of foreign investors. Environmental measures may introduce significant differences of treatment among economic operators and such differences may potentially conflict with investment disciplines. International investment law provides for a variety of non-discrimination standards, each with its own specificities and scope of operation. These standards have received ample attention in the literature and it is not my intention to embark on a general discussion of their features here.[1] Rather, after some general remarks regarding

[1] See, e.g., R. Dolzer and C. Schreuer, *Principles of International Investment Law* (Oxford University Press, 2008), pp. 178ff; C. McLachlan, L. Shore and M. Weiniger, *International Investment Arbitration: Substantive Principles* (Oxford University Press, 2007), pp. 252ff; A. K. Bjorklund, 'National Treatment', in A. Reinisch (ed.), *Standards of Investment Protection* (Oxford University Press, 2008), pp. 29ff; A. R. Ziegler, 'Most-Favoured-Nation (MFN) Treatment', in Reinisch above, pp. 59ff. On different aspects of these standards of particular relevance for this chapter, see also A. Joubin-Bret, 'Admission and Establishment in the Context of Investment Protection', in Reinisch above, pp. 9ff; F. Ortino, 'Non-Discriminatory Treatment in Investment Disputes', in P.-M. Dupuy, F. Francioni and E.-U. Petersmann (eds.), *Human Rights in International Investment Law and Arbitration* (Oxford University Press, 2009), pp. 344ff; F. Baetens, 'Discrimination on the Basis of Nationality: Determining Likeness in Human Rights and Investment Law', in S. Schill (ed.), *International Investment Law and Comparative Public Law* (Oxford University Press, 2010), pp. 279ff; J. Kurtz, 'The Merits and Limits of Comparativism: National Treatment in International Investment Law and the WTO', in Schill above, pp. 243ff; K. Miles, 'Sustainable Development, National Treatment and Like Circumstances in Investment Law', in M.-C. Cordonnier Segger, M. W. Gehring and A. Newcombe (eds.), *Sustainable Development in World Investment Law* (Alphen aan den Rijn, 2011), pp. 265ff; N. DiMascio and J. Pauwelyn, 'Nondiscrimination in Trade and Investment Treaties: Worlds Apart of Two Sides of the Same Coin?' (2008) 102 *American Journal of International Investment Law* 48.

non-discrimination standards (Section 13.1), I analyse four potential entry points for environmental considerations: differentiation at various stages of the investment cycle (Section 13.2); the issue of 'like circumstances' (Section 13.3); the fact of discrimination (Section 13.4); and possible justifications (Section 13.5).

13.1   Non-discrimination in foreign investment law

13.1.1   Conceptual distinctions

The non-discrimination standards provided in foreign investment law, and particularly investment treaties, can be conceptualised from at least four different perspectives.

A first perspective relates to the time or, more specifically, the stage of the investment cycle at which the differentiation is operated. The main distinction from this perspective is that between pre-establishment (before the investment is made in the host State) and post-establishment differentiation (after the investment is made in the host State). Although some investment treaties regulate both stages, most of them focus on post-establishment differentiation.[2] Pre-establishment differentiation remains the province of those bilateral and multilateral trade agreements that regulate services.

Second, from the perspective of the applicable comparator, one may distinguish among: (i) the most-favoured nation clause ('MFN'), where the comparator is other foreign investors;[3] (ii) the national treatment clause, where the comparator is the nationals of the host State;[4] and (iii) a broad customary non-discrimination standard, often subsumed under the international minimum standard of treatment or the fair and equitable treatment standard ('FET'), where the comparator may be either another foreign investor or a national of the host State or, still, another entity (e.g., another investor from the claimant's home State).[5]

---

[2] Joubin-Bret, 'Admission and Establishment in the Context of Investment Protection', above n. 1, 10; Dolzer and Schreuer, *Principles of International Investment Law*, above n. 1, pp. 80ff.

[3] See, e.g., Article 4(1) of the 2004 US Model BIT.

[4] See, e.g., Article 3(1) of the 2004 US Model BIT.

[5] The absence of a comparator is perhaps the reason why the claimant in *Chemtura* v. *Canada* did not ground its claim for discrimination on the MFN and national treatment clause of the NAFTA but rather sought to import an FET clause from another treaty. See *Chemtura Corporation (formerly Crompton Corporation)* v. *Government of Canada*, UNCITRAL, Award (2 August 2010) ('*Chemtura* v. *Canada*'), paras. 231–7.

A third perspective is offered by the level of specificity with which differentiation is defined. MFN and national treatment clauses routinely require that the investor and its comparator be in 'similar' or 'like' circumstances. They also refer to 'more favourable' or 'no less favourable' treatment and, in some cases, they exclude certain areas or issues from their scope.[6] Conversely, fair and equitable treatment clauses do not, as a rule, go into such considerations, which may have significant evidentiary consequences, when the level of 'similarity' or 'favourableness', or the scope of application, of the clause are in dispute.

A fourth perspective relates to the differing effects of such clauses. Whereas the MFN clause has a practically very important 'importing' power (as it allows an investor to incorporate, within certain limits, advantages granted to foreign investors of third States in other treaties[7]), national treatment and FET clauses have no such power.

13.1.2   The components of non-discrimination standards

In order for a claim for breach of the MFN or national treatment clauses to be established, three main elements must be assessed:[8] (i) whether the investor (or the investment, according to the language of the applicable treaty) was in a position similar to that of other economic operators (foreign or local) ('likeness'); (ii) whether the investor received less favourable treatment than such other economic operators (or, what is conceptually equivalent, whether such other operators were treated

---

[6] See Joubin-Bret, 'Admission and Establishment in the Context of Investment Protection' above n. 1, 13, noting that treaties with expanded MFN and national treatment clauses commonly contain 'negative lists', i.e., lists of areas where the admission commitment is excluded.

[7] See, e.g., *Bayindir Insaat Turizm Ticaret ve Sanayi AŞ* v. *Pakistan*, ICSID Case No. ARB/03/29, Award (27 August 2009) ('*Bayindir* v. *Pakistan*'), paras. 153–60. A vivid debate, still ongoing, concerns the question of whether, and to what extent, a more favourable arbitration clause from another treaty can be imported through the MFN clause. The essence of the debate is epitomised by two awards: *RosInvest Co UK Ltd* v. *Russian Federation*, SCC Case No. V079/2005, Award on Jurisdiction (5 October 2007), paras. 23–44 and 50–75; *Austrian Airlines* v. *Slovakia*, UNCITRAL, Award (9 October 2009), paras. 109–41. On this point see, e.g., Y. Banifatemi, 'The Emerging Jurisprudence on the Most-Favored-Nation Treatment in Investment Arbitration', in A. K. Bjorklund, I. Laird and S. Ripinsky (eds.), *Investment Treaty Law. Current Issues III* (London: BIICL, 2009), pp. 24ff; Z. Douglas, 'The MFN Clause in Investment Arbitration: Treaty Interpretation Off the Rails' (2010) 2 *Journal of International Dispute Settlement* 97.

[8] These three components arise from the investment case-law. See McLachlan, Shore and Weiniger, *International Investment Arbitration*, above n. 1, pp. 253–4; Bjorklund, 'National Treatment', above n. 1, p. 37.

more favourably[9]) ('treatment'); and (iii) whether the differing treatment is justified by some specific reason (other than the absence of likeness) ('justification').

From an evidentiary perspective, the general rule is that the burden of proving the first two elements lies with the claimant, whereas that of proving the third element lies with the respondent.[10] On closer examination, this basic rule is somewhat more complex. Whereas, in some cases, proving likeness (item (i)) may be sufficient, because the differential treatment arises from the face of the measure challenged[11] (e.g., a measure that makes a distinction between foreign and local investors), in other cases the fact of differentiated treatment (item (ii)) will also have to be proved. But this is not to say that investors only carry the burden of proving likeness. The confusion stems from at least two reasons. The first reason is the extrapolation of trade law into investment disputes. For example, in *Feldman v. Mexico*, the tribunal considered, following the case-law of the WTO Appellate Body, that the investor was only required to make a *prima facie* showing, after which the burden of proof shifted to the respondent.[12] However, this conclusion does not go against the general principle stated before, as the tribunal recognised that the claimant had the burden of proving likeness and differentiation.[13] The main problem with the reasoning of the *Feldman* tribunal is that a presumption (as opposed to a showing) of less favourable treatment should not be sufficient to shift the burden of proof.[14] The extrapolation of trade law into investment disputes has subsequently been excluded by tribunals hearing both environment-related[15] and other claims.[16] The second reason for the confusion is the fact that tribunals do not always make a distinction between 'likeness' and 'treatment'. They sometimes discuss issues of 'treatment' as a

---

[9] *Pope & Talbot v. Canada*, NAFTA (UNCITRAL), Interim Award on Merits II (10 April 2001) ('*Pope & Talbot* – Interim Award on Merits II'), para. 42.

[10] A. Newcombe and L. Paradell, *Law and Practice of Investment Treaties* (Alphen aan den Rijn: Kluwer Law International, 2009), p. 20.

[11] *Pope & Talbot* – Interim Award on Merits II, above n. 9, paras. 78 and 84–5.

[12] *Marvin Roy Feldman Karpa v. United Mexican States*, ICSID Case No. ARB(AF)/99/1, Award (16 December 2002) ('*Feldman v. Mexico*'), para. 177.

[13] *Ibid.*, para. 177 *in fine*.

[14] DiMascio and Pauwelyn, 'Nondiscrimination in Trade and Investment Treaties', above n. 1, pp. 85–6.

[15] *Methanex Corporation v. United States of America*, NAFTA (UNCITRAL), Award (3 August 2005) ('*Methanex v. United States*'), Part IV, Ch. B, paras. 29–30.

[16] *Bayindir v. Pakistan*, above n. 7, para. 402.

component of the analysis of 'likeness'[17] and, if they consider that likeness has been established, they shift the burden of proving justification (item (iii)) to the respondent.

This latter point raises the more general question of the relations between likeness, treatment and justification. Although these three questions are conceptually distinct, they are often related. Determining whether certain treatment is more favourable or less favourable depends on the circumstances of each investor or economic operator. A measure that, on its face, would look less favourable or more favourable may not be so if evaluated in the light of other considerations normally captured by the analysis of likeness or that of justification. Similarly, questions of justification may be discussed in the analysis of likeness or *vice versa*. After all, the fact that two economic operators are not in 'like circumstances' is a reason justifying differential treatment. From an analytical perspective, it seems useful, however, to distinguish questions of likeness, treatment and justification.

13.2   Differentiation at various stages of the investment cycle

13.2.1   Green investment protectionism

In the last several years, there has been much discussion as to whether certain unilateral environmental restrictions on trade would constitute a breach of trade disciplines under the WTO set of agreements.[18] More recently, this debate has spilled over to the relations between foreign investment and environmental measures. In one of the draft papers circulated by the OECD staff as part of the consultation process regarding the OECD's work on liberalising investment for green growth, 'green investment protectionism' is defined as follows:

Investment protectionism occurs when government policies and practices restrict the free flow of capital across the global economy and when such restrictions do not have a solid justification in safeguarding essential security

---

[17] *Ibid.*, paras. 402–11 (discussing in connection with likeness contractual terms that directly concerned the question of whether the comparator had received better treatment or not).

[18] P. Sands, *Principles of International Environmental Law* (Cambridge University Press, 2003) pp. 946ff; D. Bodansky, 'What's So Bad about Unilateral Action to Protect the Environment ?' (2000) 11 *European Journal of International Law* 339. More recently, the question has arisen in connection with carbon-intensive production processes and methods. See D. H. Regan, 'How to Think about PPMs (and Climate Change)', in T. Cottier, O. Nartova and S. Z. Bigdelli (eds.), *International Trade Regulation and the Mitigation of Climate Change* (Cambridge University Press, 2009), pp. 97ff.

interests and public order. Green investment protectionism occurs when environmental policies have this same effect and when the restrictions cannot be justified as advancing well-founded public-policy goals.[19]

The main concern underlying this definition is the potential for discrimination in granting foreign investors access to a given market. As further specified by the OECD Paper: '[f]or inward investment, this [openness] means that conditions for establishment should not discriminate against non-resident investors – that is, the rules and procedures that they must follow to establish an investment are similar to those that apply to resident investors in like circumstances'.[20]

Judging by the experience in the international trade arena, the concern raised by the OECD Paper is not theoretically unjustified,[21] as the protection of the environment may indeed serve as a useful excuse for protectionist practices. Conversely, one must not overlook the fact that the need to foster green growth can also become an excuse for liberalising capital movements in a manner that would excessively reduce the room for legitimate regulation of market access. In both respects, the main question is what should be the limit between green protectionism and legitimate regulation of market access.

Yet, in assessing the need for entry regulation, one must not conflate the realm of investment with that of trade. In the trade context basic competition problems may arise when similar products exported from States with lower environmental requirements are granted access to the domestic market. This has led to differentiation between the products exported by countries with different types of regulations or, in other words, to discrimination based on the nationality of the producers.[22] In the investment context, this type of discrimination is unlikely, because the dividing line set by screening requirements is based on the environmental impact of the producers, irrespective of their nationality. A relevant issue for both the trade and investment regimes is the protection of nascent green industries of strategic importance for the host

---

[19] K. Gordon, 'Green-Investment Protectionism: What Is it and How Prevalent is it?', 2011 ('OECD Paper'), para. 16, available at: www.oecd.org/dataoecd/8/3/46905672.pdf (accessed on 4 January 2012).

[20] Ibid., para. 17.

[21] However, as acknowledged in the OECD Paper, green investment protectionism is not yet a problem in practice. See ibid., para. 19.

[22] In the trade law context, this difficulty is epitomised by the so-called Tuna/Dolphin controversy. See M. Hurlock, 'The GATT, US Law and the Environment: A Proposal to Amend the GATT in Light of the Tuna/Dolphin Decision' (1992) 92 Columbia Law Review 2098.

State. But, even in this latter case, not every policy promoting 'green' industries based in the territory of the host State will be nationality-sensitive, as some of them are open to all resident investors.[23]

13.2.2   Pre-establishment environmental differentiation

A legitimacy conflict may arise when a State adopts an environmental measure restricting the admission of foreign investors into its territory in potential breach of an investment discipline contained in a treaty. This type of legitimacy conflict is rare, however, because investment treaties do not accord, as a rule, a right of admission.

Indeed, in most investment treaties, the regulation of entry is placed beyond the scope of investment disciplines.[24] Unless the State has consented to a limitation in the exercise of its regulatory powers, the basic principle is that the State is free to regulate admission of foreign investment into its territory. Regulation of admission can take a variety of forms, ranging from the simple prohibition of entry to more nuanced frameworks, including licensing requirements, tax arrangements, capitalisation and control requirements, requirements of local collaboration and requirements relating to the protection of the environment (most frequently the conduct of a prior environmental impact assessment).[25] Under this prevalent approach, there is ample room for differentiating among foreign investors and/or between foreign investors and local companies on the basis of environmental considerations. The only limitations will arise from specific clauses contained in investment treaties (e.g., prohibition of certain performance requirements) or from potentially applicable trade disciplines. However, as noted above, environmental screening is, as a rule, not sensitive to nationality issues. The dividing line, for admission purposes, will be between, on the one hand, clean and responsible producers, and, on the other hand, dirty and irresponsible producers.

The State's freedom to regulate entry may be significantly restricted by treaty. Some treaties extend the scope of the MFN and national treatment clauses beyond post-establishment treatment to cover the issue of admission. This less frequent approach has been followed in the investment treaty practice of Canada, the United States, Japan and,

---

[23]   OECD Paper, above n. 19, p. 22.

[24]   Joubin-Bret, 'Admission and Establishment in the Context of Investment Protection', above n. 1, p. 10.

[25]   M. Sornarajah, *The International Law on Foreign Investment* (Cambridge University Press, 2010), pp. 97–116.

more generally, in many free trade agreements.[26] The limitation of the right to regulate entry in this hypothesis comes close to the actual granting of a right of admission.[27] To assess the implications of this second approach, three observations appear useful.

First, one must distinguish between treaties containing extended MFN clauses only and treaties containing extended national treatment clauses. The incorporation of a right of admission through an extended MFN clause entirely depends on the granting of such right in an 'importable' treaty. The identification of an importable treaty raises, in turn, the question of the *eiusdem generis* principle. By way of illustration, it is unclear whether a right of admission could be imported from a free trade agreement and into an investment treaty, as the nature of the former agreement is not necessarily within the scope of the MFN clause. When a treaty contains an extended national treatment clause, these problems do not arise. In this case, the right of admission would be implicit, as such right is normally granted to the local companies of the host State.

The second observation is that the operation of such extended clauses is unclear. The legal nature of investment disciplines, such as extended national treatment clauses, cannot be equated with that of actual 'rights', such as human rights, for all practical purposes. For example, if a claim based on an extended national treatment clause cannot be brought before an arbitral tribunal (e.g., if this latter has no jurisdiction or, simply, if there is no arbitration clause), the chances for such a claim to be admissible before a domestic court of the host State would largely depend on whether or not the national treatment clause can deploy a 'direct effect' (i.e., can be directly relied on as the basis of a claim before domestic courts).[28] Whereas some provisions in human rights treaties do have a direct effect, it is unclear whether such effect

---

[26] Joubin-Bret, 'Admission and Establishment in the Context of Investment Protection', above n. 1, pp. 10 and 13–15, referring to the following treaties: (i) investment treaties: US–Egypt BIT (1992), Article 2(a); US–Georgia BIT (1994), Article 2; US–Azerbaijan BIT (2000), Article 2; US–Uruguay BIT (2005), Article 2; Canada–Peru BIT (2006), Article 3; Japan–Vietnam BIT (2003), Article 2; Japan–Republic of Korea BIT (2002), Article 2; (ii) free trade agreements: US–Morocco FTA (2004), Article 10.3; US–Republic of Korea FTA (2007), Article 11.3; US–Peru FTA (2006), Article 10.3; US–Australia FTA (2004), Article 11.3.

[27] Some treaties explicitly provide for a right of admission. See, e.g., Convention Establishing the European Free Trade Association (EFTA), 4 January 1960, 370 UNTS 3 ('EFTA Convention'), Article 23(1), referred to in Joubin-Bret, 'Admission and Establishment in the Context of Investment Protection', above n. 1, 14.

[28] E. Denza, 'The Relationship between International and National Law', in M. D. Evans (ed.), *International Law* (Oxford University Press, 2010) 411ff.

can also be ascribed to certain investment disciplines. Given their formulation as obligations of the State, it is, in fact, likely that most investment disciplines arising from a BIT will not have a direct effect. In all events, the scarcity of practice on the operation of extended MFN and national treatment clauses for entry purposes makes any conclusions on this point conjectural.[29]

Third, and most significantly for the analysis of environmental differentiation, the distinction between the pre- and post-establishment phases is mostly relevant in connection with the requirement that investments be made 'in accordance with domestic law' contained in some treaties. It is unclear whether an investment made in breach of the host State's environmental law would be protected by the investment treaty at all. It is also unclear how to deal with this issue in the context of an investment proceeding. Both issues have been discussed in some detail in Chapter 5.[30] The other relevant questions for the understanding of environmental differentiation (likeness, treatment, justification) are common to the pre- and post-establishment phases and are discussed in the following sections.

13.3   The concept of 'like circumstances' from an environmental perspective

13.3.1   'Like circumstances' in trade and investment

Before undertaking the analysis of the criteria used to determine whether the claimant is in a similar position to that of relevant comparators, it seems useful to clarify one question that has led to considerable debate in the trade law context.

The test used in trade law to assess whether two products are in like circumstances leaves limited room for taking into account the manner in which each product has been produced, the so-called 'production processes and methods' ('PPMs'). This means that granting differential treatment to two products that are similar in all respects except for their PPMs may amount to a breach of trade disciplines, unless an exception, such as Article XX of the GATT, is available.[31]

---

[29] Joubin-Bret, 'Admission and Establishment in the Context of Investment Protection', above n. 1, p. 14.

[30] See Section 5.3.2.3.

[31] On environmental exceptions in WTO law, see S. Zleptnig, *Non-Economic Objectives in WTO Law* (The Hague: Kluwer, 2010).

The situation is substantially different in the investment context. As a general matter, whereas trade is primarily about transboundary movements of goods and services and only secondarily about production, investment is mainly about production and only secondarily about transboundary movements of goods and services. Of course, production and movements are relevant for both bodies of law. Production-related measures such as export subsidies are clearly within the regulatory scope of trade law. Conversely, import or export restrictions affecting the operations of investors in the State adopting such measures are well within the scope of investment disciplines. But the difference in the emphasis of each body of law is significant for the PPMs question. Specifically, in the context of foreign investment regulation, PPMs are a primary concern of any assessment of discrimination. This is very important from an environmental perspective, as the environmental measures adopted by a host State may not only concern the composition of an end-product (e.g., a pesticide[32] or a fuel-additive[33]), but also the impact of the investor's operations (e.g., the potential harm to the environment[34]) and, more precisely, the methods of production used by the investor.[35]

This overall context must be kept in mind when analysing the approaches to 'likeness' used in investment law. From a legal perspective, one consequence is that the test for establishing likeness in the context of international trade law is not applicable in the investment context. Where reference is made to it, the trade law test must be

---

[32] See, e.g., *Chemtura* v. *Canada*, above n. 5 (measure suspending and then terminating the authorisation to produce pesticides and fungicides containing a harmful active ingredient).

[33] See, e.g., *Methanex* v. *United States*, above n. 15 (measure affecting the use of a fuel-additive based on its water-polluting potential).

[34] See, e.g., *Dillingham-Moore* v. *Murphyores* (1979) 136 CLR 1 (measures affecting a sand-mining investment with adverse impact on the Great Coral Reef); *Parkerings-Compagniet AS* v. *Republic of Lithuania*, ICSID Case No. ARB/05/8, Award (11 September 2007) ('*Parkerings* v. *Lithuania*')(measures affecting a construction project with potentially adverse impacts on a UNESCO protected site); *Glamis Gold Ltd* v. *United States of America*, NAFTA (UNCITRAL), Award (16 May 2009) ('*Glamis* v. *United States*') (measures affecting a gold mining project with potentially adverse impacts on the lands and livelihood of first nations).

[35] See, e.g., *Vattenfall AB, Vattenfall Europe AG, Vattenfall Europe Generation AG* v. *Federal Republic of Germany*, ICSID Case No. ARB/09/6, Award (11 March 2011) ('*Vattenfall* v. *Germany*') (measures affecting coal-fired power plant on environmental grounds); *Société Arcelor Atlantique et Lorraine et al.* v. *Premier Ministre, Ministre de l'Economie, des Finances et de l'Industrie, Ministre de l'Ecologie et du Développement Durable*, ECJ Case C-127/07, Judgment (16 December 2008)('*Arcelor* reference') (measures affecting a steel producer adopted on environmental grounds).

understood as mere interpretive guidance,[36] on the same footing as other tests that could potentially be derived, for example, from human rights law.[37] The difference between the trade and investment contexts has been explicitly acknowledged in the investment case-law. In *Methanex* v. *United States*, a dispute with a strong environmental component, the claimant sought to establish, by reference to WTO case-law, that a methanol producer (the claimant itself) was in like circumstances with US ethanol producers:

Methanol and ethanol are both oxygenates under US law. Methanex and other methanol producers are in 'like circumstances' with US domestic ethanol producers because they both produce the same product – oxygenates used in manufacturing reformulated gasoline – and because they both compete directly for customers in the oxygenate market.[38]

The tribunal rejected Methanex's argument noting, *inter alia*, that the test of likeness used in trade law was not applicable in the NAFTA context. According to the tribunal, the NAFTA provisions:

do not use the term of art in international trade law, 'like products', which appears in and plays a critical role in the application of GATT Article III [. . .] [t]he drafting parties were fluent in GATT law and incorporated, in very precise ways, the term 'like goods' and the GATT provisions relating to it when they wished to do so.[39]

Some paragraphs earlier, the tribunal had also noted that 'the ethanol and methanol products cannot be said to be in competition, even assuming that this trade criterion were to apply'.[40] In the same vein, the tribunal in *Bayindir* v. *Pakistan* rejected the attempt by the claimant to define likeness by reference to the WTO case-law, noting that a different test applied under a free-standing non-discrimination clause.[41]

---

[36] *Methanex* v. *United States*, above n. 15, Part IV, Ch. B, para. 37 (recognising the possibility of taking into account other treaties for interpretation purposes).

[37] See, e.g., *Lithgow and others* v. *United Kingdom*, ECtHR Application No. 9006/80, 9262/81, 9263/81, 9265/81, 9266/81, 9313/81, 9405/81, Judgment (8 July 1996), para. 177 (noting, in connection with Article 14 of the ECHR, that this provision 'safeguards persons (including legal persons) who are "placed in analogous situations" against discriminatory differences of treatment; and, for the purposes of Article 14 (art. 14), a difference of treatment is discriminatory if it "has no objective and reasonable justification", that is, if it does not pursue a "legitimate aim" or if there is not a "reasonable relationship of proportionality between the means employed and the aim sought to be realized"').

[38] *Methanex* v. *United States*, above n. 15, Part IV, Ch. B, para. 23.

[39] *Ibid.*, Part IV, Ch. B, paras. 29–30.   [40] *Ibid.*, Part IV, Ch. B, para. 28.

[41] *Bayindir* v. *Pakistan*, above n. 7, para. 402. See, also, *Occidental Exploration and Production Company* v. *Republic of Ecuador*, LCIA Case No. UN3467, Final Award (1 July 2004) ('*Occidental* v. *Ecuador*'), paras. 174–6.

13.3.2 'Like circumstances' and the relevance of environmental considerations

The most important question in assessing a discrimination claim lies in the determination of the appropriate comparator. This is a subtle and, to some extent, volatile process. A slight difference of emphasis in this assessment could potentially result in a different outcome. As noted by the tribunal in *Methanex v. United States*: 'it would be as perverse to ignore identical comparators if they were available and to use comparators that were less "like", as it would be perverse to refuse to find and to apply less "like" comparators when no identical comparators existed'.[42] In other words, there is a risk of 'comparator-shopping' with potentially significant consequences for the success of a discrimination claim.[43] In the *Methanex* case, assimilating ethanol and methanol producers could have led the tribunal to reach a different conclusion. However, the *Methanex* tribunal did not provide a clear articulation of how the comparator must be identified.

The position of investment tribunals on this question varies considerably. Perhaps the broadest interpretation was given in *Occidental v. Ecuador*, where the tribunal found that companies in totally different sectors (oil exporters, such as the claimant, and companies active in the exports of seafood, flowers, mining, lumber and even bananas) were in like circumstances.[44] At the other end of the spectrum, the tribunal in *Bayindir v. Pakistan* considered that two companies active in exactly the same business and, in fact, even in the same project (the comparator identified had been a sub-contractor of the claimant) were not in like circumstances because of differences 'in the financial terms; the constitution of the two entities; their level of experience and expertise; the scope of work; and the commitment of the two entities to progressing with the works'.[45] The claimant had argued that it had been discriminated against because more time for the completion of the works had been given to the local contractors who took over the project after the claimant was expelled. The tribunal's analysis of likeness takes this claim as a starting point and suggests that granting more time did

---

[42] *Methanex v. United States*, above n. 15, Part IV, Ch. B, Para. 17.

[43] *Ibid.*, Part IV, Ch. B, para. 19 (referring to *Pope & Talbot v. Canada* where, according to the *Methanex* tribunal, 'the tribunal selected the entities that were in the most "like circumstances" and not comparators that were in less "like circumstances"').

[44] *Occidental v. Ecuador*, above n. 41, para. 173.

[45] *Bayindir v. Pakistan*, above n. 7, paras. 402 and 403–11. On the relations between 'likeness' and 'treatment', see Section 13.1.2.

not amount, under the circumstances, to providing more favourable treatment. However, the tribunal reached this conclusion through the channel of likeness, stating that the claimant and the investor were not in like circumstances.

Many (and perhaps most) other cases take an intermediate stance. These cases include virtually all relevant investment cases with an environmental component. In *S. D. Myers* v. *Canada*, the tribunal made an important general statement in connection with the assessment of likeness:

> the interpretation of the phrase 'like circumstances' in Article 1102 must take into account the general principles that emerge from the legal context of the NAFTA, including both its concern with the environment and the need to avoid trade distortions that are not justified by environmental concerns. The assessment of 'like circumstances' must also take into account circumstances that would justify governmental regulations that treat them differently in order to protect the public interest.[46]

This statement, although it conflates to some extent questions of likeness and justification, is important because it directs tribunals to take into account, in assessing likeness, environmental provisions contained in the applicable treaty. One could think, for example, of the specific conflict norms discussed in Chapter 11 of this book. Some treaties go even further and mention the circumstances that need to be taken into account in assessing references to 'like circumstances', including 'effects on third persons and the local community' or 'effects on the local, regional or national environment, including the cumulative effects of all investments within a jurisdiction on the environment'.[47] In influencing the interpretation of investment disciplines, such norms could provide a useful tool to solve legitimacy conflicts. Also of note is the reference made by the tribunal in *S. D. Myers* v. *Canada* to other separate instruments for purposes of assessing likeness.[48] Among these, one finds not only the environmental side agreement to the NAFTA, the NAAEC,[49]

---

[46] *S. D. Myers Inc.* v. *Canada*, NAFTA (UNCITRAL), Partial Award (13 November 2000) ('*S. D. Myers* v. *Canada*'), para. 250.

[47] See COMESA Common Investment Area Agreement (COMESA CIAA)(2007), Article 17(2), referred to in S. A. Spears, 'The Quest for Policy Space in a New Generation of International Investment Agreements' (13) 4 *Journal of International Dispute Settlement* 1037, at 1058.

[48] *S. D. Myers* v. *Canada*, above n. 46, paras. 247–8.

[49] North American Agreement on Environmental Cooperation, 17 December 1992, 32 ILM 1519 ('NAAEC').

but also two soft-law instruments, the Rio Declaration on Environment and Development[50] and an OECD Declaration.[51] Eventually, however, neither the environmental clauses of the NAFTA nor the other separate instruments played a major role in the tribunal's conclusion that the claimant and the local companies engaged in the same activity were in like circumstances.[52]

An additional step was taken by the tribunal in *Parkerings* v. *Lithuania*, which concluded that two foreign investors engaged in the same type of activity (the construction of car parks) were not in like circumstances because of their different impact on a UNESCO protected site (the old town of Vilnius). The tribunal concluded that '[t]he historical and archaeological preservation and environmental protection could be and in this case were a justification for the refusal of the project' and that, as a result, the claimant's project 'was not similar with the MSCP [multi-story car park] constructed by Pinus Propius [the comparator]'.[53] This conclusion could be relevant for assessing whether high-emitting and low-emitting industries (or, more generally, highly polluting and cleaner industries) are in like circumstances.[54]

Read together, these two cases suggest that the assessment of 'like circumstances' can and indeed must take into account the environmental normative context (i.e., the applicable treaty and also separate instruments) in which the investor operates. This point was also made in *Methanex* v. *United States* in connection with the domestic regulatory environment. In this case the tribunal considered that local methanol producers were the most appropriate comparator because these producers faced a similar regulatory framework as the one applicable to Methanex.[55] This approach illustrates another form in which the analyses of likeness and treatment can be integrated. Indeed, after finding

---

[50] Rio Declaration on Environment and Development, 13 June 1992, UN Doc. A/CONF.151/26 ('Rio Declaration').

[51] OECD, Declaration on International and Multinational Enterprises, 21 June 1976.

[52] *S. D. Myers* v. *Canada*, above n. 46, para. 251.

[53] *Parkerings* v. *Lithuania*, above n. 34, para. 392.

[54] See, e.g., Miles, 'Sustainable Development, National Treatment and Like Circumstances in Investment Law', above n. 1, p. 294; Baetens, 'Discrimination on the Basis of Nationality', above n. 1, p. 305.

[55] *Methanex* v. *United States*, above n. 15, Part IV, Ch. B, paras. 18–19. See, also, *Grand River Enterprises Six Nations Ltd et al.* v. *United States of America*, NAFTA (UNCITRAL), Award (12 January 2011), paras. 164–7 (considering 'the identity of the legal regime(s) applicable to a claimant and its purported comparators to be a compelling factor in assessing whether like is indeed being compared to like for purposes of Articles 1102 and 1103 [of the NAFTA]', para. 167).

that domestic methanol producers were subject to the same environmental regulations as the claimant, the tribunal rejected the claim for lack of differential treatment.[56]

13.4   The objective test of differential treatment

For a discrimination claim to prosper, the investor needs to prove that despite being in like circumstances it received less favourable treatment than the one accorded to the comparator.[57] Several questions arise in this connection, including the definition of 'more (or less) favourable treatment',[58] the impact of this definition on evidentiary matters,[59] and the relevance of intent. The first two questions do not present any specificity in connection with environmental matters; only the latter requires additional comment.

Many environmental measures introduce de iure (e.g., subsidies to clean industries or carbon caps imposed only on certain industries) or de facto (e.g., general environmental taxation of fuels would have a stronger impact on fuel-intensive industries) differentiation for genuinely environmental purposes. Such differentiation, if established, may amount to a breach of a non-discrimination standard. Of course, as discussed in the previous Section, the differentiation must intervene among companies in like circumstances, and the State still has the possibility to justify the differential treatment (see below Section 13.5). But, if these conditions are met, the fact that the State did not have a discriminatory intent (i.e., the intention to discriminate on the basis of the nationality of the investor – with respect to local companies or to other foreign investors) may not change the result. Indeed, a consistent line of cases has held that the intent to discriminate on the basis of nationality is not necessary for a breach of a non-discrimination standard to be found.[60]

---

[56] *Methanex* v. *United States*, above n. 15, Part IV, Ch. B, para. 38.

[57] *Parkerings* v. *Lithuania*, above n. 34, para. 393; *Plama Consortium Limited* v. *Bulgaria*, ICSID Case No. ARB/03/24, Award (27 August 2008) ('*Plama* v. *Bulgaria*'), para. 223.

[58] See Bjorklund, 'National Treatment', above n. 1, pp. 48–56.

[59] In cases of de facto discrimination there may be a practical difference between proving that the investor has received less favourable treatment and establishing that others have received more favourable treatment. Gaining access to the necessary documentary evidence to prove the second hypothesis may present some additional challenges, as these documents will most likely not be in the possession, custody or control of a party to the arbitration.

[60] *Feldman* v. *Mexico*, above n. 12, para. 181 and 183; *Pope & Talbot* – Interim Award on Merits II, above n. 9, para. 79; *S. D. Myers* v. *Canada*, above n. 46, para. 254. Beyond the NAFTA context, see, e.g., *Bayindir* v. *Pakistan*, above n. 7, para. 390.

Conversely, the presence of discriminatory intent may be very important to establish a breach of a non-discrimination standard, even when
the measure also pursues an environmental objective. Intent alone is, of
course, not sufficient, as the measure must have had objectively a
differentiation effect. As noted by the tribunal in *S. D. Myers* v. *Canada*:
'intent to favour nationals over non-nationals would not give rise to a
breach of Chapter 1102 of the NAFTA if the measure in question were to
produce no adverse effect on the non-national complainant'.[61] Yet,
showing that a host State acted discriminatorily or simply disingenuously in introducing an environmental measure is a powerful technique
to deprive an environmental measure from its public legitimacy. This
line of argument was pursued by the claimants in a number of cases,
sometimes successfully and sometimes unsuccessfully. A case where this
argument was successful is *Tecmed* v. *Mexico*.[62] The investor did not argue
that it had been discriminated against in breach of an MFN or a national
treatment clause, as there was no comparator. Rather, it argued, *inter
alia*, that it had been treated unfairly and inequitably. The tribunal
concluded that the non-renewal of the operation permit of a land-fill
was not a result of genuine environmental concerns, but rather a reaction to public protests. It noted, in this connection, that:

> the ambiguity of INE's [the regulator's] actions was even greater when it resorted
> to the non-renewal of the Permit to overcome obstacles not related to the
> preservation of health and the environment although, according to the evidence
> submitted, the protection of public health and the environment is where INE's
> preventive function should be focused . . . The refusal to renew the Permit in this
> case was actually used to permanently close down a site whose operation had
> become a nuisance due to political reasons.[63]

An example of a case where this argument was unsuccessful is provided
by *Plama* v. *Bulgaria*. In this case, the tribunal referred to the fact that an
amendment to the environmental laws prejudicial to the investor had
been adopted pursuant to a recommendation of the World Bank and
was not aimed directly against the investor to conclude that there was
insufficient evidence to consider that the investor had been discriminated against.[64] Another example is given by *Chemtura* v. *Canada*.[65]

---

[61] *S. D. Myers* v. *Canada*, above n. 46, para. 254.
[62] *Técnicas Medioambientales Tecmed SA* v. *United Mexican States*, ICSID Case No. ARB(AF)/00/2,
Award (29 May 2003) ('*Tecmed* v. *Mexico*').
[63] *Ibid.*, para. 164.   [64] *Plama* v. *Bulgaria*, above n. 57, paras. 218 and 223.
[65] *Chemtura* v. *Canada*, above n. 5.

Here, the investor claimed that it had been discriminated against in several ways, most notably as compared to one of its competitors. It brought this claim under the international minimum standard of treatment (Article 1105 of the NAFTA) or, in the alternative, under an imported FET clause (allegedly available through the operation of the MFN clause in Article 1103 of the NAFTA), presumably because the relevant comparator had the same nationality as the investor. One of the main lines of argumentation used by the investor was that the Canadian regulator had acted disingenuously, adopting the measures challenged as a result of a trade irritant, and not for health or environmental reasons.[66] The tribunal rejected the claim, noting, *inter alia*, that no such disingenuous behaviour had taken place and that, in all events, no less favourable treatment was objectively established.[67]

13.5   Justifying differential treatment of similar situations

13.5.1   Rule or exception?

Even once it is established that an investor in like circumstances with a comparator has been objectively treated less favourably than such comparator by the host State, the State may still be able to justify its conduct and escape liability for breach of a non-discrimination standard.

A question of some practical importance is whether such justifying factors must be seen as an internal component of non-discrimination clauses (i.e., an additional requirement for establishing discrimination) or rather as an exception excusing the action taken by the State. This question has ramifications at two levels, namely, (i) the allocation of the burden of proof and (ii) the identification of the justifying factors available.

As far as the first difficulty is concerned, it seems now settled that the burden of proof lies with the State who invokes the justifying factor.[68] The second difficulty is less settled. Beyond specific exceptions (e.g., a specific clause contained in a treaty[69]) or general exceptions (e.g., the customary circumstances precluding wrongfulness codified in the ILC Articles on State Responsibility[70] or GATT-like exceptions), it is unclear

---

[66] *Ibid.*, paras. 126 and 195.

[67] *Ibid.*, paras. 137–8 and 217–24. See, also, *Methanex* v. *United States*, above n. 15, Part IV, Ch. B, para. 26 *in fine*.

[68] See Section 13.1.2. See, also, *Arcelor* reference, above n. 35, para. 48.

[69] See Chapter 11.

[70] Responsibility of States for Internationally Wrongful Acts, GA Res. 56/83, UN Doc. A/RES/56/83, 12 December 2001 ('ILC Articles'), Part I, Chapter V.

whether some other legal tools, such as the police powers doctrine or simply some other unspecified factors could also be sufficient to justify differential treatment. Here, I focus on three questions: the relevance of purpose (Section 13.5.2); the operation of specific exceptions contained in relevant treaties (Section 13.5.3); and the availability of some other unspecified factors that had been referred to in the case-law (Section 13.5.3). Relevant general exceptions as well as other legal tools potentially useful in this connection are analysed in Chapter 15.

13.5.2 The relevance of purpose

The purpose pursued by a measure must be distinguished from the intent underlying its adoption. For example, the purpose of an environmental measure may be to reduce greenhouse gas emissions or to limit pollution, whereas the intent underlying its adoption is to establish a level playing field or to avoid carbon and jobs leakage.

Often, purpose and intent are aligned. But sometimes they are not. As discussed in the previous section, to advance a discrimination claim, it is sufficient to establish the fact of differentiation objectively, irrespective of whether there is intent to discriminate or not. Intent to discriminate provides, however, a strong indication that the measure was adopted to introduce an objective differentiation. Similarly, a genuine environmental purpose provides a strong indication that (i) the measure was not adopted with a discriminatory intent, and therefore that (ii) even if the measure introduces an objective differentiation, such differentiation may be justified by the environmental purpose pursued by the measure. Yet, as discussed in Chapter 12 in connection with expropriation, the environmental purpose of a measure may not, alone, be sufficient to justify an objective differentiation. Purpose is mostly relevant as a component of a justifying factor.

13.5.3 Justification clauses

A number of investment treaties include justification clauses specifically in connection with non-discrimination standards.[71] Some of them expressly refer to measures pursuing certain purposes related to environmental protection.

---

[71] On exceptions, see, generally, W. W. Burke-White and A. von Staden, 'Investment Protection in Extraordinary Times: The Interpretation and Application of Non-Precluded Measures Provisions in Bilateral Investment Treaties' (2008) 48 *Virginia Journal of International Law* 307.

For example, the Protocol attached to the Germany–China BIT states, in its paragraph 4(a), that '[m]easures that have to be taken for reasons of public security and order, public health or morality shall not be deemed "treatment less favourable" within the meaning of Article 3 [of the BIT, i.e. MFN and national treatment clauses]'.[72] This provision illustrates the point made earlier regarding the impact of purpose as a component of a justification factor. In this example, if a measure is taken for the purpose of protecting public health (and, arguably, also for the protection of the environment) any objective differentiation will be disregarded as not constituting 'treatment less favourable'. As a result, the host State will not engage its liability, as there will be no breach of either the MFN or the national treatment clause in the BIT.

Another example is provided by Article 3(2) of the Uganda–Benelux BIT, according to which '[e]xcept for measures required to maintain public order, such investments shall enjoy continuous protection and security, i.e. excluding any unjustified or discriminatory measure which could hinder, either in law or in practice, the management, maintenance, use, possession or liquidation thereof'.[73] Here, measures 'required' for the purpose of maintaining public order, which could potentially include some aspects of environmental protection, are exempted from the non-discrimination disciplines provided for in Article 3(2). The term 'required' is quite characteristic of this and other exceptions. The measure must be necessary to reach the objective identified. But such 'nexus' should not be interpreted restrictively.[74]

Other justification clauses tend to have a broader scope applying generally to all the investment disciplines provided in the treaty. They will be discussed in more detail in Chapter 15.

---

[72] Agreement on the Encouraging and Reciprocal Protection of Investments, Protocol, People's Republic of China–Federal Republic of Germany, 1 December 2003 ('Germany–China BIT'), reproduced in Burke-White and von Staden 'Investment Protection in Extraordinary Times', above n. 71, 327.

[73] Agreement on the Reciprocal Promotion and Protection of Investments, Uganda–Belgium–Luxembourg, 1 February 2005 ('Uganda–Benelux BIT'), reproduced in Burke-White and von Staden, 'Investment Protection in Extraordinary Times', above n. 71, 328.

[74] Burke-White and von Staden, 'Investment Protection in Extraordinary Times', above n. 71, 344; DiMascio and Pauwelyn, 'Nondiscrimination in Trade and Investment Treaties', above n. 1, 77; A. Newcombe, 'General Exceptions in International Investment Agreements', in Cordonnier Segger, Gehring and Newcombe (eds), *Sustainable Development in World Investment Law*, above n. 1, p. 355, at 367 (quoting DiMascio and Pauwelyn with approval).

13.5.4   Other justifying factors

The existence of justifying factors other than those explicitly contemplated in the text of the treaty or in customary international law is unclear. The case-law suggests that differential treatment of companies placed in like circumstances could indeed be justified by other factors, such as proportionality.

In the *Arcelor* case, a large steel producer argued that the European Emissions Trading Directive ('ETS Directive') and the French implementing measures were in breach of the equal treatment standard[75] because they discriminated between sectors (steel, chemical and aluminium producers) that were in like circumstances. Of these three sectors, only steel producers had been included in the first phase of the cap-and-trade system established by the ETS Directive, despite the fact that the chemical and aluminium sectors also produce large emissions of greenhouse gases. This question was brought before the European Court of Justice ('ECJ') both through a reference procedure initiated by the French Conseil d'Etat[76] and through an action for annulment brought by Arcelor.[77] The Court considered that the three sectors at stake were 'in a comparable position'[78] and that they had been treated differently. Yet, it concluded that the European Community ('EC') had justified such differential treatment[79] as a valid exercise of the Community's 'broad discretion'[80] based on 'objective criteria appropriate to the aim pursued by the legislation ... taking into account all the facts and the technical and scientific data available at the time of adoption of the act in question'[81] and 'all the interests involved'.[82] The 'test' used by the ECJ provides an additional illustration of the relevance of purpose as a component of a justifying factor. As to the objective criteria mentioned in this test, the Court referred to the excessive administrative complexity that would have entailed the inclusion of the chemical sector,[83] to the fact that '[t]he difference in the levels of direct emissions between the two sectors concerned is so substantial'[84] and, more generally, to the criterion that the

---

[75] *Arcelor* reference, above n. 35, para. 23.   [76] *Ibid.*, para. 23.

[77] *Arcelor SA* v. *European Parliament and Council*, ECJ Case T-16/04, Judgment (2 March 2010) ('*Arcelor* annulment').

[78] *Arcelor* reference, above n. 35, para. 38.   [79] *Ibid.*, paras. 69 and 72.

[80] *Ibid.*, para. 57.   [81] *Ibid.*, para. 58.   [82] *Ibid.*, para. 59.

[83] The main line of argument of the EC in this regard was that, given the number of chemical installations that would be concerned (34,000), the inclusion of the chemical sector would entail excessive administrative complexity, at least for the first phase of the ETS Directive (which covered some 10,000 installations overall). The Court admitted this argument, *ibid.*, para. 68.

[84] *Ibid.*, para. 72.

EC's 'exercise of its discretion must not produce results that are manifestly less appropriate than those that would be produced by other measures that were also suitable for those objectives'.[85] As noted in Chapter 10, the reasoning of the ECJ on the latter point comes close to the views of the tribunal in *S. D. Myers* v. *Canada*, which took into account that the objective pursued by the measure challenged could have been reached by other measures with a lower impact on foreign investors.[86]

Interestingly, the test applied by the ECJ in the *Arcelor* case presents many similarities with the police powers doctrine and the margin of appreciation doctrine as applied in the investment context. These two doctrines will be analysed in Chapter 15.

---

[85] *Ibid.,* para. 59.   [86] *S. D. Myers* v. *Canada*, above n. 46, paras. 255–6.

14 Environmental measures, stability and due process

This chapter analyses a variety of legal tools used in foreign investment law for the pursuit of predictability in connection with changes in environmental regulation. The term predictability is used here to encompass the need for a stable regulatory environment but also the expectation that any changes will proceed in accordance with certain basic due process requirements. Thus understood, predictability is embodied in a number of investment disciplines, including 'stabilising' clauses *lato sensu*, umbrella clauses, fair and equitable treatment ('FET') clauses, or the denial of justice standard. As in previous chapters, my goal is not to provide a general discussion of such disciplines,[1] but only

---

[1] See (i) on stabilisation clauses: P. Weil, 'Les clauses de stabilisation ou d'intangibilité insérées dans les accords de développement économique', in *Mélanges Ch. Rousseau* (Paris: Pédone 1974), pp. 307ff; E. Paasivirta, 'Internationalisation and Stabilisation of Contracts versus State Sovereignty' (1989) 60 *British Yearbook of International Law* 315; P. Bernardini, 'The Renegotiation of the Investment Contract' (1998) 13 *ICSID Review – Foreign Investment Law Journal* 411; T. Wälde and G. N'Di, 'Stabilising International Investment Commitments' (1996) 31 *Texas International Law Journal* 215; P. Cameron, *International Energy Investment Law* (Oxford University Press, 2010) pp. 68–83; (ii) on umbrella clauses: A. Sinclair, 'The Origins of the Umbrella Clause in International Law of Investment Protection' (2004) 20 *Arbitration International* 411; J. W. Salacuse, *The Law of Investment Treaties* (Oxford University Press, 2011), Chapter 11; (iii) on FET: S. Vasciannie, 'The Fair and Equitable Treatment Standard in International Investment Law and Practice' (2000) 60 *British Yearbook of International Law* 99; I. Tudor, *The Fair and Equitable Treatment Standard in the International Law of Foreign Investment* (Oxford University Press, 2008); R. Kläger, *'Fair and Equitable Treatment' in International Investment Law* (Cambridge University Press, 2011); (iv) on denial of justice: C. de Visscher, 'Le déni de justice en droit international', in *Recueil de cours de l'Académie de droit international*, vol. 52 (1935-II), pp. 365–442; A. V. Freeman, *The International Responsibility of States for Denial of Justice* (London: Longmans Greens, 1938); and, recently, J. Paulsson, *Denial of Justice in International Law* (Cambridge University Press, 2005); C. Focarelli 'Denial of Justice', *Max Planck Encyclopaedia of Public International Law*, available at: www.mpepil.com (accessed on 4 January 2012).

to analyse their impact on the evolution of domestic environmental regulation from the perspective of legitimacy conflicts.[2] The chapter is structured into two sections, one dealing with stability-related questions (Section 14.1) and the other focusing on due process (Section 14.2).

14.1   The protection of stability and environmental regulatory change

14.1.1   The legal anatomy of stability commitments

One important approach used in international investment law to protect foreign investors is to provide some measure of stability through the use of a variety of legal techniques. These techniques have evolved over time from contractual devices to clauses enshrined in bilateral investment treaties (BITs). Some evolution has also taken place within each one of these categories. From choice-of-law clauses, to stabilisation clauses, to modern day adjustment or renegotiation clauses, the legal techniques used in investment contracts have changed significantly, but the objective pursued is fundamentally the same, namely to limit the normative power of the host State. Similarly, from the customary international minimum standard of treatment to modern treatment clauses included in BITs, such as those providing for fair and equitable treatment, full protection and security or the respect of undertakings (umbrella clauses), the tools used in international law to secure some measure of predictability for the operation of foreign investors have become increasingly sophisticated.

This said, the specific contours of the predictability granted by such contractual and treaty devices are difficult to determine in the abstract.

---

[2] On studies specifically addressing this dimension, see, e.g., L. Cotula, 'Stabilization Clauses and the Evolution of Environmental Standards in Foreign Investment Contracts' (2006) 17 *Yearbook of International Environmental Law* 111; K. Tienhaara, 'Unilateral Commitments to Investment Protection: Does the Promise of Stability Restrict Environmental Policy Development?' (2006) 17 *Yearbook of International Environmental Law* 139; L. Cotula, 'Reconciling Regulatory Stability and Evolution of Environmental Standards in Investment Contracts: Towards a Rethink of Stabilization Clauses' (2008) 1 *Journal of World Energy Law and Business* 158; Kläger, *'Fair and Equitable Treatment' in International Investment Law*, above n. 1, pp. 197ff; A. Shemberg, *Stabilization Clauses and Human Rights: A Research Project Conducted for IFC and the United Nations Special Representative to the Secretary General on Business and Human Rights*, 11 March 2008, available at: www.ifc.org (accessed on 4 January 2012); A. Sheppard and A. Crockett, 'Are Stabilization Clauses a Threat to Sustainable Development?', in M.-C. Cordonnier Segger, M. W. Gehring and A. Newcombe (eds.), *Sustainable Development in World Investment Law* (Alphen aan den Rijn: Wolters Kluwer, 2011), pp. 329ff.

This is because the wording of such clauses is not always clear (it must therefore be assessed by tribunals on a case-by-case basis) and, even when it is, their operation must be reconciled with a number of important considerations, including the inherent powers of States to regulate activities conducted within their jurisdiction and the differences between political and commercial risks (as noted by one tribunal, BITs are not insurance against bad business judgment[3] or, one may add, normal commercial risk).

These three uncertainty factors (wording, regulatory powers, type of risk) are especially acute when it comes to balancing the protection of investors with that of the environment. Environmental protection must constantly adapt to changes in the scientific understanding of environmental cycles and advances in technology. Such changes are a fact of life, particularly for investors directly exposed to these changes, such as those active in the chemical or energy industries. In brief, changes in environmental regulation cannot simply be equated to changes in tax regulations for purposes of the operation of predictability devices. In the next sections, I analyse the operation of two main predictability devices: 'stabilising' clauses (Section 14.1.2); and legitimate expectations protected under the FET standard (Section 14.1.3). The operation of another legal device, i.e. the protection of specific assurances, will be discussed in Chapter 15.

14.1.2   Stabilising clauses and environmental regulation

In this section, the term 'stabilising clauses' is used broadly to cover three types of contractual devices: choice-of-law clauses (Section 14.1.2.1); clauses 'freezing' the applicable law at a given point in time ('intangibility' or 'stabilisation clauses' *stricto sensu*)(Section 14.1.2.2); and clauses requiring the renegotiation or adjustment of certain contractual terms under some specified circumstances (Section 14.1.2.3). The relationship between some of these clauses and the so-called 'umbrella clauses' appearing in certain investment treaties will also be discussed (Section 14.1.2.4).

14.1.2.1   Choice of law clauses and environmental regulation

Choice-of-law clauses provide some measure of stability when the law chosen to govern the contract is not the one of the host State.[4] Whether

---

[3] *Maffezini v. Spain*, ICSID Case No. ARB/97/7, Award (13 November 2000), para. 64.
[4] See P. Weil, 'Problèmes relatifs aux contrats passés entre un Etat et un particulier', in Vol. 128 (1969), pp. 95, at 226–7; Paasivirta, 'Internationalisation and Stabilisation of Contracts versus State Sovereignty', above n. 1, 323.

such law is that of another State or international law or a combination of international and domestic law, the main objective remains to shield the contract from the normative power of the host State. One question that may arise in this connection is whether the environmental laws of the host State may apply despite a choice-of-law clause subjecting the contract to another law. The broader context of this issue has been analysed in Chapter 11. Two main considerations must be taken into account in answering this question: the nature of environmental law and the forum selected to hear the dispute.

Regarding the first consideration, environmental law should not be seen as a monolithic body of law. The legal protection of the environment may take different forms with different consequences as to the applicability of a given rule. In those cases where the environmental regulation in question can be characterised as an overriding mandatory rule or a '*loi de police*', its application to the investment 'situation' may indeed be commanded by the very nature of the rule. For example, Article 7 of the Rome Convention on the law applicable to contractual obligations expressly reserves the application of the 'mandatory rules' of the forum or of a third State.[5] This principle has not been incorporated as such in the Rome I Regulation ('Rome I').[6] While restating the applicability of mandatory rules of the forum, Article 9 of Rome I allows for the application of mandatory rules of third States only where such rules stem from the 'law of the country where the obligations arising out of the contract have to be or have been performed, in so far as those overriding mandatory provisions render the performance of the contract unlawful'.[7] Despite the difference in scope between Article 7(1) of the Rome Convention and Article 9(3) of Rome I, these two examples suggest that whether one adopts an expansive or a more restrictive view as to the applicability of overriding rules, the application of the environmental laws of the host State would seem to be permitted under both conceptions. In addition, such rules could also apply as part of the overriding rules of the forum, which leads to the second consideration identified above.

---

[5] See Convention on the Law Applicable to Contractual Obligations, 19 June 1980, OJ 1980 L/ 266/1, ('Rome Convention'). The origins of this rule can be traced back to the *Alnati* case, decided by the Supreme Court of the Netherlands in 1967. See M. Giuliano and P. Lagarde, 'Report on the Convention on the Law Applicable to Contractual Obligations', OJ 1980 C 282/1, ('Giuliano–Lagarde Report'), commentary ad Article 7, para. 1. The observance of overriding rules in the territory of the host State would seem *a fortiori* justified.

[6] Regulation (EC) No. 593/2008 of the European Parliament and of the Council of 17 June 2008 on the law applicable to contractual obligations ('Rome I'), OJ 2008 L 177.

[7] *Ibid.*, Article 9(3).

Whereas the application by a court of the overriding mandatory rules of the forum seems widely accepted,[8] the powers of arbitral tribunals in this connection are less clear, as the 'forum' of such tribunals depends on the legal seat of the arbitration. According to one commentator, arbitral tribunals have considerable leeway in deciding whether the environmental laws of the host State may be applied.[9] In all events, what can be derived from the preceding discussion is that choice-of-law clauses cannot insulate an investor from the application of at least certain environmental laws of the host State.

14.1.2.2   Stabilisation clauses *stricto sensu* and environmental regulation

Another important contractual device used to stabilise the framework governing the investment are clauses freezing the law of the host State applicable to a contract at a given point in time or requiring the consent of the investor as a condition for the application of any subsequent change in such law.[10] One important question in this connection is whether such clauses prevent the host State from applying subsequent environmental regulations to the investor.

This question was discussed in a number of cases in the 1970s and 1980s, and focusing on domestic regulations concerning other areas.[11] The common understanding that has developed over the years is that the State fully retains its regulatory power[12] but an exercise of such power in breach of a stabilisation clause gives rise to an obligation to

---

[8] Giuliano–Lagarde Report, above n. 5, commentary ad Article 7, para. 4.

[9] L. Radicati di Brozolo, 'Arbitrage commercial international et lois de police. Considérations sur les conflits de juridictions dans le commerce international', in *Recueil des cours de l'Académie de droit international*, Vol. 315 (2005), p. 402.

[10] Paasivirta, 'Internationalisation and Stabilisation of Contracts versus State Sovereignty', above n. 1, 323–5; Cotula, 'Reconciling Regulatory Stability' above n. 2, 159–61; Cameron, *International Energy Investment Law*, above n. 1, pp. 68–74.

[11] See, e.g., *Texaco Overseas Petroleum Company and California Asiatic Oil Company v. The Government of the Libyan Arab Republic*, Award (19 January 1977), 53 ILR 389 ('*Texaco*'); *Libyan American Oil Company (Liamco) v. The Government of the Libyan Arab Republic*, Award (12 April 1977), 62 ILR 140 ('*Liamco*'); *Revere Copper & Brass, Inc. v. Overseas Private Investment Corporation (OPIC)*, Award (24 August 1978), 56 ILR 258 ('*Revere Copper*'); *AGIP Company v. The People's Republic of the Congo*, Award (30 November 1979), 21 ILM 726 ('*AGIP v. Congo*'); *Government of Kuwait v. American Independent Oil Co*, Award (24 March 1982), 21 ILM 976 ('*Aminoil*'). See also and relatedly two domestic cases: *Rederiaktiebolaget Amphitrite v. The King* [1921] 3 KB 500; *United States of America v. Winstar Corporation et al.*, 518 US 839 (1996).

[12] *Parkerings-Compagniet AS v. Republic of Lithuania*, ICSID Case No. ARB/05/8, Award (11 September 2007) ('*Parkerings v. Lithuania*'), para. 332.

compensate the investor.[13] Some commentators have argued that this obligation could lead to 'regulatory chill' or 'regulatory distortion', dissuading States from adopting normal and necessary regulations because of the litigation risks potentially involved.[14] This challenge would be particularly significant for environmental regulation, which, by its very nature, is constantly evolving, either through new norms or measures or simply through the evolving interpretation of existing measures. Here, after a brief discussion of the question of evolving interpretation, I analyse two approaches to handle potential tensions between stabilisation clauses and environmental regulation.

Stabilisation clauses normally cover legislative or regulatory changes. It is unclear, however, whether a change in the interpretation of the same provision would also be covered. In some cases, such changes may indeed have effects similar to the enactment of a new provision.[15] For instance, most of what is usually referred to as a human rights approach to environmental protection has developed through the evolving interpretation of human rights provisions in treaties or in constitutions. The relationship between a stabilisation clause and a change in the interpretation of domestic tax law was addressed by the tribunal in *Duke Energy v. Peru*.[16] The tribunal started by noting that, normally, to demonstrate a breach of a stabilisation clause, an investor would need to prove '(i) the existence of a pre-existing law or regulation (or absence thereof) at the time the tax stability guarantee was granted, and (ii) a law or regulation passed or issued after the LSA [legal stability agreement] that changed the pre-existing regime'.[17] In the case of a change of interpretation, the tribunal considered that it would be sufficient for an investor to prove '(i) a *stable* interpretation or application at the time the tax

---

[13] Weil, 'Problèmes relatifs aux contrats passés entre un Etat et un particulier', above n. 4, p. 215; E. Jimenez de Aréchaga, 'International Law in the Past Third of a Century', in *Recueil des cours de l'Académie de droit international*, Vol. 159 (1978), p. 1, at 307; Paasivirta, 'Internationalisation and Stabilisation of Contracts versus State Sovereignty', above n. 1, 330; Cameron, *International Energy Investment Law*, above n. 1, p. 90.

[14] Cotula, 'Reconciling Regulatory Stability', above n. 2, 170; Tienhaara, 'Unilateral Commitments to Investment Protection', above n. 2, 161.

[15] See, e.g., *Glamis Gold Ltd v. United States of America*, NAFTA (UNCITRAL), Award (16 May 2009) (*'Glamis v. United States'*), paras. 758–72 (discussing a reinterpretation of the term 'undue impairment' by a US federal agency, which, according to the claimant 'disregarded "decades of settled law and practice"'. However, the question was not analysed in the light of a stabilising clause).

[16] *Duke Energy International Peru Investments No. 1 Ltd v. Republic of Peru*, ICSID Case No. ARB/03/28, Award (25 July 2008) (*'Duke v. Peru'*).

[17] *Ibid.*, para. 217.

stability guarantee was granted, and (ii) a decision or assessment after the LSA that modified that stable interpretation or application'.[18] As recognised by the tribunal, this second test was much more demanding for the investor than the first test, because it required 'compelling evidence'. As noted by the tribunal: '[c]lear case law and/or well-established practice constitute persuasive evidence on the issue of consistent meaning, as does generally accepted legal doctrine. The opinion of lawyers retained by a party does not'.[19] Moreover 'the statements or actions of a State agency that merely *imply* a specific interpretation or application of the law do not ... provide a sufficiently sound basis upon which to conclude that a stable interpretation of the law existed'.[20] Yet, where there has been insufficient time for stable interpretations to develop, because the regulations at stake are new or recent, the tribunal 'may depart from a strictly comparative analysis' and 'evaluate the decision or assessment that is impugned by Claimant against a reasonableness standard'.[21] Under this third test, the inquiry to be conducted by the tribunal is as follows:

It is not for the Tribunal to simply determine if Peruvian law was properly applied, to formulate its own theory on Peruvian law, or to determine what it would consider to be the appropriate interpretation from the variety of interpretations that one might reasonably formulate. By their very nature, laws often invite different interpretations based on fairly reasonable principles. For this reason, and in order to preserve the proper balance of fairness between the parties in this arbitration, it must be demonstrated, absent a demonstrable change of law or a change to a stable prior interpretation or application, that the application of the law to DEI Egenor was patently unreasonable or arbitrary.[22]

The tribunal eventually concluded that Peru had indeed breached the guarantee of stability given to the investor, but did so on the basis that the investor had been able to discharge its burden of proving a stable interpretation.[23] From an environmental perspective, the main contributions of this award are the second and the third tests and, more specifically, the type of 'compelling evidence' that would be needed to meet the requirements of the second test. It must be added that, as the reasons underlying changes in the interpretation of tax law and changes

---

[18] *Ibid.*, para. 218.   [19] *Ibid.*, para. 220.
[20] *Ibid.*, para. 221.   [21] *Ibid.*, para. 223.   [22] *Ibid.*, para. 226.
[23] *Ibid.*, paras. 345 and 350–66. The tribunal also concluded, albeit only for abundance of motives (see para. 379), that Peru had breached its implied duty of good faith (see para. 442).

in the interpretation of environmental law are often very different,[24] the operation of these two tests will likely be different in practice, particularly for the assessment of reasonableness or arbitrariness.

Moving now to the first approach that could be used to handle friction between stabilisation clauses and environmental law, it has been argued that States cannot contract out of certain norms, most notably those protecting human rights, either in general or with respect to the activities of certain investors who could avail themselves of a stabilisation clause.[25] This would amount to an implied exception to any stabilisation clause (or commitment). This argument has been extended to norms protecting the environment.[26] In assessing the merits of this argument, one must be careful to disentangle what reflects positive international law and what is only an attempt at progressive development. In this regard, three key considerations must be taken into account. The first consideration concerns the type of human rights or environmental norms at stake. Neither environmental law nor human rights law are monolithic bodies of law. Different norms have different standing in international and domestic law and, as a result, they have different legal implications. Most human rights treaties recognise the possibility for States to derogate from certain provisions in times of public emergency.[27] A contrario, if the conditions for derogation are not met (which is the usual situation when States conclude investment contracts), then such derogations would be legally precluded. Thus, a State cannot undertake to freeze the domestic legislation adopted pursuant to such

---

[24] At least two significant differences can be identified. First, changes in the interpretation of environmental law aim to protect health and/or the environment, whereas changes in the interpretation of tax law are not directly aimed at protecting the population. At best, one could argue that the tax revenues will be used to protect public health or the environment, but the link would only be indirect, at least where the tax measure does not expressly provide for such allocation of funds. Second, changes in the interpretation of environmental law (as regulatory changes) are inherent to the evolving nature of the object of protection, whereas changes in the interpretation of tax law are in no way 'required' by the nature of the object of protection.

[25] S. Leader, 'Human Rights, Risks, and New Strategies for Global Investment' (2006) 9 *Journal of International Economic Law* 657.

[26] Cotula, 'Reconciling Regulatory Stability', above n. 2, 172–5.

[27] See, e.g., Article 4(1) of the International Covenant on Civil and Political Rights, 16 December 1966, 999 UNTS 171 ('ICCPR'). However, no derogation is admissible with respect to core human rights identified in Article 4(2): 'No derogation from articles 6, 7, 8 (paragraphs 1 and 2), 11, 15, 16 and 18 may be made under this provision.' See also, Article 15 of the Convention for the Protection of Human Rights and Fundamental Freedoms, 4 November 1950, 213 UNTS 221 ('ECHR'); Article 27 of the American Convention on Human Rights, 22 November 1969, 1144 UNTS 123 ('ACHR').

treaties and, even if it did so, an investor could not reasonably rely on such undertaking.[28] It is, however, unclear whether, aside from certain human rights, other norms could deploy similar effects. *A priori* many environmental norms could not per se deploy these effects, but some caveats must be introduced here. As discussed in some detail in Chapters 7 to 10, international environmental law can follow either a regulatory approach or a human rights approach. In the latter case, the environmental standards introduced into human rights standards could deploy the same effects as these latter and, therefore, not be contracted out through stabilisation clauses. Also, some widely accepted environmental standards expressly preclude investors from 'seeking or accepting exemptions not contemplated in the statutory or regulatory framework related to human rights, environmental, health, safety, labour, taxation, financial incentives, or other issues'.[29] The second consideration concerns the level of realisation or fulfilment of human rights or environmental norms. One may, indeed, agree with the first consideration and, yet, disagree on whether a measure adopted by a State in breach of a stabilisation clause was actually required by the human right or environmental treaty. This goes to the 'vulnerability' of the link between domestic measures and international norms, an issue that has been analysed in Chapters 7 to 10. The third consideration relates to compensation and leads to the second approach.

Assuming that a State has agreed not to change its environmental regulation as required by an environmental treaty and that it later adopts a domestic environmental measure pursuant to this treaty, it seems clear that such a measure will indeed apply to the investor. What remains unclear is whether an obligation of compensation arises for the

---

[28] There are indeed limits to the protection of specific assurances given to investors. See *Revere Copper*, above n. 11, 271 (referring to 'undertakings and assurances given in good faith to such aliens' which excludes assurances given or received in bad faith); *Methanex Corporation* v. *United States of America*, NAFTA (UNCITRAL), Award (3 August 2005) ('*Methanex* v. *United States*'), Part IV, Ch. D, para. 7 (circumscribing the requirements for actionable specific assurances). See also, the discussion of specific assurances in Chapter 15.

[29] OECD, 'Guidelines for Multinational Enterprises', Annex I to the Declaration on International Investment and Multinational Enterprises, 25 May 2011 ('OECD Guidelines'), Chapter II, para. 5. This standard was at stake in a 'specific instance' brought before the UK National Contact Point. See 'Letter from Friends of the Earth to Wesley Scholz, Director, Office of Investment Affairs and National Contact Point for the OECD Guidelines for Multinational Enterprises, Department of State 3–8', 29 April 2003, referred to in E. Morgera, *Corporate Accountability in International Environmental Law* (Oxford University Press, 2009), p. 232.

State. As already noted, the ordinary rule is that a breach of a stabilisation clause gives rise to an obligation of compensation. But this rule does not take into account international standards such as the OECD Guidelines (Chapter II, para. 5) nor, more generally, does it specify whether there are exceptions to such an obligation. For example, an investor could not reasonably expect that a State will breach its human rights (or assimilated environmental) obligations to comply with a stabilisation clause or other stability commitments. There are limits to what a State can promise and at least some of these limits are manifest enough to require investors to be (factually or constructively) aware of them. As noted by the tribunal in *Parkerings* v. *Lithuania*:

[t]he investor will have a right of protection of its legitimate expectations provided it exercised due diligence and that its legitimate expectations were reasonable in light of the circumstances. Consequently, an investor must anticipate that the circumstances could change, and thus structure its investment in order to adapt it to the potential changes of legal environment.[30]

In the same vein, the tribunal in *Plama* v. *Bulgaria* reasoned that an investor who had not been diligent in determining the implications of the domestic environmental law applicable to its investment could not claim that its legitimate expectations have been frustrated.[31] A second related question is whether a tribunal could consider that, by entering into a stabilisation clause, a State was undertaking to compensate the investor for abiding by the human rights or environmental framework applicable within the country.[32] This may depend on the human rights/environmental framework at stake. A State could perhaps be bound to compensate an investor for the additional costs imposed by compliance with 'higher than normal' human rights or environmental standards but not with 'basic' standards.[33] The boundary between 'basic' and 'higher than normal' should be determined by reference to a variety of materials, such as human rights/environmental treaty provisions, the

---

[30] *Parkerings* v. *Lithuania*, above n. 12, para. 333.

[31] *Plama Consortium Limited* v. *Bulgaria*, ICSID Case No. ARB/03/24, Award (27 August 2008) ('*Plama* v. *Bulgaria*'), paras. 220–1.

[32] By analogy to the so-called 'compensation clauses'. See Sheppard and Crockett, 'Are Stabilization Clauses a Threat to Sustainable Development?', above n. 2, 337 (and references).

[33] According to a survey of seventy-six contracts and twelve model contracts, contracts with OECD countries tend to exclude at least some health and environmental regulations from the scope of stabilisation clauses. See Shemberg, *Stabilization Clauses and Human Rights*, above n. 2, paras. 100 and 115.

interpretation of such provisions made by human rights bodies or by the conferences of the parties of the environmental treaty in question, or, still, by any relevant case-law. As the understanding of what is 'basic' and what is 'higher than normal' will normally evolve over time, the observations of the tribunal in *Duke* v. *Peru* as to the type of materials that could be used to prove a given interpretation would also be useful here.[34] A third related question is whether, in those cases where compensation is due, the amount could be adjusted to reflect the fact that a change in environmental regulation is part of the commercial risk assumed by the investor. This question has been discussed in Chapter 5.

14.1.2.3   Renegotiation/adjustment clauses and environmental regulation

Other stabilising clauses focus on maintaining the economic equilibrium underlying the contract. Under such clauses, if a certain triggering event occurs, an obligation of renegotiation or adjustment of some terms of the contract is set in motion to restore the initial economic equilibrium. Most of what has been said in connection with stabilisation clauses *stricto sensu* also applies to renegotiation/adjustment clauses. Here, I focus on two specific issues: the extent to which triggering events of an environmental nature are taken into account in such clauses and the legal consequences associated with the occurrence of a triggering event.

Regarding the first issue, the parties to a contract are free to define such triggering events as they deem appropriate. Contractual practices follow some patterns. According to a recent study commissioned by the International Finance Corporation and the UN Special Rapporteur on Business and Human Rights, a distinction can be made between 'full economic equilibrium clauses' and 'limited economic equilibrium clauses'. These latter are characterised by the fact that 'for some type of new laws (for example, laws protecting health, the environment, individual safety, or security) compensation will not be due'.[35] Limited economic equilibrium clauses are significantly more frequent in contracts concluded by OECD countries, whereas in contracts with non-OECD countries full economic equilibrium clauses are the rule.[36] This difference may be due to the different bargaining power of OECD and non-OECD countries when they negotiate with investors as well as to

---

[34] *Duke* v. *Peru*, above n. 16, paras. 220–1.
[35] Shemberg, *Stabilization Clauses and Human Rights*, above n. 2, para. 30.
[36] *Ibid.*, 26, Figures 6.6. and 24, and Figure 6.5.

different levels of stability (and thus of political risk). Yet, from a legal perspective, the analysis conducted in the preceding sub-section as to the need to take into account the (un)-'reasonableness' of accepting stringent stability commitments that go against basic human rights or environmental protection standards remains applicable. This takes me to the analysis of the legal consequences of such clauses.

These consequences vary from one clause to another, but, generally speaking, the occurrence of a triggering event gives rise to: (i) a duty to renegotiate; (ii) an obligation to restore the economic equilibrium; and/or (iii) an obligation to compensate. Clauses triggering a duty to renegotiate may also contemplate, in case the renegotiation is unsuccessful, the obligation for the State to pay compensation. But this is not to say that the obligation to renegotiate in good faith cannot as such be breached. In *Suez v. Argentina*, Argentina was found in breach of its treaty obligations (which took the contract terms into account as part of the legitimate expectations of the investor) because of the coercive manner in which it conducted the renegotiation of the applicable tariff.[37] Obligations to restore the economic equilibrium may take different forms, including 'adjusted tariffs, extension of the concession, tax reductions, monetary compensation, or other'.[38] Economic equilibrium clauses in contracts with OECD countries sometimes distribute the risk by requiring the investor to absorb a certain level of loss before the restoration obligation is triggered or subjecting the compensation obligation to the condition that the law in question be discriminatory.[39] Shemberg refers, by way of example, to Article 14.2.1. of the UK Model Project Finance agreement, which states that:

[c]ontractors have in the past expressed concern that change of law is a risk which they cannot control and which they regard as being within the control of the Authority or wider Government. In practice, however, many Authorities (particularly local authorities) have negligible influence over legislation whereas the private sector has traditionally proved adept at managing the effects of changes of law and minimising their impact on their business. Hence it is appropriate for the Contractor to bear or share in the risk.[40]

---

[37] *Suez, Sociedad General de Aguas de Barcelona SA and Vivendi Universal SA v. The Argentine Republic*, ICSID Case No. ARB/03/19, Decision on Liability (30 July 2010) ('*Suez v. Argentina – 03/19*'), paras. 241–3.

[38] Shemberg, *Stabilization Clauses and Human Rights*, above n. 2, p. vii.

[39] *Ibid.*, paras. 98–101.

[40] UK Model Project Finance Agreement, cited in Shemberg, *Stabilization Clauses and Human Rights*, above n. 2, para. 102.

Shemberg summarises the main criteria used in this model agreement to allocate risk, namely 'the character of the law (generally applicable, specific, discriminatory) and the character of the project (whether costs can be passed on to the users of the project)'.[41] The more generally applicable is a regulation or the more the costs it entails can be passed on to users, the more it appears justified for the investor to bear the cost. Conversely, the more it is targeted and/or discriminatory, the more it seems justified for the State to compensate.

14.1.2.4   Interactions with investment treaties – the 'umbrella clause'

The preceding observations regarding certain contractual devices may also be relevant in the context of a treaty claim. The 'elevation' of contractual considerations to the level of treaty has been widely debated in foreign investment circles, one of the main points of contention being the identification of those contractual terms that can be elevated and those that cannot.[42]

For present purposes, it is not necessary to reopen this broad and, in many ways, still unresolved question. Suffice it to say that stabilising clauses tend to be seen as contractual terms capable of being elevated to treaty level. According to the tribunal in *El Paso v. Argentina*:

[an] umbrella clause … will not extend the Treaty protection to breaches of an ordinary commercial contract entered into by the State or a State-owned entity, but will cover additional investment protections contractually agreed by the State as a sovereign – such as a stabilization clause – inserted in an investment agreement.[43]

The view underlying this statement is that only the State acting as a sovereign can enter into a stabilisation clause. It remains, however, unclear whether, under this same view, a clause merely providing for compensation or allocating the costs arising from the adoption of new

---

[41] Shemberg, *Stabilization Clauses and Human Rights*, above n. 2, para. 102.

[42] Sinclair, 'The Origins of the Umbrella Clause in International Law of Investment Protection', above n. 1; Salacuse, *The Law of Investment Treaties*, above n. 1.

[43] *El Paso Energy International Company v. The Argentine Republic*, ICSID Case No. ARB/03/15, Decision on Jurisdiction (27 April 2006) ('*El Paso v. Argentina*'), para. 81. The tribunal supported its conclusion by reference to three other decisions, namely *SGS Société Générale de Surveillance SA v. Islamic Republic of Pakistan*, ICSID Case No. ARB/01/13, Decision on Jurisdiction (27 August 2003), paras. 166, 168 and 173; *Salini Costruttori SpA & Italstrade SpA v. Hashemite Kingdom of Jordan*, ICSID Case No. ARB/02/13, Decision on Jurisdiction (29 November 2004), para. 126; *Joy Machinery Limited v. Arab Republic of Egypt*, ICSID Case No. ARB/02/11, Award (6 August 2004), para. 81.

regulations would also be covered. Much will depend on the specific wording of the umbrella clause. But, in the absence of specification, the question will have to be assessed on a case-by-case basis, taking into account that when a State agrees to limit its power to adopt environmental regulation it will be most likely acting in its sovereign capacity.

In at least one case, i.e., *Plama* v. *Bulgaria*,[44] a tribunal has gone even further, considering that a regular commercial clause distributing the risk of liability for environmental damage had to be assessed in the light of the umbrella clause contained in Article 10(1) *in fine* of the Energy Charter Treaty ('ECT').[45] The tribunal rejected the claim because it found that the amendment of the domestic environmental law challenged by the investor did not violate the contract and was therefore consistent with the umbrella clause of the ECT.[46] In doing so, the tribunal assumed that the contractual term in question could indeed be elevated through the operation of the umbrella clause.

14.1.3   Legitimate expectations under the FET standard

Perhaps the most important question regarding the relations between environmental regulation and the protection of stability is the extent to which the legitimate expectations of an investor may be frustrated by the adoption of new environmental regulation. After some observations regarding the protection of stability under investment treaties (Section 14.1.3.1), I analyse the requirements for the protection of investors' legitimate expectations (Section 14.1.3.2), and then focus on some cases where this question arose in connection with environmental regulation (Section 14.1.3.3).

14.1.3.1   The protection of stability under investment treaties

There is some controversy as to the manner in which stability is protected in international investment law. Whereas some tribunals consider that it is protected as such, independently of other 'theories' of protection such as the 'legitimate expectations' of the investor, other tribunals have taken the stance that stability is protected through the intermediary of such theories, in particular the protection of 'legitimate expectations' under the fair and equitable treatment ('FET') standard.

---

[44] *Plama* v. *Bulgaria*, above n. 31.
[45] Energy Charter Treaty, 17 December 1994, 2080 UNTS 95 ('ECT').
[46] *Plama* v. *Bulgaria*, above n. 31, para. 224.

An example of the first stance is provided by the award of the tribunal in *Metalclad* v. *Mexico*. In this case, the tribunal based its conclusion that Mexico had breached the NAFTA on an apparently distinct obligation to provide a 'transparent and predictable framework' for the operations of the investor.[47] However, the award was partially set aside (on this specific point) by the Supreme Court of British Columbia on the grounds that no such distinct standard existed.[48] Other tribunals have followed a similar stance, including those in *Tecmed* v. *Mexico*[49] and *Occidental* v. *Ecuador*.[50]

Yet, this broad conception of the FET standard has come under considerable criticism.[51] Some tribunals have considered that the protection of stability must be seen as a component of the protection of the investor's legitimate expectations under FET. In *Duke* v. *Ecuador*, the tribunal referred to *Tecmed* v. *Mexico* and *Occidental* v. *Ecuador* with approval but added that '[t]he stability of the legal and business environment is directly linked to the investor's justified expectations'.[52] This statement was quoted with assent by the tribunal in *Bayindir* v. *Pakistan*, who explicitly noted that its reliance on the broad *Tecmed* standard was not unqualified.[53] Similarly, in a number of cases involving Argentina, tribunals have linked stability to the protection of legitimate expectations. For example, in *CMS* v. *Argentina*, the tribunal noted that '[i]t is not a question of whether the legal framework might need to be frozen as it can always evolve and be adapted to changing circumstances, but neither is it a question of whether the framework can be dispensed with altogether when specific commitments to the contrary have been

---

[47] *Metalclad Corporation* v. *United Mexican States*, ICSID Case No. ARB(AF)/97/1, Award (25 August 2000) ('*Metalclad* v. *Mexico*'), para. 99.

[48] *United Mexican States* v. *Metalclad*, 2001 BCSC 664, Supreme Court of British Columbia, Reasons for the Judgment (2 May 2001), paras. 67–77.

[49] *Técnicas Medioambientales Tecmed SA* v. *United Mexican States*, ICSID Case No. ARB(AF)/00/2, Award (29 May 2003) ('*Tecmed* v. *Mexico*'), para. 154.

[50] *Occidental Exploration and Production Co.* v. *Republic of Ecuador*, LCIA Case No. UN 3467, Award (1 July 2004), para. 183.

[51] See e.g., *MTD Equity Sdn Bhd and MTD Chile SA* v. *Republic of Chile*, ICSID Case No. ARB/01/7, Decision on Annulment (16 February 2007) ('*MTD* v. *Chile* – Annulment'), paras. 66–7 (criticising the conception of *Tecmed* standard); *Suez* v. *Argentina* – 03/19, above n. 37, para. 224 (quoting the critical remarks of the *MTD* Ad Hoc Committee with assent).

[52] *Duke Energy Electroquil Partners and Electroquil SA* v. *Republic of Ecuador*, ICSID Case No. ARB/04/19, Award (18 August 2008) ('*Duke* v. *Ecuador*'), paras. 339–40.

[53] *Bayindir Insaat Turizm Ticaret ve Sanayi A Ş* v. *Pakistan*, ICSID Case No. ARB/03/29, Award (27 August 2009) ('*Bayindir* v. *Pakistan*'), para. 179.

made'.[54] In the same vein, the tribunal in *Suez* v. *Argentina* framed the question of regulatory change from the perspective of legitimate expectations and quoted the remarks of the *Bayindir* tribunal with assent.[55] The approach to the protection of stability that emerges from these more recent cases has been summarised in a recent monograph on the FET standard by Kläger.[56] According to this author:

[f]air and equitable treatment is often said to require the protection of the investors' legitimate expectations. The protection of such expectations covers the abidance to promises and covenants that have been given to the investor and upon which the investor has relied. *In this context*, arbitral tribunals have also found that the protection of expectations is closely intertwined with a *certain level of stability and consistency* in the legal framework of the host State.[57]

This is not a purely academic controversy because the requirements for a breach of the FET standard in the first approach are lower than in the second approach. Specifically, the rather demanding requirements for the protection of legitimate expectations will only be relevant if one follows the second approach. In the next paragraphs, I analyse these requirements as they may apply to changes in environmental regulation.

14.1.3.2 Requirements for the protection of legitimate expectations

The protection of the investor's legitimate expectations under the FET standard is subject to some general requirements. These requirements can be identified by reference to some recent decisions. In *LG&E* v. *Argentina*, the tribunal considered that, to be protected, such expectations must be:

based on the conditions offered by the host state at the time of the investment; they may not be established unilaterally by one of the parties; they must exist and be enforceable by law; in the event of infringement by the host state, a duty to compensate the investor for damages arises except for those caused in the event of state of necessity; however, the investor's fair expectations cannot fail to consider parameters such as business risk or industry's regular patterns.[58]

---

[54] *CMS Gas Transmission Company v. Argentine Republic*, ICSID Case No. ARB/01/08, Award (12 May 2005) ('*CMS v. Argentina* – Award'), para. 277.

[55] *Suez v. Argentina* – 03/19, above n. 37, paras. 225–6.

[56] Kläger, '*Fair and Equitable Treatment' in International Investment Law*, above n. 1, pp. 151 and 164–87.

[57] *Ibid.*, p. 117 (italics added).

[58] *LG&E v. Argentina*, ICSID Case No. ARB/02/1, Decision on Liability (13 October 2006) ('*LG&E v. Argentina*'), para. 130.

Largely similar requirements were identified by the tribunal in *Parkerings* v. *Lithuania*. According to this tribunal:

[t]he expectation is legitimate if the investor received an explicit promise or guaranty from the host-State, or if implicitly, the host-State made assurances or representations that the investor took into account in making the investment. Finally, in the situation where the host-State made no assurance or representation, the circumstances surrounding the conclusion of the agreement are decisive to determine if the expectation of the investor was legitimate. In order to determine the legitimate expectation of an investor, it is also necessary to analyse the conduct of the State at the time of the investment.[59]

In a similar vein, the tribunal in *Duke* v. *Ecuador* noted, by reference to *LG&E* v. *Argentina*, that:

[t]o be protected, the investor's expectations must be legitimate and reasonable at the time when the investor makes the investment. The assessment of the reasonableness or legitimacy must take into account all circumstances, including not only the facts surrounding the investment, but also the political, socioeconomic, cultural and historical conditions prevailing in the host State. In addition, such expectations must arise from the conditions that the State offered the investor and the latter must have relied upon them when deciding to invest.[60]

These three decisions identify a largely overlapping set of requirements for the protection of the investor's legitimate expectations under the FET standard. Such expectations: (i) must be the result of State conduct; (ii) must be sufficiently clear (as a rule they must be explicit, e.g., given in a contract, but they may exceptionally be implicit in State conduct); (iii) they must arise prior to the moment when the investment is made; (iv) they must be legitimate and reasonable in the light of the overall circumstances surrounding the investment (as opposed to the purely subjective expectations of the investor); (v) the investor must specifically rely on such expectations in making its investment. The *LG&E* tribunal added that the expectations cannot be unilateral, which could be understood either as restating condition (iv) or as expressly requiring the existence of a contract (a bilateral act). The latter interpretation seems to be more consistent with the additional requirement that the expectations be enforceable by law within the domestic system.[61] As discussed next, from the perspective of environmental regulation, the most important requirement is (iv).

---

[59] *Parkerings* v. *Lithuania*, above n. 12, para. 331.
[60] *Duke* v. *Ecuador*, above n. 52, para. 340.
[61] *Glamis* v. *United States*, above n. 15, para. 767.

14.1.3.3   'Legitimacy' and 'reasonableness' from an environmental perspective

How 'reasonable' or 'legitimate' are an investor's expectations that the host State will not adopt regulations to protect the environment or amend existing ones? This question arose in *Plama v. Bulgaria*[62] in connection with an amendment of the applicable environmental laws as a result of which the investment vehicle was rendered liable for past environmental damages. The investor claimed that the amendment was in breach of several investment disciplines of the ECT, particularly the FET standard protecting the investor's legitimate expectations.

In assessing this claim, the tribunal paid much attention to the circumstances in which the investor's expectations allegedly arose. The tribunal's reasoning was premised on the following general statement:

> the Tribunal believes that the ECT does not protect investors against any and all changes in the host country's laws. Under the fair and equitable treatment standard the investor is only protected if (at least) reasonable and justifiable expectations were created in that regard.[63]

The tribunal went on to discuss whether, under the circumstances, the expectations of the investor that the environmental regulatory framework would not change were 'reasonable' or 'legitimate'. It noted that the investor 'was, of course, aware of, or should have been aware of, the state of Bulgarian law when it invested in Nova Plama' and that no 'lack of due diligence in Respondent's treatment of Claimant and its investment with regard to the environmental amendments' could be identified.[64] Interestingly, the tribunal also noted, in connection with the investor's argument that it could not be aware of the upcoming amendment because such amendment was still being debated in the Bulgarian parliament at the time the investment was made, that 'those parliamentary debates were in the public record and should have been known by [the investor's] Bulgaria advisors'.[65] On this basis, the tribunal dismissed the claim for breach of the FET standard.

Two main clarifications can be derived from the reasoning of the *Plama* tribunal. First, investors have a due diligence obligation, which covers not only (i) the basic regulations applicable to foreign investment transactions (e.g., licensing requirements and the like) but also (ii) the entire legal framework potentially applicable to the investment, and

---

[62] *Plama v. Bulgaria*, above n. 31.   [63] *Ibid.*, para. 219.
[64] *Ibid.*, paras. 220 and 222.   [65] *Ibid.*, para. 221.

even (iii) the potential changes of such framework that are foreseeable at the time the investment is made. Investors may, of course, manage regulatory risk by introducing specific provisions in their contract with the host State, but this possibility is not without limits.[66] In addition, as noted by other investment tribunals, 'reasonableness' must also be assessed in the light of other broader circumstances, including 'business risk or industry's regular patterns'[67] or 'the political, socioeconomic, cultural and historical conditions prevailing in the host State'.[68]

Second, a distinction must be introduced between those cases where only the investor has behaved negligently and those other cases where both the investor and the host State have lacked diligence. In the first hypothesis, the tribunal should in principle consider that the expectations invoked by the investor are not sufficiently 'reasonable' or 'legitimate' to be protected, as was the case in *Plama* v. *Bulgaria*. In the second hypothesis, the tribunal may simply take the investor's negligence into account in determining the amount of damages. The latter solution was followed in *MTD* v. *Chile*, where the tribunal held that 'the Claimants [had] incurred costs that were related to their business judgment irrespective of the breach of fair and equitable treatment under the BIT ... [because] [t]hey accepted to pay a price for the land with the Project without appropriate legal protection'.[69]

14.2 Environmental regulatory change and due process

14.2.1 The link between due process and environmental regulatory change

The diverse nature of the protection of due process in international law makes the connection between this concept and environmental regulatory change both easy to establish and difficult to circumscribe precisely. Due process considerations are protected by a number of investment disciplines, including the denial of justice standard, the international minimum standard of treatment or the FET standard.[70] The respect of

---

[66] OECD Guidelines, above n. 29, Chapter II, Para 5, and more generally the discussion in Section 14.1.2. above.

[67] *LG&E* v. *Argentina*, above n. 58, para. 130. In *Glamis* v. *United States*, above n. 15, para. 767.

[68] *Duke* v. *Ecuador*, above n. 52, para. 340.

[69] *MTD Equity Sdn Bhd and MTD Chile SA* v. *Republic of Chile*, ICSID Case No. ARB/01/7, Award (25 May 2004), paras. 242–3.

[70] See, e.g., Kläger, *'Fair and Equitable Treatment' in International Investment Law*, above n. 1, pp. 213–27 (discussing due process claims brought under the FET standard).

due process is also required by international human rights law, either explicitly (e.g., Article 6 of the ECHR or Articles 13 and 14(1) of the ICCPR) or implicitly (e.g., Article 8 of the ECHR[71]). More recently, the scope of protection of due process considerations has been extended to include some environmental components, most notably a certain level of transparency, participation and access to justice in connection with environmental matters.[72]

In the context of investment transactions, due process considerations may come into play in different ways. As noted by the tribunal in *Azinian* v. *Mexico*:

A denial of justice could be pleaded if the relevant courts refuse to entertain a suit, if they subject it to undue delay, or if they administer justice in a seriously inadequate way ... a fourth type of denial of justice ... [is] the clear and malicious misapplication of the law.[73]

As suggested by this quote, the focus is on cases where an investor is deprived of due process by the host State in respect of: (i) access to justice; (ii) procedural fairness; and (iii) denial of justice (procedural or substantive).[74] The most common hypothesis is the alleged mistreatment of the investor by administrative authorities in the process of issuing or renewing a permit.[75] Frequent points of contention in this regard include the lack of transparency, arbitrariness, inadequate participation and/or excessive delays. Another factual hypothesis concerns the impact on investors of proceedings brought before domestic courts for environmental damage. Most environmental litigation takes place at the domestic level. In some cases, this includes highly politicised mass claims with strong social dimensions as well as potentially significant

---

[71] *Tătar* v. *Romania*, Application No. 67021/01, ECtHR, Judgment, 27 January 2009 (Final 06/07/09), para. 69 (interpreting Article 8 of the ECHR in the light of the Convention on Access to Information, Public Participation in Decision-making and Access to Justice in Environmental Matters, 25 June 1998, 2161 UNTS 447 ('Aarhus Convention')).

[72] See Rio Declaration on Environment and Development, 13 June 1992, UN Doc. A/CONF.151/26 ('Rio Declaration'), Principle 10; Aarhus Convention, Articles 4–5 (access to environmental information), Articles 6–8 (participation) and Article 9 (access to justice).

[73] *Robert Azinian, Kenneth Davitian, and Ellen Baca* v. *United Mexican States*, ICSID Case No. ARB (AF)/97/02, Award (1 November 1999) ('*Azinian* v. *Mexico*'), paras. 102–3.

[74] R. Dolzer and C. Schreuer, *Principles of International Investment Law* (Oxford University Press, 2008), pp. 162ff.

[75] See, e.g., *Metalclad* v. *Mexico*, above n. 47; *Tecmed* v. *Mexico*, above n. 49; *Glamis* v. *United States*, above n. 15; *Chemtura Corporation (formerly Crompton Corporation)* v. *Government of Canada*, UNCITRAL, Award (2 August 2010)('*Chemtura* v. *Canada*').

consequences for foreign investors. The proper operation of domestic courts is therefore very important. In at least two cases,[76] investors have referred to deficiencies in domestic court proceedings relating to environmental liability as a basis for an investment claim.

Aside from the protection of investors, due process considerations are also important in connection with the social and environmental impact of investment transactions on local stakeholders.[77] Participation and consultation requirements are indeed receiving increasing acceptance in both international and domestic law. Such requirements may potentially collide with the standards of treatment protecting the activities of foreign investors. This third hypothesis has been discussed, as relevant, in Chapters 7 to 10.

In the following paragraphs, I analyse the first (Section 14.2.2) and second (Section 14.2.3) hypotheses identified above in the light of the relevant case law.

14.2.2   Procedural fairness under FET clauses

Claims for breach of due process are not infrequent in investment disputes. From an environmental perspective, the often heavy requirements that must be met for the issuance of environmental permits, including the conduct of an environmental impact assessment, consultation requirements and ongoing monitoring, leave significant room for administrative frictions and delays.

In addition, a challenge to the procedure is possible even when the ultimate objective of the measure is entirely justifiable. For example, in *Chemtura* v. *Canada*, the investor challenged the conduct of a special review of lindane leading to the suspension of the investor's authorisation to produce and commercialise certain pesticides, but the investor's position on the harmful character of lindane remained vague and called for the tribunal to review the process.[78]

Yet, 'pure' breaches of process are difficult to establish. A review of the case-law suggests that three considerations are particularly important in

---

[76] *Chevron Corporation and Texaco Petroleum Corporation* v. *Republic of Ecuador* PCA case No. 2009–23 (UNCITRAL), Notice of Arbitration (23 September 2009)('*Chevron* v. *Ecuador* – NoA'); *The Renco Group* v. *Republic of Peru*, US–Peru Trade Promotion Agreement, Claimant's Notice of Intent to Commence Arbitration (29 December 2010)('*Renco* v. *Peru* – NoI').

[77] F. Francioni, 'Access to Justice, Denial of Justice, and International Investment Law', in P.-M. Dupuy, F. Francioni and E.-U. Petersmann (eds.), *Human Rights in International Investment Law and Arbitration* (Oxford University Press, 2009), pp. 63, at 73ff.

[78] *Chemtura* v. *Canada*, above n. 75, para. 126.

assessing a claim for lack of procedural fairness: (i) a comparison of the administrative process challenged to one identified as 'normal' or 'regular' (Section 14.2.2.1); (ii) the mandate and scope of discretion of the administrative authority involved (Section 14.2.2.2); and (iii) the conduct of the investor (Section 14.2.2.3).

14.2.2.1   'Regular' and 'irregular' administrative conduct

The starting point of any claim for lack of procedural fairness is a factual demonstration that the relevant authorities behaved in a way that cannot be tolerated from a State organ or agency. However, as with claims for discriminatory treatment, in order to prove irregular behaviour, it is necessary to identify a comparator and to determine the level of irregularity necessary for a breach.

Regarding the first question, the comparator is seldom rendered explicit in the case-law. Instead, tribunals tend to assume an abstract comparator, a sort of 'normal' or 'diligent' administrator[79] or, alternatively, an 'accepted administrative practice' that would provide the benchmark to assess the conduct challenged.[80] In *Chemtura* v. *Canada*, the investor claimed that the Canadian environmental agency had unfairly delayed the registration of a substitute to the pesticides formerly produced by the investor. To prove its contention, it referred to the timing required for the approval of a product of one of its competitors as well as to the 'standard timeline' of the agency.[81] The tribunal rejected the claim noting, *inter alia*, that 'the operation of complex administrations is not always optimal in practice and that the mere existence of delays is not sufficient for a breach of the minimum standard of treatment'.[82] More specifically, the tribunal noted that the registration procedure before the Canadian regulatory agency took approximately the same time as the registration of the investor's product in the United States, using the US regulatory agency as a suitable comparator.[83]

---

[79] In *Tecmed* v. *Mexico*, above n. 49, para. 166, the tribunal took the perspective of a 'reasonable and unbiased observer'. Similarly, in *Waste Management Inc.* v. *United Mexican States*, ICSID Case No. ARB(AF)/00/3, Award (30 April 2004) ('*Waste Management* v. *Mexico*'), para. 93, the tribunal took the perspective of 'every reasonable and impartial man'.

[80] See, e.g., *Alex Genin, Eastern Credit Ltd Inc. and AS Baltoil* v. *Estonia*, ICSID Case No. ARB/99/2, Award (25 June 2001) ('*Genin* v. *Estonia*'), para 364 (referring to 'generally accepted banking and regulatory practice'); *Waste Management* v. *Mexico*, above n. 79, para. 93 (referring to 'international standards'); *Glamis* v. *United States*, above n. 15, para. 774 (referring to 'average time').

[81] *Chemtura* v. *Canada*, above n. 75, para. 195.   [82] *Ibid.*, para. 215.

[83] *Ibid.*, para. 220.

The second question concerns the level of irregularity. The case-law suggests that the standard for administrative due process is different from the one of judicial due process. As noted by the tribunal in *Thunderbird* v. *Mexico*: 'proceedings should be tested against the standards of due process and procedural fairness applicable to administrative officials. The administrative due process requirement is lower than that of a judicial process'.[84] Lower here means that administrative procedure admits some deviations from due process that would not be admitted in a judicial context. The extent to which procedural irregularities are admitted remains, however, to be determined. In *Glamis* v. *United States*, the tribunal referred to the exacting standards of the classic *Neer* case, stating that:

[t]he fundamentals of the *Neer* standard thus still apply today: to violate the customary international law minimum standard of treatment codified in Article 1105 of the NAFTA, an act must be sufficiently egregious and shocking – a gross denial of justice, manifest arbitrariness, blatant unfairness, a complete lack of due process, evident discrimination, or a manifest lack of reasons – so as to fall below accepted international standards and constitute a breach of Article 1105(1).[85]

By contrast, the tribunal in *Chemtura* v. *Canada* observed, also in connection with Article 1105 of the NAFTA, that it is not necessary 'that a violation ... be outrageous in order to breach such standard [international minimum standard of treatment]'.[86] Within the space left by these two views, tribunals have identified at least four specific types of conduct that may amount to a breach of procedural fairness. The first is discriminatory treatment and has been discussed at length in Chapter 13. The other three are: (i) the disregard for the right to be heard or to present its views at a stage of the procedure when it is useful to do so; (ii) the lack of sufficient reasons; and (iii) excessive delays.

With respect to the disregard for the right to be heard, an apposite example is provided by *Metalclad* v. *Mexico*. In this case, the tribunal noted that the construction permit at stake had been 'denied at a meeting of the Municipal Town Council of which Metalclad received no notice, to which it received no invitation, and at which it was given no opportunity to appear'.[87] Similarly, the tribunal in *Tecmed* v. *Mexico* considered that

---

[84] *International Thunderbird Gaming Corporation* v. *United Mexican States*, NAFTA (UNCITRAL), Award (26 January 2006) ('*Thunderbird* v. *Mexico*'), para. 198.
[85] *Glamis* v. *United States*, above n. 15, para. 616.
[86] *Chemtura* v. *Canada*, above n. 75, para. 215.
[87] *Metalclad* v. *Mexico*, above n. 47, para. 91.

the investor had not been granted an adequate opportunity to express its position with regard to certain infringements of the domestic regulations raised by the Mexican authorities and, more importantly, that the investor had not been made aware of the potential consequences of such infringements for the non-renewal of its operating permit.[88] One question that arises in this regard is whether such a material procedural flaw may be cured by subsequent action. The tribunal in *Glamis* v. *United States* considered that a procedural error can indeed be corrected thereby excluding a characterisation of 'a complete lack of due process'.[89] Another difficult question is whether such right of participation must be granted in all administrative procedures or only in some of them. The tribunal in *Bayindir* v. *Pakistan* retained this latter solution considering that certain internal procedures (*in casu* the internal decision-making procedure regarding the management of a contract for the construction of a motorway) are not governed by the due process requirement to provide contractors participatory rights other than in the limits of contractual specifications.[90] Interestingly, investors could potentially derive some additional participatory rights from environmental instruments, such as Articles 6 to 8 of the Aarhus Convention.[91]

Concerning the lack of sufficient reasons, it is an argument frequently advanced in investment disputes. The argument was admitted in two early cases applying a broad conception of the FET standard, namely *Metalclad* v. *Mexico*[92] and *Tecmed* v. *Mexico*.[93] It was rejected in *Glamis* v. *United States*[94] and *Chemtura* v. *Canada*.[95] From an environmental perspective, the difficulties entailed by the assessment of a claim for lack of sufficient reasons are further amplified by the limits of tribunals regarding a review of the scientific basis of regulatory action. This issue has been discussed in Chapter 5 in connection with evidentiary matters and is also analysed in Chapter 15 in the context of the margin of appreciation doctrine.

---

[88] *Tecmed* v. *Mexico*, above n. 49, paras. 161–2. See, also, *Rumeli Telekom AS and Telsim Mobil Telekomunikasyon Hizmetleri AS* v. *Kazakhstan*, ICSID Case No. ARB/05/16, Award (29 July 2008)('*Rumeli* v. *Kazakhstan*'), para. 617. This decision withstood an application for annulment. See *Rumeli* v. *Kazakhstan*, Decision of the Ad Hoc Committee (25 March 2010).

[89] *Glamis* v. *United States*, above n. 15, para. 771.

[90] *Bayindir* v. *Pakistan*, above n. 53, paras. 343–8.

[91] Aarhus Convention, above n. 71.   [92] *Metalclad* v. *Mexico*, above n. 47, paras. 92–3.

[93] *Tecmed* v. *Mexico*, above n. 49, paras. 162–4. See, also, *Rumeli* v. *Kazakhstan*, above n. 88, para. 617 (referring to 'a three and a half pages decision, summarily reasoned . . . [concluding] that the Contract was lawfully terminated and that there were no grounds for its restoration').

[94] *Glamis* v. *United States*, above n. 15, para. 764.

[95] *Chemtura* v. *Canada*, above n. 75, paras. 153–4.

Regarding delays, the mere existence of them is not, as such, a sufficient ground for a breach of the FET standard. As mentioned above, the tribunal in *Chemtura* v. *Canada* expressly noted that 'the operation of complex administrations is not always optimal in practice and that the mere existence of delays is not sufficient for a breach of the minimum standard of treatment'.[96] An additional element seems therefore required for a delay to become a breach. In *Tecmed* v. *Mexico*, such additional element was the disingenuous behaviour underlying the delays.[97] Another element that could potentially play a role is the economic impact of the irregularity. The tribunal in *Chemtura* v. *Canada* looked at this element and concluded that the low economic impact of the delay suggested that the irregularity did not amount to a breach of the NAFTA.[98] On the other hand, there are certain elements that may justify procedural delays, including the action of the investor, the complexity of the issue, the number of stakeholders or even the litigation risk faced by the State.[99]

14.2.2.2   Mandate and discretionary powers

Mandate and discretionary powers were two key considerations in *Genin* v. *Estonia*. In this case, the regulatory authorities had briskly revoked the operating licence of the investor's bank because the latter had failed to comply with certain information requests. *In casu*, the tribunal considered that, despite the differences between Estonian banking laws and international practice, the banking regulator had acted within its mandate and discretion and, as a result, there was no breach of international law.[100]

Although the preceding case does not concern environmental measures, it nevertheless sheds light on questions relevant to environment-related cases. Conduct exceeding an agency's mandate, either explicitly or implicitly, has been seen as an important indication of procedural unfairness. For example, in *Tecmed* v. *Mexico*, the tribunal noted that, in refusing the renewal of the investor's operating permit, the Mexican regulatory agency had taken into account political reasons instead of 'the protection of public health and the environment ... where INE's preventive function should be focused'.[101]

---

[96] *Ibid.*, para. 215. See, also, *Glamis* v. *United States*, above n. 15, para. 774.
[97] *Tecmed* v. *Mexico*, above n. 49, para. 161.
[98] *Chemtura* v. *Canada*, above n. 75, para. 223.
[99] *Glamis* v. *United States*, above n. 15, para. 774.
[100] See *Genin* v. *Estonia*, above n. 80, paras. 355 and 363–5.
[101] *Tecmed* v. *Mexico*, above n. 49, para. 164.

Conversely, when action is taken in accordance with an agency's mandate, this is seen as an indication of consistency with regulatory fairness. Thus, in *Chemtura* v. *Canada*, the tribunal looked at the mandate and discretionary powers of the Canadian environmental agency in assessing the launching of a special review of lindane and the subsequent deregistration of the investor's pesticides. Mandate and discretion played a significant role in connection with the margin of appreciation and police powers doctrines.[102] These two doctrines are analysed in Chapter 15.

14.2.2.3   The conduct of the investor

Another important element in assessing the merits of a claim for breach of procedural fairness is the conduct of the investor. Like claims for frustration of legitimate expectations, claims for breach of due process are sensitive to the investor's due diligence.

In *Genin* v. *Estonia*, the tribunal acknowledged that the authorities had disregarded the investor's right to be heard;[103] yet, it rejected the claim for breach of the applicable treaty because the revocation of the banking licence had been consistent with the mandate of the authority and, more significantly for present purposes, because it seemed justified in light of the conduct of the investor. The tribunal noted, indeed, that:

> the decision taken by the Bank of Estonia must be considered in its proper context – a context comprised of serious and entirely reasonable misgivings regarding EIB's management, its operations, its investments and, ultimately, its soundness as a financial institution.[104]

Another example is provided by *Chemtura* v. *Canada*. The investor claimed that the Canadian environmental agency had failed to clarify the importance of certain aspects of the review of lindane (occupational risks), thus depriving the investor of the possibility to express its views on this question. The tribunal rejected this argument on the grounds that, as a sophisticated registrant, the investor should have known the importance of occupational risk,[105] and that, in all events, the investor had been made aware of this issue.[106]

---

[102] *Chemtura* v. *Canada*, above n. 75, paras. 138 and 266. See, also, *Glamis* v. *United States*, above n. 15, para. 763 (noting that a legal opinion issued by a federal authority was 'arguably within the scope of Solicitor Leshy's [the authority's] powers and foreseeable actions').

[103] *Genin* v. *Estonia*, above n. 80, para. 358.   [104] *Ibid.*, para. 361.

[105] *Chemtura* v. *Canada*, above n. 75, para. 149.   [106] *Ibid.*, para. 150.

14.2.3   Denial of justice

As noted above, in at least two cases, i.e., *Chevron* v. *Ecuador* and *Renco* v. *Peru*,[107] the initiation of judicial proceedings relating to environmental damage has led to investment disputes. The basic facts underlying these claims are interesting because they suggest that this type of claim could become more frequent in the future.

14.2.3.1   Factual configurations

Typically, one important term of investment contracts is the distribution of the burden of environmental remediation and of environmental liability arising from claims brought by third parties.

Such terms are common when the investment takes the form of an acquisition of a local company with unknown but potentially high environmental liability. This factual configuration was present in *Plama* v. *Bulgaria*,[108] where the tribunal had to assess whether the distribution of environmental liability in the investment contract, particularly after an amendment of the domestic environmental laws, put the burden on the investor or on the host State. It is also present in *Renco* v. *Peru*, where the investor acquired a metallurgical complex under a set of agreements that, according to the investor, allocated the burden of environmental liability arising from claims brought by third parties to the seller as well as to Peru.[109]

When the investment takes the form of a new structure (a joint venture), environmental liability will also need to be distributed among the different participants in the consortium, either at the beginning of the operations or at the end. This factual configuration is present in *Chevron* v. *Ecuador*, where the investor claims that it was released from all environmental liability arising from its participation in a joint venture for the exploration and production of oil in the Amazonian jungle, by virtue of a set of agreements concluded at the end of the operations.[110]

The legal issues raised by these two factual configurations have already been analysed in the Sections relating to stabilising clauses and legitimate expectations. Additional factual elements must be present for such situations to give rise to a claim for denial of justice. Even the additional factual elements advanced by the investor in *Renco* v. *Peru* (i.e., the lawsuits

---

[107] See *Chevron* v. *Ecuador* – NoA, above n. 76, para. 4; *Renco* v. *Peru* – NoI, above n. 76, para. 57 (in this case, the argument that Peruvian courts are biased is not clearly spelled out).
[108] Above n. 31.   [109] *Renco* v. *Peru* – NoI, above n. 76, paras. 2–9.
[110] *Chevron* v. *Ecuador* – NoA, above n. 76, paras. 1–2.

brought against it before US courts and an allegedly bogus claim brought by Peru in the context of bankruptcy proceedings open against the investor) would not be sufficient for a claim of denial of justice to be brought. An additional element – an allegation of improper behaviour by the courts of the host State – would still be needed.

14.2.3.2   Claims for denial of justice

The additional step identified above has been made in *Chevron* v. *Ecuador*, where the investor claims that:

> Ecuador's judicial branch has conducted the . . . [domestic environmental litigation against the investor] in total disregard of Ecuadorian law, international standards of fairness, and Chevron's basic due process and natural justice rights, and in apparent coordination with the executive branch and the . . . plaintiffs.[111]

Irrespective of the merits of this (still pending) claim, the case provides an interesting set of facts to assess the potential legitimacy conflict between the denial of justice standard (as a component of the FET standard) and domestic environmental litigation. The main questions raised by this hypothesis are not related to the merits of the domestic litigation or to the position adopted by the State in such proceedings but only to the conduct of the domestic judiciary. With respect to such conduct, three main issues arise.

First, what is the proper analytical unit for the assessment of judicial impropriety (a specific judge; a given judicial district; the entire judiciary of a country)? The answer to this question is, in principle, that the extent of judicial impropriety must be assessed at the level of the specific proceeding allegedly in breach of international law.[112] The assessment of claims for denial of justice, whether in the context of environmental litigation or of other proceedings, is necessarily fact-specific and cannot be based on broad extrapolations from media reports or general political conditions, although these latter may have some evidentiary impact.[113]

---

[111] *Ibid.*, para. 4.

[112] *Loewen Group, Inc. and Raymond L. Loewen* v. *United States of America*, ICSID Case No. ARB (AF)/98/3, Award on Merits (26 June 2003)('*Loewen* v. *United States*'), para. 45; *Petrobart Ltd* v. *Kyrgyzstan*, SCC Case No. 126/2003, Award (29 March 2005) ('*Petrobart* v. *Kyrgyzstan*'), para. 131 (analysing collusion between the executive and judicial branches at the level of the specific order issued by the Bishkek court).

[113] *Solomon Case (United States* v. *Panama)*, (1955) 6 RIAA 370, at 373 (referring to the influence of 'strong popular feeling' on the domestic courts, but grounding the decision on specific examples of judicial impropriety during the proceedings).

Second, to what extent is the claim subject to the traditional require-ment to exhaust local remedies?[114] As noted by one commentator '[d]enial of justice requires, as a rule, the exhaustion of local remedies, given that when local remedies are still effectively available the judicial ill-treatment may still be corrected by higher courts'.[115] However, this customary rule operates differently in different areas of international law. Whereas human rights treaties normally require the exhaustion of local remedies as a condition for the admissibility of a claim, this requirement is sometimes waived in investment treaties.[116] Yet, even when there is a waiver, the exhaustion of local remedies remains a substantive requirement for a claim of denial of justice to be estab-lished.[117] The tribunal in *Loewen* v. *United States* made this distinction when it stated that 'it would be very strange if a State were to be confronted with liability for a breach of international law committed by its magistrate or low-ranking judicial officer when domestic avenues of appeal are not pursued, let alone exhausted'.[118]

Third, and related, if the claimant seeks to set aside this substantive requirement by arguing that the judicial remedies in a country are not reasonably available or are ineffective, it is again necessary to identify the proper unit of analysis (a specific judge; a given judicial district; the entire judiciary of a country). An investor may seek to do so for a variety of reasons, including, as in *Chevron* v. *Ecuador*, to pre-empt the outcome of domestic proceedings. At this third level, it seems uncontroversial that the unit of analysis must be the judicial system as a whole since, as noted by two commentators, 'what fails here is the *system* of justice and not the individual judge'.[119]

---

[114] See, generally, J. Crawford and T. Grant, 'Exhaustion of Local Remedies', *Max Planck Encyclopaedia of Public International Law*, available at: www.mpepil.com (accessed on 4 January 2012).

[115] Focarelli, 'Denial of Justice', above n. 1, para. 29.

[116] *Ibid.*, para. 30.

[117] *Ibid.*, para. 30; Crawford and Grant, 'Exhaustion of Local Remedies', above n. 114, para. 41.

[118] *Loewen* v. *United States*, above n. 112, para. 162.

[119] Crawford and Grant, 'Exhaustion of Local Remedies', above n. 114, para. 41.

15 Defence arguments based on environmental considerations

This final chapter analyses the operation of certain 'defence arguments' that have often been used in international litigation to justify the adoption of environmental measures. The terminology used to refer to each one of them varies somewhat. Whereas the term 'doctrine' is often used in connection with the exercise of police powers or discretion by a State, necessity and emergency clauses are most often characterised as exceptions, defences, circumstances precluding wrongfulness or, still, excuses. The choice of a term to describe the legal nature of these defence arguments has some practical relevance, particularly with respect to the allocation of the burden of proof among the parties as well as to the effects to be derived from their successful invocation.[1] To avoid taking an implicit stance on such terminological debates, I will refer to them as 'defence arguments'.

The most important defence arguments that can be mobilised on the basis of environmental considerations are the police powers doctrine (Section 15.1), the margin of appreciation doctrine (Section 15.2) and emergency and necessity clauses (Section 15.3). The following discussion focuses on how each of these three defence arguments has, in practice, been applied in connection with environmental issues.

---

[1] V. Lowe, 'Precluding Wrongfulness or Responsibility: A Plea for Excuses' (1999) 10 *European Journal of International Law* 405; A. Newcombe, 'General Exceptions in International Investment Agreements', in M.-C. Cordonnier Segger, M. W. Gehring and A. Newcombe (eds.), *Sustainable Development in World Investment Law* (Alphen aan den Rijn: Wolters Kluwer, 2011), pp. 355, at 362–3.

15.1 The police powers doctrine

15.1.1 Sources

The police powers doctrine as it is applied in international investment law seems to have developed from two main sources: one rooted in North American scholarship and practice and the other in general international law.

Regarding the first source, as noted by one commentator writing in 1953, the police powers doctrine was seen as a necessary implication of the State's duty to maintain public order:

> In the United States, lotteries, the manufacture of oleo-margarine and 'pool halls' were abolished without compensation, and in the latter case the taking of property in anticipation of an 'evil' was spoken of. The best known example is, however, the prohibition of the manufacture and sale of alcoholic liquor, introduced in 1926, which resulted in considerable injury to private property rights. When Mexico protested against this measure, the United States Secretary of State, Kellogg, replied that it was an exercise of the 'police powers' of the State and could not, therefore, be the subject of a diplomatic protest.[2]

The doctrine also appears in the codification efforts undertaken by the American Law Institute ('ALI'). Section 197(1)(a) of the Restatement (Second) of the Law of Foreign Relations of the United States provides indeed that '[c]onduct attributable to a state and causing damage to an alien does not depart from the international standard of justice indicated in § 165 if it is reasonably necessary for ... the maintenance of public order, safety, or health'.[3] In the same vein, the commentary to Section 712 of the third Restatement notes that:

> [a] state is not responsible for loss of property or for other economic disadvantage resulting from bona fide general taxation, regulation, forfeiture for crime, or other action of the kind that is commonly accepted as within the police power of states, if it is not discriminatory ... and is not designed to cause the alien to abandon the property to the state or sell it at a distress price. As under United States constitutional law, the line between 'taking' and 'regulation' is sometimes uncertain.[4]

---

[2] S. Friedman, *Expropriation in International Law* (London: Stevens & Sons, 1953), p. 51.

[3] ALI, Restatement (Second) of the Law of Foreign Relations of the United States, 1965, Section 197(1)(a).

[4] ALI, Restatement (Third) of the Law of Foreign Relations of the United States, 1986, Section 712, commentary, letter (g).

The specific requirements for the application of the police powers doctrine have been spelled out in other codification efforts. Article 10(5) of the so-called 'Harvard Draft' provides that:

[a]n uncompensated taking of property of an alien or a deprivation of the use or enjoyment of property of an alien which results from the execution of the tax laws; from a general change in the value of currency; from the action of the competent authorities of the State in the maintenance of public order, health, or morality; or from the valid exercise of belligerent rights; or is otherwise incidental to the normal operation of the laws of the State shall not be considered wrongful, provided:

(a) it is not a clear and discriminatory violation of the law of the State concerned;
(b) it is not the result of a violation of any provision of Articles 6 to 8 of this Convention;
(c) it is not an unreasonable departure from the principles of justice recognized by the principal legal systems of the world; and
(d) it is not an abuse of the powers specified in this paragraph for the purpose of depriving an alien of his property.[5]

This North American source has influenced the case-law of the Iran–United States Claims Tribunal and of arbitral tribunals constituted under the NAFTA Chapter Eleven.[6]

With respect to the second source of the doctrine, according to Brownlie, the rule that takings of alien property is lawful upon payment of prompt, adequate and effective compensation is subject to a number of exceptions, including 'a legitimate exercise of police power ... seizure by way of taxation or other fiscal measures; loss caused indirectly by health and planning legislation and concomitant restrictions on the use of property'.[7] Similarly, Christie notes that 'the operation of a State's tax laws, changes in the value of a State's currency, actions in the interest of the public health and morality, will all serve to justify actions which

---

[5] L. B. Sohn and R. R. Baxter, 'Draft Convention on the International Legal Responsibility of States for Injuries to Aliens' (1961) 55 *American Journal of International Law* 545 ('Harvard Draft 1961'), Article 10(5).

[6] G. H. Aldrich, 'What Constitutes a Compensable Taking of Property? The Decisions of the Iran–United States Claims Tribunal' (1994) 88 *American Journal of International Law* 585; M. Kinnear, A. K. Bjorklund and J. F. G. Hannaford, *Investment Disputes under NAFTA. An Annotated Guide to NAFTA Chapter 11* (Alphen aan den Rijn: Kluwer Law International, 2006), commentary ad Article 1110, pp. 49–55. See, also, *Fireman's Fund Insurance Company v. United Mexican States*, ICSID Case No. ARB(AF)/02/1, Award (14 July 2006), para. 176(j).

[7] I. Brownlie, *Principles of Public International Law* (Oxford University Press, 2008), pp. 533–6; A. Newcombe 'The Boundaries of Regulatory Expropriation in International Law' (2005) 20 *ICSID Review – Foreign Investment Law Journal* 1.

because of their severity would not otherwise be justifiable'.[8] Yet, the international recognition of the doctrine of police powers or, in other words, the international source of this doctrine, is a result of a generalisation of municipal practice.

As is apparent from the above references, the police powers doctrine has mostly been discussed and applied in connection with non-compensable expropriations. However, its effect is not to exclude compensation but, more plainly, to exclude a qualification of expropriation. Moreover, this doctrine has increasingly permeated the drafting of model investment treaties in the last few years[9] and, as seen next, it has also been discussed and applied in the specific context of environmental regulations adverse to the interests of foreign investors.

15.1.2   The use of the police powers doctrine to justify environmental measures

The police powers doctrine has been invoked in a number of investment disputes to justify the adoption of regulatory and targeted environmental measures.[10] The case-law on this issue has evolved over the years.

In *S. D. Myers* v. *Canada*,[11] the tribunal referred to the idea underlying the police powers doctrine in connection with the distinction between expropriation and regulation (in this case, the adoption of administrative orders preventing the export of toxic waste across the border between Canada and the United States):

The general body of precedent does not treat regulatory action as amounting to expropriation. Regulatory conduct by public authorities is unlikely to be the subject of legitimate complaint under Article 1110 [expropriation] of the NAFTA, although the Tribunal does not rule out that possibility ... Expropriations tend to involve the deprivation of ownership rights; regulations a lesser interference. The distinction between expropriation and regulation screens out most potential cases of complaints concerning economic intervention by a state and reduces the risk that governments will be subject to claims as they go about their business of managing public affairs.[12]

---

[8] G. C. Christie, 'What Constitutes a Taking of Property under International Law' (1962) 38 *British Yearbook of International Law* 307, at 331.

[9] See, e.g., Canada Model BIT 2004, Annex B 13(1); US Model BIT 2004, Annex B. Both reproduced in OECD, *International Investment Law: Understanding Concepts and Tracking Innovation*, 2008 ('*OECD 2008 Study*'), pp. 179 and 184–5.

[10] See Chapter 12.

[11] *S. D. Myers Inc.* v. *Canada*, NAFTA (UNCITRAL), Partial Award (13 November 2000) ('*S. D. Myers* v. *Canada*').

[12] *Ibid.*, paras. 281–2.

A clear statement of the potential operation of the police powers in an environment-related dispute was made by the tribunal in *Tecmed v. Mexico*.[13] Analysing whether the measure challenged by the claimant (a refusal to renew the claimant's operational permit) amounted to an expropriation, the tribunal noted that that '[t]he principle that the State's exercise of its sovereign powers within the framework of its police power may cause economic damage to those subject to its powers as administrator without entitling them to any compensation whatsoever is undisputable'.[14] Although this statement was proffered only as an *obiter dictum*, as the tribunal excluded *in casu* the application of the police powers doctrine, it is nevertheless worthy of note because of the confidence shown by the tribunal in the international recognition of this principle.

In a subsequent environment-related case, *Methanex v. United States*,[15] the tribunal offered a more nuanced view. The claimant argued that its rights had been expropriated as a result of a measure adopted by the Californian authorities banning a fuel additive, methyl tertiary-butyl ether (MTBE), which had been found to be a ground-water pollutant. The claimant was not a producer of MTBE but rather of a feedstock, methanol, used in the production of MTBE.[16] The tribunal rejected the claim on the basis that the Californian regulations had been adopted as part of the use of the State's police powers, and made the following statement:

[A]s a matter of general international law, a non-discriminatory regulation for a public purpose, which is enacted in accordance with due process and, which affects, inter alios, a foreign investor or investment is not deemed expropriatory and compensable unless specific commitments had been given by the regulating government to the then putative foreign investor contemplating investment that the government would refrain from such regulation.[17]

This statement has been subsequently confirmed in another investment dispute, albeit not related to environmental regulation, where the tribunal considered, by reference to the *Methanex* award, that 'the principle that a State does not commit an expropriation and is thus not liable to pay compensation to a dispossessed alien investor when it adopts

---

[13] *Técnicas Medioambientales Tecmed SA v. United Mexican States*, ICSID Case No. ARB(AF)/00/2, Award (29 May 2003) ('*Tecmed v. Mexico*').

[14] *Ibid.*, para. 119.

[15] *Methanex Corporation v. United States of America*, NAFTA (UNCITRAL), Award (3 August 2005) ('*Methanex v. United States*').

[16] *Ibid.*, Part IV, Ch. D, para. 1.   [17] *Ibid.*, Part IV, Ch. D, para. 7.

general regulations that are "commonly accepted as within the police powers of States" forms part of customary law today'.[18] In turn, the *Saluka* award was used as authority by the tribunal in *Chemtura* v. *Canada*. Paragraph 266 of this award provides the clearest formulation of the police powers doctrine in the context of environmental regulation so far:

[T]he Tribunal considers in any event that the measures challenged by the Claimant constituted a valid exercise of the Respondent's police powers. As discussed in detail in connection with Article 1105 of NAFTA, the PMRA took measures within its mandate, in a non-discriminatory manner, motivated by the increasing awareness of the dangers presented by lindane for human health and the environment. A measure adopted under such circumstances is a valid exercise of the State's police powers and, as a result, does not constitute an expropriation.[19]

This strong statement leaves no doubt as to the effects of the police powers doctrine. Importantly, the tribunal did not refer to this doctrine in an *obiter dictum*, but it actually applied it to justify a targeted environmental measure. In addition, this paragraph is also an implicit acknowledgement of the formulation of the police powers doctrine contained in the Harvard Draft of 1961, although another contemporary decision has nuanced this conclusion.[20]

Summarising, in principle, where a legitimacy conflict arises between a domestic environmental measure and an investment discipline in a treaty, the former would 'prevail' if it is not *ultra vires*, pursues a public purpose and is not discriminatory, unless the host State has given specific assurances to the investor that such regulation would not be adopted. The latter requirement calls for further comment.

15.1.3   Specific assurances and environmental measures

The question of specific assurances is particularly important for the analysis of potential conflicts between investment disciplines and environmental measures. As a general matter, it must be noted that

---

[18] See *Saluka Investments BV* v. *The Czech Republic*, UNCITRAL, Partial Award (17 March 2006) ('*Saluka* v. *Czech Republic*'), para. 262.

[19] *Chemtura Corporation (formerly Crompton Corporation)* v. *Government of Canada*, UNCITRAL, Award (2 August 2010) ('*Chemtura* v. *Canada*'), para. 266, referring to para. 262 of *Saluka* v. *Czech Republic*, above n. 18.

[20] See *Suez, Sociedad General de Aguas de Barcelona SA and InterAguas Servicios Integrales del Agua SA* v. *The Argentine Republic*, ICSID Case No. ARB/03/17, Decision on Liability (31 August 2010)('*Suez* v. *Argentina* – 03/17 – Liability'), para. 147.

the exercise of the State's regulatory powers (and more specifically the application of the police powers doctrine) is not subordinated, in customary international law, to the absence of specific assurances. This is evidenced among others by the sources referred to in Section 15.1.1, which make no reference to specific assurances. The legal grounding of this requirement is given by considerations of good faith.[21]

In the investment case-law, the absence of specific assurances was initially formulated as a requirement for the operation of the police powers in *Methanex* v. *United States*. In this case, the tribunal referred, *inter alia*, to another environment-related dispute, *Waste Management* v. *Mexico*,[22] where the tribunal had considered that in assessing a potential breach of Article 1105 of the NAFTA 'it is relevant that the treatment is in breach of representations made by the host State which were reasonably relied on by the claimant'.[23] Similar reasoning can be found in a previous case, *Metalclad* v. *Mexico*,[24] in connection with the refusal by the local Mexican authorities to issue a construction permit on environmental grounds. The *Metalclad* tribunal considered that such refusal was *ultra vires* and contrary to the previous assurances received by the investor from the federal Mexican authorities.[25] However, the award was subsequently set aside by a Canadian court on the grounds that the tribunal had improperly introduced an obligation of transparency in Article 1105 of the NAFTA and then decided the dispute on this basis.[26]

Another case addressing the impact of specific assurances is *MTD* v. *Chile*[27] where the tribunal concluded that Chile had breached the fair and equitable treatment standard of the applicable BIT by reason of the incoherent behaviour of its authorities. The Chilean Foreign Investment Commission (FIC) had approved the investment plan of the investor, but the zoning changes required to proceed with the scheme were rejected by the Minister of Urban Development because the project

---

[21] See, e.g., *Revere Copper & Brass Inc.* v. *Overseas Private Investment Corporation ('OPIC')*, Award (24 August 1978), 56 ILR 258.

[22] *Waste Management Inc.* v. *United Mexican States*, ICSID Case No. ARB(AF)/00/3, Award (30 April 2004)('*Waste Management II*').

[23] *Ibid.*, para. 98.

[24] *Metalclad Corporation* v. *United Mexican States*, ICSID Case No. ARB(AF)/97/1, Award (25 August 2000)('*Metalclad* v. *Mexico*').

[25] *Ibid.*, para. 79–101.

[26] *United Mexican States* v. *Metalclad*, 2001 BCSC 664, Supreme Court of British Columbia, Reasons for the Judgment (2 May 2001) ('*United Mexican States* v. *Metalclad*'), paras. 67–77.

[27] *MTD Equity Sdn Bhd and MTD Chile SA* v. *Republic of Chile*, ICSID Case No. ARB/01/7, Award (25 May 2004)('*MTD* v. *Chile* – *Award*').

was inconsistent with the applicable urban development policy. Significantly, the investor had not conducted a due diligence inquiry into the feasibility of its project from the perspective of zoning. In its argumentation, the respondent heavily relied on a meeting where, allegedly, the investor had been made aware of the fact that the project was contrary to planning regulations. The tribunal did not resolve this factual issue. Instead, it focused on the assurances given by the FIC, which it found decisive to allocate regulatory risk between the investor and the host State. It thus concluded that Chile had breached the applicable BIT:

[T]he Tribunal agrees that it is the responsibility of the investor to assure itself that it is properly advised, particularly when investing abroad in an unfamiliar environment. However, in the case before us, Chile is not a passive party and the coherent action of the various officials through which Chile acts is the responsibility of Chile, not of the investor. Whether the Claimants acted responsibly or diligently in reaching a decision to invest in Chile is another question ... Chile claims that it had no obligation to inform the Claimants and that the Claimants should have found out by themselves what the regulations and policies of the country were. The Tribunal agrees with this statement as a matter of principle, but Chile also has an obligation to act coherently and apply its policies consistently, independently of how diligent an investor is. Under international law (the law that this Tribunal has to apply to a dispute under the BIT), the State of Chile needs to be considered by the Tribunal as a unit.[28]

Chile sought annulment of the award arguing, *inter alia*, that the tribunal had confused attribution and breach. The Ad Hoc Committee agreed that 'to mix up attribution and breach would require explanation and would indicate confusion' but concluded that there was no cause for annulment.[29]

These cases stress the importance of specific assurances given to a foreign investor, even when the State authorities act *ultra vires* or when the investor does not exercise due diligence. It is unclear, however, how far such reasoning should go. Specifically, one may ask whether an investor should be allowed to rely on specific assurances when the circumstances of the case suggest that freezing the environmental regulatory framework was not a reasonable expectation. In order to answer this question, it is necessary to circumscribe the scope of the specific assurances exception.

---

[28] *Ibid.*, paras. 164–5.
[29] *MTD Equity Sdn Bhd and MTD Chile SA* v. *Republic of Chile*, ICSID Case No. ARB/01/7, Decision on Annulment (16 February 2007) ('*MTD* v. *Chile* – Annulment'), para. 89.

15.1.4 Circumscribing the scope of specific assurances

As noted in Chapter 12, in practice, specific assurances raise three distinct issues: (i) what type of declaration or commitment qualifies as a specific assurance; (ii) which party has the burden to prove the existence and content of specific assurances; and (iii) whether, when established, such assurances necessarily lead to a finding of breach.

What exactly qualifies as an actionable specific assurance or a specific commitment is still subject to debate. In *Methanex v. United States*,[30] the tribunal identified five conditions: (i) that the assurance is given by the regulating government (i.e., by the environmental regulator and not by another governmental agency); (ii) to the foreign investor itself (i.e., neither to a third party nor, more generally, to any potential investor); (iii) at the time the investor is contemplating making the investment (i.e., the investor must specifically rely on this commitment when deciding to enter the market[31]); (iv) the commitment must be specific (i.e., it is not sufficient to state that the government will refrain from adopting adverse regulations; instead, the assurance must concern a specific regulation); and (v) the assurance must be given in good faith (i.e., an assurance given by a corrupt official may not be reasonably relied upon by the investor).[32] This is the definition that seems to prevail in connection with expropriation claims. In the context of other investment disciplines, tribunals have given broader characterisations of these 'assurances' or 'commitments' or 'expectations'.[33]

---

[30] *Methanex v. United States*, above n. 15, Part IV, Ch. D, para. 7.

[31] *Waste Management II*, above n. 22, para. 98 (referred to by the tribunal in *Methanex v. United States*, above n. 15, Part IV, Ch. D, para. 8, although the paragraph quoted concerns a discussion of the application of the fair and equitable treatment standard).

[32] *OPIC*, above n. 21 (referred to by the tribunal in *Methanex v. United States*, above n. 15, Part IV, Ch. D, para. 8).

[33] See the similarly restrictive conception of such commitments developed by the Ad Hoc Committee in *CMS v. Argentina*, in the context of its discussion of the umbrella clause. *CMS Gas Transmission Company v. Argentine Republic*, ICSID Case No. ARB/01/08, Decision on Annulment (25 September 2007) ('*CMS v. Argentina* – Annulment'), para. 95. See also the broader conception developed by the tribunal in *LG&E v. Argentina* in the context of its discussion of the claim for breach of the fair and equitable treatment standard (admitting that the regulatory framework is, as such, a basis on which the investor can form legitimate expectations). *LG&E v. Argentine Republic*, ICSID Case No. ARB/02/1, Decision on Liability (13 October 2006), para. 133 ('*LG&E* – Liability'). This broader understanding is to some extent controversial. The award in *Metalclad v. Mexico*, which had adopted a broad view of the investor's expectations in connection with the fair and equitable treatment standard (see *Metalclad v. Mexico*, above n. 24, para. 89), was partially annulled by a Canadian court for its excessively broad understanding of this standard (specifically, the existence of an obligation of transparency. See *United Mexican States v. Metalclad*, above n. 26,

Regarding the second issue, it seems clear that, as recognised by the tribunal in *Methanex v. United States*, the burden of proving the existence of such specific commitments lies with the claimant.[34] As to the standard of proof, it will depend on how the investor frames its claim. Investors sometimes advance 'conspiracy theories' in order to be allowed to establish their case on the basis of inferential evidence. These attempts are normally unsuccessful.[35] This position is understandable not only because bad faith should not be easily established, but also because, as discussed in Chapter 12, showing that the measure challenged is in glaring contradiction with prior specific assurances may lead to a finding of expropriation even when such measure is part of the investor's normal commercial risk.

This takes me to the third issue, namely the effects of establishing the existence of prior specific commitments. If the foundations of such an additional requirement lie in considerations of good faith, one must take into account that there is some regulatory space between the two extremes represented by, on one side of the spectrum, a bad faith measure and, on the other side, measures adopted in the absence of specific commitments. A State may indeed be led, even after giving specific assurances to a foreign investor, to change its regulations for important environmental or health reasons. Would such measure amount to a regulatory expropriation? The answer to this question must be based on an assessment of (i) the diligence and reasonableness of the investor, (ii) the nature of the market and (iii) the importance of the goal pursued by the adverse measure. Regarding the first item, it seems clear that an investor that has lacked diligence and/or reasonableness in doing its investment (e.g., because it relied on an unsupported statement of an official, or because it did not perceive the entire regulatory framework applicable to its investment, or, still, because it should have known that the regulatory framework would normally change[36]) should not be allowed to recover (at least not in full[37]) for what

---

paras. 67–77). Similarly, the tribunal in *Continental Casualty* v. *Argentina* took a restrictive view of the concept of specific commitments in the context of the fair and equitable treatment standard. See *Continental Casualty* v. *Argentine Republic*, ICSID Case No. ARB/03/9, Award (5 September 2008) ('*Continental Casualty* v. *Argentina*'), para. 261.

[34] *Methanex* v. *United States*, above n. 15, Part IV, Ch. D, paras. 13–14.

[35] *Ibid.*, Part IV, Ch. D, paras. 13–14; *Bayindir Insaat Turizm Ticaret ve Sanayi A Ş* v. *Pakistan*, ICSID Case No ARB/03/29, Award (27 August 2009)('*Bayindir* v. *Pakistan*'), paras. 223–58 (particularly 239); *Chemtura* v. *Canada*, above n. 19, para. 137.

[36] *Bayindir* v. *Pakistan*, above n. 35, paras. 193–4; *Methanex* v. *United States*, above n. 15, Part IV, Ch. D, para. 9; *Chemtura* v. *Canada*, above n. 19, para. 149.

[37] *MTD* v. *Chile* – Award, above n. 27, paras. 242–3.

is little more than an unsuccessful business venture. With respect to the nature of the market, even when the investor has been diligent and reasonable, some markets are, by their very nature, subject to frequent and even radical changes.[38] Investors operating in such markets cannot expect that, if the harmful character of a substance they produce is unveiled, the State will not take action. This should apply even in the event that specific assurances have been given to the investor because such assurances are not to be construed as an insurance against obsolete lines of business. Host States would, of course, remain subject to a requirement to honour their prior commitments within the limits of proportionality, for instance, by offering phase out periods or other processes. Third, depending on the regulatory interests at stake, States may also need to compensate the investor. For instance, if a State gives specific assurances to an investor that it will maintain a certain purchase price of the electricity provided by the investor from renewable sources, the State could not disregard this commitment simply because a better and cheaper way to produce low-emissions electricity has been found. The State may, of course, decide to stop purchasing electricity from the initial investor, but it will have to pay compensation. Variations in the amount of compensation may then be introduced to take into account the investor's commercial risk (i.e., the availability of better sources of clean electricity sooner rather than later).

15.2   The margin of appreciation doctrine

15.2.1   Sources

Another expression of the State's regulatory powers is the so-called 'margin of appreciation doctrine' developed by the ECtHR[39] on the basis of the practice of several European civil law jurisdictions[40] and subsequently adopted by other international bodies.[41] This doctrine was initially formulated in the context of derogations from human rights standards in accordance with Article 15 of the ECHR,[42] and it was later

---

[38] *Methanex v. United States*, above n. 15, Part IV, Ch. D, para. 9; *Chemtura v. Canada*, above n. 19, para. 149.

[39] Y. Arai-Takahashi, *The Margin of Appreciation Doctrine and the Principle of Proportionality in the Jurisprudence of the ECHR* (Antwerp: Intersentia, 2002).

[40] *Ibid.*, pp. 2–3.

[41] In particular, the Inter-American Court of Human Rights and the United Nations Human Rights Committee, see *ibid.*, p. 4.

[42] *Ireland v. United Kingdom*, ECtHR Application No. 5310/71, Judgment (18 January 1978), A 25, para. 207, quoted in Arai-Takahashi, *The Margin of Appreciation Doctrine and the Principle of Proportionality in the Jurisprudence of the ECHR*, above n. 39, p. 5.

used in the assessment of the scope of the individual rights granted under Articles 6 (due process) and 8 (right to private and family life, extended to cover environmental aspects) of the Convention, and Article 1 (right to private property) of the First Protocol.

The underlying rationale of this doctrine was formulated in the *Handy-side* case as follows:

[I]t is not possible to find in the domestic law of the various Contracting States a uniform European conception of morals. The view taken by their respective laws of the requirements of morals varies from time to time and from place to place, especially in our era which is characterised by a rapid and far-reaching evolution of opinions on the subject. By reason of their direct and continuous contact with the vital forces of their countries, State authorities are in principle in a better position than the international judge to give an opinion on the exact content of these requirements as well as on the 'necessity' of a 'restriction' or 'penalty' intended to meet them ... This margin is given both to the domestic legislator ('prescribed by law') and to the bodies, judicial amongst others, that are called upon to interpret and apply the laws in force.[43]

Thus, the margin of appreciation is, in essence, a standard of deference given to the national authorities to assess a situation because of their better position to understand it. As discussed next, this rationale is particularly significant for environment-related disputes where a regulatory agency focusing on health or environmental protection takes measures that are subsequently challenged by an investor as being in breach of international investment law.

15.2.2 Applicability in the context of investment disputes

Among the different questions raised by the margin of appreciation doctrine, perhaps the most basic one for the purposes of the present study is whether such doctrine is applicable in the context of investment disputes.

This seems to be the case, if one judges by the reasoning of the tribunals in *Methanex* v. *United States*[44] and *Glamis* v. *United States*.[45] In both cases, the tribunals considered that their role was not to judge the scientific conclusions on which the measures challenged by the

---

[43] *Handyside* v. *United Kingdom*, ECtHR Application No. 5493/72, Judgment (7 December 1976), A 24, para. 48, quoted in Arai-Takahashi, *The Margin of Appreciation Doctrine and the Principle of Proportionality in the Jurisprudence of the ECHR*, above n. 39, pp. 7–8.

[44] *Methanex* v. *United States*, above n. 15, Part III, Ch. A, para. 101.

[45] See *Glamis Gold Ltd* v. *United States of America*, NAFTA (UNCITRAL), Award (16 May 2009) ('*Glamis* v. *United States*'), para. 779.

investors were based, but only the acceptability of the process followed to reach such conclusions. This stance received some support in *Chemtura* v. *Canada*,[46] although, in this case, the tribunal took a more nuanced position on whether its scope of review was limited by a margin of appreciation. The tribunal noted, indeed, that:

In assessing whether the treatment afforded to the Claimant's investment was in accordance with the international minimum standard, the Tribunal must take into account all the circumstances, including the fact that certain agencies manage highly specialized domains involving scientific and public policy determinations. This is not an abstract assessment circumscribed by a legal doctrine about the margin of appreciation of specialized regulatory agencies. It is an assessment that must be conducted *in concreto*.[47]

The language used by the tribunal in *Chemtura* v. *Canada* as to the actual operation of the margin of appreciation doctrine in the investment context raises an additional question, namely that of the tribunal's scope of review regarding the determinations of domestic specialised agencies.

Part of the answer to this second question has already been given in connection with the first question. Tribunals must not focus on the science but on the process. However, questions of science and process are sometimes difficult to disentangle.[48] Moreover, focusing only on process may sometimes lead to unsatisfactory solutions as, under some circumstances, it could be unreasonable to penalise a State that took a decision based on sound science but through a procedurally inefficient process. Assuming the result of the regulatory process to be the same, mere procedural breaches would be relevant only where and to the extent that they have imposed an unnecessarily heavy burden on the investor. In other terms, the articulation between science and process must leave some room to accommodate proportionality considerations. For instance, in *Chemtura* v. *Canada*, the tribunal considered that the delays in the registration process of a lindane-free replacement pesticide submitted by the claimant did not amount to a violation of Article 1105 of the NAFTA.[49]

---

[46] *Chemtura* v. *Canada*, above n. 19, paras. 133–4.

[47] *Ibid.*, para. 123.

[48] In *Methanex* v. *United States*, the tribunal made explicit what it gathered from the discussion of scientific evidence. See *Methanex* v. *United States*, above n. 15, Part III, Ch. A, para. 102.

[49] *Chemtura* v. *Canada*, above n. 19, paras. 217–20.

15.2.3 Margin of appreciation and police powers

An additional question that arises in connection with the margin of appreciation doctrine concerns the differences between this doctrine and the police powers doctrine. Although the concepts underlying these two doctrines overlap to some extent, at least four differences of emphasis can be identified.

The first difference was highlighted by the tribunal in *Suez* v. *Argentina* – 03/17. It noted that the police powers doctrine would be relevant only in connection with expropriation because the same considerations underlying this doctrine are already taken into account in the definition and scope of other investment disciplines, such as the fair and equitable treatment standard. According to the tribunal:

the application of the police powers doctrine as an explicit, affirmative defense to treaty claims *other* than for expropriation is inappropriate, because in judging those claims and applying such principles as full protection and security and fair and equitable treatment, both of which are considered in subsequent sections of this Decision, a tribunal must take account of a State's reasonable right to regulate. Thus, if a tribunal finds that a State has violated treaty standards of fair and equitable treatment and full protection and security, it must of necessity have determined that such State has exceeded its reasonable right to regulate. Consequently, for that same tribunal to make a subsequent inquiry as to whether that same State has exceeded its legitimate police powers would require that tribunal to engage in an inquiry it has already made. In short, a decision on the application of the police powers doctrine in such circumstance would be duplicative and therefore inappropriate.[50]

The second difference rests on the reasons for deferring to State authorities. Whereas the police powers doctrine is based on the inherent duty of States to regulate certain questions, the margin of appreciation doctrine, as applied so far in the investment context,[51] seeks rather to avoid second guessing the scientific or technical assessment conducted by a specialised agency.

The third difference is that the police powers doctrine concerns liability, whereas the margin of appreciation doctrine concerns factual analysis. Indeed, if the police powers doctrine is found to apply, the result is that the measure challenged is not in breach of investment disciplines. By contrast, the deference to the scientific assessment conducted by

---

[50] See *Suez* v. *Argentina* – 03/17 – Liability, above n. 20, para. 148.

[51] In the context of the ECtHR, the doctrine serves much broader purposes, including the adaptation of the European Convention standards to the cultural and political specificities of each State party to the Convention. See above n. 39.

State authorities is only a finding of fact (e.g., that a given substance is harmful) and, as such, it is not necessarily dispositive of the issue of liability.

A fourth difference, that flows from the one just mentioned, concerns the room for proportionality reasoning within the two doctrines, which seems to be larger within the margin of appreciation doctrine. Thus, in a case where a measure has been adopted for environmental reasons, the application of the police powers doctrine would tend to be more favourable to the host State, as it would in principle exempt it from liability. By contrast, the application of the margin of appreciation doctrine may allow a tribunal to defer to the environmental assessment conducted by the State authorities while considering that the measures taken on that basis were not proportional.

The latter difference may be clarified by an example. In *Tecmed* v. *Mexico*,[52] the tribunal analysed the refusal by the local authorities to renew a licence for the operation of a landfill facility in the light of both the police powers and the margin of appreciation doctrines. The tribunal subjected the characterisation of a measure as legitimate under the police powers doctrine to domestic (instead of international) law.[53] This preliminary (and debatable) step allowed the tribunal to make some additional room for assessing the conformity of the measures with the applicable investment treaty, paying less attention to the (social and economic) reasons that led to the adoption of the measure challenged.[54] Thus, it placed itself under the margin of appreciation doctrine. The tribunal noted that even those regulations that have a legitimate public purpose, such as environmental protection, could fall under the expropriation clause of the treaty.[55] It then proceeded to a proportionality analysis, borrowed from the case-law of the ECtHR:

[A]fter establishing that regulatory actions and measures will not be initially excluded from the definition of expropriatory acts, in addition to the negative financial impact of such actions or measures, the Arbitral Tribunal will consider, in order to determine if they are to be characterized as expropriatory, whether such actions or measures are proportional to the public interest presumably protected thereby and to the protection legally granted to investments, taking into account that the significance of such impact has a key role upon deciding the proportionality. *Although the analysis starts at the due deference owing to the State*

---

[52] *Tecmed* v. *Mexico*, above n. 13.   [53] *Ibid.*, para. 119.   [54] *Ibid.*, para. 120.

[55] *Ibid.*, para. 121, referring to a controversial conclusion in *Compañía del Desarrollo de Santa Elena SA* v. *Republic of Costa Rica*, ICSID Case No. ARB/96/1, Award, 17 February 2000 ('*CDSE* v. *Costa Rica*').

when defining the issues that affect its public policy or the interests of society as a whole, as well as the actions that will be implemented to protect such values, such situation does not prevent the Arbitral Tribunal, without thereby questioning such due deference, from examining the actions of the State in light of Article 5(1) of the Agreement to determine whether such measures are reasonable with respect to their goals, the deprivation of economic rights and the legitimate expectations of who suffered such deprivation. There must be a reasonable relationship of proportionality between the charge or weight imposed to the foreign investor and the aim sought to be realized by any expropriatory measure. To value such charge or weight, it is very important to measure the size of the ownership deprivation caused by the actions of the state and whether such deprivation was compensated or not.[56]

This paragraph suggests that, under the margin of appreciation doctrine, the link between deference and exemption of liability is mediated by the concept of proportionality, whereas, under the police powers doctrine, proportionality plays a role only with respect to whether the doctrine is applicable or not. Once applied, the police powers doctrine excludes liability. This difference has also some bearing in connection with issues of compensation, as discussed in Chapter 5.

15.3 Emergency and necessity clauses

15.3.1 Sources

Another expression of the State's regulatory powers is provided by emergency and necessity clauses. Although some of the traditional hypotheses covered by both the police powers and the margin of appreciation doctrines were situations of public emergency, the legal sources and operation of emergency and necessity clauses are clearly distinct.

Despite considerable controversy throughout the rather long period of its codification,[57] the customary basis of the necessity defence, as defined in Article 25 of the ILC Articles on State Responsibility,[58] is nowadays widely acknowledged.[59] According to this provision:

---

[56] *Tecmed* v. *Mexico*, above n. 13, para. 122 (emphasis added), referring to the decision of ECtHR *James and others* v. *United Kingdom*, ECtHR Application No. 8793/79, Judgment (21 February 1986), 63, 24 ('*James* v. *United Kingdom*').

[57] S. Heathcote, 'Circumstances Precluding Wrongfulness in the ILC Artices on State Responsibility: Necessity', in J. Crawford, A. Pellet, S. Olleson and K. Parlett (eds.), *The Law of International Responsibility* (Oxford University Press, 2010) pp. 491, at 492–4.

[58] Responsibility of States for Internationally Wrongful Acts, GA Res. 56/83, UN Doc. A/Res/ 56/83, 12 December 2001 ('ILC Articles').

[59] *Gabčíkovo-Nagymaros Project (Hungary* v. *Slovakia)*, ICJ Rep 1997 ('*Gabčíkovo-Nagymaros*'), paras. 50–2 (referring to Article 33 of the previous draft on State responsibility); *Legal*

1. Necessity may not be invoked by a State as a ground for precluding the wrongfulness of an act not in conformity with an international obligation of that State unless the act:
    (a) is the only way for the State to safeguard an essential interest against a grave and imminent peril; and
    (b) does not seriously impair an essential interest of the State or States towards which the obligation exists, or of the international community as a whole.
2. In any case, necessity may not be invoked by a State as a ground for precluding wrongfulness if:
    (a) the international obligation in question excludes the possibility of invoking necessity; or
    (b) the State has contributed to the situation of necessity.

As it will be discussed in the next Section, this provision has been addressed in a growing number of investment disputes.

Regarding emergency clauses, their source must be found in specific treaty provisions, as there are no customary circumstances precluding wrongfulness beyond those identified in the ILC Articles, nor any customary rules for the suspension or termination of treaties other than those identified in the Vienna Convention on the Law of Treaties.[60] Several examples could be given of such emergency clauses, although it is estimated that only a few BITs (less than thirty BITs out of more than 3,000) contain such clauses.[61] One approach, followed in Canadian treaty practice, is the inclusion of general exception clauses similar to Article XX of the GATT:

1. Subject to the requirement that such measures are not applied in a manner that would constitute arbitrary or unjustifiable discrimination between investments or between investors, or a disguised restriction on international trade or investment, nothing in this Agreement shall be construed to prevent a Party from adopting or enforcing measures necessary:
    (a) to protect human, animal or plant life or health;

Consequences of the Construction of a Wall in the Occupied Palestinian Territory, Advisory Opinion, *ICJ Reports* 2004, 136, at para. 140; *CMS Gas Transmission Company* v. *Argentine Republic*, ICSID Case No. ARB/01/08, Award (12 May 2005)('*CMS* v. *Argentina* – Award'), para. 315. On necessity see S. Heathcote, *State of Necessity and International Law*, unpublished Ph.d. thesis, Graduate Institute of International Studies (IUHEI) Geneva (2005).

[60] ILC Articles, above n. 58, Commentary *ad* Chapter V, para. 9; *Gabčíkovo-Nagymaros*, above n. 59, para. 47.

[61] Newcombe, 'General Exceptions in International Investment Agreements', above n. 1, p. 358.

(b)   to ensure compliance with laws and regulations that are not inconsistent with the provisions of this Agreement; or

(c)   for the conservation of living or non-living exhaustible natural resources.[62]

Another example, of particular relevance for the analysis conducted in this chapter, is Article XI of the Argentina–US BIT.[63] This provision states that the treaty 'shall not preclude the application by either Party of measures necessary for the maintenance of public order, the fulfilment of its obligations with respect to the maintenance or restoration of international peace or security or the protection of its own essential security interests'. Other more specific examples are discussed in Chapters 11 and 13 above.

15.3.2   Asserting the defence

Both emergency and necessity clauses can be treated as 'defences' for the purpose of allocating the burden of proof. This means that the *onus probandi* lies with the party invoking the defence.[64] In this connection, two main difficulties arise.

The first concerns the interpretation of such clauses. Some tribunals have considered that exceptions or defences must be interpreted restrictively,[65] which sets a higher standard of proof for the respondent. There is, however, no basis for such an assertion. The general principle that limitations to the sovereignty of States are to be interpreted restrictively[66] or neutrally (according to the more recent trend concerning arbitration clauses)[67] entails that the scope of protection of investment disciplines may not be inflated through teleological interpretation. In other words,

---

[62] Reproduced in *ibid.*, p. 359.

[63] Treaty between the United States of America and the Argentine Republic concerning the Reciprocal Encouragement and Protection of Investment, 14 November 1991, 31 ILM 124 ('Argentina–US BIT').

[64] See above n. 1 and Chapter 5.

[65] *Canfor Corporation* v. *United States of America* and *Terminal Forest Products Ltd* v. *United States of America*, NAFTA (UNCITRAL), Decision on Preliminary Question (6 June 2006), para. 187; *Enron and Ponderosa Assets* v. *Argentine Republic*, ICSID Case No. ARB/01/3, Award (22 May 2007)('*Enron* v. *Argentina* – Award'), para. 331, referred to in Newcombe, 'General Exceptions in International Investment Agreements', above n. 1, p. 363.

[66] See, e.g., *SS Wimbledon*, PCIJ, Series A, No. 1 (17 August 1923), at 24–5; *SS Lotus*, PCIJ, Series A, No. 10 (7 September 1927), at 18; *Free Zones of Upper Savoy and the District of Gex*, PCIJ, Series A/B, No. 46 (7 June1932), at 167.

[67] *Austrian Airlines* v. *Slovakia*, UNCITRAL, Award (9 October 2009), paras. 119ff. (referring to previous investment cases either supporting a restrictive interpretation of consent – in accordance with the traditional view – or adopting a neutral interpretation approach).

the exceptions that tend to preserve sufficient room for the State to exercise its inherent regulatory powers must not be interpreted restrictively but neutrally, as other provisions of investment treaties. One reason explaining the confusion surrounding this issue is the improper extrapolation of private law reasoning into treaty interpretation. Another reason is that it is often overlooked that the restrictive character of some exceptions lies in the stringent requirements set to their availability and not in the restrictive interpretation of each of those requirements. Still another reason contributing to this confusion is the fact that some defences are formulated negatively (e.g., the customary rule of necessity codified in Article 25 of the ILC Articles[68]). However, many defences and exceptions are formulated in a positive manner (e.g., 'nothing in this treaty shall be construed to prevent a party from adopting or enforcing measures ...'), which further undermines the argument in favour of restrictive interpretation. In addition, as noted by some commentators, in the WTO context, tribunals have increasingly leaned towards a 'softer' interpretation of the 'necessity' requirement included in Article XX of the GATT.[69]

The second (related) difficulty lies in the identification of the requirements for the admission of each of these defences. Unless an emergency clause in a treaty explicitly provides for the same conditions as the customary necessity defence, the requirements for establishing each of these defences are clearly distinct. As discussed next, this question arose in the practice of investment tribunals with important practical consequences.

15.3.3   Environmental justifications between emergency and necessity

The potential application of the necessity defence for the protection of environmental interests was recognised for the first time in the *Gabčíkovo-Nagymaros* case, before the International Court of Justice ('ICJ').[70] In this case, the Court expressly admitted that 'the concerns expressed by

---

[68] See above n. 58.

[69] N. DiMascio and J. Pauwelyn, 'Nondiscrimination in Trade and Investment Treaties: Worlds Apart of Two Sides of the Same Coin?' (2008) 102 *American Journal of Investment Law* 48, at 77; Newcombe, 'General Exceptions in International Investment Agreements', above n. 1, p. 367 (quoting DiMascio and Pauwelyn with approval); W. W. Burke-White and A. von Staden, 'Investment Protection in Extraordinary Times: The Interpretation and Application of Non-Precluded Measures Provisions in Bilateral Investment Treaties' (2008) 48 *Virginia Journal of International Law* 307, at 344.

[70] *Gabčíkovo-Nagymaros*, above n. 59. On the so-called 'ecological necessity' see A. K. Bjorklund, 'The Necessity of Sustainable Development', in Cordonnier Segger, Gehring and Newcombe, *Sustainable Development in World Investment Law*, above n. 1, p. 373.

Hungary for its natural environment in the region affected by the Gabčíkovo-Nagymaros Project related to an "essential interest" of that State, within the meaning given to that expression in Article 33 of the Draft of the International Law Commission'.[71] Hungary had raised concerns relating, *inter alia*, to the potential effects of the construction projects contemplated in a treaty of 1977 on the aquifer providing Budapest with freshwater. While recognising the importance of environmental protection, the ICJ rejected Hungary's argument on the grounds that some of the conditions for the admissibility of the customary necessity defence were not met.

Public emergency clauses and the necessity defence have been invoked together in the context of a series of investment disputes relating to the Argentine crisis of 2001–3.[72] Although most of these cases do not concern environmental issues, they remain relevant to assess the potential operation of emergency and necessity clauses in connection with such issues. The first case in which the tribunal admitted an argument of necessity to justify the breach of an investment treaty is *LG&E* v. *Argentina*.[73] The respondent had argued that the measures challenged by the investor were justified under both the customary rule on necessity and Article XI of the Argentina–US BIT. The tribunal found that the specific circumstances that had prevailed in Argentina from 2001 to 2003 met the requirements for the application of Article XI:

While unemployment, poverty and indigency rates gradually increased from the beginning of 1998, they reached intolerable levels by December 2001. Unemployment reached almost 25%, and almost half of the Argentine population was living below poverty. The entire healthcare system teetered on the brink of collapse. Prices of pharmaceuticals soared as the country plunged deeper into the deflationary period, becoming unavailable for low-income people. Hospitals suffered a severe shortage of basic supplies. Investments in infrastructure and

---

[71] *Gabčíkovo-Nagymaros*, above n. 59, para. 53.

[72] See *Continental Casualty* v. *Argentina*, above n. 33; *Metalpar* v. *Argentine Republic*, ICSID Case No. ARB/03/5, Award (6 June 2008) ('*Metalpar* v. *Argentina*'); *Sempra Energy* v. *Argentine Republic*, ICSID Case No. ARB/02/16, Award (28 September 2007)('*Sempra* v. *Argentina* – Award'), Decision on Annulment (29 June 2010)('*Sempra* v. *Argentina* – Annulment'); *Enron* v. *Argentina* – Award, above n. 65, and Decision on Annulment (30 July 2010) ('*Enron* v. *Argentina* – Annulment'); *LG&E* – Liability, above n. 33, Award (25 July 2007) ('*LG&E* – Award'); *CMS* v. *Argentina* – Award, above n. 59; *CMS* v. *Argentina* – Annulment, above n. 33. For a discussion of some of these awards, see C. Leben, 'L'état de nécessité dans le droit international de l'investissement' (2005) 3 *Les Cahiers de l'arbitrage* 47; J. E. Viñuales, 'State of Necessity and Peremptory Norms in International Investment Law' (2008) 14 *NAFTA: Law and Business Review of the Americas* 79.

[73] *LG&E* – Liability, above n. 33.

equipment for public hospitals declined as never before. These conditions prompted the Government to declare the nationwide health emergency to ensure the population's access to basic health care goods and services. At the time, one quarter of the population could not afford the minimum amount of food required to ensure their subsistence. Given the level of poverty and lack of access to healthcare and proper nutrition, disease followed. Facing increased pressure to provide social services and security to the masses of indigent and poor people, the Government was forced to decrease its per capita spending on social services by 74% ... By December 2001, there was widespread fear among the population that the Government would default on its debt and seize bank deposits to prevent the bankruptcy of the banking system. Faced with a possible run on banks, the Government issued on 1 December 2001 Decree of Necessity and Emergency No. 1570/01. The law triggered widespread social discontent. Widespread violent demonstrations and protests brought the economy to a halt, including effectively shutting down transportation systems. Looting and rioting followed in which tens of people were killed as the conditions in the country approached anarchy. A curfew was imposed to curb lootings ... By 20 December 2001, President De la Rúa resigned. His presidency was followed by a succession of presidents over the next days, until Mr. Eduardo Duhalde took office on 1 January 2002, charged with the mandate to bring the country back to normal conditions ... All of these devastating conditions – economic, political, social – in the aggregate triggered the protections afforded under Article XI of the Treaty to maintain order and control the civil unrest.[74]

It then confirmed its reasoning by reference to the customary rule on necessity, but without technically applying it.[75]

The second case in which a necessity argument was admitted in the context of the Argentine crisis is *Continental Casualty* v. *Argentina*.[76] Although both the customary and the treaty-based defence were invoked by Argentina, the decision of the tribunal admitting the defence was, again, based on Article XI of the Argentina–US BIT only.[77] The tribunal clearly spelled out how the operation of Article XI would simply exclude the existence of a breach instead of excusing an existing breach, as would arguably be the case of the customary necessity defence.[78] More specifically, the tribunal described Article XI as a safeguard in the

---

[74] *Ibid.*, paras. 234–7.

[75] *Ibid.*, para. 245. This *modus operandi* is important because it contrasts with the reasoning of the tribunal in *CMS* v. *Argentina*, which applied both the treaty provision and the customary requirements for the admissibility of necessity together (see *CMS* v. *Argentina* – Award, above n. 59, paras. 357–8). On annulment, the CMS tribunal was severely criticised for having proceeded in this manner. See *CMS* v. *Argentina* – Annulment, above n. 33, paras. 131–2.

[76] *Continental Casualty* v. *Argentina*, above n. 33.

[77] *Ibid.*, para. 162.   [78] *Ibid.*, para. 164.

meaning usually given to this term in the international trade context.[79]
This had the important consequence of making the availability of such
emergency clause less exceptional than the customary necessity defence.
As noted by the tribunal:

> [I]n view of these differences between the situation regulated under Art. 25 ILC
> Articles and that addressed by Art. XI of the BIT, the conditions of application are
> not the same. The strict conditions to which the ILC text subjects the invocation
> of the defence of necessity by a State is explained by the fact that it can be
> invoked in any context against any international obligation. Therefore 'it can
> only be accepted on an exceptional basis.' This is not necessarily the case under
> Art. XI according to its language and purpose under the BIT. This leads the
> Tribunal to the conclusion that invocation of Art. XI under this BIT, as a specific
> provision limiting the general investment protection obligations (of a 'primary'
> nature) bilaterally agreed by the Contracting Parties, is not necessarily subject to
> the same conditions of application as the plea of necessity under general inter-
> national law.[80]

Moreover, in determining the scope of the term 'essential security interests' used in Article XI, the tribunal retained a fairly broad understanding encompassing the protection of the environment.[81] This conclusion
could be relevant for pending or future disputes under the Argentina–
US BIT. The protection of environmental interests would be technically
possible under both the customary necessity defence and at least some
public emergency clauses.

The latter point was later confirmed in two water-related investment
cases involving Argentina.[82] In these two cases, the customary necessity
defence was discussed in connection with the right to water by both the
respondent and the *amici curiae*. The *amicus* brief referred, *inter alia*, to the
observation of the *LG&E* tribunal that 'a state of necessity is identified by
those conditions in which a State is threatened by a serious danger. . . to the
possibility of maintaining its essential services in operation'.[83] However,
whereas the necessity defence was well articulated by the respondent, its
application seems to have been excluded by the *amici curiae*. This point
is noteworthy because it underlines the ambiguities of the distinction

---

[79] *Ibid.*, para. 164.   [80] *Ibid.*, para. 167.   [81] *Ibid.*, para. 175.

[82] *Suez v. Argentina – 03/17 – Liability*, above n. 20; *Suez, Sociedad General de Aguas de Barcelona, SA and Vivendi Universal, SA v. The Argentine Republic*, ICSID Case No. ARB/03/19, Decision on Liability (31 August 2010) ('*Suez v. Argentina – 03/19 – Liability*')

[83] *Suez, Sociedad General de Aguas de Barcelona, SA and Vivendi Universal SA v. Argentine Republic*, ICSID Case No. ARB/03/19, *Amicus Curiae* Submission, 4 April 2007 ('*Suez – Amicus* brief'), available at: www.ciel.org, 27–8 (last accessed on 4 January 2012).

between primary and secondary norms in the law of State responsibility, particularly in the context of circumstances precluding wrongfulness.[84] Indeed, the *amici* emphasised that 'necessity does not apply to human rights treaties that provide guarantees to human rights in times of national emergency'.[85] The purpose of this assertion is not entirely clear. First, the *amicus* brief itself referred to provisions encompassing the right to water in instruments that do not impose such limitations on their relevant primary norms.[86] Second, even in those instruments that do impose limitations on their primary norms, not every primary norm can be limited in a public emergency. For instance, Article 6(1) of the International Covenant on Civil and Political Rights, referred to by the *amici* as encompassing the right to water,[87] is one of the provisions from which it cannot be derogated on grounds of public emergency. Third, irrespective of whether the scope of primary norms is limited or not, these norms may entertain with the necessity defence a more subtle relationship than the one envisaged in the *amicus* brief, for instance, by attaching importance to an interest and thereby facilitating its characterisation as an essential interest. Primary norms have already played such a role in connection with the crystallisation of environmental protection as an essential interest in the meaning of the customary necessity rule.[88] Eventually, the necessity defence was rejected in the two *Suez* v. *Argentina* cases. However, the tribunals acknowledged that '[t]he provision of water and sewage services... certainly was vital to the health and well-being of [the population] and was therefore an essential interest of the Argentine State'.[89]

The rejection of the necessity defence in two other cases[90] has been considered as a ground for annulment by the Ad Hoc Committees

---

[84] E. David, 'Primary and Secondary Rules', in Crawford *et al.*, *The Law of International Responsibility*, above n. 57, pp. 29ff.

[85] *Suez* – *Amicus* brief, above n. 83, 28.

[86] *Ibid.*, 4, referring, *inter alia*, to Articles 11(1) and 12 of the International Covenant on Economic, Social and Cultural Rights, 16 December 1966, 993 UNTS 3 (entered into force on 3 January 1976) ('ICESCR'), which does not impose such limitations.

[87] *Suez* – *Amicus* brief, above n. 83, 7, referring, *inter alia*, to Article 6(1) of the International Covenant on Civil and Political Rights, 16 December 1966, 999 UNTS 171 (entered into force on 23 March 1976) ('ICCPR'). Article 4(2) of the ICCPR expressly prohibits derogations, even in times of public emergencies, from Article 6.

[88] J. E. Viñuales, 'The Contribution of the International Court of Justice to the Development of International Environmental Law: A Contemporary Assessment' (2008) 32 *Fordham International Law Journal* 232, at 248–9.

[89] *Suez* v. *Argentina* – 03/17 – Liability, above n. 20, para. 238; *Suez* v. *Argentina* – 03/19 – Liability, above n. 82, para. 260.

[90] *Sempra* v. *Argentina* – Award, above n. 72, paras. 344–54 and 364–91; *Enron* v. *Argentina* – Award, above n. 65, paras. 303–13 and 331–42.

constituted to review the awards.[91] Although the reasoning of the Committees on this point is debatable, the fact remains that a threat to an environmental interest may potentially trigger the customary necessity defence or a public emergency clause.

15.3.4   Effects

After an emergency or a necessity defence has been successfully asserted, an important practical question is whether damages are due. The answer to this question seems relatively clear in the case of an emergency clause contained in the treaty, such as Article XI of the Argentina–US BIT. In this case, no breach has occurred and, as a result, no compensation is due. Depending on the wording of the clause, the situation may be similar to a legitimate use of the police powers doctrine, which excludes liability irrespective of the duration of the measure challenged, or, alternatively, it may only exclude liability for a certain period during which the requirements of the clause were met. Beyond that specific period, damages may be due. This latter solution was retained by the tribunal in *LG&E* v. *Argentina*.[92]

The answer is less clear with respect to the customary necessity defence. Article 27 of the ILC Articles indeed leaves open the possibility that a State may have an obligation to pay damages despite having availed itself of a circumstance precluding wrongfulness. According to this provision '[t]he invocation of a circumstance precluding wrongfulness in accordance with this chapter is without prejudice to: ... (b) the question of compensation for any material loss caused by the act in question'.[93] Shortly before the adoption of this provision in its final version, the Special Rapporteur on this topic, Professor James Crawford, wrote that conduct covered by the necessity defence is 'in some sense wrongful, although there may be an excuse for it' and referred, in this connection, to 'the possibility of compensation in cases of necessity'.[94] This comment echoes an idea already present in the *Gabčíkovo-Nagymaros* case, where the Court had pointed out that Hungary had 'expressly

---

[91] *Sempra* v. *Argentina* – Annulment, above n. 72, paras. 186–219 (ground: manifest excess of powers for not applying Article XI of the Argentina–US BIT); *Enron* v. *Argentina* – Annulment, above n. 72, paras. 355–95 (grounds: failure to state reasons and manifest excess of powers in connection with the application of the customary necessity defence), paras. 400–5 (ground: manifest excess of powers for not applying Article XI of the Argentina–US BIT).

[92] *LG&E* – Liability, above n. 33, para. 261.   [93] ILC Articles, above n. 58, Article 27.

[94] J. Crawford, 'Revising the Draft Articles on State Responsibility' (1999) 10 *European Journal of International Law* 435, at 444.

acknowledged that, in any event, ... a state of necessity would not exempt it from its duty to compensate its partner'.[95] Yet, this idea was not clearly couched in the final draft of the ILC Articles, which indicates that it was not viewed as an entirely accurate reflection of customary law. Thus, while it seems clear that necessity, as a customary defence, does not preclude the need to compensate, it is also clear that no obligation to compensate arises from customary law. In practice, much will depend on the circumstances. Payment of some form of compensation would seem fair because a State acting under necessity is prioritising its own interests over those of other States. But in the case of investors based in the territory of the State concerned, it would also seem fair that all those that find themselves on the same boat when the storm hits do some sort of burden sharing. In other words, if the tribunal concludes that compensation must be paid to the investor, it would seem unfair to use the standards of compensation as in cases of unexcused breach. The tribunal would indeed have to take into account, in adjusting the amount of compensation, both (i) that the requirements of necessity have been met and (ii) that some burden sharing must be carried out.[96] Instead of applying 'fair market value' as the appropriate standard of compensation, a tribunal faced with this hypothesis may apply a different standard, such as the actual loss suffered by the investor,[97] or the unjust enrichment, if any, of the State, or, still, some other standard.

---

[95] *Gabčíkovo-Nagymaros*, above n. 59, para. 48.

[96] *James* v. *United Kingdom*, ECtHR Application No. 8793/79, Judgment (21 February 1986); *Tecmed* v. *Mexico*, above n. 13, para. 122.

[97] Bjorklund, 'The Necessity of Sustainable Development', above n. 70, p. 400 (referring to Crawford's second report).

Concluding observations

Some general conclusions can be drawn from the analysis conducted in the preceding chapters. The first conclusion concerns the evolving relationship between foreign investment and environmental law. The growing role assigned to the private sector in global environmental strategies – particularly in the context of the transition to a green economy – is, to a limited extent, mirrored by the growing space left for environmental considerations in investment and free trade agreements (IIAs). Concretely, however, the synergies between foreign investment and environmental protection are only now starting to be seriously explored. Chapter 3 provided an overview of the legal mechanisms that are giving shape to these synergies. But, as discussed in Chapters 1 and 4, the interactions between these two terms are not always synergistic or mutually supportive in practice. Over the years, several 'soft' control mechanisms have been developed to keep foreign investment within certain environmental bounds, including social and environmental standards, contractual devices and an array of accountability mechanisms. Yet, the effectiveness of these mechanisms tends to be rather limited. When the analysis is taken a step further to cover 'hard' accountability mechanisms – adjudicatory and quasi-adjudicatory mechanisms – the focus of the discussion gradually shifts to the assessment of the room left for environmental protection in IIAs and investment disputes. This shift introduces a subtle bias, namely that environmental protection can only evolve within the bounds left to it by investment law.

The second conclusion relates to the underpinnings of this shift. The analysis conducted in this book shows that the aforementioned bias has no legal grounding in international law. As discussed in detail in Part II, one may consider that international environmental law sets bounds for the operation of foreign investment much in the same way as IIAs do for environmental protection measures (Part III). More importantly, as a matter of principle there is no pre-determined hierarchy between an international environmental obligation and an investment discipline arising from an IIA. The conception that environmental protection can only take place within the bounds of investment disciplines is not based on law; rather, it is the result of two practical considerations. On the one hand, the rather vague formulation of many international environmental standards makes their application more difficult. On the other hand, unlike foreign investment law, international environmental law lacks a system of specialised tribunals ensuring its practical application. Yet, on closer examination, there are a number of indications that the challenges posed by these two practical considerations are being increasingly addressed.

Regarding the impact of environmental norms, the impetus given in the last several years to environmental concerns is gradually changing both the formulation and the understanding of international environmental standards. From little more than 'dormant clauses', many of these standards are now being perceived and applied as international obligations that require specific implementation at the national level. As the link between domestic environmental measures and the international environmental obligations of States becomes more visible, environmental protection initiatives at the domestic level are less and less framed as 'protectionist' or 'unilateral' to become 'co-ordinated' or 'multilateral' environmental measures. This, in turn, changes the legal framework applicable to the analysis of their relations with investment disciplines. The relevant conflict norms are no longer those applicable to legitimacy conflicts (Chapter 11) but those applicable to normative conflicts (Chapter 6). In other words, no pre-determined hierarchy is accorded to either international investment law or to international environmental law. Both are treated as specialised fields of one and the same legal order, international law.

In order for this shift to deploy its full effects, a change of mindset in how investment tribunals perceive environmental law would also be necessary. The question is: are investment tribunals likely to give more room to environmental law in deciding investment disputes? The present study provides two indications that this change of mindset is not unreachable. First, as more cases with environmental components are brought before investment tribunals (Chapter 1), environmental reasoning is likely to be increasingly integrated into investment disputes; in turn, as environmental reasoning becomes less 'unusual', it is also likely to become more widespread or 'mainstreamed'. The proliferation of environmental reasoning in other adjudicatory and quasi-adjudicatory mechanisms (Chapters 7–10) illustrates how this main-streaming process could unfold in the context of investment tribunals. Second, an intermediate stage of this mainstreaming process is already discernible in the case-law of investment tribunals addressing legitimacy conflicts. Indeed, as discussed in Chapters 12–15, some additional space for the adoption of purely domestic environmental measures is being carved out in investment disciplines through a variety of legal avenues, including the police powers and the margin of appreciation doctrines, emergency and necessity clauses, a broader understanding of the concept of 'like circumstances' in non-discrimination standards or a higher threshold in the assessment of the reasonableness of the investor's expectations.

Whether investment tribunals will go beyond this intermediate stage to openly address normative conflicts will depend, to a considerable extent, on how much space can be carved out in investment disciplines for environmental protection. As discussed in Chapters 12–15, there is a link between the operation of concepts such as the police powers doctrine or that of 'like circumstances' and international environmental law. The link between a domestic environmental measure and an environmental treaty may facilitate its characterisation as an exercise of the police powers doctrine. Similarly, reference to international environmental law may assist in establishing that two investments are not in like circumstances. In the context of the broad theoretical question identified in the Introductory Observations, the general finding of the foregoing analysis is that, irrespective of whether the integration of environmental protection is achieved through the struggle described in Part III rather than the one discussed in Part II, it will be achieved. Environmental protection can no longer be considered as a marginal component of foreign investment operations. In contemporary international law, environmental protection is a basic component of the commercial risk of foreign investment ventures.

Bibliography

Books

Alchourrón, C. E. and E. Bulygin, *Normative Systems* (New York: Springer, 1971).

Aldrich, G. H., *The Jurisprudence of the Iran–United States Claims Tribunal* (Oxford: Clarendon Press, 1996).

Anaya, J., *Indigenous Peoples in International Law* (Oxford University Press, 2004).

Anzilotti, D., *Cours de droit international* (Paris: Sirey, 1929).
  Scritti di diritto internazionale pubblico (Padova: Cedam, 1956).

Appleton, A. (ed.), *Environmental Labelling Programmes: Trade Law Implications* (London: Kluwer International, 1997).

Arai-Takahashi, Y., *The Margin of Appreciation Doctrine and the Principle of Proportionality in the Jurisprudence of the ECHR* (Antwerp: Intersentia, 2002).

Baer, P., T. Athanasiou, S. Kartha and E. Kemp-Benedict, *The Right to Development in a Climate Constrained World* (Berlin: Heinrich Boll Stiftung, 2008).

Batiffol, H. and P. Lagarde, *Droit international privé*, 2 vols. (Paris: LGDJ, 1971–4).

Birnie, P., A. E. Boyle and C. Redgwell, *International Law and the Environment* (Oxford University Press, 3rd edn, 2009).

Bishop, D., J. Crawford and M. Reisman, *Foreign Investment Disputes: Cases, Materials and Commentaries* (The Hague: Kluwer Law International, 2005).

Bodansky, D., J. Brunnée and E. Hey (eds.), *The Oxford Handbook of International Environmental Law* (Oxford University Press, 2007).

Bogdanovic, S., *International Law of Water Resources: Contribution of the International Law Association* (London: Kluwer Law International, 2001).

Bowman, M., P. Davies and C. Redgwell, *Lyster's International Wildlife Law* (Cambridge University Press, 2nd edn, 2010).

Brown, C., *A Common Law of International Adjudication* (Oxford University Press, 2007).

Brown Weiss, E., 'The Evolution of International Water Law', in *Recueil des cours de l'Académie de droit international*, Vol. 331 (2007) pp. 161–404.

Brownlie, I., *Principles of Public International Law* (Oxford University Press, 2008).

Burns, W. C. G. and H. M. Osofsky, *Adjudicating Climate Change: Sub-National, National, and Supra-National Approaches* (Cambridge University Press, 2010).

Cameron, P., *International Energy Investment Law: The Pursuit of Stability* (Oxford University Press, 2010).

Caponera, D., *Principles of Water Law and Administration: National and International* (London: Taylor & Francis, 2nd edn, 2007).

Caron, D., L. M. Caplan and M. Pellonpaa, *The UNCITRAL Arbitration Rules. A Commentary* (Oxford University Press, 2006).

Carson, R., *Silent Spring* (Boston, MA: Houghton Mifflin, 1962).

Commoner, B., *The Closing Circle: Nature, Man, and Technology* (New York, NY: Alfred Knopf, 1971).

Cordonnier Segger, M.-C., M. W. Gehring and A. Newcombe (eds.), *Sustainable Development in World Investment Law* (Alphen aan den Rijn: Wolters Kluwer, 2011).

Cottier, T., O. Nartova and S. Z. Bigdelli (eds.), *International Trade Regulation and the Mitigation of Climate Change* (Cambridge University Press, 2009).

Craig, L., W. W. Park and J. Paulsson, *International Chamber of Commerce Arbitration* (Dobbs Ferry, NY: Oceana Publications, 2000).

de Visscher, C., 'Le déni de justice en droit international', in *Recueil des cours de l'Académie de droit international*, Vol. 52, (1935) pp. 365–442.

Depledge, J., 'Tracing the Origins of the Kyoto Protocol: An Article-by-Article Textual History', Technical Paper, FCCC/TP/2000/2 (2000).

Dobson, A., *Fairness and Futurity: Essays on Environmental Sustainability and Social Justice* (Oxford University Press, 1999).

Dolzer, R. and C. Schreuer, *Principles of International Investment Law* (Oxford University Press, 2008).

Douglas, Z., *The International Law of Investment Claims* (Cambridge University Press, 2009).

Dupuy, P.-M., F. Francioni and E.-U. Petersmann (eds.), *Human Rights in International Investment Law and Arbitration* (Oxford University Press, 2009).

Dupuy, P.-M. and J. E. Viñuales (eds.), *Harnessing Foreign Investment to Promote Environmental Protection: Incentives and Safeguards* (Cambridge University Press, forthcoming).

Fitzmaurice, M., 'International Protection of the Environment', in *Recueil des cours de l'Académie de droit international*, Vol. 293, (2001) pp. 9–488.

Forest Trends, The Katoomba Group and United Nations Environment Programme, *Payments for Ecosystem Services. Getting Started: A Primer* (Nairobi: UNON/Publishing Services Section, 2008).

Forster, C., *Science and Precautionary Principle in International Courts and Tribunals* (Cambridge University Press, 2011).

Francioni, F. (ed.), *The 1972 Heritage Convention. A Commentary* (Oxford University Press, 2008).

Francioni, F. and M. Scheinin (eds.), *Cultural Human Rights* (Leiden: Martinus Nijhoff, 2008).

Freeman, A. V., *The International Responsibility of States for Denial of Justice* (London: Longmans Greens, 1938).

Freeman, C., C. Heydenreich and S. Lillywhite, *Guide to the OECD Guidelines for Multinational Enterprises' Complaints Procedure: Lessons from Past NGO Complaints* (2006), available at: www.oecdwatch.org.

Freestone, D. and C. Streck (eds.), *Legal Aspects of Carbon Trading* (Oxford University Press, 2009).

Friedman, S., *Expropriation in International Law* (London: Stevens & Sons, 1953).

Gaillard, E., *La jurisprudence du CIRDI*, 2 vols. (Paris: Pédone, 2004–10).

Gillespie, A., *Protected Areas and International Environmental Law* (Leiden: Martinus Nijhoff, 2007).

Grisel, F., *L'arbitrage international ou le droit contre l'ordre juridique*. Ph.D. dissertation, Université Paris I – Panthéon-Sorbonne (2010).

Happ, R. and N. Rubins, *Digest of ICSID Awards and Decisions 2003–2007* (Oxford University Press, 2009).

Harris, D. J., M. O'Boyle, E. P. Bates and C. M. Buckley, *Law of the European Convention on Human Rights* (Oxford University Press, 2nd edn, 2009).

Heathcote, S., *State of Necessity and International Law,* Ph.D. thesis, Graduate Institute of International Studies (IUHEI), Geneva (2005).

International Council on Human Rights Policy (ICHRP), *Climate Change and Human Rights: A Rough Guide* (2008).

Jasanoff, S. (ed.), *Learning from Disaster: Risk Management after Bhopal* (Philadelphia: University of Pennsylvania Press, 1994).

Jimenez de Aréchaga, E., 'International Law in the Past Third of a Century', in *Recueil des cours de l'Académie de droit international*, Vol. 159 (1978), p. 1.

Kelsen, H., 'Les rapports de système entre le droit interne et le droit international', in *Recueil des cours de l'Académie de droit international*, Vol. 14, (1926) pp. 227–332.

Kinnear, M., A. K. Bjorklund and J. F. G. Hannaford, *Investment Disputes under NAFTA. An Annotated Guide to NAFTA Chapter 11* (Alphen aan den Rijn: Kluwer Law International, 2006).

Kläger, R., *'Fair and Equitable Treatment' in International Investment Law* (Cambridge University Press, 2011).

Kornicker, E., *Ius cogens und Umweltvölkerrecht. Kriterien, Quellen und Rechtsforgen zwingender Völkerrechtsnormen und deren Anwendung auf das Umweltvölkerrecht* (Basel: Helbing & Lichtenhahn, 1997).

Landolt, P., *Modernised EC Competition Law in International Arbitration* (London: Kluwer, 2006).

Lewis-Lettington, R. and S. Mwanyiki, *Case Studies on Access and Benefit Sharing* (Rome: International Plant Genetic Resources Institute, 2006).

McCaffrey, S., *The Law of International Watercourses* (Oxford University Press, 2007).

McLachlan, C., L. Shore and M. Weiniger, *International Investment Arbitration: Substantive Principles* (Oxford University Press, 2007).

Meadows, Donnella H., Dennis L. Meadows, J. Randers and W. W. Berens, *The Limits to Growth: A Report for the Club of Rome's Project on the Predicament of Mankind* (New York, NY: Universe Books, 1972).

Morgera, E., *Corporate Accountability in International Environmental Law* (Oxford University Press, 2009).

Muchlinsky, P., F. Ortino and C. Schreuer (eds.), *The Oxford Handbook of International Investment Law* (Oxford University Press, 2008).

Newcombe, A. and L. Paradell, *Law and Practice of Investment Treaties* (Alphen aan den Rijn: Kluwer Law International, 2009).

Nicholson, M., *The Environmental Revolution: A Guide for the New Masters of the World* (London: Hodder & Stoughton, 1969).

O'Faircheallaigh, C., *Environmental Agreements in Canada: Aboriginal Participation, EIA Follow-up and Environmental Management of Major Projects* (Calgary AB: Canadian Institute of Resources Law, 2006).

Orakhelashvili, A., *Peremptory Norms in International Law* (Oxford University Press, 2006).

Organisation for Economic Co-operation and Development, *International Investment Law: Understanding Concepts and Tracking Innovation* (Paris: OECD, 2008).

Orts, E. W. and K. Deketelaere (eds.), *Environmental Contracts: Comparative Approaches to Regulatory Innovation in the United States and Europe* (The Hague: Kluwer Law International, 2001).

Paulsson, J., *Denial of Justice in International Law* (Cambridge University Press, 2005).

Pauwelyn, J., *Conflict of Norms in Public International Law: How WTO Law relates to other Rules of International Law* (Cambridge University Press, 2003).

Racine, J.-B., *L'arbitrage commercial international et l'ordre public* (Paris: LGDJ, 1999).

Radicati di Brozolo, L., 'Arbitrage commercial international et lois de police. Considérations sur les conflits de juridictions dans le commerce international', in *Recueil des cours de l'Académie de droit international*, Vol. 315 (2005), pp. 265–502.

Richardson, B. J., *Socially Responsible Investment Law: Regulating the Unseen Polluters* (Oxford University Press, 2008).

Robert-Cuendet, S., *Droits de l'investisseur étranger et protection de l'environnement: Contribution à l'analyse de l'expropriation indirecte* (Leiden: Martinus Nijhoff, 2010).

Roucounas, E., 'Engagements parallèles et contradictoires', in *Recueil des cours de l'Académie de droit international*, Vol. 206 (1987), pp. 9–288.

Sadat-Akhavi, S. A., *Methods of Resolving Conflicts between Treaties* (Leiden: Martinus Nijhoff, 2003).

Salacuse, J. W., *The Law of Investment Treaties* (Oxford University Press, 2011).

Sands, P., *Principles of International Environmental Law* (Cambridge University Press, 2003).

Santulli, C., *Droit du contentieux international* (Paris: Montchrestien, 2005).

Sasson, M., *Substantive Law in Investment Treaty Arbitration. The Unsettled Relationship between International Law and Municipal Law* (Alphen aan den Rijn: Kluwer Law International, 2010).

Schill, S., *The Multilateralization of International Investment Law* (Cambridge University Press, 2009).

Schreuer, C., L. Malintoppi, A. Reinisch and A. Sinclair, *The ICSID Convention. A Commentary* (Cambridge University Press, 2nd edn, 2009).

Schrijver, N., 'The Evolution of Sustainable Development in International Law: Inception, Meaning and Status', in *Recueil des cours de l'Académie de droit international*, Vol. 329, (2008) pp. 217–412.

Shemberg, A., *Stabilization Clauses and Human Rights: A Research Project Conducted for IFC and the United Nations Special Representative to the Secretary General on Business and Human Rights*, 11 March 2008.

Sornarajah, M., *The International Law on Foreign Investment* (Cambridge University Press, 3rd edn, 2010).

Stephens, T., *International Courts and Environmental Protection* (Cambridge University Press, 2009).

Tienhaara, K., *The Expropriation of Environmental Governance* (Cambridge University Press, 2009).

Treves, T., L. Pineschi, A. Tanzi, C. Pitea, C. Ragni and F. Romanin Jacur (eds.), *Non-Compliance Procedures and Mechanisms and the Effectiveness of International Environmental Agreements* (The Hague: T.M.C. Asser Press, 2009).

Triepel, H., 'Les rapports entre le droit interne et le droit international', in *Recueil des cours de l'Académie de droit international*, Vol. 1, (1923) pp. 73–122.
    Völkerrecht und Landesrecht (Leipzig: Hirschfeld, 1899).

Tudor, I., *The Fair and Equitable Treatment Standard in the International Law of Foreign Investment* (Oxford University Press, 2008).

United Nations Environment Programme, *Towards a Green Economy: Pathways to Sustainable Development and Poverty Eradication* (UNEP, 2011).

Weil, P., 'Problèmes relatifs aux contrats passés entre un Etat et un particulier', in *Recueil des cours de l'Académie de droit international*, Vol. 128 (1969) pp. 95–240.

Weiler, T. (ed), *International Investment Law and Arbitration: Leading Cases from the ICSID, NAFTA, Bilateral Treaties and Customary International Law* (London: Cameron May, 2005).

Wolfrum, R. and N. Matz, *Conflicts in International Environmental Law* (Berlin: Springer Verlag, 2003).

Yamin, F. and J. Depledge, *The International Climate Change Regime* (Cambridge University Press, 2004).

Zerk, J. *Multinationals and Corporate Social Responsibility* (Cambridge University Press, 2006).

Zleptnig, S., *Non-Economic Objectives in WTO Law* (The Hague: Kluwer, 2010).

Articles and chapters

Abi-Saab, G., 'Les sources du droit international: essai de deconstruction' in R. Rama Montaldo (ed.), *International Law in an Evolving World. Liber Amicorum Jiménez de Aréchaga*, Vol. I (Montevideo: Fundación de Cultura Universitaria, 1994), pp. 29–49.

Affolder, N., 'Mining and the World Heritage Convention: Democratic Legitimacy and Treaty Compliance' (2007) 24 *Pace Environmental Law Review* 35.

'Rethinking Environmental Contracting' (2010) 21 *Journal of Environmental Law and Practice* 115.

Alchourrón, C. E., 'Conflicts of Norms and the Revision of Normative Systems' (1991) 10 *Law and Philosophy* 417.

Aldrich, G. H., 'What Constitutes a Compensable Taking of Property? The Decisions of the Iran–United States Claims Tribunal' (1994) 88 *American Journal of International Law* 585.

Anzilotti, D., 'Il diretto internazionale nei giudizi interni', in D. Anzilotti (ed.), *Scritti di diretto internazionale pubblico*, Vol. 1 (Padova: Cedam, 1956).

Baeteus, F., 'Discrimination on the Basis of Nationality: Determining Likeness in Human Rights and Investment Law', in S. Schill (ed.), *International Investment Law and Comparative Public Law* (Oxford University Press, 2010), pp. 279–315.

'The Kyoto Protocol in Investor-State Arbitration: Reconciling Climate Change and Investment Protection Objectives', in M.-C. Cordonnier Segger, M. W. Gehring and A. Newcombe (eds.), *Sustainable Development in World Investment Law* (Alphen aan den Rijn: Wolters Kluwer, 2011), pp. 683–715.

Banifatemi, Y., 'The Emerging Jurisprudence on the Most-Favoured-Nation Treatment in Investment Arbitration', in A. K. Bjorklund, I. Laird and S. Ripinsky (eds.), *Investment Treaty Law. Current Issues III* (London: BIICL, 2009), pp. 24ff.

Baughen, S., 'Expropriation and Environmental Regulation: The Lessons of NAFTA Chapter Eleven (2006) 18 *Journal of Environmental Law* 207.

Been, V. and J. Beauvais, 'The Global Fifth Amendment? NAFTA's Investment Protections and the Misguided Quest for an International "Regulatory Takings" Doctrine' (2003) 78 *New York University Law Review* 30.

Bernardini, P., 'The Renegotiation of the Investment Contract' (1998) 13 *ICSID Review – Foreign Investment Law Journal* 411.

Bernhardt, R., 'Article 103', in B. Simma (ed.), *The Charter of the United Nations: A Commentary* (Oxford University Press, 2nd edn, 2002), pp. 1293–302.

Bjorklund, A. K., 'National Treatment', in A. Reinisch (ed.), *Standards of Investment Protection* (Oxford University Press, 2008), pp. 29–58.

'The Necessity of Sustainable Development', in M.-C. Cordonnier Segger, M. W. Gehring and A. Newcombe (eds.), *Sustainable Development in World Investment Law* (Alphen aan den Rijn: Wolters Kluwer, 2011).

Bodansky, D., 'Deconstructing the Precautionary Principle', in D. Caron and H. N. Scheiber (eds.), *Bringing New Ocean Waters* (Leiden: Martinus Nijhoff, 2004), pp. 381–91.

'The United Nations Framework Convention on Climate Change: A Commentary' (1993) 18 *Yale Journal of International Law* 451.

'What's So Bad about Unilateral Action to Protect the Environment?' (2000) 11 *European Journal of International Law* 339.

Bodansky, D. and J. C. Lawrence, 'Trade and Environment', in D. Bethlehem, D. McRae, R. Deufeld and I. van Damme (eds.), *The Oxford Handbook of International Trade Law* (Oxford University Press, 2009), pp. 505–38.

Boisson de Chazournes, L., 'Technical and Financial Assistance', in D. Bodansky, J. Brunéi and E. Hey (eds.), *The Oxford Handbook of International Law* (Oxford University Press, 2007), pp. 947–73.

Boulding, K. E., 'The Economics of the Coming Spaceship Earth', in H. Jarrett (ed.), *Environmental Quality in a Growing Economy* (Baltimore, MD: Johns Hopkins University Press, 1966), pp. 3–14.

Brower, C., 'International Decisions: S. D. Myers Inc. v. Canada' (2004) 98 *American Journal of International Law* 339.

Brower, C. and J. Wong, 'General Valuation Principles: The Case of Santa Elena', in T. Weiler (ed.), *International Investment Law and Arbitration: Leading Cases from the ICSID, NAFTA, Bilateral Treaties and Customary International Law* (London: Cameron May, 2005), pp. 747–75.

Brown Weiss, E., 'Water Transfers and International Trade Law' in E. Brown Weiss, L. Boisson de Chazournes and N. Bernasconi-Osterwalder (eds.), *Fresh Water and International Economic Law* (Oxford University Press, 2005), pp. 61–89.

Brunnee, J., 'COPing with Consent: Law-making under Multilateral Environmental Agreements' (2002) 15 *Leiden Journal of International Law* 1.

Burke-White, W. W. and A. von Staden, 'Investment Protection in Extraordinary Times: The Interpretation and Application of Non-Precluded Measures Provisions in Bilateral Investment Treaties' (2008) 48 *Virginia Journal of International Law* 307.

Christie, G. C., 'What Constitutes a Taking of Property under International Law' (1962) 38 *British Yearbook of International Law* 307.

Clemençon, R., 'What Future for the Global Environmental Facility' (2006) 15 *The Journal of Environment and Development* 50.

Coe, J. and N. Rubins, 'Regulatory Expropriation and the Tecmed Case: Context and Contributions', in T. Weiler (ed.), *International Investment Law and Arbitration: Leading Cases from the ICSID, NAFTA, Bilateral Treaties and Customary International Law* (London: Cameron May, 2005), pp. 597–667.

Coonrod, S., 'The United Nations Code of Conduct for Transnational Corporations' (1977) 18 *Harvard International Law Journal* 273.

Coughlin, M. D. 'Using the Merck-INBio agreement to clarify the Convention on Biological Diversity' (1993) 31 *Columbia Journal of Transnational Law* 337.

Cotula, L., 'Reconciling regulatory stability and evolution of environmental standards in investment contracts: Towards a rethink of stabilization clauses' (2008) 1 *Journal of World Energy Law and Business* 158.

'Stabilization Clauses and the Evolution of Environmental Standards in Foreign Investment Contracts' (2006) 17 *Yearbook of International Environmental Law* 111.

Crawford, J., 'Revising the Draft Articles on State Responsibility' (1999) 10 *European Journal of International Law* 435.

Crawford, J. and T. Grant, 'Exhaustion of Local Remedies', *Max Planck Encyclopaedia of Public International Law*, available at: www.mpepil.com.

Cullet, P. and A. Gowlland-Gualtieri, 'Local Communities and Water Investments', in E. Brown Weiss, L. Boisson de Chazournes and N. Bernasconi-Osterwalder (eds.), *Fresh Water and International Economic Law* (Oxford University Press, 2005), pp. 303–30.

David, E., 'Primary and Secondary Rules', in J. Crawford, A. Pellet and S. Olleson (eds.), *The Law of International Responsibility* (Oxford University Press, 2010).

Dellapenna, J., 'Treaties as Instruments for Managing Internationally-Shared Water Resources: Restricted Sovereignty vs. Community of Property' (1994) 26 *Case-Western Reserve Journal of International and Comparative Law* 27.

Dellapenna, J. and J. Gupta, 'Toward Global Law on Water' (2008) 13 *Global Governance* 437.

Denza, E., 'The Relationship between International and National Law', in M. D. Evans (ed.), *International Law* (Oxford University Press, 2010), pp. 411–38.

DiMascio, N. and J. Pauwelyn, 'Nondiscrimination in Trade and Investment Treaties: Worlds Apart or Two Sides of the Same Coin?' (2008) 102 *American Journal of International Law* 48.

Dolzer, R., 'Indirect Expropriation of Alien Property' (1986) 1 *ICSID Review – Foreign Investment Law Journal* 41.

Dombrowsky, I., 'Integration in the Management of International Waters: Economic Perspectives on a Global Policy Discourse' (2008) 14 *Global Governance* 455.

Douglas, Z., 'The MFN Clause in Investment Arbitration: Treaty Interpretation Off the Rails' (2010) 2 *Journal of International Dispute Settlement* 97.

Dupuy, P.-M., 'Formation of Customary International Law and General Principles', in D. Bodansky, J. Brunnée and E. Hey (eds.), *The Oxford Handbook of International Environmental Law* (Oxford University Press, 2007), pp. 449–66.

Fauchald, O. K., 'International Investment Law and Environmental Protection' (2006) 17 *Yearbook of International Environmental Law* 3.

Firestone, J., W. Kempton, A. Krueger and C. E. Loper, 'Regulating Offshore Wind Power and Aquaculture: Messages from Land and Sea' (2004) 14 *Cornell Journal of Law and Public Policy* 71.

Firger, D. M. and M. B. Gerrard, 'Harmonizing Climate Change Policy and International Investment Law' (2010/11) 3 *Yearbook of International Investment Law and Policy* 517.

Focarelli, C., 'Denial of Justice', *Max Planck Encyclopaedia of Public International Law*, available at: www.mpepil.com.

Fitzmaurice, M., 'The Human Right to Water' (2007) 18 *Fordham Environmental Law Review* 537.

Fortier, Y. and S. Drymer, 'Indirect Expropriation in the Law of International Investment: I Know It When I See It, or Caveat Investor' (2004) 19 *ICSID Review – Foreign Investment Law Journal* 293.

Francioni, F., 'Access to Justice, Denial of Justice, and International Investment Law', in P.-M. Dupuy, F. Francioni and E.-U. Petersmann (eds.), *Human Rights in International Investment Law and Arbitration* (Oxford University Press, 2009), pp. 63–81.

'International Human Rights in an Environmental Horizon' (2010) 21 *European Journal of International Law* 41.

Francioni, F. and F. Lenzerini, 'The Destruction of the Buddhas of Bamiyan and International Law' (2003) 14 *European Journal of International Law* 619.

Gaillard, E. and Y. Banifatemi, 'The Meaning of "and" in Article 42(1), second sentence, of the Washington Convention: The Role of International Law in the ICSID Choice of Law Process' (2003) 18 *ICSID Review – Foreign Investment Law Journal* 375.

Gaines, S., 'The Masked Ball of NAFTA Chapter 11: Foreign Investors, Local Environmentalists, Government Officials, and Disguised Motives', in J. Kirton and V. MacLaren (eds.), *Linking Trade, Environment, and Social Cohesion: NAFTA Experiences, Global Challenges* (Aldershot: Ashgate, 2002), pp. 103–29.

Ghaleigh, N. S., 'Emissions Trading before the European Court of Justice: Market Making in Luxembourg', in D. Freestone and C. Streck, *Legal Aspects of Carbon Trading* (Oxford University Press, 2009), pp. 367–88.

Gillespie, A., 'The Management of Protected Areas of International Significance' (2006) 10 *New Zealand Journal of Environmental Law* 93.

Gordon, K. and J. Pohl, 'Environmental Concerns in International Investment Agreements: A Survey' (2011) *OECD Working Papers on International Investment* No. 2011/1.

Gowlland Gualtieri, A., 'The Environmental Accountability of the World Bank to Non-State Actors: Insights from the Inspection Panel' (2001) 72 *British Yearbook of International Law* 213.

Grisel, F. and J. E. Viñuales, 'L'amicus curiae dans l'arbitrage d'investissement (2007) 22 *ICSID Review – Foreign Investment Law Journal* 380.

Harper, F. V. and E. D. Etherington, 'Lobbyists before the Court' (1953) 101 *University of Pennsylvania Law Review* 1172.

Heathcote, S., 'Circumstances Precluding Wrongfulness in the ILC Artices on State Responsibility: Necessity', in J. Crawford, A. Pellet, S. Olleson and K. Parlett (eds.), *The Law of International Responsibility* (Oxford University Press, 2010), pp. 491–501.

Hobley, A. and C. Robers, 'Joint Implementation Transactions: An Overview', in D. Freestone and C. Streck (eds.), *Legal Aspects of Carbon Trading* (Oxford University Press, 2009), pp. 195.

Howse, R., 'The Appellate Body Rulings in the Shrimp/Turtle Case: A New Legal Baseline for the Trade and Environment Debate' (2002) 27 *Columbia Journal of Environmental Law* 491.

Hurlock, M., 'The GATT, US Law and the Environment: A Proposal to Amend the GATT in Light of the Tuna/Dolphin Decision' (1992) 92 *Columbia Law Review* 2098.

Jacobson, J. L., 'International Fisheries Law in the Year 2010' (1985) 45 *Louisiana Law Review* 1161.

Jessup, P., 'Confiscation' (1933) 21 *American Society of International Law Proceedings* 40.

Johnson, L., 'International Investment Agreements and Climate Change: The Potential for Investor-State Conflicts and Possible Strategies for Minimizing It' (2009) 39 *Environmental Law Reporter* 11147.

Joubin-Bret, J., 'Admission and Establishment in the Context of Investment Protection', in A. Reinisch (ed.), *Standards of Investment Protection* (Oxford University Press, 2008), pp. 9–28.

Kaufmann-Kohler, G., 'Arbitral Precedent: Dream, Necessity or Excuse?' (2007) 23 *Arbitration International* 357.

Kekic, L., 'The Global Economic Crisis and FDI Flows to Emerging Markets' (October 2009) *Columbia FDI Perspectives* No. 15.

Kelsen, H., 'La transformation du droit international en droit interne' (1936) 43 *Revue générale de droit international public* 5.

King, B., 'The UN Global Compact: Responsibility for Human Rights, Labour Relations, and the Environment in Developing Nations' (2001) 34 *Cornell International Law Journal* 481.

Knight, C., 'A Regulatory Minefield: Can the Department of Interior say "No" to a Hardrock Mine?' (2002) 73 *University of Colorado Law Review* 619.

Krislov, K., 'The Amicus Curiae Brief: From Friendship to Advocacy' (1963) 72 *Yale Law Journal* 694.

Kulovesi, K., E. Morgera and M. Muñoz, 'The EU's Climate and Energy Package: Environmental Integration and International Dimensions', *Working Paper Series of the Europa Institute*, University of Edinburgh, available at: www.law.ed.ac.uk/europa/.

Kurtz, J., 'The Merits and Limits of Comparativism: National Treatment in International Investment Law and the WTO', in S. Schill (ed.), *International Investment Law and Comparative Public Law* (Oxford University Press, 2010), pp. 243–78.

Laird, S. and R. Wynberg, Access and Benefit-Sharing in Practice: Trends in Partnerships across Sectors, *CBD Technical* Series No. 38, 2008.

Lalive, P., 'Ordre public transnational (ou réellement international) et arbitrage international' (1986) 3 *Revue de l'arbitrage* 329.

Lalive, P. and L. Halonen, 'On the Availability of Counterclaims in Investment Treaty Arbitration' (2011) 2 *Czech Yearbook of International Law* 141.

Lawrence, J., 'Chicken Little Revisited: NAFTA Regulatory Expropriations after Methanex' (2006) 41 *Georgia Law Review* 261.

Leader, S., 'Human Rights, Risks, and New Strategies for Global Investment' (2006) 9 *Journal of International Economic Law* 657.

Leben, C., 'L'état de nécessité dans le droit international de l'investissement' (2005) 3 *Les cahiers de l'arbitrage* 47.

Lester, S., 'A Framework for Thinking about the "Discretion" in the Mandatory/Discretionary Distinction' (2011) 14 *Journal of International Economic Law* 369.

Lin, J., 'Private Actors in International and Domestic Emissions Trading Schemes', in D. Freestone and C. Streck (eds.), *Legal Aspects of Carbon Trading* (Oxford University Press, 2009), pp. 134–54.

Lowe, V., 'Precluding Wrongfulness or Responsibility: A Plea for Excuses' (1999) 10 *European Journal of International Law* 405.

Magraw, D. B. and L. D. Hawke, 'Sustainable Development', in D. Bodansky, J. Brunnée and E. Hey (eds.), *The Oxford Handbook of International Environmental Law* (Oxford University Press, 2007), pp. 613–38.

Manciax, S., 'Chronique des sentences arbitrales' (2011) 138 *Journal de droit international* 565.

Mayer, P., 'Lois de police étrangères' (1981) 108 *Journal du droit international* 277.

McLachlan, C., 'The Principle of Systemic Integration and Article 31 3) c) of the Vienna Convention' (2005) 54 *International and Comparative Law Quarterly* 279.

Metcalf, G. E. and D. Weisbach, 'The Design of a Carbon Tax' (2009) 33 *Harvard Environmental Law Review* 499.

Miles, K., 'Arbitrating Climate Change: Regulatory Regimes and Investor-State Disputes' (2010) 1 *Climate Law* 63.

'Sustainable Development, National Treatment and Like Circumstances in Investment Law', in M.-C. Cordonnier Segger, M. W. Gehring and A. Newcombe (eds.), *Sustainable Development in World Investment Law* (Alphen aan den Rijn: Wolters Kluwer, 2011), pp. 265–94.

Miller, A. S., 'The Global Environmental Facility and the Search for Financial Strategies to Foster Sustainable Development' (1999–2000) 24 *Vermont Law Review* 1229.

Morgera, M., 'An Environmental Outlook on the OECD Guidelines for Multinational Enterprises: Comparative Advantage, Legitimacy, and Outstanding Questions in the Lead Up to the 2006 Review' (2006) 18 *Georgetown International Environmental Law Review* 751.

'Significant Trends in Corporate Environmental Accountability: The New Performance Standards of the International Financial Corporation' (2007) 18 *Colorado Journal of International Law and Policy* 151.

Newcombe, A., 'The Boundaries of Regulatory Expropriation in International Law' (2005) 20 *ICSID Review – Foreign Investment Law Journal* 1.

'General Exceptions in International Investment Agreements', in M.-C. Cordonnier Segger, M. W. Gehring and A. Newcombe (eds.), *Sustainable Development in World Investment Law* (Alphen aan den Rijn: Wolters Kluwer, 2011), pp. 355–70.

Nikken, P., 'Balancing of Human Rights and Investment Law in the Inter-American System of Human Rights', in P.-M. Dupuy, F. Francioni and E.-U. Petersmann (eds.), *Human Rights in International Investment Law and Arbitration* (Oxford University Press, 2009), pp. 246–71.

Ong, D., 'The Impact of Environmental Law on Corporate Governance: International and Comparative Perspectives' (2001) 12 *European Journal of International Law* 685.

Orellana, M., 'The Role of Science in Investment Arbitrations Concerning Public Health and the Environment' (2006) 17 *Yearbook of International Environmental Law* 48.

Ortino, F., 'Non-Discriminatory Treatment in Investment Disputes', in P.-M. Dupuy, F. Francioni and E.-U. Petersmann (eds.), *Human Rights in International Investment Law and Arbitration* (Oxford University Press, 2009), pp. 344–66.

Paasivirta, E., 'Internationalisation and Stabilisation of Contracts versus State Sovereignty' (1989) 60 *British Yearbook of International Law* 315.

Paparinskis, M., 'Regulatory Expropriation and Sustainable Development', in M.-C. Cordonnier Segger, M. W. Gehring and A. Newcombe (eds.), *Sustainable Development in World Investment Law* (Alphen aan den Rijn: Wolters Kluwer, 2011), pp. 299–327.

Paulsson, J., 'Arbitration without Privity' (1995) 10 *ICSID Review – Foreign Investment Law Journal* 232.

Pavoni, R., 'Mutual Supportiveness as a Principle of Interpretation and Law-Making: A Watershed for the "WTO-and-Competing-Regimes" Debate?' (2010) 21 *European Journal of International Law* 649.

Perrot-Maître, D., 'The Vittel Payments for Ecosystem Services: A "Perfect" PES Case?', *IISD Project Paper No. 3* (2006).

Peterson, L. E. and R. Garland, 'Bilateral Investment Treaties and Land Reform in Southern Africa', Report prepared for Rights & Democracy (June 2010).

Redgwell, C., 'The International Law of Public Participation: Protected Areas, Endangered Species, and Biological Diversity', in D. N. Zillman, A. R. Lucas and G. Pring (eds.), *Human Rights in Natural Resource Development* (Oxford University Press, 2002), pp. 187–214.

Regan, D. H., 'How to Think about PPMs (and Climate Change)', in T. Cottier, O. Navorta and S. Z. Bigdelli (eds.), *International Trade Regulation and the Mitigation of Climate Change* (Cambridge University Press, 2009).

Reiner, C. and C. Schreuer, 'Human Rights and International Investment Arbitration', in P.-M. Dupuy, F. Francioni and E.-U. Petersmann (eds.), *Human Rights in International Investment Law and Arbitration* (Oxford University Press, 2009), pp. 82–96.

Reisman, M. and R. Sloane, 'Indirect Expropriation and its Valuation in the BIT Generation' (2003) 74 *British Yearbook of International Law* 115.

Revesz, R. L., 'Rehabilitating Interstate Competition: Rethinking the Race-to-the-Bottom Rationale for Federal Environmental Regulation' (1992) 67 *New York University Law Review* 1210.

Richardson, B. J., 'The Equator Principles: The Voluntary Approach to Environmentally Sustainable Finance' (2005) 14 *European Environmental Law Review* 280.

  'Financing Sustainability: The New Transnational Governance of Socially Responsible Investment' (2006) 17 *Yearbook of International Environmental Law* 73.

Rukundo, O. and J. Cabrera, 'Investment Promotion and Protection in the UNCBD: An Emerging Access and Benefit Sharing Regime', in

M.-C. Cordonnier Segger, M. W. Gehring and A. Newcombe (eds.), *Sustainable Development in World Investment Law* (Alphen aan den Rijn: Wolters Kluwer, 2011), pp. 721–43.

Sand, P. H., 'The Evolution of International Environmental Law', in D. Bodansky, J. Brunée and E. Hey (eds.), *The Oxford Handbook of International Environmental Law* (Oxford University Press, 2007).

Salacuse, J. W., 'The Treatification of International Investment Law' (2007) 13 *NAFTA: Law and Business Review of the Americas* 155.

Shelton, D., 'Normative Hierarchy in International Law' (2006) 100 *American Journal of International Law* 291.

  'The Participation of Nongovernmental Organizations in International Judicial Proceedings' (1994) 88 *American Journal of International Law* 611.

Sheppard, A. and A. Crockett, 'Are Stabilization Clauses a Threat to Sustainable Development?', in M.-C. Cordonnier Segger, M. W. Gehring and A. Newcombe (eds.), *Sustainable Development in World Investment Law* (Alphen aan den Rijn: Wolters Kluwer, 2011), pp. 329–50.

Shihata, I., 'Implementation, Enforcement and Compliance with International Environmental Agreements – Practical Suggestions in Light of the World Bank's Experience' (1996–7) 9 *Georgetown International Environmental Law Review* 37.

Shue, H., 'Subsistence Emissions and Luxury Emissions' (1993) 15 *Law & Policy* 39.

Simonetti, S. and R. de Witt Wijnen, 'International Emissions Trading and Green Investment Schemes', in D. Freestone and C. Streck (eds.), *Legal Aspects of Carbon Trading* (Oxford University Press, 2009), pp. 157–175.

Sinclair, A., 'The Origins of the Umbrella Clause in International Law of Investment Protection' (2004) 20 *Arbitration International* 411.

Sohn, L. B. and R. R. Baxter, 'Draft Convention on the International Legal Responsibility of States for Injuries to Aliens' (1961) 55 *American Journal of International Law* 545.

Soloway, J., 'Environmental Expropriation under NAFTA Chapter 11: The Phantom Menace', in J. Kirton and V. MacLaren (eds.), *Linking Trade, Environment, and Social Cohesion: NAFTA Experiences, Global Challenges* (Aldershot: Ashgate, 2002), pp. 131–44.

Spears, S. A., 'The Quest for Policy Space in a New Generation of International Investment Agreements' 2010 13 (4) *Journal of International Dispute Settlement* 1037.

Spiermann, O., 'Applicable Law', in P. Muchlinsky, F. Ortino and C. Schreuer (eds.), *The Oxford Handbook of International Investment Law* (Oxford University Press, 2008), pp. 89–116.

Stern, B., 'Civil Society's Voice in the Settlement of International Economic Disputes' (2007) 22 *ICSID Review – Foreign Investment Law Journal* 280.

Stewart, R. B., 'A New Generation of Environmental Regulation' (2001) 29 *Capital University Law Review* 21.

Streck, C., 'The Global Environmental Facility – A Role Model for International Environmental Governance?' (2001) 1 *Global Environmental Politics* 71.

'The World Summit on Sustainable Development: Partnerships as New Tools in Environmental Governance' (2002) 13 *Yearbook of International Environmental Law* 63.

Tienhaara, K., 'Unilateral Commitments to Investment Protection: Does the Promise of Stability Restrict Environmental Policy Development' (2006) 17 *Yearbook of International Environmental Law* 139.

Triggs, G., 'The Rights of Indigenous Peoples to Participate in Resource Development: An International Legal Perspective', in D. N. Zillman, A. R. Lucas and G. Pring (eds.), *Human Rights in Natural Resource Development* (Oxford University Press, 2002), pp. 123–54.

Tschanz, P.-Y. and J. E. Viñuales, 'Compensation for Non-Expropriatory Breaches of International Investment Law – The Contribution of the Argentine Awards' (2009) 6 *Journal of International Arbitration* 729.

Vasciannie, S., 'The Fair and Equitable Treatment Standard in International Investment Law and Practice' (2000) 60 *British Yearbook of International Law* 99.

Verdross, A., 'Jus dispositivum and jus cogens in International Law' (1966) 60 *American Journal of International Law* 55.

Viñuales, J. E., 'Conflit de normes en droit international: normes environnementales vs. protection des investissements', in Société française pour le droit international (SFDI), *Le droit international face aux enjeux environnementaux* (Paris: Pédone, 2010), p. 407.

'The Contribution of the International Court of Justice to the Development of International Environmental Law: A Contemporary Assessment' (2008) 32 *Fordham International Law Journal* 232.

'Du bon dosage du droit international: les négociations climatiques en perspective' (2010) 56 *Annuaire français de droit international* 437.

'Foreign Investment and the Environment in International Law: An Ambiguous Relationship' (2009) 80 *British Yearbook of International Law* 244.

'Legal Techniques for Dealing with Scientific Uncertainty in Environmental Law' (2010) 43 *Vanderbilt Journal of Transnational Law* 437.

'Managing Compliance with Standards for the Protection of the Environment', in A. Cassese (ed.), *Realizing Utopia* (Oxford University Press, forthcoming), Chapter 29.

'State of Necessity and Peremptory Norms in International Investment Law' (2008) 14 *NAFTA: Law and Business Review of the Americas* 79.

Viñuales, J. E. and S. Chuffart, 'From the Other Shore: Economic, Social and Cultural Rights from an International Environmental Law Perspective', in E. Reidel, C. Golay, C. Mahon and G. Giacca (eds.), *Contemporary Issues in the Realization of Economic, Social and Cultural Rights* (Oxford University Press, forthcoming).

Viñuales, J. E. and F. Grisel, 'L'amicus curiae dans l'arbitrage d'investissement' (2007) 22 *ICSID Review – Foreign Investment Law Journal* 380.

van Aaken, A., 'Fragmentation of International Law: The Case of International Investment Law' (2006) 17 *Finnish Yearbook of International Law* 91.

van Zeben, J., 'The European Emissions Trading Scheme Case Law' (2009)
    18 *Review of European Community and International Environmental Law* 119.
Verdross, A., 'Jus dispositivum and jus cogens in International Law' (1966) 60
    American Journal of International Law 55.
von Wright, G. H., 'Deontic Logic' (1951) 60 *Mind* 1.
  'A Note on Deontic Logic and Derived Obligation' (1956) 65 *Mind* 507.
  'Is There a Logic of Norms?' (1991) 4 *Ratio Juris* 270.
Wälde, T. and A. Kolo, 'Environmental Regulation, Investment Protection and
    "Regulatory Taking" in International Law' (2001) 50 *International and
    Comparative Law Quarterly* 811.
Wälde, T. and G. N'Di, 'Stabilising International Investment Commitments'
    (1996) 31 *Texas International Law Journal* 215.
Wara, M., 'Measuring the Clean Development Mechanism's Performance and
    Potential' (2007) 55 *UCLA Law Review* 1759.
Weil, P., 'Les clauses de stabilisation ou d'intangibilité insérées dans les accords
    de développement économique', in *Mélanges offerts è Charles Rousseau:
    La communauté internationale* (Paris: Pédone, 1974), pp. 301–28.
  'Towards Relative Normativity in International Law?' (1983) 77 *American Journal
    of International Law* 413.
Weiler, T., 'Good Faith and Regulatory Transparency: The Story of Metalclad
    v. Mexico', in T. Weiler (ed.), *International Investment Law and Arbitration:
    Leading Cases from the ICSID, NAFTA, Bilateral Treaties and Customary International
    Law* (London: Cameron May, 2005), pp. 701–45.
Wirth, D., 'Hazardous Substances and Activities', in D. Bodansky, J. Brunnée and
    E. Hey (eds.), *The Oxford Handbook of International Environmental Law* (Oxford
    University Press, 2007), pp. 394–422.
Wolf, A. and J. Hammer, 'Patterns in International Water Resource Treaties:
    The Transboundary Freshwater Dispute Database' (1998) 9 *Colorado Journal of
    International Environmental Law and Policy* 157.
Wyman, K. M., 'The Property Rights Challenge in Marine Fisheries' (2008)
    50 *Arizona Law Review* 511.
Ziegler, A. R., 'Most-Favoured-Nation (MFN) Treatment', in A. Reinisch (ed.),
    Standards of Investment Protection (Oxford University Press, 2008), pp. 59–86.

Index